social problems

social problems
Values and Interests in Conflict

ROBERT J. ANTONIO
University of Kansas

GEORGE RITZER
University of Maryland

GEORGE RITZER
Consulting Editor

Allyn and Bacon, Inc.
Boston • London • Sydney

Library of Congress Cataloging in Publication Data

Antonio, Robert J   comp.
  Social problems.

  Includes bibliographical references.
    1. Social problems—Addresses, essays, lectures.
2. Social conflict—Addresses, essays, lectures.
3. Social values—Addresses, essays, lectures.
4. United States—Social conditions—Addresses, essays,
lectures. I. Ritzer, George, joint comp. II. Title.
HN60.A58   309.1 '73   74–30023

ISBN 0–205–04713–0

CONTENTS

PREFACE

Most anthologies in social problems provide a diverse selection of articles grouped under a number of divergent topic headings. The topic headings refer to general problem areas while the articles illustrate some of the varied dimensions of the problems. Because of the immense number of social problems and the almost equally large number of approaches to each problem, it is impossible for social problems anthologies to provide complete coverage. Most editors are cognizant that completeness is an impossible ideal and they simply try to provide broad coverage of many problems in as stimulating a fashion as possible. However stimulating, most of these anthologies lack a clear and consistent analytic framework. Because of this students find it difficult to mentally organize the book's diverse factual knowledge and are unable to establish logical connections between the numerous ideas and social criticisms. These problems stem from the fact that the included articles often share only a topical relation. For example, a section on drugs might include an article on methadone treatment, another on the social dimensions of the marijuana experience, still another on middle-class abuse of stimulants and depressants, and finally one on alcoholism on skid-row. Such a presentation provides the student with general descriptive information about social problems, but it does little to generate a coherent sociological perspective.

Some recent anthologies in social problems have adopted a more theoretical stance. A number of these advocate the conflict approach, which assumes that social problems in industrial society are perpetuated by societal divisions and competing interests. Such anthologies usually include a preponderance of articles focusing upon conflict processes in oppressive social relations and in the transcendence of such relations. However, the choice of articles in conflict oriented books often express only the reformist or radical perspective. Although we are not antagonistic to this position, we feel that a conflict oriented anthology should portray social problems as conflict situations. To do so it must include articles that give sympathetic presentations of the positions of the various groups in conflict.

In this anthology an attempt is made to avoid the problems implied above. First, we present in the introductory essay a conflict theory of social problems.

This approach provides structure to the book and logical relation to the articles in each section. The articles in these sections "speak to one another"— that is they constitute debates or controversies about particular social problems. Thus they should be integrated and meaningful units to the student.

This anthology was constructed to promote conceptualization and analysis of social problems as conflicts of values and interests. An attempt was made to go beyond simple presentation of descriptive data about social problems. Instead, we intend it to communicate a way of looking at social problems. The articles present contrasting and sometimes even contradictory analyses. These are supposed to represent different values and interests and sensitize the student to the role of conflict in social problems. At the end of each controversy is a brief section intended to draw out further the conflicting values and interests and their social significance.

It is hoped that this anthology will upset naive conceptions of social problems as objective breakdowns of social order with objective technical solutions. Social problems always concern the "quality of life" or threats to it. Such concerns must always be interpreted in the light of subjective factors, because social problems are never fully technical in nature. Furthermore, the meaning of "quality of life" varies with the location of persons in the various strata of society. For example, possible solutions to the crime problem and even definitions of it vary between social workers, police, urban ghetto dwellers and suburban housewives. Conflicting attitudes reflect the realities of separate, but overlapping worlds. It is only in the context of these conflicts that the nature of social problems and their difficult solutions are understandable.

We would like to thank Susan Raymos for her help in acquiring permissions for the selections. Also we are greatly appreciative to David Dickens for his help in numerous problems and tasks related to the book. Our gratitude is also extended to Carol Pennington who typed much of the manuscript. Finally, we are deeply indebted to Dr. Norman Yetman who did considerable editing, provided superb criticism, and most importantly, offered his friendship and support.

ROBERT J. ANTONIO
GEORGE RITZER

social problems

INTRODUCTORY ESSAY

Social Problems:
A Conflict Approach

Robert J. Antonio

Sociologists tend to treat social problems as objective realities that threaten the social order. The following discussion of the different theories of social problems illustrates the persistence of the *objectivist orientation.* This orientation will be contrasted with the approach that provides the rationale for this book—which characterizes social problems as more subjective phenomena that must be seen in the context of intergroup conflict. The *subjectivist orientation* results in a mode of conceptualizing, analyzing, and resolving social problems that is different in crucial respects from the more traditional objectivist approach.

The study of social problems has been a central concern of sociologists since the establishment of sociology as an independent discipline. Nineteenth century sociologists made serious attempts to investigate the social dislocations and turmoil that accompanied the transformation of the Western world from a rural, agricultural society to an urban, industrial one. Sociology first developed as a science in response to the social problems generated by industrialization, urbanization, and rapid social change. Because of their overwhelming significance for society, analysis pertinent to social problems was frequently included in the sociologist's more general theorizing about the social order.

Initially, sociological thought was dominated by *evolutionary organicism.* Society was portrayed as an organism with mutually dependent parts analogous to the bodily parts of a biological organism. Each part was believed to contribute to the organism's adaptation to environmental conditions. For example, the educational institution was thought to provide the same kind of guidance and intellectual direction to society as the brain supplies to advanced biological organisms. This perspective suggested that biological nature and social nature were similarly structured and, moreover, similarly governed by systematic processes. Evolution was considered the most rudimentary of these processes.

Both biological and social organisms were thought to evolve from the simple to the complex. Biological development was said to begin with simple one-celled organisms and end with man, a highly complex creature possessing highly specialized aggregations of cells. The evolution of the social organism was thought to parallel that of the biological organism. Thus according to the evolutionary organicist position, social evolution begins with small, simply organized primitive societies that have few social roles, institutions, and types of groups. In these primitive societies there is little specialization and everyone carries out similar tasks. Stated simply, this type of social organization lacks complexity. In contrast to the primitive one, industrial society, which was conceived to be the highest product of social evolution, is heterogeneous and complicated. This results from its highly differentiated social roles, vastly specialized labor force, large number of institutions, and many different social groups. Thus early society stands in the same relation to modern society, as primitive organisms do to man.

Early evolutionary sociologists argued that the existence of specific values, rules, and institutions was the result of natural selection. They asserted that social patterns promoting survival of society were maintained, while those that reduced its capacity for survival disappeared. Early sociologists suggested that the industrialization and urbanization of the nineteenth century increased the adaptation of modern society. However, they feared certain trends. They felt that modern man had intervened too often and too extensively in the evolutionary process and his attempts to direct social change were upsetting the natural evolutionary process and resulting in "maladaptive" social forms.

The evolutionary organicists were especially concerned with the possibility that the heightened productive capacity of modern society would increase the chances for survival of the "weaker segments" of the population. They asserted that modern affluence and charity insures the survival of almost everyone, including the "defective" individuals who would have perished in other historical epochs. The evolutionary organicists argued that the increased incidence of crime, mental disorder, civil disobedience, and poverty were empirical evidence that this process was already occurring. Again borrowing from the biological sciences, they conceptualized social problems as *social pathologies*—disorders resembling the diseases and disabilities of biological organisms. They believed that if these problems were to go unchecked, it could eventually result in the destruction of the social organism.

Few nineteenth century sociologists proposed ameliorative programs to eliminate social problems, although many favored more severe punishments for those plagued with the problems. For example, they argued that public welfare to the poor was socially destructive and should be discontinued. They believed that welfare programs allowed the poor to prosper and reproduce even larger numbers of poor people. Evolutionary organicists advocated that instead of being given public welfare benefits, poor people should be required to work to meet their subsistence needs. They implied that people who refused to work or were in other ways defective should be made to suffer deprivation. Furthermore, individuals who used illicit means to acquire necessities would be subject to stiff punitive measures. Early sociologists believed that if man avoided intervening in the evolutionary process and allowed the weak to perish, then social problems would eventually be diminished in number and intensity. The organicists theorized that if evolution were allowed to unfold naturally, destructive social forces would diminish because the groups that cause them would be eliminated through natural selection.

Evolutionary organicism came under heavy criticism in the early twentieth century. Critics argued that societal components cannot be equated with the structural units of a biological organism. They asserted that there is much more interdependence between the units of a real organism than between the parts of a society. *Social evolution* and *social pathology* were discarded as analytic concepts because they resulted in the evaluation of social forms in terms of progress, health, and sickness. Critics asserted that application of these terms led to value-laden interpretations. The sociologists who used them often viewed traditions and institutions consistent with their own values as progressive and healthy, while those conflicting with their values as regressive and pathological.

In the 1920s sociology rapidly gained respectability as a scientific discipline. The extensive work of scholars at the University of Chicago, who became known as the Chicago School of Sociology, was instrumental in promoting the status of sociology. The Chicago School retained the intense interest in the processes of industrialization and urbanization that characterized the earlier evolutionary approach. They focused on the city because they considered it to be the focal point of modern social change. They were actively concerned with the social problems of the city and how they might be eliminated; they not only analyzed how the city was structured, but they attempted to reveal the causes of breakdowns in this structure. In extending their theories, these sociologists utilized the concept of *social organization* to replace social organism and the concept of *social disorganization* to replace social pathology.

The following quotation illustrates how sociologists of the early Chicago School of Sociology conceptualized social organization:

> *Out of the commonality of human experience, man has adopted habits of thinking which he has crystallized into institutions and systems of social control. By common assent the traditions, mores, laws and institutions become the rules in the game of life. Existence takes on an "essential orderliness" and assumes a mechanized and routinized aspect which the average individual seldom questions . . . behavior falls into established grooves.*[1]

This quotation suggests that social organization structures group life so that it takes on a predictable and orderly quality that the individual does not

[1] *Mabel A. Elliot and Frances E. Merrill,* Social Disorganization *(New York: Harper Brothers, 1934), p. 5.*

question. People derive a sense of security from the social agreement or consensus upon which social order is predicated. According to this model, even the stability of the self-concept is dependent upon the social group transmitting to the individual a consistent and orderly conception of the social world.

The approach of the Chicago School suggested that social organization requires a correspondence between individual and group definitions of reality. In short, the individual must learn and conform to group values and rules. When social organization is strong, people seldom experience ambiguity. They know what behavior is expected and proper for a situation and they act accordingly. Groups with a high level of social organization operate more efficiently than groups that are not well-organized. When agreement on and conformity to rules exists, people are able to cooperate in tasks that fulfill both individual and group needs. On the other hand, poorly organized groups have difficulty accomplishing these tasks.

Social disorganization occurs when the actions of individuals are not oriented by group norms and values. The individual experiences ambiguity because his *definition of situation* does not reflect group definitions. In this case the consensus, or agreement, that cements people into viable groups breaks down and results in the disintegration of the orderliness and security of organized society. People no longer know what behaviors to expect from others, and they are unsure of the behaviors others expect from them. When this occurs, cooperative activity diminishes, conflict intensifies, and the very existence of the group may be imperiled. Furthermore, social disorganization generates feelings of uncertainty and fear that are sometimes expressed in self-destructive, maladjusted, or anti-social behaviors. Thus, the early Chicago School believed social disorganization generated personal disorganization. They interpreted the various forms of rule-breaking activity that were increasing in urban areas during this period to be a product of intensifying social disorganization.

The Chicago School equated social problems with social disorganization. Furthermore, they implied that urban life is inherently characterized by social disorganization, for it is in the city that people from different groups come together. In contrast to rural people, urban inhabitants are less likely to share common values and common definitions of their social roles. Because of diverse group affiliations, urban people often have different and sometimes conflicting definitions of appropriate behavior. As a result, according to the Chicago School, urban life is more disorganized and has higher rates of crime, delinquency, addictions, and poverty than rural areas.

The concept of social disorganization came under criticism as had the idea of social pathology that preceded it. Critics asserted that it constituted an anti-urban bias because it supported the contention that the city is doomed to the chaos of social disorganization. Also, sociologists became skeptical of the empirical accuracy of the approach. It was probably William F. Whyte's study of an urban lower-class Italian community in Boston that dealt the most damaging blow to the viability of this model as an analytic tool. Advocates of the social disorganization approach expected a community of this nature to be highly disorganized. However, Whyte's study proved this prediction inaccurate. He showed that the members of this community shared common definitions of situation and acted in accordance with them. Whyte's study suggested that even urban, ethnic communities can be highly organized. However, the rules and values upon which this organization is based differ from those of the middle-class, Anglo-American sociologist; and again, many sociologists who applied the concept of social disorganization judged social conditions and behaviors that conformed to their own values as organized, while labeling those that did not as disorganized. For these reasons and others, sociologists generally concluded that the concept of social disorganization had limited utility in the analysis of social problems.

Functionalism is the dominant theoretical orientation in modern American sociology. Functionalists, like the organicists of the nineteenth century, consider society as consisting of an interdependent set of related units. However, functionalists do not compare society to a biological organism. Instead, they generally assert that the laws governing social life are uniquely social and are not determined by those that govern biological reality. The functionalists view society as a social system of interrelated actors and institutions. The system runs smoothly as long as the actors are bound by consensus to common norms and values.

The social system has certain requirements that have to be fulfilled if it is to be perpetuated. For example, to maintain order the society's rules and values must be transmitted uniformly to all actors. The family is the social unit primarily responsible for this function. The continued existence of the social system depends on the family socializing the child for his eventual adoption of the roles that fulfill various system needs. For example, the system requires a productive network that provides for the material needs of its actors. The family must instill in the child the values and knowledge that enable and motivate him to play a role in this network. It is important to stress the interdependency of the functional units of the social system. The family trains actors for roles in the productive network, which, in turn, provides the material goods that help perpetuate the family. Both institutions promote each other's existence and the existence of the system as a whole.

The functionalists conceptualize social problems as *dysfunctions*. Dysfunction refers to the consequences that result from a behavior, belief, or group activity that interferes with the functional requirements of the social system. For example, actor conformity to system rules is the most basic requirement of all social systems. Widespread or systematic violation of these rules is disruptive and dysfunctional since it serves to undermine the order and consensus that perpetuates the social system. For this reason, action must be taken to control rule-breaking behavior.

From the earliest sociological analysis of social groups to the present, there has been a tendency to conceptualize social problems as "objective" breakdowns of the organization of a society. *Social pathology, social disorganization,* and *dysfunction,* the principal concepts that sociologists have used to analyze social problems, all characterize social problems as breakdowns in social order. For this reason they fail to capture the value and conflict factors that are inherent in social problems.

The style of thought discussed above is not incompatible with the ideas that many laymen express concerning social problems. They often maintain that social problems are recognized, defined, publicized, and acted upon according to the degree of objective threat they pose to society. This position, whether held by laymen or sociologists, implies that people, regardless of their position in society, share a common set of interests. Social problems are the objective conditions that threaten these interests.

However, a number of sociologists have vigorously criticized the theoretical assumptions of the objectivistic approach to social problems. They argue that there is far less consensus in society than this approach suggests. The critics feel that the objectivist model is especially inappropriate for advanced industrial societies, like our own, where heterogeneous groups with divergent interests predominate.

Essays by Waller[2] and Fuller and Myers[3] provided a framework for the subjectivist approach to social problems. They asserted that culturally created values define certain conditions as undesirable. Social problems became the social conditions that conflict with the values of a considerable portion of the members of a group. Thus, according to this approach, social problems appear when there is a gap between the values defining what "should be" and the way things actually are. Social problems are intensified when there is a lack of consensus about their definition and solution, and this often occurs because people from different groups with different values disagree about what "should be." Persistent social problems are unfavorable social conditions perpetuated by conflicting values that prevent concerted action to eliminate them. For example, the lowly socioeconomic position of black Americans is perceived as a social problem because their condition conflicts with the values that most Americans have about equality. However, Americans differ in their ideas of an effective solution to the problem. Some people argue that welfare programs should be cut because they destroy motivation for work. Others assert the need for vastly increased welfare programs. Finally, some people call for a revolution that would eliminate the institutions that oppress blacks. These differences are indicative of the considerable value-conflict that exists with respect to this problem; and this lack of consensus helps prevent the development of effective programs to deal with the problem.

This approach, which became known as the *value-conflict* perspective, suggests that the sociologist perform a practical role in resolving social problems. Its advocates assert that he should isolate and define the conflicting values related to the social problem in question. Furthermore, he should clarify the points of opposition and agreement between the various groups that are concerned about the problematic condition. Finally, the sociologist should be able to suggest to social planners and policymakers the attitude and value changes that would be necessary to bring disagreeing groups into consensus so that conflict could be eliminated and the problem situation resolved.

Kitsuse and Spector[4] assert that presently the field of social problems

2 *Willard Waller, "Social Problems and the Mores,"* American Sociological Review, (*Dec. 1936*) *922–33.*

3 *Richard C. Fuller and Richard R. Myers, "Some Aspects of a Theory of Social Problems,"* American Sociological Review, 6 (*Feb. 1941*), *24–32.*

4 *John I. Kitsuse and Malcolm Spector, "Toward a Sociology of Social Problems: Social Conditions, Value Judgements, and Social Problems,"* Social Problems, *20 (Spring 1973) , 407–19.*

lacks a well defined and distinctive subject matter. They attempt to correct this situation in a revised statement of the subjectivist approach.

> *The central problem for a theory of social problems, so defined, is to account for the* emergence and maintenance of claim-making and responding activities. *Such a theory should comprehend the activities of any group making claims on others for ameliorative action, material remuneration, alleviation of social, political, legal, economic disadvantage or other consideration.*

Instead of stressing value-conflict, Kitsuse and Spector are suggesting that emphasis must focus on the interests and activities of groups that are concerned about social problems. They assert that the very existence of social problems is dependent upon those groups and agencies that stimulate the awareness of certain conditions as social problems and who generate actions to eliminate or ameliorate the problems. Kitsuse and Spector suggest that the unique subject matter that should be the focus of social problems theory is not objective breakdowns of social order, but is instead the way groups create a consciousness or awareness of social problems and the responses this awareness evokes.

I shall refer to the emergent perspective to social problems that is the focus of this essay as the *conflict-of-interests* approach. This characterizes social problems as conditions, situations, or behaviors that conflict with the interests of specific segments of society. These group interests may be material or symbolic objects, conditions or situations that are deemed desirable and rewarding by a group—in other words, all those diverse elements that a group may define as constituting the "good life." Social conditions that interfere with attempts by group members to acquire or maintain these goods are likely to be considered social problems.

The conflict-of-interests approach has its origins in Karl Marx's theory of law. Marx suggested that the rich and powerful have the most influence in creating law, and they do so in such a way that the law perpetuates their advantaged social position. Howard Becker,[5] in less radical terms, argues the same point. He says, "Rules are the products of someone's initiative and we can think of the people who exhibit such enterprise as *moral entrepreneurs.*" He suggests that rules do not originate from the will of *all* the people, but from the action of individuals and groups who desire their creation and enforcement, and have power to implement them. Richard Quinney[6] states this position most clearly when he asserts that law is a product of conflict oriented social relations: "*Criminal definitions describe behaviors that conflict with the interests of the segments of society that have the power to shape public policy.*"

This approach is easily extended to the analysis of social problems, in general. Laws, rules, and sanctions can be viewed as the most formal means a group has of dealing with social conditions or potential social conditions that threaten its interests. However, these social conditions must be considered problematic before a group bothers to initiate the formal procedures of

[5] *Howard Becker,* Outsiders (*New York: Free Press, 1963*) , *p. 147.*
[6] *Richard Quinney,* The Social Reality of Crime (*Boston: Little, Brown and Company, 1970*) , *p. 16.*

establishing rules or laws. In other words, the definition of social problems precedes the formulation of rules; interests affect the awareness of social problems in the same way that they are said to affect the devising of rules and laws.

Social problems should be analyzed as conflicts-of-interest. This means that the definitions of certain phenomena as social problems are not the product of the society acting as a whole recognizing a common threat but are instead the result of enterprising groups actively promoting the definitions that reflect their own interests. These groups call on everyone in the society to support programs to alter or eliminate a given social condition. *Social problems are conditions that are defined negatively by certain interest groups who have convinced, or are trying to convince, a significant number of people in the society or community that the conditions should be changed in order to improve the group's quality of life and insure its well-being.* As this definition suggests, to actually stimulate extensive attempts to bring change, the active interest group must gain considerable agreement among other groups that the condition to be changed is in fact a social problem. The ability to do this depends on how well the active interest group communicates its position to the rest of society. This ability is, in turn, conditioned by the degree of power the group has, its proximity to the political structure of the society, and its affect on the media.

Social problems are defined by groups acting on the basis of their interests. Modern industrial society is comprised of many different groups with diverse, and often conflicting, sets of interests. It is understandable, then, why there is such a high level of disagreement about social problems in American society. For instance, the New York City banker is likely to see social problems in a way that is radically different from an impoverished Indian in New Mexico. Even if they agree on the definition of a social problem, they are likely to disagree about the possible solutions. For example, both the banker and the Indian might agree that poverty is an important social problem. However, the banker may consider poverty to be the result of the poor person's lack of skills or his laziness. He might suggest as a solution to the problem the development of new educational programs that train the poor in basic work skills and in the values of work. On the other hand, the Indian might argue that poverty is brought about by exploitation and discrimination. He might insist on the need for massive aid programs and guaranteed jobs for the poor. In both cases their proposals reflect the interests of their respective groups.

Disagreements over the definitions of, and solutions to, social problems also derive from the fact that in many cases one group defines certain aspects of another group's life-style as a social problem. For example, the heterosexual members of a society may define the sexual practices of the homosexual members of the society as undesirable. In this case, what is undesirable to one group is a central focus of life for another group. In this kind of disagreement, the following applies, "He who has the bigger stick has the better chance of imposing his definitions of reality."[7] In other words, many social problems are defined by the wealthy and powerful groups who call

---

[7] *Peter L. Berger and Thomas Luckmann,* The Social Construction of Reality *(New York: Anchor Books, 1967)* , *p. 109.*

for changes in groups that are in a less advantageous social position.

This approach does not define social problems as breakdowns in social organization. In fact it suggests that social problems can be created by an efficiently functioning social organization. For example, some social critics argue that poverty is a structural necessity in a capitalist society—an inherent product of the normal functioning of this type of economic structure. According to this view, the elimination of poverty requires dismantling the economic structure rather than repairing it. This approach also points out that serious threats to social organization may at some times not be considered social problems at all. Groups that are most aware of these threats may have an interest in preventing their exposure. For example, the management of an industry might be very aware of the environmental implications of pouring tons of pollutants into the water and air. They might even be cognizant of the fact that this pollution could destroy humanity. However, their concern for maintenance of their profit margin might outweigh their concern for the environment. In this case, the industry might even struggle against opposing interest groups that consider the environment as their first priority. There may even be some conscious attempts to withhold pertinent information from the public about pollution.

It should be recognized that having something defined as a social problem and acting to eliminate it sometimes results in counterproductive consequences. The attempt to change negatively defined social conditions could have destructive implications. To illustrate this point, let us consider the case of the prohibition of alcohol in the 1920s. Prohibition did little to alleviate the national drinking problem, but it did help stimulate the development of organized crime. It is generally accepted that prohibition did more to intensify social dislocations than to resolve them. Today many sociologists argue that making heroin illegal for addicts creates problems that are more dangerous than heroin use itself. They assert that the prohibition has stimulated the growth of a viable illicit trade that makes the drug available, but at very high prices. This drives addicts into secondary crime to support their habits. Some critics believe that urban property crimes in some areas could be reduced by as much as 80 percent, if the heroin were made available to addicts cheaply and legally.

Finally, it should be stressed that programs designed to deal with social problems reflect group interests and are often the source of conflict. Definition of a social problem always implies that certain conditions should be transformed to insure or to improve social welfare. However, significant social change threatens some interest groups because it almost always upsets, to some degree, the existing distribution of power and wealth. For example, many people consider the state of poverty as a most pressing social problem and demand higher levels of welfare for the poor. However, there are numerous groups that feel that the resulting tax burdens would directly contradict their interests. Thus, attempts to raise welfare levels results in debate and conflict between opposing groups. If one accepts this orientation towards social problems, then the great dissensus over the definition of, and solution for, contemporary social problems is understandable. Social problems by definition become conflict situations between groups located in the different strata of society.

Having presented the conflict-of-interests approach, what kind of analysis is it likely to generate? How would its application differ from the more traditional, objectivistic modes of analysis? The sociologist's traditional role has been to provide reliable information about social problems and how they might be alleviated. He is supposed to collect and organize this information so that it can be made available to the public and to policy-makers for possible use in the formulation of programs to diminish social breakdown. The sociologist also makes recommendations for or provides criticism of specific ameliorative programs.

Advocates of the traditional role often assert that the sociologist should be neutral or "value-free" in his study of social problems. However, if he accepts popular definitions of social problems and acts in accordance with these definitions, the sociologist does not remain value-free. Instead, he becomes aligned with those who possess sufficient power to have these issues defined as social problems. I am not suggesting that the traditional sociologist consciously plots with powerful groups to maintain the established order. I am stating simply that the sociologist who sets out to collect data about social problems without questioning their definition makes himself vulnerable to becoming the unwitting advocate of narrowly defined interests.

In *Blaming the Victim*,[8] William Ryan points out that studies of social problems are often biased in favor of the interests of the powerful and the rich. He suggests that sociological analysis tends to focus on the victims of social problems rather than the victimizers. For example, Ryan asserts that the poverty of black Americans, a popular topic of sociological inquiry, has been explained in terms of a variety of different characteristics of the black population—illegitimacy, matriarchy, culture of poverty, and cultural deprivation. Ryan argues that such interpretations beg the question by focusing on the *effects* of poverty rather than the *causes*. Furthermore, they isolate the problem in the impoverished black population, while tending to ignore the exploitation of a white dominated economy and white racism. Studies of this nature support social policy oriented to changing the victim rather than one that copes with the agents of victimization. They have provided intellectual legitimization for the many programs instituted to change the values or life-style of blacks rather than being an impetus for basic institutional change.

Ryan[9] states that "Every important social problem—crime, mental illness, civil disorder, unemployment—has been analyzed within the framework of the victim—blaming ideology." He characterizes this analysis as ideological because he believes it helps perpetuate the interests of society's dominant groups by transforming social problems into victim problems and therefore precluding any possible disturbance of the status quo.

How does the sociologist avoid the ideological abuses that Ryan asserts occur frequently? There is no way of assuring that one's analysis of a social problem will be ideologically pure and absolutely impartial. On the other hand, the sociologist can avoid the worst abuses of this nature by expressing a healthy scepticism towards popular definitions of social problems. This means

8 *William Ryan*, Blaming the Victim *(New York: Vantage, 1971)* .
9 *Ibid., p. 6.*

that he should not be limited merely to an information-gathering role,
but should be actively engaged in questioning those definitions. The
conflict-of-interests approach is structured to generate this sceptical
perspective; social problems would be viewed as conflict situations rather
than as "objective" breakdowns of social order. Therefore, it becomes
necessary to question all perspectives toward the problem. Study would then
be directed toward discovery of how the social condition was initially defined
as a social problem, the relevant interests of the different groups effected
by the problem, the agreements and conflicts between these groups, and the
relative merits of policy proposed by the groups. Carried out properly, this
analysis would prevent naive acceptance of the popular conceptions of a
social problem.

Those using the conflict-of-interests approach to study black poverty
would not simply adopt the dominant group definition of a "Negro problem"
and search for characteristics of the black population that bring it about.
Instead, he would consider this definition as one perspective generated by a
particular set of interests. The sociologist would be equally concerned with
the black person's perception of a "white problem" generated by white
institutions. Furthermore, the role of various group interests might also be
considered. For example, government agencies, community agencies, and
charitable organizations might represent different sets of relevant interests,
definitions, and policies. The object of investigation would be to expose
the clashing interest groups concerned with black poverty, and also determine
how policy formulated to deal with this problem relates to these diverse
interests.

A case is not being made for extreme neutrality on the part of the
sociologist. Sociologists cannot disassociate themselves from the social groups
they belong to and therefore cannot be free of interests and values, which
will likely color their perceptions of the various positions toward a social
problem. However, in my opinion, it is advisable for the sociologist to try
according to the best of his ability to make himself, and others whom he
might advise, cognizant of his values and the interests they reflect.

Earlier I stated that the purpose of this essay is to explicate the perspective
that provides the organizing framework of this book. How then, does this
conflict-of-interests approach relate to the diverse collection of articles
presented here? The articles that comprise each section represent different
and often conflicting positions towards a specific social problem. These
controversies are intended to express the clashing interests related to each
issue. For example, in the section on crime, Inbau and Carrington present
the argument that crime is a most serious social problem that should be
dealt with by tougher police measures and more stringent correctional
programs. In other words, they suggest that we must simply incarcerate
more lawbreakers. Zeisel and Clark, in their articles, also consider crime
an important social problem, but they both assert that the "get tougher"
policies of Inbau and Carrington will do little to reduce crime. Instead, they
believe that liberal social reform and improvement of prison conditions
are the best methods of coping with the problem. Finally, David M. Gordon
suggests that the basic structure of America's social and economic institutions
are the major problem, while most crime is only an acquisitive behavior

generated by these institutions. He calls for the complete transformation of the institutional structure of capitalist society.

These articles express conservative, liberal, and radical positions toward criminal behavior and reflect interests located in different strata of society. They raise questions not only about crime but also about protection of life and property, rights of the accused, treatment of the convicted, reform, and even social revolution.

The student using this book should be sensitized to three factors. First, all of the articles are intended to impart important factual material about the respective social problems. However, authors tend to provide only that data supporting their position. This problem is somewhat diminished by the fact that articles representing different perspectives towards each problem are presented. To derive maximum benefit from them, the student is urged to withhold judgment until each of the articles in an entire section is thoroughly considered. Second, it is important to point out that the specific interests reflected in the various controversies are not always easily apparent. Authors are often unwilling to present themselves as representatives of specific interest groups. For example, advocates of some positions characterize themselves as objective, disinterested observers. Some authors who claim to be "value free" are really partisans trying to give their arguments the force and legitimacy that neutrality provides. Other individuals may truly believe that they are impartial but are oblivious to the fact that they are representatives of a certain position and a particular interest. Finally, others may not be directly associated with particular groups, but still present positions supportive of their interests. But the problem of the precise interests represented is not a major one, for the goal of this book is not to define precisely for the student all the diverse interests related to each issue. This would have been an impossible task for a book of this nature. Instead, an attempt is made to present the student with information about social problems from a diverse set of perspectives, with the hope that it will result in his perceiving social problems as conflict issues while also leading him to reflect upon the diverse interests that generate in these conflicts. A third and final qualification is that the articles presented were not originally written for inclusion in this book. Thus, it is not the fault of the contributors if the approaches to the issues are not always completely parallel or all-inclusive.

1

Social Problems and Individual Deviance

1

MENTAL DISORDER:

Illness or Social Stigma?

Today mental disorder is conceptualized as a medical problem. It is usually considered a disease and the affected person is said to be ill. The mentally ill person is viewed as the victim of an internal breakdown, or psychological dysfunctioning, that is expressed in observable symptoms. These symptoms are manifested in the person's cognitive life, emotional condition and social behavior. Like those with other diseases, the mentally ill are given specialized treatment (e.g. hospitalization, psychotherapy, drugs, electroshock) by licensed medical practitioners.

Widespread medical treatment of the mentally disordered is a rather recent historical development appearing only in the past hundred years. Since its advent, there have been a rapidly increasing number of mental health personnel, a vast increase in the number of mental hospitals, and an ever-growing number of behaviors that are considered symptomatic of mental illness. Most people accept the idea that medical treatment of the mentally disordered marks a vast improvement over earlier times when the "mad" were not given any treatment at all, or even worse, when they were punished as evil people. However, in recent years the medical definition of mental disorder has been challenged. Critics argue that medical treatment does little to help the troubled person and often even contributes to his problems. Moreover, the critics assert that the real goal of the therapist is not treatment, but merely control of the person's rule-breaking acts.

Mental disorder is a social problem of major proportions. More than two million Americans have, at some time, supposedly suffered from the severest form of mental disorder—schizophrenia. If we accept the definition of mental illness, and consider it in all its forms, it is probably the most common and costly disease in contemporary society. We have no accurate measure for determining the extent of mental disorder in America. However, some investigators have argued that up to 50 percent of our population have at least mild psychological impairments.

The first article in this section is one of the classic statements against the growing mental health establishment. Thomas Szasz is a passionate advocate of patient's rights and a bitter critic of involuntary treatment and involuntary commitment procedures. He argues that there is no such condition as mental illness. Szasz asserts, instead, that mental illness is a label applied to people who express unacceptable ideas in an unusual idiom. This is not to say that the mentally disordered are free of problems. They have problems, but these are social and ethical rather than medical. Szasz believes that attempts to resolve such problems by medical means are fruitless. Instead, they must be resolved by treatment that is appropriate to their social and ethical nature. Furthermore, he suggests that the very concept of mental illness indicates a tendency of the modern world to avoid facing human conflict realistically and on its own terms. Szasz also feels that the medical model of social behavior promotes a growing unwillingness to accept responsibility for our own actions.

In the second article, David Ausubel criticizes Szasz's position. Ausubel asserts that mental disorder is a disease that requires medical treatment. He admits that symptoms are expressed in social behavior, but he feels these to be manifestations of the internal disease. Ausubel believes that the mentally ill are precisely those people who cannot cope with socially and ethically defined problems of life. He feels psychiatric treatment is helpful to such individuals. Ausubel asserts that if we heed Szasz's advice and cast out the concept of mental illness, and cease treatment based upon it, the care of the mentally disordered will be set back 2,500 years. He feels that the mentally disordered would once again be treated as evil. Ausubel implies that this would result in a less scientific and dehumanized form of treatment for the insane.

In his paper, James S. Gordon discusses both traditional psychiatry and its radical alternative as expressed in the theory and practice of R. D. Laing. Laing conceptualizes mental disorder as a distorted reflection of the pervasive social and political madness of modern society. According to Laing, mental disorder is a reaction to the poverty and alienation of normalcy. He suggests that breakdown can result in liberation from the stultifying effects of conformity. Laing sees psychiatry as a miserable failure because it seeks to return people to conformity and normal alienation, rather than seeking health and growth. Gordon effectively relates how Laing's theory has been put into practice. He discusses his visit to Kingsley Hall, a treatment center run by Laing and his colleagues. Gordon indicates that an existential and social alternative to traditional medical treatment of mental disorder is a desirable and realizable possibility.

In the last article of this section David Rosenhan raises important questions about the definitions of sanity and madness. In his study, eight sane people or pseudopatients gained admission to twelve mental hospitals. Each of these individuals went to the admissions office complaining that they heard voices that said "empty," "hollow," or "thud." They gave false names and vocations, but they accurately described their experiences, feelings, and interpersonal relationships. All of these persons were admitted to the hospitals and all were diagnosed as being severely mentally ill. Once in the hospital they acted normally and asserted that they no longer heard voices. The pseudopatients were not discovered by the hospital staffs. In fact, after stays that ranged from seven to fifty-two days, all but one patient was diagnosed as having schizophrenia in remission.

Rosenhan discusses another part of the experiment where he warned the staff of a hospital that he would try to get one pseudopatient or more admitted to it. After a period of three months, in which 193 new patients were admitted, the staff was asked to determine who the pseudopatients were. Forty-one patients were alleged, with high confidence, to be pseudopatients by at least one member of the staff. One psychiatrist suspected twenty-three pseudopatients. Rosenhan's findings bring into question the accuracy of psychiatric diagnoses and should lead to even graver questions about the nature of forced treatment and involuntary commitment procedures.

The Myth of Mental Illness

THOMAS S. SZASZ

My aim in this essay is to raise the question "Is there such a thing as mental illness?" and to argue that there is not. Since the notion of mental illness is extremely widely used nowadays, inquiry into the ways in which this term is employed would seem to be especially indicated. Mental illness, of course, is not literally a "thing"—or physical object —and hence it can "exist" only in the same sort of way in which other theoretical concepts exist. Yet, familiar theories are in the habit of posing, sooner or later—at least to those who come to believe in them—as "objective truths" (or "facts"). During certain historical periods, explanatory conceptions such as deities, witches, and microorganisms appeared not only as theories but as self-eviden *causes* of a vast number of events. I submit that today mental illness is widely regarded in a somewhat similar fashion, that is, as the cause of innumerable diverse happenings. As an antidote to the complacent use of the notion of mental illness—whether as a self-evident phenomenon, theory, or cause—let us ask this question: What is meant when it is asserted that someone is mentally ill?

Note: Thomas S. Szasz, "The Myth of Mental Illness," *American Psychologist*, Vol. 15, 1960, pp. 113–118. Copyright 1960 by the American Psychological Association, and reproduced by permission.

In what follows I shall describe briefly the main uses to which the concept of mental illness has been put. I shall argue that this notion has outlived whatever usefulness it might have had and that it now functions merely as a convenient myth.

MENTAL ILLNESS AS A SIGN OF BRAIN DISEASE

The notion of mental illness derives its main support from such phenomena as syphilis of the brain or delirious conditions— intoxications, for instance—in which persons are known to manifest various peculiarities or disorders of thinking and behavior. Correctly speaking, however, these are diseases of the brain, not of the mind. According to one school of thought, *all* so-called mental illness is of this type. The assumption is made that some neurological defect, perhaps a very subtle one, will ultimately be found for all the disorders of thinking and behavior. Many contemporary psychiatrists, physicians, and other scientists hold this view. This position implies that people *cannot* have troubles— expressed in what are *now called* "mental illnesses"—because of differences in personal needs, opinions, social aspirations, values, and so on. *All problems in living* are attributed to physicochemical processes which in due time will be discovered by medical research.

"Mental illnesses" are thus regarded as basically no different than all other diseases (that is, of the body). The only difference, in this view, between mental and bodily diseases is that the former, affecting the brain, manifest themselves by means of mental symptoms; whereas the latter, affecting other organ systems (for example, the skin, liver, etc.), manifest themselves by means of symptoms referable to those parts of the body. This view rests on and expresses what are, in my opinion, two fundamental errors.

In the first place, what central nervous system symptoms would correspond to a skin eruption or a fracture? It would *not* be some emotion or complex bit of behavior. Rather, it would be blindness or a paralysis of some part of the body. The crux of the matter is that a disease of the brain, analogous to a disease of the skin or bone, is a neurological defect, and not a problem in living. For example, a *defect* in a person's visual field may be satisfactorily explained by correlating it with certain definite lesions in the nervous system. On the other hand, a person's *belief* —whether this be a belief in Christianity, in Communism, or in the idea that his internal organs are "rotting" and that his body is, in fact, already "dead"—cannot be explained by a defect or disease of the nervous system. Explanations of this sort of occurrence—assuming that one is interested in the belief itself and does not regard it simply as a "symptom" or expression of something else that it *more interesting*—must be sought along different lines.

The second error in regarding complex psychosocial behavior, consisting of communications about ourselves and the world about us, as mere sypmtoms of neurological functioning is *epistemological*. In other words, it is an error pertaining not to any mistakes in observation or reasoning, as such, but rather to the way in which we organize and express our knowledge. In the present case,

the error lies in making a symmetrical dualism between mental and physical (or bodily) symptoms, a dualism which is merely a habit of speech and to which no known observations can be found to correspond. Let us see if this is so. In medical practice, when we speak of physical disturbances, we mean either signs (for example, a fever) or symptoms (for example, pain). We speak of mental symptoms, on the other hand, when we refer to a patient's *communications about himself, others, and the world about him.* He might state that he is Napoleon or that he is being persecuted by the Communists. These would be considered mental symptoms *only* if the observer believed that patient was *not* Napoleon or that he was *not* being persecuted by the Communists. This makes it apparent that the statement that "X is a mental symptom" involves rendering a judgment. The judgment entails, moreover, a covert comparison or matching of the patient's ideas, concepts, or beliefs with those of the observer and the society in which they live. The notion of mental symptom is therefore inextricably tied to the *social* (including *ethical*) *context* in which it is made in much the same way as the notion of bodily symptom is tied to an *anatomical* and *genetic context* (Szasz, 1957a, 1957b).

To sum up what has been said thus far: I have tried to show that for those who regard mental symptoms as signs of brain disease, the concept of mental illness is unnecessary and misleading. For what they mean is that people so labeled suffer from diseases of the brain; and, if that is what they mean, it would seem better for the sake of clarity to say that and not something else.

MENTAL ILLNESS AS A NAME FOR PROBLEMS IN LIVING

The term "mental illness" is widely used to describe something which is very different than a disease of the brain. Many people today take it for granted that living is an arduous process. Its hardship for modern man, moreover, derives not so much from a struggle for biological survival as from the stresses and strains inherent in the social intercourse of complex human personalities. In this context, the notion of mental illness is used to identify or describe some feature of an individual's so-called personality. Mental illness—as a deformity of the personality, so to speak—is then regarded as the *cause* of the human disharmony. It is implicit in this view that social intercourse between people is regarded as something *inherently harmonious,* its disturbance being due solely to the presence of "mental illness" in many people. This is obviously fallacious reasoning, for it makes the abstraction "mental illness" into a *cause,* even though this abstraction was created in the first place to serve only as a shorthand expression for certain types of human behavior. It now becomes necessary to ask: "What kinds of behavior are regarded as indicative of mental illness, and by whom?"

The concept of illness, whether bodily or mental, implies *deviation from some clearly defined norm.* In the case of physical illness, the norm is the structural and functional integrity of the human body. Thus, although the desirability of physical health, as such, is an ethical value, what health *is* can be stated in anatomical and physiological terms. What is the norm, deviation from which is regarded as mental illness? This question cannot be easily answered. But whatever this norm might be, we can be certain of only one thing: namely, that it is a norm that must be stated in terms of *psychosocial, ethical,* and *legal* concepts. For example, notions such as "excessive repression" or "acting out an unconscious impulse" illustrate the use of psychological concepts for judging (so-called) mental health and illness. The idea that chronic hostility, vengefulness, or divorce are indicative of mental illness would be illustrations of the use of ethical norms (that is, the desirability of love, kindness, and a stable marriage relationship). Finally,

the widespread psychiatric opinion that only a mentally ill person would commit homicide illustrates the use of a legal concept as a norm of mental health. The norm from which deviation is measured whenever one speaks of a mental illness is a *psychosocial and ethical one.* Yet, the remedy is sought in terms of *medical* measures which—it is hoped and assumed—are free from wide differences of ethical value. The definition of the disorder and the terms in which its remedy are sought are therefore at serious odds with one another. The practical significance of this covert conflict between the alleged nature of the defect and the remedy can hardly be exaggerated.

Having identified the norms used to measure deviations in cases of mental illness, we will now turn to the question: "Who defines the norms and hence the deviation?" Two basic answers may be offered: (*a*) It may be the person himself (that is, the patient) who decides that he deviates from a norm. For example, an artist may believe that he suffers from a work inhibition; and he may implement this conclusion by seeking help *for* himself from a psychotherapist. (*b*) It may be someone other than the patient who decides that the latter is deviant (for example, relatives, physicians, legal authorities, society generally, etc.). In such a case a psychiatrist may be hired by others to do something *to* the patient in order to correct the deviation.

These considerations underscore the importance of asking the question "Whose agent is the psychiatrist?" and of giving a candid answer to it (Szasz, 1956, 1958). The psychiatrist (psychologist or nonmedical psychotherapist), it now develops, may be the agent of the patient, of the relatives, of the school, of the military services, of a business organization, of a court of law, and so forth. In speaking of the psychiatrist as the agent of these persons or organizations, it is not implied that his values concerning norms, or his ideas and aims concerning the proper nature of remedial action, need to coincide exactly with those of his employer. For example, a patient in individual psychotherapy may believe that his salvation lies in a new marriage; his psychotherapist need not share this hypothesis. As the patient's agent, however, he must abstain from bringing social or legal force to bear on the patient which would prevent him from putting his beliefs into action. If his *contract* is with the patient, the psychiatrist (psychotherapist) may disagree with him or stop his treatment; but he cannot engage others to obstruct the patient's aspirations. Similarly, if a psychiatrist is engaged by a court to determine the sanity of a criminal, he need not fully share the legal authorities' values and intentions in regard to the criminal and the means available for dealing with him. But the psychiatrist is expressly barred from stating, for example, that it is not the criminal who is "insane" but the men who wrote the law on the basis of which the very actions that are being judged are regarded as "criminal." Such an opinion could be voiced, of course, but not in a courtroom, and not by a psychiatrist who makes it his practice to assist the court in performing its daily work.

To recapitulate: In actual contemporary social usage, the finding of a mental illness is made by establishing a deviance in behavior from certain psychosocial, ethical, or legal norms. The judgment may be made, as in medicine, by the patient, the physician (psychiatrist), or others. Remedial action, finally, tends to be sought in a therapeutic— or covertly medical—framework, thus creating a situation in which *psychosocial, ethical,* and/or *legal deviations* are claimed to be correctable by (so-called) *medical action.* Since medical action is designed to correct only medical deviations, it seems logically absurd to expect that it will help solve problems whose very existence had been defined and established on nonmedical grounds. I think that these considerations may be fruitfully applied to the present use of tranquilizers and, more generally, to what might be expected of drugs of whatever type in regard to the amelioration or solution of problems in human living.

THE ROLE OF ETHICS IN PSYCHIATRY

Anything that people *do*—in contrast to things that *happen* to them (Peters, 1958) — takes place in a context of value. In this broad sense, no human activity is devoid of ethical implications. When the values underlying certain activities are widely shared, those who participate in their pursuit may lose sight of them altogether. The discipline of medicine, both as a pure science (for example, research) and as a technology (for example, therapy), contains many ethical considerations and judgments. Unfortunately, these are often denied, minimized, or merely kept out of focus; for the ideal of the medical profession as well as of the people whom it serves seems to be having a system of medicine (allegedly) free of ethical value. This sentimental notion is expressed by such things as the doctor's willingness to treat and help patients irrespective of their religious or political beliefs, whether they are rich or poor, etc. While there may be some grounds for this belief—albeit it is a view that is not impressively true even in these regards—the fact remains that ethical considerations encompass a vast range of human affairs. By making the practice of medicine neutral, in regard to some specific issues of value, need not, and cannot, mean that it can be kept free from all such values. The practice of medicine is intimately tied to ethics; and the first thing that we must do, it seems to me, is to try to make this clear and explicit. I shall let this matter rest here, for it does not concern us specifically in this essay. Lest there be any vagueness, however, about how or where ethics and medicine meet, let me remind the reader of such issues as birth control, abortion, suicide, and euthanasia as only a few of the major areas of current ethicomedical controversy.

Psychiatry, I submit, is very much more intimately tied to problems of ethics than is medicine. I use the word "psychiatry" here to refer to that contemporary discipline which is concerned with *problems in living* (and not with diseases of the brain, which are problems for neurology). Problems in human relations can be analyzed, interpreted, and given meaning only within given social and ethical contexts. Accordingly, it *does* make a difference—arguments to the contrary notwithstanding—what the psychiatrist's socioethical orientations happen to be; for these will influence his ideas on what is wrong with the patient, what deserves comment or interpretation, in what possible directions change might be desirable, and so forth. Even in medicine proper, these factors play a role, as for instance, in the divergent orientations which physicians, depending on their religious affiliations, have toward such things as birth control and therapeutic abortion. Can anyone really believe that a psychotherapist's ideas concerning religious belief, slavery, or other similar issues play no role in his practical work? If they do make a difference, what are we to infer from it? Does it not seem reasonable that we ought to have different psychiatric therapies—each expressly recognized for the ethical positions which they embody—for, say, Catholics and Jews, religious persons and agnostics, democrats and communists, white supremacists and Negroes, and so on? Indeed, if we look at how psychiatry is actually practiced today (especially in the United States), we find that people do seek psychiatric help in accordance with their social status and ethical beliefs (Hollingshead & Redlich, 1958). This should really not surprise us more than being told that practicing Catholics rarely frequent birth control clinics.

The foregoing position which holds that contemporary psychotherapists deal with problems in living, rather than with mental illnesses and their cures, stands in opposition to a currently prevalent claim, according to which mental illness is just as "real" and "objective" as bodily illness. This is a confusing claim since it is never known exactly what is meant by such words as "real" and "objective." I suspect, however, that what is intended by the proponents of this view is to create the idea in the popular mind that mental illness is some sort of disease entity, like an infection or a malignancy. If this were true, one could *catch* or *get* a "mental illness," one might *have* or *harbor* it, one might *transmit* it to others, and finally one could get *rid* of it. In my opinion, there is not a shred of evidence to support this idea. To the contrary, all the evidence is the other way and supports the view that what people now call mental illnesses are for the most part *communications* expressing unacceptable ideas, often framed, moreover, in an unusual idiom. The scope of this essay allows me to do no more than mention this alternative theoretical approach to this problem (Szasz, 1957c).

This is not the place to consider in detail the similarities and differences between bodily and mental illnesses. It shall suffice for us here to emphasize only one important difference between them: namely, that whereas bodily disease refers to public, physicochemical occurrences, the notion of mental illness is used to codify relatively more private, sociopsychological happenings of which the observer (diagnostician) forms a part. In other words, the psychiatrist does not stand *apart* from what he observes, but is, in Harry Stack Sullivan's apt words, a "participant observer." This means that he is *committed* to some picture of what he considers reality—and to what he thinks society considers reality—and he observes and judges the patient's behavior in the light of these considerations. This touches on our earlier observation that the notion of mental symptom itself implies a comparison between observer and observed, psychiatrist and patient. This is so obvious that I may be charged with belaboring trivialities. Let me therefore say once more that my aim in presenting this argument was expressly to criticize and counter a prevailing contemporary tendency to deny the moral aspects of psychiatry (and psychotherapy) and to substitute for them allegedly value-free medical considerations. Psychotherapy, for example, is being widely practiced as though it entailed nothing other than restoring the patient from a state of mental sickness to one of mental health. While it is generally accepted that mental illness has something to do with man's social (or interpersonal) relations, it is paradoxically maintained that problems of values (that is, of ethics) do not arise in this process.[1] Yet, in one sense, much of psychotherapy may revolve around nothing other than the elucidation and weighing of goals and values—many of which may be mutually contradictory—and the means whereby they might best be harmonized, realized, or relinquished.

The diversity of human values and the methods by means of which they may be realized is so vast, and many of them remain so unacknowledged, that they cannot fail but lead to conflicts in human relations. Indeed, to say that human relations at all levels—from mother to child, through husband and wife, to nation and nation—are fraught with stress, strain, and disharmony is, once again, making the obvious explicit. Yet, what may be obvious may be also poorly understood. This I think is the case here. For it seems to me that—at least in our scientific theories of behavior—we have failed to *accept* the simple fact that human relations are inherently fraught with difficulties and that to make them even relatively harmonious requires much patience and hard work. I submit that the idea of mental illness is now being put to work to obscure certain difficulties which at present may be inherent—not that they need be unmodifiable—in the social intercourse of persons. If this is true, the concept functions as a disguise; for instead of calling attention to conflicting human needs, aspirations, and values, the notion of mental illness

[1] Freud went so far as to say that: "I consider ethics to be taken for granted. Actually I have never done a mean thing" (Jones, 1957, p. 247). This surely is a strange thing to say for someone who has studied man as a social being as closely as did Freud. I mention it here to show how the notion of "illness" (in the case of psychoanalysis, "psychopathology," or "mental illness") was used by Freud—and by most of his followers—as a means for classifying certain forms of human behavior as falling within the scope of medicine, and hence (by *fiat*) outside that of ethics!

provides an amoral and impersonal "thing" (an "illness") as an explanation for *problems in living* (Szasz, 1959). We may recall in this connection that not so long ago it was devils and witches who were held responsible for men's problems in social living. The belief in mental illness, as something other than man's trouble in getting along with his fellow man, is the proper heir to the belief in demonology and witchcraft. Mental illness exists or is "real" in exactly the same sense in which witches existed or were "real."

CHOICE, RESPONSIBILITY, AND PSYCHIATRY

While I have argued that mental illnesses do not exist, I obviously did not imply that the social and psychological occurrences to which this label is currently being attached also do not exist. Like the personal and social troubles which people had in the Middle Ages, they are real enough. It is the labels we give them that concerns us and, having labelled them, what we do about them. While I cannot go into the ramified implications of this problem here, it is worth noting that a demonologic conception of problems in living gave rise to therapy along theological lines. Today, a belief in mental illness implies—nay, requires—therapy along medical or psychotherapeutic lines.

What is implied in the line of thought set forth here is something quite different. I do not intend to offer a new conception of "psychiatric illness" nor a new form of "therapy." My aim is more modest and yet also more ambitious. It is to suggest that the phenomena now called mental illnesses be looked at afresh and more simply, that they be removed from the category of illnesses, and that they be regarded as the expressions of man's struggle with the problem of *how* he should live. The last mentioned problem is obviously a vast one, its enormity reflecting not only man's inability to cope with his environment, but even more his increasing self-reflectiveness.

By problems in living, then, I refer to that truly explosive chain reaction which began with man's fall from divine grace by partaking of the fruit of the tree of knowledge. Man's awareness of himself and of the world about him seems to be a steadily expanding one, bringing in its wake an ever larger *burden of understanding* (an expression borrowed from Susanne Langer, 1953). *This burden*, then, *is to be expected and must not be misinterpreted.* Our only *rational* means for lightening it is *more understanding*, and appropriate *action* based on such understanding. The main alternative lies in acting as though the burden were not what in fact we perceive it to be and taking refuge in an outmoded theological view of man. In the latter view, man does not fashion his life and much of his world about him, but merely lives out his fate in a world created by superior beings. This may logically lead to pleading nonresponsibility in the face of seemingly unfathomable problems and difficulties. Yet, if man fails to take increasing responsibility for his actions, individually as well as collectively, it seems unlikely that some higher power or being would assume this task and carry this burden for him. Moreover, this seems hardly the proper time in human history for obscuring the issue of man's responsibility for his actions by hiding it behind the skirt of an all-explaining conception of mental illness.

CONCLUSIONS

I have tried to show that the notion of mental illness has outlived whatever usefulness it might have had and that it now functions merely as a convenient myth. As such, it is a true heir to religious myths in general, and to the belief in witchcraft in particular; the role of all these belief-systems was to act as *social tranquilizers*, thus encouraging the hope that mastery of certain specific problems may be achieved by means of substitutive (symbolic-magical) operations. The notion of mental illness thus serves mainly to obscure the everyday fact that life for most people is a continuous struggle, not for biological survival, but for a "place in the sun," "peace of mind," or some other human value. For man aware of himself and of the world about him, once the needs for preserving the body (and perhaps the race) are more or less satisfied, the problem arises as to what he should do with himself. Sustained adherence to the myth of mental illness allows people to avoid facing this problem, believing that mental health, conceived as the absence of mental illness, automatically insures the making of right and safe choices in one's conduct of life. But the facts are all the other way. It is the making of good choices in life that others regard, retrospectively, as good mental health!

The myth of mental illness encourages us, moreover, to believe in its logical corollary: that social intercourse would be harmonious, satisfying, and the secure basis of a "good life" were it not for the disrupting influences of mental illness or "psychopathology." The potentiality for universal human happiness, in this form at least, seems to me but another example of the I-wish-it-were-true type of fantasy. I do believe that human happiness or well-being on a hitherto unimaginably large scale, and not just for a select few, is possible. This goal could be achieved, however, only at the cost of many men, and not just a few being willing and able to tackle their personal, social, and ethical conflicts. This means having the courage and integrity to forego waging battles on false fronts, finding solutions for substitute problems—for instance, fighting the battle of stomach acid and chronic fatigue instead of facing up to a marital conflict.

Our adversaries are not demons, witches, fate, or mental illness. We have no enemy whom we can fight, exorcise, or dispel by "cure." What we do have are *problems in living*—whether these be biologic, economic, political, or sociopsychological. In this essay

I was concerned only with problems belonging in the last mentioned category, and within this group mainly with those pertaining
to moral values. The field to which modern
psychiatry addresses itself is vast, and I made
no effort to encompass it all. My argument
was limited to the proposition that mental
illness is a myth, whose function it is to
disguise and thus render more palatable the
bitter pill of moral conflicts in human relations.

REFERENCES

HOLLINGSHEAD, A. B., & REDLICH, F. C. *Social class
and mental illness.* New York: Wiley, 1958.

JONES, E. *The life and work of Sigmund Freud.*
Vol. III. New York: Basic Books, 1957.

LANGER, S. K. *Philosophy in a new key.* New
York: Mentor Books, 1953.

PETERS, R. S. *The concept of motivation.* London: Routledge & Kegan Paul, 1958.

SZASZ, T. S. Malingering: "Diagnosis" or social
condemnation? *AMA Arch Neurol. Psychiat.,*
1956, 76, 432–443.

SZASZ, T. S. *Pain and pleasure: A study of bodily
feelings.* New York: Basic Books, 1957. (a)

SZASZ, T. S. The problem of psychiatric nosology:
A contribution to a situational analysis of
psychiatric operations. *Amer. J. Psychiat.,*
1957, 114, 405–413. (b)

SZASZ, T. S. On the theory of psychoanalytic treatment. *Int. J. Psycho-Anal.,* 1957, 38, 166–
182. (c)

SZASZ, T. S. Psychiatry, ethics and the criminal
law. *Columbia law Rev.,* 1958, 58, 183–198.

SZASZ, T. S. Moral conflict and psychiatry, *Yale
Rev.,* 1959, in press.

Personality Disorder Is Disease

DAVID P. AUSUBEL

In two recent articles in the *American Psychologist,* Szasz (1960) and Mowrer (1960) have argued the case for discarding the concept of mental illness. The essence of Mowrer's position is that since medical science lacks "demonstrated competence . . . in psychiatry," psychology would be wise to "'get out" from "under the penumbra of medicine," and to regard the behavior disorders as manifestations of sin rather than of disease (p. 302). Szasz' position, as we shall see shortly, is somewhat more complex than Mowrer's, but agrees with the latter in emphasizing the moral as opposed to the psychopathological basis of abnormal behavior.

For a long time now, clinical psychology has both repudiated the relevance of moral judgment and accountability for assessing behavioral acts and choices, and has chafed under medical (psychiatric) control and authority in diagnosing and treating the personality disorders. One can readily appreciate, therefore, Mowrer's eagerness to sever the historical and professional ties that bind clinical psychology to medicine, even if this means denying that psychological distur-

bances constitute a form of illness, and even if psychology's close working relationship with psychiatry must be replaced by a new rapprochement with sin and theology, as "the lesser of two evils" (pp. 302–303). One can also sympathize with Mowrer's and Szasz' dissatisfaction with prevailing amoral and nonjudgmental trends in clinical psychology and with their entirely commendable efforts to restore moral judgment and accountability to a respectable place among the criteria used in evaluating human behavior, both normal and abnormal.

Opposition to these two trends in the handling of the behavior disorders (i.e., to medical control and to nonjudgmental therapeutic attitudes), however, does not necessarily imply abandonment of the concept of mental illness. There is no inconsistency whatsoever in maintaining, on the one hand, that most purposeful human activity has a moral aspect the reality of which psychologists cannot afford to ignore (Ausubel, 1952, p. 462), that man is morally accountable for the majority of his misdeeds (Ausubel, 1952, p. 469), and that psychological rather than medical training and sophistication are basic to competence in the personality disorders (Ausubel, 1956, p. 101), and affirming, on the other hand, that the latter disorders are genuine manifestations of illness. In recent years psychology has been steadily moving away from the formerly fashionable stance of ethical neutrality in the behavioral sciences; and in spite of strident medical claims regarding superior professional qualifications and preclusive legal responsibility for treating psychiatric patients, and notwithstanding the nominally restrictive provisions of medical practice acts, clinical psychologists have been assuming an increasingly more important, independent, and responsible role in treating the mentally ill population of the United States.

It would be instructive at this point to examine the tactics of certain other medically allied professions in freeing themselves from medical control and in acquiring independent, legally recognized professional status. In no instance have they resorted to the devious stratagem of denying that they were treating diseases, in the hope of mollifying medical opposition and legitimizing their own professional activities. They took the position instead that simply because a given condition is defined as a disease, its treatment need not necessarily be turned over to doctors of medicine if other equally competent professional specialists were available. That this position is legally and politically tenable is demonstrated by the fact that an impressively large number of recognized diseases are legally treated today by both medical *and* nonmedical specialists (e.g., diseases of the mouth, face, jaws, teeth, eyes, and feet). And there are few convincing reasons for believing that psychiatrists wield that much more political power than physicians, maxillofacial surgeons, ophthalmologists, and orthopedic surgeons, that they could be successful where these latter specialists have failed, in legally restricting practice in their particular area of competence to holders of the medical degree. Hence, even if psychologists were not currently managing to hold their own vis-à-vis psychiatrists, it would be far less dangerous and much more forthright to press for the necessary ameliorative legislation than to seek cover behind an outmoded and thoroughly discredited conception of the behavior disorders.

THE SZASZ-MOWRER POSITION

Szasz's (1960) contention that the concept of mental illness "now functions merely as a convenient myth" (p. 118) is grounded on four unsubstantiated and logically untenable propositions, which can be fairly summarized as follows:

1. Only symptoms resulting from demonstrable physical lesions qualify as legitimate manifestations of disease. Brain pathology is a type of physical lesion, but its symptoms, properly speaking, are neurological rather than psychological in nature. Under no circumstances, therefore, can mental symptoms be considered a form of illness.
2. A basic dichotomy exists between *mental* symptoms, on the one hand, which are subjective in nature, dependent on subjective judgment and personal involvement of the observer, and referable to cultural-ethical norms, and *physical* symptoms, on the other hand, which are allegedly objective in nature, ascertainable without personal involvement of the observer, and independent of cultural norms and ethical standards. Only symptoms possessing the latter set of characteristics are genuinely reflective of illness and amenable to medical treatment.
3. Mental symptoms are merely expressions of problems of living and, hence, cannot be regarded as manifestations of a pathological condition. The concept of mental illness is misleading and demonological because it seeks to explain psychological disturbance, in particular, and human disharmony, in general, in terms of a metaphorical but nonexistent disease entity, instead of attributing them to inherent difficulties in coming to

grips with elusive problems of choice and responsibility.

4. Personality disorders, therefore, can be most fruitfully conceptualized as products of moral conflict, confusion, and aberration. Mowrer (1960) extends this latter proposition to include the dictum that psychiatric symptoms are primarily reflective of unacknowledged sin, and that individuals manifesting these symptoms are responsible for and deserve their suffering, both because of their original transgressions and because they refuse to avow and expiate their guilt (pp. 301, 304).

Widespread adoption of the Szasz-Mowrer view of the personality disorders would, in my opinion, turn back the psychiatric clock twenty-five hundred years. The most significant and perhaps the only real advance registered by mankind in evolving a rational and humane method of handling behavioral aberrations has been in substituting a concept of disease for the demonological and retributional doctrines regarding their nature and etiology that flourished until comparatively recent times. Conceptualized as illness, the symptoms of personality disorders can be interpreted in the light of underlying stresses and resistances, both genic and environmental, and can be evaluated in relation to *specifiable* quantitative and qualitative norms of appropriately adaptive behavior, both cross-culturally and within a particular cultural context. It would behoove us, therefore, before we abandon the concept of mental illness and return to the medieval doctrine of unexpiated sin or adopt Szasz's ambiguous criterion of difficulty in ethical choice and responsibility, to subject the foregoing propositions to careful and detailed study.

Mental Symptoms and Brain Pathology

Although I agree with Szasz in rejecting the doctrine that ultimately some neuroana-

tomic or nurophysiologic defect will be discovered in *all* cases of personality disorder, I disagree with his reasons for not accepting this proposition. Notwithstanding Szasz's straw man presentation of their position, the proponents of the extreme somatic view do not really assert that the *particular nature* of a patient's disordered beliefs can be correlated with "certain definite lesions in the nervous system" (Szasz, 1960, p. 113). They hold rather that normal cognitive and behavioral functioning depends on the anatomic and physiologic integrity of certain key areas of the brain, and that impairment of this substrate integrity, therefore, provides a physical basis for disturbed ideation and behavior, but does not explain, except in a very gross way, the particular kinds of symptoms involved. In fact, they are generally inclined to attribute the *specific* character of the patient's symptoms to the nature of his pre-illness personality structure, the substrate integrity of which is impaired by the lesion or metabolic defect in question.

Nevertheless, even though this type of reasoning plausibly accounts for the psychological sypmtoms found in general paresis, various toxic deleria, and other comparable conditions, it is an extremely improbable explanation of *all* instances of personality disorder. Unlike the tissues of any other organ, brain tissue possesses the unique property of making possible awareness of and adjustment to the world of sensory, social, and symbolic stimulation. Hence by virtue of this unique relationship of the nervous system to the environment, diseases of behavior and personality may reflect abnormalities in personal and social adjustment, quite apart from any structural or metabolic disturbance in the underlying neural substrate. I would conclude, therefore, that although brain pathology is probably not the most important cause of behavior disorder, it is undoubtedly responsible for the incidence of *some* psychological abnormalities *as well as* for various neurological signs and symptoms.

But even if we completely accepted Szasz's view that brain pathology does not account for any symptoms of personality disorder, it would still be unnecessary to accept his assertion that to qualify as a genuine manifestation of disease a given symptom must be caused by a physical lesion. Adoption of such a criterion would be arbitrary and inconsistent both with medical and lay connotations of the term "disease," which in current usage is generally regarded as including any marked deviation, physical, mental, or behavioral, from normally desirable standards of structural and functional integrity.

Mental versus Physical Symptoms

Szasz contends that since the analogy between physical and mental symptoms is patently fallacious, the postulated parallelism between physical and mental disease is logically untenable. This line of reasoning is based on the assumption that the two categories of symptoms can be sharply dichotomized with respect to such basic dimensions as objectivity-subjectivity, the relevance of cultural norms, and the need for personal involvement of the observer. In my opinion, the existence of such a dichotomy cannot be empirically demonstrated in convincing fashion.

Practically all symptoms of bodily disease involve some elements of subjective judgment—both on the part of the patient and of the physician. Pain is perhaps the most important and commonly used criterion of physical illness. Yet, any evaluation of its reported locus, intensity, character, and duration is dependent upon the patient's subjective appraisal of his own sensations and on the physician's assessment of the latter's pain threshold, intelligence, and personality structure. It is also a medical commonplace that the severity of pain in most instances of bodily illness may be mitigated by the administration of a placebo. Furthermore, in taking a meaningful history the physician must not only serve as a participant observer but also as a skilled interpreter of human behavior. It is the rare patient who

does not react psychologically to the signs of physical illness; and hence physicians are constantly called upon to decide, for example, to what extent precordial pain and reported tightness in the chest are manifestations of coronary insufficiency, of fear of cardiac disease and impending death, or of combinations of both conditions. Even such allegedly objective signs as pulse rate, BMR, blood pressure, and blood cholesterol have their subjective and relativistic aspects. Pulse rate and blood pressure are notoriously susceptible to emotional influences, and BMR and blood cholesterol fluctuate widely from one cultural environment to another (Dreyfuss & Czaczkes, 1959). And anyone who believes that ethical norms have no relevance for physical illness has obviously failed to consider the problems confronting Catholic patients and/or physicians when issues of contraception, abortion, and preferential saving of the mother's as against the fetus's life must be faced in the context of various obstetrical emergencies and medical contraindications to pregnancy.

It should now be clear, therefore, that symptoms not only do not need a physical basis to qualify as manifestations of illness, but also that the evaluation of *all* symptoms, physical as well as mental, is dependent in large measure on subjective judgment, emotional factors, cultural-ethical norms, and personal involvement on the part of the observer. These considerations alone render no longer tenable Szasz' contention (1960, p. 114) that there is an inherent contradiction between using cultural and ethical norms as criteria of mental disease, on the one hand, and of employing medical measures of treatment on the other. But even if the postulated dichotomy between mental and physical symptoms were valid, the use of physical measures in treating subjective and relativistic psychological symptoms would still be warranted. Once we accept the proposition that impairment of the neutral substrate of personality can result in behavior disorder, it is logically consistent to accept the corollary proposition that other kinds of manipulation of the same neutral substrate can conceivably have therapeutic effects, irrespective of whether the underlying cause of the mental symptoms is physical or psychological.

Mental Illness and Problems of Living

"The phenomena now called mental illness," argues Szasz (1960), can be regarded more forthrightly and simply as "expressions of man's struggle with the problem of how he should live"(p. 117). This statement undoubtedly oversimplifies the nature of personality disorders; but even if it were adequately inclusive it would not be inconsistent with the position that these disorders are a manifestation of illness. There is no valid reason why a particular symptom cannot both reflect a problem in living *and* constitute a manifestation of disease. The notion of mental illness, conceived in this way, would not "'obscure the everyday fact that life for most people is a continuous struggle . . . for a 'place in the sun,' 'peace of mind,' or some other human value" (p. 118). It is quite true, as Szasz points out, that "human relations are inherently fraught with difficulties" (p. 117), and that most people manage to cope with such difficulties without becoming mentally ill. But conceding this fact hardly precludes the possibility that some individuals, either because of the magnitude of the stress involved, or because of genically or environmentally induced susceptibility to ordinary degrees of stress, respond to the problems of living with behavior that is either seriously distorted or sufficiently unadaptive to prevent normal interpersonal relations and vocational functioning. The latter outcome—gross deviation from a designated range of desirable behavior variability—conforms to the generally understood meaning of mental illness.

The plausibility of subsuming abnormal behavioral reactions to stress under the general rubric of disease is further enhanced by the fact that these reactions include the same three principal categories of symptoms found in physical illness. Depression and catastrophic impairment of self-esteem, for example, are manifestations of personality disorder which are symptomologically comparable to edema in cardiac failure or to heart murmurs in valvular disease. They are indicative of underlying pathology but are neither adaptive nor adjustive. Symptoms such as hypomanic overactivity and compulsive striving toward unrealistically high achievement goals, on the other hand, are both adaptive and adjustive, and constitute a type of compensatory response to basic feelings of inadequacy, which is not unlike cardiac hypertrophy in hypertensive heart disease or elevated white blood cell count in acute infections. And finally, distortive psychological defenses that have some adjustive value but are generally maladaptive (e.g., phobias, delusions, autistic fantasies) are analogous to the pathological situation found in conditions like pneumonia, in which the excessive outpouring of serum and phagocytes in defensive response to pathogenic bacteria literally causes the patient to drown in his own fluids.

Within the context of this same general proposition, Szasz repudiates the concept of mental illness as demonogical in nature, i.e., as the "true heir to religious myths in general and to the belief in witchcraft in particular" (p. 118) because it allegedly employs a reified abstraction ("a deformity of personality") to account in causal terms both for "human disharmony" and for symptoms of behavior disorder (p. 114). But again he appears to be demolishing a straw man. Modern students of personality disorder do not regard mental illness as a cause of human disharmony, but as a co-manifestation with it of inherent difficulties in personal adjustment and interpersonal relations; and insofar as I can accurately interpret the literature, psychopathologists do not conceive of mental illness as a cause of particular behavioral symptoms but as a generic term under which these symptoms can be subsumed.

Mental Illness and Moral Responsibility

Szasz's final reason for regarding mental illness as a myth is really a corollary of his previously considered more general proposition that mental symptoms are essentially reflective of problems of living and hence do not legitimately qualify as manifestations of disease. It focuses on difficulties of ethical choice and responsibility as the particular life problems most likely to be productive of personality disorder. Mowrer (1960) further extends this corollary but asserting that neurotic and psychotic individuals are responsible for their suffering (p. 301), and that unacknowledged and unexpiated sin, in turn, is the basic cause of this suffering (p. 304). As previously suggested, however, one can plausibly accept the proposition that psychiatrists and clinical psychologists have erred in trying to divorce behavioral evaluation from ethical considerations, in conducting psychotherapy in an amoral setting, and in confusing the psychological explanation of unethical behavior with absolution from accountability for same, *without* necessarily endorsing the view that personality disorders are basically a reflection of sin, and that victims of these disorders are less ill than responsible for their symptoms (Ausubel, 1952, pp. 392–397, 465–471).

In the first place, it is possible in most instances (although admittedly difficult in some) to distinguish quite unambiguously between mental illness and ordinary cases of immorality. The vast majority of persons who are guilty of moral lapses knowingly violate their own ethical precepts for expediential reasons—despite being volitionally capable at the time, both of choosing the more moral alternative and of exercising the necessary inhibitory control (Ausubel, 1952, pp. 465–471). Such persons, also, usually do not exhibit any signs of behavior disorder. At crucial choice points in facing the problems of living they simply choose the opportunistic instead of the moral alternative. They are not mentally ill, but they are clearly accountable for their misconduct. Hence, since personality disorder and immorality are neither coextensive nor mutually exclusive conditions, the concept of mental illness need not necessarily obscure the issue of moral accountability.

Second, guilt may be a contributory factor in behavior disorder, but is by no means the only or principal cause thereof. Feelings of guilt may give rise to anxiety and depression; but in the absence of catastrophic impairment of self-esteem induced by *other* factors, these symptoms tend to be transitory and peripheral in nature (Ausubel, 1952, pp. 362–363). Repression of guilt is more a consequence than a cause of anxiety. Guilt is repressed in order to avoid the anxiety producing trauma to self-esteem that would otherwise result if it were acknowledged. Repression per se enters the causal picture in anxiety only secondarily—by obviating "the possibility of punishment, confession, expiation, and other guilt reduction mechanisms" (Ausubel, 1952, p. 456). Furthermore, in most types of personality disorder other than anxiety, depression, and various complications of anxiety such as phobias, obsessions, and compulsion, guilt feelings are either not particularly prominent (schizophrenic reactions), or are conspicuously absent (e.g., classical cases of inadequate or aggressive, antisocial psychopathy).

Third, it is just as unreasonable to hold an individual responsible for symptoms of behavior disorder as to deem him accountable for symptoms of physical illness. He is no more culpable for his inability to cope with sociopsychological stress than he would be for his inability to resist the spread of infectious organisms. In those instances where warranted guilt feelings *do* contribute to personality disorder, the patient is accountable for the misdeeds underlying his guilt, but is hardly responsible for the symptoms brought on by the guilt feelings or for unlawful acts committed during his illness. Acknowledgment of guilt may be therapeutically beneficial under these circumstances, but punishment for the original misconduct should obviously be deferred until after recovery.

Lastly, even if it were true that all personality disorder is a reflection of sin and that people are accountable for their behavioral symptoms, it would still be necessary to deny that these symptoms are manifestations of disease. Illness is no less real because the victim happens to be culpable for his illness. A glutton with hypertensive heart disease undoubtedly aggravates his condition by overeating, and is culpable in part for the often fatal symptoms of his disease, but what reasonable person would claim that for this reason he is not really ill?

CONCLUSIONS

Four propositions in support of the argument for discarding the concept of mental illness were carefully examined, and the following conclusions were reached:

First, although brain pathology is probably not the major cause of personality disorder, it does account for *some* psychological symptoms by impairing the neural substrate of personality. In any case, however, a symptom need not reflect a physical lesion in order to qualify as a genuine manifestation of disease.

Second, Szasz's postulated dichotomy between mental and physical symptoms is untenable because the assessment of *all* symptoms is dependent to some extent on subjective judgment, emotional factors, cultural-ethical norms, and personal involvement of the observer. Furthermore, the use of medical measures in treating behavior disorders—irrespective of whether the underlying causes are neural or psychological—is defensible on the grounds that if inadvertent impairment of the neural substrate of personality can have distortive effects on behavior, directed manipulation of the same substrate may have therapeutic effects.

Third, there is no inherent contradiction in regarding mental symptoms both as ex-

pressions of problems in living *and* as manifestations of illness. The latter situation results when individuals are for various reasons unable to cope with such problems, and react with seriously distorted or maladaptive behavior. The three principal categories of behavioral symptoms—manifestations of impaired functioning, adaptive compensation, and defensive overreaction—are also found in bodily disease. The concept of mental illness has never been advanced as a demonological cause of human disharmony, but only as a co-manifestation with it of certain inescapable difficulties and hazards in personal and social adjustment. The same concept is also generally accepted as a generic term for all behavioral symptoms rather than as a reified cause of these symptoms.

Fourth, the view that personality disorder is less a manifestation of illness than of sin, i.e., of culpable inadequacy in meeting problems of ethical choice and responsibility, and that victims of behavior disorder are therefore morally accountable for their symptoms, is neither logically nor empirically tenable. In most instances immoral behavior and mental illness are clearly distinguishable conditions. Guilt is only a secondary etiological factor in anxiety and depression, and in other personality disorders is either not prominent or conspicuously absent. The issue of culpability for symptoms is largely irrelevant in handling the behavior disorders, and in any case does not detract from the reality of the illness.

In general, it is both unnecessary and potentially dangerous to discard the concept of mental illness on the grounds that only in this way can clinical psychology escape from the professional domination of medicine. Dentists, podiatrists, optometrists, and osteopaths have managed to acquire an independent professional status without rejecting the concept of disease. It is equally unnecessary and dangerous to substitute the doctrine of sin for illness in order to counteract prevailing amoral and nonjudgmental trends in psychotherapy. The hypothesis of repressed guilt does not adequately explain most kinds and instances of personality disorder, and the concept of mental illness does not preclude judgments of moral accountability where warranted. Definition of behavior disorder in terms of sin or of difficulties associated with ethical choice and responsibility would substitute theological disputation and philosophical wrangling about values for specific quantitative and qualitative criteria of disease.

REFERENCES

Ausubel, D. P. *Ego development and the personality disorders.* New York: Grune & Stratton, 1952.

Ausubel, D. P. Relationships between psychology and psychiatry: The hidden issues. *Amer. Psychologist,* 1956, 11, 99–105.

Dreyfuss, F., & Czaczkes, J. W. Blood cholesterol and uric acid of healthy medical students under the stress of an examination. *AMA Arch. Intern. Med.,* 1959, 103, 708.

Mowrer, O. H. "Sin," the lesser of two evils. *Amer. Psychologist,* 1960, 15, 301–304.

Szasz, T. S. The myth of mental illness. *Amer. Psychologist,* 1960, 15, 113–118.

Who Is Mad? Who Is Sane?
R. D. Laing: In Search of a New
Psychiatry

JAMES S. GORDON

*"To increasing numbers of readers—psy-
chiatrists as well as patients; political activists and dropouts; the hardly literate,
searching young; as well as middle-class
artists and intellectuals— R. D. Laing is the
guide who most clearly elucidates the disordered surfaces and depths of their own
lives."*

In a working-class area of London's East
End, near where the River Lem flows over
marshes, past the gasworks, and into the
Thames, stands a three-story, sixty-year-old,
dusty brick building called Kingsley Hall.
Nearby are dismal rows of modern apartments. The rest of the neighborhood is composed of Victorian homes, converted to
multiple dwellings. A few blocks away are
pubs, grocery stores, and other shops. Across
the street from the Hall, which stands alone,
is a small open space.

Note: James S. Gordon, "Who Is Mad? Who Is Sane?
R. D. Laing: In Search of a New Psychiatry," *Atlantic
Monthly,* Jan. 1971, pp. 50–53, 56–66. Copyright ©
1970, by The Atlantic Monthly Company, Boston,
Mass. Reprinted with permission. James S. Gordon,
M.D., is a psychiatrist with the National Institute of
Mental Health.

Sixty years ago, two wealthy spinster sisters
with social-work inclinations established
Kingsley Hall as a settlement house. In time,
the sisters died and left the building to a
foundation, the Kingsley Hall Association.
Over the years the building served as a center
for social, religious, and pacifist activities in
the East End.

In 1931, while he negotiated India's fate
with Britain, Mahatma Gandhi slept on a
straw mat in one of the tiny cells on the
roof of the building. He kept a goat in his
room and milked it for food. Cabinet ministers, puzzled by his choice of location, came
there to talk with him. On the wall outside
Kingsley Hall, a blue and white plaque com-
memorates Gandhi's visit.

In 1965 the building was leased to the
Philadelphia Association (Philadelphia
means, literally, "brotherly love") , a group
of Londoners, headed by the Glasgow-born
psychiatrist Ronald D. Laing, who are dedicated to "relieving" and investigating "mental illness of all descriptions." Though the
lease ended last May, the consequences of the
Philadelphia Association's five-year tenure
could be as important for the therapy of

schizophrenia, indeed for our conceptions of sanity and madness, as Gandhi's visit was for the future of India.

In January, 1970, I went to London to visit Kingsley Hall and to speak with R. D. Laing and some of his co-workers. I had just been appointed a chief resident (administrator, and instructor of doctors and medical students taking psychiatric training) on a psychiatric ward in New York, and it seemed to be the time to take a trip that had been brewing in me for four years, since I had read Laing's first book, *The Divided Self.*

Four years ago, although he had already written several books, Laing's name was known only to a small number of people who were interested in existential psychiatry and the phenomenology of schizophrenia. It was only with the publication of *The Politics of Experience* in 1967 that he began to be regarded as a major cultural and social critic. Like Norman O. Brown and Herbert Marcuse, he drew on psychoanalytic insights to make a radical critique of Western society. But where Marcuse and Brown are theoretical and speak in generalities, Laing is immediate and personal. He speaks directly from his own experience to that of his readers. He speaks both as a therapist with "mad" patients and as a man groping for sanity in a mad world.

In *The Politics of Experience* the reader is constantly made aware of Laing's own uncertainties. Illuminations are shadowed by doubt. The book begins by questioning its own existence: "Few books today are forgiveable. Black on canvas, silence on the screen, an empty white sheet of paper, are perhaps feasible." After seven chapters which attempt to lay bare the truth of the madman's delusions and the delusions at the heart of accepted truths, the book ends with a series of Blake-like images which Laing calls "The Bird of Paradise." The last incantatory words of this section are as ironic as they are fitting: "If I could turn you on, if I could drive you out of your wretched mind, if I could tell you I would let you know." Analytic con-

clusions are embedded in the ambiguous, tortured processs of discovery.

In *The Divided Self* Laing observed that "Freud was a hero who descended to the 'Underworld' and met there stark terrors." But, he continues, Freud "carried with him his theory as a Medusa's head which turned these terrors to stone." Laing has set himself the task of "surviving without using a theory that is in some measure an instrument of defense." To increasing numbers of readers —psychiatrists as well as patients; political activists and dropouts; the hardly literate, searching young; as well as middle-class artists and intellectuals—Laing is the guide who most clearly elucidates the disordered surfaces and depths of their own lives.

During my own psychiatric training, I was deeply dissatisfied with the theoretical models psychiatrists applied to their patients and appalled by the supposedly therapeutic techniques that these models dictated or permitted. I was also disturbed by the hospital psychiatrist's institutionalized position as the guardian and enforcer of received social values. In *The Divided Self,* I found a perspective which helped me to understand and experience my patients directly, without the distorting prism of diagnostic classification. In Laing's later works, I began to perceive the outlines of a new, broader conception of sanity and madness and of the role of the psychiatrist. In these books he had begun to examine the familial and societal conditions which produced mental patients. He had come to see individual madness as the distorted reflection of a pervasive social and political madness, of which psychiatry was itself a part. He felt that only through a re-evaluation of our socially and institutionally defined ideas about sanity and madness could he arrive at any conception of true sanity, any true therapy for madness. Only in a new setting, where all previous definitions and roles could be called into question, could this re-evaluation proceed. At Kingsley Hall, for five years, he and his co-workers, together with a number of people who had been "mental patients," were embarked on this venture. I hoped that what they had learned there could guide me in my own undertaking.

In order to understand the originality and significance of what happened at Kingsley Hall, it is necessary first to present some of the more traditional ideas about madness and its treatment, and the critique that Laing makes of them.

There have always, and in all cultures, been some people whose behavior was regarded by others as different and unusual. But these people, however deviant or "mad," were not always thought to be "sick." It is only during the last two centuries, in Western Europe and America, that the madman—no longer considered as possessed or saintly, annoying or amusing—has come to be seen primarily as sick.

The reasons why madness came to be regarded as a disease are complicated. Thomas Szasz, an American psychiatrist, points to the fact that in the industrial era the traditional Christian categories of sin and salvation were displaced by the scientific-medical ones of disease and health.

Advances in pathology in the nineteenth century did indeed show a relationship between some mad behavior and damage to the brain. Neurosyphilis, chronic alcoholism, and arteriosclerosis all caused people to speak and behave in a mad fashion, and all produced identifiable pathologic lesions. But the brains of people with the most prevalent form of modern madness, schizophrenia (by conservative estimates one to two percent of all Americans will be diagnosed as schizophrenic at some point during their lifetime), show no pathologic lesions. Nor, at this time, has any genetic defect or biochemical abnormality been conclusively demonstrated in their bodies. Nevertheless, psychiatrists treat people who act and speak strangely as if they were diseased. And they look for the signs and symptoms of schizophrenia just as a specialist in internal medicine searches for sugar in the urine of a suspected diabetic.

Madness is a personal experience and social fact. Schizophrenia is a medical artifact.

But the assumption that schizophrenia is a disease dictates that physicians declare who has it, and care for those so diagnosed. It provides the rationale for trying to cure the schizophrenic by the medical means of tranquilizers and electroshock therapy and, with fortunately diminishing frequency, surgical intervention in the form of a lobotomy.

The creation of mental hospitals institutionalized this convergence of social fact and medical artifact. In *Madness and Civilization,* French historian of culture Michel Foucault points out that with the decline of leprosy at the end of the Middle Ages, madmen took the place of lepers as social scapegoats. During the Renaissance, madmen were expelled from their native cities and confined to boats, the "ships of fools." These ships served to isolate and exclude the socially disruptive and sometimes frightening madman from his fellow citizens. At present, within a medical framework, mental hospitals serve the same function. One half of all the hospital beds in America are in mental hospitals, and more than one half of these beds are occupied by diagnosed schizophrenics.

Medical students and young physicians who are beginning training in psychiatry are taught to classify their most bizarre patients according to categories which owe their origin to a late-nineteenth-century German psychiatrist, Emil Kraepelin. Kraepelin adopted his French contemporary Morel's term *"Démence précoce"* ("precocious or early insanity") and placed under this rubric, catatonic, hebephrenic, and paranoid psychoses. In his discussion he emphasized the onset of these conditions in young people and their usual progression to a state of mental deterioration.

In 1911, the Swiss psychiatrist Eugen Bleuler, emphasizing the patient's state of mind rather than the outcome of his disease, coined the term schizophrenia ("split-mind" or "split-soul"). Bleuler outlined what he called the primary and secondary symptoms of schizophrenia. The primary symptoms include the "4 A's" that still form the basis for first lectures on schizophrenia: distortions of Affect (for example, the patient is laughing when the situation should call for crying); loose Associations (use of words and phrases which do not seem to connect with one another); Ambivalence (a constant uncertainty or changing of mind); and Autism (an apparent preoccupation with internal concerns and a lack of relatedness to the environment). Secondary symptoms, often quite obvious and bizarre, but not essential to the diagnosis, include hallucinations, negativism, delusions, and stupor.

The psychiatrist's initial task involves observing or elucidating these symptoms in a patient and coming to a diagnosis. And a considerable amount of time and energy is devoted to perfecting one's ability in this process. In *The Divided Self*, Laing points out the wrongheadedness of this enterprise. He tries to show how the medical model, with its assumption of the doctor's scientific objectivity, prevents rather than facilitates his understanding of the patient.

Laing sees rigid diagnostic and psychodynamic ways of regarding people as a perpetuation, through the verbal and conceptual means of psychiatry, of the same dehumanizing attitudes which precipitated their emotional dilemmas. He points out that the language of psychiatric description is a "vocabulary of denigration." People who behave and speak in ways the psychiatrist cannot understand are said to be "maladaptive," "out of contact with reality," "lacking in insight." The psychiatrist sees the patient through a filter of diagnostic criteria which do violence to a two-sided interpersonal situation. The patient is reduced to an organism to be dissected, the psychiatrist to a judgmental anatomist. Bleuler, Laing reminds his reader, stated that "when all is said and done [his patients] were stranger to him than the birds in his garden."

Laing demonstrates the classical clinical psychiatric attitude in his discussions of an interview of Kraepelin's with a boy who would be diagnosed as schizophrenic:

The patient I will show today has almost to be carried into the room . . . [he] sits with his eyes shut and pays no attention to his surroundings. He does not look up even when he is spoken to, but answers beginning in a low tone, and gradually becoming louder and louder. When asked where he is, he says, "You want to know that too? I tell you who is being measured and is measured and shall be measured. I know all that, and could tell you, but I do not want to." When asked his name, he screams, "What is your name? What does he shut? He shuts his eyes. What does he hear? He does not understand; he understands not. How? Who? Where? When? What does he mean? When I tell him to look he does not look properly. You there, just look!"

Kraepelin notes the young man's "inaccessibility" and asserts that his talk was "only a series of unconnected sentences having no relation whatever to the general situation." From Kraepelin's point of view the young man exhibits the "signs of catatonic excitement." (Post-Bleulerian psychiatrists might note inappropriate affect, autism, loose associations, negativism, and perhaps auditory hallucinations.) But Laing suggests that from the young man's perspective, his words are perhaps a "dialogue between his own parodied version of Kraepelin and his own defiant rebelling self." Laing concludes: "What is the boy's experience of Kraepelin? He seems to be tormented and desperate. What is he about in speaking and acting this way? He is objecting to being measured and tested, he wants to be heard." The situation, it seems, has two sides. Kraepelin wants information, the boy wants understanding. They operate at cross-purposes, and potential communication is ruptured.

Freud, who created psychoanalysis, emphasized the necessity for the psychiatrist to understand his patient's experience of the world. Through the medium of free associations the analyst could gain access to the hidden, unconscious parts of his patients' minds. Once brought to light, unconscious conflicts could come under the influence of conscious directive activity. But Freud felt his techniques were not applicable to the treatment of psychotic patients (schizophrenia is the major psychosis). He thought these patients too absorbed in the inner workings of their minds—too narcissistic—to establish a working relationship with a therapist.

In the 1920s, however, a group of American psychiatrists, including William Alanson White and Harry Stack Sullivan, undertook the psychoanalytically oriented treatment of schizophrenic patients. Sullivan saw his patients' apparently strange speech and behavior not as the signs and symptoms of a disease, but as evidence of "difficulties in living." He felt that the schizophrenic, in the context of a warm interpersonal relationship with a therapist, could come to understand these difficulties. Both he and his followers, including Frieda Fromm-Reichman (the psychiatrist in Hannah Green's celebrated autobiographical novel *I Never Promised You a Rose Garden*), Harold Searles, and Otto Will, have emphasized the two-sidedness of the therapeutic encounter. And they were willing to admit, as the medically oriented psychiatric establishment often is not, that valid insight and experience are not merely the property of the psychiatrist. Fromm-Reichman observed that "mentally disturbed persons who have withdrawn from their environment are refreshingly intolerant of all kinds of cultural compromises. Hence they inevitably hold the mirror of the hypocritical aspects of the culture in front of society."

The mental hospitals I have worked in, as medical student, intern, and psychiatric resident, have had special teaching wards which are among the most "advanced" in this country. Patients received intensive individual therapy, and a great deal of lip service was paid to "understanding" them. At the same time, therapists were told that they really knew better than their patients what was good for the latter. We exercised a power over their daily lives and their thoughts which seemed to contradict our attempts to understand them and win their confidence.

We were told not to argue with a patient's hallucinations or delusions. But at the same time, our superiors and ward staff insisted that we give patients tranquilizers to make these symptoms go away. If a patient felt he wanted to leave the hospital, it was up to us to decide whether or not he was ready. If he was speaking or acting bizarrely, we had the power to keep him from leaving. We could lock the ward door, put the patient in a seclusion room, or deprive him of his clothes— all this in his own best interest.

If at any point I resisted using these sanctions, I was told that I was depriving my patients of the best possible care: "Patients need controls"; "Medication improves thought disorders"; "They'll never get better if you don't set limits." I found myself feeling guilty for going along with these measures. And I felt guilty, or at least beleaguered by a frightened and angry ward staff, when I refused.

Under less auspicious circumstances, those that most people who are hospitalized are subjected to, the experience is a disaster from beginning to end. The institutional drama of degradation and misunderstanding often starts in a city hospital emergency room. For example: a man comes in, pursued, as he believes, by demons. A psychiatric resident takes a history from whoever brought him in, the police or perhaps his family, listens politely to the man, and, unable to grasp much of what he is saying, begins to examine his "mental status." To determine whether or not he is "schizophrenic," he is asked to interpret proverbs and to subtract seven from one hundred, and seven from that, and so on. If his thinking is "concrete"—as opposed to abstract— if in the psychiatrist's opinion his affect is "inappropriate" and his associations are loose, he is schizophrenic. The man is terrified, and he is injected with a numbing tranquilizer, deprived of his clothes, and hustled off to a locked ward.

The next morning, in a room with other people present, a ward doctor sees the man for ten or fifteen minutes. The doctor asks him a few questions—when were you last in the hospital? are you suicidal? homicidal? do you hear voices? do you think people are after you? is there anyone at home to take care of you?—and dismisses him. The doctor prescribes more medication. For the next few days the man, treated perfunctorily and often condescendingly by the nurses and attendants, wanders around an overcrowded ward in a daze. If at the end of this time he is acting more "normal," he will probably be sent back to the family which a week before hospitalized him. If not, commitment proceedings will be instituted, and he will be sent to a state hospital.

Laing's approach to people that psychiatrists describe as schizophrenic presents an important alternative. Drawing on an existential-phenomenological as well as a psychoanalytic framework, he views madness not as a disease to be cured, but as the breakdown of a precariously maintained split between an outer false self and an inner true self. This split and these terms reflect the patient's own way of experiencing himself, rather than the psychiatrist's attempts at classification.

In the "sane, schizoid state," writes Laing, a false outer self has arisen "in compliance with the intentions and expectations of the other or with what one imagines to be the other's intentions and expectations." That state is grounded in the body and manifest in action and social intercourse. But the inner, true self feels the perceptions and manifestations of this socially adjusted, outwardly visible, false self to be unreal, alien, and meaningless. The true self, fearful and detached, has retreated from the consequences of being embodied and responsible. It is preoccupied with observation and fantasy, a last refuge of hopes, love, anger, and despair. From a position "transcendent and unembodied" the true self views the behavior of the false self. Terrified of participation in actions that seem like betrayals, the true self gradually becomes more and more isolated from the outer world, which could, potentially, infuse it with life.

Originally, the split arose as a consequence of intolerably conflicted and confusing life situations. It was a means of preserving oneself from the ravages of others, and from the unacceptable reactions they provoked. For instance, a two-year-old who withholds his feces is given frequent and painful enemas by a mother to whom he looks for love and sustenance. The boy gradually detaches himself from the bodily pain and emotional confusion which these assaults provoke. He gives his body up to the mother; he represses the anger which his mother has punished or ignored. Now the mother is violating *only* the child's body, removing only feces; the child's feelings of anger and resentment, his disappointment at the mother's hurtfulness, are no longer manifest.

This kind of interaction, repeated innumerable times and in a variety of situations, gives rise to a more or less stable split between outer and inner, false and true self. The child grows into an adult who sees the outer world of his body and other people as necessary but threatening. He relates to it in ways that appear acceptable, but all the while maintains himself aloof from his relatedness. In later life his existential truth may be that he is not having intercourse with another person, even while his body goes through the motions. He is not feeling friendly even though he is smiling.

Laing feels that "what is called psychosis (an acute schizophrenic episode—'a nervous breakdown') is sometimes simply the sudden removal of the veil of the false self which had been serving to maintain an outer behavioral normality that may long ago have failed to be any reflection of the state of affairs in the secret self. Then the self [will] pour out accusations of persecution [the observed, though often disguised and distorted, paranoid ideas] at the hands of the person with whom the false self has been complying for years."

Viewed from this perspective, treatment by tranquilizers, ward restrictions, and "controls" represents an attempt to restore the split between true and false selves, to produce outward compliance and deny the validity and acceptability of the inner self's accusations and aspirations. In psychiatric jargon, one hopes for "a restoration of the pre-morbid personality."

Laing, on the other hand, feels the psychotic episode may present an opportunity for a person to begin to heal the division into true and false selves which has deformed his life. Therapy involves encouraging and guiding the person in the exploration of the "inner time and space" into which psychosis has plunged him: "In this journey there are many occasions to lose one's way, for confusion, partial failure, even final shipwreck; many terrors, demons to be encountered, that may not be overcome.... There are very few of us who know the territory in which he is lost, who knows how to reach him, and how to find the way back."

In a paper entitled "Metanoia: Some Experiences at Kingsley Hall" (metanoia is, literally, change of mind), Laing lays the intellectual groundwork for his therapeutic venture:

> The setting of a psychiatric clinic and mental hospital promotes in staff and patients the set best designed to turn the metanoiac voyage from a voyage of discovery into self of a potentially revolutionary nature into a catastrophe; into a pathological process from which the person requires to be cured. We asked what could happen if we began by changing our set and setting, to regard what was happening as a potential healing process through which the person may be guided and during which he is guarded.

At Kingsley Hall he and his co-workers "changed the paradigm: someone is involved in a desperate strategy of liberation within the micro-social situation in which he finds himself. We try to follow the movement of what is called 'an acute schizophrenic episode' instead of arresting it."

A brochure put out by the Philadelphia Association describes some of the features of Kingsley Hall and present statistics. The reference point is the traditional mental hospital. The statistics represent an attempt to demonstrate the therapeutic success, even in traditional terms, of Kingsley Hall:

> At Kingsley Hall everyone's actions could be challenged by anyone.
>
> With no staff and no patients—with the ultimate breakdown of the binary role system of the institution—no resident has been given by any other resident any tranquilizers or sedatives. Experience and behavior which could not be tolerated in most families or psychiatric institutions made heavy but finally tolerable demands on the community.
>
> Members of households [there were several other small communities similar to Kingsley Hall which the Philadelphia Association established in London] determined the structure of their days. The context they thus establish fits their experience rather than that of a superimposed "ideal," and results eventually in people going into society at large. Members of households get up or stay in bed as they wish, eat what they want when they want, stay alone or be with others and generally make their own rules. DESPITE GLOOMY PREDICTIONS there have been no suicides to date. [When Kingsley Hall closed there still had been no suicides.] Kingsley Hall accommodates 14 people. From June 1965 to November 30, 1968, 104 people have stayed there.

About 85 percent of the residents were between twenty and forty years old, and about two thirds were men. Sixty-five out of the 104 people were classified as patients. More than half of them had been previously hospitalized. Three quarters of all the "patients" who lived there had been diagnosed as schizophrenic. Only nine of the sixty-five have been hospitalized since leaving Kingsley Hall.

But the quality of the lived experience at Kingsley Hall cannot be measured by statistics. Kingsley Hall provided troubled people with an alternative to hospitalization, an opportunity to live and grow through their madness. It was a place for "doctors" and "patients" to shed their restrictive roles and help and learn from one another immediately, without the distorting mediation of a hierarchical medical structure, without coercion. It was a place where people could simply be. It was simultaneously an experiment in psychotherapy and an attempt at communal living.

Going to London was a pilgrimage for me, but one fraught with anxiety and uncertainty. If Laing did not in some way live up to the profoundly sympathetic voice of his books, if Kingsley Hall were not somehow successful, I felt that the source of much of my own conviction would disappear.

I had written to Laing several weeks before going to England, had told him how important his books were to me, and asked if I could speak with him and visit Kingsley Hall. But I left for London without having received a reply.

It was more than a week before I actually got to Kingsley Hall. To some degree this was because many of the people who lived there had grown tired of having visitors. It was their home, and they had begun to resent the succession of reporters, psychiatrists, and curiosity seekers who wanted to visit.

When I first telephoned I was told that I couldn't possibly understand what the place was about in two weeks. My telling the man at the other end of the phone that I wanted to set up a similar community in an American hospital didn't excite him. He thought that my effort, like that of Laing's colleague David Cooper, who had tried to restructure a mental hospital ward in England, would be doomed. He didn't tell me to come or stay away, just to "keep trying." "Perhaps someone else will invite you." Then I called Laing's office and discovered that I already had an appointment to see him.

I had heard disturbing rumors about Laing, that he was periodically admitting himself to the mental hospitals that he publicly attacked; that he was likely to be abrupt and inconsiderate, perhaps sloppy drunk. A woman who had met him described him as frightening, "demonic." An American psychoanalyst who knew him fairly well felt that he was a charming man, perhaps the most original and creative psychiatric thinker since

Frued. But another, who had met him at the same time, called him "a brilliant and seductive paranoid schizophrenic."

My first surprise was his office. It was in a town house not far from Harley Street, where many of London's rich and fashionable specialists have theirs. It's hard to say what I expected, perhaps an ornate but seedy mansion on a deserted street. Nothing so ordinary and solid. His name, together with several other physicians', was on the door, engraved on a brass plate.

A secretary answered my ring, and showed me into a waiting room on the ground floor. I sat in a straight-backed Victorian chair facing an electric heater that glowed in the fireplace. Across from me an attractive blond girl was reading a fashion magazine.

After a few minutes, R. D. Laing appeared in the doorway. He greeted me, shook hands, and led the way, three steps at a time, up two long winding flights.

Laing's consultation room has none of the studied elegance with which most analysts surround themselves. It is simple, bare, functional. Two well-stuffed armchairs with end tables face each other across several feet of space. On one long wall there is a daybed with a drab spread. On the other, bookshelves with a few dozen titles. I noticed Erik Erikson's book on Gandhi and foreign-language translations of Laing's own books. There is an uncluttered desk near the windows, a hot plate in one corner.

Laing sat back in his chair, crossed his legs, and waited. In his dress there was a kind of careless sobriety: a dark jacket and pants which seemed just to miss matching, a black turtleneck shirt, and scuffed black loafers. In contrast, his face was pale, handsome, rugged, dominated by a high broad forehead; brown hair, longish, graying, strayed in back over his collar. His light, deep-set eyes seemed to gaze somewhere beyond my chair.

I nervously repeated what I had said in my letter to him, then talked about my own discomfort at being there. I lit a cigarette as I spoke, and he held up a pack of Gauloises smiling, showing me we smoked the same brand. His eyes went distant again, as I began to ask questions about Kingsley Hall and his relation to it. After a while I stopped, and he began to talk, slowly at first, then with relish. A strong Scots burr crept into his voice in reflective or ironic moments:

"Seven of us, the original members of the Philadelphia Association, obtained the building five years ago. There were psychiatrists and a social worker. One woman had been a psychiatric nurse, and one of the men was, by profession, a businessman. We planned to live at Kingsley Hall communally and work things out among ourselves. But even before we took over the building, we began to promise people who were in trouble that they could move in." When the building opened in the summer of 1965, it was already a new kind of community. People who earned their living as therapists lived communally with those who had been legally certified as patients.

When he moved into Kingsley Hall, Laing, like most of the other members of the community, left his family behind. He stayed in a ten-by-sixteen-foot room on the building's ground floor, which was formerly a library and has since served as a meditation room and darkroom. Except for about twenty-five hours each week when he saw patients in his office, he spent virtually all of his time at Kingsley Hall.

Though he felt "at ease" in the place, the physical and emotional pace was torrid. During a typical day Laing would return from seeing private patients, spend time with troubled members of the household, discuss communal problems, and preside over an hours-long dinner discussion which often turned into a seminar or spontaneous theater event. Going to bed at two or three in the morning, he would awaken at six or seven, write for several hours, and return to his office. After more than a year, he felt physically tired, emotionally "drained," and he moved out. He needed more privacy, wanted to devote more time to his theoretical writings. Still, he maintained close contact with Kingsley Hall, was visiting several times a

month, publicizing and raising money for the community, and serving as a consultant and adviser in times of stress.

During the first four years of its existence, a number of other therapists lived in Kingsley Hall. Laing mentioned David Cooper, and Aaron Esterson, co-author with him of *Sanity, Madness and the Family,* as well as Sid Briskin, a social worker. Four young psychiatrists, Leon Redler, Joseph Berke, Morton Schatzman, and Jerome Liss, emigrated from America to work with Laing. They lived at Kingsley Hall and stayed on after he left. Psychiatrists, sociologists, poets, painters, writers, and musicians from England, America, and the Continent were visitors for varying periods of time. Seminars in political, social, and therapeutic aspects of psychiatry were held regularly. Dancing, painting, weaving, yoga, poetry reading, lectures, and films were integral parts of life in Kingsley Hall. There was an atmosphere of continual personal, creative, and intellectual quest.

People "on the run" from mental hospitals, about to have a breakdown, or simply interested in taking part in a new experiment in communal living came to Kingsley Hall. They had read Laing's books, or knew someone who lived in Kingsley Hall, or had just heard about the place. The people who lived in the Hall decided, if there was room, who could move in, with preference given to those who seemed most in need of it. Laing emphasized that he never insisted that a given person be allowed to come, that it was purely the community's decision.

Once there, those who needed help came together with those who felt they could be of help on a basis of personal affinity, without constraint, without fees. Those who felt like it or needed money worked outside during the day. Others lived on National Assistance. All paid about three pounds a week (seven dollars) into a common fund for room and board. Each of the fourteen people who stayed there at any one time had his own tiny room, which he could share if he wanted.

Kingsley Hall, Laing explained, was always changing. He felt that what I would see would be quite different from what it had been like several years ago. That winter there was a general feeling of depression. Friction with neighbors, many of whom regarded the inhabitants of Kingsley Hall as dangerous and subversive, had caused the Kingsley Hall Foundation to refuse to renew the lease. There was little substance to the neighbors' charges, but random incidents disquieted them: a man who, at a neighboring green-grocer's, had a habit of biting into an occasional piece of fruit and replacing it on a pile; another who wandered into peoples' houses and sat in their living rooms. On one Friday night drunken workmen had broken in, shouting obscenities at the "perverts," "loonies," and "lay-abouts." Boys from the neighborhood once smashed down the front door with an ax. Now the building was in a state of disrepair. Windows broken by children and replaced had been broken again and left unmended. The large rooms were rarely used. In four months the building itself would be vacated.

Laing got up from his chair, put a kettle on the hot plate, and heated water for tea; he opened a bag of dried fruit and placed it on the table next to me. He moved easily around the room, preparing tea, emptying ashtrays, continuing to talk. His careful domesticity puzzled me; I had hardly expected it from the oracular author of *The Politics of Experience*.

I asked Laing about his attitude toward peoples' delusions; toward the ideas they have about themselves and the world, with which virtually everyone else disagrees, and which are often the most obvious and provocative aspect of schizophrenia. For example, someone's belief that he is Christ, or that the television is sending him messages, or that there is a worldwide plot against him.

Laing replied, "I often differ with people, but do not feel that it is incumbent on me to impose a particular viewpoint on anyone." He spoke about the personal and cultural origins of the "delusions" of several people he knew. Then, after asking if I had read the fifteenth-century *Malleus Maleficarum*, he

began to tell what first appeared to be an unrelated story about the Inquisition. "It seems that the Inquisition dealt with a number of problems that are today regarded as the province of psychiatry. They found that the causes of these problems lay in the fact that black magic had been practiced on the sufferer. If a man complained of impotence with his wife, the Inquisition would find the man's former mistress and torture her until she admitted she had practiced black magic. If, however, someone came along and proposed a naturalistic or psychological explanation for the man's impotence, he was regarded as a heretic. Now, however, someone who claims that black magic is being practiced on him is regarded as deluded. His belief is a symptom for which psychiatrists seek a naturalistic explanation, and often prescribe a pharmacological cure."

I listened to his narrative in rapt silence, wondering if he was putting me on. Certainly he was pointing out that ideas which once made up a dominant "therapeutic" ideology, the Inquisition's demonology, would now be regarded as "psychotic delusions." But did he also mean that psychiatric thought was, itself, a delusional system, no different in essence from the Inquisition's demonology? Perhaps he did. I'm still not sure. At any rate, he went on to say that "delusions are as culturally relative as life-style and family structure," and that there was no absolute way of determining their validity. Some were culturally sanctioned and validated, others not. He had, in his story, provided a larger framework for the consideration of the whole problem of delusions, psychiatrists' as well as patients'. The anecdote was a kind of mental judo, turning my question back on itself.

I asked Laing other questions about his own writings. Was the "Bird of Paradise" the record of an LSD trip? I knew that Laing had used LSD and that he found it helpful in psychotherapy and as a means of self-exploration. "No," he replied. "It was merely a description of some of the things that make up my own inner life." He reminded me that

Freud in *The Interpretation of Dreams* and *The Psychopathology of Everyday Life* had written about himself, and Laing contrasted his accessibility with the self-imposed anonymity of modern "Freudian" analysts. Freud, Laing added, was still "the best of psychiatric writers."

Before I left the office Laing gave me the names of several people who had spent time at Kingsley Hall, and during the next few days I contacted them.

Somehow, I felt unsatisfied with my first discussion with Laing. I wanted something more from him than a glimpse of how his mind worked and a description of Kingsley Hall. I wasn't exactly sure what it was. Thinking I might get closer to him if I gathered material for a biographical sketch, I asked if I could record our next session. He reluctantly agreed; then, later, changed his mind.

Perhaps Laing sensed my craving for more intimate knowledge, because when I next came to him he asked if I wanted to sit in on an interview that he was conducting with a family.

The parents were elderly lower-middle-class people, from a provincial town, whose son had been diagnosed as schizophrenic and hospitalized. Through Laing's widely publicized BBC broadcasts on schizophrenia, they had heard of his work and had come to him after a series of resigned, dismal prognoses from local psychiatrists. Their son was currently on large does of tranquilizers, and saw a doctor once monthly to get them.

The parents, growing old, were worried about what would happen to him after their death. Terribly anxious, heavily medicated, he seemed incapable of caring for himself. The parents sat on the daybed, the son in the chair opposite Laing. The interview was marked by a courteous ease on Laing's part and a remarkable openness in all members of the family. Laing is sometimes regarded as being very hostile to parents and as glorifying the madness of their children. Yet, though his writings depict the absurd and sometimes Christ-like suffering of the chil-

dren of confused and confusing homes, he does not vilify the parents. His descriptions, as in *Sanity, Madness and the Family,* are quite dispassionate. But the maneuvers by which children are driven mad, the connections between the shape of the resultant madness and the structure of the family interaction, are inescapable. In extreme and untenable situations, extreme measures of evasion and compliance—the signs and symptoms of "mental illness"—are necessary to survive.

Laing enabled each member of the family to tell his side of the story. He asked few questions, yet received much information. He was able, by a shifting glance or direct question, to interrupt what appeared to be deeply ingrained family patterns easily, without challenge or rancor, and without alienating any of the family members. The son had clearly found someone who could understand his predicament, and this understanding helped him build a bridge of communication to his parents. Laing helped him divest his fears and felt inadequacies of their frightening and bizarre quality. They were revealed as responses to family stress which the family could now begin to understand. Laing patiently discussed the details of the son's starting therapy with one of his colleagues. He talked with the parents about train schedules, fees, living accommodations in London, and the possibility of their son's moving into Kingsley Hall.

Afterward, Laing and I talked for a while about the interview. This discussion felt very different from the first one. Laing had let me see how he worked. A degree of intimacy had been broached, one which I hesitantly advanced when I asked him why he hadn't wanted me to use a tape recorder. "I don't want to make a public statement," he said, "to speak to all people at all times. The message I have to convey is from one person to another. I would rather speak to *you,* so that when you write something it will be about *your* experience of me and of London." I wondered whether what he had said was merely a rationalization for not permitting a

tape recorder. But it *felt* as if he were helping to transform our meeting from an "interview" into a personal encounter. He didn't
seem to have much to hide.

I asked his opinion of the body therapy
of Wilhelm Reich and his followers. Laing
felt that "one could work with emotional
problems by dealing with their physical
manifestations." He mentioned his occasional
use of the techniques of sensory awareness
and of yoga. He told me about a psychoanalyst in London who believed that an entire analysis could be conducted by dealing
with how someone stood up from a chair.
While I sat, smilingly surprised, Laing stood
up from his own chair, mechanically, emphasizing each movement; then he did so
more smoothly. He added that his own interests were, in general, "more verbal and intellectual." As a young man he had wanted to
write stories. At present he is fascinated by
attempts to delineate the structures of cultures, by the work of the anthropologist
Claude Lévi-Strauss, and by Michel Foucault's attempt to write a comprehensive intellectual history of the last 300 years in
Europe.

At my insistence he spoke of his own career. Laing was born to a poor family in
Glasgow in 1927 and grew up there, attending state-supported grammar and secondary
schools. He was graduated from Glasgow
University with a Doctor of Medicine degree
in 1951, and then served in the British Army
for two years. After his discharge, he worked
as a psychiatrist in a mental hospital. He set
about to see whether by changing the way
some of his patients were treated he could
change the nature of the "mental illness"
they were diagnosed as having. At that time,
the early 1950s, he still believed schizophrenia was possibly a genetic or biochemical
disorder or that it was secondary to an innate
lowered threshold to certain kinds of stress.

He described, with amused tolerance for
his own "scientific procedure," the socio-
metric process by which he had selected the
twelve most "out-of-contact" chronic schizophrenic patients on his ward. He had two

nurses each day take the twelve who were
chosen to a pleasant room in another part of
the hospital. There, with decent occupational and recreational facilities, treated simply as human beings, they could do whatever
they pleased. On the first day, the patients,
many of whom had hardly moved or spoken
in years, had to be wheeled or pushed off the
ward. "On the second day," he recalled, "an
hour before the ward door opened, they had
gathered around it talking, laughing, jumping up and down: it was enormously moving."

Within eighteen months all twelve, many
of whom had been hospitalized for ten or
fifteen years, were out of the hospital and
back to their families. Within another year
they were all back in the hospital.

To Laing this suggested, first, that "a
change in the way schizophrenics were
treated could radically alter the nature of
their schizophrenia," and, second, that the
family creates the "disease" in the individual.
Interest in individual schizophrenics gave
way to studies of the families of schizophrenics. He conducted these in association with
the psychoanalytically oriented Tavistock
Clinic. He went on to an elaboration of a
theory of interpersonal relations based on
models derived from psychoanalysis, phenomenology, and communications theory.

And this work in turn led to his critiques
of a society which, he says, produces, and is
maintained by, destructive families and
warped interpersonal relations. And ultimately to the creation of Kingsley Hall.

There, in the context of a new family and
society, the diagnosed schizophrenic could
rediscover and begin to redefine himself.
"My interests," he said, "fell into line like
a row of skittles." For the present, his interests have taken him somewhat away from
Kingsley Hall. He is devoting much of his
time to theoretical writings—right now, "an
attempt to revise Freud's theory of defenses."

I wanted to get some idea of Laing's politics. How did he reconcile his position as a
psychiatrist with his own sweeping criticisms
of the society which produces and maintains

psychiatrists? Didn't he feel that he—and by implication I and other psychiatrists—should be more directly active in helping to shock what he describes in *The Politics of Experience* as the "often fibrillating heartland of a senescent capitalism"?

Laing spoke only for himself: he said that he was "not an activist in the ordinary sense of the word." "Living in England," he observed, "made radical activism less pressing than in America." Besides, he felt that he was "temperamentally not very well suited for it." His own energies are devoted to what he calls "microrevolutions," profound changes in individuals, families, hospitals, and other small institutions. These changes may, in turn, bring about others, not through dramatic confrontation but by personal contact. Kingsley Hall, it is clear, is one such microrevolution.

Our time was up, and Laing led me down the stairs to the door. We stood outside for a moment. "You can tell your friends in America," he said, grinning, "that I'm not in a mental hospital." We both laughed. "Good luck in your scene back there."

When I left Laing's office, I felt satisfied. Even if he didn't have "the answers," he was unafraid of pursuing his questions and living with the contradictions they brought. He is a dedicated professional with revolutionary ideas, a staunch opponent of our civilization's "abdication of ecstasy," who produces careful scholarly books; a distant and ironic person who can make intense felt contact with others; a man accustomed to the depths of despair and the many faces of alienation, who prepares tea and treats visitors with politeness. I had no nagging doubts about his "sanity," and the rumors regarding his hospitalizations seem trivial.

In the days that followed, in speaking to people who were close to Laing, I found no hint of confirmation for these rumors. I can only attribute their persistence, and the fascination they hold for many of Laing's readers, to the degree of discomfort that his ideas have engendered. The parallel that comes to mind is the response of the medical establishment to Freud's early work. Freud pointed out that the intensity with which his contemporaries vilified him and his theories of infantile sexuality was evidence of the strength of their defenses against their own childhood sexual experiences. Laing, who has sought to point out the madness in much of our "normal" life, including accepted psychiatric practice, is suspected by tentative admirers, and accused by his psychiatric colleagues, of being himself mad.

That afternoon I took the long tube ride out to Kingsley Hall. During the preceding week I had telephoned twice more, but couldn't get a definite invitation from the people who answered the phone. Finally, through Laing's colleague Joe Berke, I had contacted Mary Barnes, who cheerfully agreed to talk with me.

By this time I was well prepared for disappointment. Everyone I had spoken to told me that the people at Kingsley Hall were depressed and angry at having to leave the building. One psychiatrist I met thought the building symbolized Laing's body, its present state of neglect the community's fury about what was happening, directed at Laing. On top of that, an article that appeared in the *Evening Standard* had provoked them. When I read it, it seemed simpleminded but generally favorable. But it called Kingsley Hall a "mental hospital," and some of the people who lived there were outraged.

I paused for a moment outside the building, looked at the plaque commemorating Gandhi's visit and at the array of broken windows. I was reminded of an abandoned parochial school. I sat on a bench across the street and tried to imagine what it would be like inside. A girl came out of the front door and walked in my direction. "You must be here to see Mary," she said. I said I was. "She's left the door open. The bell doesn't work. The children have broken it." She walked away, and I got up, crossed the street, and pushed open the scarred double doors.

I entered a large dark room which was about as cold as the January day outside. It looked as if it had once been a chapel or auditorium, but was now without pews or chairs. On one side, dozens of canvases leaned against the wall; to the right were stone stairs. At the head of the stairs, next to a pay telephone, was a door with a tree painted on it. The branches looked like arms. This was where Mary Barnes had lived for over three years.

While I was wondering whether I had arrived too early, Mary came up behind me. She led the way back downstairs, through the auditorium and into "the library," the room where Laing had lived. "I'll like living in Ronnie's old room," Mary told me. "Besides, it's larger than mine was." She apologized for the condition of the room as we pushed aside piles of clothes, paint tubes, scrapbooks, and glass jars. We sat on the floor, Mary in a pink quilted housecoat and slippers, her thick dark hair, framing a broad, deeply lined face, flowing over her shoulders, her knees drawn up against her chest; me shifting occasionally from one position to another when, during the next three or four hours, my body let me know I was uncomfortable.

There are, in the literature of psychotherapy, some remarkable first-person accounts of human growth achieved through madness. Hannah Green's *I Never Promised You a Rose Garden* and Marguerite Secheheye's and her patient Renee's *Autobiography of a Schizophrenic* are two. To me, the story of Mary Barnes, a forty-seven-year-old Roman Catholic and former nurse, who is now a painter and author of children's stories, is even more striking.

Unlike almost all psychiatric patients, Mary has been allowed and encouraged to experience "the natural healing process" of madness, the "initiation ceremonial through which the person will be guided with full social sanction into inner space and time" of which Laing speaks in *The Politics of Experience.* Mary's experience is crucial to Laing's model of therapy in the same way that Freud's early hysterical patients were to psychoanalysis. It is quite unlikely that it could have taken place anywhere but Kingsley

Hall, and even there a great strain was felt by the other inhabitants.

As she talked of the two periods of months during which she was quite mad, of the slow evolution of her trust in Joe Berke, who became her therapist, and of the discovery of herself as a painter, the light gradually faded from the room until we were sitting in darkness. After a while, Mary lit a candle. In the light of the candle I could see changes flicker across her face as she spoke of her life: the shy child who had been told she was awkward and untalented, the embarrassed adolescent, the constricted nursing instructor barely holding on to her sanity, the frenzied adult smearing feces on the walls, and the gentle wise woman who was able, in the calm born of great suffering, to tell me straightforwardly what she had gone through.

Mary's speech is quiet, direct, melodious, and modest. She uses some expressions often: "going down" for plunges into madness; "it went in on me" for anger that she turned against herself; "baby" as an adjective; "out" for people who are sociable—"he was very out"—and "in" for those who are feeling introspective.

Since I took notes and want to convey as directly as possible the quality of Mary's experience and her language, some of what follows is quoted from a paper of Laing's, some from Morton Schatzman's chapter "Madness and Morals," included in Joe Berke's book of essays on counterculture, and some directly from Mary's own writing.

Through Dr. James Robertson of the Tavistock Clinic, Mary had gone to Laing in 1963 to ask for help. She had been in a mental hospital in 1953 for a year with a diagnosis of schizophrenia, and had maintained herself since then as a nursing tutor in a general hospital. But she saw her daily life as a rigid, anxiety-laden, and constricted facade. She began to sense "that I had lost myself sometime in my life a long time ago." She felt she was on the verge of another psychotic episode, but this time, instead of the padded cells and shock therapy of the mental hospital, she wanted "to go back to before I was born and come up again." Laing told her that he was trying to establish a place where she could live through this experience, and Mary agreed to try to "hold on" until he could do so. During this time Mary continued to work at her job. Severe anxiety attacks were frequent. At night, with great effort, she pulled herself together for the next day's work. Periodically she visited Laing.

Nineteen months later Kingsley Hall opened, and Mary Barnes moved in: "At first so great was my fear I forgot what I had come for. Quite suddenly, I remembered, 'I've come here to have a breakdown, to go back to before I was born, and come up again.'" She continued to work for two weeks, but each night when she came to Kingsley Hall she "regressed." "Life became quite fantastic. Every night at Kingsley Hall I tore off my clothes, feeling I had to be naked. Lay on the floor with my shits and water, smeared the walls with feces. Was wild and noisy about the house or sitting in a heap on the kitchen floor. Half aware that I was going mad, there was the terror that I might not know what I was doing, away, outside of Kingsley Hall." She wrote to the hospital resigning her position and then took to bed, "went down" into her madness and back in time to infancy.

"The tempo was increasing. Down, down, oh, God, would I never break?"

She stopped eating solids, was fed milk from a bottle by Joe, by Laing, and by others. She rarely spoke and lay immobile for hours at a time. "In bed I kept my eyes shut so I didn't see people but I heard them. Touch was all important. Sometimes my body seemed apart, a leg or an arm across the room. The wall became hollow, and I seemed to go into it as into a big hole. Vividly aware of people, I was physically isolated in my room."

During this time there were several crises. Joe recalled that at one point Mary stopped sucking, urinating, and defecating; she was returning to a completely womblike state. She lost weight, grew weaker. The community met and decided that they couldn't let her continue this way, and that at Kingsley Hall they felt uneasy about putting in the feeding tube and catheter that would be necessary. They told Mary their decision, and gradually she began to suck again. Somewhat later the smell of the feces she smeared on the walls became annoying: Mary's room was next to the kitchen. Again the community debated. Eventually it was decided to let Mary continue. Each time a crisis came up the members of the community came together to decide what to do. Each step on Mary's journey was also a step in the community's development.

As Mary "came up" out of the madness she put on trousers, played ball, and danced, as she had never been allowed to as a child. Joe gave her some grease crayons, and in November, 1965, after five months at Kingsley Hall, she began to "scribble black breasts all over the walls of the hall. Suddenly a picture emerged, a woman kneeling with a baby at her breast."

"About the house, left over from decorating, were old tins of paints and brushes. On the walls of my room I painted moving figures, on my door twining stems and leaves, and on the table an orange bird appeared. Finding odd lengths of wallpaper I made picture stories. Then on strips of wallpaper backing, and on the walls of the house, I painted big, very big, at high speed. Through the spring of 1966 work poured out, all my insides were loose, the painting, like lightning, was streaking from the storm of me. Joe suggested 'paint the Crucifixion'; I did, again and again; hungry for life I wanted the cross."

Joe was with Mary every day, talking, playing with her, taking her shopping. For a long time she felt "Joe and I are not separate." But there were frequent crises of trust. Mary told me that once when they were eating together, Joe put salt on his food. She was desolate: "Joe," she said, "what have I done that you had to punish yourself?"

In June, 1966, "feeling it go in on me," Mary took to her bed again, but with the support of the community she was up in a few months. "In the autumn, with oil pastels and a sketchbook, I made more stories with pictures, including 'The Hollow Tree' for Ronnie's birthday and 'The King and the Donkey.' "

Since then, Mary has been painting and writing steadily. She has had four shows of her work and was preparing for another when I saw her. The paintings—dozens of which she showed me after we had talked, on canvas, boards, sheets of wrapping paper, and the walls—reminded me of a hybrid of Munch and Rouault. I bought two from her, vivid, powerful renderings of Saul struck down by God on the way to Damascus, emblems to me of the blinding force of Mary's own transformation.

Laing's introduction to the catalogue of her Camden Art Center exhibits seems apt: "In her painting Mary puts outside herself with a minimum of meditation what is inside her. Paintings are executed with her finger not because she cannot use a brush, but because she prefers (often) not to. She is not professionally proficient in the art of composition, not because of the failure to master the means for this end, but because hers is not the end that this is a means towards. We must take her on her terms. . . ."

Mary still feels that in many ways she is "not very grown up." She continues to see Joe in therapy, continues to learn more about herself. Though she could have lived elsewhere, she preferred, until its closing, to stay at Kingsley Hall, which she regarded as home. There, according to other members of the community, she was a highly valued therapist. Having gone so deeply down and come out, she is unafraid of others' madness. A terrified girl would speak with no one else but came to Mary, slept in her room for days, and drank the mixture of warm milk and honey that Mary prepared for her. When Mary was "down" Joe had given it to her.

After I looked at some of her paintings, Mary showed me around Kingsley Hall: the large rooms, now not regularly used, where communal meals were eaten, seminars and entertainment held; the roof garden; and some of the individual rooms where people I had met had lived. After a while we came to "the flat," a living room on the third story of the house. Several people sat around an electric heater sipping tea, chatting, and reading. Just off this room, in a small kitchen, someone was cooking. Mary introduced me to a couple of people and left to continue her packing.

I sat down close to the heater, beside a young man who held his head in his hands. The wall above him was covered with graffiti. One read "Harold Pinter was here with his friend Franz Kafka." Further up were black three-quarter circles, solid sweeps of pigment, the breasts that Mary had first painted. After a while, the girl I had seen on the street came out of the kitchen and offered me tea. We sat in silence for a while, I grew uncomfortable and asked a polite, inane question. Abruptly, she got up. I felt alone, an awkward snooper.

A meticulously dressed man of about thirty-five came over and introduced himself as David. I told him I recognized his voice from the telephone, and he smiled with satisfaction: "So you've finally got here." He began to talk animatedly about the *Evening Standard* article: "Kingsley Hall is not a hospital, and we are not Laing's patients unless we choose to be." He said he was thinking of suing the *Standard,* and was sending copies of the article to the members of the Philadelphia Association.

David went on to describe the vitriolic public attacks that members of the organic and behaviorist Establishment had recently launched against Laing and Kingsley Hall. He said that William Sargant, the chief psychiatrist at London's St. Thomas's Hospital, and one of those quoted in the *Standard,* had complained of having to "take care of Laing's failures." He also suggested I read "an absurd article" in which the psychologist H. J. Eysenck, long a critic of psychoanalysis, accuses Laing (and David Cooper) of "using these poor suffering victims as a platform for pseudo-philosophical arguments."

A tall young man, long-haired, bearded,

wide-eyed—a figure out of Saxon legends—
wandered by, grimacing, folding and unfold-
ing his arms. He said something about
"Green helmets" and "Princeton, New Jersey." I sat very seriously, uncomprehending,
in my best listener's posture.

Everyone else continued about his business. In the kitchen there was a discussion
about the proper way to cook a Christmas
pudding. The voices grew louder, more argu-
mentative. An older man left the kitchen,
silent, obviously angry. His advice, at first
solicited, had been rejected.

David was carefully mounting copies of
the *Standard* article on heavy paper. The girl
returned to the room, sat down again with a
magazine. The man next to me was looking
into the electric flame of the heater, warm-
ing his hands.

Suddenly the bearded man burst out laughing. I started to laugh too, aware of my own
self-conscious seriousness. He told me that
he was "in the ionosphere," and that the
"air [was] thin." I asked if it was "lonely,"
and he said, serious now, that it was and that
he "could come down but am not sure if I
want to." Feeling closer to him, I let go of my
psychiatric demeanor, and for a while,
through puns, mimicry, and self-caricature,
we carried on a conversation. He poured
some more tea for me.

During the two day-long visits I made to
Kingsley Hall, I spent about half my time
with Mary, talking, helping her move five
years' of possessions from her old to her new
room, and looking at her paintings. The rest
of the time I sat around the flat. The people
who passed in and out became accustomed
to my presence as I relaxed in theirs. I was
questioned about psychoanalysis and lec-
tured on electrical energy.

Feeling more comfortable, I asked some
people about their attitude toward Laing's
theories. A few, like Mary, were unabashedly
enthusiastic. But many, to my surprise, were
somewhat skeptical. One man wryly observed
that "previous encounters with psychiatrists
and mental hospitals have numbed me to
theoretical arguments."

Kingsley Hall, almost everyone seemed to
agree, was a good place—Peter, Mary Barnes's
brother, and a newcomer, strenuously objected to the lack of private cooking facilities—a home, or a haven in stormy times.
Laing's writings interested people less than
Laing himself, toward whom there seemed
to be a deep but grudging warmth. Even
though he no longer stayed there, and
couldn't stop the lease from running out,
he, and the rest of the Philadelphia Association, still cared and still fought for Kingsley
Hall: against family-sponsored health officers, bent on dragging erring relatives back
to mental hospitals; against public attacks
from other psychiatrists; and against an often
hostile neighborhood.

Mary told me that with the building soon
to be vacated, no psychiatrist in residence,
and the future uncertain, people were reluctant to "go down." She saw the community
as wary, its members self-protective, inclined
to keep their defenses up. She said that several people were in therapy with Laing and
the others with psychiatrists who had lived
in Kingsley Hall, and that any community
member could get help free or at low cost.
But it seemed unlikely that anyone would
now risk the profound journey into himself
that Mary and others took in the earlier
years.

Still, the dozen people at Kingsley Hall,
many of whom had been diagnosed schizophrenic, some among them having been for
long periods on mental hospital back wards,
were finding a way to live with one another:
free from restraints and coercion, not needing tranquilizers and shock therapy, independent of "ward administrators," and
without benefit of rules and regulations.

An American medical student who had
been at Kingsley Hall the year before told
me that even if *she* couldn't understand what
people were saying to each other *they* obviously understood one another. In two days
I couldn't really understand what the community was saying to itself. But I knew that
it spoke in accents of mutual acceptance and
open disagreement, in deeds of kindness and

"appropriate" impoliteness—in anguish and humor and guarded hope.

Just before I went to say good-bye to Mary, the young man who sat by the heater told me that he was afraid to loosen his tortured and precarious hold on his "normality" to seek a new, more stable kind of sanity. He said he felt "like a ship on the edge of darkness." The image seemed appropriate for Kingsley Hall as well. Soon the building would be returned to the pacifists who had lent it, five years ago, to Laing and his friends.

But Mary Barnes was pretty sure that new Kingsley Halls would be created, new places, which, as she put it, would be "good enough to take all the shit of all the people." Places where people could go back to where they had "gone wrong" and make a new start. I left her, late at night, looking through a pile of sketches. She told me to "come back any-time."

The Kingsley Hall experience is the central node, Laing the master switch in a "Network" of men and women who are dedicated to practicing and living a new kind of psychiatry. Energy seems to flow from him and his writings, touching in others sources of creativity which spark their own projects. Excitement, discoveries, information are passed in all directions.

The young psychiatrists who lived there over the past five years found at Kingsley Hall the same kinds of possibilities for growth and change as did the former "mental patients" who came there. The psychiatrists' paths of discovery were less agonizing than their patients', but they were more fraught with toe-stubbing ironies. The first problem, very difficult for even the most relaxed acolyte, was to unlearn the role of doctor, to drop the self-protective, self-defeating guise of the sane man in the midst of lunatics.

Joe Berke, the huge black-bearded bear of a man who worked so tirelessly with Mary Barnes, described how this process began for him: when he arrived at Kingsley Hall, recently graduated from medical school, he met a young man named "Andrew" who had spent nine of his twenty-one years in a men-

tal hospital. "Andrew" had been diagnosed as a catatonic schizophrenic and presumed beyond help. He shuffled around Kingsley Hall speaking to himself under his breath. When he wanted to talk to someone, he put his face right up against theirs and spoke, often incomprehensibly. This unnerved Joe, who, for weeks, in spite of his good intentions, had continued to regard "Andrew" as "that nut." One morning Joe rose early and went down to the dining room. "Andrew" came in at about the same time. Standing there, in the early morning light, half asleep, off-guard, they smiled at each other. After that, "Andrew" was just Andrew, and he and Joe began to get to know one another.

The others described similar experiences, meetings, and friendships with people who had been previously given up by psychiatrists as "hopelessly dilapidated, burnt-out schizophrenics." Sometimes their relationships turned into somewhat more formal psychotherapeutic ones, often not.

When I visited last January, none of the psychiatrists lived at Kingsley Hall anymore. Cramped, cold quarters and the arrival of wives who felt the need for more privacy precipitated their leaving. But all were still actively involved in Kingsley Hall.

To Leon, whose wife had just had a child, Kingsley Hall was itself a "baby," with whose growth and development he was intimately concerned. Like Laing, and Mary Barnes, he viewed its closing in May as merely the end of its first phase.

When Kingsley Hall did close, Mary Barnes took an apartment of her own, the first she has ever had, and there she paints and writes. Most of the others, whom I met in January moved into two condemned buildings which Leon managed to rent from the local council. Joe and Morty are in the process of organizing another household, and Laing himself described plans for eventually opening up a larger, more comfortable therapeutic center to which psychiatrists and others could come for training.

But the Network has spread well beyond this central core. It comprises eighty to a hundred other people, predominately in England, but also on the Continent and in America. Leon, who edits the *Network Newsletter,* described it in the first issue as a "London-based group of people concerned with liberation particularly in the context of human experience and behavior; of making sense of one's experience of oneself, the other, the world; of liberation from institutional psychiatric thought and practice; of healing and making whole, mind-body-soul; of being."

Already two new households on the Kingsley Hall model are in the process of opening in America, one in New Haven, the other in San Jose, California. Members of the Network have begun to publish books on their experience. Leon is editing a book of writings by people who stayed at Kingsley Hall. Joe and Mary are finishing a book entitled *Mary Barnes: Two Accounts of a Journey Through Madness,* which will be published here this year. Others who spent time at Kingsley Hall are writing about it and trying to set up similar communities.

As I spent time with members of the Network, I began for the first time to feel part of a larger personal and professional context which made sense to me. In spite of geographical and professional isolation, I had really been part of it for several years. Joe said, half-jokingly, that "if the Network is in you, you are in it." I was reminded, first, of the League in Hesse's *Journey to the East* and then, more concretely, of the missionary excitement that pervaded Freud's early circle.

A new way of looking at madness has given birth to a new kind of therapy. Patients' and therapists' strategies of liberation have be-

gun to coincide. New places for them to "work things out," to "discover the wholeness of being human between them," are being created. The insights won from understanding madness are being used to transform the social worlds of the "mad" patient and the "sane" doctor. Kingsley Hall, the Network, and the new communities in America are among the first of these transformations. These new developments in psychiatric theory and practice, sometimes referred to as Anti-Psychiatry, parallel and catalyze developments in the larger society.

At Kingsley Hall the barrier between the "sane" doctor and the "mad" patient was removed. In his writings, Laing, starting with an attempt to describe madness, ultimately questions the sanity of the society which erected this barrier: "A little girl of seventeen told me she was terrified because the Atom Bomb was inside her. That is a delusion. The statesmen of the world who boast and threaten that they have Doomsday weapons are far more dangerous and far more estranged from 'reality' than any of the people to whom the label 'psychotic' is affixed."

Laing holds up to his readers a vision of a world in which all of us are "bemused and crazed creatures, strangers to our true selves, to one another, and to the spiritual and material world." He insists that the way out of this pervasive madness is through profound personal and social transformation.

The metanoiac voyage that took place at Kingsley Hall must become possible for all who need and wish to embark on it. Perhaps "mental hospitals," reversing history, can become ships of sanity.

On Being Sane in Insane Places

D. L. ROSENHAN

If sanity and insanity exist, how shall we know them?

The question is neither capricious nor itself insane. However much we may be personally convinced that we can tell the normal from the abnormal, the evidence is simply not compelling. It is commonplace, for example, to read about murder trials wherein eminent psychiatrists for the defense are contradicted by equally eminent psychiatrists for the prosecution on the matter of the defendant's sanity. More generally, there are a great deal of conflicting data on the reliability, utility, and meaning of such terms as "sanity," "insanity," "mental illness," and "schizophrenia" (1). Finally, as early as 1934, Benedict suggested that normality and abnormality are not universal (2). What is viewed as normal in one culture may be seen as quite aberrant in another. Thus, notions of normality and abnormality may not be quite as accurate as people believe they are.

To raise questions regarding normality and abnormality is in no way to question

the fact that some behaviors are deviant or odd. Murder is deviant. So, too, are hallucinations. Nor does raising such questions deny the existence of the personal anguish that is often associated with "mental illness." Anxiety and depression exist. Psychological suffering exists. But normality and abnormality, sanity and insanity, and the diagnoses that flow from them may be less substantive than many believe them to be.

At its heart, the question of whether the sane can be distinguished from the insane (and whether degrees of insanity can be distinguished from each other) is a simple matter: do the salient characteristics that lead to diagnoses reside in the patients themselves or in the environments and contexts in which observers find them? From Bleuler, through Kretchmer, through the formulators of the recently revised *Diagnostic and Statistical Manual* of the American Psychiatric Association, the belief has been strong that patients present symptoms, that those symptoms can be categorized, and, implicitly, that the sane are distinguishable from the insane. More recently, however, this belief has been questioned. Based in part on theoretical and anthropological considerations, but also on philosophical, legal, and therapeutic ones, the view has grown that psychological cate-

Note: D. L. Rosenhan, "On Being Sane In Insane Places," *Science,* Vol. 179, Jan. 1973, p. 250–259. Copyright 1973 by the American Association for the Advancement of Science. Reprinted with permission.

gorization of mental illness is useless at best and downright harmful, misleading, and pejorative at worst. Psychiatric diagnoses, in this view, are in the minds of the observers and are not valid summaries of characteristics displayed by the observed (3–5).

Gains can be made in deciding which of these is more nearly accurate by getting normal people (that is, people who do not have, and have never suffered, symptoms of serious psychiatric disorders) admitted to psychiatric hospitals and then determining whether they were discovered to be sane and, if so, how. If the sanity of such pseudopatients were always detected, there would be prima facie evidence that a sane individual can be distinguished from the insane context in which he is found. Normality (and presumably abnormality) is distinct enough that it can be recognized wherever it occurs, for it is carried within the person. If, on the other hand, the sanity of the pseudopatients were never discovered, serious difficulties would arise for those who support traditional modes of psychiatric diagnosis. Given that the hospital staff was not incompetent, that the pseudopatient had been behaving as sanely as he had been outside of the hospital, and that it had never been previously suggested that he belonged in a psychiatric hospital, such an unlikely outcome would support the view that psychiatric diagnosis betrays little about the patient but much about the environment in which an observer finds him.

This article describes such an experiment. Eight sane people gained secret admission to 12 different hospitals (6). Their diagnostic experiences constitute the data of the first part of this article; the remainder is devoted to a description of their experiences in psychiatric institutions. Too few psychiatrists and psychologists, even those who have worked in such hospitals, know what the experience is like. They rarely talk about it with former patients, perhaps because they distrust information coming from the previously insane. Those who have worked in psychiatric hospitals are likely to have adapted so thoroughly to the settings that they are insensitive to the impact of that experience. And while there have been occasional reports of researchers who submitted themselves to psychiatric hospitalization (7), these researchers have commonly remained in the hospitals for short periods of time, often with the knowledge of the hospital staff. It is difficult to know the extent to which they were treated like patients or like research colleagues. Nevertheless, their reports about the inside of the psychiatric hospital have been valuable. This article extends those efforts.

PSEUDOPATIENTS AND THEIR SETTINGS

The eight pseudopatients were a varied group. One was a psychology graduate student in his 20's. The remaining seven were older and "established." Among them were three psychologists, a pediatrician, a psychiatrist, a painter, and a housewife. Three pseudopatients were women, five were men. All of them employed pseudonyms, lest their alleged diagnoses embarrass them later. Those who were in mental health professions alleged another occupation in order to avoid the special attentions that might be accorded by staff, as a matter of courtesy or caution, to ailing colleagues (8). With the exception of myself (I was the first pseudopatient and my presence was known to the hospital administrator and chief psychologist and, so far as I can tell, to them alone), the presence of pseudopatients and the nature of the research program was not known to the hospital staffs (9).

The settings were similarly varied. In order to generalize the findings, admission into a variety of hospitals was sought. The 12 hospitals in the sample were located in five different states on the East and West coasts. Some were old and shabby, some were quite new. Some were research-oriented, others not. Some had good staff-patient ratios, others were quite understaffed. Only one was a strictly private hospital. All of the others were supported by state or federal funds or, in one instance, by university funds.

After calling the hospital for an appointment, the pseudopatient arrived at the admissions office complaining that he had been hearing voices. Asked what the voices said, he replied that they were often unclear, but as far as he could tell they said "empty," "hollow," and "thud." The voices were unfamiliar and were of the same sex as the pseudopatient. The choice of these symptoms was occasioned by their apparent similarity to existential symptoms. Such symptoms are alleged to arise from painful concerns about the perceived meaninglessness of one's life. It is as if the hallucinating person were saying, "My life is empty and hollow." The choice of these symptoms was also determined by the *absence* of a single report of existential psychoses in the literature.

Beyond alleging the symptoms and falsifying name, vocation, and employment, no further alterations of person, history, or circumstances were made. The significant events of the pseudopatient's life history were presented as they had actually occurred. Relationships with parents and siblings, with spouse and children, with people at work and in school, consistent with the aforementioned exceptions, were described as they were or had been. Frustrations and upsets were described along with joys and satisfactions. These facts are important to remember. If anything, they strongly biased the subsequent results in favor of detecting sanity, since none of their histories or current behaviors were seriously pathological in any way.

Immediately upon admission to the psychiatric ward, the pseudopatient ceased simulating *any* symptoms of abnormality. In some cases, there was a brief period of mild nervousness and anxiety, since none of the pseudopatients really believed that they would be admitted so easily. Indeed, their shared fear was that they would be immediately exposed as frauds and greatly embarrassed. Moreover, many of them had never visited a psychiatric ward; even those who had, nevertheless had some genuine fears about what might happen to them. Their nervousness, then, was quite appropriate to the novelty of the hospital setting, and it abated rapidly.

Apart from that short-lived nervousness, the pseudopatient behaved on the ward as he "normally" behaved. The pseudopatient spoke to patients and staff as he might ordinarily. Because there is uncommonly little to do on a psychiatric ward, he attempted to engage others in conversation. When asked by staff how he was feeling, he indicated that he was fine, that he no longer experienced symptoms. He responded to instructions from attendants, to calls for medication (which was not swallowed), and to dining-hall instructions. Beyond such activities as were available to him on the admissions ward, he spent his time writing down his observations about the ward, its patients, and the staff. Initially these notes were written "secretly," but as it soon became clear that no one much cared, they were subsequently written on standard tablets of paper in such public places as the dayroom. No secret was made of these activities.

The pseudopatient, very much as a true psychiatric patient, entered a hospital with no foreknowledge of when he would be discharged. Each was told that he would have to get out by his own devices, essentially by convincing the staff that he was sane. The psychological stresses associated with hospitalization were considerable, and all but one of the pseudopatients desired to be discharged almost immediately after being admitted. They were, therefore, motivated not only to behave sanely, but to be paragons of cooperation. That their behavior was in no way disruptive is confirmed by nursing reports, which have been obtained on most of the patients. These reports uniformly indicate that the patients were "friendly," "cooperative," and "exhibited no abnormal indications."

THE NORMAL ARE NOT DETECTABLY SANE

Despite their public "show" of sanity, the pseudopatients were never detected. Admitted, except in one case, with a diagnosis of schizophrenia (10), each was discharged with a diagnosis of schizophrenia "in remission." The label "in remission" should in no way be dismissed as a formality, for at no time during any hospitalization had any question been raised about any pseudopatient's simulation. Nor are there any indications in the hospital records that the pseudopatient's status was suspect. Rather, the evidence is strong that, once labeled schizophrenic, the pseudopatient was stuck with that label. If the pseudopatient was to be discharged, he must naturally be "in remission"; but he was not sane, nor, in the institution's view, had he ever been sane.

The uniform failure to recognize sanity cannot be attributed to the quality of the hospitals, for, although there were considerable variations among them, several are considered excellent. Nor can it be alleged that there was simply not enough time to observe the pseudopatients. Length of hospitalization ranged from 7 to 52 days, with an average of 19 days. The pseudopatients were not, in fact, carefully observed, but this failure clearly speaks more to traditions within psychiatric hospitals than to lack of opportunity.

Finally, it cannot be said that the failure to recognize the pseudopatients' sanity was due to the fact that they were not behaving sanely. While there was clearly some tension present in all of them, their daily visitors could detect no serious behavioral consequences—nor, indeed, could other patients. It was quite common for the patients to "detect" the pseudopatients' sanity. During the first three hospitalizations, when accurate counts were kept, 35 of a total of 118 patients on the admissions ward voiced their suspicions, some vigorously. "You're not crazy. You're a journalist, or a professor [referring to the continual note-taking]. You're check-ing up on the hospital." While most of the patients were reassured by the pseudopatient's insistence that he had been sick before he came in but was fine now, some continued to believe that the pseudopatient was sane throughout his hospitalization (11). The fact that the patients often recognized normality when staff did not raises important questions.

Failure to detect sanity during the course of hospitalization may be due to the fact that physicians operate with a strong bias toward what statisticians call the type 2 error (5). This is to say that physicians are more inclined to call a healthy person sick (a false positive, type 2) than a sick person healthy (a false negative, type 1). The reasons for this are not hard to find: it is clearly more dangerous to misdiagnose illness than health. Better to err on the side of caution, to suspect illness even among the healthy.

But what holds for medicine does not hold equally well for psychiatry. Medical illnesses, while unfortunate, are not commonly pejorative. Psychiatric diagnoses, on the contrary, carry with them personal, legal, and social stigmas (12). It was therefore important to see whether the tendency toward diagnosing the sane insane could be reversed. The following experiment was arranged at a research and teaching hospital whose staff had heard these findings but doubted that such an error could occur in their hospital. The staff was informed that at some time during the following 3 months, one or more pseudopatients would attempt to be admitted into the psychiatric hospital. Each staff member was asked to rate each patient who presented himself at admissions or on the ward according to the likelihood that the patient was a pseudopatient. A 10-point scale was used, with a 1 and 2 reflecting high confidence that the patient was a pseudopatient.

Judgments were obtained on 193 patients who were admitted for psychiatric treatment. All staff who had had sustained contact with or primary responsibility for the patient—attendants, nurses, psychiatrists, physicians, and psychologists—were asked to make judgments. Forty-one patients were alleged, with high confidence, to be pseudopatients by at least one member of the staff. Twenty-three were considered suspect by at least one psychiatrist. Nineteen were suspected by one psychiatrist *and* one other staff member. Actually, no genuine pseudopatient (at least from my group) presented himself during this period.

The experiment is instructive. It indicates that the tendency to designate sane people as insane can be reversed when the stakes (in this case, prestige and diagnostic acumen) are high. But what can be said of the 19 people who were suspected of being "sane" by one psychiatrist and another staff member? Were these people truly "sane," or was it rather the case that in the course of avoiding the type 2 error the staff tended to make more errors of the first sort—calling the crazy "sane"? There is no way of knowing. But one thing is certain: any diagnostic process that lends itself so readily to massive errors of this sort cannot be a very reliable one.

THE STICKINESS OF PSYCHODIAGNOSTIC LABELS

Beyond the tendency to call the healthy sick—a tendency that accounts better for diagnostic behavior on admission than it does for such behavior after a lengthy period of exposure—the data speak to the massive role of labeling in psychiatric assessment. Having once been labeled schizophrenic, there is nothing the pseudopatient can do to overcome the tag. The tag profoundly colors others' perceptions of him and his behavior.

From one viewpoint, these data are hardly surprising, for it has long been known that elements are given meaning by the context in which they occur. Gestalt psychology made this point vigorously, and Asch (*13*) demonstrated that there are "central" personality traits (such as "warm" versus "cold") which are so powerful that they markedly color the meaning of other information in forming an impression of a given personality (*14*). "Insane," "schizophrenic," "manic-depressive," and "crazy" are probably among the most powerful of such central traits. Once a person is designated abnormal, all of his other behaviors and characteristics are colored by that label. Indeed, that label is so powerful that many of the pseudopatients' normal behaviors were overlooked entirely or profoundly misinterpreted. Some examples may clarify this issue.

Earlier I indicated that there were no changes in the pseudopatient's personal history and current status beyond those of name, employment, and, where necessary, vocation. Otherwise, a veridical description of personal history and circumstances was offered. Those circumstances were not psychotic. How were they made consonant with the diagnosis of psychosis? Or were those diagnoses modified in such a way as to bring them into accord with the circumstances of the pseudopatient's life, as described by him?

As far as I can determine, diagnoses were in no way affected by the relative health of the circumstances of a pseudopatient's life. Rather, the reverse occurred: the perception of his circumstances was shaped entirely by the diagnosis. A clear example of such translation is found in the case of a pseudopatient who had had a close relationship with his mother but was rather remote from his father during his early childhood. During adolescence and beyond, however, his father became a close friend, while his relationship with his mother cooled. His present relationship with his wife was characteristically close and warm. Apart from occasional angry exchanges, friction was minimal. The children had rarely been spanked. Surely there is nothing especially pathological about such a history. Indeed, many readers may see a similar pattern in their own experiences, with no markedly deleterious consequences. Observe, however, how such a history was translated in the psychopathological context, this from the case summary prepared after the patient was discharged.

> This white 39-year-old male . . . manifests a long history of considerable ambivalence in close relationships, which begins in early childhood. A warm relationship with his mother cools during his adolescence. A distant relationship to his father is described as becoming very intense. Affective stability is absent. His attempts to control emotionality with his wife and children are punctuated by angry outbursts and, in the case of the children, spankings. And while he says that he has several good friends, one senses considerable ambivalence embedded in those relationships also. . . .

The facts of the case were unintentionally distorted by the staff to achieve consistency with a popular theory of the dynamics of a schizophrenic reaction (15). Nothing of an ambivalent nature had been described in relations with parents, spouse, or friends. To the extent that ambivalence could be inferred, it was probably not greater than is found in all human relationships. It is true the pseudopatient's relationships with his parents changed over time, but in the ordinary context that would hardly be remarkable—indeed, it might very well be expected. Clearly, the meaning ascribed to his verbalizations (that is, ambivalence, affective instability) was determined by the diagnosis: schizophrenia. An entirely different meaning would have been ascribed if it were known that the man was "normal."

All pseudopatients took extensive notes publicly. Under ordinary circumstances, such behavior would have raised questions in the minds of observers, as, in fact, it did among patients. Indeed, it seemed so certain that the notes would elicit suspicion that elaborate precautions were taken to remove them from the ward each day. But the precautions proved needless. The closest any staff member came to questioning these notes occurred when one pseudopatient asked his physician what kind of medication he was receiving and began to write down the response. "You needn't write it," he was told gently. "If you have trouble remembering, just ask me again."

If no questions were asked of the pseudopatients, how was their writing interpreted? Nursing records for three patients indicate that the writing was seen as an aspect of their pathological behavior. "Patient engages in writing behavior" was the daily nursing comment on one of the pseudopatients who was never questioned about his writing. Given that the patient is in the hospital, he must be psychologically disturbed. And given that he is disturbed, continuous writing must be a behavioral manifestation of that disturbance, perhaps a subset of the compulsive behaviors that are sometimes correlated with schizophrenia.

One tacit characteristic of psychiatric diagnosis is that it locates the sources of aberration within the individual and only rarely within the complex of stimuli that surrounds him. Consequently, behaviors that are stimulated by the environment are commonly misattributed to the patient's disorder. For example, one kindly nurse found a pseudopatient pacing the long hospital corridors. "Nervous, Mr. X?" she asked. "No, bored," he said.

The notes kept by pseudopatients are full of patient behaviors that were misinterpreted by well-intentioned staff. Often enough, a patient would go "berserk" because he had, wittingly or unwittingly, been mistreated by, say, an attendant. A nurse coming upon the scene would rarely inquire even cursorily into the environmental stimuli of the patient's behavior. Rather, she assumed that his upset derived from his pathology, not from his present interactions with other staff members. Occasionally, the staff might assume that the patient's family (especially when they had recently visited) or other patients had stimulated the outburst. But never were the staff found to assume that one of themselves or the structure of the hospital had anything to do with a patient's behavior. One psychiatrist pointed to a group of patients who were sitting outside the cafeteria entrance half an hour before lunchtime. To a group of young residents he indicated that such behavior was characteristic of the oral-acquisitive nature of the syndrome. It seemed not to occur to him that there were very few things to anticipate in a psychiatric hospital besides eating.

A psychiatric label has a life and an influence of its own. Once the impression has been formed that the patient is schizophrenic, the expectation is that he will continue to be schizophrenic. When a sufficient amount of time has passed, during which the patient has done nothing bizarre, he is considered to be in remission and available for discharge. But the label endures beyond discharge, with the unconfirmed expectation that he will behave as a schizophrenic again. Such labels, conferred by mental health professionals, are as influential on the patient as they are on his relatives and friends, and it should not surprise anyone that the diagnosis acts on all of them as a self-fulfilling prophecy. Eventually, the patient himself accepts the diagnoses, with all of its surplus meanings and expectations, and behaves accordingly (5).

The inferences to be made from these matters are quite simple. Much as Zigler and Phillips have demonstrated that there is enormous overlap in the symptoms presented by patients who have been variously diagnosed (16), so there is enormous overlap in the behaviors of the sane and the insane. The sane are not "sane" all of the time. We lose our tempers "for no good reason." We are occasionally depressed or anxious, again for no good reason. And we may find it difficult to get along with one or another person—again for no reason that we can specify. Similarly, the insane are not always insane. Indeed, it was the impression of the pseudo-patients while living with them that they were sane for long periods of time—that the bizarre behaviors upon which their diagnoses were allegedly predicated constituted only a small fraction of their total behavior. If it makes no sense to label ourselves perma-

nently depressed on the basis of an occasional depression, then it takes better evidence than is presently available to label all patients insane or schizophrenic on the basis of bizarre behaviors or cognitions. It seems more useful, as Mischel (17) has pointed out, to limit our discussions to *behaviors*, the stimuli that provoke them, and their correlates.

It is not known why powerful impressions of personality traits, such as "crazy" or "insane," arise. Conceivably, when the origins of and stimuli that give rise to a behavior are remote or unknown, or when the behavior strikes us as immutable, trait labels regarding the *behavior* arise. When, on the other hand, the origins and stimuli are known and available, discourse is limited to the behavior itself. Thus, I may hallucinate because I am sleeping, or I may hallucinate because I have ingested a peculiar drug. These are termed sleep-induced hallucinations, or dreams, and drug-induced hallucinations, respectively. But when the stimuli to my hallucinations are unknown, that is called craziness, or schizophrenia—as if that inference were somehow as illuminating as the others.

THE EXPERIENCE OF PSYCHIATRIC HOSPITALIZATION

The term "mental illness" is of recent origin. It was coined by people who were humane in their inclinations and who wanted very much to raise the station of (and the public's sympathies toward) the psychologically disturbed from that of witches and "crazies" to one that was akin to the physically ill. And they were at least partially successful, for the treatment of the mentally ill *has* improved considerably over the years. But while treatment has improved, it is doubtful that people really regard the mentally ill in the same way that they view the physically ill. A broken leg is something one recovers from, but mental illness allegedly endures forever (18). A broken leg does not threaten the observer, but a crazy schizophrenic? There is by now a host of evidence that attitudes toward the mentally ill are characterized by fear, hostility, aloofness, suspicion, and dread (*19*). The mentally ill are society's lepers.

That such attitudes infect the general population is perhaps not surprising, only upsetting. But that they affect the professionals—attendants, nurses, physicians, psychologists, and social workers—who treat and deal with the mentally ill is more disconcerting, both because such attitudes are self-evidently pernicious and because they are unwitting. Most mental health professionals would insist that they are sympathetic toward the mentally ill, that they are neither avoidant nor hostile. But it is more likely that an exquisite ambivalence characterizes their relations with psychiatric patients, such that their avowed impulses are only part of their entire attitude. Negative attitudes are there too and can easily be detected. Such attitudes should not surprise us. They are the natural offspring of the labels patients wear and the places in which they are found.

Consider the structure of the typical psychiatric hospital. Staff and patients are strictly segregated. Staff have their own living space, including their dining facilities, bathrooms, and assembly places. The glassed quarters that contain the professional staff, which the pseudopatients came to call "the cage," sit out on every dayroom. The staff emerge primarily for caretaking purposes—to give medication, to conduct a therapy or group meeting, to instruct or reprimand a patient. Otherwise, staff keep to themselves, almost as if the disorder that afflicts their charges is somehow catching.

So much is patient-staff segregation the rule that, for four public hospitals in which an attempt was made to measure the degree to which staff and patients mingle, it was necessary to use "time out of the staff cage" as the operational measure. While it was not the case that all time spent out of the cage was spent mingling with patients (attendants, for example, would occasionally emerge to watch television in the dayroom), it was the only way in which one could gather reliable data on time for measuring.

The average amount of time spent by attendants outside of the cage was 11.3 percent (range, 3 to 52 percent). This figure does not represent only time spent mingling with patients, but also includes time spent on such chores as folding laundry, supervising patients while they shave, directing ward cleanup, and sending patients to off-ward activities. It was the relatively rare attendant who spent time talking with patients or playing games with them. It proved impossible to obtain a "percent mingling time" for nurses, since the amount of time they spent out of the cage was too brief. Rather, we counted instances of emergence from the cage. On the average, daytime nurses emerged from the cage 11.5 times per shift, including instances when they left the ward entirely (range, 4 to 39 times). Late afternoon and night nurses were even less available, emerging on the average 9.4 times per shift (range, 4 to 41 times). Data on early morning nurses, who arrived usually after midnight and departed at 8 a.m., are not available because patients were asleep during most of this period.

Physicians, especially psychiatrists, were even less available. They were rarely seen on the wards. Quite commonly, they would be seen only when they arrived and departed, with the remaining time being spent in their offices or in the cage. On the average, physicians emerged on the ward 6.7 times per day (range, 1 to 17 times). It proved difficult to make an accurate estimate in this regard, since physicians often maintained hours that allowed them to come and go at different times.

The hierarchical organization of the psychiatric hospital has been commented on before (*20*), but the latent meaning of that kind of organization is worth noting again. Those with the most power have least to do with patients, and those with the least power are most involved with them. Recall, however, that the acquisition of role-appropriate behaviors occurs mainly through the obser-

TABLE 1. *Self-initiated contact by pseudopatients with psychiatrists and nurses and attendants, compared to contact with other groups.*

Contact	Psychiatric hospitals		University campus (nonmedical)	University medical center		
				Physicians		
	(1) Psychiatrists	(2) Nurses and attendants	(3) Faculty	(4) "Looking for a psychiatrist"	(5) "Looking for an internist"	(6) No additional comment
Responses						
Moves on, head averted (%)	71	88	0	0	0	0
Makes eye contact (%)	23	10	0	11	0	0
Pauses and chats (%)	2	2	0	11	0	10
Stops and talks (%)	4	0.5	100	78	100	90
Mean number of questions answered (out of 6)	*	*	6	3.8	4.8	4.5
Respondents (No.)	13	47	14	18	15	10
Attempts (No.)	185	1283	14	18	15	10

* Not applicable.

vation of others, with the most powerful having the most influence. Consequently, it it understandable that attendants not only spend more time with patients than do any other members of the staff—that is required by their station in the hierarchy—but also, insofar as they learn from their superiors' behavior, spend as little time with patients as they can. Attendants are seen mainly in the cage, which is where the models, the action, and the power are.

I turn now to a different set of studies, these dealing with staff response to patient-initiated contact. It has long been known that the amount of time a person spends with you can be an index of your significance to him. If he initiates and maintains eye contact, there is reason to believe that he is considering your requests and needs. If he pauses to chat or actually stops and talks, there is added reason to infer that he is individuating you. In four hospitals, the pseudopatient approached the staff member with a request which took the following form: "Pardon me, Mr. [or Dr. or Mrs.] X, could you tell me when I will be eligible for grounds privileges?" (or ". . . when I will be presented at the staff meeting?" or ". . . when I am

likely to be discharged?"). While the content of the question varied according to the appropriateness of the target and the pseudopatient's (apparent) current needs the form was always a courteous and relevant request for information. Care was taken never to approach a particular member of the staff more than once a day, lest the staff member become suspicious or irritated. In examining these data, remember that the behavior of the pseudopatients was neither bizarre nor disruptive. One could indeed engage in good conversation with them.

The data for these experiments are shown in Table 1, separately for physicians (column 1) and for nurses and attendants (column 2). Minor differences between these four institutions were overwhelmed by the degree to which staff avoided continuing contacts that patients had initiated. By far, their most common response consisted of either a brief response to the question, offered while they were "on the move" and with head averted, or no response at all.

The encounter frequently took the following bizarre form: (pseudopatient) "Pardon me, Dr. X. Could you tell me when I am eligible for grounds privileges?" (physician)

"Good morning, Dave. How are you today?" (Moves off without waiting for a response.)

It is instructive to compare these data with data recently obtained at Stanford University. It has been alleged that large and eminent universities are characterized by faculty who are so busy that they have no time for students. For this comparison, a young lady approached individual faculty members who seemed to be walking purposefully to some meeting or teaching engagement and asked them the following six questions.

1) "Pardon me, could you direct me to Encina Hall?" (at the medical school: ". . . to the Clinical Research Center?").

2) "Do you know where Fish Annex is?" (there is no Fish Annex at Stanford).

3) "Do you teach here?"

4) "How does one apply for admission to the college?" (at the medical school: ". . . to the medical school?").

5) "Is it difficult to get in?"

6) "Is there financial aid?"

Without exception, as can be seen in Table 1 (column 3), all of the questions were answered. No matter how rushed they were, all respondents not only maintained eye contact, but stopped to talk. Indeed, many of the respondents went out of their way to direct or take the questioner to the office she was seeking, to try to locate "Fish Annex," or to discuss with her the possibilities of being admitted to the university.

Similar data, also shown in Table 1 (columns 4, 5, and 6), were obtained in the hospital. Here too, the young lady came prepared with six questions. After the first question, however, she remarked to 18 of her respondents (column 4), "I'm looking for a psychiatrist," and to 15 others (column 5), "I'm looking for an internist." Ten other respondents received no inserted comment (column 6). The general degree of cooperative responses is considerably higher for these university groups than it was for pseudopatients in psychiatric hospitals. Even so, differences are apparent within the medical school setting. Once having indicated that she was looking for a psychiatrist, the degree of cooperation elicited was less than when she sought an internist.

POWERLESSNESS AND DEPERSONALIZATION

Eye contact and verbal contact reflect concern and individuation; their absence, avoidance and depersonalization. The data I have presented do not do justice to the rich daily encounters that grew up around matters of depersonalization and avoidance. I have records of patients who were beaten by staff for the sin of having initiated verbal contact. During my own experience, for example, one patient was beaten in the presence of other patients for having approached an attendant and told him, "I like you." Occasionally, punishment meted out to patients for misdemeanors seemed so excessive that it could not be justified by the most radical interpretations of psychiatric canon. Nevertheless, they appeared to go unquestioned. Tempers were often short. A patient who had not heard a call for medication would be roundly excoriated, and the morning attendants would often wake patients with, "Come on, you m——f——s, out of bed!"

Neither anecdotal nor "hard" data can convey the overwhelming sense of powerlessness which invades the individual as he is continually exposed to the depersonalization of the psychiatric hospital. It hardly matters *which* psychiatric hospital—the excellent public ones and the very plush private hospital were better than the rural and shabby ones in this regard, but, again, the features that psychiatric hospitals had in common overwhelmed by far their apparent differences.

Powerlessness was evident everywhere. The patient is deprived of many of his legal rights by dint of his psychiatric commitment (21). He is shorn of credibility by virtue of his psychiatric label. His freedom of movement is restricted. He cannot initiate contact with the staff, but may only respond to such over-

tures as they make. Personal privacy is minimal. Patient quarters and possessions can be
entered and examined by any staff member,
for whatever reason. His personal history and
anguish is available to any staff member
(often including the "grey lady" and "candy
striper" volunteer) who chooses to read his
folder, regardless of their therapeutic relationship to him. His personal hygiene and
waste evacuation are often monitored. The
water closets may have no doors.

At times, depersonalization reached such
proportions that pseudopatients had the
sense that they were invisible, or at least unworthy of account. Upon being admitted, I
and other pseudopatients took the initial
physical examinations in a semipublic room,
where staff members went about their own
business as if we were not there.

On the ward, attendants delivered verbal
and occasionally serious physical abuse to
patients in the presence of other observing
patients, some of whom (the pseudopatients)
were writing it all down. Abusive behavior,
on the other hand, terminated quite abruptly
when other staff members were known to be
coming. Staff are credible witnesses. Patients
are not.

A nurse unbuttoned her uniform to adjust her brassiere in the presence of an entire
ward of viewing men. One did not have the
sense that she was being seductive. Rather,
she didn't notice us. A group of staff persons
might point to a patient in the dayroom and
discuss him animatedly, as if he were not
there.

One illuminating instance of depersonalization and invisibility occurred with regard
to medications. All told, the pseudopatients
were administered nearly 2100 pills, including Elavil, Stelazine, Compazine, and Thora-
zine, to name but a few. (That such a variety
of medications should have been administered to patients presenting identical symptoms is itself worthy of note.) Only two were
swallowed. The rest were either pocketed or
deposited in the toilet. The pseudopatients
were not alone in this. Although I have no
precise records on how many patients re-

jected their medications, the pseudopatients
frequently found the medications of other
patients in the toilet before they deposited
their own. As long as they were cooperative,
their behavior and the pseudopatients' own
in this matter, as in other important matters,
went unnoticed throughout.

Reactions to such depersonalization among
pseudopatients were intense. Although they
had come to the hospital as participant observers and were fully aware that they did
not "belong," they nevertheless found themselves caught up in and fighting the process
of depersonalization. Some examples: a graduate student in psychology asked his wife to
bring his textbooks to the hospital so he
could "catch up on his homework"—this
despite the elaborate precautions taken to
conceal his professional association. The
same student, who had trained for quite
some time to get into the hospital, and who
had looked forward to the experience, "remembered" some drag races that he had
wanted to see on the weekend and insisted
that he be discharged by that time. Another
pseudopatient attempted a romance with a
nurse. Subsequently, he informed the staff
that he was applying for admisison to graduate school in psychology and was very likely
to be admitted, since a graduate professor
was one of his regular hospital visitors. The
same person began to engage in psychotherapy with other patients—all of this as a way
of becoming a person in an impersonal
environment.

THE SOURCES OF DEPERSONALIZATION

What are the origins of depersonalization?
I have already mentioned two. First are attitudes held by all of us toward the mentally
ill—including those who treat them—attitudes
characterized by fear, distrust, and horrible
expectations on the one hand, and benevolent intentions on the other. Our ambiva-

lence leads, in this instance as in others, to avoidance.

Second, and not entirely separate, the hierarchical structure of the psychiatric hospital facilitates depersonalization. Those who are at the top have least to do with patients, and their behavior inspires the rest of the staff. Average daily contact with psychiatrists, psychologists, residents, and physicians combined ranged from 3.9 to 25.1 minutes, with an overall mean of 6.8 (six pseudopatients over a total of 129 days of hospitalization). Included in this average are time spent in the admissions interview, ward meetings in the presence of a senior staff member, group and individual psychotherapy contacts, case presentation conferences, and discharge meetings. Clearly, patients do not spend much time in interpersonal contact with doctoral staff. And doctoral staff serve as models for nurses and attendants.

There are probably other sources. Psychiatric installations are presently in serious financial straits. Staff shortages are pervasive, staff time at a premium. Something has to give, and that something is patient contact. Yet, while financial stresses are realities, too much can be made of them. I have the impression that the psychological forces that result in depersonalization are much stronger than the fiscal ones and that the addition of more staff would not correspondingly improve patient care in this regard. The incidence of staff meetings and the enormous amount of record-keeping on patients, for example, have not been as substantially reduced as has patient contact. Priorities exist, even during hard times. Patient contact is not a significant priority in the traditional psychiatric hospital, and fiscal pressures do not account for this. Avoidance and depersonalization may.

Heavy reliance upon psychotropic medication tacitly contributes to depersonalization by convincing staff that treatment is indeed being conducted and that further patient contact may not be necessary. Even here, however, caution needs to be exercised in understanding the role of psychotropic drugs.

If patients were powerful rather than powerless, if they were viewed as interesting individuals rather than diagnostic entities, if they were socially significant rather than social lepers, if their anguish truly and wholly compelled our sympathies and concerns, would we not *seek* contact with them, despite the availability of medications? Perhaps for the pleasure of it all?

THE CONSEQUENCES OF LABELING AND DEPERSONALIZATION

Whenever the ratio of what is known to what needs to be known approaches zero, we tend to invent "knowledge" and assume that we understand more than we actually do. We seem unable to acknowledge that we simply don't know. The needs for diagnosis and remediation of behavioral and emotional problems are enormous. But rather than acknowledge that we are just embarking on understanding, we continue to label patients "schizophrenic," "manic-depressive," and "insane," as if in those words we had captured the essence of understanding. The facts of the matter are that we have known for a long time that diagnoses are often not useful or reliable, but we have nevertheless continued to use them. We now know that we cannot distinguish insanity from sanity. It is depressing to consider how that information will be used.

Not merely depressing, but frightening. How many people, one wonders, are sane but not recognized as such in our psychiatric institutions? How many have been needlessly stripped of their privileges of citizenship, from the right to vote and drive to that of handling their own accounts? How many have feigned insanity in order to avoid the criminal consequences of their behavior, and, conversely, how many would rather stand trial than live interminably in a psychiatric hospital—but are wrongly thought to be mentally ill? How many have been stigmatized by well-intentioned, but nevertheless erroneous, diagnoses? On the last point, recall again that a "type 2 error" in psychiatric diagnosis does not have the same consequences it does in medical diagnosis. A diagnosis of cancer that has been found to be in error is cause for celebration. But psychiatric diagnoses are rarely found to be in error. The label sticks, a mark of inadequacy forever.

Finally, how many patients might be "sane" outside the psychiatric hospital but seem insane in it—not because craziness resides in them, as it were, but because they are responding to a bizarre setting, one that may be unique to institutions which harbor nether people? Goffman (4) calls the process of socialization to such institutions "mortification"—an apt metaphor that includes the processes of depersonalization that have been described here. And while it is impossible to know whether the pseudopatients' responses to these processes are characteristic of all inmates—they were, after all, not real patients—it is difficult to believe that these processes of socialization to a psychiatric hospital provide useful attitudes or habits of response for living in the "real world."

SUMMARY AND CONCLUSIONS

It is clear that we cannot distinguish the sane from the insane in psychiatric hospitals. The hospital itself imposes a special environment in which the meanings of behavior can easily be misunderstood. The consequences to patients hospitalized in such an environment—the powerlessness, depersonalization, segregation, mortification, and self-labeling—seem undoubtedly countertherapeutic.

I do not, even now, understand this problem well enough to perceive solutions. But two matters seem to have some promise. The first concerns the proliferation of community mental health facilities, of crisis intervention centers, of the human potential movement, and of behavior therapies that, for all of their own problems, tend to avoid psychiatric labels, to focus on specific problems and behaviors, and to retain the individual in a relatively nonpejorative environment. Clearly, to the extent that we refrain from sending the distressed to insane places, our impressions of them are less likely to be distorted. (The risk of distorted perceptions, it seems to me, is always present, since we are much more sensitive to an individual's behaviors and verbalizations than we are to the subtle contextual stimuli that often promote them. At issue here is a matter of magnitude. And, as I have shown, the magnitude of distortion is exceedingly high in the extreme context that is a psychiatric hospital.)

The second matter that might prove promising speaks to the need to increase the sensitivity of mental health workers and researchers to the *Catch 22* position of psychiatric patients. Simply reading materials in this area will be of help to some such workers and researchers. For others, directly experiencing the impact of psychiatric hospitalization will be of enormous use. Clearly, further research into the social psychology of such total institutions will both facilitate treatment and deepen understanding.

I and the other pseudopatients in the psychiatric setting had distinctly negative reactions. We do not pretend to describe the subjective experiences of true patients. Theirs may be different from ours, particularly with the passage of time and the necessary process of adaptation to one's environment. But we can and do speak to the relatively more objective indices of treatment within the hospital. It could be a mistake, and a very unfortunate one, to consider that what happened to us derived from malice or stupidity on the part of the staff. Quite the contrary, our overwhelming impression of them was of people who really cared, who were committed and who were uncommonly intelligent. Where they failed, as they sometimes did painfully, it would be more accurate to attribute those failures to the environment in which they, too, found themselves than to personal callousness. Their perceptions and behavior were controlled by the situation, rather than being motivated by a malicious disposition. In a more benign environment, one that was less attached to global diagnosis, their behaviors and judgments might have been more benign and effective.

REFERENCES AND NOTES

1. P. Ash, *J. Abnorm. Soc. Psychol.* 44, 272 (1949); A. T. Beck, *Amer. J. Psychiat.* 119, 210 (1962); A. T. Boisen, *Psychiatry* 2, 233 (1938); N. Kreitman, *J. Ment. Sci.* 107, 876 (1961); N. Kreitman, P. Sainsbury, J. Morrisey, J. Towers, J. Scrivener, *ibid.*, p. 887; H. O. Schmitt and C. P. Fonda, *J. Abnorm. Soc. Psychol.* 52, 262 (1956); W. Seeman, *J. Nerv. Ment. Dis.* 118, 541 (1953). For an analysis of these artifacts and summaries of the disputes, see J. Zubin, *Annu. Rev. Psychol.* 18, 373 (1967); L. Phillips and J. G. Draguns, *ibid.*, 22, 447 (1971).

2. R. Benedict, *J. Gen. Psychol.* 10, 59 (1934).

3. See in this regard H. Becker, *Outsiders: Studies in the Sociology of Deviance* (Free Press, New York, 1963); B. M. Braginsky, D. D. Braginsky, K. Ring, *Methods of Madness: The Mental Hospital as a Last Resort* (Holt, Rinehart & Winston, New York, 1969); G. M. Crocetti and P. V. Lemkau, *Amer. Sociol. Rev.* 30, 577 (1965); E. Goffman, *Behavior in Public Places* (Free Press, New York, 1964); R. D. Laing, *The Divided Self: A Study of Sanity and Madness* (Quadrangle, Chicago, 1960); D. L. Phillips, *Amer. Sociol. Rev.* 28, 963 (1963); T. R. Sarbin, *Psychol. Today* 6, 18 (1972); E. Schur, *Amer. J. Sociol.* 75, 309 (1969); T. Szasz, *Law, Liberty and Psychiatry* (Macmillan, New York, 1963); *The Myth of Mental Illness: Foundations of a Theory of Mental Illness* (Hoeber Harper, New York, 1963). For a critique of some of thse views, see W. R. Gove, *Amer. Sociol. Rev.* 35, 873 (1970).

4. E. Goffman, *Asylums* (Doubleday, Garden City, N.Y., 1961).

5. T. J. Scheff, *Being Mentally Ill: A Sociological Theory* (Aldine, Chicago, 1966).

6. Data from a ninth pseudopatient are not incorporated in this report because, although his sanity went undetected, he falsified aspects of his personal history, including his marital status and parental relationships. His experimental behaviors therefore were not identical to those of the other pseudopatients.

7. A. Barry, *Bellevue Is a State of Mind* (Harcourt Brace Jovanovich, New York, 1971); I. Belknap, *Human Problems of a State Mental Hospital* (McGraw Hill, New York, 1956); W. Caudill, F. C. Redlich, H. R. Gilmore, E. B. Brody, *Amer. J. Orthopsychiat.* 22, 314 (1952); A. R. Goldman, R. H. Bohr, T. A. Steinberg, *Prof. Psychol.* 1, 427 (1970); unauthored, *Roche Report* 1 (No. 13), 8 (1971).

8. Beyond the personal difficulties that the pseudopatient is likely to experience in the hospital, there are legal and social ones that, combined, require considerable attention before entry. For example, once admitted to a psychiatric institution, it is difficult, if not impossible, to be discharged on short notice, state law to the contrary notwithstanding. I was not sensitive to these difficulties at the outset of the project, nor to the personal and situational emergencies that can arise, but later a writ of habeas corpus was prepared for each of the entering pseudopatients and an attorney was kept "on call" during every hospitalization. I am grateful to John Kaplan and Robert Bartels for legal advice and assistance in these matters.

9. However distasteful such concealment is, it was a necessary first step to examining these questions. Without concealment, there would have been no way to know how valid these experiences were; nor was there any way of knowing whether whatever detections occurred were a tribute to the diagnostic acumen of the staff or to the hospital's rumor network. Obviously, since my concerns are general ones that cut across individual hospitals and staffs, I have respected their anonymity and have eliminated clues that might lead to their identification.

10. Interestingly, of the 12 admissions, 11 were diagnosed as schizophrenic and one, with the identical symptomatology, as manic-depressive psychosis. This diagnosis has a more favorable prognosis, and it was given by the only private hospital in our sample. On the relations between social class and psychiatric diagnosis, see A. deB. Hollingshead and

F. C. Redlich, *Social Class and Mental Illness: A Community Study* (Wiley, New York, 1958).

11. It is possible, of course, that patients have quite broad latitudes in diagnosis and therefore are inclined to call many people sane, even those whose behavior is patently aberrant. However, although we have no hard data on this matter, it was our distinct impression that this was not the case. In many instances, patients not only singled us out for attention, but came to imitate our behaviors and styles.

12. J. Cumming and E. Cumming, *Community Ment. Health* 1, 135 (1965); A. Farina and K. Ring, *J. Abnorm. Psychol.* 70, 47 (1965); H. E. Freeman and O. G. Simmons, *The Mental Patient Comes Home* (Wiley, New York, 1963); W. J. Johannsen, *Ment. Hygiene* 53, 218 (1969); A. S. Linsky, *Soc. Psychiat.* 5, 166 (1970).

13. S. E. Asch, *J. Abnorm. Soc. Psychol.* 41, 258 (1946); *Social Psychology* (Prentice-Hall, New York, 1952).

14. See also I. N. Mensh and J. Wishner, *J. Personality* 16, 188 (1947); J. Wishner, *Psychol. Rev.* 67, 96 (1960); J. S. Bruner and R. Tagiuri, in *Handbook of Social Psychology*, G. Lindzey, Ed. (Addison-Wesley, Cambridge, Mass., 1954), vol. 2, pp. 634–654; J. S. Bruner, D. Shapiro, R. Tagiuri, in *Person Perception and Interpersonal Behavior*, R. Tagiuri and L. Petrullo, Eds. (Stanford Univ. Press, Stanford, Calif., 1958), pp. 277–288.

15. For an example of a similar self-fulfilling prophecy, in this instance dealing with the "central" trait of intelligence, see R. Rosenthal and L. Jacobson, *Pygmalion in the Classroom* (Holt, Rinehart & Winston, New York, 1968).

16. E. Zigler and L. Phillips, *J. Abnorm. Soc. Psychol.* 63, 69 (1961). See also R. K. Freudenberg and J. P. Robertson, *A.M.A. Arch. Neurol. Psychiatr.* 76, 14 (1956).

17. W. Mischel, *Personality and Assessment* (Wiley, New York, 1968).

18. The most recent and unfortunate instance of this tenet is that of Senator Thomas Eagleton.

19. T. R. Sarbin and J. C. Mancuso, *J. Clin. Consult. Psychol.* 35, 159 (1970); T. R. Sarbin, *ibid.* 31, 447 (1967); J. C. Nunnally, Jr., *Popular Conceptions of Mental Health* (Holt, Rinehart & Winston, New York, 1961).

20. A. H. Stanton and M. S. Schwartz, *The Mental Hospital: A Study of Institutional Participation in Psychiatric Illness and Treatment* (Basic, New York, 1954).

21. D. B. Wexler and S. E. Scoville, *Ariz. Law Rev.* 13, 1 (1971).

22. I thank W. Mischel, E. Orne, and M. S. Rosenhan for comments on an earlier draft of this manuscript.

Analysis of Values
and
Conflicts of Interest

Thomas Szasz's position is consistent with the interests of many who favor the conservative position. He prefers that the existing social system be maintained, but with increased safeguards against autocratic or bureaucratic interventions in the lives of individuals. This position rests on the idea that the "good society" is one in which the sanctity of the individual is the first priority. Conservatives believe that increasing centralization of power in the modern state threatens this sanctity. They are especially concerned about expansion of paternalistic welfare-state institutions, supported by liberals, that insist on caring for the individual regardless of the person's wishes. The conservative position not only represents the interests of sincere libertarians like Szasz, but is also used by many individuals and groups who object to paying taxes supporting welfare-state institutions.

Szasz believes that psychiatry usurped responsibility for the mentally disordered when it defined mental disorder as an illness. This gave the psychiatrist legitimation to examine, label, treat, and institutionalize people against their will. As Rosenhan asserts, the definition of mental illness is vague and diagnosis is difficult. For this reason Szasz feels that mental illness becomes a residual category applicable to many different types of nonconformists. According to Szasz, psychiatry armed with the concept of mental illness is a dangerous threat to the individual—it wields a weapon to maintain conformity.

Szasz not only represents the broader interests discussed above, but also those of therapists who oppose socialized medicine or other public treatment programs. Szasz argues that federally sponsored mental health projects, community psychiatry, and public mental institutions do little to help people, sometimes harm them and always threaten their freedom. This position not only has moral and political implications, but it is also supportive of the economic interests of those who desire to keep therapy private and financially lucrative for the therapist.

In discussing the ideas of R. D. Laing, James S. Gordon also characterizes psychiatry as a threat to the individual. However, Laing, a radical, represents those who feel that society must be reorganized to meet human needs more fully. He believes that traditional psychiatry helps prevent this. Laing argues that people should feel alienated, because the institutions of contemporary society are oppressive and hostile. He suggests that alienation channeled outward toward its sources, the institutions, would bring change, but that psychiatry, by treating the alienated as sick, directs them inward to see the problem in themselves. Laing wants to develop a psychiatry that would sensitize people to alienative social relations and oppressive institutions, so they can take an active role in changing them.

Laing, like Szasz, also reflects more specific interests—those of the many psychiatrists who want to undermine the existing hierarchy of orthodox therapists who now control the psychiatric profession. Such change would not only promote the nontraditional psychiatrists' professional careers, but would also allow them to institute, on a wider scale, the therapeutic innovations they believe necessary.

The Rosenhan article is included to emphasize the empirical relevance of the Szasz and Laing critiques. However, it is important to emphasize that even experimental studies are not detached from values and interests. The problem one chooses to study and the way the problem is conceptualized is affected by the researcher's values and interests. For example, if Rosenhan was not initially skeptical of psychiatry he might have conducted a study that produced data showing that mental hospitals perform important therapeutic functions. The fact that even empirical research is not value-free does not mean that social science is doomed to inaccurate and biased analyses. Once the problem is defined and research is carried out, the researcher should report his findings objectively. For example, Rosenhan was obligated to describe the results of his experiment accurately, even if the findings contradicted his value position. Findings of this nature are always possible and often occur. Sometimes they even lead the researcher to rearrange his values and realign his interests.

Ausubel's position supports persons who are engaged in the traditional practice of psychiatry. This includes many of a liberal persuasion who feel that psychiatric treatment provides a reasonable and more humanistic alternative to punitive measures for coping with rule-breakers. Ausubel very clearly represents the interests of the psychiatric profession since the work of most psychiatrists is predicated on the idea that insanity is an illness and that psychiatrists have the expertise to treat it. Ausubel does not assert that psychiatry is completely effective, but he does believe it provides the best and most humanistic method now available for treating mental disorder.

2

DRUGS:
Are the Present Drug Laws Effective?

In recent years drug abuse has spread at an alarming rate through diverse segments of the American population. Some people refer to widespread drug abuse as a drug epidemic. Throughout this period federal, state, and local law enforcement agencies have escalated their efforts to stop the flow of illicit drugs. However, these efforts have done little to cut down on the availability or use of these drugs. The drug abuser and drug pusher have not been discouraged by the fact that their chances of being arrested and prosecuted have increased due to these efforts.

In considering the problem of drug abuse several questions must be asked. First, does the drug do physical or psychological harm to the person? Does it foster incapacitating dependencies? Does it interfere with his work or his interpersonal relationships? Then we must consider the effects of the use of the drug on others. What are the costs to the user's family and community? Once these are answered, questions should be posed about what actions (if any) should be taken to control or to prohibit the use of the drug. Finally, one must ask whether these means of control are effective and whether they have any destructive effects upon the user or others. The articles in this section illustrate that there are no simple and unequivocal solutions to these problems.

In the first article John Ingersoll, former director of the Bureau of Narcotics and Dangerous Drugs, calls for the maintenance of public commitment in the battle against marijuana and heroin. He suggests that, despite the increasing effectiveness of measures to control the use of marijuana and heroin, many people would rather "cop out" and cease fighting the problems. Ingersoll states that the report of the National Marijuana Commission exemplifies this tendency. He asserts that the commission admits that marijuana might be dangerous. However, the report calls for the elimination of all legal penalties for possession and personal use of the drug. Also it suggests lessening the penalties for sale of small amounts of the drug. Ingersoll contends that the adoption of this proposal would eliminate any possibility of cutting marijuana traffic and restoring it to its former nuisance level. Instead, marijuana would be permanently institutionalized and would become more widely available. Ingersoll states that this proposal is a result of a desire to save the young from the stigma of arrest and incarceration. He believes that this is a misguided and emotional proposal that would, if heeded, create a more serious social problem.

Ingersoll also attacks the proponents of heroin maintenance for addicts. He asserts that advocates of such a proposal have little scientific evidence of its workability. He contends that the advocates of heroin maintenance believe that it would serve to reduce urban crime rates. However, he claims that the rates of addict crime have been exaggerated and legal heroin for addicts would do little to reduce these rates. Ingersoll asserts that heroin maintenance would serve to weaken the social barriers against heroin, and would make it cheaper and more attractive to nonusers. He concludes that such a program would lead to increased rates of addiction. Ingersoll believes that we must maintain the prohibitions against marijuana and heroin—to become more permissive means surrender to a pernicious social problem.

Joel Fort argues that marijuana is relatively harmless. He believes that penalties against the use and sale of the drug are oppressive. He discusses several comprehensive studies of the use of marijuana, all of which conclude that marijuana has negligible deleterious physical, psychological, and social effects on the user. Fort points out that the marijuana laws were passed in a climate of public hysteria generated by self-serving law enforcement officials and irresponsible journalists. Totally unsubstantiated claims linking marijuana to crime, violence, insanity, and other antisocial acts convinced lawmakers to pass very restrictive laws prohibiting the use or sale of marijuana. These laws have been inconsistently enforced. However, many people have served long jail sentences or have been stigmatized needlessly for mere possession of marijuana. Fort believes that the marijuana laws are unjust and suggests that "Bad law is the worst form of tyranny." He calls for the full legalization of marijuana, because its prohibition is irrational, impractical, unjust, and alienating. Fort asserts that legalization would not lead to an epidemic of marijuana use because most Americans have already indicated their preference for the use of alcohol. Furthermore, the effects of marijuana are subtle and might not be attractive to people who expect stronger effects.

Edgar May is an advocate of the British system of heroin maintenance. He argues that this approach to the heroin problem has been highly effective, even though most American law enforcement officials categorically reject it. He admits that there was a significant increase in British drug addiction in the 1960s. However, this was due to a flaw in the distribution system that made it easy for doctors to overprescribe. Thus, unscrupulous doctors sold prescriptions and the surplus heroin was sold on the street. Since that time, the program has been modified to permit only doctors at specified clinics to prescribe the drug. This new mode of distribution is strictly controlled by the government. As a result of these measures the upward spiral of addiction rates seems to have been checked. Furthermore, monthly amounts of prescribed heroin have declined and the majority of addicts are being changed over to methadone, a substitute for heroin that has less potent psychological effects.

In Britain one hundred tablets of heroin cost $2.16, while in New York City the same amount is worth a $1000 or more. The British addict, unlike his American counterpart, does not have to engage in crime to support his habit. This is an important consideration because statistics indicate that a great deal of urban property crime is carried out by addicts. For example, May states that in Washington, D.C. police believe that up to 80 percent of serious property crime is addict initiated. May points out that addicts in Britain have a chance to lead a decent and productive life because they are not engaged in a constant struggle to acquire the drug. He concludes that the heroin maintenance program in Britain has some flaws, but that it is far superior to the way in which Americans have tried to deal with the heroin problem.

James Markham is an opponent of the heroin maintenance program. He believes that it is dangerous to extrapolate from the British experience and suggests that it is highly debatable how well this system would work in the United States. Markham implies that it would be foolish to implement this measure to cut down on crime because we are unsure of the degree of addict-related crime. Furthermore, many addict criminals have established their criminal life styles before they ever used heroin. These individuals would probably continue to engage in criminal activity regardless of the cost of the drug. Markham argues that the British themselves are moving away from heroin maintenance. He asserts that their clinics are pushing addicts into methadone maintenance as a substitute for heroin. Methadone can be taken orally, has longer lasting effects and does not cause the psychological ups and downs that interfere with the addict's daily activities. Markham also points out that heroin maintenance would be prohibitively expensive in America. For example, six nurses are needed to supervise injections for every thirty to sixty addicts. This would be extremely costly since we have several hundred thousand addicts and a shortage of trained nurses.

Markham believes that heroin maintenance is portrayed as an overly simple solution to a very complex problem. He suggests that experimenting with heroin maintenance could be a disastrous venture. He cites one expert who estimates that there would soon be three to four million American addicts if we adopted the British system. Markham suggests that the prohibition must be maintained and a diversified set of techniques should be adopted that would use all available means to deal with the problem (e.g. methadone, group therapy, and law enforcement).

The Effect of Legalizing Marihuana & Heroin

JOHN E. INGERSOLL

In my position as Director of the Federal Government's principal drug law enforcement agency, I necessarily have many public appearances to make. Because the problem with which I deal is one in which so many other professional groups—doctors, psychiatrists, educators and scientists—are equally concerned, I find I am often addressing people who have little understanding of what law enforcement is trying to do in this area. It is, for this reason, a genuine pleasure when I have the opportunity to address a group of fellow professionals.

Whenever I am being interviewed, the first question that is usually asked is, "Where are we in the fight against illegal narcotics and drug abuse?"

To answer this question I am often tempted to quote the opening lines from Charles Dickens' "Tale of Two Cities"—"It was the best of times, it was the worst of times."

While this may be a poetic answer, and an accurate one, it never seems to satisfy reporters. So today I want to talk to you about the good news and the bad news.

When we find a noticeable shortage of

Note: John E. Ingersoll, "The Effect of Legalizing Marihuana & Heroin," *Vital Speeches*, Oct. 1972, pp. 24–27. Reprinted by permission of Vital Speeches of the Day.

heroin throughout the Eastern Seaboard and particularly, in Maryland—that's good news—the best of times.

When our agents in the Baltimore Regional Office have no opportunity to purchase bulk heroin for the past two months and others report a severe shortage of bulk heroin—that's the best of times.

When the street price of bags in Maryland increased from $8 to $10 during June and from $12 to $15 in July and the purity of heroin seized by Baltimore City Police is down two per cent—that's the best of times.

And when we combine all these events, we can arrive at the conclusion that increased enforcement activities, seizures, arrests and current active investigations have either neutralized or driven underground many of the major suppliers in the Baltimore area. That's the best of times.

Events on the national and international scene have been equally encouraging.

Not long ago the enforcement of drug laws was something in which most police departments lacked either knowledge or experience. Resources were not simply inadequate, they were nonexistent. When I took over the leadership of the Bureau of Narcotics and Dangerous Drugs in 1968, we had a combined staff of less than 900 with fewer than 600 agents, and a budget of slightly more than $14 million. It was also the year in which the Law Enforcement Assistance Administration was established as a Federal effort to help provide additional financial support to State and local police units.

Since then, much has transpired. Our budget has risen to approximately $74 million and our agent force has nearly reached 1,600; the total staff is almost 3,000 engaged in investigations of criminal activity, inspections of legitimate drug production and distribution, prevention and education programs, training of police around the world, and scientific and technological development. We have established a complete network of forensic drug laboratories.

We have tripled our overseas offices and increased the number of positions five times over in foreign countries. We have secured agreement with Turkey to get out of opium production. The budget of LEAA has increased from $300 million to $850 million for FY 1973. A respectable chunk of this money has been earmarked for drug law enforcement at State and local level, through MEG programs and other ways.

All of this increase in resources offers reason for encouragement. Most important yet, are some of the great enforcement achievements.

In Fiscal Year 1972 our agency alone removed 5,107 pounds of heroin and heroin equivalents from the illicit traffic. The French have been moving especially after stimulus from the President and the Attorney General; and in a single case, as you know, seized a half ton of heroin on a fishing trawler, the largest such seizure in history. They have also eliminated five heroin labs since the first of the year.

State and local activities are reflected in that 346,412 arrests were made for drug law violations in calendar year 1970. We recently concluded a survey which showed that 15 per cent of the personnel of all of the law enforcement agencies responding had received at least some training in drug law enforcement, and there are probably some 21,000 police narcotic specialists in the country.

That's a brief rundown on the overall national picture.

While I don't want to foster false hopes nor lead anyone to believe that we have enough manpower or resources to do the job, the progress which the references suggest are truly impressive.

Now let's talk about the bad news—"The worst of times."

From the actions of the President, the Congress and the support we in law enforcement have received, the message should be loud and clear that we have a national commitment and determination to cope with illegal narcotics traffic and drug abuse. In plain and simple language we are waging a global war on narcotics and dangerous drugs in cooperation with most of the rest of the countries of the world.

Yet at the very time when we should be encouraged, there are powerful voices and personalities who would have us "cop out" on that commitment and surrender our determination.

There are two outstanding examples which I will use to illustrate this danger. Both of which would have the practical effect of nullifying the very purpose of enforcing the drug laws, which is to reduce the severity and frequency of drug abuse.

First let us consider the report of the National Marihuana Commission chaired by Governor Shafer of Pennsylvania.

This Commission in its report stated clearly that it disapproved of the abuse of marihuana, felt that the drug could be dangerous, and concluded that nothing should be done which would in any way encourage its use.

Having indulged itself in this rhetoric, the Commission went on to set forth recommendations which, if followed to the letter, would be bound to encourage the use of marihuana and destroy any purpose which enforcement of remaining laws might have.

The Commission would eliminate all offenses for possession of marihuana for personal use and weaken prohibitions on the "casual distribution of small amounts of marihuana for no remuneration, or insignificant remuneration"—whatever that means.

In other words, both the use of and petty traffic in the drug would be legally condoned. Thus, the basic level of consumer demand, as well as the tail end of the distribution chain on which all the larger drug traffic rests, would be legally and permanently assured.

It is, therefore, impossible to speak of removing the prohibition against the possession of marihuana without encouraging its abuse. This problem was considered by the Congress when the laws against possession of LSD and other dangerous drugs were advanced in 1968. One of the reasons for finally settling on a possession penalty was to "counter the feeling among some young people that abuse of dangerous drugs is not detrimental to them" since there was no law against it.

In other words, if these proposals are adopted, any hopes of drying up marihuana traffic and restoring use of this drug to former nuisance level would be lost forever.

In the long run we would simply have to learn to live with abuse of drugs in the same calloused fashion that we have been taught to live with the problems of alcoholism or automobile fatalities.

Marihuana would simply be another one of life's hazards from which we try to protect ourselves and our families. In time, the next step would be to recognize traffic and sale of the drug as equally legitimate and the vice would be permanently institutionalized.

If marihuana is safe enough for recommendation that would encourage its use, why did the Commission adopt the position that its use should be discouraged?

In the 19th Century this fence straddling was called "mugwumping"—an act denoting a person sitting on the fence, his "mug" on one side and his "wump" on the other.

How could sensible men of great reputation lead themselves into rationalizing this obviously contradictory report—disapproving of marihuana, desiring to discourage its use, and at the same time, laying the ground work for its permanent incorporation within our culture?

It should be noted that the recommendations in many ways go beyond the wildest proposals of most marihuana advocates. Those recommendations would not distinguish between the leaves of the plant and the resins—hashish. Even liquid hash with a potency approaching LSD would be "legalized." They would not only recognize possession and use by adults, but children as well.

I believe that more than any single motive in the recommendations of this report was the Commission's desire to save young people from the stigma of the arrest and criminal justice process even though provisions now exist to clear records in such cases.

This is an entirely misguided and emotional approach. Consider, for example, that in 1971, 62,977 persons under the age of 18 were arrested for marihuana violations. This is far less than the number arrested for automobile thefts which was approximately 69,000; or for loitering which was approximately 102,000; or for disorderly conduct at 134,000; or vandalism at 87,000; or even liquor violations at 82,000. Should this concern for keeping kids out of jail not equally extend to such categories? Is the risk of jail to a juvenile less if he is involved in these offenses?

To save these multitudes of persons from the criminal justice system, should we then legalize all of these offenses? Should we conclude that anything that large numbers of people do should simply be permitted?

The difficulty with the Commission report is that it failed to generate alternatives. It looked at the situation simply and said, "Either these people are arrested and go to jail, or we change the laws." In most cases neither of these alternatives is suitable. There may be need for improvement. There may be room for change. It may be desirable that we design some alternatives in addition to or in place of incarceration. But it is not desirable that we simply solve this problem by changing all of our laws and thereafter permanently playing ostrich with major social problems.

The Commission's recommendations toll a

knell of despair that would lead us from a national commitment to simplistic solutions that could lead to the furthering of the drug subculture that sprang up in the 1960s.

That is the "worst of times" and I am not about to buy that type of solution. I think we can find better ways.

The second era of concern to all of us is a new program to use heroin to maintain addicts' habits.

As I have stated, the quantities of heroin being removed from illicit traffic both in the United States and abroad are of unprecedented volume. In fact, in Europe alone, they are approaching the estimated annual American consumption rate. At the same time programs for the treatment and rehabilitation of heroin addicts are also expanding at an unprecedented rate. The programs under Dr. Jaffe's office in the White House have just been funded by the Congress at a level of $1 billion over the next three years.

Just when these programs are promising to cope with the situation, we are once again hearing of proposals for the establishment of heroin maintenance clinics.

We had first-hand opportunity to review a so-called research proposal of this kind and quickly discovered that it had virtually no support within the knowledgeable scientific community and that most of those advocating this approach had already made up their minds as to the conclusions which will be derived. They persist in subscribing to an idealized view of the so-called British system which the British authorities themselves will not support.

These programs would provide intravenous injections of heroin including a lounge or "nodding room" reminiscent of the opium dens of a by-gone century. There is no credible pretext of treatment in this. On the contrary, everyone will admit that the only purpose of such programs is to eliminate crime and not addiction. But, how valid is the assumption, and what is the price we would have to pay?

According to most authorities who have studied the point, the typical heroin addict's involvement in crime preceded his involvement with heroin. Addiction seems more often to be one of several manifestations of antisocial behavior. Alternatively, it may occur due to availability of the drug and inquisitive nature of young people coming together, with the result that behavior is thereafter shaped by the drug.

We recently concluded a study of some 1,900 persons arrested for non-drug violations in six cities across the nation—Los Angeles, New York, San Antonio, Chicago, New Orleans and St. Louis. We found, as had been expected, that heroin addicts were largely involved in property-type crimes and accounted for a far smaller number of violent crimes than either non-drug users or users of other kinds of drugs. In this study, we found that of all the robberies committed by drug users, 20 per cent were committed by heroin addicts. Of burglaries, 23 per cent; of automobile thefts, 14 per cent; of larceny, 26 per cent.

This is not to suggest that the cost of a heroin habit does not contribute to crime. It does. But the point is that this entire generalization has been greatly overstated and, in too many cases, I am sad to say, by people who should know better: police chiefs.

Free heroin is not going to solve the crime problem in the United States. What is going to contribute to its solution is the elimination of heroin addiction.

What is the price we would have to pay for legalizing heroin in this fashion? First, it would be a virtual announcement of medical surrender on the treatment of addiction and would amount to consigning hundreds of thousands of our citizens to the slavery of heroin forever. The availability of free heroin would almost invariably result in driving out bona fide forms of treatment.

It would be a travesty of the medical profession and an ethical tragedy for the Government to involve itself in the gradual day-by-day poisoning of individuals simply because it represents their expressed desire. But, some hard-nosed people who have given up on addicts from long experience, say it is of their own choosing and that we should "put them on an island and give them all the heroin they desire." This may not be a very humane approach to the problem, but it would do one thing that the current proposals would not. It would isolate the addict from the rest of society so that his contagion cannot be spread.

Under a plan of free heroin, addicts would simply come and go as they wished, partaking of the clinic's drugs and buying in the illicit traffic when they desire, out of reasons of convenience or otherwise. Addiction would be much cheaper than before, social barriers to it would be much reduced, and the addict would still be at large to spread his habit to others.

There would be no scientific way to determine when and how often an addict used illegal heroin as opposed to legitimate heroin.

In summary, we would have succeeded in doing the following things:

1. Giving up on efforts to treat addiction,
2. Rendering addiction less costly, more attractive, and more socially acceptable,
3. Freeing additional supplies of heroin to further feed newcomers to the drug without the compensating benefit of having cured any heroin addicts,
4. Establishing a so-called "legitimate" use for heroin which would make our international goal of eliminating opium cultivation contradictory and unrealistic,
5. Discouraging bona fide treatment efforts which would be unable to compete with free heroin, and
6. Reducing by an unknown number some property crimes, though it is unlikely that these would be of significance since a heroin-maintained addict would continue in his usual incapacitated state of euphoria and be unable to make a normal working wage.

In view of this, it is inconceivable that the establishment of free heroin clinics could even be considered when bona fide treatment facilities are still woefully lacking. In New York City alone, more than 8,000 addicts are still on the waiting list to get into programs. It is hard for me to understand why anyone should be willing to give up the treatment effort before it has ever been attempted.

I also want to remind you that we have now had two or three years' experience with large-scale methadone programs. Many will say that methadone is no better a drug than heroin, but I would dispute this, even though it is a narcotic that can be abused exactly like heroin. When given in good programs, it does eliminate some of the worst aspects of addiction. Individuals can be stabilized, can be weaned from the needle, and their physical and mental condition can be improved.

But, in addition to this, there is one other thing we have learned in these brief years of experience. We have not succeeded in controlling the drug and keeping it in programs and off the street. We have a growing problem of illicit methadone and methadone addiction. Six per cent of the sample of 1,900 felons that I mentioned in our study were users of methadone compared to 24 per cent who were users of heroin. If it is difficult to control the pilferage and diversion of methadone, just imagine how that problem would be multiplied with heroin.

Looking around this room, I see dedicated men who committed their lives to the spirit of the law. You have been part of the front line cadre who have waged the battle against the drug traffickers and every other form of criminal.

And today I can assure you that your efforts have the full support of President Nixon. Recently we held a news conference with members of the Congress to oppose any plan which would allow addicts to receive heroin to maintain their habit. Following the meeting, President Nixon sent a letter to Congressman Peter Peyser of New York and I would like to briefly quote the President's words:

The concept of heroin maintenance represents a concession to weakness and defeat in the drug abuse struggle, a concession which would surely lead to the erosion of our most cherished values for the dignity of man. Heroin maintenance would condemn an undetermined number of our citizens, desperately in need of help, to a lifetime of degradation and addiction at the very time when other, more positive methods of treatment and rehabilitation are rapidly becoming available throughout the country.

The President continued:

As I have often stated, drug abuse—especially the terrible scourge of heroin addiction—is this nation's Public Enemy Number One. We have a solemn obligation to ourselves and to our children to rid drug addiction from America.

As you can see, the President is with us all the way in opposition to heroin maintenance programs.

Now as the Administration, the Congress and the public have come to your support and we are just beginning to forge ahead in our struggle, there are those who would throw up their hands and surrender.

If we let this happen and marihuana is legalized and heroin is administered to addicts, have we not lost altogether?

Could we justify prohibition of any drug use?

Would we not have opened the door to an age of recreational drug use that would make the "swinging sixties" look puritanical?

Each of you in your communities has not only the right but the obligation to become a spokesman against those who would throw in the towel of surrender. We must be active in our opposition on these crucial issues.

As I said earlier, we could consider this the "Best of times or the worst of times"— How do you want it?

Pot: A Rational Approach

JOEL FORT

There are an estimated 10,000,000 Americans who smoke marijuana either regularly or occasionally, and they have very obvious reasons for wishing that pot were treated more sensibly by the law. As one of the 190,000,000 who have never smoked marijuana, I also favor the removal of grass from the criminal laws, but for less personal reasons. It is my considered opinion, after studying drug use and drug laws in 30 nations and dealing with drug-abuse problems professionally for 15 years, that the present marijuana statutes in America not only are bad laws for the offending minority but are bad for the vast majority of us who never have lit a marijuana cigarette and never will.

That some changes in these laws are coming in the near future is virtually certain, but it is not at all sure that the changes will be improvements .

On May 19, 1969, the U.S. Supreme Court, in an 8–0 vote, declared that the Marijuana Tax Act of 1937 was unconstitutional. This decision delighted the defendant, Timothy

Note: Joel Fort, "Pot: A Rational Approach," *Playboy*, Oct. 1969, pp. 131, 154, 216, 218, 220, 222, 225, 227–28. Originally appeared in *Playboy* magazine; copyright © 1969 by Playboy. Joel Fort, M.D., founder-leader, National Center for Solving Special Social and Health Problems—FORTHELP, San Francisco; author, *The Pleasure Seekers: The Drug Crisis, Youth and Society,* and *Alcohol: Our Biggest Drug Problem.*

Leary, and was no surprise at all to lawyers who specialize in the fine points of constitutional law. It had long been recognized that the Marijuana Tax Act was "vulnerable"—a polite term meaning that the law had been hastily drawn, rashly considered and railroaded through Congress in a mood of old-maidish terror that spent no time on the niceties of the Bill of Rights, scientific fact or common sense.

Celebrations by marijuanaphiles and lamentations by marijuanaphobes, however, are both premature. The Court, while throwing out this one inept piece of legislation, specifically declared that Congress has the right to pass laws governing the use, sale and possession of this drug (provided these laws stay within the perimeter of the Constitution) .

And, of course, state laws against pot, which are often far harsher than the Federal law, still remain in effect.

There were two defects found by the Supreme Court in the Federal anti-marijuana law—a section that requires the suspect to pay a tax on the drug, thus incriminating himself, in violation of the Fifth Amendment; and a section that assumes (rather than requiring proof) that a person with foreign-grown marijuana in his possession knows it is smuggled. These provisions were perversions of traditional American jurisprudence, no less than the remaining parts of the law that are bound to fall when challenged before the Supreme Court. These forthcoming decisions will, inevitably, affect the anti-marijuana laws of the individual states as well. However, the striking down of the old laws does not guarantee that the new ones will be more enlightened; it merely invites more carefully drawn statutes that are less vulnerable to judicial review. In fact, in a message to Congress, President Nixon specifically demanded harsher penalties for marijuana convictions. But every sane and fair-minded person must be seriously concerned that the new laws are more just and more in harmony with known fact than the old ones. In my opinion, such new laws must treat marijuana no more harshly than alcohol is presently treated.

It is ironic that our present pot laws are upheld chiefly by the older generation, and flouted and condemned by the young; for it is the senior generation that should understand the issue most clearly, having lived through the era of alcohol prohibition. They saw with their own eyes that the entire nation—not just the drinkers and the sellers of liquor—suffered violent moral and mental harm from that particular outbreak of armed and rampant puritanism. They should certainly remember that attempts to legislate morality result only in widespread disrespect for law, new markets and new profits for gangsters, increased violence and such wholesale bribery and corruption that the Government itself becomes a greater object of contempt than the criminal class. Above all, they should be able to see the parallel between the lawless Twenties and the anarchic Sixties and realize that both were produced by bad laws—laws that had no right to exist in the first place.

"Bad law," it has been said, "is the worst form of tyranny." An open tyranny breeds open rebellion, and the issues are clear-cut; bad law, in an otherwise democratic nation, provokes a kind of cultural nihilism in which good and evil become hopelessly confused and the rebel, instead of formulating a single

precise program, takes a perverse delight in anything and everything that will shock, startle, perplex, anger, baffle and offend the establishment. Thus it was during alcohol prohibition and thus it is under marijuana prohibition. The parallel is not obvious only because there were already millions of whiskey drinkers when the Volstead Act became law in 1919, leading to immediate flouting of "law and order" by vast hordes—whereas the use of marijuana did not become extensive until the early 1950s, more than 13 years after the Government banned pot in 1937. But the results, despite the delay, are the same: We have bred a generation of psychological rebels.

Banning marijuana not only perpetuates the rebelliousness of the young but it also establishes a frightening precedent, under which puritanical bias is more important to our legislators than experimentally determined fact—something every scientist must dread. Dr. Philip Handler, board chairman of the National Science Foundation, bluntly told a House subcommittee investigating drug laws, "It is our puritan ethics . . . rather than science" that say we should not smoke marijuana.

Consider the most recent study of the effects of marijuana, conducted under careful laboratory conditions and reported in *Science*. This is the research performed by Drs. Norman E. Zinberg and Andrew T. Weil at Boston University in 1968. This study was "double-blind"; that is, neither the subjects nor the researchers knew, during a given session, whether the product being smoked was real marijuana (from the female Cannabis plant) or an inactive placebo (from the male Cannabis plant). Thus, both suggestibility by the subjects and bias by the experimenters were kept to the scientific minimum. The results were:

1. Marijuana causes a moderate increase in heartbeat rate, some redness of the eyes and virtually no other physical effects. Contrary to the belief of both users and policemen, pot does not dilate the pupils

—this myth apparently derives from the tradition of smoking Cannabis in a darkened room; it is the darkness that dilates the pupils.

2. Pot does not affect the blood-sugar level, as alcohol does, nor cause abnormal reactions of the involuntary muscles, as LSD often does, nor produce any effects likely to be somatically damaging. In the words of Zinberg and Weil, "The significance of this near absence of physical effects is twofold. First, it demonstrates once again the uniqueness of hemp among psychoactive drugs, most of which strongly affect the body as well as the mind. . . . Second, it makes it unlikely that marijuana has any seriously detrimental physical effects in either short-term or long-term usage."

3. As sociologist Howard Becker pointed out long ago, on the basis of interviews with users, the marijuana "high" is a learned experience. Subjects who had never had Cannabis before simply did not get a "buzz" and reported very minimal subjective reactions, even while physically "loaded" with very high doses, while experienced users were easily turned on.

4. The hypothesis about "set and setting" strongly influencing drug reactions was confirmed. The pharmacological properties of a psychoactive drug are only one factor in a subject's response: equally important—perhaps more important—are the set (his expectations and personality type) and the setting (the total emotional mood of the environment and persons in it).

5. Both inexperienced subjects and long-time users did equally well on some tests for concentration and mental stability, even while they were on very high doses. On tests requiring a higher ability to focus attention, the inexperienced users did show some temporary mental impairment, but the veterans sailed right on, as if they were not high at all. In short, experienced potheads do not have even a *temporary* lowering of the intelligence while they are high, much less a permanent mental impairment.

6. On some tests, the experienced users scored even higher while stoned than they did when tested without any drug.

7. Not only alcohol but even tobacco has more adverse effects on the body than marijuana does.

As Zinberg and Weil noted sardonically in a later article in *The New York Times Magazine,* there is a vicious circle operating in relation to marijuana: "Administrators of scientific and Government institutions feel that marijuana is dangerous. Because it is dangerous, they are reluctant to allow [research] to be done on it. Because no work is done, people continue to think of it as dangerous. We hope that our own study has significantly weakened this trend."

One slight sign that the trend may have been weakened was the appearance last June of a study by the Bureau of Motor Vehicles in the state of Washington concerning the effects of Cannabis on driving ability. Using driving-traffic simulators, not only did the study find that marijuana has less adverse effect on driving ability than alcohol—which many investigators have long suspected—but also, as in the Boston study, the evidence indicated that the only detrimental effect is on inexperienced users. Veteran potheads behave behind the wheel as if they were not drugged at all.

In short, we seem to have a drug here that makes many users very euphoric and happy—high—without doing any of the damage done by alcohol, narcotics, barbiturates, amphetamines or even tobacco.

But we didn't have to wait until 1968 to learn that pot is relatively harmless. Some research has been done in the past, in spite of the vicious circle mentioned by Zinberg and Weil. As far back as 1942, the mayor of New York City, Fiorello La Guardia, alarmed by sensational press stories about "the killer drug, marijuana" that was allegedly driving people to rape and murder, appointed a commission to investigate the pot problem in his city. The commission was made up of 31 eminent physicians, psychiatrists, psycologists, etc., and six officers from the city's narcotics bureau. If there was any bias in that study, it must have been directed against marijuana, considering the presence of the narcotics officers, not to mention psychiatrists and M. D.s, who were then, as now, rather conservative groups. Nevertheless, after two years of hard study, including psychological and medical examinations of users, electroencephalograms to examine for brain damage, sociological digging into the behavior patterns associated with marijuana use and intelligence tests on confirmed potheads, the commission concluded:

> Those who have been smoking marijuana for a period of years showed no mental or physical deterioration which may be attributed to the drug. . . . Marijuana is not a drug of addiction, comparable to morphine. . . . Marijuana does not lead to morphine or heroin or cocaine addiction. . . . Marijuana is not the determining factor in the commission of major crimes. . . . The publicity concerning the catastrophic effects of marijuana smoking in New York City is unfounded.

Even earlier, a study of marijuana use in the Panama Canal Zone was undertaken by a notably conservative body, the United States Army. Published in 1925, the study concluded, "There is no evidence that marijuana as grown here is a habit-forming drug" and that "Delinquencies due to marijuana smoking which result in trial by military court are negligible in number when compared with delinquencies resulting from the use of alcoholic drinks which also may be classed as stimulants or intoxicants."

What may be the classic study in the whole field goes back further: to the 1893–1894 report of the seven-member Indian Hemp Drug Commission that received evidence from 1193 witnesses from all regions of the country (then including Burma and Pakistan), professionals and laymen, Indians and British, most of whom were required to answer in writing seven comprehensive questions covering most aspects of the subject. The commission found that there was no connection between the use of marijuana and "social and moral evils" such as crime, violence or bad character. It also concluded that occasional and moderate use may be beneficial; that moderate use is attended by no injurious physical, mental or other effects; and that moderate use is the rule: "It has been the most striking feature of this inquiry to find how little the effects of hemp drugs have intruded themselves on observation. The large numbers of witnesses of all classes who profess never to have seen them, the very few witnesses who could so recall a case to give any definite account of it and the manner in which a large proportion of these cases broke down on the first attempt to examine them are facts which combine to show most clearly how little injury society has hitherto sustained from hemp drugs." This conclusion is all the more remarkable when one realizes that the pattern of use in India included far more potent forms and doses of Cannabis than are presently used in the United States. The commission, in its conclusion, stated:

> Total prohibition of the hemp drugs is neither necessary nor expedient in consideration of their ascertained effects, of the prevalence of the habit of using them, of the social or religious feelings on the subject and of the possibility of its driving the consumers to have recourse to other stimulants [alcohol] or narcotics which may be more deleterious.

Ever since there have been attempts to study marijuana scientifically, every major investigation has arrived at, substantially, the same conclusions, and these directly contradict the mythology of the Federal Bureau of Narcotics. In contrast with the above facts, consider the following advertisement, circulated before the passage of the 1937 Federal anti-marijuana law:

Beware! Young and Old—People in All Walks of Life! This [picture of a marijuana cigarette] may be handed you by the *friendly stranger*. It contains the Killer Drug "Marijuana"—a powerful narcotic in which lurks *Murder! Insanity! Death!*

Such propaganda was widely disseminated in the mid-1930s, and it was responsible for stampeding Congress into the passage of a law unique in all American history in the extent to which it is based on sheer ignorance and misinformation.

Few people realize how *recent* anti-marijuana legislation is. Pot was widely used as a folk medicine in the 19th Century. Its recreational use in this country began in the early 1900s with Mexican laborers in the Southwest, spread to Mexican Americans and Negroes in the South and then the North, and then moved from rural to urban areas. In terms of public reaction and social policy, little attention was paid to pot until the mid-1930s (although some generally unenforced state laws existed before then). At that time, a group of former alcohol-prohibition agents headed by Harry J. Anslinger, who became head of the Federal Bureau of Narcotics, began issuing statements to the public (via a cooperative press) claiming that marijuana caused crime, violence, assassination, insanity, release of anti-social inhibitions, mental deterioration and numerous other onerous activities.

In what became a model for future Federal and state legislative action on marijuana, Congressional hearings were held in 1937 on the Marijuana Tax Act. No medical, scientific or sociological evidence was sought or heard; no alternatives to criminalizing users and sellers were considered; and the major attention was given to the oilseed, birdseed and paint industries' need for unrestrained access to the hemp plant from which marijuana comes. A U.S. Treasury Department witness began his testimony by stating flatly that "Marijuana is being used extensively by high school children in cigarettes with deadly effect," and went on to introduce as further "evidence" an editorial from a Washington newspaper supposedly quoting the American Medical Association as having stated in its journal that marijuana use was one of the problems of greatest menace in the United States. Fortunately for historical analysis, a Dr. Woodward, serving as legislative counsel for the American Medical Association, was present to point out that the statement in question was by Anslinger and had only been reported in the A.M.A. journal.

Dr. Woodward deserves a posthumous accolade for his singlehanded heroic efforts to introduce reason and sanity to the hearing. Most importantly, the doctor (who was also a lawyer) criticized the Congressmen for proposing a law that would interfere with future medical uses of Cannabis and pointed out that no one from the Bureau of Prisons had been produced to show the number of prisoners "addicted" to marijuana, no one from the Children's Bureau or Office of Education to show the nature and extent of the "habit" among children and no one from the Division of Mental Hygiene or the Division of Pharmacology of the Public Health Service to give "direct and primary evidence rather than indirect and hearsay evidence." Saying that he assumed it was true that a certain amount of "narcotic addiction" existed, since "the newspapers have called attention to it so prominently that there must be some grounds for their statements," he concluded that the particular type of statute under consideration was neither necessary nor desirable. The Congressmen totally ignored the content of Dr. Woodward's testimony and attacked his character, qualifications, experience and relationship to the American Medical Association, all of which were impeccable. He was then forced to admit that he could not say with certainty that no problem existed. Finally, his testimony was brought to a halt with the warning, "You are not cooperative in this. If you want to advise us on legislation, you ought to come here with some constructive proposals rather than criticism, rather than trying to throw obstacles in the way of something that the Federal Government is trying to do."

A similar but shorter hearing was held in the Senate, where Anslinger presented anecodotal "evidence" that marijuana caused murder, rape and insanity.

Thus, the Marijuana Tax Act of 1937 was passed—and out of it grew a welter of state laws that were, in many cases, even more hastily ill conceived.

The present Federal laws impose a two-to-ten-year sentence for a first conviction for possessing even a small amount of marijuana, five to twenty years for a second conviction and ten to forty for a third. If Congress is not forced to recognize scientific fact and basic civil liberties, these penalties will be retained when the new Federal law is written without the sections declared invalid in the Leary case. The usual discretion that judges are given to grant probation or suspended sentences for real crimes is taken from them by this (and state) law as is the opportunity for parole. For sale or "dissemination," no matter how small the quantity of marijuana involved, and even if the dissemination is a gift between friends, the Federal penalty for first-offense conviction is five to twenty years; for a second offense, it's ten to forty.

The state laws, as I stated, are even hairier. Here are two real, and recent, cases: In Texas, Richard Dorsey, a shoe-shine-stand operator in a bowling alley, sold a matchbox full of marijuana (considerably less than an ounce) to a Dallas undercover policeman, for five dollars. His sentence: 50 years.

In Michigan, for selling five dollars' worth of grass to another police agent, Larry Belcher was sentenced to 20 to 30 years in prison. This case is worth noting as an example of how the marijuana laws actually function in many instances. Belcher is the only individual in Grand Traverse County to receive this sentence in the past two years; 25 other marijuana arrestees were all placed on probation within that time. Belcher, it appears, was the author of a column called "Dope-O-Scope" in a local underground

newspaper and had presented there some of the same scientific facts incorporated into this article. People who publicly oppose the marijuana laws and marijuana mythology of our narcotics police have an unusually high arrest record.

There is no consistency in these laws from state to state. Until 1968, South Dakota had the nation's lowest penalty for first-offense possession—90 days (it has since been raised to two to five years); however, if you crossed the state line to North Dakota, the picture changed abruptly. North Dakota had (and still has) the nation's highest penalty for first-offense possession—*99 years at hard labor*. In New York state, in spite of the revelatory work of the La Guardia commission, the penalties have increased since the Forties. Today, in that state, selling or transferring marijuana to anyone under 21 carries a penalty of one to 25 years, even if the transfer is by somebody who is also under 21 and is a gift to a friend. (The state legislature recently tried to raise this penalty to 15 years to life, but Governor Rockefeller vetoed the bill.) In Louisiana, a minor selling to a minor is subject to five to fifteen years' imprisonment, while an adult selling to a minor may receive the death penalty. Finally, in Georgia, the penalty for a first conviction for selling to a minor is life imprisonment. If the offender is paroled or his sentence suspended, and he is convicted again, he can be sentenced to death.

The barbarity of such penalties in relation to pot's relative harmlessness is even beginning to be recognized in Washington, despite incessant and quite unscientific efforts to maintain the old mythology, emanating from the Federal Bureau of Narcotics. In 1963, President Kennedy's Advisory Commission on Narcotic and Drug Abuse called into question some of the prevailing beliefs about marijuana and recommended lighter sentences for possession. In 1967, President Johnson's Commission on Law Enforcement and the Administration of Justice took a similar view, recommending more flexible penalties; more significantly, it stated that marijuana has virtually nothing in common with true narcotics or opiates—the first time that fact was publicly admitted by a U.S. Government agency. And in 1967, Dr. James Goddard, while commissioner of the U.S. Food and Drug Administration, was quoted as saying that it would disturb him less if his teenage daughter smoked one marijuana cigarette than if she drank an alcoholic beverage. (Faced with a predictable outcry from conservatives in Congress, Goddard said he had been misquoted—but quite honestly added that the known facts did not support the opinion that marijuana is more dangerous than alcohol.)

Not only is marijuana comparatively harmless on the face of all the evidence but there are even reasons to believe it may be beneficial in some cases. In many countries, Cannabis has been used medicinally for as long as 5000 years and is regarded as a sovereign remedy for a variety of ills. There are references to medicinal uses of marijuana in American medical journals (mostly of the 19th Century) where doctors reported it as useful as an analgesic, appetite stimulant, anti-spasmodic, anti-depressant, tranquilizer, anti-asthmatic, topical anesthetic, childbirth analgesic and antibiotic. My own investigations in areas of the world where this folk medicine still flourishes and my study of 20th Century scientific literature lead me to believe that marijuana would be useful for treating depression, loss of appetite, high blood pressure, anxiety and migraine.

An English psychiatrist who employed marijuana in the therapy of depressive patients, Dr. George T. Stockings, concluded that it "might be more effective than any tranquilizer now in use." Dr. Robert Walton of the University of Mississippi has also suggested its use for certain gynecological and menstrual problems and in easing childbirth. We should not let lingering puritanical prejudices prevent us from investigating these areas further. As Dr. Tod Mikuriya, a psychiatrist formerly associated with the National Institute of Mental Health, notes, "The fact that a drug has a recreational

history should not blind us to its possible other uses. Morton was the first to use ether publicly for anesthesia after observing medical students at 'ether frolics' in 1846." While such speculations about the benefits of pot must await further research before a final answer is given, there can be no doubt that a grave injustice has been suffered by those currently in prison because of laws passed when the drug was believed to incite crime and madness.

Even the Federal Bureau of Narcotics and its propagandists have largely given up the "steppingstone theory" (that marijuana smoking leads to use of addictive drugs) and the "degeneracy theory" (that it leads to crime or "bad character"). They have recently rallied around the oldest, and most discredited, canard of all—the legend that marijuana causes insanity. To shore up this crumbling myth, they cite recent research at the Addiction Research Center in Lexington, Kentucky, where 30 former opiate addicts were given high doses of synthetic THC (the active ingredient in marijuana) or concentrated Cannabis extract. Most of the subjects showed marked perceptual changes, which the experimenter chose to describe as "hallucinations" and "psychotic reactions." This, of course, merely confirms a basic axiom of pharmacology; i.e., with increasing doses of any drug, different and more dangerous responses will occur; you could obtain some spectacularly adverse reactions with horse doctors' doses of aspirin, coffee or even orange juice. (With ordinary doses of THC or marijuana, the subjects experienced the same "high" found in normal, social marijuana smoking.)

A more serious defect in this research lies in the loaded terminology with which the experimenter, Dr. Harris Isbell, reported his results. Psychiatrist Thomas Szasz, a crusader for reform in the mental-health field, points out that a "psychotic reaction" is not something *in* an individual, Mr. A, like cancer; rather, it is a label that a second individual, Mr. B (more often, Dr. B), pins on Mr. A. The *fact* is that the subjects experienced perceptual changes; it is not a fact but merely an *opinion* whether one wants to call these changes "consciousness expansion" and "transcendence of the ego" (with Timothy Leary) or "hallucinations" and "psychotic reactions" (with Dr. Isbell).

Sociologist Howard Becker—the observer who first noted the effect of "learning" on the marijuana experience—has researched medical literature from the early 1930s to the present in search of reported cases of "marijuana psychosis." He found none after 1940, a remarkable fact, considering the pyramiding acceleration of marijuana use during the Forties, Fifties and Sixties. Becker concluded that persons who were diagnosed as "marijuana psychotics" in the Thirties were simply anxious and disoriented because they hadn't learned yet how to use the drug. Dr. Isbell's subjects, almost certainly, were not advised about the effects of the drug; and his experiment is really just another proof of the effect of "set and setting" as well as high doses on drug experience.

A 1946 study examined 310 persons who had been using marijuana for an average of seven years each. There was no record of mental-hospital commitment among any of them.

The marijuanaphobes also cite studies from the Near East to prove that marijuana is associated with psychosis. In the first place, many of the people in these studies smoked hashish, not marijuana; and while hashish is derived from the same plant, Cannabis sativa, it is otherwise a considerably stronger form of the drug. One might compare the two Cannabis drugs with two alcohol drugs as follows: Smoking a pipe of hashish is equivalent to drinking a fifth of vodka; smoking the same pipe of marijuana is about like drinking a bottle of beer. However, the studies themselves do not deserve such careful rebuttal; they are scientifically worthless. They prove only that, in countries where most of the population regularly use Cannabis, many of the patients in mental hospitals also have a history of Cannabis use. Usually the proportion of users in the institution is less than that in the general population, leading to a possible conclusion that it is psychologically beneficial. In fact, however, there are no scientifically valid statistics or records kept at these facilities. The testimony turns out, on examination, to be impressionistic and anecdotal rather than scientific and precise. The diagnosis of psychosis and its attribution to Cannabis is often made by a ward attendant. In short, we are faced with the kind of "evidence" that the Indian Hemp Drug Commission discarded in 1893. I have visited the mental hospitals of several of the countries involved in the "Cannabis psychosis" and none of the record keeping involved meets the minimum requirements demanded of freshman scientific reports in American colleges.

Perhaps the last bastion of marijuanaphobia is the argument by uncertainty. "Who knows?" this line goes. "Maybe, in the future, marijuana might be discovered, by further research, to have dangerous side effects that haven't been noted yet." This argument, of course, is unanswerable; but it applies equally well to such diverse objects as diet pills and bubble gum. One cannot prove that the future will not discover new things; but does such a fact—science's lack of clairvoyance—justify our present marijuana laws? It clearly does not. No drug, including marijuana, will ever be found to be totally harmless; and no drug, particularly marijuana, will ever be found to be as dangerous as the hydrogen bomb (once claimed by Anslinger). Social policy should not be determined by this anyway. The possible risks should be dealt with by education. What is unacceptable is locking a man up for 99 years for possessing something of far less proven danger than tobacco, alcohol, automobiles and guns.

Instead of decreasing marijuana usage, our present laws have created the contempt for Government about which I spoke earlier. In addition to continuing to disobey the law, hordes of young people have begun to flout it publicly. There have been smoke-ins

—masses who gather in a public park, where those in the inner core of the group light up, while the outer perimeter obstruct and slow down the police until the evidence is consumed—at Berkeley, in Boston and elsewhere. Planting marijuana in conspicuous places has become a fad; among the notable seedings have been the center strip of Park Avenue in New York City, the lawn in front of a police station in ultrarespectable Westchester County, the UN Building and (twice recently) in front of the state capital in Austin, Texas.

But the American marijuana tragedy is even worse than I have indicated. Like other crimes-without-victims, pot smoking is a private activity and involves no harm to anyone else. Remember: The police do not have to engage in cloak-and-dagger activities to find out if there have been any banks or grocery stores robbed lately—the bankers and store owners (the victims) call them immediately. But since there is no victim in the "crime" of smoking marijuana, nobody is going to call the police to report it—except, very rarely, a neighbor who finds the evidence. Hence, the entire apparatus of the police state comes into existence as soon as we attempt to enforce anti-grass legislation; and by the nature of such legislation, totalitarian results must ensue. We cannot police the private lives of the citizenry without invading their privacy; this is an axiom.

That a man's home is his castle has long been a basic principle of Anglo-American jurisprudence, and some of us can still recall the near poetry of the great oration by William Pitt in which he says, "The poorest man may in his cottage bid defiance to the force of the Crown. It may be frail, its roof may shake; the wind may blow through it; the storms may enter; the rain may enter; but the King of England cannot enter—all his forces dare not cross the threshold of the ruined tenement!" This principle goes back to the Magna Charta and is firmly entrenched in the Fourth Amendment to our own Constitution, guaranteeing the people "the right . . . to be secure in their persons, houses, papers and effects, against unreasonable searches and seizures."

This libertarian tradition is a great hindrance to the police when they attempt to enforce sumptuary laws—laws concerning the private morals of the citizens. And, in fact, the enforcement of the marijuana law requires pernicious police behavior.

For instance, the *Chicago Sun-Times* told, in 1967, how the police of that city obtain search warrants for use in legalizing raids that otherwise would be mere "fishing expeditions"—intolerable to any American court. In dealing with the organized-crime cartel usually called "the Syndicate," the police have obtained from the courts the right to use what are called "blank warrants"—warrants in which the witness who alleges he has seen the crime is permitted to sign a false name. This is supposedly necessary to protect informers against the wrath of the reputedly all-seeing and all-powerful Syndicate. Once this dangerous precedent was set, the police began applying it to marijuana users as well. As the *Sun-Times* noted:

> Those methods are dubious. . . . We refer to the method of obtaining search warrants. The informer signs a search-warrant complaint, with an assumed name, alleging perhaps that he bought illicit drugs from a certain person, at a certain place. The police do not have to disclose the name of the informer or the time when the drugs were bought. There is also a device known as constructive possession: The police can arrest anybody found in the vicinity of prohibited drugs, whether he's an innocent visitor or the real culprit. The frameup is easy. Plant the drugs, get the search warrant, grab everybody in sight. It could happen to you and you'd never have the right to face your accuser.

William Braden, a *Sun-Times* reporter, also uncovered one informer, a heroin addict, who admitted signing dozens of such warrants without the names of the accused on them. The narcotics squad could then type in the name of any individual whose apartment they wanted to raid and it would be perfectly "legal" in form—but a terrifying distance in spirit from the actual meaning of the Constitution. Such raids, of course, violate the Sixth Amendment—guaranteeing the right "to be confronted with the witnesses" against you—as well as the Fourth (no "unreasonable searches") ; and they occur everywhere in the nation.

Most of us never hear of such things, because reporters routinely print the police version of the raid, without interviewing the arrested "dope fiends." It is also standard practice for the police to multiply the quantity of drugs seized in such a raid by a factor of two (and the price by a factor of ten) when giving the news to the press. This makes for impressive headlines; it also contributes to the growing tendency toward "trial by newspaper," which worries civil libertarians.

Some types of entrapment are regarded as legal in America today—although some still are not. In my opinion, *all* forms of entrapment are profoundly immoral, whether technically legal or illegal; but my opinion is, perhaps, immaterial. The results of this practice, however, are truly deplorable from the point of view of anyone who has any lingering affection for the spirit of the Bill of Rights.

Here is a specific case: John Sinclair, a poet, leader of the Ann Arbor hippie community and manager of a rock group called MC-5, became friendly, around October 1966, with Vahan Kapagian and Jane Mumford, who presented themselves to him as members of the hippie-artist-mystic subculture that exists in all of our large cities. Over a period of two months, they worked to secure his confidence and friendship and several times asked him to get them some marijuana. Finally, on December 22, Sinclair, apparently feeling that he could now trust them, gave two marijuana cigarettes to Miss Mumford—one for her and one for Kapagian. He was immediately arrested; his "friends" were police undercover agents.

Sinclair has been convicted of both "pos-

sessing" and "dispensing" marijuana and faces a minimum of 20 years under each statute, and a maximum of life for the sale. If his appeal is not upheld, the very smallest sentence he could receive is 40 years. As his lawyers pointed out in his appeal, "The minimum sentence to which [Sinclair] is subject to imprisonment is 20 times greater than the minimum to which a person may be imprisoned [in Michigan] for such crimes as rape, robbery, arson, kidnapping or second-degree murder. It is more than 20 times greater than the minimum sentence of imprisonment for any other offense in Michigan law, except first-degree murder."

That illegal wire tapping has also been widely used by the narcotics police was an open secret for years; now it is no secret at all—and not illegal, either. The 1968 Omnibus Crime Bill authorizes such wire tapping for suspected marijuana users. Since this usage has spread to all classes and all educational levels, such suspicion can be directed at virtually anyone (after all, the nephew and the brother of one of President Nixon's closest friends were recently busted on pot charges) ; thus, almost any American can now have his phone tapped legally. Considering the elastic interpretation police usually give to such Congressional authorization, an anonymous tip by any crank in your neighborhood would probably be enough to get a tap on your phone by tomorrow morning. Why not? As *Chicago Daily News* columnist Mike Royko recently wrote, "There is a democratic principle in injustice. If enough people support it, they'll all get it."

With the doctrine of "constructive possession," anyone who has a pot-smoking friend is subject to marijuana laws if he walks into the friend's house at the wrong time. In California two years ago, a woman was sentenced to sterilization for being in the same room with a man who was smoking grass. The fact that a higher court overturned this sentence does not lessen its frightening implications.

And a new wrinkle has been added. According to a story in the *San Francisco Chronicle* last June 20, the Government is planning "an unpleasant surprise for marijuana smokers—'sick pot.'" The article goes on to explain how an unspecified chemical can be sprayed on Mexican marijuana fields from a helicopter, whereupon "just a puff or two produces uncontrollable vomiting that not even the most dedicated smoker could ignore."

This, I submit, could come from the morbid fantasy of Kafka, Burroughs or Orwell. The Government, in its holy war against a relatively harmless drug, is deliberately creating a very harmful drug. Nor is the *Chronicle* story something dreamed up by a sensation-mongering reporter. A call to the Justice Department in Washington has confirmed that this plan has been discussed and may go into operation in the near future.

Consider, now, the actual social background in which this crusade against Cannabis is being waged. America is not the Victorian garden it pretends to be; we are, in fact, a drug-prone nation. Parents and other adults after whom children model their own behavior teach them that every time one relates to other human beings, whether at a wedding or at a funeral, and every time one has a pain, problem or trouble, it is necessary or desirable to pop a pill, drink a cocktail or smoke a cigarette. The alcohol, tobacco and over-the-counter pseudo-"sedative" industries jointly spend more than $2,000,000 a day in the United States alone to promote as much drug use as possible.

The average "straight" adult consumes three to five mind-altering drugs a day, beginning with the stimulant caffeine in coffee, tea or Coca-Cola, going on to include alcohol and nicotine, often a tranquilizer, not uncommonly a sleeping pill at night and sometimes an amphetamine the next morning to overcome the effects of the sedative taken the evening before.

We have 80,000,000 users of alcohol in this country, including 6,000,000 alcoholics;

50,000,000 users of tobacco cigarettes; 25,000,000 to 30,000,000 users of sedatives, stimulants and tranquilizers; and hundreds of thousands of users of consciousness alterers that range from heroin and LSD to cough syrup, glue, nutmeg and catnip—all in addition to marijuana use.

Drs. Manheimer and Mellinger, surveying California adults over 21, found that 51 percent had at some time used sedatives, stimulants or tranquilizers (17 percent had taken these drugs frequently) and 13 percent had at some time used marijuana.

Further underlining the extent of use of the prescription drugs is the estimate from the National Prescription Audit that 175,000,000 prescriptions for sedatives, stimulants and tranquilizers were filled in 1968. Also enough barbiturates (Nembutal, Seconal, phenobarbital) alone are manufactured to provide 25 to 30 average doses per year for every man, woman and child in this country.

In the light of this total drug picture, the persecution of potheads seems to be a species of what anthropologists call "scapegoatism"—the selection of one minority group to be punished for the sins of the whole population, whose guilt is vicariously extirpated in the punishment of the symbolic sacrificial victims.

Meanwhile, my criticisms—and those of increasing numbers of writers, scientific and popular—continue to bounce off the iron walls of prejudice that seem to surround Congress and state legislatures. It is quite possible that our new, post-Leary pot laws will be as bad as the old ones. If there is any improvement, it is likely to come, once again, from the courts.

Several legal challenges to our anti-pot mania are, in fact, working their way upward toward the Supreme Court, and the issues they raise are potentially even more significant than those involved in the Leary case.

First is the challenge raised by attorney Joseph Oteri in his defense of two Boston University students. Oteri's case cites the

equal-protection clause of the Constitution
—grass is less harmful than booze, so you
can't outlaw one without the other. He also
argues that the marijuana statute is irrational and arbitrary and an invalid exercise of police power because pot is harmless
and wrongly defined as a narcotic, when it
is, technically, not a narcotic. This is not
mere hairsplitting. It is impossible, under
law, to hang a man for murder if his actual
crime was stealing hubcaps; it should be
equally impossible to convict him of "possession of a narcotic" if he was not in possession of a narcotic but of a drug belonging
to an entirely different chemical family.

And marijuana, decidedly, is not a narcotic—although just what it should be called
is something of a mystery. The tendency
these days is to call it a "mild psychedelic,"
with the emphasis on mild; this is encouraged both by the Tim Leary crowd—to
whom psychedelic is a good word, denoting
peace, ecstasy, non-violent revolution, union
with God and the end of all neurotic hang-
ups of Western man—and by those to whom
psychedelic is a monster word denoting hallucinations, insanity, suicide and chaos. I
doubt the psychedelic label very much and
think it is as off base as narcotic. Since marijuana has very little in common with LSD
and the true psychedelics, but much in common with alcohol and other sedatives, and a
certain similarity also to amphetamine and
other stimulants, I prefer to call it a sedative-
stimulant as it is classified by Dr. Frederick
Meyers, who also notes its resemblance to
laughing gas (nitrous oxide). Dr. Leo Hollis-
ter finds enough resemblance to LSD to call
it a sedative-hypnotic-psychedelic. *Goodman
and Gilman,* the orthodox pharmacological
reference, dodges the issue entirely by listing
marijuana as a "miscellaneous" drug. In any
case, it is not a narcotic, and anyone arrested
for having a narcotic in his possession when
he actually has marijuana definitely is being
charged with a crime he hasn't committed.

A second challenge, raised by Oteri and
also being pressed by two Michigan attorneys,
is based on the prohibition of "cruel and

unusual punishments" in the Eighth Amendment. The courts have held, in the past, that
a law can be struck down if the punishments
it requires are cruel and unusual in comparison with the penalties in the same state
for similar or related crimes. For instance, the
statute against chicken stealing was made
quite harsh in the early days of Oklahoma,
apparently because the offense was common
and provoked great public indignation. As a
result, a man named Skinner was threatened
with the punishment of sterilization under
one section of this law. He appealed to the
Supreme Court, which struck down the Oklahoma statute because similarly harsh penalties were not provided for other forms of
theft. Obviously, in the states where the penalty for possession of marijuana is higher
than the penalty for armed robbery, rape,
second-degree murder, etc., the law is vulnerable to legal attack as cruel and unusual.

There is also the "zone of privacy" argument, originally stated in the Connecticut
birth-control decision and more recently invoked by the Kentucky supreme court, in
striking down a local (Barbourville, Kentucky) ordinance making it a crime to smoke
tobacco cigarettes. The court ruled that "The
city . . . may not unreasonably interfere with
the right of the citizen to determine for himself such personal matters." The zone of
privacy was also cited by the U.S. Supreme
Court in invalidating the Georgia law
against possession (not sale) of pornography.

The drug police and their legislative allies
have been experimenting with our liberties
for a long time now. The Leary decision,
however, shows that it is not too late to reverse the trend, and the issues raised by the
constitutional questions discussed above show
how the erosion of our liberties can, indeed,
be reversed.

A compelling medical, sociological and
philosophical case exists for the full legalization of marijuana, particularly if legalization
is the only alternative to the present crimi-
nalization of users. But an even more substantial case exists for ending all criminal
penalties for possession or use of the drug,

while still exercising some caution. I would recommend, for example, that to prevent the sale of dangerously adulterated forms of the drug, marijuana be produced under Federal supervision, as alcohol is. Furthermore, sellers of the drug should be licensed, and they should be prohibited from selling to minors. If there are infractions of these laws, the penalties should be directed at the seller, not the user. I would also strongly recommend that all advertising and promotion of marijuana be prohibited, and that packages of the drug carry the warning: CAUTION: MARIJUANA MAY BE HARMFUL TO YOUR HEALTH.

If marijuana were to be legalized, what would happen? According to the marijuana-phobes, the weed will spread into every American home; people will become lazy and sluggish, sit around all day in a drugged stupor and talk philosophy when they talk at all; we will sink into the "backward" state of the Near Eastern and Asian nations.

There are good, hard scientific reasons for doubting this gloomy prognostication.

1. Most Americans have already found their drug of choice—alcohol—and there is more conditioning involved in such preferences than most people realize. The average American heads straight for the bar when he feels the impulse to relax; a change in the laws will not change this conditioned reflex. When the Catholic Church allowed its members to eat meat on Friday, the majority went right on following the conditioned channel that told them, "Friday is fish day."

2. Of the small minority that will try pot (after it is legalized) in search of a new kick, most will be vastly disappointed, since (a) it doesn't live up to its sensational publicity, largely given to it by the Federal Narcotics Bureau; and (b) the "high" depends, as we have indicated, not only on set and setting but, unlike alcohol, on learning.

This involves conditioning and the relationship of the actual chemistry of the two drugs to the total *Gestalt* of our culture. What pot actually does—outside mythology—is produce a state midway between euphoria and drowsiness, like a mild alcohol high; ac-

celerate and sharpen the thoughts (at least in the subjective impression of the user), like an amphetamine; and intensify sound and color perception, although not nearly as much as a true psychedelic. It can also enhance sexual experience, but not create it—contrary to Mr. Anslinger, pot is not an aphrodisiac. It is, in short, the drug of preference for creative and contemplative types—or, at least, people with a certain streak of that tendency in their personality. Alcohol, on the other hand, depresses the forebrain, relaxes inhibitions, produces euphoria and drowsiness and, while depleting some functions, such as speech and walking, does not draw one into the mixture of sensuality and introspection created by pot. It is the drug of preference for aggressive and extroverted types. Therefore, the picture of pot spreading everywhere and changing our culture is sociologically putting the cart before the horse; our society would first have to change basically before pot could spread everywhere.

3. Even if, against all likelihood, marijuana were to sweep the country, this would not have dire consequences. Marijuana has no specifically anti-machine property in it; it would not make our technology go away, like a wave of an evil sorcerer's wand. Nor does it dull the mental faculties, as we have seen in reviewing the scientific evidence. (I might add, here, that the highest honor students at certain Ivy League colleges are frequently pot users, and one study at Yale found more marijuana smokers at the top of the class than at the bottom.)

4. Finally, the whole specter of America sinking into backwardness due to pot is based upon totally false anthropological concepts. The Near East is not tribal, preindustrial, superstitious, and so forth, merely because Mohammed banned alcohol in the Koran but forgot to exclude Cannabis drugs also; a whole complex of historical and cultural factors is involved, not the least of which is the continuous intervention of Western imperialism from the Crusades onward. Other factors are the rigid structure of the Islamic religion and the lack of a scientific minority

that can effectively challenge these dogmas; the Western world was equally backward—please note—when the Christian religion was not open to scientific dissent and criticism. Backwardness is a relative concept, and, although pot has been used in the Arabic countries for millenniums, they have several times been ahead of the West in basic science (the most famous example being their invention of algebra). The populations of these nations are not "lazy" due to marijuana nor to any other cause; they are merely underemployed by a feudalistic economic system. The ones lucky enough to find work usually toil for longer hours, in a hotter sun, than most Americans would find bearable.

Thus, treating marijuana in a sane and rational way presents no threat to our society, whereas continuing the present hysteria will alienate increasing numbers of the young while accelerating the drift toward a police state. I take no pleasure in the spread of even so mild a drug as marijuana, and I am sure (personally, not scientifically) that in a truly open, libertarian and decent society, nobody would be inclined to any kind of drug use. While I agree with the psychedelic generation about the absurdity and injustice of our criminal laws relating to drugs, I am not an apostle of the "turn on, tune in, drop out" mystique. I recognize that drugs can be an evasion of responsibility, and that there is no simple chemical solution to all the psychic, social and political problems of our time. My own program would be: Turn on to the life around you, tune in to knowledge and feeling, and drop *in* to changing the world for the better. If that course could prevail, the adventurous young, no longer haunted by the anxiety and *anomie* of the present system, would probably discover that love, comradeship, music, the arts, sex, meaningful work, alertness, self-discipline, real education (which is a lifelong task) and plain hard thought are bigger, better and more permanent highs than any chemical can produce.

But, meanwhile, I must protest—I will continue to protest—against the bureaucrat who stands with cocktail in one hand and cigarette in the other and cries out that the innocent recreation of pot smoking is the major problem facing our society, one that can be solved only by raising the penalty to castration for the first offense and death for the second. He would be doing the young people—and all the rest of us—a true favor if he forgot about marijuana for a while and thought, a few minutes a day, about such real problems as racism, poverty, starvation, air pollution and our stumbling progress toward World War Three and the end of life on earth.

It is an irony of our time that our beloved George Washington would be a criminal today, for he grew hemp at Mount Vernon, and his diary entries, dealing specifically with separating the female plants from the male before pollination, show that he was not harvesting it for rope. The segregation of the plants by sex is only necessary if you intend to extract "the killer drug, marijuana" from the female plant.

Of course, we have no absolute evidence that George turned on. More likely, he was using marijuana as many Americans in that age used it: as a medicine for bronchitis, chest colds and other respiratory ailments. (Pot's euphoric qualities were not well known outside the East in those days.) But can you imagine General Washington trying to explain to an agent of the Federal Narcotics Bureau, "I was only smoking it to clear up my lumbago"? It would never work; he would land in prison, perhaps for as long as 40 years. He would be sharing the same cruel fate as several thousand other harmless Americans today. As it says in the book of *Job,* "From the dust the dying groan, and the souls of the wounded cry out."

Drugs Without Crime

EDGAR MAY

"What the hell's that guy doing in the front seat?" the cab dispatcher asked at Kennedy airport. "He's my protection," the driver said. "It's a new cab, see, and I don't have no screen installed yet between me and the back. He's my son. I won't drive at night without him."

I had just landed in New York after months of investigating the British approach to narcotic addiction for an American foundation. Although I now worked in Europe, I had gone to public school in this city and to one of its universities—but I felt like a stranger. In my cab I was far from the haunts of the addict, but not from the terror he provoked. And the vignettes of fear continued.

The first of three keys needed to enter the building where a friend loaned me an apartment . . . the safety lock that wouldn't budge . . . the crinkled metal signature of the crowbar used the last time the place was robbed . . . the neighbor's door with the decal of a helmeted heroine radiating jagged lightning and the message: "This home is protected electronically" . . . the next morning's embarrassment when I was forced off a bus be-

cause I didn't know drivers no longer carry money to make change . . . the armed guard in the midtown office building and his intercom announcement: "There's a man here who *says* he's got an appointment."

Later, whenever I mentioned the drug problem, someone would offer his personal anecdote of a burglarized apartment, a vandalized car, a neighbor's purse snatched. The illustrations even had slipped into the wry humor of the young.

"You can't get anybody to play the outfield in Central Park anymore," a friend's son told me. "They're afraid of getting mugged."

In England I was with addicts daily, with their neighbors and those who work with them, but fear was not among the emotions I observed. There was pity, disgust, sorrow, and sometimes scorn. But the English are not afraid of the addict. They don't label him a criminal. They believe he is sick.

In contrast, decade after decade we have proclaimed his problem a sin not a sickness and have spent ever-increasing law-enforcement millions to snare him, while "shielding" him from a continuously expanding smuggling, processing, and pushing network whose magnitude—and profits for some—surpasses the bootlegging operations of Prohibition. Meanwhile, nine out of ten American drug addicts are without any medical help at all.

Note: Edgar May, "Drugs Without Crime," *Harper's,* July 1971, pp. 60–65. Copyright © 1971 by Harper's Magazine. Reprinted from the July 1971 issue by special permission.

Compared with ours, the British drug problem is minuscule. There are slightly fewer than 3,000 narcotic addicts in England, while our estimates range from 100,000 to 250,000. However, in Britain heroin use increased so rapidly a few years ago that drug-control officials felt it had reached epidemic proportions. In the middle Sixties heroin addicts in Great Britain doubled every sixteen months. When the count soared from 237 to 2,240, a visiting American drug expert predicted that it would shortly reach 10,000. This will never happen.

England has stopped the narcotic-addiction spiral. In 1968 almost 1,000 new heroin addicts were counted. But in 1969 there were only ninety-nine additional heroin and other narcotic addicts. Since then, monthly additions have been falling, and the 1970 report is expected to show a reversal—the first drop since the heroin crisis began in the Sixties.

This achievement has made few headlines in England and virtually none in the United States, where all addiction indicators are going the other way. In part this is because the British approach to addiction is far more complex and problem-filled than a Home Office tally sheet shows. But much more likely, the statistics have been overshadowed by the controversy which surrounds the basic ingredient of the English drug program: government clinics which give free heroin and other narcotics to addicts.

Critical vision has often been not only blurred but distorted. Americans, particularly, tend to dismiss the British experience categorically, sometimes with a tinge of sadness that the usually sensible English should have made such an unfortunate mistake. A U.S. Government drug pamphlet issued last year says flatly: "The British system is considered a failure and has been modified to meet the increasing problem of addiction."

The press, more often than not, hasn't done much better. While the statistics may seem unduly optimistic, the litany of bizarre anecdotes published in the past conveys more despair than is justified.

In the new kaleidoscope that is Piccadilly Circus, the scene is as distorted as the spasmodic electric messages which flash above the throng. The anecdotes are all there. The young, wan addict, staggering out of a doorway to panhandle enough for a fix . . .furtive glances at the passerby while pills or other drugs are exchanged . . . a jab of a needle in the toilet of the Underground . . . a spurt of blood on a soiled white shirt . . . a young girl collapsing on the sidewalk after a barbiturate injection. This may have become part of the tourist attraction of London's Times Square, but it doesn't reflect accurately the addiction problem in England. What does?

Between the statistics and the anecdotes there are no unassailable conclusions. No one trumpets about a British drug program "success"; no one talks of "cures." Neither word has much relevance in the contemporary addiction dictionary on either side of the Atlantic. In Britain, as in America, treatment methods are debated. Furthermore, the label "addict" includes not just the heroin user but an addicted population which injects methadone and barbiturates, often during the same week, if not the same day. And that's only the hard-drug user.

Behind him is a far larger turn-on army of the young who dabble with LSD and amphetamines, and lose themselves in clouds of marijuana and hashish. No one disputes that this second division of drug abusers is increasing.

But in England, as in the United States, the paramount public concern has been with the casualties in the first rank—the narcotic addict. And in Britain this rising toll has been halted. Since the government clinics began, the monthly amounts of prescribed heroin have continued to drop. The majority of heroin addicts have been weaned over to methadone, a synthetic narcotic substitute developed by the Germans in World War II. But the drop in heroin hasn't been matched by an equivalent rise in methadone.

The most significant contrast with America's drug problem, however, is that in England there is no direct connection between addiction and crime. No one—from the toughest London detective to the most liberal-minded physician—suggests that sticking a needle into your arm propels you into the robber and burglar fraternity. "There is no concrete evidence to connect any particular criminal activity with those dependent on the 'hard' drugs," Scotland Yard said in one of its reports.

In Washington, D. C., on the other hand, police blame up to 80 per cent of serious property crime on drug users. In New York City annual addict thievery is estimated at anywhere from a low of $250 million to a high of nearly $2 billion. No one has counted the people who are terrorized or those who are maimed and killed.

In Britain, different investigators have found that addicts are likely to commit *fewer* crimes after they are hooked than before. British prison psychiatrist Ian Pierce James showed that in those categories where U.S. addicts predominate—larceny, housebreaking, and robbery—his English sample had fewer convictions after addiction.

What all the British studies show is that a track record in court often is established before tracks are found on a subject's arm. Addicts are likely to have a whole series of antisocial "hang-ups," and addiction is just another form, rather than the cause, of delinquent behavior. This tends to support the theory, fairly widely held in the United States, that the gang wars which plagued our cities in bygone years ceased not so much because of street-worker efforts, but because drugs became a substitute for the rumble.

For a major clue to the difference in the addict-crime relationship in the two countries, you have to go back to Piccadilly Circus. There, amid the medicine shelves of Boots the Chemist, the all-night drugstore, you find heroin tablets in small bottles in a locked cabinet. A printed-in-red retail price list says: Heroin 100 tablets 90 Pence or $2.16. On New York City's streets, the retail price for the same amount of heroin can run to $1,000 or more.

America's crime problem, to be sure, is far more complex than the difference between these two price tags. But one thing is clear. Only a tiny fraction of America's addicts can legitimately earn the $300 to $500 a week it takes to support a full-blown heroin habit. In England, their equivalents have a luxurious option; they don't have to steal. Even if the British National Health Service insisted that they dig into their own pockets, it would make little difference. Pure British-made heroin costs the government no more than a daily tin of aspirin for each addict.

However, this is one English bargain not available to the tourist. For all but the clinic-confined addicts, heroin is no more legal in England than picking up samples at the British Museum. Possession without a precription means a maximum seven-year jail sentence: the penalty for trafficking, recently increased, could be as much as fourteen years. And British drug laws have been getting tougher. Until three years ago any doctor could write a prescription for heroin. With addiction figures soaring, the government stopped this and limited prescribing to special treatment centers which it aided regional hospital areas to set up. But even with these restrictions, the British never lost sight of the fact that they were talking about medicine. The "addict," said the distinguished panel which urged the clinic approach, "should be regarded as a sick person, he should be treated as such and not as a criminal, provided that he does not resort to criminal acts." [1]

Much of the narcotics crisis of the Sixties is blamed on a very small segment of the

[1] Ironically, the clinics the panel recommended were tried in the United States a long time ago. After World War I, some forty short-lived narcotic-maintenance clinics existed to cope with the wave of morphine and heroin addiction brought home by the doughboys. More recently, several prestigious committees have suggested reviving the maintenance clinics on an experimental basis. For example, in 1955 the New York Academy of Medicine urged another attempt and suggested that earlier efforts were stopped not because they had failed, but because they ran against "the prevailing philosophy of a punitive approach."

British medical profession. Some physicians carelessly overprescribed; a few, working like pushers, made huge quantities of heroin available to dissatisfied youths seeking the drugged dream of escape.

For these junkie doctors, it was a lucrative enterprise. In 1962, for example, one prescribed six kilos of heroin, enough to support 822 American addicts with a daily $20 habit for an entire year. Another physician, when addicts were not coming to his office fast enough, made house calls to prod the laggards. A former patient told me he could count on a visit whenever the doctor had a bad day at the races. He was issuing prescriptions from a taxi parked in front of the Baker Street tube station when he was finally caught, fined, jailed, and barred from medicine.

Many addicts luxuriating in this narcotic largesse not only revved themselves up to ever-higher doses, but often sold their surplus to eager novices who soon were welded to the habit. There was so much of the drug around that, despite inflation, black-market heroin—the overprescribed surplus—remained at a constant $2.40 a grain.

It was to end this chaos that the government launched its clinics. And almost immediately some critics launched their onslaught on the new British "system." The very word is wrong. Contrary to the widespread American view, the British National Health Service is not a monolith which dictates everything from aspirin dispensing to appendix removal. And the Ministry of Health has approached physicians both inside and outside the drug clinics with the circumspection of an impresario dealing with a skittish diva. Each clinic director is doing "his own thing." In common with his colleagues, he is a psychiatrist who treats addicts and prescribes narcotics. The important medical "how" is left up to him, and to his local hospital board which holds his purse strings.

There are fourteen clinics in London, which has four-fifths of the country's addicts. Elsewhere an addict may obtain drugs at thirteen special facilities or at forty-two hospital outpatient departments.

Some clinics have hospital beds for withdrawal "cures," many mix social-work services with their drugs, some provide extensive psychiatric service to addicts, some put the top premium on addict employment (almost 40 per cent of all clinic-attending addicts work) —other clinics don't have these extra services. Almost all clinics permit addicts to inject drugs away from the premises, but at least two insist that a nurse administer them twice a day.

Physical facilities also vary greatly. In the naval-base city of Portsmouth, the clinic is in a large general hospital tucked behind a door marked "Dental Waiting Room." In East London the center is in its own building on the grounds of a mental hospital. In the Denmark Hill area it's part of the hospital's general outpatient department, and if you visit St. Giles Clinic in the Church of England Community Center you are reminded of an Alec Guinness movie. Dr. James H. Willis, a young psychiatrist, holds court, resplendent in white medical coat, in a lecture hall where he sits behind a large wooden table flanked by two pianos and a bass fiddle. He took refuge behind these church walls after neighborhood people prevented him from occupying a newly constructed clinic, because they believed that his commuting addicts would infect their children.

At none of these facilities can an individual simply walk in and sign up for a government-sponsored fix. A detailed form is sent to the Home Office for comparison with the master list of known addicts to avoid duplicate registration. New patients generally receive at least two interviews with a social worker or one or more psychiatrists. One, and sometimes several, urine tests are demanded, usually two or three days apart. Drug-positive urine tests are the chief tools to determine the kind of drug, if any, the addict is taking.

All doctors I interviewed agreed that confirming addiction—and particularly prescribing the correct amount—is the toughest part of their job. They used words like "haggling" and "bargaining" to describe the process. Mistakes were not uncommon in the hectic opening months of the clinics in 1968. "A drug addict presented himself and said he needed six grains of heroin a day," Dr. John Denham of St. Clement's clinic recalled. "We thought he could do with two, but that he would settle for four. It was as haphazard as that."

Dr. Philip H. Connell, clinic director and one of the pioneers in the drug field, candidly admitted that the *clinic* had addicted some previously "clean" patients. "Eleven individuals with negative urines were mistakenly prescribed an opiate," he wrote in a British medical publication. Another clinic, on an addict's tip, discovered a dozen others who were collecting a double narcotic bounty by enrolling at a second center.

Once accepted, the addict doesn't receive his drugs from the clinic. A week's prescription is mailed directly to his neighborhood druggist, but the patient can pick it up only in daily doses.

The size and particularly the content of these prescriptions have changed radically since the clinics began. All but several hundred addicts have been converted to using only, or at least some, methadone. The use of this alternate narcotic, however, generally is very different from the treatment approach pioneered in America by Drs. Vincent Dole and Marie Nyswander. They provide methadone mixed in orange juice, in an effort to block the heroin craving. While some English addicts drink methadone, three-fourths of the prescriptions are for mainlining it like heroin. Clinic physicians believe patients often are almost as addicted to the hypodermic as to the narcotic itself—and few volunteer to give it up. Furthermore, many doctors are skeptical that methadone, no matter how it is taken, will eliminate the taste for heroin.

Their patients fall into four rough groups: those who inject heroin only; those who inject both heroin and methadone; those who inject methadone only; and those who drink the alternate narcotic. Many doctors believe

shifting an addict through these categories is progress, even though none has recorded any dramatic differences between methadone and heroin. Some favor methadone because its longer-lasting quality requires fewer daily injections. Second, as a liquid preparation, unlike the heroin tablet, it doesn't have to be mixed with water, which frequently is a contributor to infection in the addict's self-administered fix. Finally there is a nonmedical incentive. The clinics were established specifically to stop the heroin explosion, and the government keeps and circulates a record of each clinic's monthly heroin prescriptions, a clearly implied measure of performance.

Although most addicts report weekly to the clinic, there is seldom enough staff to provide intensive social work or psychiatric counseling. In one London clinic the lone and part-time social worker has a caseload of thirty addicts out of the near one hundred total. She estimated she had what she called "a deep relationship with a half-dozen. They get a good half-hour a week. I think," she added. "I do first aid a lot."

Some clinic directors have purposely ruled out therapy sessions. "If they chose drugs, they get drugs," Dr. Ian Christie, who runs the Portsmouth clinic, said. He offers the addict three options: he can enter the hospital for withdrawal ("everyone who has tried that has relapsed"); he can continue on drugs by reporting to the clinic twice a day for intramuscular but not intravenous injections; or he can sign up for an eighteen-month tour in a therapeutic community modeled after New York's Phoenix House. Dr. Christie is encouraged by his experience with those who make the last choice and is expanding the program even though the dropout rate has been very high, as in America.

Most English workers in the field do not believe that even the most skilled and intense psychological cajoling, or, for that matter, harassment, will move a patient away from drugs until he has made the decision himself. Both the American and British drug scenes are littered with the failures which support this view. It is the recognition that many addicts don't want to be cured—no matter how much society wishes it were otherwise—that is a key rationale for giving free narcotics at clinics. "We at least have the addicts under some responsible medical supervision, and not just those who will volunteer for an oral methadone program or a therapeutic community," said Dr. Martin Mitcheson, a clinic director and drug researcher. "This gives the doctor some chance to learn how to motivate even the more hopeless junkies toward a more lasting cure than prison ever will enforce."

In the two dozen doctor-addict interviews I was permitted to observe, I heard little sermonizing. Occasionally, the results are encouraging. There was, for instance, the young boy with a narcotic history dating back to one of the celebrated junkie doctors. His blond girlfriend had accompanied him to the session. After the preliminaries about how he was feeling and how his job was going, there was a momentary silence. The boy fidgeted and his eyes focused on the girl. "Next week," he said softly, "cut back my script."

While the more glaring mistakes of the clinics' early days are now a thing of the past, the clinics often cannot persuade their clients to stick to the prescribed drug diet. Like their American counterparts, many abuse more than one drug. Others sell, loan, or exchange some of their own allotment. This traffic would be reduced if drugs were administered directly at the clinics, a practice most of the doctors do not favor.

London drug-squad detectives do favor it. They want fewer clinics, open around the clock, providing drugs on the spot and nowhere else. While they acknowledge that illicit heroin has been drastically reduced, they are uncertain about how much bootleg methadone has replaced it. Since price reflects scarcity, illicit heroin's cost has jumped at least sixfold since the days of the junkie doctors. And illegal methadone isn't much cheaper. But the black market where they are sold might more accurately be called the

narcotic surplus market, fueled principally by clinic addicts hawking a portion of their prescriptions. While some Hong Kong heroin is imported, there is no large-scale underworld-dominated operation. What the black market does provide is an entrance for those who want to dabble with narcotics.

One thing is clear, however. No policeman I interviewed was prepared to scrap the clinics. London detectives may grumble about doctors who overprescribe. On the other hand, the head of Southhampton's drug squad went on TV earlier this year to criticize the local clinic doctor's stingy policies, which he blamed for an increase in pharmacy burglaries.

In neighboring Portsmouth, the respected head of the drug squad offered an unqualified endorsement. "Make no mistake about it," said Detective Sergeant Alan Russell. "People forget that a few years ago this country had a serious heroin problem. You've got to accept the fact they've knocked a hole in it."

There is, unfortunately, no computer printout on overall clinic performance. Yet a cautious note of optimisim is sounded by many of the doctors involved. "Much to my surprise, we have stabilized the addicts—they're not dead and they are better," said Dr. Margaret Tripp, who directs an East London clinic. "Their drug use has gone down, they work longer, and they are less of a nuisance to everybody."

"I'm pleased that the frightening curve of heroin addiction has leveled off, but I'm disturbed that methadone and barbiturates have risen," says Dr. Philip Connell. "The clinics have provided some treatment services where none have existed, but in terms of research they are a failure.

"But all of the terrible prognostications [for the clinics] of American workers in the drug field have been unfounded."

To document these subjective judgments, there are the national addiction statistics. While they may be incomplete, no one believes that there is a huge, hidden group of unreported addicts. The downward trend is reflected in British prisons. In London's version of New York City's Tombs, Ian Pierce James saw one-third fewer addicts in 1970 than he had in 1969. All three London centers, the number of addicts holding jobs almost doubled over two years. In these same clinics, a series of urine tests given a year apart showed that while many addicts still were taking more and different drugs than those prescribed, such misuse had been reduced. In yet another survey, there were fewer arrests a year after addicts were with a clinic than before.

No one, however, claims that the British are on their way toward eliminating man's centuries-old dilemma of drugged escape. So it is easy to dismiss the British drug approach and say it simply doesn't apply to the American scene. The countries are just too different. Not only do some key narcotic laws point in opposite directions, but each society's traditions, youth culture, and race problems are so disparate that what works in the row houses of London could not possibly work in the walk-ups of New York.

A soon-to-be-published study gives an explosive jolt to such blanket judgments. For the first time, a comparison has been made of the lives of addicts in a society which says they are criminals against another which says they are sick. Jim Zacune, a social psychologist with the Addiction Research Unit of London's Institute of Psychiatry, studied the performance of twenty-five Canadian addicts at home and in England, where they migrated in the early Sixties. He diplomatically says that his findings should not be used to pillory one country's addiction approach while praising another's and cautions that his sample may have included the most stable of the Canadians who packed up their syringes for England. However polite and academically sound the qualifiers, his findings are startling:

At home the Canadians spent 25 per cent of their addicted years in jail; in England, less than 2 per cent.
At home this meant a combined total of 141 years and 2 months in prison; in England, 2 years and 5 months.
At home they compiled 182 offenses; in England, 27.
At home, in the high addict crime category of theft, which also included robbery and burglary, they committed 88; in England, 8.

In Britain many onetime "hustlers" became jobholders and often led fairly normal lives on a daily heroin dosage three and a half times that of London addicts. In Canada, only one claimed to have worked steadily while addicted. In England, thirteen worked full-time and four worked part-time. Six had held the same job for at least three years. Seven had semi-skilled or skilled manual jobs; two were office workers; one in sales; and the rest worked as croupier, housewife, and student.

"For once we could work and live like humans," the addicts said. The interviews repeat again and again their personal and pragmatic assessments. "There is less trouble from the police . . . we don't constantly have to be paranoid . . . there is less pressure . . . there is no need to steal."

How many American addicts today would find "no need to steal" and "could work and live like human beings" if they had a choice?

The British approach to addiction raises many questions, but for an American the most painful may be this: what has the United States accomplished in all these years of viewing narcotic addiction largely as a criminal, instead of a medical, problem?

With all its imperfections and shortcomings, the British effort confirmed for me that America never will make significant headway with the drug problem until it puts in charge the man who ultimately will have to solve it: the doctor, not the policeman.

Skilled and specially licensed physicians should be permitted to prescribe the widest range of medical possibilities. For some this may mean traditional hospital withdrawal; for others a therapeutic community; and for many, a drug-maintenance program, administered and supervised within a medical facility. These doctors should be permitted not only to experiment with different ways of using methadone, but, when other treatment approaches have failed, to experiment with heroin.

The choice is not between the doctor and the police. It is a matter of priorities. Which discipline comes first. Unauthorized narcotics must be illegal and the wholesale purveyors of this disease must be hounded with every resource of police science.

At the same time, to suggest a blanket export order of England's clinics to America is as irrational as the blanket dismissals they have suffered in the past. Different models are desirable. Greater safeguards are both possible and required. Even with them, some mistakes will be made. Some innocent youths may be infected. A few charlatans will have to be exposed. And still some more addicts will die of needless overdoses.

Callous? Maybe. But what about the cabby who needs his "protection," the elderly lady who tonight will be terrorized, and the millions of innocent Americans who want and deserve the right to live in our urban centers without having to fear them as jungles?

How long will it be before our national policy is changed?

How long will a flourishing opiate black market continue—daily infecting others because of the astronomical profits that spur an ever-widening clientele?

How long will American addicts be a banished subculture, morally exiled, often from the very medical help they so desperately need, but always present in the criminal countdown of the larger society which has had to safety-lock itself behind so many doors for the luxury of guarding an unworkable dogma?

What's All This Talk About Heroin Maintenance?

JAMES M. MARKHAM

At 10 P.M. on March 3, Atsushi Kurahara, a 35-year-old Japanese advertising executive, was stabbed in the heart and robbed of $40 on 103rd Street between Broadway and West End Avenue. The murder, which received little notice in New York, caused a stir in Japan. "Dear Mayor Lindsay, I heard that when you visited Tokyo last year you expressed a particular interest in the subject of Japan's public peace and order," wrote Mrs. Kurahara from Japan, asking for an explanation of the senseless killing. "I think now I have a deeper insight into what you might have meant at the time.

"Can you permit this sort of thing to happen in New York," she asked, "the very city associated with progress and civilization in the world? Would you please explain to me what is happening to America's, and New York's, public peace and order?"

In response to Mrs. Kurahara's letter, Mayor Lindsay wrote: "Murder is actually less common in our city than in many other American cities, but this is small comfort. The fact is that America has become one of the most violent free nations on earth."

He then informed Mrs. Kurahara that three heroin addicts had been arrested as suspects in the murder, "and the law is taking its course."

The connection between heroin addiction and street crime has been noted frequently enough. Patrick V. Murphy, New York's Police Commissioner, estimates that at least 25 per cent of the city's crime is committed by addicts. "Informal estimates," reports an American Bar Association study, "attribute 33 to 50 per cent of the holdups, burglaries, muggings and thefts committed in the nation's 34 major urban centers to heroin addicts." Another study reckons that 350,000 American addicts steal $2.4-billion yearly and earn another $457-million from prostitution. In dollar terms it is probably imposible to figure the price of police involvement in the flourishing heroin market; in terms of distrust and apathy in black and Hispanic neighborhoods, the price of even limited corruption has been massive. Unhappily, no one truly knows if any of these estimates—or the wildly varying estimates of

Note: James M. Markham, "What's All This Talk About Heroin Maintenance?" New York Times Magazine, July 2, 1972. © 1972 by The New York Times Company.

the numbers of addicts alleged to be roaming the streets—are accurate. But there is a tendency to *believe* the worst of them.

And so, with many urban Americans terrified they will die Mr. Kurahara's irrational death, responsible men are offering a simple, pragmatic solution, based on a syllogism. It goes like this: Addicts steal, mug, maim and murder because heroin is illegal; if we make heroin available to addicts—that is, maintain them on the drug—then they won't steal, mug, maim or murder. The syllogism's conclusion goes against a longstanding, rather moralistic American tradition of treating opiate addiction as a criminal matter. At the same time, it has the beauty of simplicity—though a simple solution may not be the answer to a complex problem.

The idea of heroin maintenance is behind a complicated, controversial plan that has been put out by the Vera Institute of Justice. Vera stresses that its proposal is for *temporary* heroin maintenance. Instead of freely giving away heroin to addicts, the Vera experiment would use short-term heroin maintenance as a "bait" or "lure" for hard-core addicts who might not otherwise be induced to enter rehabilitative treatment.

The Vera proposal, which in its final form was polished up by two psychiatrists from the Yale University School of Medicine, envisages a four-year experiment that would cost about $1-million. In the first year, operating out of a clinic in a nonresidential quarter of lower Manhattan, researchers would attempt to see if 30 male addicts between 21 and 40 years old who failed on methadone maintenance could be lured to a heroin-maintenance program. They would be required to come to the clinic seven days a week for their heroin injections—four or five time a day—to prevent any diversion of clinic heroin to the black market. After 12 months, participants would be eased into methadone maintenance, or onto a narcotic antagonist such as cyclazocine (which blocks the euphoric effects of heroin but, unlike methadone, is not

addictive and does not satisfy the addict's "drug hunger"), or into a therapeutic, drug-free community.

If the initial 30 participants could in fact be stabilized on heroin—maintained at a nonescalatory dosage—and switched to methadone or some other form of treatment, then a similar two-and-a-half year experiment with 100 methadone failures would be initiated. (If it proved impossible to move a majority of the initial 30 addicts off heroin and onto some alternate treatment, the second experiment would be called off.) For the anticipated second stage of the experiment, a control group of another 100 methadone failures would be reintroduced to methadone to provide a comparison with their heroin-maintained counterparts. Intensive psychiatric and vocational counseling would be integral parts of all three groups of treated addicts.

The man who hopes to launch this experiment, Herbert Jay Sturz, director of the Vera Institute of Justice, is a tall, earnest 41-year-old with a self-effacing, slightly shambling manner who, in the past, has devised a batch of schemes to help those at the bottom of society. The schemes include a messenger service for methadone-maintained addicts, a cleanup squad of former Bowery derelicts, a bail-reform program that has eliminated pretrial jailing for many. The Vera Institute, a gadflyish, activist think-tank in New York, gets a good deal of its funding from the Ford Foundation.

Sturz concedes that methadone and drug-free therapy are preferable to heroin as rehabilitative tools, but he points to the vast population of addicts who remain outside the reach of current efforts. As a current target population for his experiment, he cites the 20 to 50 per cent of addicts who drop out of, or are tossed out of, methadone-maintenance programs.

At present, Sturz concedes the advantages of oral methadone over heroin as a maintenance drug. Both are addictive, but oral methadone lasts 24 to 36 hours while heroin, which must be injected, lasts only four to six hours, requiring repeated injections. A heroin addict soars on a high, then sinks to a low; an addict maintained on oral methadone coasts on a single level and can lead a relatively normal life once he has built up a tolerance to the drug. Sturz, however, foresees a possible role for a hypothetical, long-lasting heroin.

Above all, Sturz insists on the research character of his proposal. "It's entirely possible that we may learn from this program that the idea of heroin maintenance is absolutely absurd in this culture," he says. "We may find that we cannot stabilize people, that they are always supplementing on the outside." Opponents of the proposal—particularly vocal black leaders—charge that the Vera undertaking is simply a "wedge in the door" that would ultimately lead to full-blown heroin-maintenance programs. Sturz denies this. "Our goal," he says, "is not heroin maintenance. Ideally, everyone should be drug-free." Pointing out that the notion of heroin maintenance is becoming increasingly popular—and that some people see it as a magical solution to all the problems—he argues that it is better for Vera to undertake a dispassionate experiment before more ambitious experiments are started by those who have already decided that heroin maintenance is the answer.

The debate over heroin maintenance comes at a moment of great impatience and some disillusionment with current efforts to halt the spread of heroin addiction. Drug-free, therapeutic communities have not been able to rescue a significant number of addicts. Civil commitment to state rehabilitation centers has proved monumentally expensive and unsuccessful. Methadone holds out some hope, but, those who favor heroin maintenance argue, why push Brand B when addicts prefer Brand A?

Politically, that reasoning can be explosive. Last summer, when an initial Vera proposal which was being considered by the Mayor's Narcotics Control Council was leaked to *The New York Times,* black leaders were outraged. They charged that the Establishment's scheme for dealing with heroin addicts—who are overwhelmingly black and Puerto Rican—was to vegetablize them, give them their junk, keep them passive and on the nod. Harlem Congressman Charles Rangel asserted that heroin-maintenance reflected "a colonialist type of thinking in dealing with the natives' problems." Commissioner Graham S. Finney of the city's Addiction Services Agency warned Mayor Lindsay that the Vera suggestion was a political time-bomb. Lindsay, fearful of further erosion of his black constituency, backed off from the idea, urging a "full discussion." Heroin maintenance, it seemed, had been interred.

But it had not. While Sturz continued to push the idea softly, within and without the council, Howard Samuels, chairman of the Off-Track Betting Corporation and father of a drug-problem son, proclaimed the message of heroin maintenance at meetings large and small. "We've already got heroin maintenance on the streets of New York," was Samuels' theme. He urged that the criminal approach to the addict be replaced by a medical one, that every addict be placed under care—whether in methadone, drug-free or heroin-maintenance programs.

Environmental Protection Administrator Jerome Kretchmer, an early advocate of methadone, began talking up heroin maintenance. "I've been talking about—and toying with—the idea of a much wider experiment [than the Vera proposal] to get people's reactions," says Kretchmer. "And you'd be surprised at the reaction it gets. To people, it no longer seems such a distant proposal." Police Commissioner Murphy, when asked, allowed that he was not opposed to a carefully controlled experiment. Assemblyman Antonio Olivieri introduced a bill that would simply establish dispensaries, a rash step which has no chance of being approved in Albany and which has aroused Sturz's opposition.

After the final Vera proposal was unveiled in May at a press conference attended by its two godfathers—Sturz and Samuels—

Lindsay appointed a special committee, heavily populated with blacks and Puerto Ricans, to help the council consider it. While the committee is deliberating, Sturz hopes to engage opponents of the plan in discussion and to explain the short-term aspect of the heroin-maintenance phase of the experiment. If he and others can defuse black opposition to the project, it stands a chance of being aproved by the Mayor—some of whose aides are urging that New York City not fail to be "first" with heroin maintenance. Sturz has shown himself an agile maneuverer. For example, he restricted the program to methadone failures, removing from the initial proposal the idea of "luring" addicts who had never volunteered for any treatment and thus propitiating methadone advocates. "This way we can press for expansion of methadone programs, and we pick up the failures," he says.

Vera does not think it will need new legislation to authorize use of heroin in an experimental program, although it will need the approval of several Federal agencies. Even if the city balks at underwriting the Vera proposal, Sturz says he plans to seek funding for it, probably from the Federal Government.

But the guardian of Federal drug-treatment funds, Dr. Jerome Jaffe, head of the Special Action Office for Drug Abuse Prevention, is definitely skeptical about heroin maintenance. He is also skeptical about—though not formally oposed to—"experiments" in heroin maintenance. His job obliges him, he says, to worry not only about addicted Americans but also about the many more who are not addicted. "We have to be careful so that we don't pull the wrong lever," he says, yanking his right hand, "and out tumble the guts of the country."

Dispensaries, he says, cannot control the spread of heroin if the drug is already available on the street. "As long as you admit people [to maintenance clinics] if they're addicted, the problem grows. People who are curious will buy heroin on the black market because the clinics won't give it to

them. And once they're strung out, they'll come to the clinics." It is unlikely that society would tolerate giving out heroin to minors. "So what do you do with the 17-year-old who's been buying and shooting heroin for three years—tell him, "Keep going for three years, son, and we'll take you into our legitimate program?" "

As for suggestions like the Vera proposal which would administer heroin in the clinic to avoid diversion to the black market, Jaffe notes this means the addict will have to come to the clinic four or five times a day. "Who will accept this kind of regimen? Maybe people who live behind the clinic. Is there going to be a penalty for missing a shot?"

The idea is to keep addicts in a tightly controlled program. Yet the addicts in the Vera experiment would be men who have failed to adhere to the much looser discipline of a methadone-maintenance program, which at the most requires a single daily visit.

Suppose, Jaffe continues, that a five-visit-a-day clinic system were established, that it did begin to cut into the black market, that the price of illegal heroin did in fact begin to drop? Then what would happen? The addict would find it more convenient to go back to the street. What would the clinics then do to retain their addict-patients? Give them heroin to take home and risk diversion to the black market and a further spread of addiction? Pay them to come to the clinics?

Jaffe notes another obstacle to a large-scale heroin-maintenance program: It would be enormously expensive, far more costly than methadone-maintenance since supervision of injections would be required. He estimates that six nurses would be needed for every 30 to 60 addicts—at a time when there is a national shortage of nurses. The topic of injections brings Jaffe back to his own experiences with hundreds of addicts in the respected Illinois Drug Abuse Treatment Program, where he developed the so-called "multimodality" approach to addiction treatment. "There's an ethical question, too. I've seen quite a few addicts. At some point, you see, they run out of veins. Are you going to let them shoot up in the neck or the femoral?"

Although Vera would appear to be breaking virgin ground, heroin maintenance has been tried in the United States, early in this century. But the experience, in New York and elsewhere, was short-lived and contributes little beyond a growing mythology to the current debate.

One of the few living links to the time when some U.S. cities tried such a program is Leroy Street, a dapper little New Yorker who is now 77. In 1910, when Street was 15, he became hooked on heroin after an older, Bohemian figure named John Devon offered him a "blow" of the drug as he sat with friends one night under flickering gas lamps in Greenwich Village. The son of working-class parents, Street soon lost his interest in baseball—he had been the best pitcher on the local sandlot team—and eventually dropped out of high school, where he had developed a tendency to nod off in class.

Although Leroy Street never had to mug anyone to support his habit, he did a lot of petty thievery; ripping fire extinguishers off Mercer automobiles was his specialty. Since restrictions on the sale of narcotic drugs were minimal in those days, Street and his fellow addicts had for some time been able to purchase heroin through venal "scrip" (prescription) doctors in Greenwich Village, who employed bouncers to keep order in their congested waiting rooms, or from a particular pharmacist on Avenue B. For $325. Street could buy 60 grains of heroin, which today would fetch $1,500. But by 1919 the Treasury Department was putting pressure on pharmacists and physicians, and the stuff was getting hard to come by.

The Harrison Narcotic Act, a tax bill passed in 1914 with the modest intention of regulating the domestic drug traffic and bringing it into the open, was gradually interpreted by the Treasury Department as a tool to stamp out dispensation of morphine, heroin and opiate-laden medications.

By selectively interpreting a series of somewhat conflicting Supreme Court decisions, the T-men succeeded in making it uncomfortable—and even dangerous—for physicians to maintain opiate addicts. The crackdown was a reflection of the national mood; amid wartime anti-Kaiser hysteria, countless scare stories told of the Hun's nefarious efforts to addict the nation's young and martial best.

A short-lived experiment with narcotics clinics grew out of the emergency created by the sudden clampdown on doctors. Addicts suddenly had nowhere to go for their drugs. Thus, on April 10, 1919, the New York Health Department opened the city's first narcotics-dispensing clinic, at a pivotal moment in the history of America's treatment of the addict. The clinic, which was at 139 Centre Street and later, 145 Worth Street, was one of 44 opened around the country.

Although he did not join the clinic the first day—he suspected it might be a clever "dragnet"—Leroy Street eventually joined the motley crowd of addicts who queued up for their day's dosage of free heroin, morphine or cocaine. Others who came included a brakeman from the New York Central Railroad, who had obtained 90 days' leave "to take the cure," housewives who had unwittingly become addicted to patent medicines and, according to *The Times,* a "number of young men who declared they had formed the drug habit at dance halls, taking the stimulant in order to have 'more pep,' as they expressed it."

"When it came my turn," Street later wrote, "a doctor asked me how much drug I used, and when I exaggerated as usual and also told him my habit was heroin, he explained that the tapering off—detoxification—would be done with morphine. After the doctor had signed my dosage chart, I took it to a long counter at the rear of the hall where several pharmacists were kept busy compounding the prescriptions. Few of the addicts waited until they were outside to get the drug into them. They could be seen in corners of various anterooms off the main hall cooking up a quick shot. As I was preparing mine, I saw a woman hand her infant to another female addict to hold while she crouched over to sink a needle into her thigh. Then she took back the baby and immediately began to nurse it. I saw this scene repeated several times before I learned that the babies born of addict mothers and fed on their milk speedily acquired a habit too, and would wail endlessly if the mother was long deprived of her drug."

The New York clinic, which was by far the largest in the country, finally reached 5,882 men and 1,582 women. Health Commissioner Royal S. Copeland first opened it as an emergency clinic to keep addicts away from pushers, but he gradually developed the notion of hospitalizing and detoxifying them at Riverside Hospital on North Brother Island. About 1,600 addicts were detoxified, but when the vast majority of them returned to street heroin Copeland became frustrated and began talking of locking up the city's addicts in a drug-free environment. He was unable to find any neighborhood that would accept a horde of "dope fiends"; residents of Pelham Bay in the Bronx and Seaview on Staten Island were outraged when they were mentioned as possible hosts. Finally, on March 6, 1920, with fewer than 100 addicts on his rolls, Copeland closed down his experiment.

Leroy Street stayed in Copeland's clinic for about six months but, like many of his addict friends, he was forced to seek more dope in the streets when the clinic started detoxifying him by gradually lowering his dosage. "The problem was," Street says, "they were trying to round up the addicts and 'cure' them at the same time. They should have waited longer, till the black market dried up. Then start to cure them." But for two months Street was able to hold down a job—as a "sheet writer" in a department store delivery room—thanks to the clinic. Today, 53 years later, he believes that heroin maintenance is the only answer to

America's addiction problem: "Definitely. It's better than the millions they're spending on so-called cures."

Street is now preparing a monograph describing his clinic experience and his own recommendations for action. It is a slightly academic document, for in 1928 he fell in love and kicked the habit. "In my neighborhood," he recalls, "there were 17 kids who fell for the drugs. I'm the only one who's still alive."

In an inquisitorial campaign, the Treasury Department forced the clinics in the U.S. to close by 1922 (although one in Shreveport, La., managed to hold out until early 1923). But the clinics remain an important touchstone in the debate over addiction. Proponents of heroin maintenance argue that a benighted law-and-order attitude snuffed out a promising experiment that, if continued, would have spared us the crisis we face today. Opponents argue that the clinics merely abetted the spread of addiction, a contention that was supported by the American Medical Association's Committee on Narcotic Drugs, in a 1921 report.

The committee stated that any treatment "which permits the addicted person to dose himself with the habit-forming narcotic drugs placed in his hands for self-administration begets deception, extends the abuse of habit-forming narcotic drugs, and causes an increase in crime." The committee therefore urged the closing of such "so-called ambulatory methods of treatment." It added, somewhat ambiguously, that "the only proper and scientific method of treating drug addiction" was the dispensation of drugs under the direct supervision of a physician, so that the patient could neither sell his allotted dosage nor buy any more on the outside. A recommendation in effect, for maintenance in confinement.

While the U.S. experience with narcotics dispensaries was really too brief to be conclusive, the British experience has lasted longer and been better documented. Indeed, the most frequently invoked evidence in the heroin-maintenance debate—invoked by both the prosecution and the defense—emerges from the so-called British system.

There is general agreement on a few facts. From the beginning, for one thing, England has managed to approach addiction as a medical, not a criminal, problem. From 1924 to 1926, a committee headed by Sir Humphrey Rolleston reviewed the British narcotics problem. At a time when the addict in America was becoming an outlaw, the Rolleston Committee recommended that physicians could administer heroin or morphine to the small number of addicts who were undergoing withdrawal or were incapable of functioning without them.

The Rolleston Committee recommendations remained the cornerstone of British drug policy through the end of World War II, when the public first began to note addiction as a growing problem. In 1959, Lady Frankau, a psychiatrist, received a good deal of publicity after she began treating a half-dozen Canadian addicts in Britain by prescribing heroin. Her approach caught on among other doctors. At the same time, the number of cocaine and opiate addicts began to rise. In the 20-to-34 age bracket, the Home Office annual figures for the number of addicts between 1959 and 1968, went up like this: 50, 62, 94, 132, 184, 257, 347, 558, 906, 1,530. Teen-age addiction increased spectacularly: 0, 1, 2, 3, 17, 40, 145, 329, 395, 764.

By American standards, of course, the British figures were—and remain—small. But the sudden, steep rise in addiction, which coincided with the liberal prescribing of opiates, caused concern. A committee headed by Sir Russell Brain reported in 1965 that six or seven irresponsible doctors had abetted the spread of addiction by over-prescribing heroin, either out of naiveté or venality. In 1962, for example, one million tablets of heroin were prescribed; 600,000 of them were prescribed by a single physician. On one day the same doctor prescribed 900 tablets to one addict; three days later he prescribed 600 more tablets to "replace pills lost in accident."

To prevent such abuses, the second Brain Committee recommended that clinics be established, that only clinic doctors be permitted to prescribe heroin or cocaine to addicts, and that a strict system of addict-registration be adopted. By 1968, 17 clinics had been established, and the British "system" was in being. But, as has been frequently noted, the loosely structured "system" allows for some variety in approach by the individual clinics. A few maintain addicts exclusively or heavily on heroin; others have switched many addicts to injectable methadone; a few doctors have experimented with oral methadone. Generally, however, the trend is away from heroin in the clinics. While Americans are talking about heroin maintenance, the British are now moving toward a system of methadone maintenance. The emphasis is currently on injectable methadone, which curbs withdrawal symptoms for roughly half as long as oral methadone and, unlike oral methadone, produces a heroin-like euphoria in a tolerant individual. Its principal advantage over heroin is its longer-lasting effect.

The British, it is true, treat addiction as a medical problem. The British addict has been given his narcotic under medical auspices and, lately, in some clinics has been encouraged to move from heroin, to injectable methadone, to oral methadone, to abstinence.

But abstinence remains a distant goal for the great majority of British addicts. And there has been precious little rehabilitation in the sense of vocational training, group therapy and psychiatric counseling. In those areas, paradoxically, America is ahead of England.

The gradually diminishing number of new addicts reported by the Home Office would indicate that the British have succeeded in containing the spread of heroin addiction. But England is now, like America, plagued with polydrug abuse: heroin is no longer the country's main drug problem. Methadone is the most frequently used drug in English clinics today. And, just as new addicts were addicted to heroin when physicians were giving out heroin, today new addicts tend to be addicted to methadone.

For all the arguments it provides to partisans in the heroin-maintenance debate, the British experience is ultimately as inconclusive as America's brief experiment in the early twenties. Comparing policies in different cultures is a hazardous enterprise. Why, for example, choose the British experience? Why not the Italian? The Italians have a repressive drug policy quite similar to America's, and yet have a minuscule addiction problem, one far smaller than Britain's. Britain, despite cultural similarities with the United States, is a different society, happily lacking, among other things, America's Faustian ethos of instant gratification—of which the American addict is so often a pathetic caricature.

The British have demonstrated, however, that when heroin is made readily available —as it was during the liberal-prescription period of the sixties—addiction spreads at an epidemic rate. As a result of this experience, the British have been moving gradually toward a more restrictive approach. Last year, the Conservative Government passed the Misuse of Drugs Act, which further restricts the rights of physicians to prescribe certain dangerous drugs, hoists the penalty for trafficking to a maximum af 14 years and permits an unlimited fine.

Part of the syllogism at the outset of this article suggested that addicts steal and mug because heroin is illegal—give the heroin to them and they wouldn't act that way. How well does this stand up under scrutiny?

Enough impartial research has been done on the character of American addicts to show that many, possibly a majority, were criminals well before they became addicts, that addiction is simply a continuation of their antisocial life-styles. James Vorenberg, director of the Harvard Law School Center for Criminal Justice, found in a study of methadone-maintained addicts that those who became addicted while very young were rarely charged with aggressive crimes, while those who became addicted at the age of 23 or older were arrested for such crimes five times more frequently. Among the early-addicted group, speculates Vorenberg, "we find the classic drug-dependency crime syndrome. But addicts who started out later are often criminal deviants who have come to accept drug use."

Lawrence Kolb, a psychiatrist who pioneered the study of the American addict, found that "a criminal addict was, in the vast majority of cases, a criminal before he became addicted." Kolb asserts: "If there was not one addict in the United States, all categories of crime, except violation of narcotic laws, would be just about what they are now except in the area of stealing and possibly prostitution, where there would be small, immeasurable decreases." To the extent that we have a criminal-addict population, the premise of the syllogism—that addicts steal because heroin is illegal—is weakened. Support the addiction of a criminal-addict and he may steal less often, but he will continue to steal.

In England, Lady Frankau who helped popularize the eventually disastrous liberal-prescription policy, conceded in 1964 that she had been unable to help her criminal-addicts. We might well find the same thing in the U.S.

One of the hardest-dying myths is that the dope pusher is the person most responsible for spreading addiction among the young. "He gives the kids free samples," sang Tom Lehrer, misleadingly, "for he knows full well—that today's young innocent faces will be tomorrow's clientele." By now we do know that the biggest culprit is not the pusher, who plays a back-up role, but the youthful, enthusiastic addict who thinks he's onto a good thing and wants to share it with his friends. This applies to many different drug addictions, but when it comes to heroin, initiation in the use of the needle is an important ritual that requires one addict to teach another. As long as there are young, enthusiastic, contagious addicts constantly enlarging the addict population, heroin maintenance is no weapon against the spread of addiction—since society is presumably unwilling to supply teen-agers with an addictive drug. And as long as the vast teen-age market exists, the black market for heroin will exist.

In a now-classic study, R. De Alarcón considered the spread of heroin use in Crawley New Town, 35 miles from London. From 1962 to 1965, De Alarcón found, a small number of youths from Crawley experimented with heroin while living in other towns. By 1966, a nucleus of heroin addicts had gathered in Crawley and began converting others to the drug. Then, suddenly, heroin use expanded "explosively," as proselytizers created a total of 58 addicts in less than a year.

Nils Bejerot, a Swedish psychiatrist, notes that it was no coincidence that the Crawley phenomenon occurred when British physicians were still permitted to prescribe heroin and rates of addiction were rising in several suburban centers. In his own country, Bejerot has plotted the explosion of amphetamine-mainlining, from a tiny group of Stockholm poets and Bohemians in 1949 to a runaway epidemic claiming 12,000 addicts today. After studying a variety of epidemic addictions—alcoholism among the ancient Israelites and the 7th-century Arabs, ether-sniffing among the 19th-century Irish, opium-smoking in China, amphetamine-mainlining in post-war Japan and, of course, America's heroin epidemic—Bejerot has found they have certain common characteristics. Drug epidemics, he finds, are spread by "personal initiation from established addicts"; they begin within certain defined class or ethnic boundaries, and then spread outward into the larger society. The debut age is low, there are usually three to six male addicts for every female addict and, most alarmingly, epidemics spread "by geometric progression if other conditions remain unchanged."

In a conclusion confirmed by other researchers, Bejerot says the one factor that correlates most highly with the epidemic spread of addiction is availability of the drug in question. Heroin may be fairly available today; make it more available and there will be more junkies—many more junkies. "You could easily get up to three or four million addicts in five years," said Bejerot when asked what might happen if the United States adopted the British system. He points to Sweden as a case in point.

Between 1949 and 1965 the Swedish Government pursued a relatively restrictive policy and the number of amphetamine addicts doubled roughly every 30 months. Then, after a press campaign by "a noisy group of drug liberals," as Bejerot calls them, Sweden began to experiment with prescription of amphetamines and opiates. At the height of this experiment, the number of addicts doubled in 12 months. In 1967 the Government returned to its old policy, and the rate of increase declined. "Heroin maintenance?" Bejerot asked incredulously on a recent visit to New York. "Only those who don't know anything about addiction can discuss it."

Surveying the partisans of heroin maintenance, one cannot help noting that there are very few specialists in the field of addiction among them. Many lawyers, yes; law enforcement officials, yes; politicians, yes, especially in a city eager to be "first" in everything and overblessed with putative mayoral candidates. But, experts in addiction, no. Such an *ad hominem* assessment is likely to infuriate many. Aren't the "experts" just grinding axes, defending their own lack of success?

To be sure, heroin maintenance is anathema to those with an emotional investment in drug-free therapy; its supporters are also threatening to outflank the methadone establishment. And, it is true, specialists in drug-abuse treatment are rarely in agreement with each other. Thus, Judianne Densen-Gerber, the psychiatrist-attorney who heads Odyssey House, a drug-free program: "Heroin maintenance is at least an honest admission that you can't do anything. Heroin is giving up. Methadone is a lie." But the point is not that addiction is a mysterious subject that only yields up its secrets to the initiate; rather, that it is a very complicated subject, in which a little learning can be a very dangerous thing.

To argue against the Vera proposal is to put one in the awkward position of seeming to oppose the very idea of research, which is all the Vera undertaking purports to be. But, just as the early methadone experiments were in some ways a stunning success, so, too, the Vera experiment *might*— considering the intensive personal attention that will be lavished on the addict-patients— succeed. A majority of the addicts might be successfully stabilized on clinic heroin and, through a sensitive process of negotiation, moved onto another form of treatment. With the announcement of these successes, politicians, questing for a quick solution, would press for adoption of the Vera model on a broad scale. But which aspects of the model? Heroin-maintenance? Transference to another treatment?

The discussion would begin to move out of the control of dispassionate researchers. Then, just as methadone programs have sprawled across the land, many of them becoming dispensaries which shuck the misnamed "ancillary" services so critical to the initial methadone successes, so, too, the initial Vera model might be expanded—with similar results. It is conceivable that in time the idea of short-term maintenance would be abandoned as "unrealistic"; it might become "pragmatic" for short-handed programs to avoid moving addicts too quickly onto methadone or some other form of treatment; the supportive services would gradually become diluted; as with methadone, certain addicts would soon be found "trustworthy" and given their heroin to take home, no longer required to come to the clinic five times a day. Addiction, mysteriously, would continue to rise—at an even faster rate. Black and Puerto Rican leaders would cry "genocide," but no one would listen. Crime would not abate. Suburban communities that had never known the

kind of addiction Harlem knows would be struck. For some, the word "epidemic" would acquire a fresh, terrible meaning.

The Vera proposal, so far, is only a proposal. But already, in some parts of New York, the word is out on the streets—the Man is going to give out smack, for free! Street workers and drug-program administrators report that the limited publicity given to the Vera proposal alone has persuaded some young addicts to hold back from treatment, to bide their time and await the incredible millennium.

What is to be done? The question is rightly asked of those who throw stones at others' suggestions. The first thing is to put America's heroin epidemic in some perspective. The comparison has become somewhat time-worn, but heroin addiction is as intractable a malady as heart disease or cancer. Yet, after years of research into those diseases, no one is demanding an instant cure. By comparison, research into heroin addiction is in its infancy. A little patience is called for. There is no magic solution.

Methadone has many drawbacks. Far too many programs permit their patients to retail methadone on the street, creating a black market for the drug that is responsible for a rising number of overdose deaths among nontolerant individuals. Sloppily run programs risk the spawning of a new variety of addict—the methadone addict who has never tried heroin. Moreover, too few programs—in fact, hardly any at all—are moving their patients toward abstinence.

For the moment, however, methadone programs should be carefully expanded until it can be shown they have reached a saturation point and are no longer attracting new addicts. Already there are 65,000 methadone-maintained addicts in the country. This is a large figure, particularly if the true number of heroin addicts is lower than the huge "statistics" sometimes cited.

Methadone, then, is an interim measure. Some people in the drug field place great hopes in opiate antagonists, which block the euphoric effects of heroin but, unlike methadone, are not addictive. Promising research is being done, but even if the ideal antagonist is developed—one that is long-lasting and has no side-effects—the problem remains of persuading an addict or addiction-prone youth to take it. Studies of methadone-maintained addicts indicate that the drug's success stems not from its reputed blocking effect—its antagonist properties—but from its satisfaction of "drug hunger."

Antagonists, which do not satisfy an addict's craving, may therefore prove to be of little help to the addicted. As prophylactics, they might conceivably help the addiction-prone—the joy-popper of Bedford-Stuyvesant—but to get people to take them would present logistical and civil liberties dilemmas of major proportions. And drug abusers, if denied one drug, will typically turn to another. Deny them opiates and they turn to barbiturates, for which no antagonist exists.

Gradually, despite the vicious infighting that goes on among partisans of different truths, a consensus is emerging in favor of a multimodality approach. Ideally, in this kind of a system, every known treatment would be made available—methadone, antagonists, group-therapy oriented drug-free programs, psychiatrically oriented drug-free programs, religious programs, even civil-commitment programs. To make this catholic approach more than a bargain basement, moreover, sound initial diagnosis is required to fit the addict—be he schizophrenic, criminal-deviant, hustle-weary, peer-group pressured—to the most appropriate program.

With more money than is now around, it would be possible to mount an ambitious quarantine-treatment program that would attempt to register every addict in the country, to know what he is up to. A combination of therapeutic and law enforcement pressures could squeeze the addict, confronting him with the choice of going straight or going to jail. Studies have shown —one thinks particularly of the important work of George E. Vaillant at Harvard—that addicts placed on strict probation after lengthy imprisonment have a rather good chance of reaching permanent abstinence. The chances are enhanced by employment, and thus more jobs must be opened up if rehabilitation is to have any meaning.

An addict who stays drug-free for a year has about a 50-50 chance of making it, Vaillant found in a 20-year study of 100 addicts; after three years of abstinence the addict is almost home free. A no-nonsense, three-year parole system for addicts convicted of crimes (that is, most addicts) —not the ineffectual, cost-hampered one of the New York State Narcotic Addiction Control Commission—might well reap encouraging results. Such a program would require expanded, professional drug-free programs, and a system for keeping in close touch with the recently "rehabilitated" ex-prisoner, helping him to find work and—most important—reminding him that a relapse into drug-taking and antisocial behavior would mean renewed confinement.

This, too, is not *the* answer to the problem. There is no single answer.

Analysis of Values
and
Conflicts of Interest

John Ingersoll's article reflects the concern of many Americans who consider drug abuse a costly, widespread, and pernicious problem. Ingersoll believes that the drug problem is growing rapidly worse, in part, because people are unwilling to support measures severe enough to control it. He asserts that proposals to legalize marijuana and to make heroin available to addicts through doctor's prescriptions reflect this lenient mentality. He believes that if such proposals were realized they would have disastrous consequences.

Ingersoll's argument is not only representative of all those people who believe that stiffer controls are needed to limit drug abuse, it also reflects the more narrow interests of police and control agencies who are constantly seeking better means with which to deal with the drug problem. For their programs to be effective they need the support and cooperation of the general public. In fact, the very existence of these agencies depends on the public being sensitized to the extent and danger of drug abuse. Maintenance or expansion of their resources is directly related to their ability to convince the public of the severity of this problem. Ingersoll, former director of the Bureau of Narcotics and Dangerous Drugs, represents an interest group that was created specifically to deal with drug abuse. Obviously his ideas about the drug problem are influenced by his role in this group.

Joel Fort's perspective reflects interests antithetical to Ingersoll's. Fort believes that laws prohibiting marijuana use and the agencies that enforce these laws are more dangerous than the use of the drug itself. He suggests that prohibition of marijuana and the draconian laws that enforce its restriction are the result of the enterprise of agencies such as the Bureau of Narcotics and Dangerous Drugs, which by disseminating inaccurate information were instrumental in generating and maintaining an erroneous public conception of the "marijuana problem." Consequently, Fort does not consider marijuana use a social problem; rather he believes that the real social problem results from the measures devised to control its use.

Fort's ideas concur with many reform oriented groups who believe that police and other agencies of the state should not intervene in private behaviors that do not victimize other persons. Finally, Fort's position supports the interests of marijuana users and, especially, those users who have formed pressure groups attempting to bring about decriminalization of the drug.

Both Edgar May and James Markham are concerned with finding a solution to the problem of heroin addiction. May believes that laws preventing the addict from getting legal and inexpensive heroin are responsible for much of the criminal behavior, physical degeneration, and human degradation associated with heroin addiction. May, like Fort, believes existing regulative laws contribute to the drug problem. However, May still considers heroin use a social problem that should be eliminated. He believes that allowing the addict to obtain heroin inexpensively and legally from doctors would eventually cut addiction rates. May advocates maintenance of very stiff penalties against the illegal use and sale of heroin. This would keep risks high both for the nonaddict wanting to try heroin and for the dealer wanting to sell it. The illicit market would be reduced because addicts would get their heroin cheaply and legally. As a consequence, heroin would be less available to nonaddicts so there would be few new addicts to replace those who die or are rehabilitated. May's position is representative of groups desiring reform of drug laws and addicts. However, even some urban police groups feel that this reform is in their interests because it is fashioned to reduce drug-related crimes.

Markham disagrees with May about the practicality of legalizing heroin for addicts. However, he advocates other therapeutic programs rather than stiffer penal measures. Markham probably does not reflect values and interests that are appreciatively different from May, although addicts would probably favor May's position over Markham's. It is possible that the disagreement between May and Markham rests more on empirical factors than on values and interests. In researching a social problem, it is possible for people with similar values and interests to come up with conflicting findings that lead them to advocate different measures to deal with the problem. However, relatively few of the major debates over social problems derive from such conflicts.

3

CRIME:

"Hard Line" or "Soft Line"?

Although many people have been victimized by criminals, many more suffer from the effects of crime without ever being affected directly. Millions of dollars are lost every year by individuals, businesses, and institutions as a result of criminal activity. A great deal of tax money is expended in law enforcement, the apprehension of criminals, the administration of justice, and the maintenance of the correctional system. There is also the less tangible, but still very evident effect of the crime threat on our everyday life. Many Americans, afraid of being victimized, avoid certain neighborhoods, stay off the streets of their own neighborhoods at night, or carry out their daily activities in a state of fear.

The nation probably has never been as conscious of the problem of crime as it is today. This has been generated not only by the objective threat of crime, but also by a news media that focuses upon "crime in the streets," and by politicians who promise to get the criminal off the street. It is ironic that the Nixon administration having made extensive use of this issue in the early 1970s found itself embroiled in the "Watergate scandal." While asserting the necessity of imposing "law and order," these politicians engaged in what appears to have been the most widespread political crimes of any administration in American political history. Thus, the public's consciousness of white-collar crime has also been expanded. The articles in this section present opposing views on the issue of crime.

Inbau and Carrington argue that serious crime has been increasing at an alarming rate. They point out that in the 1960s the population increased 13 percent, while serious crime increased 148 percent. They argue that this increase in crime is, at least in part, due to the growing number of safeguards for the accused and overall permissiveness towards criminals. Their solution involves a "hard line" approach to crime aimed at getting criminals off the streets and behind bars. Inbau and Carrington believe that people who

refer to such a tactic as "racist" or "anti-poor" are insensitive to the fact
that it is the minorities and the poor who are most often the victims of crime.
Relatedly, they assert that a "hard line" approach to crime should not
replace, but should be carried out in concert with, attempts to uncover the
breeding factors of crime.

Inbau and Carrington believe that we have to *apprehend more
criminals*. To do so, more police must be hired. Furthermore, the police
must be given massive citizen support. This means mobilizing public
sentiment against civilian review boards and court decisions that inhibit the
police in their action against the suspected criminal. Inbau and
Carrington argue that we must *convict more criminals*. They argue that the
legal tide favoring the accused must be turned so that conviction of the
guilty is not hampered by unreasonable barriers. Trials must focus less on
police propriety and more on the guilt or innocence of the criminal. Inbau
and Carrington also assert that we must *incarcerate more criminals*. They
imply that judges must impose tougher sentences on known criminals and
should be accountable for overly permissive decisions that turn criminals
loose in the community.

In the second article Hans Zeisel takes to task the "hard line" approach
explicated by Inbau and Carrington. He does *not* believe that the answer to
the rising crime rate is increased law enforcement. He argues that we
presently apprehend only 15 percent to 20 percent of the people that commit
serious criminal acts. Even if we doubled the size of our police forces, which
in Zeisel's view is costly and impractical, the percentage of crimes cleared by
arrest would not increase significantly. Zeisel disagrees with those who insist
that increased deterrents or stiffer sentencing will reduce the crime rate. He
points out that we have already more severe penalties for most crimes than
the European countries, yet our crime rate is still much higher. In any case,
Zeisel asks why, if deterrents were really effective, most of those who have
been released from prison eventually end up back in prison for the commission
of other crimes? Zeisel suggests that it is naive to believe that criminals base
their criminal acts upon a rational calculus where they evaluate the benefits
of the act, the chances of being apprehended, and the severity of the penalty
for being caught. He concludes that more police and stiffer sentences will
not reduce the crime rates.

Zeisel asserts that the job of crime reduction should not be left to the
law enforcers. He suggests alternatives for attacking the crime problem:
prison reform geared at rehabilitation and reduction of recidivism,
elimination of sanctions for victimless crime (e.g. gambling and prostitution)
that diverts massive numbers of police away from more important work,
consideration of the legalization of heroin for addicts so they would not have
to resort to secondary crime to pay for their habit, the imposition of strict
gun control laws to keep handguns out of the hands of potential criminals,
and the promotion of equality of opportunity so that the poor and minorities
would have reduced motivation for street crimes.

In his article, David Gordon argues that crime is ubiquitous among
all classes of people in this country. However, most emphasis in law
enforcement is put upon crimes of the poor and the young. On the other
hand, white collar crime (e.g., tax evasion, price fixing, embezzlement,

swindling, and consumer fraud) , which often carries more harmful social costs, is considered less offensive and is treated more permissively. Gordon asserts that we have a dual system of justice that sends the poor to prison and the affluent to psychiatrists.

Gordon asserts that most crime in the United States reflects a rational response to the competitiveness, insecurity, and inequality promoted by capitalist institutions. He maintains that in our society the state protects the interests of the rich and powerful. Thus, it is not surprising that crimes of the corporate class go unpunished while the crimes of the working class are dealt with severely. He argues that reform is impossible because most crime stems from the very nature of our present form of social organization. He says that the present selective enforcement of the law supports the dominant ideology that it is individuals rather than institutions that are to blame for the present state of things. Also, crime keeps a large number of people out of the already glutted labor market.

Many people argue that the deplorable conditions of our prisons provide a breeding ground for crime. In the final article of this section, Ramsey Clark presents this position. He asserts that 95 percent of the money alloted for corrections goes to custody (bars, walls, and guards) , while only 5 percent goes to health, services, education, and employment training. Violence pervades prison life and erodes the inmates sense of dignity. Beatings, murders, suicides, and homosexual rape are common occurrences. Prison work is trivial; medical and dental care are abominable; living conditions are degrading; and educational opportunity is limited. Clark argues that 80 percent of all felonies are carried out by recidivists, many of whom are embittered by their prison experience. He argues that in recent years as police budgets swelled, prison budgets were cut. This is self-defeating since these prisons, oriented exclusively toward punishment, promote rather than eliminate crime. Clark asserts the need to alter prison goals in the direction of rehabilitation rather than retribution. This would require a significant monetary investment and would necessitate a broad restructuring of the present penal system. However, Clark believes that this is a needed investment that would pay off in reduced crime rates.

The Case for the So-Called "Hard Line" Approach to Crime

FRED E. INBAU AND
FRANK G. CARRINGTON

Abstract: Crime is caused by criminals. This is the main thesis of this article, admittedly a "hard line" idea, but one which must be recognized if we are to do anything constructive about the problem of lawlessness and violence which besets this nation. The intolerable picture of crime in this country is described, particularly the extent to which the poor and the racial minorities pay for crime. The basic reason for crime in this country is simply that there are too many criminals on the street. The reasons that this condition exists are threefold: failure to apprehend criminals, failure to convict criminals, and failure to incarcerate criminals. These three "failures" are discussed and specific responses to each—based on a massive outpouring of citizen concern for and action against our crime problem— are described. The authors believe that only with such active involvement by the members of the law-abiding majority can the problem be solved.

The problem propounded by the topic of how to mount an effective crackdown on crime can be brought into perspective by considering two phenomena of the decade 1960 through 1969. They are: (a) during that ten year period, safeguards for the criminal accused and permissiveness toward lawless, violent acts reached heights in the United States such as no other nation has ever witnessed; and (b) in the same span of time, while our population increased by 13 percent, *serious crimes increased by 148 percent.*[1] The two are not coincidental. In any society, the incidence of lawlessness is directly related to the number of criminally inclined individuals who are at liberty to prey upon others, and it is precisely the permissiveness shown toward criminals in this country which has resulted in their being

Note: Fred E. Inbau and Frank G. Carrington, "The Case for the So-Called 'Hard Line' Approach to Crime," *The Annals of the American Academy,* Sept. 1971, pp. 19–27. Reprinted with permission of The American Academy of Political and Social Science.

[1] Based on the Uniform Crime Reports of the Federal Bureau of Investigation for the year 1969. Serious crimes are, for FBI reporting purposes, murder, rape, robbery, aggravated assault, larceny over $50, and auto theft.

free to practice their depredations to an unprecedented extent.

Crime is caused by criminals; the fact is as simple as that. When a strong-arm robber slugs his victim in order to relieve him of his watch and wallet, he has committed a crime. No amount of elaboration on the question of whether or not the assailant came from an environment of poverty or a broken home makes the robbery itself any less a crime. Likewise, when a youthful demonstrator, intolerant of this country's pace in solving its social problems, throws a rock that strikes a policeman on the head, an aggravated assault has been committed. Apologists for criminal behavior may wring their hands as much as they like about the robber "striking out at a society which has brutalized him" or the demonstrator "merely expressing his idealistic young concern"; the fact remains that both are criminals.

THE HARD-LINE POSITION

The answer, then, to the question of how to mount an effective crackdown on crime lies basically in first recognizing that crime is committed by criminals, and second, in getting as many criminals as possible out of circulation so that they are no longer free to victimize the law-abiding.

This position is called the "hard line" on crime. It is not fashionable among certain liberal social scientists, who have been characterized by Attorney General Mitchell as being able to ". . . explain the motivations of the criminal, but who can do little to protect the innocent against the mugger or armed robber." [2] To these individuals, the "hard-liner" is "simplistic," or "lacking in compassion." We suggest that neither of these appellations is valid, and that, instead, he may be better described as one who takes

[2] From a speech before the International Association of Chiefs of Police at Miami Beach, Florida, September 29, 1969.

a realistic position with regard to the crime problem.

It is quite true that there is nothing particularly compassionate toward a law violator in advocating that he be locked up; yet it would seem that the worthy object of compassion would be the victim rather than the assailant, the oppressed rather than the oppressor. If a 75-year-old woman on a ghetto street is knocked to the pavement because she has the temerity to struggle with a husky 18-year-old purse-snatcher—the result being a broken hip which, at her age, may never mend—the most elementary concepts of fairness would seem to dictate that the victimized woman is more deserving of our sympathy than her attacker.

When liberality dictates that the lawless remain free to victimize others, it is clearly misplaced. This, in short, is the hard-line position that we believe to be both realistic and valid; it favors consideration for the victims of crime and for public safety above that for the offender himself.

Let us consider, then, the hard-line approach to the problem of crime in light of our stated aim of suggesting how to mount an effective crackdown on the criminal. First, we shall sketch the dimensions of the crime picture in this country with special emphasis on the truly intolerable extent to which crime victimizes the poor. Next, we will glance briefly at public opinion about crime —the line the law-abiding majority of our citizens want taken. We then turn to the specifics—why we are not safe from the criminal and, more importantly, what can be done about it.

Before proceeding to this analysis, however, one point must be made. Just because we favor a hard-line approach, it does not mean that we are insensitive either to the factors in our society which breed criminals or to the tremendous importance of the rehabilitation of those who have been convicted and are amenable to rehabilitation. The breeding factors of crime—environmental, hereditary, educational, social, and economic—are, of course, elements which go into the making of a criminal. Anyone who is seriously concerned with the over-all problem, be he a hard-liner or not, must recognize the importance of these breeding factors, and he must also subscribe to the view that once a person has committed a crime every feasible effort should be made to rehabilitate him. But there is nothing incompatible between an acceptance of those two positions and a recognition of the need to make our society reasonably free from criminal harm—especially between now and the time when we are able to make effective progress toward those two general objectives. Moreover, we must not lose sight of the fact that even if we should achieve a society free of poverty, and even if we should develop effective rehabilitation facilities and procedures, we will still have a serious crime problem unless we recognize the need for effective criminal sanctions.

Unless the Almighty changes the nature of man himself, we will always have some criminals among us. Reflect, if you will, upon the criminal offenders you know, or know about, who never experienced poverty, and also the fact that there was far more poverty years ago, and yet there was far less crime. Too, it would be sheer fantasy to believe that all persons who commit crime will be responsive to even the best rehabilitation efforts.

THE CRIME PICTURE

The right to be safe from criminal harm—particularly among the poor and the racial minorities—has become an illusion. They are the ones who are most often the victims of crimes of violence—murder, rape, robbery, and aggravated assault. These crimes have increased 130 percent during the past decade, and the upward trend continues undiminished.

Professor Herbert L. Packer of Stanford University reported in 1970 that street crime victimizes ghetto dwellers at least 100 times more than it afflicts the affluent citizens who live in the suburbs.[3] A recent story, "Black Crime Preys on Black Victims," released by the Associated Press, described the problem:

> Between 70 and 80 percent of major big city crime is harbored in Negro or predominantly Negro precincts. Little is visited upon whites. On police maps, the colored pins flock gregariously in ghetto neighborhoods detailing the rapes and robberies.[4]

The undeniable fact is that the poor pay for crime in a most usurious way.

It is highly fashionable nowadays for white liberals who live in fairly safe neighborhoods or in the suburbs to decry as "racist" those who call for law and order, since so many crimes are in fact committed by blacks. We submit that this attitude, which embodies the idea that perhaps crime should or must thrive in the ghetto, is the vilest kind of racism imaginable. Winston Moore, the tough black Director of Corrections at Chicago's Cook County Jail, has responded to this false racist accusation in these words:

> The bleeding liberals who have so much guilt that they can justify blacks killing blacks because we're immature [are] the ones who want to keep you immature. Quit justifying why I kill my buddies on Saturday night and try to stop me from doing it.[5]

The extent to which the threat of crime permeates the ghetto can be illustrated by a report issued by a committee of the New York chapter of the NAACP in 1968. It struck out at ". . . the reign of criminal terror in Harlem."[6] While vowing to "continue

[3] Noted in *Crime Control Digest*, March 25, 1970, p. 7.
[4] See "Black Crime Preys on Black Victims," *Denver Post*, August 23, 1970.
[5] See *Newsweek*, "Justice on Trial," March 8, 1971, p. 27.
[6] Reported in the Criminal Law Reporter, December 25, 1968, p. 2269.

to fight police brutality through litigation, exposure, and public interest," the committee called for a hard-line approach to the problem. It called for "the use of whatever force is necessary to stop a crime or to apprehend a criminal." It also recommended a minimum penalty of five years in prison for strong-arm robbery, without the possibility of probation or parole even for first offenders, and a 10-year minimum for the sale of narcotics.

More dramatic than statistics on crime is the manner in which the lives of all of us, particularly the poor and members of minority groups, have had to be adjusted because of the ever-present threat of violent crime. In most of our cities, the law-abiding citizens have had to surrender possession of the streets after dark to the robber and those who may even bludgeon someone out of sheer delight. Many persons are literally afraid to leave the sanctuary of their homes for fear that they will fall victim to some form of violent attack; and for those who must be out on the streets, protective measures, unheard of ten years ago, are being used. Taxicab drivers, for example, no longer favor their passengers with opinions because the customer cannot hear the driver through the two-inch thickness of bulletproof glass which separates the front and rear seats of most taxicabs today. Bus riders must prepare themselves with the exact amount of their fares because, nowadays, bus drivers do not carry change in order to discourage robberies. In short, we have been forced to accommodate our lives to the spectre of criminal terror.

Although the human misery and the physical and mental suffering inflicted upon the victims of crime are the most hideous aspects of the picture, the devastating economic impact of crime, upon victim and non-victim alike, must also be considered. The total annual price tag for all forms of lawlessness in the country has been estimated to exceed 51 billion dollars.[7] It takes very

little imagination to conceive of what could be done with that kind of money toward alleviating some of the social ills that beset this country.

This, then, is our crime picture, viewed from several angles. It is a grim one. Lawlessness is rampant in this country and it is growing at an unchecked rate; it is a constant source of fear, anxiety, inconvenience, and discomfort. Simply put, the right to be safe has, for many, ceased to exist.

CRIME AND PUBLIC OPINION

If one single statement concerning the over-all crime picture in this country can be said to be sweepingly accurate, it is that public outrage against lawlessness has reached an all-time high. The public is demanding a hard line on crime. This can be illustrated by recent polls.

In February of 1969, a Gallup survey reported that 75 percent of those queried felt that the courts did not deal harshly enough with criminals, while only 2 percent felt the courts dealt too harshly.[8] Significantly—as evidence that the make-up of the law-abiding majority crosses color lines—this poll specifically stated that on the question of the treatment of criminals by the courts, the views of whites and Negroes differed very little. More recently, another Gallup survey published in a special article on crime in a national magazine made this finding:

> The survey shows that most Americans now want a tougher system of justice—and they are willing to grant the police broad new power to get it. Fully three-quarters of the sample feel that the system's most serious failure is that criminals receive insufficient punishment, and 62 percent find this far more disturbing than the prospect that constitutional rights may be inadequately protected.[9]

[7] U.S. News and World Report, October 26, 1970, p. 30.

[8] See "Public Wants Hard Line to Win War on Crime," Denver Post, February 16, 1969.
[9] Newsweek, "Justice on Trial," March 18, 1971, p. 39.

This is the voice of the majority—the law-abiding majority—a group which now demands a hard line on crime and which is clearly willing to turn away from the contrived rights of the criminal in order to vindicate the overriding right of every citizen: the right to be safe.

WHY WE ARE NOT SAFE

Why is our crime picture as horrendous as it is, despite overwhelming public opinion against lawlessness? The answer lies in the fact that in many—far too many—cases, the law enforcement processes in this country have broken down, with the result that more and more criminals are free to prey upon the law-abiding. This breakdown is three-fold, and stems from:

1. Failure to apprehend criminals.
2. Failure to convict criminals.
3. Failure to incarcerate criminals.

When we analyze each of these failures, it becomes apparent why we are not safe and why a hard line is needed.

Failure to Apprehend

The deficiency of failure to apprehend in our criminal justice system is related to the law-enforcement function, but this in no wise means that it is the fault of our police departments. By and large, the caliber of law enforcement, man for man, has never been higher than it is today; yet, more and more often the police find themselves at a tremendous disadvantage in their efforts to apprehend criminals. One reason for this is the shortage of policemen, particularly in the core cities where they are needed most.

Few major cities have enough men to do the job, and recruitment is difficult. With crime rising to unprecedented heights, the police line has never been stretched thinner.[10] In addition, and all too often, the already meager police strength in certain cities is being diverted away from the proper police function—the apprehension of criminals—to peace-keeping duties at demonstrations, sit-ins, and sundry other "protest" activities. It is axiomatic that a police officer "baby-sitting" at a rally of one sort or another is unavailable to watch for the burglar and the robber and perhaps thus, by the very visibility of his presence, deter the commission of crime.

Another reason for underpolicing in some areas of large cities is the understandable reluctance of police officers to subject themselves to the risk of assassination while on patrol. As this article was being written, four police officers in New York City were shot, two of them dying as a result, simply because they were policemen, although in the minds of the assassins they were, of course, "fascist pigs."

All police officers accept the risk of being killed in the prevention of serious crime and in the course of apprehending criminals, but it is asking too much of them to incur the increasing risk of an assassin's bullet.

Police are also becoming more reluctant to make arrests at the scene of a crime or disturbance out of fear that they will perhaps attract a crowd and touch off a riot, or for fear that an arrest of certain individuals or groups of individuals will result in allegations of "police brutality" or other false charges.

Court-imposed restrictions of an unrealistic nature—which in our opinion were not constitutionally or practically required—serve to further inhibit the conscientious police officer; for instance, the Miranda rule[11] requiring a litany of advice about

[10] See the President's Commission on Law Enforcement and Administration of Justice, Task Force Report: The Police (1967), "Availability of Manpower," p. 9.

[11] *Miranda v. Arizona*, 384 U.S. 436 (1966).

legal rights before the interrogation of an apprehended suspect can be conducted.

Failure to Convict

Even if a criminal is arrested, the likelihood is great that he will not be convicted. According to Senator John L. McClellan of Arkansas, in recent years verdicts of not guilty in robbery cases have increased 23 percent, and in burglary cases 53 percent.[12] The hedge of procedural safeguards which the Warren Court erected around the person accused of a criminal offense and the efforts of the judiciary to "police the police" have created such a maze of technical requirements for police conduct that, in case after case, obviously guilty persons must be freed because an officer neglected to act with the propriety demanded by the Court. Senator McClellan has characterized this situation as one in which the Court's rulings have threatened "to alter the nature of the criminal trial from a test of the defendant's guilt or innocence to an inquiry into the propriety of the policeman's conduct."[13]

At the core of the barrier which has been erected between the factual guilt of a person and the legal proof of guilt is the so-called "exclusionary rule." This rule, which was made a part of the jurisprudence of this nation by a Supreme Court in 1961,[14] holds that no evidence, regardless of how relevant or probative it may be, can be used against a defendant if it was improperly obtained. For instance, if a dope pusher has been found in possession of narcotics but the search of his person, automobile, or room which revealed the narcotics is held to have been illegal *for any reason,* the narcotics cannot be used as evidence against him. Thus, the upshot of the exclusionary rule is that the *question of actual guilt or innocence is completely disregarded;* if the policeman has blundered in the slightest, the guilty party must be released—returned to society, free to continue his career of crime. The same is true of a defendant whose confession is rejected because the police-interrogator failed to tell him that he had a right to remain silent, that whatever he says can be held against him, that he is entitled to have a lawyer present, and that if he could not afford a lawyer one would be provided free. Compounding the handicap is the fact that once a lawyer comes on the scene the standard advice is to tell the client to keep his mouth shut.

If all police work consisted of willful or wanton disregard for the legal rights of criminal suspects, the exclusionary rule might have some validity; but even then, the way to keep the police in line is by direct action against them, and not through the route of setting the criminal free in order to teach the police a lesson. The exclusionary rule works to return the criminal to the street, with an absolute and total disregard for the rights of those whom the newly released criminal may decide to victimize next.

Some measure of the damage which the Warren Court has done to elementary concepts of the public's right to be free from criminal harm may be found in that Court's phenomenal record of reversals of criminal convictions. Between 1960 and 1969 the Court reversed 63 out of 112 federal criminal convictions and 113 out of 144 state criminal convictions.[15] In many instances the reversals resulted not only in the convicted violators themselves being freed, but also, in case after case, the Court laid down such technical "ground rules" circumscribing police behavior that countless criminal suspects in trial court cases had to be freed as well. There are better ways of controlling police performance than by this costly process.

Failure to Incarcerate

On one recent day in Chicago—identified in a local newspaper editorial as a red-letter

---

[12] 115 Congressional Record 59565 (daily ed., August 11, 1969).
[13] Ibid.
[14] *Mapp v. Ohio,* 367 U.S. 643.

[15] Ibid., fn. 14.

day for convicted criminals—the following events occurred:

A sixteen-year-old killer of another teenager was found guilty of murder. He was placed on probation for five years because it was his "first offense."

A seventeen-year-old pleaded guilty to setting fire to a police car, striking a policeman, throwing rocks and bottles at policemen, and grabbing a policeman's gun while resisting arrest. He, too, received probation. This was his "first offense."

Three Black Panthers pleaded guilty to buying machine guns and hand grenades for the party's arsenal. Each one was given three years' probation, even though two of them had been fugitives and one had been convicted of assault and battery growing out of the shooting of a policeman.

These cases are illustrative of one of the reasons why the streets are no longer safe.

Contrary to the general belief that, since crime and population have both increased considerably within the past ten years, our state and federal penitentiaries must be bulging with inmates, the number of prison inmates is just about the same, if not slightly less than it was in 1960. Twenty-nine states have experienced a decrease in prison inmate population as of March, 1971. Consider the situation in three of our largest states. In New York, the prison population in 1960 was 17,207; last March it was 14,554 —*down* 2,653. In Pennsylvania there were 7,802 prison inmates in 1960; in March, 1971, there were 6,422—*down* 1,380. In Illinois, 9,064 in 1960; 7,206 in March, 1971— a *decrease* of 1,858.[16]

The federal inmate population decreased by 3,699 during the period 1960–1967, the latest year for which officially released figures are available.[17]

[16] Bureau of Prisons, National Prisoner Statistics Bulletin No. 44, July, 1969 (the latest available), and updated figures procured from prison officials by the authors.
[17] Ibid.

Thus we see one of the most logical reasons for rampant crime: even after they have been convicted, criminals are returned to the streets because some judges simply will not incarcerate them, no matter how vicious or depraved their crime.

WHAT CAN BE DONE?

The answer to what can be done lies, in our opinion, in a massive outpouring of active citizen concern and involvement. The attitude of the law-abiding majority (and again we stress the fact that this majority crosses all lines of color and class) is definitely hard-line, but it must be translated into action. When that is done, the crime picture in the United States will improve.

1. *In the area of failure to apprehend criminals,* there must be massive citizen support for the policeman when he is doing his job properly. This will create a climate under which police recruiting will be enhanced and officers will not hesitate to do their job for fear of civil suits by vocal pressure groups such as the American Civil Liberties Union and other "police watcher" organizations. A strong public sentiment against civilian review boards, and demonstrable public outrage against attacks on the police— as opposed to grumbling in country club locker rooms and at cocktail parties— would do more toward overcoming the problems of shortages of policemen and "underpolicing" than any other single thing.

2. *In the area of failure to convict criminals,* public outcry and pressure are necessary to curtail drastically those contrived "rights" of criminal suspects which serve only to protect the guilty without any compensating benefits. This can be done without diminishing the basic rights of all citizens. For instance, the Fourth Amendment's guarantee of freedom from

unreasonable search and seizure must be preserved, but it can be done without the use of an exclusionary rule that turns so many guilty persons loose; moreover, it is ineffectual, anyway, as a police disciplinary measure.

The exclusionary rule should be removed from our criminal justice system and replaced by procedures for dealing directly with the officer who willfully violates a person's constitutional rights. Great Britain has never had the automatic exclusionary rule as we know it, and that country has never been turned into a police state.

3. *In the area of failure to incarcerate,* there are those who believe that the sentencing process is nobody's business but the judge's. This is not true. It is the function of a judge to sentence a convicted criminal; but the sentence itself—the determination of whether, or how soon, a potentially dangerous felon will be released into the community—is clearly the business of the community whose safety is involved. Just as the President, a governor, or a state or national legislator is accountable to the people in the final analysis, so is a judge, whether elected directly or appointed by elected officials. In this area, citizen concern can be translated into action, as has been done already in several jurisdictions, by citizens'

groups who follow a judge's sentencing record and then report, pro or con, to their fellow citizens.

CONCLUSION

Our suggested solutions to the crime problem are admittedly "hard line," but we believe that such an approach must be taken. If crime is to be significantly diminished, the concern of the law-abiding citizen will have to be translated into constructive action. Lawlessness threatens to engulf this country, and a firm stand is necessary to stem the tide. Nonpartisan educational groups can be formed to inaugurate and follow through on projects that will harness citizen support for proper, non-abusive law enforcement. Particularly in the appellate courts it has been found effective to file "friend of the court" (*amicus curiae*) briefs in support of the law enforcement side of the question in important criminal law cases.[18] With citizen action such as this on the scene against crime, the future is encouraging.

18 See, for example, *amicus curiae* briefs filed by Americans for Effective Law Enforcement in support of the law enforcement position in such cases as *Terry v. Ohio,* 392 U.S. 1 (1968) and *United States v. Roosevelt Hudson Harris,* ——U.S.——, No. 30 October 1970 Term & U.S. Supreme Court, decided June 28, 1971.

Crime and Law-and-Order

HANS ZEISEL

There is some doubt about whether our rate of serious crime is on the increase or not. But there can be no doubt that our crime rate is very high and has been so for a long time.

I speak, of course, of the crime that we are all primarily concerned with: robbery, mugging, burglary, rape, assault, homicide—the crime that makes our cities dangerous and us afraid of walking the streets. I am not talking about the occasional violent crimes for political motives, not because they do not form a grave problem, but rather because they form a different problem—one that I believe can be more easily cured than the problem of hard crime.

Many of us know from personal experience that our crime rate is high, but just in case you have been lucky enough not to have such firsthand evidence, let me tell you a little story, and then give you a couple of illuminating figures.

Some years ago, my wife had to travel to a remote corner of India to do some design work in a ceramic factory, and, in some concern, I inquired of an Indian colleague of

Note: Hans Zeisel, "Crime and Law-and-Order," *The American Scholar,* Vol. 40, No. 4, Autumn 1971, pp. 624–633. Reprinted from the American Scholar, copyright © 1971 by the United Chapters of Phi Beta Kappa. By permission of the publishers.

mine, a distinguished statistician, at the University of Chicago, how dangerous it was for a woman to live alone in that faraway spot. He thought for a minute, and then said: "Being a statistician, I should say that it is about one-tenth as dangerous as walking at noon in one of our big cities here."

I discovered the following statistics when I recently did some consulting work for my old friends in Austria. The capital, Vienna, is a city of two million inhabitants; its 1968 number of willful homicides was forty-two. Chicago is a city of about twice that size; its 1970 number of willful homicides was eight hundred and ten. These are the kinds of figures that illustrate the magnitude of the difference between crime in the United States and in other Western countries.

As to the cure, tradition has it, and many a politician tells us, that we must look to the police, the courts, the jails—in short, to what we call our system of criminal justice. It is, we are told, their job to protect us, and if they can't, we are easily persuaded that the fault lies with our system of law enforcement and criminal justice, and that what is needed is simply more *law and order*.

Yet such belief is essentially misdirected. What we are being told is that the Supreme Court has been leaning backward in dealing with our criminals; that it cares more for the rights of these criminals than for those of their victims, and thereby hampers our police; that our courts are not strict enough, or too slow; that there are too many legal loopholes for the criminals; in short, that crime would very quickly subside if we were to allow *law and order* to reign with more authority. All that is needed to reduce the crime rate, some politicians keep telling us, is to make this crime business sufficiently unattractive. Catch more of these crooks, administer to them swift and strict justice, and all will be well. The criminals will learn quickly, the hard way, that crime does not pay.

I wish it were that simple, but I am afraid things are much more complicated.

Let us first talk about the catching. It is fairly easy to catch people who commit aggravated assault or even those who commit homicide. Why is this relatively easy? Because these crimes, as a rule, do not occur between strangers but between people who are fairly close, sometimes very close: lovers, married couples, triangles, acquaintances—all relationships that are easy to trace. But the burglars and robbers and muggers, and rapists—the real ones, not the friendly rapists, as some lawyers call them—are very difficult to catch. Only fifteen to twenty percent of such reported crime ends in arrest. To be sure, the percentage of arrested criminals is a bit larger (although not by much), because a man often performs more than one crime. But that low arrest rate is not the fault of our police. Nowhere do they catch substantially more. It is a fact of life in our big anonymous cities that you cannot catch many more, unless you increase the police force to quite unrealistic numbers. If we were to double our police force, I suppose we could get this figure up to perhaps twenty-five percent. But would that be good enough? And our already overloaded courts would do an even poorer job.

Next comes the reproach that our courts are dilatory. And, indeed, some of them are. On the average it takes six to eight months before a serious criminal case is disposed of,

and perhaps it should be less. But anybody who thinks that reducing that interval would substantially reduce our exorbitant crime rate is misinformed. Even if our courts could be brought up to date, this would have only minor impact. A careful study made by the National Bureau of Standards proved this beyond any doubt, somewhat to the chagrin of the sponsor of that study, our Department of Justice.

Third, we hear that our courts are too lenient. Some people complain that sentences just are not stiff enough; if they were, there would be less crime. To give you a feeling about where we stand on this point, let me quote a European criminologist, who visited here recently. On the subject of our sentences, he observed, "What for us in Europe is a month, is for you here a year." So you see, our sentences are already very high, and Europe, with its lower sentences, has nevertheless a lower crime rate. Still, some people will not be much impressed, and will even say that we should hang more people than we do. Yet even if we were to turn the clock back, more hangings would not help. As late as 1800, England had one hundred and eighty-three capital crimes and the crime rate was high. And then, when it was about to reduce the list of capital crimes, fearful warnings were heard of an impending flood of new crime. Yet nothing whatsoever happened, except that fewer persons were hanged.

The truth is that, roughly speaking, our criminal justice system probably works not much worse than that of any Western country, and yet we are easily led to believe that the cure must come from an improved system of law enforcement and criminal justice.

It is a deeply imbedded notion that to deal with crime is the job of criminal justice. As long as there is not much crime, nobody thinks much about the forces that keep it in check. But when the crime rate is as high as ours, then it becomes obvious that criminal justice is just not sufficient to cope with the crime problem. Beyond a certain minimum point it has little effect. To be sure, we need a criminal justice system, and it ought to function as well as possible. But to believe that by improving it we could significantly affect our exorbitant crime rate is just naïve. First of all, criminal justice, quite obviously, does not deter sufficiently. If it did, we would have less crime. Most of us at one time nourished the idea that if we caught a criminal and punished him sufficiently, we would not only set a deterrent example for others, but especially also for him. Well, prison sentences do not even do the job for *him*. Our statistics on this point are, unfortunately, rather deficient. Nevertheless, we know that a fair portion of first prisoners do not come back. But too many do return, and as a result some seventy percent of our present inmates have been there before, most of them not much longer than three years before. And if our system does not deter the people it has already put into prison, why should it deter the ones who have not been there yet?

Now, why is it that deterrence does not operate? First, too many crimes are committed out of hate and love, or what seem to be hate and love if one is drunk, and such states of the mind are not easily deterred. Then, legitimate society itself operates often too close to the borderline beyond which we call things criminal. Third, there is a great amount of secondary crime by drug addicts, who cannot be deterred from burglarizing or robbing because drug addiction creates much too strong a motive. Fourth, criminals are on the whole not very intelligent; they are emotionally unstable, and to expect them to engage in a rational calculus as to risks and rewards is not realistic. Even businessmen often deviate from the postulates of economic man, and criminals are much more unreasonable. Last but not least, criminals are a conservative lot; once they have become habitual criminals they stick to their calling. But in this respect, too, there is ample precedent among normal people. In the twenties, for instance, the British coal industry lived through a major depression; but, in spite of years of suffering, the miners did not move. They stayed where they were, although they could have moved elsewhere in Great Britain, or emigrated to Australia or Canada, and even to the United States. Yet they did not go; they wanted to stay miners. So if normal people are so stubborn and unreasonable in their disregard of risks and rewards, how can one hope that criminals will be more reasonable?

But, one may ask, do not our reformatories do some good? To judge by the speed with which the inmates return, the emphasis is, at best, on the word *some*. On the whole, reformatories do not do much reforming.

Thus, if whatever we have of *law and order* in our system fails so abominably, why should more of the same succeed? But, you will object, there must be *some* improvement in the crime rate that we could bring about by improving our law enforcement system. Indeed we could, but it will be useful to see the possible impact of such reforms in proper perspective; the law can do here relatively little.

A somewhat related example will help us to see this. Consider the problem of reducing highway fatalities. If you have the law-and-order mentality you will say that it is a simple enough problem. All we need is more cops and stiffer sentences, and that will do it. Well, it will not. And the people who have actually reduced highway fatalities went about it in a very different way. To be sure, somewhere down the ladder, they also studied their law enforcement system, but it was not their first concern. First, they straightened their roads and built overpasses, thereby removing some dangerous curves and crossings. Then they improved their ambulance service; and only in the third place did they do something about the law. Similarly, the crime problem has many dimensions of which the law is only one and, perhaps, not even the most important.

Paradoxically, the first move to consider, therefore, might be that of taking the job of crime reduction away from the law-enforcement agencies. There is another good reason for such a move. Criminal justice has a narrow scope: its job is to catch the criminal, and to give him his just desert. The question that concerns the system is whether the people they catch *are* criminals; *why* they became criminals is beyond its scope. Indeed, that is probably as it should be; anything more complicated would make the system unmanageable.

Yet unless we ask and answer the *why*, we are powerless. But are we not told, primarily by the men of *law and order,* that to understand all is to condone all? Nothing is more false: even if we understand the most terrible of crimes, it need not diminish our horror and our disapproval. What is true is that looking at crime only at its point of impact, without caring to understand how it came about, will not get us far.

Whom should we put in charge of crime reduction? Not a lawyer, and not a professional do-gooder. I would suggest that the post be given to a member of that distinguished subspecies of the Homo Americanus, to one of those thoughtful, ingenious, aggressive businessmen who have proved that they can solve problems, however difficult and tricky, in the marketplace.

Where will our man begin? I suppose he will begin by trying to find out where crime comes from, where it breeds; he will want to find out why ex-convicts return so quickly to those horror chambers from which they have so recently been released. He will, therefore, take a closer look at our two major breeding grounds of mass crime: the primary one, our urban ghettos, and the secondary one, our prisons. And since our man might rightly conclude that it will be easier and less costly to begin with our prisons, he will first turn his attention to them.

In some never fulfilled hope, we call our prisons penitentiaries or reformatories. Nice names, but what our prisons do to many of their inmates is something quite different. However bad a man is when he enters prison, he will leave it a worse man. Breeding grounds of idleness, of hatred of society, of sexual perversion, prisons weld their inmates ever firmer to the community of criminals. Why is that so?

One would think that if there is anything to give a prisoner, it is work and opportunity to learn: to raise him to a level that will enable him to make an honest living once he comes out. What we do is, as a rule, the opposite. There are exceptions, to be sure, but their number grows slowly. Under pressure from us, the "honest" people, in this case primarily from the labor unions, few prisoners are trained for jobs, or even allowed to engage in meaningful work; as a rule, the work amounts to little more than sewing prison garb or mail bags, or stamping license plates or quarrying stones. And even this is sometimes too much. The State of Illinois, for instance, has, or had until recently, a law forbidding the use in public buildings of stones quarried by convicts. To be sure, I sympathize with the workers, now suffering from an ever-rising unemployment rate, who ask, if so many honest men cannot get jobs, why should they tolerate competition from the prisons. I have sympathy with this view, yet the hard fact remains that unless we make serious work-training for qualified jobs part of the prison discipline, we will not even have taken a first step.

If you ever visit one of our prisons, you will see that work is but one of its many unsolved problems. To be sure, there are some hopeful signs. Some prisons try to improve, and we are now attempting to remedy a small part of the damage our prisons inflict, by creating so-called halfway houses, temporary homes for men released from prison and so obviously unfit to join the non-criminal world.

In this broader context, is there not something the law can contribute to make things better? To be sure there is. One useful action would be to distinguish between real crimes and what one might call artificial crimes because they have no victim. We might begin with our gambling laws. What a hypocrisy they represent. Betting is legal on the tracks, but illegal off the tracks; in Pennsylvania, to place a bet is legal, but to accept one is a crime, so that the jurors who sit on the jury may have placed a bet with the bookie they have to try; gambling is legal in Nevada, and illegal everywhere else, and so it goes. And thus our gambling laws at best divert our law enforcement people from coping with more serious crimes, and at worst present a source of corruption for them. They also produce, incidentally, the black market on which the syndicate crime flourishes, about which our politicians howl after having artificially created the market in the first place.

And the situation is similar with respect to drugs. To be sure, this is a more complicated problem, but remember that the amount of secondary crime by drug addicts —and I mean real hard drug addicts, not the youngsters who smoke some weed—is one of the major contributions to our crime rate. In England, if you are a registered drug addict, you go every morning to the clinic, get your shot and go to your job; it costs you a few pennies and you need not rob somebody to pay the pusher. So far, we have preferred to deal with this problem differently, and we all know with what success.

One more example of how changing the law might help. In preparing the President's Report on Firearms and Violence, on which I had the honor of working under Milton Eisenhower, we discovered a few interesting facts. Do you know how many hand guns we have in this country? Twenty-four million pistols and revolvers, forty for every hundred families, eight times as many as in *any* other Western industrialized country. Their owners will tell you that they bought the guns for self-protection, yet the evidence shows that, for all practical purposes, possession of a hand gun does not protect from anything; rather, it is a menace to the owner and his family. Mr. Eisenhower told the present Administration and Congress: Do at least what New York City and Massachusetts did; enact a restrictive gun licensing law—not for long guns, not for hunting guns, which are not as often tools of crime —but for hand guns. Over ninety percent of all gun robberies are committed with hand guns. The city of New York, however bad it may be in other respects, has relatively fewer criminal gun attacks than other major cities: it has a strict gun law, under which a man who wants a gun permit must prove that he *needs* a gun. One may infer from this how much more gun crime could be averted if other communities could have such laws, and hence make gun bootlegging more difficult. In most other states, the law works the other way around: only if you are a criminal or a drug addict, or the like, are you officially prevented from buying a gun.

Has the present Administration heeded Mr. Eisenhower's counsel and asked for a gun law? If you ever walk by the majestic building of the National Rifle Association in Washington, D.C., you will understand better why there is so little enthusiasm for such a law, although this law would clearly reduce our rate of homicide. Indeed, in these days we hear more about laws against pornography. I think twenty-four million guns are a greater danger.

As you can see, I have left the primary and basic problem of crime reduction— what to do about our ghettos—until last, partly, of course, because the job amounts to nothing less than correcting some of the basic shortcomings of our society. In the ghettos women have not yet been liberated, and only a few of them commit crimes— mostly such minor ones as petty theft—but a young man, growing up without a family, or in a broken home, and without a job for some time (about fifteen percent of the ghetto youngsters are jobless), faces odds of something like one in two of becoming a felon.

There is something frightfully concrete and perturbing in the knowledge that if you were born into such ghetto conditions—over which you had neither power nor say—your chances of becoming a felon are *twenty times as high* as those of someone who was born into a nice suburban family. Ironically, the very concentration of crime in and radiating from our ghettos is one of the reasons we are so blind as to the right road to crime prevention. It makes it too easy to divide people neatly into two groups: *they* who are the criminals, and *we,* the decent people.

Some dent is made in this simplistic thinking when crime comes closer to home, as it sometimes does these days, when the crime rate is so high that the middle and upper classes—*our* classes—are infiltrated. When an offense occurs in our own world, it helps us to understand that the world of crime is not totally separated from ours, that in an indirect way we all are responsible for everybody, and that only by a common effort can we heal the wounds. The notion of the good guys in the white hats *versus* the bad guys in black hats is good enough for television; for the real world, it will not do.

What we must attempt is to enlarge our notion of justice. In the narrower sense, justice is what our police, courts and jails mete out to those who have broken the law and been caught. In the larger sense, justice must begin earlier; it means not more, but also not less, than equal opportunity for all, the notion that ranks so high in our patriotic vocabulary, but not quite so high among our deeds. In a truly just society, equal opportunity must begin at birth. This seems not as short a route to crime reduction as the *law and order* path so many politicians recommend, but it is the only one that can bring us there.

To be sure, even with equal opportunity some men will fail where others will succeed. But some hope comes from interesting recent studies with identical twins and adopted children. Studies have shown that far more important than the genetic inheritance, race or I.Q. are the surroundings in which a child grows up. This is a consoling message, because it allows us to hope that if we broaden our idea of justice, we may indeed succeed in reducing crime.

To move toward this larger justice will require not only much money but also a change of minds, and of hearts. But if you think how much aggravation and terror and unhappiness all these evil-doers cause to themselves and their families (not to speak of their victims), to our pride as a nation, and thereby to our esteem in the world, you may think it worth some sacrifices.

These thoughts are a far cry from the shouting for more *law and order.* But they are neither very odd nor very new. As a matter of fact, in about thirty years the foundation from which they stem will be exactly two thousand years old.

Capitalism, Class, and Crime in America

DAVID M. GORDON

Conventional public analyses of crime, both conservative and liberal, begin with the assumption that crimes are committed by irrational individuals who constitute a threat to a rational social order. Sharing that initial assumption, conservatives and liberals diverge in their policy approaches to deterring criminality. Some recent orthodox economic analyses of crime, having begun to relax the assumption, view crime as a process of rational choice by criminals; they offer the possibility of "optimal" crime prevention policies through the application of conventional economic models.

A radical economic analysis of crime, which this paper tries to formulate, suggests that the present character of crime in America flows almost inevitably from the structure of our social and economic institutions. Many kinds of crime represent perfectly rational responses to the conditions of competition and inequality fostered in capitalism; examples of this rationality are white-collar crime, organized crime, and ghetto crime. Many of the most important differences among crimes flow from the duality of our systems of justice and law enforcement, and that duality in turn reflects the biases of the State in capitalist societies. It seems unlikely that we shall be able to solve the problem of crime in this country without first effecting a radical redistribution of power in our basic institutions.

Like a brush fire, crime in the United States has seemed recently to be raging out of control. The public, the government, and the experts have all raced to cool the blaze. In one way or another, we have all been drawn into the fight. With slogans and occasional compassion, with weapons, courts, prisons, and patrols, especially with perplexity and confusion, we have probably served in the end to frustrate our own good intentions, to fan the flames rather than douse them. We seem to have as much trouble understanding the problem of crime as we do effecting its solution.

Meanwhile, amidst the confusion, orthodox economists have been striding elegantly to our rescue. Cool, fearless, the perfect picture of professionalism, they have been promising to guide us toward "optimal" crime prevention and control. Off with our silliness! Off with our psychological muddleheadedness! Gary Becker, a sort of guru

Note: David M. Gordon, "Capitalism, Class, and Crime in America," *Crime and Delinquency,* April 1973, pp. 163–185. Reprinted with permission of the National Council on Crime and Delinquency.

among them, explains how easily we can understand it all:

> A useful theory of criminal behavior can dispense with special theories of anomie, psychological inadequacies, or inheritance of special traits and simply extend the economist's usual analysis of choice." [1]

As I have read and thought recently about the problem of crime in the United States, I've found myself returning over and over to the same conclusions—that the public's understanding of the problem is mistaken, that the government's policy responses are misguided, and that the recent orthodox economic analyses have been misleading. This paper attempts to amplify those impressions. I have not tried to present a detailed brief against the conventional wisdom and the orthodox economic view. Instead, I intend to articulate my differences with those positions by formulating an alternative, radical analysis of criminal behavior and by evoking an alternative normative view of an appropriate social response to crime.

The paper has five sections. The first offers a brief descriptive summary of the nature and extent of crime in the United States. The second surveys some conventional public perspectives on the problem of crime, while the third outlines recent orthodox economic approaches to the problem. In the fourth section, I sketch the framework of a radical economic analysis of crime in the United States. In the final section, I amplify an alternative normative view of the appropriate social response to criminal behavior. [2]

[1] Gary Becker, "Crime and Punishment: An Economic Approach," *Journal of Political Economy*, March-April 1968, p. 170.

[2] I am not an expert on crime and I have not pursued extensive research about the problem. The thoughts in this paper draw mainly on some limited elementary reading; as a layman in the field, I offer these thoughts with considerable hesitation, which has especially affected my style of argument. Since I do not speak with authority, I have tried wherever possible to include quotes from respected and respectable "authorities" to support my arguments.

CRIME IN AMERICA

To compare analytic approaches to the problem of crime, one must first clarify its empirical dimensions. Several useful summaries of the nature and extent of American crime are easily available, especially in the summary report by the President's Crime Commission and in Ramsey Clark's recent book. [3] Relying primarily on the basic facts documented in those sources, I have tried in the following paragraphs to outline the most important questions about the problem of crime which any analysis must try to resolve.

It seems important to emphasize, first of all, that crime is ubiquitous in the United States. Our laws are so pervasive that one must virtually retire to hermitage in order to avoid committing a crime. According to a national survey conducted in 1965 by the President's Crime Commission, 91 per cent of all adult Americans "admitted that they had committed acts for which they might have received jail or prison sentences." [4] The Crime Commission also found that in 1965 "more than two million Americans were received in prisons or juvenile training schools, or placed on probation"—well over 2 per cent of the labor force. Criminal be-

[3] President's Commission on Law Enforcement and Administration of Justice, *The Challenge of Crime in a Free Society* (Washington, D.C.: U.S. Government Printing Office, 1967) ; Ramsey Clark, *Crime in America* (New York: Simon and Schuster, 1970). For some useful summaries of the basic data, see the first two reading selections in the chapter on crime in David M. Gordon, ed., *Problems in Political Economy: An Urban Perspective* (Lexington, Mass.: D. C. Heath, 1971). Another useful summary of information about "urban crime" can be found in Marvin E. Wolfgang, "Urban Crime," in James Q. Wilson, ed., *The Metropolitan Enigma* (Cambridge, Mass.: Harvard University Press, 1968). For much more detailed information, see the appendices to President's Commission, *op. cit. supra, Corrections* (1967), *The Courts* (1967), and *Crime and Its Impact—An Assessment* (1967). For some interesting comments on the Crime Commission Report, see James Q. Wilson, "Crime in the Streets," *The Public Interest*, No. 5, Fall 1966.

[4] President's Commission, *Challenge of Crime, op. cit. supra* note 3, p. v.

havior, it appears, is clearly a norm and not an aberration.[5]

Given that ubiquity, it seems equally important to emphasize our extraordinary selectivity in our attention to the problem of crime. We focus all our nearly paranoid fears about "law 'n' order" and "safe streets" on a limited number of crimes while we altogether ignore many other kinds of crime, equally serious and of much greater economic importance.

One can sketch the dimensions of this selectivity quite easily. The crimes on which the public *does* concentrate its fears and cannons are often lumped together as "urban" or "violent" crimes. These crimes can be usefully summarized by those for which the FBI accumulates a general statistical index. Seven "Index Crimes" are traced in the Bureau's periodic Crime Report: willful homicide, forcible rape, aggravated assault, robbery, burglary, larceny (of more than $50), and motor vehicle theft. Together, these seven crimes encompass the raging fire in fear of which we hide inside our homes.

Some basic facts about these seven fearsome crimes are well known. The measured incidence of the Index Crimes has been increasing rapidly in the United States in the past ten to fifteen years.[6] The Index Crimes occur twice as frequently in large cities as they do on an average throughout the country. Within large cities, they occur most frequently in ghetto areas. The threat and tragedy of violent crime notwithstanding, almost all of these crimes are economically motivated; as Clark notes quite simply, "their main purpose is to obtain money or property." [7] Seven-eighths of them are crimes against property; only one-eighth are crimes against the person, and many of the relatively few "violent" crimes actually occur inadvertently in the process of committing crimes against property.

A large part of the crime against property is committed by youth. Clark concludes from the scattered statistics that half of all property crime is committed by persons under twenty-one.[8] Certainly more important in considering the evolution of public attitudes, blacks commit disproportionate numbers of these seven Index Crimes (and are also disproportionately the victims of the same crimes) . Although arrest rates bear an obviously spurious relationship to the actual incidence of crime, some of the figures seem quite astonishing.[9] In 1968, for instance, official statistics indicate that 61 per cent of those arrested for robbery were black and nearly half of those arrested for aggravated assault were black, despite the fact that blacks constitute only 12 per cent of the population. As astonishing as those figures sometimes seem, however, the public exaggerates them further; public attitudes often apear to presume that *all* of the Index Crimes are committed by blacks and that every black male is on the verge of committing a crime.

The crimes to which the public and the media choose to pay almost no attention seem just as obvious. Many kinds of relatively hidden profitable crimes, most of

---

[5] One should add, of course, that these figures refer only to those harmful acts which actually violate some law. Many other tangibly harmful acts, like faulty manufacture of automobiles or certain kinds of pollution, have not yet been declared illegal.

[6] Clark also notes, *op. cit. supra* note 3, that the increase may be misleading, simply because many kinds of crime are much more likely to be reported these days than were comparable crimes, say, thirty years ago.

[7] *Id.,* p. 38.

[8] *Id.,* p. 54. Violent crimes, on the other hand, are more frequently committed by adults. As Clark explains it (p. 55), "It takes longer to harden the young to violence."

[9] The reason that the arrest rates may be spurious is that, as Clark (*op. cit. supra* note 3) and Ronald Goldfarb ("Prison: The National Poorhouse," *The New Republic,* November 1969) have especially noted, blacks are much more likely than whites to be arrested whether they have committed a crime or not. Despite that immeasurable bias in the arrest statistics, it is nonetheless assumed that blacks commit a larger percentage of most crimes than their share of urban populations.

them called "white-collar" crimes, occur with startling frequency. Tax evasion, price fixing, embezzlement, swindling, and consumer fraud capture billions of dollars every year.

> Illicit gains from white-collar crime far exceed those of all other crime combined. . . . One corporate price-fixing conspiracy criminally converted more money each year it continued than all of the hundreds of thousands of burglaries, larcenies, or thefts in the entire nation during those same years. Reported bank embezzlements cost ten times more than bank robberies each year.[10]

The selectivity of public opinion is matched, moreover, by the biases of our governmental system for the enforcement and administration of justice, which prosecutes and punishes some crimes and criminals heavily while leaving others alone. Some defenders of the system occasionally argue that it concentrates most heavily on those crimes of the greatest magnitude and importance, but the data do not support this view: the Index Crimes on which the system focuses account for small proportions of the total personal harm and property loss resulting from crime in the United States. For example, deaths resulting from "willful homicide" are one-fifth as frequent as deaths from motor vehicle accidents; although many experts ascribe nearly half of motor vehicle accidents to mechanical failure, the system rarely pays attention to those liable for that failure. The economic loss attributable to Index Crimes against property—robbery, burglary, and so on—are one-fifth the losses attributable to embezzlement, fraud, and unreported commercial theft, and yet the system concentrates almost exclusively on the former.

One can much more reasonably argue, as many have in other contexts, that the selectivity of our police, courts, and prisons corresponds most closely to the relative *class status* of those who perpetrate different

crimes. We seem to have a dual system of justice in this country, as both the Crime Commission and Goldfarb have most clearly shown.[11] The public system concentrates on crimes committed by the poor, while crimes committed by the more affluent are left to private auspices. Our prisons function, as Goldfarb notes, like a "national poorhouse," swallowing the poor, chewing them up, and occasionally spitting them back at the larger society. When the more affluent get in trouble, in contrast, private psychiatric and counseling assistance supplant prosecution: "In the classes of offenses committed by rich and poor *equally*, it is rarely the rich who end up behind bars."[12]

Finally, none of the system's selectivity works as intended. The public seems to think that concentration on a few crimes will at least improve the effectiveness of the system in controlling those few crimes—leading to greater prevention and deterrence and perhaps to greater rehabilitation. Buoyed by that hope, the various governments in the United States spent roughly $4.2-billion on police, prisons, and the courts in 1965, while private individuals and corporations spent an additional $1.9-billion on prevention and insurance. And yet, despite those billions, our systems of enforcement and administration of justice appear considerably to exacerbate the criminality they seek selectively to control. The prisons in particular, as Clark notes, are veritable "factories of crime": "Jails and prisons in the United States today are more often than not manufacturers of crime. Of those who come to jail undecided, capable either of criminal conduct or of lives free of crime, most are turned to crime."[13] More generally, very few of those who get started in

---

[10] Clark, *op. cit. supra* note 3, p. 38.

[11] President's Commission, *op. cit. supra* note 3, and Goldfarb, *supra* note 9.
[12] Goldfarb, *supra* note 9, p. 312 (emphasis in the original). It is one thing to cite this "duality" as fact, of course, and quite another thing to explain it. I cite it now as a phenomenon requiring explanation and shall try to explain it later.
[13] Clark, *op. cit. supra* note 3, p. 313.

crime ever actually leave it as a result of the system's deterrent or rehabilitative effects. According to Clark's statistical summaries, roughly half of those released from prison eventually return, and fully 80 per cent of serious crime is committed by "repeaters"— by those who have been convicted of crime before.[14]

These very brief descriptive observations clearly suggest the questions an economic analysis must seek to answer about the problem of crime: *Why* is there so much crime? Why do the public and government concentrate so selectively on such a small part of the criminal activity in this country? And why do all our billions of dollars fail so miserably in curbing even that small part of the total problem?

CONVENTIONAL PUBLIC ANALYSES

Conventional public analyses of crime divide roughly into two views—"conservative" and "liberal"—the specific features of which correspond to more general "conservative" and "liberal" perspectives on social problems. The two perspectives begin from some relatively common general views of society and its governments, diverging more and more widely as they debate the specifics of crime prevention and control.[15]

The conservative perspective on crime has an appealing simplicity.[16] Since conservatives believe that the social "order" is ultimately rational and is adequately reflected in the laws of our governments, they also believe

that those who violate it can be regarded as irrational citizens and social misfits. As such, criminals should be punished regardless of the social forces that may well have produced their criminality; they represent a threat to the safety and property of those who act with civility and reason, and they should be isolated until society can be sure of their good behavior. The more violent the crimes, the more seriously we must regard their consequences.

Since criminals (and especially violent ones) act irrationally, we can deter and prevent their actions only by responding to them with comparably irrational actions— principally by the threat or application of raw force. Toward that end, conservatives engage in two kinds of policy calculations. First, they discuss the potential deterrence of a variety of crime-prevention techniques: if only enough deterrent force could be mustered, they assume, crime could be stopped; typically, they urge more police and more equipment to prevent crime. Second, they tend to favor preventive detention as a necesary means of protecting the social order from the threat of probable criminality; they make their argument, normally, on relatively pragmatic grounds.[17]

Liberals tend to agree with conservatives,

[14] *Id.*, p. 55.

[15] For an easy reference to the differences between the general "liberal" and "conservative" views, see "General Perspectives—Radical, Liberal, Conservative" in Gordon, *op. cit. supra* note 3, Ch. 1. For a good example of traditional discussion of the problem, see Edwin H. Sutherland, *Principles of Criminology*, 6th ed. (Philadelphia: Lippincott, 1960).

[16] For the clearest exposition of the conservative view on crime, see the chapter on crime in Edward C. Banfield, *The Unheavenly City* (Boston: Little, Brown, 1970).

[17] Banfield (*id.*, p. 184) has clearly formulated the conservative equation: "In any event, if abridging the freedom of persons who have not committed crimes is incompatible with the principles of free society, so, also, is the presence in such society of persons who, if their freedom is not abridged, would use it to inflict serious injuries on others. There is, therefore, a painful dilemma. If some people's freedom is not abridged by law-enforcement agencies, that of others will be abridged by law breakers. The question, therefore, is not whether abridging the freedom of those who may commit serious crimes is an evil—it is—but whether it is a lesser or a greater one than the alternative."

For the increasing tendency of the Nixon Administration to apply the conservative perspective in its policies toward crime, see Richard Harris, *Justice* (New York: Dutton, 1970). For a superb analysis of the legal aspects of the major Nixon crime legislation, see Herbert Packer, "Nixon's Crime Program and What It Means," *New York Review of Books*, Oct. 22, 1970.

ultimately, that the social order tends toward rationality. They are more likely to pay attention to imperfections in the social order, however, and are therefore more likely to favor government action to correct those imperfections. As a justification for government action, they usually rely on what has been called the "pluralistic" view of democratic governments—that those governments generally act in everyone's interests because they are constantly checked and balanced by the competition of many different interest groups for the favors of government action.[18]

Given those general predilections, liberals tend to regard the problem of criminal activity as a much more complicated dilemma than do their conservative counterparts.[19] Since the social order can be viewed as an ultimately rational state, those who violate it can indeed be regarded as "irrational." At the same time, however, liberals regard the interactions of individuals with society as extremely complex processes, fraught with imperfections in the allocation and distribution of social rewards. Through those imperfections, some individuals are much more likely than others to be *pushed* toward the irrationality of criminal behavior. Criminality should be regarded as irrationality, but we should nonetheless try to avoid *blaming* criminals for their irrational acts. And since different individuals are pushed in very different ways by different social circumstances, there is a wide variety of behavior among criminals. As the Crime Commission concludes:

[18] For a summary of the general liberal perspective, see Ch. 1 in Gordon, *op. cit. supra* note 3. For a good statement of the pluralist argument, see Arnold Rose, *The Power Structure: Political Process in America* (New York: Oxford University Press, 1968).

[19] The clearest expressions of the liberal view of crime are contained in three reports of Presidential commissions published in the late 1960's: President's Commission, *The Challenge of Crime, op. cit. supra* note 3; National Advisory Commission on Civil Disorders, *Report* (New York: Bantam Books, 1968); National Commission on the Causes and Prevention of Violence, *To Establish Justice, To Insure Domestic Tranquility* (New York: Bantam Books, 1970).

"No single formula, no single theory, no single generalization can explain the vast range of behavior called crime."[20]

Some of these heterogeneous crimes are more serious than others, liberals continue, because they are more violent and therefore more threatening. Liberals tend to agree with conservatives and the FBI that the FBI Crime Index adequately encompasses the potentially most violent crimes. But liberals tend to disagree with conservatives in arguing that these kinds of relatively violent crimes cannot simply be prevented by force, that they cannot ultimately be curbed until the social imperfections which underlie them are eliminated. The prevalence of "violent" crime among youth, blacks, and ghetto residents derives from the diseases of poverty and racism in American society, most liberals have finally concluded. Given those basic social imperfections, as the Crime Commission argues, "it is probable that crime will continue to increase . . . unless there are drastic changes in general social and economic conditions."[21]

Can we do nothing about crime until we eliminate the sores of poverty and racism? Liberals respond on two different levels. On the one hand, they argue that we can marginally improve our prevention of crime and our treatment of criminals if we can at least marginally rationalize our system of enforcement and administration of justice. We need more research, more analysis, more technology, more money, better administration, and more numerous and professional personnel.[22] And since liberals place considerable faith in the dispassionate beneficence of the government, they expect that the government's re-

[20] *Op. cit. supra* note 3, p. v.

[21] *Id.*, p. 5.

[22] Wolfgang writes (*supra* note 3, p. 275), "Urban crime might be reduced by significant proportions if more talent, time, and funds were put into public use to produce the kind of research findings necessary to make more rational informed decisions." The Commission on Violence concluded (*op. cit. supra* note 19, p. 40), "We reiterate our previous recommendations that we double our national investment in the criminal justice process. . . ."

sponses to crime can be improved simply by urging the government to make those improvements.

On another level, liberals argue strongly—and in relatively sharp opposition to many conservatives—that we should not tolerate abridgements of civil liberties while we wait for ultimate solutions to the problems of crime. Though a bit confused and rarely articulated with any real coherence, the liberals' defense of civil liberties appears to derive from the high priorities they conventionally place on social equality and justice, while conservatives seem to be more swayed by their own concern for social order and the preservation of the integrity of private property. However confused its sources, this debate between liberals and conservatives cannot easily be ignored. "A coincidence of events has heightened the traditional tensions between the forces of enforcement and of justice, and has greatly increased the likelihood of a constitutional crisis somewhere down the line."[23]

In short, the conventional liberal and conservative analyses of crime pose fairly simple answers to the most important questions about crime. They argue that criminals are essentially irrational, with liberals adding that such irrationality sometimes seems, in one sense or another, partially justified. They agree that we should concentrate most heavily on trying to prevent the most violent crimes, and they both conclude that the admitted selectivity of public opinion and governmental response roughly corresponds to the degree of violence latent or manifest in different kinds of crime. Conservatives suspect that we have failed to curb those especially violent kinds of crimes because we

have not been willing to apply enough force to deter and punish those kinds of criminals. Liberals suspect that we have failed because poverty and racism are deeply rooted in our society but that we can at least marginally improve our enforcement and administration of justice in the short run through more rational public policies and that we can ultimately curb crime through public action to eliminate the basic social causes of crime.

ORTHODOX ECONOMIC ANALYSIS

In the past few years, redressing a historic neglect, several orthodox economists have tried to clarify our analysis of criminal behavior and our evaluation of alternative public policies to combat it.[24] Although a few nineteenth-century classical economists like Jeremy Bentham had originally applied economics to the analysis of the problem of crime, economists since then have generally left the problem to sociologists and psychologists. Recent advances in neo-classical micro-economic theory permit us, we are now told, to "extend the economist's usual analysis of choice" to an analysis of criminal behavior and its "optimal" prevention and punishment. Since each of the recent applications of orthodox economics outlines the mode of analysis rather clearly and since the approach so directly reflects the more general predispositions of orthodox micro-economics, a few brief observations about its underlying

[23] Fred P. Graham, "Black Crime: The Lawless Image," *Harper's*, September 1970, p. 68. This debate, indeed, has some fascinating historical roots, for both the liberal and conservative positions have borrowed in very different ways from classic nineteenth-century liberalism, especially from the work of John Stuart Mill. For one of the clearest comparisons of the two perspectives and their common legacies, see Robert Paul Wolff, *The Poverty of Liberalism* (Boston: Beacon Press, 1968).

[24] For the most notable pieces of the recent literature, see Becker, *supra* note 1; George Stigler, "The Optimum Enforcement of Laws," *Journal of Political Economy*, May-June 1970; Lester C. Thurow, "Equity and Efficiency in Justice," *Public Policy*, Summer 1970; and Gordon Tullock, *General Standards: The Logic of Law and Ethics*, Virginia Polytechnic Institute, 1968, unpublished manuscript, and "An Economic Approach to Crime," *Social Science Quarterly*, June 1969. Some attempts have been made to apply the orthodox analysis empirically; for one such attempt, still unpublished at the time of writing, see William Landes, "An Economic Analysis of the Courts," National Bureau of Economic Research, 1970, unpublished manuscript.

assumptions are sufficient in order to clarify its differences from both the "public perspectives" outlined above and the radical analysis developed below.

The central and most important thrust of the orthodox analysis is that criminal behavior, like any other economic activity, is eminently rational; in this important respect, the economists differ fundamentally with conventional liberal and conservative public analyses. Becker formulates this central contention quite simply:

> A person commits an offense if the expected utility to him exceeds the utility he could get by using his time and other resources at other activities. Some persons become "criminals," therefore, not because their basic motivation differs from that of other persons, but because their benefits and costs differ.[25]

More specifically, individuals are assumed to calculate the returns to and the risks of "legitimate" employment and "criminal" activity and base their choices between those two modes of activity on their cost/benefit calculations. Stigler adds: "The details of occupational choice in illegal activity are not different from those encountered in the legitimate occupations."[26]

Given those assumptions of rationality, orthodox economists argue that we can construct some "optimal" social policies to combat crime. They assume, first of all, that there is a social calculus through which the costs and benefits of criminal offenses to each member of society can be translated into a common metric—the calculus is conveniently expressed in terms of a "social welfare function." Society (through its several governments) should then try to minimize the "social loss" from criminal offenses as measured by the social welfare function. In their formulation of the parameters of these calculations, they hypothesize that criminals respond quite sensitively in their own deci-

sion-making to variations in the level and probability of punishment. They also assume that, as Becker puts it, "the more that is spent on policemen, court personnel, and specialized equipment, the easier it is to discover offenses and convict offenders."[27] They then proceed to the final argument: we can choose (through our governments) some combination of punishment levels and social expenditures—with expenditures determining the probability of capture and conviction—which will minimize our social losses from crime subject to the revenue constraints in our public and private budgets.

Behind the orthodox economic analysis lie two fundamental assumptions. First, although the assumption is rarely made explicit, the economists obviously assume that, in a democratic society, everyone's preferences have an equal chance of influencing the final outcome and that public policy formulations can adequately reflect the costs and benefits of criminal offenses to all individuals in society. Without that assumption, the basis for minimization of social "losses" through a social welfare function is undercut.[28]

Second, the orthodox economists assume some simple and identifiable relationships among the amount of money we actually spend on prevention and enforcement, the amount of prevention and enforcement we would *like to achieve*, and the amount of prevention and enforcement we can *actually*

[25] *Supra* note 1, p. 176.
[26] Stigler, *supra* note 24, p. 530.

[27] *Supra* note 1, p. 174.
[28] Becker admits (*supra* note 1, p. 209) that the analysis is hampered by "the absence of a reliable theory of political decision-making." Tullock is the only one who makes the underlying political assumption precise and explicit. He writes (*op cit supra* note 24, *General Standards*, p. II–2) : "My first general assumption, then, is that the reader is not in a position to assure himself of special treatment in any legal system. That is, if I argue that the reader should favor a law against theft, one of the basic assumptions will be that he does not have a real opportunity to get a law enacted which prohibits theft by everyone else but leaves him free to steal himself." He adds that this assumption "will . . . underlie all of the specific proposals" he makes in his manuscript.

achieve. This involves the assumption, noted above, that larger expenditures automatically increase the probability of apprehension and conviction. It also involves another, related assumption—that the level of government expenditures on prevention and punishment accurately reflects society's desired level of prevention and enforcement instead of, for example, the influence of vested interests in maximizing expenditures. If a state or locality spends more on its police, courts, and prisons, *ceteris paribus,* orthodox economists assume that they do so because they seek to deter crime more effectively through the expected increase in the probability of arrest and punishment.

A RADICAL ANALYSIS

This section outlines the structure of a radical analysis of crime in the United States. Many points in the argument will seem quite obvious, simple elaborations of common sense. Other points will bear some important similarities to one or another of the views described in the preceding sections. Taken all together, however, the arguments in the following analysis seem to me to provide a more useful, coherent, and realistic interpretation than the more conventional models. In the analysis, I have tried as simply as possible to apply some general hypotheses of radical economic analysis to a discussion of the specific problem of crime in this country. My intention, quite clearly is to argue that we cannot realistically expect to "solve" the problem of crime in the United States without first effecting a fundamental redistribution of power in our society.

I have divided the analysis into five separate parts. The first sketches the major hypotheses of the general radical framework through which I have tried to view the problem of crime. The second tries to explain a basic behavioral *similarity* among all the major kinds of crime in the United States. Given that fundamental similarity, the third

part seeks to explain the most important dimensions of *difference* among various crimes in this country. Given a delineation of the sources of difference among crimes, the fourth part attempts a historical explanation of the origins of those sources of difference— an analysis, as it were, of the underlying causes of some immediate causes of difference. The fifth part argues that we cannot easily reverse history, cannot easily alter the fundamental social structures and trends that have produced the problem of crime today. A final paragraph provides a brief summary of the central hypotheses of the entire argument.

Some General Assumptions

The radical analysis of crime outlined in this section applies several basic radical assumptions or hypotheses.[29] It presumes, first of all, that the basic structure of social and economic institutions in any society fundamentally shapes the behavior of individuals in that society and, therefore, that one cannot in fact understand the behavior of individuals in a society like the United States without first understanding the structures and biases of the basic "system-defining" institutions in this country. It argues, furthermore, that the "social relations of production" in capitalist societies help define an economic class structure and that one cannot therefore adequately understand the behavior of individuals unless one first examines the structure of institutionally determined opportunities to which members of the respective economic classes are more or less confined.[30] The analysis depends, at another

[29] For a summary of those basic perspectives in richer detail, see my introduction to Ch. 1 in Gordon, *op. cit. supra* note 3, and the selection by Edwards and MacEwan in Richard Edwards, Arthur MacEwan, et al., "A Radical Approach to Economics," *American Economic Review,* May 1970 (reprinted in Gordon, *ibid.*) .

[30] For an amplification of these contentions, see Gordon, *op. cit. supra* note 3, and especially Edwards and MacEwan, *supra* note 29. There is some confusion, admittedly, about the proper definition of the

level, on the radical theory of the State, according to which radicals hypothesize that the activities of the State in capitalist societies serve primarily to benefit members of the capitalist class—either directly, by bestowing disproportionate benefits upon them, or indirectly, by helping preserve and solidify the structure of class inequalities upon which capitalists so thoroughly depend.[31] The radical analysis expects, finally, that various social problems in capitalist societies, although they may not have been created by capitalists, cannot easily be solved within the context of capitalist institutions because their solution would tend to disrupt the functioning of the capitalist machine. If the disruptive potential of solutions to such problems therefore inclines the State to postpone solution, one can expect to solve those problems only by changing the power relationships in society so that the State is forced to serve other interests than those of the capitalist class.[32]

Each of these general hypotheses underlies all of the more specific hypotheses about crime which follow.

Competitive Capitalism and Rational Crime

Capitalist societies depend, as radicals often argue, on basically competitive forms of social and economic interaction and upon substantial inequalities in the allocation of social resources. Without inequalities, it would be much more difficult to induce workers to work in alienating environments. Without competition and a competitive ideology, workers might not be inclined to struggle to improve their relative income and status in society by working harder. Finally, although rights of property are protected, capitalist societies do not guarantee economic security to most of its individual members. Individuals must fend for themselves, finding the best available opportunities to provide for themselves and their families. At the same time, history bequeaths a corpus of laws and statutes to any social epoch which may or may not correspond to the social morality of that epoch. Inevitably, at any point in time, many of the "best" opportunities for economic survival open to different citizens will violate some of those historically determined laws. Driven by the fear of economic insecurity and by a competitive desire to gain some of the goods unequally distributed throughout the society, many individuals will eventually become "criminals." As Adam Smith himself admitted, "Where there is no property, . . . civil government is not so necessary."[33]

---

concept of class in the radical literature, in part because Marx himself used the term in several different meanings. For a useful discussion of the different kinds of meaning of the concept, see Stanislaw Ossowski, *Class Structure in the Social Consciousness* (New York: Free Press, 1963), trans. by Sheila Patterson. For a clear description, however short, of the analytic link in the Marxist analysis between the "social relations of production" and the definition and determination of "economic class," see Robert Tucker, *The Marxian Revolutionary Idea* (New York: W. W. Norton, 1969).

[31] For a useful discussion of the radical theory of the state, see Paul Sweezy, "The State," ch. XIII of *The Theory of Capitalist Development* (New York: Monthly Review Press, 1968), partially reprinted in Gordon, *op. cit. supra* note 3; and Ralph Milliband, *The State in Capitalist Society* (New York: Basic Books, 1969).

[32] The argument is best illustrated by the "problems" of racism and sexism in capitalist societies. Capitalists did not create the problems but the phenomena of rasicm and sexism serve useful functions in the United States through their pervasiveness. They help forge large pools of cheap labor and help divide the labor force into highly stratified competitive groups of workers, among whom united worker opposition to capitalists becomes relatively more difficult to develop. If one somehow erased the phenomena of racism and sexism by creating a perfect equality of opportunities among the races and sexes, the process through which capitalists are able

to accrue their profits and keep the working class divided would be substantially threatened. In that respect, one can hardly expect capitalists to favor the eradication of racism and sexism spontaneously, although they might be forced to move toward their eradication if the costs of not doing so become too high. For more on this kind of reasoning, see the chapters on employment, education, and poverty in Gordon, *op. cit. supra* note 3.

[33] Adam Smith, *The Wealth of Nations* (New York: Modern Library, 1937), p. 670.

In that respect, therefore, radicals argue that nearly all crimes in capitalist societies represent perfectly *rational* responses to the structure of institutions upon which capitalist societies are based. Crimes of many different varieties constitute functionally similar responses to the organization of capitalist institutions, for those crimes help provide a means of survival in a society within which survival is never assured. Three different kinds of crime in the United States provide the most important examples of this functionally similar rationality among different kinds of crime: ghetto crime, organized crime, and corporate (or "white-collar") crime.[34]

It seems especially clear, first of all, that ghetto crime is committed by people responding quite reasonably to the structure of economic opportunities available to them. Only rarely, it appears, can ghetto criminals be regarded as raving, irrational, antisocial lunatics.[35] The "legitimate" jobs open to many ghetto residents, especially to young black males, typically pay low wages, offer relatively demeaning assignments, and carry the constant risk of layoff. In contrast, many kinds of crime "available" in the ghetto often bring higher monetary return, offer even higher social status, and—at least in some cases like numbers running—sometimes carry relatively low risk of arrest and punishment.[36] Given those alternative opportunities, the choice between "legitimate" and "illegitimate" activities is often quite simple. As Arthur Dunmeyer, a black hustler from Harlem, has put it:

> In some cases this is the way you get your drug dealers and prostitutes and your numbers runners. . . . They see that these things are the only way that they can compete in the society, to get some sort of status. They realize that there aren't any real doors open to them, and so, to commit crime was the only thing to do, they can't go back.[37]

The fact that these activities are often "illegal" sometimes doesn't really matter; since life out of jail often seems as bad as life in-

[34] This is not meant to imply, obviously, that there would be no crime in a communist society in which perfectly secure equal support was provided for all. It suggests, quite simply, that one would have to analyze crime in such a society with reference to a different set of ideas and a different set of institutions.

[35] Our knowledge of ghetto crime draws primarily from the testimony of several ex-ghetto criminals, as in Claude Brown, *Man-child in the Promised Land* (New York: Macmillan, 1965); Eldridge Cleaver, *Post-Prison Writings and Speeches* (New York: A Ramparts Book by Random House, 1969); George Jackson, *Soledad Brother* (New York: Bantam Books, 1970); and Malcolm X, *Autobiography* (New York: Grove Press, 1964). For more analytic studies, see Clifford Shaw and Henry McKay, *Juvenile Delinquency and Urban Areas* (Chicago: University of Chicago Press, 1969); and Marvin E. Wolfgang and Franco Ferracuti, *The Subculture of Violence* (New York: Barnes and Noble, 1967). For interesting evidence on the different attitudes toward crime of poor and middle-class youth, see Leonard Goodwin, "Work Orientations of the Underemployed Poor," *Journal of Human Resources,* Fall 1969. For a bit of "analytic" evidence on the critical interaction between job prospects and rates of recidivism, see Robert Evans, Jr., "The Labor Market and Parole Success," *Journal of Human Resources,* Spring 1968.

[36] For more on the structure of jobs available, see Ch. 2 in Gordon, *op. cit. supra* note 3. One often finds informal support for such contentions. A Manhattan prostitute once said about her crimes, "What is there to say. We've got a living to earn. There wouldn't be any prostitution if there weren't a demand for it." Quoted in the *New York Times,* May 29, 1970. A black high school graduate discussed the problem at greater length with an interviewer in Herb Goro, *The Block* (New York: Random House, 1970), p. 146: "That's why a lot of brothers are out on the street now, stinging, robbing people, mugging, 'cause when they get a job, man, they be doing their best, and the white man get jealous 'cause he feels this man could do better than he doing. 'I got to get rid of him!' So they fire him, so a man, he lose his pride. . . . They give you something, and then they take it away from you. . . . And people tell you jobs are open for everybody on the street. There's no reason for you to be stealing. That's a lie! If you're a thief, I'd advise you to be a good thief. 'Cause you working, Jim, you ain't going to succeed unless you got some kind of influence."

[37] Claude Brown and Arthur Dunmeyer, "A Way of Life in the Ghetto," in Gordon, *op. cit. supra* note 3, p. 292.

side prison, the deterrent effect of punishment is negligible. Dunmeyer expresses this point clearly as well:

> It is not a matter of a guy saying, "I want to go to jail [or] I am afraid of jail." Jail is on the street just like it is on the inside. The same as, like when you are in jail, they tell you, "Look, if you do something wrong you are going to be put in the hole." You are still in jail, in the hole or out of the hole. You are in jail in the street or behind bars. It is the same thing. . . .[38]

In much the same way, organized crime represents a perfectly rational kind of economic activity.[39] Activities like gambling and prostitution are illegal for varieties of historical reasons, but there is a demand for those activities nonetheless. As Donald Cressey writes: "The American confederation of criminals thrives because a large minority of citizens demands the illicit goods and services it has for sale."[40] Clark makes the same point, arguing that organized crimes are essentially "consensual crimes . . . , desired by the consuming public."[41] The simple fact that they are both illegal and in great demand provides a simple explanation for the secrecy, relative efficiency, and occasional violence of those who provide them. In nearly every sense the organization of the heroin industry, for example, bears as rational and reasonable a relationship to the nature of the product as the structures of the tobacco and alcoholic beverages industries bear to the nature of their own products.[42]

Finally, briefly to amplify the third example, corporate crime also represents a quite rational response to life in capitalist societies. Corporations exist to protect and augment the capital of their owners. If it becomes difficult to perform that function one way, corporate officials will quite inevitably try to do it another. When Westinghouse and General Electric conspired to fix prices, for instance, they were resorting to one of many possible devices for limiting the potential threat of competition to their price structures. Similarly, when Ford and General Motors proliferate new car model after new car model, each differing only slightly from its siblings, they are choosing to protect their price structures by what economists call "product differentiation." In one case, the corporations were using oligopolistic power quite directly; in the other, they rely on the power of advertising to generate demand for the differentiated products. In the context of the perpetual and highly competitive race among corporations for profits and capital accumulation, each response seems quite reasonable. Sutherland made the same points about corporate crime and linked the behavior of corporations to lower-class criminality:

> I have attempted to demonstrate that businessmen violate the law with great frequency. . . . If these conclusions are correct, it is very clear that the criminal behavior of businessmen cannot be explained by poverty, in the usual sense, or by bad housing or lack of recreational facilities or feeblemindedness or emotional instability. Business leaders are capable, emotionally balanced, and in no sense pathological. . . .

---

[38] *Id.*, p. 293. A friend of Claude Brown's made a similar point about the ineffectiveness of the threat of jail (Brown, *op. cit. supra* note 35, p. 412): "When I go to jail now, Sonny, I live, man. I'm right at home. . . . When I go back to the joint, anywhere I go, I know some people. If I go to any of the jails in New York, or if I go to a slam in Jersey, even, I still run into a lot of cats I know. It's almost like a family."

[39] For two of the best available analyses of organized crime, see Donald Cressey, *Theft of the Nation: The Structure and Operations of Organized Crime* (New York: Harper & Row, 1969); and Norval Morris and Gordon Hawkins, *The Honest Politician's Guide to Crime Control* (Chicago: University of Chicago Press, 1969).

[40] Cressey, *op. cit. supra* note 39, p. 294.

[41] Clark, *op. cit. supra* note 3, p. 68.

[42] As Cressey (*op. cit supra* note 39) points out, for instance, it makes a great deal of sense in the heroin industry for the supplier to seek a monopoly on the source of the heroin but to permit many individual sellers of heroin at its final destination, usually without organization backing, because the risks occur primarily at the consumers' end.

The assumption that an offender must have some such pathological distortion of the intellect or the emotions seems to me absurd, and if it is absurd regarding the crimes of businessmen, it is equally absurd regarding the crimes of persons in the lower economic class.[43]

Class Institutions and Differences among Crimes

If most crime in the United States in one way or another reflects the same kind of rational response to the insecurity and inequality of capitalist institutions, what explains the manifold differences among different kinds of crimes? Some crimes are much more violent than others, some are much more heavily prosecuted, and some are much more profitable. Why?

As a first step in explaining differences among crimes, I would apply the general radical perspective in a relatively straightforward manner and argue quite simply that many of the most important differences among different kinds of crime in this country are determined by the *structure of class institutions* in our society and by the *class biases* of the State. That argument has two separate components.

First, I would argue that many of the important differences among crimes in this society derive quite directly from the different socio-economic classes to which individuals belong. Relatively affluent citizens have access to jobs in large corporations, to institutions involved in complicated paper transactions involving lots of money, and to avenues of relatively unobtrusive communication. Members of those classes who decide to break the law have, as Clark puts it, "an easier, less offensive, less visible way of doing wrong."[44] Those raised in poverty, on the other hand, do not have such easy access to money. If they are to obtain it criminally, they must impinge on those who already

have it or direct its flow. As Robert Morgenthau, a former federal attorney, has written, those growing up in the ghetto "will probably never have the opportunity to embezzle funds from a bank or to promote a multi-million dollar stock fraud scheme. The criminal ways which we encourage [them] to choose will be those closest at hand—from vandalism to mugging to armed robbery."[45]

Second, I would argue that the biases of of our police, courts, and prisons *explain* the relative violence of many crimes—that many of the differences in the degree of violence among different kinds of crime do not cause the selectivity of public concern about those crimes but *are* in fact *caused by* that selectivity. For a variety of historical reasons, as I noted above, we have a dual system of justice in this country; the police, courts, and prisons pay careful attention to only a few crimes. It is only natural, as a result, that those who run the highest risks of arrest and conviction may have to rely on the threat or commission of violence in order to protect themselves. Many kinds of ghetto crimes generate violence, for instance, because the participants are severely prosecuted for their crimes and must try to protect themselves however they can. Other kinds of ghetto crimes, like the numbers racket, are openly tolerated by the police, and those crimes rarely involve violence. It may be true, as Clark argues, that "violent crime springs from a violent environment,"[46] but violent environments like the ghetto do not always produce violent crimes. Those crimes to which the police pay attention usually involve violence, while those which the police tend to ignore quite normally do not. In similar ways, organized crime has become violent historically, as Cressey especially argues,[47] principally because its participants are often prosecuted. As long as that remains true, the suppliers of illegal goods require

---

[43] Edwin H. Sutherland, "The Crime of Corporations," in Gordon, *op. cit. supra* note 3, p. 310.
[44] Clark, *op. cit. supra* note 3, p. 38.

[45] Robert Morgenthau, "Equal Justice and the Problem of White Collar Crime." *The Conference Board Record*, August 1969.
[46] Clark, *op. cit. supra* note 3, p. 39.
[47] Cressey, *op. cit. supra* note 39.

secrecy, organization, and a bit of violence to protect their livelihood. Completely in contrast, corporate crime does not require violence because it is ignored by the police; corporate criminals can safely assume they do not face the threat of jail and do not therefore have to cover their tracks with the threat of harming those who betray them. When Lockheed Aircraft accountants and executives falsified their public reports in order to disguise cost overruns on the C-5A airplane in 1967 and 1968, for instance, they did not have to force Defense Department officials at knifepoint to play along with their falsifications. As Robert Sherrill reports in his investigation of the Lockheed affair, the Defense Department officials were entirely willing to cooperate.[48] "This sympathy," he writes, "was reflected in orders from top Air Force officials to withhold information regarding Lockheed's dilemma from all reports that would be widely circulated." If only local police were equally sympathetic to the "dilemmas" of street-corner junkies, the violent patterns of drug-related crimes might be considerably transformed.[49]

In short, it seems important to view some of the most important differences among crimes—differences in their violence, their style, and their impact—as fundamental outgrowths of the class structure of society and the class biases of our major institutions, including the State and its system of enforcement and administration of justice. Given that argument, it places a special burden on attempts to explain the historical sources of the duality of the public system of justice in this country, for that duality, coupled with the class biases of other institutions, plays an important role in determining the patterns of American crime.

[48] Robert Sherrill, "The Convenience of Being Lockheed," *Scanlan's Monthly*, August 1970, p. 43.
[49] It is possible to argue, as this point suggests, that heroin addicts would not be prone either to violence or to crime if heroin were legal and free. The fact that it is illegal and that the police go after its consumers means that a cycle of crime and violence is established from which it becomes increasingly difficult to escape.

The Sources of Duality

One can explain the duality of our public system of justice quite easily, it seems to me, if one is willing to view the State through the radical perspective. The analysis involves answers to two separate questions. First, one must ask why the State ignores certain kinds of crimes, especially white-collar crimes and corporate crimes. Second, given that most crimes among the poor claim the poor as their victims, one must ask why the State bothers to worry so incessantly about those crimes.

The answer to the first question draws directly from the radical theory of the State. According to the radical theory, the government in a capitalist society like the United States exists primarily to preserve the stability of the system which provides, preserves, and protects returns to the owners of capital. As long as crimes among the corporate class tend in general to harm members of other classes, like those in the "consuming" class, the State will not spontaneously move to prevent those crimes from taking place. On the other hand, as Paul Sweezy has especially argued,[50] the State may be pressured to prosecute the wealthy if their criminal practices become so egregiously offensive that their victims may move to overthrow the system itself. In those cases, the State may punish individual members of the class in order to protect the interests of the entire class. Latent opposition to the practices of corporations may be forestalled, to pick several examples, by token public efforts to enact and enforce antitrust, truth-in-lending, antipollution, industrial safety, and auto safety legislation. As James Ridgeway has most clearly shown in the case of pollution,[51] however, the gap between the enactment of the statutes and their effective enforcement seems quite cavernous.[52]

[50] Sweezy, *supra* note 31.
[51] James Ridgeway, *The Politics of Ecology* (New York: Dutton, 1970).
[52] This rests on an assumption, of course, that one learns much more about the priorities of the state

The answer to the second question seems slightly more complicated historically. Public responses to crime among the poor have changed periodically throughout American history, varying according to changes in the patterns of the crimes themselves and to changes in public morality. The subtlety of that historical process would be difficult to trace in this kind of discussion. But some patterns do seem clear.

Earlier in American history, as Clark has pointed out,[53] we intended to ignore many crimes among the poor because those crimes rarely impinged upon the lives of the more affluent. Gambling, prostitution, dope, and robbery seemed to flourish in the slums of the early twentieth century, and the police rarely moved to intervene. More recently, however, some of the traditional patterns of crime have changed. Two dimensions of change seem most important. On the one hand, much of the crime has moved out of the slums: "Our concern arose when social dynamics and population movements brought crime and addiction out of the slums and inflicted it on or threatened the powerful and well-to-do."[54] On the other hand, the styles in which ghetto criminals have fulfilled their criminal intent may have grown more hostile since World War II, flowing through what I have elsewhere called the "promised land effect."[55] As Claude Brown points out, second-generation Northern blacks—the slum-born sons and daughters of Southern migrants—have relatively little reason to hope that their lives will improve. Their parents migrated in search of better times, but some of those born in the North probably believe that their avenues for escape from poverty have disappeared.

> The children of these disillusioned colored pioneers inherited the total lot of their parents—the disappointments, the anger. To add to their misery, they had little hope of deliverance. For where does one run to when he's already in the promised land?[56]

Out of frustration, some of the crime among younger ghetto-born blacks may be more vengeful now, more concerned with sticking it to whitey. Coupled with the spread of ghetto crime into other parts of the city, this symbolic expression of vengefulness undoubtedly heightens the fear that many affluent citizens feel about ghetto crime. Given their influence with the government, they quite naturally have moved toward increasing public attention to the prevention and punishment of crimes among the poor.

Once the patterns of public duality have been established, of course, they acquire a momentum and dynamic all their own. To begin with, vested interests develop, deriving their livelihood and status from the system. The prison system, like the defense industry, becomes a power of its own, with access to public bureaucracies, with workers to support, and with power to defend. Eldridge Cleaver has made special note of this feature of our public system:

> The only conclusion one can draw is that the parole system is a procedure devised primarily for the purpose of running people in and out of jail—most of them

---

by looking at its patterns of enforcement than by noting the nature of its statutes. This seems quite reasonable. The statutory process is often cumbersome, whereas the patterns of enforcement can sometimes be changed quite easily. (Stigler, *supra* note 24, makes the same point.) Furthermore, as many radicals would argue, the State in democratic societies can often support the capitalist class most effectively by selective enforcement of the laws rather than by selective legislation. For varieties of relatively complicated historical reasons, selective enforcement of the law seems to arouse less fear for the erosion of democratic tradition than selective legislation itself. As long as we have statutes which nominally outlaw racial inequality, for instance, inadequate enforcement of those laws seems to cause relatively little furor: before we had such laws in this country, protests against the selective statutes could ultimately be mounted.

[53] Clark, *op. cit. supra* note 3, pp. 55–56.
[54] *Id.*, p. 55.

[55] Gordon, *op. cit. supra* note 3.
[56] Gordon, *op. cit. supra* note 3, p. 8.

black—in order to create and maintain a lot of jobs for the white prison system. In California, which I know best—and I'm sure it's the same in other states—there are thousands and thousands of people who draw their living directly or indirectly from the prison system; all the clerks, all the guards, all the bailiffs, all the people who sell goods to the prisons. They regard the inmates as a sort of product from which they all draw their livelihood, and the part of the crop they keep exploiting most are the black inmates.[57]

In much the same way, the police become an interest and a power of their own.[58] They are used and manipulated by the larger society to enforce the law selectively: "We send police to maintain order, to arrest, to jail—and to ignore vital laws also intended to protect life and to prevent death. . . ."[59] As agents of selective social control, the police also inevitably become the focus of increasing animosity among those they are asked selectively to control. Manipulated by the larger society, hated by those at the bottom, the police tend to develop the mentality of a "garrison."[60] They eventually seek to serve neither the interests of the larger society nor the interests of the law but the interests of the garrison. One reaches the point, finally, where police interests interject an intermediate membrane screening the priorities of the state and society on the one hand and the

interests of their victims on the other. "When enforcement of the law conflicts with the ends of the police, the law is not enforced. When it supports the ends of the police, they are fully behind it. When it bears no relation to the ends of the police, they enforce it as a matter of routine."[61]

The Implausibility of Reform

One needs to ask, finally, whether these patterns can be changed and the trends reversed. Can we simultaneously eradicate the causes of crime and reform our dual system of justice? At the heart of that question lies the question posed at the beginning of this essay, for it simultaneously raises the necessity of explaining the failures of our present system to prevent the crime it seeks most systematically to control.

I would argue, quite simply, that reform is implausible unless we change the basic institutions upon which capitalism in the United States depends. We cannot legitimately expect to eradicate the initial causes of crime for two reasons. First, capitalism depends quite substantially on the preservation of the conditions of competition and inequality. Those conditions, as I argue above, will tend to lead quite inevitably to relatively pervasive criminal behavior; without those conditions, the capitalist system would scarcely work at all. Second, as many have argued, the general presence of racism in this country, though capitalists may not in fact have created it, tends to support and maintain the power of the capitalists as a class by providing cheap labor and dividing the working class. Given the substantial control of capitalists over the policies and priorities of the State, we cannot easily expect to prod the State to eliminate the fundamental causes of racism in this country. In that respect, it seems likely that the particular inequalities facing blacks and their consequent attraction to the opportunities available in crime seem likely to continue.

---

57 Cleaver, *op. cit. supra* note 35, p. 185.
58 For some useful refrences on the police, see Paul Chevigny, *Police Power* (New York: Pantheon, 1969); William Westley, *Violence and Police* (Cambridge, Mass.: M.I.T. Press, 1970); and James Q. Wilson, *Varieties of Police Behavior* (New York: Basic Books, 1969). For a review of that literature, with some very interesting comments about the police, see Murray Kempton, "Cops," *New York Review of Books*, Nov. 5, 1970. For one discussion of the first hints of evidence that there may not, in fact, be any kind of identifiable relationship between the number of police we have and their effectiveness, see Richard Reeves, "Police: Maybe They Should Be Doing Something Different," *New York Times*, Jan. 24, 1971.
59 William Westley, *Violence and Police*. Cambridge, Mass.: M.I.T. Press, 1970.
60 Westley, *op. cit. supra* note 58.

61 *Supra* note 58.

Given expectations that crime will continue, it seems equally unlikely that we shall be able to reform our systems of prosecution and punishment in order to mitigate their harmful effects on criminals and to equalize their treatment of different kinds of crime. First and superficially, as I noted above, several important and powerful vested interests have acquired a stake in the current system and seem likely to resist efforts to change it. Second and more fundamentally, the cumulative effect of the patterns of crime, violence, prosecution, and punishment in this country plays an important role in helping legitimize and stabilize the capitalist system. Although capitalists as a class may not have created the current patterns of crime and punishment, those patterns currently serve their interests in several different ways. We should expect that the capitalists as a class will hardly be able to push reform of the system. Given their relative reluctance to reform the system, we should expect to be able to push reform only in the event that we can substantially change the structure of power to which the state responds.

The current patterns of crime and punishment support the capitalist system in three different ways.

First, the pervasive patterns of selective enforcement seem to reinforce a prevalent ideology in this society that individuals, rather than institutions, are to blame for social problems. Individuals are criminally prosecuted for motor accidents because of negligent or drunken driving, for instance, but auto manufacturers are never criminally prosecuted for the negligent construction of unsafe cars or for their roles in increasing the likelihood of death through air pollution. Individual citizens are often prosecuted and punished for violence and for resisting arrest, equally, but those agents of institutions, like police and prison guards, or institutions themselves, like Dow Chemical, are never prosecuted for inflicting unwarranted violence on others. These patterns of selectivity reinforce our pervasive preconceptions of the invulnerability of institutions, leading us to blame ourselves for social failure; this pattern of individual blame, as Edwards and MacEwan have especially argued,[62] plays an important role in legitimizing the basic institutions of this kind of capitalist society.

Second, and critically important, the patterns of crime and punishment manage "legitimately" to neutralize the potential opposition to the system of many of our most oppressed citizens. In particular, the system serves ultimately to keep thousands of men out of the job market or trapped in the secondary labor market by perpetuating a set of institutions which serves functionally to feed large numbers of blacks (and poor whites) through the cycle of crime, imprisonment, parole, and recidivism. The system has this same ultimate effect in many different ways. It locks up many for life, first of all, guaranteeing that those potentially disaffected souls keep "out of trouble." As for those whom it occasionally releases, it tends to drive them deeper into criminality, intensifying their criminal and violent behavior, filling their heads with paranoia and hatred, keeping them perpetually on the run and unable, ultimately, to organize with others to change the institutions which pursue them. Finally, it blots their records with the stigma of criminality and, by denying them many decent employment opportunities, effectively precludes the reform of even those who vow to escape the system and to go "straight."[63]

The importance of this neutralization should not be underestimated. If all young black men in this country do not eventually become criminals, most of them are conscious of the trap into which they might fall. The late George Jackson wrote from prison: "Black men born in the U.S. and fortunate enough to live past the age of eighteen are conditioned to accept the inevitability of

---

[62] *Supra* note 29.

[63] For the most devastating story about how the neutralization occurs to even the most innocent of ghetto blacks, see Eliot Asinof, *People vs. Blutcher* (New York: Viking, 1970).

prison. For most of us, it simply looms as the next phase in a sequence of humiliations."[64] And once they are trapped, the cycle continues almost regardless of the will of those involved. Prison, parole, and the eventual return to prison become standard points on the itinerary. Cleaver has written:

> I noticed that every time I went back to jail, the same guys who were in Juvenile Hall with me were also there again. They arrived there soon after I got there, or a little bit before I left. They always seemed to make the scene. In the California prison system, they carry you from Juvenile Hall to the old folks' colony, down in San Luis Obispo, and wait for you to die. Then they bury you there. . . . I noticed these waves, these generations . . . graduating classes moving up from Juvenile Hall, all the way up.[65]

And those who succeed finally in understanding the trap and in pulling themselves out of it, like Malcolm X, Claude Brown, Eldridge Cleaver, and George Jackson, seem to succeed precisely because they understood how debilitating the cycle becomes, how totally dehumanizing it will remain. Another black ex-con has perfectly expressed the sudden insight which allowed him to pull out of the trap:

> It didn't take me any time to decide I wasn't going back to commit crimes. Because it's stupid, it's a trap, it only makes it easier for them to neutralize you. It's hard to explain, because you can't say it's a question of right and wrong, but of being free or [being] trapped.[66]

If the system did not effect this neutralization, if so many of the poor were not trapped in the debilitating system of crime and punishment, they might gather the strength to oppose the system that reinforces their

misery. Like many other institutions in this country, the system of crime and punishment serves an important function for the capitalist class by dividing and weakening those who might potentially seek to overthrow the capitalist system. Although the capitalists have not created the system, in any direct sense, they would doubtlessly hate to have to do without it.[67]

The third and perhaps most important functionally supportive role of the current patterns of crime and punishment is that those patterns allow us to ignore some basic issues about the relationships in our society between institutions and individuals. By treating criminals as animals and misfits, as enemies of the state, we are permitted to continue avoiding some basic questions about the dehumanizing effects of our social institutions. We keep our criminals out of sight, so we are never forced to recognize and deal with the psychic punishment we inflict on them. Like the schools and the welfare system, the legal system turns out, upon close inspection, to be robbing most of its "clients" of the last vestiges of their personal

---

[64] Jackson, op. cit. supra note 35.

[65] Cleaver, op. cit. supra note 35, pp. 154–55.

[66] Bell Gale Chevigny, "After the Death of Jail," Village Voice, July 10, 1969; partially reprinted in Gordon, op. cit. supra note 3.

[67] One should not underestimate the importance of this effect for quantitative as well as qualitative reasons. In July 1968, for instance, an estimated 140,000 blacks were serving time in penal institutions at federal, state, and local levels. If the percentage of black males in prison had been as low as the proportions of white men (by age groups), there would have been only 25,000 blacks in jail. If those extra 115,000 black men were not in prison, they would likely be unemployed or intermittently employed. In addition, official labor force figures radically undercount the number of blacks in the census because many black males are simply missed by the census-taker. In July 1968, almost one million black males were "missed" in that way. On the conservative assumption that one-fifth of those "missing males" were in one way or another evading the law, involved in hustling, or otherwise trapped in the legal system, a total of 315,000 black men who might be unemployed were it not for the effects of the law were not counted in "measured" unemployment statistics. Total "measured" black male unemployment in July 1968 was 317,000, so that the total black unemployment problem might be nearly twice as large as we "think" it is were it not for the selective effects of our police, courts, and prisons on black men.

dignity. Each one of those institutions, in its own way, helps us forget about the responsibilities we might alternatively assume for providing the best possible environment within which all of us could grow and develop as individuals. Cleaver sees this "role" of the system quite clearly:

> Those who are now in prison could be put through a process of real rehabilitation before their release. . . . By rehabilitation I mean they would be trained for jobs that would not be an insult to their dignity, that would give them some sense of security, that would allow them to achieve some brotherly connection with their fellow man. But for this kind of rehabilitation to happen on a large scale would entail the complete reorganization of society, not to mention the prison system. It would call for the teaching of a new set of ethics, based on the principle of cooperation, as opposed to the presently dominating principle of competition. It would require the transformation of the entire moral fabric. . . .[68]

By keeping its victims so thoroughly hidden and rendering them so apparently inhuman, our system of crime and punishment allows us to forget how sweeping a "transformation" of our social ideology we would require in order to begin solving the problem of crime. The more we forget, the more protected the capitalists remain from a thorough re-examination of the ideological basis of the institutions upon which they depend.

It seems useful to summarize briefly the analysis outlined in this section, in order both to emphasize the connections among its arguments and to clarify its differences with other "models" of crime and punishment. Most crimes in this country share a single important similarity—they represent rational responses to the competitiveness and inequality of life in capitalist societies. (In this emphasis on the rationality of crime, the analysis differs with the "conventional public analyses" of crime and resembles the

[68] Cleaver, *op. cit. supra* note 35, pp. 179, 182.

orthodox economic approach.) Many crimes seem very different at the same time, but many of their differences—in character and degree of violence—can usefully be explained by the structure of class institutions in this country and the duality of the public system of the enforcement and administration of justice. (In this central deployment of the radical concepts of class and the class-biased State, the analysis differs fundamentally with both the "public" and the orthodox economic perspectives.) That duality, in turn, can fruitfully be explained by a dynamic view of the class-biased role of public institutions and the vested interests which evolve out of the State's activities. For many reasons, finally, it seems unlikely that we can change the patterns of crime and punishment, for the kinds of changes we would need would appear substantially to threaten the stability of the capitalist system. If we managed somehow to eliminate ghetto crime, for instance, the competitiveness, inequalities, and racism of our institutions would tend to reproduce it. And if, by chance, the pattern of ghetto crime was not reproduced, the capitalists might simply have to invent some other way of neutralizing the potential opposition of so many black men, against which they might once again be forced to rebel with "criminal acts." It is in that sense of fundamental causality that we must somehow change the entire structure of institutions in this country in order to eliminate the causes of crime.

A NORMATIVE VIEW OF CRIME

Strangely enough, I find it easiest to evoke an alternative normative view of crime and to compare it with our current social responses to the problem by drawing on a recent exchange in the legal literature.

In a widely heralded article written in 1964, Herbert Packer, a leading American legal expert on criminal process, argued that most legal discussion of criminal procedure involves a conflict (or dialogue) between two different models of the criminal process. He called one of these the "Crime Control Model" and the other the "Due Process Model." The emphases embodied in each model closely resemble the difference in emphasis between the general conservative and liberal views of crime, respectively, as described in the second section of this article. The Crime Control Model, according to Packer, "is based on the proposition that the repression of criminal conduct is by far the most important function to be performed by the criminal process." The Due Process Model, on the other hand, derives from the "concept of the primacy of the individual and the complementary concept of limitation on official power."[69]

In reply to Packer's article, John Griffiths argued that Packer's two models represent qualitatively similar views of the relationship between the criminal and society, deriving from some common ideological assumptions about the law.[70] Griffiths calls this set of shared assumptions the "Battle Model of the Criminal Process." He argues that both the "conservative" and "liberal" views derive from a common vision of conflict and hostility between the aberrant, deviant individual on the one hand and the social "order" on the other. To illustrate the communality of the two models proposed by Packer, Griffiths suggests a third "model" which closely resembles what I presume to be the radical vision of how society should respond to its "criminals." He calls this the "Family Model of the Criminal Process," suggesting that society's treatment of criminals could easily be patterned after the treatment by families of those family members who betray the family trust. The Family Model begins from an assumption, Griffiths writes, of "reconcilable— even mutually sup-

portive—interests, a state of love."[71] In contrast to the Battle Model, the Family Model would propose that "we can make plain that while the criminal has transgressed, we do not therefore cut him off from us; our concern and dedication to his well-being continue. We have punished him and drawn him back in among us; we have not cast him out to fend for himself against our systematic enmity." As in the best families, society would work actively, supportively, and lovingly to restore the state of trust and mutual respect upon which the family and society should both be based. Rather than forcing the criminal to admit his failure and reform himself, we would all admit our mutual failures and seek to reform the total community—in which effort the criminal would play an important, constructive, and educative role.

The Battle Model, as Griffiths describes it, obviously reflects not only "liberal" and "conservative" views of crime but the manifest reality of our social treatment of criminals in this country; it is reflected exactly in a psychiatrist's recent description of the ideology underlying the California prisons:

> The people who run these places . . . believe that the way to get a man's behavior to change is to impose very strict controls and take away everything he values and make him work to get it back. But that doesn't make him change. It just generates more and more rage and hostility.[72]

The Family Model, in contrast, illustrates the fundamentally different priorities which might motivate institutional responses to criminal behavior in a radically different kind of society, one in which human needs were served and developed by social institutions rather than sacrificed to the interests of a single dominant class. That vision of social response may seem like a very distant dream in this country, but it seems like a dream worthy of all our most determined pursuit.

[69] Herbert Packer, "Two Models of the Criminal Process," *University of Pennsylvania Law Review,* November 1964.

[70] John Griffiths, "Ideology in Criminal Procedure, or a Third 'Model' of the Criminal Process," *Yale Law Journal,* January 1970.

[71] *Id.,* p. 371.

[72] Quoted in the *New York Times,* Feb. 7, 1971, p. 64.

When Punishment Is a Crime

RAMSEY CLARK

Dostoevsky called the book he wrote about his years in prison in Siberia *The House of the Dead* with reason. If he died and awoke in hell, he wrote, he would expect it to be no worse than the prisoners' bathhouse—a filthy, stinking hole filled with dense steam and hundreds of naked bodies. On his last night in prison, walking along the fence that had confined him for four years, he concluded that, on the whole, the men there were not better and no worse than people generally. Among them were exceptionally strong and gifted people; the waste of their lives was an intolerable cruelty. From this experience he defined man as "a creature that can become accustomed to anything."

It sometimes seems that prisons try to disprove Dostoevsky's definition by brutalizing beyond the ability of man to bear. Here in the United States, jails and prisons are usually little more than warehouses of human degradation. More often than not, they manufacture crime rather than discourage it. Ninety-five percent of all the expenditures in the entire field of correction in this country goes for custody— iron bars, stone walls, guards. Five percent goes for

health services, education, developing employment skills—for hope.

A look at prison custody at its worst was afforded by the 1968 investigation of the Cummins and Tucker prison farms in Arkansas. Discipline was maintained largely by prisoners themselves—trusties with shotguns—working under a handful of paid employees. It was alleged that inmates were beaten, shot, murdered. Broken bodies were uncovered in shallow graves. Food unfit to eat was regularly served. Forced homosexuality was openly tolerated. Wardens allegedly extorted money and sexual favors from inmates' families. Prisoners were reportedly tortured with such bizarre devices as the "Tucker telephone"—components of which were an old telephone, wiring and a heavy duty battery: After an inmate was stripped, one wire was fastened to his penis, the other to a wrist or ankle, and electric shocks were sent through his body until he was unconscious.

It would be difficult to devise a better method of draining the last drop of compassion from a human being than confinement in most prisons as they exist today. In many of them, there are largely dormitory rooms with 100 beds or more, where guards do not venture at night. Violence cannot be controlled in such an area. Beatings, deaths and suicides are frequent. Rape and homosexual cultures involve most of the inmates by choice or force. In a climate of fear and violence, many wardens work only to avoid the general disorder that can wreck their prisons. They are so relieved to see the most dangerous and violent prisoners go that they sometimes release such men in disregard of public safety.

If prisons offer any work at all, it is generally meaningless or obsolete. Most prisoners in youth centers are school dropouts, yet only a few have a chance to continue their schooling while imprisoned. Studies have shown that most prisoners suffer from some mental disturbance at the time they commit their crime, but treatment for mental illness in prisons is virtually nonexistent. More men have mental-health problems on leaving prison than on entering. Psychotics are frequently left for the inmates to control, and sometimes it is the psychotics who control.

Simple physical illnesses generally are poorly treated in prison, if they are treated at all. For example, because they have been poor, most prisoners have never had any dental work and badly need it, but few get adequate attention in prison. Personalities are shaped by such factors as the loss of teeth. While that loss is but one of many disadvantages and only a part of a dehumanizing existence, it adds its measure of brutalization. Human dignity is lost. Finally, drug usage is common in prison and many men become addicted there.

It is one of the greater ironies of our time that, concerned as we are about crime, we so neglect the one area within the whole system of criminal justice that offers the best opportunity to cut the crime rate. The most important crime statistic is that 80 percent of all felonies are committed by repeaters. That is, four fifths of our major crimes are committed by people who are already known to the criminal-justice system. We have demonstrated that we can cut recidivism—the repetition of crime by individuals—in half where we make the effort to do so. In fact, under

the best of conditions, we could cut recidivism far more than that. If we are truly concerned about crime—if we really care about our own character—how can we fail to make the massive effort called for?

Correction, in its entire range of services—from pretrial detention in jail through the parole system—has been debilitated by neglect. In general, our local jails are manned by untrained people. Prisons are usually located in remote areas, where it is difficult to attract personnel with professional skills or to retain those that do have them. In both jails and prisons, salaries are so low, working conditions so unpleasant and opportunity for advancement so limited that few people want to work in them. Many of those who could accomplish the most in correction are frightened away by the present deplorable conditions. Some of those attracted to guard duty today have an unhealthy urge for authority over people; many more prison guards are gradually made brutal by the environment of the prison itself, something that might happen to anyone.

As public concern over crime rises, prison budgets are cut while police budgets swell. The best leaders in the California prison system resigned after Governor Ronald Reagan cut already inadequate budgets while he sought increases for the state police. The Federal Bureau of Prisons—probably the most effective correction system in the nation—is responsible for all 20,000 Federal civilian prisoners. Yet its budget for 1968, including the cost of owning, maintaining and operating expensive prison facilities, was $77,000,000, while the FBI, one of the more than 20 substantial Federal investigative and enforcement agencies, had a budget of nearly $200,000,000. Every year, the prison budget is the first of those in the Department of Justice that Congress cuts. The FBI budget is often increased above its own request. The Bureau of Prisons struggles to keep old facilities operational. Only two Federal prisons have been built since World War II and as recently as 1965, the only all-female Federal prison had no toilets in many units; the inmates used jars. Twenty psychiatrists are available for the entire Federal correction system. When Congress reviewed the Manpower Development Training Act for budget savings in 1968, the first cut—and the only 100 percent cut—was for prisoner training.

During the Congressional debate of the Omnibus Crime Control and Safe Streets Act of 1968, self-styled tough crime fighters such as Senators John McClellan of Arkanas and Strom Thurmond of South Carolina tried to limit funds available for correction under the bill to five percent, although correction nationwide receives about 25 percent of all funds provided for the criminal justice process. The Senators joked in public hearings about going as high as $7\frac{1}{2}$ percent for correction. Could the reason have been that they knew the jails and prisons of their states and many others are filled with Negroes? Fortunately, such a tragic limitation was avoided, and up to 20 percent of the act's funds were expendable for correction. Yet this figure must be compared with a 30-percent allocation for police to combat organized crime and an additional 30 percent for police to control riots. Correction remains the stepchild of the criminal justice process: The hard-liners have no interest in correction; they want punishment.

In earlier times, among small, closely knit groups threatened by nature and warring tribes, those individuals who broke society's rules by their actions or their words were confined, maimed or killed in a spirit of vengeance. Punishment was a matter of balancing accounts. In a way, the spirit of vengeance proves how much, how emotionally, people care: But the day, if there ever was one, when punishment driven by vengeance had any moral justification passed centuries ago. The sheer multitudes of people in modern society make the idea of a balancing out between the offender and the many offended a meaningless form of retribution. Slowly, civilization came to see that action by the state could not be compared with action by individuals. The state had to act justly, coolly, rationally, deliberately and systematically. No human emotion or disability, no intoxicant could overwhelm it.

Centuries before vengeance as an admitted motive passed from general practice in the most advanced nations, it was recognized as an aggravant of crime. It caused crime. At a time when civilized men could hope to create a gentle, nonviolent, humane society, vengeance served as a brutalizing throwback and proof of the full horror of man's inhumanity.

The modern penitentiary grew from another theory of penology. The very name is rooted in the Latin word that gives us *penitence*. To seek divine forgiveness, to repent, to be sorry for one's sins, to be alone to contemplate the pity of one's own wrongdoing—this was the theory, if not the practice, of the early penitentiary. For the Puritan conscience, penance may have been a powerful regimen. In our mass culture, it is rarely relevant. Those few who commit crime and are then stricken with overpowering remorse pose little threat to society. But so many of our prison inmates are sick in mind and body, full of frustration and despair; their entire life experience provides them with little grist for constructive contemplation. Indeed, any serious contemplation is more likely to cause anger at society's sins than remorse for their own.

Finally, there is a theory of penology that sees punishment as the desired end. Punishing for punishment's sake is itself a crime in our times. The crime of punishment, as Karl Menninger has shown in his works, is suffered by all society, because punishment regularly gives rise to subsequent criminal acts inflicted on the public. The use of prisons to punish only causes crime.

We practice no theory of penology in America today. We do what we do. And what we do has almost no relationship to what we say we do. Essentially, we use penology to confine as inexpensively as possible and thus separate from society people who have committed crime. Simultaneously, if incidentally, we punish by providing an unpleasant experience. The combination tends to turn the prisoner from concern for anyone but himself. In prison, abuse of the individual's integrity and personality has been almost total. When men leave this environment, no other individual seems very important to them. They will take what they want or need. Hanging over most all released men there lingers a personal disorganization, an emotional instability and the threat—almost the expectation—of returning to prison. So most return. We almost seem to want it to happen this way.

The goal of modern correction must be not revenge, not penance, not punishment, but rehabilitation. The theory of rehabilitation is based on the belief that healthy, rational people will not injure others. Rehabilitated, an individual will not have the capacity—will not be able to bring himself—to injure another nor to take or destroy property. Rehabilitation is individual salvation. What achievement can give society greater satisfaction than to afford the offender the chance, once lost, to live at peace, to fulfill himself and to help others? Rehabilitation is also the one clear way that the criminal justice system can significantly reduce crime. We know who the most frequent offenders are; there is no surprise when they strike again. Even if nothing but selfish interest impelled us, rehabilitation would be worth the effort. When it works, it reduces crime, reduces the cost of handling prisoners, reduces the cost of the criminal justice system and even relieves pressure to provide the basic and massive reforms that are necessary to affect the underlying causes of crime.

From the moment a person is charged with crime, correction personnel should work toward the day he will return to unrestrained community life. Accused persons should be released pending trial. They may need help and can be given it, including supervision that protects the public and that is not inconsistent with their presumed innocence. Many of the personal problems pushing a person toward crime are visible long before the first arrest. They were having trouble in school

and dropped out or were unemployed, running with a gang, drinking too much, taking dope, or were obviously mentally unstable. Once the individual is arrested, these problems should immediately be identified; counseling, guidance and treatment can then begin.

Following a conviction, an analysis of the individual's physical, mental, emotional, family and social condition must be made. The prisoner should be allowed to review this analysis, which will be the basis for the design of his individual program. It should be available to the judge and carefully analyzed before sentencing.

Many judges dread the day they must impose sentence. It may look easy for them in the courtroom. They may seem stern, even indifferent; but many sleep little the night before they impose sentences. They are, after all, exerting a greater influence on the life of another man in a single moment than most men do in a lifetime. They must try to guess what period of confinement will rehabilitate someone they will never know, under unknown future conditions they cannot control or even affect. Some judges sentence long, some short. Two young men fail to report for military induction—one is sentenced to five years in prison, the other gets probation. One judge, because of his personal values, thinks homosexuality the most heinous of crimes and gives long sentences for it. Another hates prostitution. A third judge would never jail juveniles for either offense.

For many offenders, a program of rehabilitation can consist simply of the effort to communicate clearly the reasons for society's rule of law and the purposes of its penalties. Young men who refuse induction into the military service because they oppose war often believe they adhere to a higher moral standard. They may. Certainly, from the standpoint of their potential for violence or property crime, there is no quality in their character requiring rehabilitation. But they should understand that the rule of law is not mindless, that it has a purpose and that if the system is to have integrity, the purpose must be fulfilled, or changed by law. But for society to waste years, or even days, of the lives of these young men in prison idleness and brutality is tragically wasteful and desperately wrong. Until the laws can be reformed, a sensitive correction system will afford the hundreds of young men serving sentences for violating the Selective Service Act the chance to make constructive contributions outside the prison environment.

The young boy convicted of smoking a marijuana cigarette and the young girl in prison for having had an abortion present difficult challenges, as does the drunken driver who has caused a fatal accident. Confining such people in prison or placing them in an irrelevant program designed to rehabilitate persons who have deliberately committed serious crimes against others is senseless. Special programs for such offenders can protect the public without the waste and injury risked by imprisonment, while law reform considers whether or not criminal sanctions should apply at all.

Some crimes are acts of momentary irrationality by people who will never commit another serious crime. Murder is often such an act. Occurring most often within families and between friends and neighbors, it is sometimes the result of an uncontrollable impulse, of sudden overwhelming anger—spontaneous, unpredictable and nonrecurrent. Placing the tormented people who have committed such a crime among men who lead lives of crime can be cruel and senseless.

If rehabilitation is the goal, only the indeterminate sentence should be used in all cases. Such a sentence sets an outer limit beyond which the state may no longer restrain the liberty of the individual. The prisoner may be unconditionally released or gradually released under restrictive conditions designed to assure rehabilitation at any time within the period of the sentence. Techniques of release may begin with family visits of a few hours' duration. Later, a man may be able to take on part-time or full-time employment or attend school in a community correction center. Overnight visits with the family might follow and, finally, the conditional release, requiring continued schooling with good performance, employment at a productive level or a stable family situation.

What motivation does a prisoner condemned to seven certain years have in the first, the second or even the fifth year? He is waiting. A program designed to rehabilitate him must wait also. There is no incentive. But even in the early months of the long indeterminate sentence—say for a maximum period of ten years—the prisoner can see the chance to work days, to attend school, to learn trade, to visit home, to move to a community correction location. The light at the end of the tunnel is visible and it always looks good. It can be a goal—perhaps the first goal of a lifetime.

The day of the indeterminate sentence is coming, but slowly. The practice is less than 15 years old in the Federal system, but the number of indeterminate sentences given in the system doubled between 1964 and 1969 and today the sentence is used in more than 20 percent of all convictions to prison. Yet there remain entire Federal judicial districts where an indeterminate sentence has never been given, while some enlightened Federal judges give little else.

No correctional system in the country is yet staffed to make effective use of the indeterminate sentence, but this is hardly an argument against it. In any system where professional skills are available, they would be put to better use. Even in those systems with no skills, the change to indeterminate sentencing would at least give the prisoner the chance, however remote, of release at any time.

There are risks, of course, in the use of the indeterminate sentence, as there are in any technique. And it does not, obviously guarantee rehabilitation. It is only the beginning—only an opportunity. Parole authorities and prison personnel can abuse this additional power, use it arbitrarily or fail to use it through timidity. But we must reform personnel standards and techniques in the system anyway, and any flagrant abuses could be expected to come under judicial review.

Meaningful vocational training in high-employment fields is the best program for many. Throughout the history of Federal correction, most prisoners have been faced with two choices—remaining in the total custody of a prison or being released to the community with insignificant parole supervision. While the Federal Prison Industries program trained and meaningfully employed some, their projects took place within the prison environment and the skills learned were minimal and often in trades in which employment was hard to find. In the early days, it was agriculture, still a dominant occupation in some state prison systems. Later, textile work, bricklaying, tire recapping, auto repair and metalwork were offered some. Now automatic data processing and white-collar training are afforded a few.

In 1965, in what seemed a bold step, the Federal prison system first placed prisoners in normal community employment situations. A work-release program authorized by Congress permitted prisoners to leave in the morning for a place of employment, work there during the day and return to prison when the workday ended. Prisoners were cautiously selected and assigned to the program, nearly always during the last months of their incarceration. Other inmates often made it clear to those chosen that they had better not abuse the opportunity. Among the first jobs offered prisoners in the program were carpentry, auto repair and bookkeeping. One young man traveled 60 miles a day by commercial bus from the Federal institution at Seagoville, Texas, worked a half day in the dean's office at a state college, took three courses and made three A's.

The strain was great on these men, of course. The meaning of imprisonment had never been so clear. Some admitted the great difficulties in returning to prison at night. But by the end of 1968, thousands of men had been through the program and fewer than one in twenty had failed to comply with all the conditions. Alcohol was the cause of failure in nearly two thirds of the cases; the tavern simply looked too inviting after work and the prospect of returning to prison too dismal. We should hardly be surprised that five percent failed: With no program, 50 percent of all prisoners fail when finally released. As to the five percent who sought to escape, all were caught and returned to prison, where they served more time. People do not really escape from prison successfully. In the history of the Federal Bureau of Prisons, hundreds of thousands have been imprisoned and thousands have escaped, but fewer than 20 have not been recaptured or otherwise accounted for.

The most discouraging thing about work release is the timidity of the program and the opposition it arouses. It is a small, late and uncertain step in a direction in which we should be moving boldly. Even so, the hard-liners—those who would control crime by long, brutalizing penitentiary sentences and the fear of eternal damnation—have attacked work release as if it caused crime. Blind to the fact that prisoners will soon be released anyway, they prefer six more months of incarceration to a chance to test the personal stability of the individual in community life. What perversity so deprives such critics of compassion that they will not give a prisoner a chance?

From work release, men can move back into society with a job and a history of having worked at it. Many have said that they felt human for the first time in years. A typical releasee in the very first group that began in the late fall of 1965 worked on a construction crew in Texarkana, Texas. He liked the men he worked with and they liked him. When he was kidded with "How about going fishing with us Saturday?" he would answer, "Wait until spring." They slapped him on the back; it had been a long time since anyone had done that. He said he felt like a man again. Before, he had been alone against the world. His family, on relief for five years, went off relief and moved to Texarkana. He was supporting them. He could send them money. He was going to live and work in Texarkana. He would be the best carpenter there, he said. He would work hard and raise his family. He may.

Work release, halfway houses, pre-release guidance centers—these are only the beginnings. Community supervision is the future of correction. Whenever competent authorities decide that prisoners have reached a reasonable level of rehabilitation, they should be moved from conventional prisons to such community facilities as a floor of a Y.M.C.A., a wing in an apartment building or a house. In such settings, men can learn to live in an environment approaching the kind to which they must adjust before being released. Their freedom, their associations, their schedules can be controlled, as necessary, to help achieve rehabilitation. Family visits can begin, followed by church attendance, if desired, perhaps a movie or a date and later a whole weekend.

As with any pioneer endeavor, our experience with community correction is hardly definitive. There have been successes and failures, but we know that it is a vast improvement over conventional detention. The California Youth Authority experimented with young offenders chosen at random from all except those convicted of the most serious crimes. One group was confined in conventional prison facilities. A second was sent to the celebrated California Forest Camps that were built in the Thirties. It was thought that the fresh air and the dignity and solemnity of the forests might make decent citizens of kids from the slums of Oakland. A third group was treated in small community centers near areas in which they would live when released. From there, they were slowly worked back into the communities. The test began in 1960 in three counties and involved hundreds of youngsters. By 1967, recidivism among those who had been in the conventional facilities or had gone to the forest camps ran about 54 percent. Among those who had been in the community correctional program, the recidivism rate was 29 percent.

The efforts of correctional agencies must be directed primarily at the youngest of-

fenders, those from backgrounds and with personal histories that indicate emotional instability and the probability of continuing and increasing antisocial activities. If we try, we can help many before they err. They commit most of the common crimes of violence and most burglaries, larcenies and thefts. Thousands of crimes are caused by the neglect of the mentally retarded children of the poor, for example. Mental retardation is approximately five times more common in the ghetto; 25 percent of the inmates in some state penitentiaries, such as Texas, are mentally retarded. Had society truly cared, the physically or mentally deficient youngster could have been helped. Instead, a handicap that did not of itself make him antisocial alienated him from all love and he became antisocial. In time, he committed criminal acts.

Many youngsters—retarded or not—come to prison so disorganized and so lacking in self-control that they cannot focus on any subject for more than a few moments. Their attention span is too short to permit training. Before they begin their rehabilitation, they must live in a calm, orderly atmosphere in which they can learn to concentrate. For many, this is the highest hurdle. It is something they have never known. Born in bedlam, physically abused in infancy and childhood, they have lived amid chronic violence, fear and confusion. Their physical and mental illnesses—alcoholism and drug addiction are very often present—must be professionally treated and dealt with as the medical problems they are.

As soon as possible, schooling should be resumed for those capable of it. In Federal youth centers, some 90 percent of the inmates are high school and junior high school dropouts. Without special tutoring to get them somewhere near their appropriate grade level, their chances for a life free of crime are slight.

America is a nation with the skills and resources to provide the necessary elements of rehabilitation: Physical and mental health, all the education a youngster can absorb, vocational skills for the highest trade he can master, a calm and orderly environment away from anxiety and violence, life among people who care, who love—with these, a boy can begin again. With these, he can regain a reverence for life, a sense of security and self-assurance amid all the pressures of modern community life. These attitudes will not be developed in a laboratory. They must be developed in the community itself —first, sometimes, in the prison community, but finally in the open society in which the individual must make his way by himself.

Indeterminate sentences, work-release programs and community supervision all will have a much greater chance of success if there is an across-the-board reform of prison administration. Some 125,000 full-time employees are scattered through an impossible maze of jurisdictions throughout the country. Jails across the street from each other— one run by the county, the other by the city— are still commonplace. The waste in manpower and resources available for rehabilitation effort is outrageous in such situations. Even in the biggest city, there should be but one jail system. It would need many facilities and varied programs, but it should manage all correctional activities in the area. Persons in pretrial detention, whether charged with Federal, state or local crime, could be boarded in the facility best suited to their needs and most convenient to the courts and other agencies that might require frequent contact with them. A single agency serving all jurisdictions would have greater resources. Different courts could insist on good performance, as Federal courts have often demanded that a county jail provide regular and decent meals, beds for all inmates and separation of youngsters and first offenders from hardened criminals. Excellence could be attained with one comprehensive service, if properly funded. Today, there are usually several bad ones, none with enough, qualified personnel or proper rehabilitation programs. Someone mugged by a teenager just released from county jail can derive little

comforts from reports that the Federal youth center is doing a marvelous job.

In fact, city and county jail systems should be abolished in favor of statewide systems. Local prisons do not have the staff, the range of skills nor sometimes even the numbers of prisoners necessary to provide all of the services required. They are even less able to provide the special services needed by female and juvenile offenders.

The Federal system itself has too few women prisoners to offer adequate services to them. There are fewer than 800 Federal female inmates. They come from all over the United States to the women's reformatories at Alderson, West Virginia, and Terminal Island, California. How many will have visitors while serving their sentences? What will happen to their children, whom they will not see during the entire imprisonment? Indeed, the whole system of correction for women needs analysis. Prisons for women began by analogy to male prisons after the penitentiary system developed in the 19th Century. Techniques have been refashioned only slightly to reflect the very great differences in the conduct of male and female prisoners. Women are rarely violent. They are not a threat to the public. Confinement will not break a drug habit nor train a girl for employment nor make less likely her return to prostitution. Nearly all women inmates need mental-health services that their institutions rarely provide. The only possible benefit for many women is the calming influence of what can be, but in most women's prisons is not, a quiet, orderly, attractive environment. Regular meals and a clean private room can be shown as life possibilities. Such amenities—and the habits they imply—can soon become desirable, but iron bars will not speed the process.

There should be a drastic shift in manpower from prisons to community services. Eighty percent of all correction manpower guards jails and prisons. The 800,000 men on probation and parole—twice as many individuals as there are in prison—are serviced by only one fifth of the total national correctional personnel, to the extent that they are serviced at all. Surveys have turned up Federal judicial districts where probation service officers carry four or five times the case load of 50 persons that the National Council on Crime and Delinquency considers desirable. Some officers devote up to 85 percent of their time preparing presentence reports for judges and are therefore left with only minutes a day in which to supervise hundreds of recent parolees.

When a man is released on parole after confinement of perhaps many years' duration, he needs help desperately. He may not know it and he may not want it, but he needs advice, careful supervision, a voice with his employer and fellow workers, a friend to eat dinner with once in a while, a visit with a family. The early months are the hardest; once he gets through them, his chances for making it all the way are much higher. But instead of help, most of his supervision takes the form of routine office visits, spot phone checks, pointless report writing, all of it often surrounded by an aura of mistrust.

No effort within the criminal-justice system holds a fraction of the potential for reducing crime offered by a vigorous, thoughtful correction program. Not even efforts directed at the underlying causes of crime, such as health services, education, employment or decent housing, offer the same immediate potential at anywhere near the cost. Correction focuses directly on the highly distilled mainstream of criminal conduct. If all of our research and learning about human behavior, if all the teaching in our great universities of medical science, mental health, psychiatry, psychology and sociology have any applicability to real life, it is in the field of correction. Yet the people who need these lessons and skills the most almost never get them. If we care for our character, we must revolutionize our approach to correction.

Analysis of Values
and
Conflicts of Interest

Inbau and Carrington assert that crime is a major social problem. They
believe it requires urgent attention because it incurs great and rapidly
increasing costs. Their program for solving the crime problem involves an
increase in resources, power, and public support for social control agencies.
In short, Inbau and Carrington want to enable these agencies to put more
law-breakers in prison. In asserting the need for apprehension of more
criminals, they do not consider the inequities of the law, of law enforcement,
or of the administration of the justice. Instead, they consider only factors
that would expedite police work. Their article represents a plea for increased
citizen support of the police. This is most apparent in their call for public
indignation of legal and judicial practices that hamper police work by
extending the rights of the accused. Inbau and Carrington are primarily
concerned with the preservation of social order. Their avid and unquestioning
support of the police and the existing legal structure aligns them with
groups that are influential in creating and maintaining law. However, Inbau
and Carrington also represent the values and interests of a large number of
citizens who are disturbed by high crime rates. These people agree with the
authors that locking up more criminals is the only way to reduce these rates.

Zeisel and Clark also consider crime a major social problem. However,
they disagree with the "hard line" approach. Instead, they call for progressive
changes in law, prison, and the social structure—changes that reflect the
liberal position toward crime and that coincide with programs proposed by a
variety of reform groups. The liberal perspective, like the position of Inbau
and Carrington, serves narrow as well as broad interests. Welfare agencies,
therapeutic groups, and other ameliorative organizations generally use the
liberal position as an operating ideology. It validates their practice and
legitimates their claims to resources. Even social scientists should be considered
an interest group that benefits from public acceptance of the liberal
perspective. The liberal approach generally asserts that research should

precede social change; and since social scientists are best equipped to carry out this research, the liberal position tends to validate the role of the social scientist and support his claims for research funds.

David Gordon does not consider crime a major social problem. Instead he believes that the problem resides in the social and economic institutions of capitalist society. He argues that crime is generated by these institutions and cannot be eliminated until the institutions are transformed. Gordon's article supports the position of revolutionary groups that seek radical alteration of the existing social order. Although these groups often claim to be acting in the interests of the powerless and the poor, they are themselves interest groups acting on the basis of conceptions that promote their desires and welfare.

4

ABORTION:

Right to Abort or Right to Life?

The Supreme Court decision declaring that state laws restricting early abortion were unconstitutional should have resolved the legal debate surrounding abortion. However, that is clearly not the case—given legal efforts in various states to maintain or to reinstitute at least limited anti-abortion statutes. Thus, the legal issue remains, although it has been altered somewhat by the action of the Supreme Court. However, the legal debate rests on a deeper moral issue. Those who favor abortion argue that women should have the right to control their own bodies. Also they believe that no child should be brought into the world unwanted. Those who oppose abortion assert that the fetus is a living being with a right to life. They believe that no one has the moral right to expunge that life.

In her article, Gratz discusses the cases of illegal abortion that ended in mutilation or death of the mother. She compares these abortions with legal abortion carried out by competent doctors. In this setting, abortion is a relatively safe operation since care is taken to avoid harming the mother physically or psychologically. Gratz feels that women must not be faced with the choice of bearing an unwanted child or facing the butchery and stigma of illegal abortion. They must have the option of a safe, legal abortion if they so desire.

The article by Gratz was written after the Supreme Court decision declared state laws restricting early abortion unconstitutional. However, she remains concerned with problems that persist despite this judicial action. She expresses the following views:

1. Dignified and safe abortions are still not available to all who want them.
2. The price is so high that the poor cannot afford abortion.

3. Anti-abortionists are engaged in "ingenious maneuverings that are already being tried to forestall compliance."
4. Condescending physicians are making women feel guilty about having an abortion.
5. State laws remain on the abortion issue.
6. Abortion is still not treated in the same respect as any other medical matter.

Thus, in addition to the moral issue, Gratz expresses concern with a number of practical problems that remain for women in spite of the action of the Supreme Court.

Gordon Zahn takes what he calls the "religious pacifist" position against abortion. Zahn finds "free abortion on demand" abhorrent and immoral. He does not accept seriously the feminist claim that a woman's body is her own property. He compares this to the argument that the slumlord should be allowed to do whatever he wants with his property since it belongs to him. Further, he finds the feminist discussion of the body as property as degrading since it is precisely the same position taken by prostitutes in treating their bodies as property available for "use." Zahn feels that others have rights as far as an unborn child is concerned, in particular, the child himself and the father of the child. He sees it not as an issue of property rights, but human rights. It is his view that a child's rights begin at the moment of conception, but at this point the fetus is unable to defend itself. Therefore he sees it as the obligation of others to defend the fetus against the efforts of those who want to "kill" it. Zahn speaks for the absolute right to life. He even feels that a woman who is impregnated by a rapist should have the child, although he recognizes that society, rather than the mother, might have to take responsibility for it after it is born.

Mary Daly replies to Zahn and other males within the Catholic Church who have spoken out on the abortion issue. It is her thesis that anti-abortion sentiment is part of the sexual hierarchy that exists within both society and the Catholic Church. It is a hierarchy organized with a caste structure in which women stand at the bottom with less access to ". . . goods, services, prestige and well-being." Given this caste-like structure, Daly argues that men such as Zahn cannot possibly share or comprehend the position of women in society.

Daly likens priests to rapists since both seek to manipulate women. While the rapist does it physically, the priest manipulates the woman psychologically. In attacking Zahn and others, Daly says she is attacking the sexist, conservative, male-dominated Church and society.

Zahn, of course, does not agree with Daly's position. In his reply to her, he reverses the argument and accuses her of sexism for asserting that men cannot understand women's problems. Also he feels that Daly exaggerates the oppression of women as a caste in society. Finally, he suggests, that by encouraging abortion, women are engaging in absolute oppression against the unborn child.

Never Again

ROBERTA BRANDES GRATZ

In January, the Supreme Court partially rewarded the long and courageous fight for women's right to choose by ruling that the state laws restricting early abortion were unconstitutional. The proper implementation of this ruling will mean much less suffering in the future. But the many, many women whose lives have been lost or tragically damaged in the past cannot be brought back to life.

We must not forget. Now that a part of the battle is over, it is important to honor its victims and heroines.

Moreover, the Supreme Court victory will not be complete until dignified and safe abortions are available to all who seek them, poor women as well as those who can afford the current inflated price; until we have defeated the ingenious maneuverings that are already being tried to forestall compliance; until women will no longer be made to feel guilty by condescending doctors; until all state laws pertaining to abortion are wiped off the books, and abortion is no longer treated differently from other medical matters.

Note: Roberta Brandes Gratz, "Never Again," *Ms.*, April 1973, pp. 44–46, 48. Reprinted with permission from *Ms.* magazine. Portions of this article referring to a photograph appearing in the original article have been omitted.

But that is still a long way off. For the time being, we must deal with the questions raised by the Supreme Court decision. For example, to what extent will health codes limit where abortion may be performed after the first 12 weeks—in hospitals only, or in clinics and doctors' offices as well? And what will happen to the doctors and nurses across the country who either have been jailed or had their medical licenses revoked for performing abortions?

And what about the costs for abortions? Can they truly be made free while the rest of the health system is so inequitable? The Supreme Court has given the states the option of specifying that only doctors may perform abortions. This comes at a time of increasing use of paramedics and midwives in birth deliveries and other areas of medicine. If only doctors may perform abortions, it will be more difficult to keep the cost down.

Clearly, a large part of the judicial question has been resolved, but the regulatory, economic, and ideological issues are a long way from being resolved.

The whole abortion debate has always been as much emotional as legal. For the patriarchal structure to give up control of women, especially the most fundamental control of women's bodies as the means of production, means the loss of an emotional and actual sense of superiority. (Indeed, the opposition to the new situation is so strong that some abortion foes are trying the only remaining legal tactic: a Constitutional amendment specifically against abortion.) The situation has been illogical from the start: a surrealistic nightmare of rhetoric in which everything appears in the reverse, or out of proportion, or upside down.

Politicians quaked before the shrill outcries of the vocal Right-to-Life groups, and ignored the fact that a 1972 Gallop poll showed 64 percent of the general population and 56 percent of the Catholic population to be in favor of a woman's right to choose. Those in favor of repealing or reforming repressive abortion laws were accused of advocating abortion when, in fact, they were really advocating an individual woman's freedom to decide for or against.

Antiabortion officials stood up before male-dominated legislatures and displayed bottled fetuses and wept for life, but they ignored the growing children who are starved, abandoned, and variously abused. (There were also brave men, a few of them in Congress or the state legislatures, who risked their political careers to support women's right. They are to be recognized and rewarded for their stand.) Often, the most vocal advocates of the unborn were and are the same legislators who vote against welfare programs and school lunch appropriations for children already born. They wept for the sanctity of life but shed no tears for the children and adults we have killed in Indochina. They ignored the fact that women have never advocated abortion as a form of birth control, that most women who seek abortions are those who already have children, and that the decision to have an abortion is never made lightly.

Indeed, these contradictions continue. Even after the Supreme Court decision, resistance and statements of outrage continue—as if the objecting groups were trying to compensate for their small number and for their humiliating defeat.

What makes it all even less logical is that neither the resistant legislators nor the Right-to-Lifers ever asked the women who were undegoing illegal abortions what they were thinking. Liberal male legislators who work among the poor, the black, the youth, and the elderly learning about "their needs," rarely asked women about their need for abortion. Though they rarely tell those other constituents that their needs are unconscionable or immoral, they did and do imply as much to women.

They continue to visit veterans' centers, factories, and child-care centers, but do they visit hospitals where women who have had illegal abortions fight for their lives? Do they care about knitting-needle techniques, past or present; about other barbarisms that desparate women might resort to? Certainly, the danger of self-destruction in the well-publicized and just-as-illegal drug scene has been an area of far more concern.

In a way, legislators were shielded from confronting the gruesome consequences of restrictive laws: though regularly treated to horrifying displays—bottled fetuses, magnified photographs of aborted fetuses, and the like. Freedom-of-choice groups all refrained from duplicating such "gutter tactics." They chose instead to fight irrationality with rationality, ignorance with fact, misrepresentation with truth; a noble motive, though one that resulted in obscuring women's real suffering.

But then New York's liberal law was saved from repeal only by Governor Nelson Rockefeller's veto. The Michigan referendum on abortion was defeated and nearly buried by the Nixon landslide. The Catholic Church and other conservative forces poured a fortune into the highly visible Right-to-Life campaigns. And thousands of abortions were performed daily, more or less safely on the women who could afford them, and very unsafely on the poor.

Finally, the pro-choice groups were ready to take the gloves off, to fight fire with fire. It is one of the many ironies of the abortion fight that just when abortion defenders were beginning to unveil the gruesome photos of butchered abortion victims, deformed fetuses, and battered babies, the Supreme Court intervened.

Dr. Barbara Roberts, who works on a volunteer basis at Pre-Term, Inc., a non-profit abortion clinic in Washington, D.C., has many first-hand stories of women whose suffering was never reported.

Dr. Roberts recalls that, in 1967 when she was a medical student at Miami's Jackson Memorial Hospital, "a woman was brought into the emergency room in shock, practically dead with a black mass coming out of her vagina. We didn't know what it was until we got her to surgery. She had had an illegal abortion, and her uterus was perforated in several places. Through one of the perforations had come several feet of small bowels, which then worked their way out through the vagina and were actually hanging out between her legs. This was a woman who had already had children and who couldn't get a legal abortion. She had to have a hysterectomy, but there was a time when we didn't think she would survive at all."

On another occasion at the same hospital, Dr. Roberts, a nonpracticing Catholic herself, overheard two Catholic doctors discussing a patient who had requested a therapeutic abortion. The patient, a chronic alcoholic with four children, had rheumatic heart disease. She was brought into the hospital with an infection of the heart valves. She was also in the early stages of pregnancy, and a conference of hospital officials was scheduled to consider a therapeutic abortion.

"The two doctors I overheard," Dr. Roberts recalls, "were plotting to make sure the abortion request was presented before a mainly Catholic group. I couldn't find out the details at the time, but a few months later when I was no longer with the hospital, a friend told me that the abortion had been denied—and that the woman had died of heart failure in her sixth or seventh month of pregnancy. This woman was actually murdered because of other people's religious convictions."

To Dr. Roberts, these are the real horror stories. About the horror stories of the Right-to-Lifers, she says: "A fetus doesn't experience pain. Pain is a learned response." And, she adds, "antiabortion groups often claim to be displaying an aborted fetus when, in fact, it is a stillborn or an eight-month-fetus; in other words, a much more developed growth.

"The real point is that a fetus is part of a woman's body until it is born," Dr. Roberts says. "Antiabortion laws give fetuses rights that living people don't enjoy. No human's right to life includes the use of another human being's body and life-support systems against that individual's will."

The belief in fetal rights and the state's right to regulate the production of humans has resulted in much unnecessary anguish for the following women:

• The 47-year-old grandmother who discovered she was pregnant three weeks before her second child's wedding. Raising children was not something she had ever looked upon lightly. She had given it her all, and now she simply did not have the strength to start again.

• There was the middle-aged mother whose own doctor told her to stop taking the Pill for health reasons and then refused to abort her resultant pregnancy.

• The mother of five who was told she had a 50-50 chance to survive her sixth pregnancy.

• The 14-year-old who doesn't want to be a mother while still a child.

• The Catholic mother of two, soon-to-be-divorced but presently pregnant. In spite of a religious upbringing that deeply prejudiced her against divorce, she decided that the Church could not impose permanent unhappiness upon her. Now she is forced into another battle of principle. While the Church may care more for her unborn fetus, she now feels she must care more about her own life and the children she already has.

• The 34-year-old mother of a 6-year-old boy and a 5-year-old girl. A widow, she was about to remarry when she became pregnant. She was going to marry the father of the child. "We both wanted the baby," she says, "but I just couldn't very well say to my kids: 'Well, kiddies, in seven months you're going to have a baby sister or brother'—a new father and a new baby would be too much at once. And that's not the way to start any marriage."

• The pregnant mother of a mildly retarded toddler who is told that her child's chances for normal growth would be severely jeopardized by the entry of a second child into the family.

• Then there are the unmarried college students and the young working-woman who have no desire to take the shotgun approach to marriage, and the scores of married women who are not ready to start a family, or who already have more children than they can handle, or who would face dire economic hardship were there another mouth to feed.

All these are real cases, and all these women are still suffering the effects of the past.

But now there is Cindy, one of the lucky ones. Cindy is 18 and lives in a blue-collar suburb in New York, one of the few states to have liberalized its abortion law before the Supreme Court ruling. Last spring, two months before high school graduation, Cindy discovered she was pregnant. It had been her first experience with sex.

Cindy loves children. She worked in summer camp jobs, and as a babysitter to save money for a future education as a nursery school teacher. But she says simply, "I'm just too young to be a mother, and I won't fall into the trap my mother did. She married at eighteen and never left her hometown and kitchen."

There was no way, Cindy believes, that she could have told her parents of her condition. "They barely understand why I wear blue jeans and want to go to college."

So without a word to them, Cindy contacted a nearby Planned Parenthood office and was given the name and number of a clinic. She phoned, made an appointment ("no questions asked," she adds gratefully), and was told the fee would be $150.

At 9:30 the next morning, she went to the clinic. By 12:30, she was on her way home feeling great. "Everyone was so nice there I couldn't believe it," Cindy recalls. "They congratulated me when I arrived at having the courage to do it, explained in full what would be done [the aspirator technique], and asked me if I wanted a local or total anesthetic. I chose local.

"I didn't have to wait more than a few minutes. After it was over—it went very quickly—they let me rest for a couple of hours in a very pleasant recovery room. There was another girl in there with me, a public school teacher, and we talked about how wonderful everyone had been."

Amazing, the contrast between Cindy's experience and the experience of an illegal abortion; the difference between a law that gives women a free choice and one that restricts the course of women's lives. It's unlikely that any of the women described here *wanted* to have an abortion, or that they looked upon the operation lightly. Regardless of what Right-to-Lifers argued or what male legislators chose to believe, women have rarely advocated abortion. They have never said, "It's the form of birth control we choose." Instead, the message has been free choice—that if and when a woman finds herself in a position where abortion is the plausible option to a diminished life, then she and she alone should decide her own fate.

A Religious Pacifist Looks at Abortion

GORDON C. ZAHN

Prudence, if nothing else, would seem to dictate that a celibate male, especially one committed to pacifism, should avoid getting embroiled in controversy with the women's liberation crowd. Ordinarily I would be all set to go along with this and not only for reasons of such prudential restraint. I am in general agreement with the movement's objectives and principles and more than ready to give it the benefit of almost every doubt—even though I do wish at times that its principal spokesmen (?) could be a little more, if not "ladylike," at least gentlemanly in their rhetoric and tone. But these are minor reservations.

There is one point of substance, however, on which I must register strong disagreement, and that is the increasing emphasis being placed on "free abortion on demand" as a principal plank in the liberationists' platform. From my perspective as a religious pacifist, I find this proposal thoroughly abhorrent; and I am disturbed by the willingness of so many who share my political and theological approach in most respects to go along with or condone a practice which so

Note: Gordon C. Zahn, "A Religious Pacifist Looks at Abortion," *Commonweal,* May 1971, pp. 279–282. Reprinted with permission of Commonweal Publishing Co., Inc.

clearly contradicts the values upon which that aproach is based.

In the past I have criticized "establishment" Christians, in particular official Catholic ecclesiastical and theological spokesmen, for the hypersensitivity to the evil of killing the unborn and their almost total disregard of the evil of "post-natal" abortion in the form of the wholesale destruction of human life in war. The argument works both ways and with equal force: those of us who oppose war cannot be any less concerned about the destruction of human life in the womb.

In discussing this issue from a pacifist standpoint I do not intend to enter upon two controversies which, though clearly related to the problem of abortion, are somewhat peripheral to my essential concern for life and the reverence for life. Thus, the whole question of the morality of contraception, obviously one of the alternatives to abortion as a means of population control, involves moral principles of an altogether different order. More closely related but also excluded from consideration here is the legal question, that is whether or not anti-abortion legislation now on the statute books should be repealed, modified, or retained. One can argue, as I shall here, that abortion is immoral and still recognize compelling practical and theoretical reasons for not using state authority to impose a moral judgment that falls so far short of universal acceptance within the political community. On the other hand, there are equally compelling arguments upholding legal prohibition of what has long been considered by many to be a form of murder; and this takes on added force to the extent that repeal of laws already in effect will be interpreted as official authorization of the hitherto forbidden practice. Since the intention here is to discuss the objections to abortion itself, this very important legal question will be left for others to debate and resolve.

Nor will I comment upon what I consider the tactical blunder on the part of the liberationists to "borrow trouble" by making so touchy an issue—on emotional as well as moral grounds—a central part of their program. I must, however, reject the rationale that is usually advanced to support their demands, the "property rights" line which holds that because a woman's body is "her own," she and she alone must be left free to decide what is to be done about the developing fetus. Leaving aside the obvious fact that the presence of the fetus suggests a decision that could have been made earlier, this line of argument represents a crude reversion to the model of *laissez-faire* economics Catholics of a liberal or radical persuasion have long since repudiated. Even if one were to accept the characterization of a woman's body as "property" (is it not one of the liberationists' complaints that men and man-made laws have reduced her to that status?), the claim to absolute rights of use and disposal of that property could not be taken seriously. The owner of a badly needed residential building is not, or at least *should not be,* free to evict his tenants to suit a selfish whim or to convert his property to some frivolous or non-essential use. In such a case we would insist upon the traditional distinction which describes property as private in ownership but social in use.

To use another example, the moral evil associated with prostitution does not lie solely, perhaps not even primarily, in the illicit sex relationship but, rather, in the degradation of a person to precisely this status of a "property" available for "use" on a rental or purchase basis. It is a tragic irony that the advocates of true and full personhood for women have chosen to provide ideological justification for attitudes which have interfered with recognition of that personhood in the past.

This is not to say, of course, that a woman does not have prior rights over her own body but only that the exercise of those rights must take into account the rights of others. In monogamous marriage this would preclude a wife's "freedom" to commit adultery (a principle, it should be unnecessary to add, which applies to the husband as well). Similarly, in the case of a pregnancy in wedlock, the husband's rights concerning the unborn child must be respected too; indeed, even in a pregnancy out of wedlock, the putative father retains parental rights to the extent that he is ready to assume his share of responsibility for the child's future needs. In both cases, and this is the crux of the argument, of course, the rights of the unborn child, perhaps the most important claimant of all, must be respected and protected.

HUMAN RIGHTS

These categories of rights, I insist, are not to be put in any "property rights" or similar economic frame of reference. They represent elementary human rights arising out of an intimacy of union between responsible persons which transcends purely utilitarian or proprietary considerations. The governing consideration as far as the unborn child is concerned is simply this: when do these rights come into existence? The answer offered here, and I think it is the only answer compatible with a pacifist commitment, is that they exist at the moment of conception marking the beginning of the individual's life processes.

This has nothing to do with the old thelogical arguments over whether or not the soul can be said to be present at conception; it rests completely upon the determination of whether or not there is now something "living" in the sense that, given no induced or spontaneous interferences, it will develop into a human person. We know for certain that this fertilized ovum is not going to develop into a dog or cat or anything else: whatever its present or intervening states, it will at the end emerge as a human child. One need only consider the usual reaction to a spontaneous or accidental termination of a *wanted* pregnancy. The sorrow of the prospective parents, a sorrow shared by friends and relatives alike, testifies not only to the fact that something has "died" but, also, that this "something" was human.

So, too, with the medical arguments over when the fetus becomes "viable" and, therefore, eligible for birth. It is the life that is present, not the organism, which should concern us most. Once we agree that society's origin and purpose lie in the fulfillment of human capacities and needs, we have established the basis for a reverence for life which goes far beyond such purely technical determination. Should a life once begun be terminated (whether before or after the point of viability) because the prospective mother did not have adequate food and care or because she was forced by the demands of her social or economic condition to undergo excessive physical or psychological strain, we would have no problem about charging society with a failure to meet its responsibility. There is no reason to change this judgment when the termination is brought about by deliberate act, either to avoid some personal inconvenience or to serve what may be rationalized into the "greater good" of the family unit or, as the eugenicist might put it, society as a whole. Just as rights begin with the beginning of the life process,

so does society's obligation to protect them.

Recently a new and somewhat terrifying "viability" test has been proposed in arguments supporting abortion. No longer is it to be the stage of physiological development which determines whether or not life is to be terminated but rather the degree to which "personhood" has emerged or developed. Although strict logic might suggest that personhood can be established only after the fetus has entered upon its extra-uterine existence (that is, after the child has been born) advocates of this new test are apparently willing to extend it back into the later weeks of pre-natal development as well.

Two objections to this test should be immediately obvious. In the first place (and the "generous allowance" of pre-natal personhood serves as a good illustration of this point), we are caught up with the same old problems of judgment that plagued the older viability standards: if the fetus is to be considered viable at x-weeks, what about the day before that period is completed? If personhood can be manifested in the pre-natal period when, let us say, fetuses can be compared in terms of differential activity, what about the hour before such differences can be noticed? Is more activity a sign that personhood is advanced, or might the absence of much activity be a sign of equal, though different, emergence of personhood?

The second objection is even more troubling. Under the old notion of physiological viability, the child once born was unquestionably viable. The same may not be true—or may not remain so in the face of changing social definitions—once the emergence or development of personhood is the measure. My experience as a conscientious objector in World War II doing alternate service in a home for mental deficients introduced me to literally hundreds of individuals whose state of retardation was such that they could be described as "animals" or even "vegetables" by members of the institutional staff. Later, working in a hospital for mental diseases, I attended paretic and senile patients who had reached the state of regression and psychological deterioration at which the same terms could be applied to them and their behavior. However ardent and sincere the disclaimers may be, applying the test of personhood to the unborn is certain to open the way to pressures to apply that same test to the already born. In this sense, then, abortion and euthanasia are ideological twins.

In the old theological formulations of the problem, the condemnation of abortion was justified in terms of the "sanctity" or the "intrinsic worth" of human life. Today much of the argument supporting abortion rests upon similar abstractions applied now to the intrinsic worth of the prospective mother's life or of siblings whose living standards and life-chances might be threatened by the additional pregnancy. These are valid concerns and deserve serious and sympathetic understanding; and society does have a responsibility to find answers to these problems that do not involve the sacrifice of the human life that has begun. Pacifism and opposition to abortion converge here, for both find their ultimate justification in the Christian obligation to revere human life and its potential and to respect all of the rights associated with it.

The developmental model used by those who propose emergence of personhood as the test is basically sound, but as used by by the advocates of abortion it becomes a logical enormity arguing for a development from an undefined or unstipulated beginning. A more consistent approach would see human life as a continuity from the point of clinically determined conception to the point of clinically determined death. This physiological life-span is then convertible to an existential framework as a developmental pattern of dependence relationships: at the earliest stages of a pregnancy the dependence is total; as the fetus develops, it takes on some of its own functions; at birth, its bodily functions are physiologically independent, but existential dependency is still the child's dominant condition. The rest of

the pattern is obvious enough. As the individual matures and achieves the fullness of personhood, both functional and behavioral independence become dominant (though never total; culture and its demands must be taken into account). Finally, advanced age and physical decline returns him to a state of dependency which may, at the end, approximate that of his earliest childhood.

Society's responsibilities to the individual stand in inverse relationship to the growth and decline of his independence and autonomy. It would follow, then, that the immorality of abortion (and euthanasia as well) lies precisely in the fact that they propose to terminate the life process when the dependency is most total, that it would do so with the approval or authorization of society, that it would seek to justify this betrayal of society's responsibility on purely pragmatic grounds. The various claims made for the social utility of abortion (reducing the threat of over-population and now pollution; sparing the already disadvantaged family the strain of providing for yet another mouth; etc.) or the even less impressive justifications in terms of personal and all too often selfish benefits to the prospective parent(s) have to be put in this context; and once they are, they lose much of their force.

The earlier reference to the sorrow caused by the loss through miscarriage of a wanted child does not obscure the fact that most abortion proposals are concerned with preventing the birth of unwanted children. No one will deny that being regarded as an unwanted intruder in the family circle will be psychologically if not always physically harmful, but there should be other solutions to this problem than "sparing" the intruder this unpleasantness by denying him life in the first place. If a child is "unwanted" before conception, science has provided sufficient means for avoiding the beginning of the life process.

Since the sexual enlightenment burst upon us a generation or so ago, we have replaced the old Victorian notions about "the mystery of sex" with a kind of mechanistic assumption that man is the helpless victim of his chemistry and unconscious impulses, an assumption which reduces sexual intercourse to a direct, natural, and almost compulsive response to stimuli and situations. The other side of this particular coin is the not so hidden danger that man himself will be redefined in strictly biological terms, a largely accidental event brought into being by the union of two adult organisms acting in response to that irresistible urge. This is reflected in many of the statements made by advocates of abortion in their references to the conceived child as a "fertilized ovum." The term is perfectly accurate in the strictly physiological sense; in the Christian perspective, however, it leaves something to be desired.

The act of intercourse, like any other human act, is and must remain subject to human responsibility. This means that those who enter upon it should consider the possible consequences of the act and acknowledge responsibility for those consequences if and when they come to pass. Ideally this would mean that unwanted children would not be conceived; where the ideal is not achieved—or where the participants change their minds after the child is conceived—it will be society's obligations to assume the responsibility for the new life that has been brought into being.

Unwanted pregnancies resulting from a freely willed and voluntary act of sexual intercourse are one thing; those resulting from rape require special consideration. Even here, I would hope, the reverence for life which forms the basis of this pacifist rejection of abortion would preclude the intentional termination of the life process begun under such tragic circumstances. The apparent harshness of this position may be mitigated somewhat by reflecting that pregnancies attributable to true rape (or incest) represent a small proportion of the unwanted. Certainly they do not constitute a large enough proportion to justify the emphasis placed upon them by proponents of

abortion. This provides small consolation to the victim who has already undergone the physically and psychologically traumatic experience of the assault itself and must still suffer the consequences of an act for which she bears no active responsibility. Nevertheless, the life that has begun is a human life and must be accorded the same rights and protection associated with the life resulting from normal and legitimate conceptions. Here again society must do what it can to provide all possible assistance to the victim including compensation (if one can speak of "compensation" in this context!) for the sacrifice she has been called upon to make. In most cases we must assume the mother will not want to keep the child after birth, at which point society's responsibility for its future development will become complete. If a mother does decide to keep her child, society will still have the obligation to make some continuing provision for adequate care and support.

The position I have outlined here has been described as unrealistic and even irresponsible in that it absolutizes the right of every "fertilized ovum" to develop, as one critic put it, "in a planet which can no longer support that kind of reproduction and where it threatens the possibility of realizing the lives which exist." The adjectives unrealistic and irresponsible do not trouble me; they are fairly standard descriptions of the pacifist approach, and this is a pacifist case against abortion. What does trouble me is the rest of the criticism. The ability or inability of the planet to support present and projected population totals is still a contested issue, and even if the prospects were as desperate as the statement suggests, the question would still remain as to whether the termination of unborn life is a desirable or acceptable solution. And as for the "realization" of the life which exists, it is essential to face the prior question of who is to determine what that involves and by what standards. How long, we must ask, before the quotas now being set in terms of "zero population growth" and similar *quantitative* formulae are refined by eugenic selectionists into *qualitative* quotas instead? This is not an idle fear, and one would think that a movement dedicated to the elimination of long-standing inequalities based on the qualitative distinction of sex should be particularly sensitive to the possibility.

Beyond this there is that matter of "absolutizing" the right to life, and to this I am ready to plead guilty. At a time when moral absolutes of any kind are suspect and the fashions in theological and ethical discourse seem to have moved from situationalism to relativism and now to something approximating indifferentism, it strikes me as not only proper but imperative that we proclaim the value of every human life as well as the obligation to respect that life wherever it exists—if not for what it is at any given moment (a newly fertilized ovum; a convicted criminal; the habitual sinner) at least for what it may yet, with God's grace, become.

It is not just a matter of consistency; in a very real sense it is the choice between integrity and hypocrisy. No one who publicly mourns the senseless burning of a napalmed child should be indifferent to the intentional killing of a living fetus in the womb. By the same token, the Catholic, be he bishop or layman, who somehow finds it possible to maintain an olympian silence in the face of government policies which contemplate the destruction of human life on a massive scale, has no right to issue indignant protests when the same basic disregard for human life is given expression in government policies permitting or encouraging abortion.

Abortion and Sexual Caste

MARY DALY

In panels and discussions on religion and abortion I frequently have cited my favorite set of statistics: one hundred percent of the bishops who oppose the repeal of anti-abortion laws are men and one hundred percent of the people who have abortions are women. These "statistics" have the double advantage of being both irrefutable and entertaining, thereby placing the speaker in an enviable situation vis-à-vis the audience. More important than this, however, is the fact that this simple juxtaposition of data suggests something of the context in which problems concerning the morality of abortion and the repeal of anti-abortion laws should be understood. That is, I'm proposing that the issue of the repeal of anti-abortion laws should be seen within the wide context of the oppression of women in sexually hierarchical society.

Society as we know it is characterized by a sexual caste system in which men and women constitute birth-ascribed, hierarchically ordered groups, having unequal access to "goods, services, prestige, and well-being" (from Berreman's description of caste). There is already available abundant researched material demonstrating the exist-

ence of such social inequality of the sexes in all basic areas: access to income, occupational specialization, prestige, self-esteem, behavior, sexual privileges, and institutional power. All of this is enforced through sex role segregation, which in some ways is more devastating than spatial segregation (as in a ghetto), for it prevents comparisons and masks inequalities.

Patriarchal religion—in its various forms with their varying degrees of intensity—functions to legitimate sexual caste, affirming that it is in harmony with "nature" and "God's plan." It does this in a number of interrelated ways, and I am proposing that rigidity on the abortion issue should be seen as part of the syndrome. It is less than realistic to ignore the evidence suggesting that within Roman Catholicism the "official" opposition to the repeal of anti-abortion laws is profoundly interconnected—on the level of motivations, basic assumptions, and style of argumentation—with positions on other issues. Such interconnected issues include birth control, divorce, the subordination of women in marriage and in religious life, and the exclusion of women from the ranks of the clergy.

The fact that all of the major ethical studies of the abortion problem have been done by men is itself symptomatic of women's op-

Note: Mary Daly, "Abortion and Sexual Caste," Commonweal, Feb. 1972, pp. 415–419. Reprinted with permission of Commonweal Publishing Co., Inc.

pressed condition. The concepts, terminology, and modes of questioning and reasoning in theology and philosophy all have been devised by men under the conditions of patriarchy. As Simone de Beauvior pointed out, women have been obliged to exhaust themselves just in the process of survival and, in the case of feminists, of breaking through the barriers imposed upon their sex. They have had little energy left for developing a real opposition to the prevailing culture. Moreover, as is the case in all oppressed groups, women suffer from a duality of consciousness, having internalized the consciousness of the superordinate group. Divided within themselves and against themselves, women by and large have not been able to challenge the value system of the dominant elite, even in matters vitally affecting their own lives.

Since the condition of sexual caste has been camouflaged so successfully by sex role segregation, it has been difficult to perceive anti-abortion laws and anti-abortion ethical arguments within this context. Yet it is only by perceiving them within this total environment of patriarchial bias that it is possible to assess realistically how they function in society. If, for example, one-sided arguments using such loaded terminology as "the *murder* of the unborn *child*" are viewed as independent units of thought unrelated to the kind of society in which they were formulated, then they may well appear plausible and cogent. However, once the fact of sexual caste and its implications have been unveiled, such arguments and the laws they attempt to justify can be recognized as consistent with the rationalizations of a system that oppresses women but incongruous with the experience and needs of women.

A number of male-authored essays on abortion that have appeared recently in liberal publications (including *Commonweal*) have been praised for their "clarity" and "objectivity." Yet in many cases, I suggest, such articles give the illusion of clarity precisely because they concentrate upon some selected facts or data while leaving out of consideration the assumptions, attitudes, stereotypes, customs and arrangements which make up the fabric of the world in which the problem of abortion arises. Moreover, upon closer examination, their "objectivity" can be seen as the detachment of an external judge who a) does not share or comprehend the experience of the women whose lives are deeply involved and b) has by reason of his privileged situation within the sexual caste system a built-in vested interest opposed to the interest of those most immediately concerned.

Illustrative of this problem is an article by Professor George Huntston Williams of Harvard in which the author proposes as model for the politics of abortion a "sacred condominium" in which the progenitors and the "body politic" "share sovereignty in varying degrees and in varying circumstances." As he develops his thesis, it becomes evident, I think, that the woman's judgment is submerged in the condominium, and that the theory's pretensions to offer reasonable solutions are belied by the realities of sexual politics in the society in which we actually live. Basically, Professor Williams' theory ignores the fact that since men and women are not social equals, the representatives of the male-dominated "body politic" cannot be assumed to judge without bias. It also overlooks the fact that the "progenitors" do not have equal roles in the entire reproductive process, since it is obviously the woman who has the burden of pregnancy and since under prevailing social conditions the task of upbringing is left chiefly and sometimes solely to the woman. It disregards the fact that the male sometimes deserts his wife or companion (or threatens desertion) in a situation of unwanted pregnancy.

The inadequacies of Professor Williams' approach are evident in his treatment of the problem of abortion in the case of rape. He writes:

Society's role . . . would be limited to ascertaining the validity of the charge of rape.

Here the principals in the condominium could be at odds in assessing the case and require specialized arbitration. If this were the case the medical and legal professions could be called upon together with that of social work. But *even if rape is demonstrable* (italics mine) the mother may surely assent to the continuance of the misplaced life within her . . . (from "The Sacred Condominium," in *The Morality of Abortion,* edited by John Noonan).

What is left out in this eloquent, multisyllabic, and seemingly rational discussion? First, it does not take into consideration the bias of a society which is male-controlled and serves male interests. Second, (and implied in the first point), it leaves out the fact that it is very difficult to prove rape. In New York State, for example, one must have corroborating evidence to convict a man of rape. In some states, if the man accused of rape was known previously by the woman, this fact can be used in his defense. According to the laws of many states, it is impossible for a man to rape his wife. Moreover, women who have been raped and who have attempted to report the crime to the police frequently have reported that the police treated them with ridicule and contempt, insinuating that they must have worn provocative clothing or invited the attack in some way. The whole mechanism of "blaming the victim" thus works against them, adding to the trauma and suffering already endured. Nor are the police alone in taking this view of the situation. Their judgment reflects the same basic attitude of sexist society which is given physical expression in the rapist's act.

The kind of spiritual counseling that women frequently receive within the "sacred condominium" is exemplified in an article by Fr. Bernard Häring. Writing of the woman who has been raped, he says:

We must, however, *try to motivate her* [italics his] to consider the child with love because of its subjective innocence, and to bear it in suffering through to birth, where-

upon she may consider her *enforced maternal obligation fulfilled* [italics mine] and may give over the child to a religious or governmental agency, after which she would try to resume her life with the sanctity that she will undoubtedly have achieved through the great sacrifice and suffering (from "A Theological Evolution," in *The Morality of Abortion,* edited by John Noonan).

Fr. Häring adds that if she has already "yielded to the violent temptation" to rid herself of the effects of her experience, "we can leave the judgment of the degree of her sin to a merciful God." Those who are familiar with "spiritual counseling" have some idea of what could be implied in the expression "try to motivate her." Despite Fr. Häring's intention to be compassionate, his solution, I submit, is not adequate. The paternalistic and intimidating atmosphere of "spiritual counseling" is not generally conducive to free and responsible decision-making, and can indeed result in "enforced maternal obligation." The author does not perceive the irony of his argument, which is visible only when one sees the "environment" of the woman's predicament. She lives in a world in which not only the rapist but frequently also the priest view her as an object to be manipulated—in one case physically, and in the other case psychologically. *Machismo* religion, in which only men do spiritual counseling, asks her to endure a double violation, adding the rape of her mind to that of her body. As Mrs. Robinson of the once popular hit song knew: "Any way you look at it, you lose."

Feminist ethics—yet to be developed because women have yet to be free enough to think out their *own* experience—will differ from all of this in that it will refuse to give attention merely to the isolated physical act involved in abortion, and will insist upon seeing this within its social context. Christian moralists generally have paid attention to context when dealing with such problems as killing in self-defense and in war. They have found it possible to admit the existence of a "just war" within which the concept of "murder" generally does not apply, and have permitted killing in self-defense and in the case of capital punishment. They have allowed to pass unheeded the fact that by social indifference a large proportion of the earth's population is left to die of starvation in childhood. All of these situations are viewed as at least more complex than murder. Yet when the question of abortion is raised, frequently it is only the isolated material act that is brought into focus. The traditional maxim that circumstances affect the morality of an action is all but forgotten or else rendered non-operative through a myopic view of the circumstances. Feminists perceive the fact of exceptional reasoning in the case of abortion as related to the general situation. They ask the obviously significant (but frequently overlooked) question: Just *who* is doing the reasoning and *who* is forced to bear unwanted children?

Feminist ethics, as I envisage it, will see a different and more complex human meaning in the act of abortion. Rather than judging universally in black and white categories of "right" and "wrong" it will be inclined to make graded evaluations of choices in such complex situations as those in which the question of abortion concretely arises. It will attempt to help women to orchestrate the various elements that come into play in the situation, including the needs of the woman as a person, the rights of women as an oppressed class, the requirements of the species in adapting to changing conditions, such as overpopulation, the positive obligations of the woman as the mother of other children or as a professional, the negative aspects of her situation in a society which rewards the production of unwanted children with shame and poverty. It will take into consideration the fact that since the completely safe and adequate means of birth control does not yet exist, women are at the mercy of their reproductive systems.

As I have indicated elsewhere (*Commonweal*, March 12, 1971) the women's movement is bringing into being a new consciousness which is beginning to challenge the symbols and the ethics of patriarchal religion. The transvaluation of values which is beginning to take place affects not only thinking on abortion, but the whole spectrum of moral questions. The ethic emerging from the movement has as its primary emphasis not self-abnegation but self-affirmation in community with others. The kind of suffering that it values is that which is endured in acting to overcome an oppressive situation rather than that which accompanies abject submission to such a situation.

Although repudiation of the passive ethic of authoritarian religion is not new, what is new is the fact that women are giving expression to it, personally, corporately and politically. Those who have been socialized most profoundly to live out the passive ethic are renouncing it and affirming instead a style of human existence that has existential courage as its dominant motif. In challenging the patriarchal authority structure, women are developing in themselves the quality of courage required to face the ambiguities of the human situation. This courage implies taking intellectual and moral risks. It is qualitatively different from the "fortitude" extolled in authoritarian society and epitomized in the attitude of the soldier who faces death in blind obedience to his superior's command. The kind of attitude it inspires is not likely to be appreciated by the military-industrial complex.

At this moment in history the abortion issue has become a focal point for dramatic conflict between the ethic of patriarchal authoritarianism and the ethic of courage to confront ambiguity. When concrete decisions have to be made concerning whether or not to have an abortion, a complex web of circumstances demands consideration. There are no adequate textbook answers. Essentially women are saying that because there is ambiguity surrounding the whole question and because sexually hierarchical society is stacked against women, abortion is not appropriately a matter of criminal law. In our society as it is, no laws can cover the situation justly. Abortion "reform" generally works out in a discriminatory way and is not an effective deterrent to illegal abortions. Thousands of women who have felt desperate enough to resort to criminal abortions have been subjected to psychological and physical barbarities, and sometimes these have resulted in death.

At this point it may be appropriate to consider the "pacifist" argument concerning abortion presented by Gordon Zahn ("A Religious Pacifist Looks at Abortion," *Commonweal*, May 28, 1971). In its own way, this article is also illustrative of non-comprehension of women's situation. The response of *Commonweal* readers to it was apparently positive, praising its lucidity and logic. At least this would seem to be indicated by most of the letters that were printed, all of which were from men, with one exception, which was from a nun. However, it is unlikely that many feminists would be impressed. Indeed, the article is particularly enigmatic because Professor Zahn, in addressing his critique to what he imagines to be the women's liberationists' point of view, by his own admission refuses to deal with "the legislative question." This leads to considerable mystification since the issue being raised by the women's movement is precisely *the repeal of anti-abortion laws*. There is not merely one single view of the morality of abortion among feminists. Yet there is an almost universal consensus that it should be removed from criminal law. Pacifists such as Gordon Zahn are free to refuse to defend themselves if physically attacked, but a legal system that would condemn taking the necessary means for self-defense would be inappropriate to the human condition. So also a women may take a "pacifist" position in regard to an unwanted pregnancy and refuse to have an abortion. However, a woman also might reasonably decide that, in her circumstances, having an abortion would be the better part of valor. Attempting to exclude such decisions by legislation is, I think, unrealistic and inappropriate. It is generally unwise to try to legislate heroism. Feminists point out, more-over, that bringing an unwanted child into the world is even a questionable form of heroism. It would seem particularly unwise to try to enforce through criminal law a species of self-sacrifice whose consequences are dubious at best, and often tragic.

Women—many of them victims also of economic and racial oppression—have just begun to cry out publicly about their rights over their own bodies. That academics find this language unsatisfactory as a complete moral methodology is understandable. Their inability to listen to what is being said, however, is deplorable. Women are making explicit the dimension that traditional morality and abortion legislation simply have not taken into account: the realities of their existence as an oppressed caste of human beings. I think the fact that Professor Zahn just does not hear these voices of experience is indicated by a number of statements. For example, his claim that science has provided sufficient means for avoiding the beginning of the life process is out of touch with the realities of individual situations. His admonition that one should acknowledge the consequences of the sex act is of high moral tone, but it doesn't have much meaning when applied after the fact to the case of an economically and culturally deprived adolescent. As for the "rights of the putative father"— Professor Zahn really should speak to a few young women who would be willing to tell it to him like it is.

As the movement for the repeal of anti-abortion laws gains momentum, we are rapidly moving into a situation in which open war is declared between feminism in this country and official Roman Catholicism. I use the word "official" advisedly, since this position hardly represents the thinking of all Catholics. The anti-feminine discriminations within the Church have, of course, been known in a general way by feminists, but these for the most part have seemed irrelevant to their own lives. As this issue surfaces more and more, however, women are seeing the Church as their enemy. For its part, the institutional Church is focusing its tremendous lobbying power on the issue. As one woman pointed out, it is well organized and has plenty of money to spend.

Women did not arbitrarily choose abortion as part of their platform. It has arisen out of the realities of their situation. On its deepest level, I think the issue is not as different from the issue of birth control as many, particularly liberal Catholics, would make it appear. There are deep questions involved which touch the very meaning of human existence. Are we going to let "nature" take its course or take the decision into our own hands? In the latter case, who will decide? What the women's movement is saying is that decisions will be made affecting the processes of "nature," and that women as individuals will make the decisions in matters most intimately concerning themselves. I think that this, on the deepest level, is what authoritarian religion fears. Surely its greatest fear is not the destruction of life, as its record on other issues reveals.

Declaration of war between the women's movement and the official Church should come as no surprise. Yet there are certain deep ironies and tragic conflicts here, for there is widespread spiritual consciousness in the movement. Among its leaders and theoreticians are women who are spiritual expatriates. Having seen through the idolatries and the oppressive bias of patriarchal religion, they have found that their sense of transcendence and creative hopes can be expressed within the movement but not in the institutional Churches. For such women the movement functions as "space" set apart —a province primarily of the mind—in which they experience authenticity and freedom. It is the space where they need not go through the mendacious contortions of mind, will and imagination demanded of them by sexist society and sexist religion. It is a charismatic community, and its mission is based upon the promise within women themselves, their undeveloped potential. The women's movement is anti-Church in the sense of being in conflict with sexist religion *as sexist*. At the same time, it is expressing dimensions of human truth that the institutional Churches have failed to incarnate and express.

What can be the role of a living, healing, prophetic Church in this situation? I suggest that the work of such a community, wherever that may exist—underground, above-ground, "inside" or "outside" the official Church—will not be to cut off the possibility for women to make free and courageous decisions, either by lobbying to prevent the repeal of anti-abortion laws or by psychological manipulation. I think that it will try to *hear* what women are saying and to support their demands for the repeal of unjust laws.

In addition to this, and more importantly, I suggest that a living Church will try to point beyond abortion to more fundamental solutions. That is, it will work toward the development of a social context in which the problem of abortion will not arise. As catalyst for social change, it will foster research into more adequate and safer means of birth control. As educative force, it will make available information about the better means now in existence, for example, vasectomy. Most fundamentally, as a prophetic and healing community it will work to eradicate sex-role socialization and the sexual caste system itself, which in many ways works toward the entrapment of women in situations of being burdened with unwanted pregnancies. I think it should be clear that authentic religion will point beyond abortion, not by instilling fear and guilt, but by inspiring the kind of personal, social and technological creativity that can, in the long run, make abortion a non-problem.

Reply to Daly

GORDON C. ZAHN

It is a losing game to engage in a discussion in which one knows his views are going to be dismissed as those of someone who doesn't know (*and really can't know*) the score or, even worse, who is merely defending a "built-in vested interest." When these incapacities are linked to nothing more than one's maleness, we have an interesting variant of the sexist thinking Prof. Daly, ["Abortion and Sexual Caste," Feb. 4] and other feminist spokeswomen so rightly condemn in others.

I did not develop the legislative question in my article because it was peripheral to my concern about abortion as an imposed termination of the life process and its total incompatibility with pacifism or any other position based on a reverence for life. Since the new feminism has become the principal vehicle for open advocacy of abortion and has placed so much emphasis upon the woman's "property rights" in her own body as deserving priority over the personal rights of the human being whose life process has begun, it was on this level that I chose to argue the case. The legislation issue is too complex to be summarized this briefly but, since the objection has been raised, this

Note: From a letter published in *Commonweal*, Feb. 18, 1972. Gordon Zahn, "Reply to Daly," *Commonweal*, Feb. 1972, pp. 470–71. Reprinted with permission of Commonweal Publishing Co., Inc.

would by my general position: I probably would oppose the introduction of new anti-abortion legislation because I do not feel that punitive legislation is the most appropriate channel for dealing with moral questions; on the other hand, I probably would oppose repeal of existing legislation because such repeal would carry with it (as it clearly has done in New York) implications of social approval and authorization. If the laws are repealed or, as seems increasingly likely, invalidated by court decisions, I would not consider this a moral or legal disaster. However, I do reject the argument that the existing laws by being "sex specific" are unjust instruments of female oppression, just as I do not regard laws against rape—"sex selective" too, in their application at least—as vehicles for the unjust oppression of males. Both have to do with extreme violations of basic human rights, and that is justification enough for formal social concern.

To respond fully to the Daly article would require a recapitulation of my earlier article. Some points cannot be ignored, however. The flippant dismissal of the rights of a putative father does Ms. Daly's argument little justice especially if, as I would assume, she is not prepared to be equally flippant about society's efforts, imperfect as they admittedly are, to establish his responsibilities, financial and otherwise. Second, and much more critical, is her failure to address herself to the crucial question of the nature and rights of the intended victims of abortion (about fifty percent of whom, if I may suggest an additional statistic worthy of note, are likely to be female) .

This latter omission has **an** important bearing upon her overall case. I happen to feel that the author's description of the total oppression of women is exaggerated and that the use of "caste"—a sociological concept implying no prospect of upward mobility whatsoever across fixed status boundaries—is in fact belied by her own distinguished career and the positions attained by other feminist leaders. Inequity and discrimination are beyond question and should be opposed, but the picture of inflexible and structured oppression she presents as the condition of women today is open to challenge. By a supreme irony, her article does touch upon a form of oppression that she apparently fails to recognize. The real measure of oppression is the extent to which an individual and his actions are subject to the command of another and his very existence made dependent upon the pleasure, the whims, the convenience or the self-determined "necessity" of that other. The radical feminists with their advocacy of abortion on demand—and, Dr. Daly notwithstanding, this is the real force behind the agitation for repeal of existing laws—are in effect claiming rights which would reach the absolute in oppression, "rights" which would give them the arbitrary power to destroy a human being at those stages of development when its dependency is greatest.

Analysis of Values
and
Conflicts of Interest

Feminists Gratz and Daly believe that only the pregnant woman has the right to decide whether she will bear a child or not. They feel that anti-abortion sentiment is the product of a male-dominated society and they therefore refuse to accept what they consider a form of sexist oppression. They argue that rescinded anti-abortion laws, which immorally subjected women to emotional and physical harm, were an affront to all women.

Anti-abortion laws had an especially deleterious impact upon poor and working-class women. In most cases the wealthy could afford the expense of a willing, competent doctor capable of performing a safe abortion. However, less fortunate women were often forced to patronize untrained and incompetent abortionists, who frequently administered abortions under unsanitary conditions. The consequences were sometimes mutilation or death. Other women unable to afford an inexpensive abortion sometimes hurt or mutilated themselves while attempting to induce a miscarriage or in self-administered abortion. The articles by Gratz and Daly support the position of women's groups throughout the country who desire to liberate women from the constrictions of her traditional role. These feminist organizations usually consider abortion on demand to be a right that all women should have. However, Gratz and Daly should not be considered as representatives of only these groups. They also reflect the interests of all women who are potential victims of the conditions discussed above.

Numerous groups of both men and women favoring abortion do not couch their support in feminist terms. For example, many assert that the state has no right to interfere in a person's private decision to terminate a pregnancy. Others believe that abortion is a humanistic alternative to bringing an unwanted child into the world. Others favor abortion as an essential means to curb population growth. The papers by Gratz and Daly give at least indirect support to all these positions.

Zahn, a priest, is a spokesman for the Catholic Church. The doctrine of the Catholic Church establishes conception as the time when we become human and possess the natural rights of all other humans. Consequently, the Catholic Church considers abortion murder. If one accepts the Catholic definition of humanity, then Zahn is not only a representative of the Church, but also is acting in the interests of the unborn child.

Many "right to life" groups throughout the country are applying moral, political, and legal pressures to repeal the laws permitting abortion on demand. Although spearheaded by Catholics, many of the movement's supporters are not Catholic but concur in Catholic conceptions of fetal rights. Today there is a lack of consensus about the point at which we become human. Many people, Catholics and non-Catholics alike, feel that the human fetus is a person that has an inalienable right to life. Furthermore, they argue that legal abortion represents a trend toward dehumanization. Those opposing abortion on these grounds feel that it is a harbinger of a "brave new world," where life is no longer sacred. They assert that persons must take a moral stand for life if this condition is to be averted. Even though Zahn is a Catholic expressing the position of his Church, his ideas are also supportive of these broader interests opposed to abortion.

5

PORNOGRAPHY:

Should it Be Tolerated?

The issue concerning the censorship of pornography has been debated
vigorously for many years. Recently it has drawn even greater public
interest because of the Supreme Court decision that allows communities to
establish their own legal standards defining pornography and to prosecute
people who violate them. Persons who advocate censorship often argue that
pornography encourages sexually deviant acts and impedes healthy sexual
adjustment. Those who argue against censorship claim that there is no
empirical evidence for such assertions and that pornography can sometimes
even provide an outlet for sexual needs. This position concludes that if these
needs are left unmet they could be manifested in destructive, sexually
aggressive acts. However, there is a related concern of more profound
importance. This involves a possible conflict between individual freedom and
the preservation of the moral order of society. If we dedicate ourselves to the
former we are likely to argue against censorship because it represents a threat
to artistic and intellectual expression. If we commit ourselves to the latter,
we are likely to support censorship as a defense against the erosion of the
moral values that provide a foundation for society.

In the first article, the recommendations of the Commission on Obscenity
and Pornography are presented. The commission argues the case against the
censorship of pornography. It asserts that adults should have full freedom
to read or obtain any sexual material that they desire, regardless of its nature.
It suggests that sexual problems in our society are likely to result from the
secrecy that provides sex with a magical aura, rather than from materials
that deal with sex explicitly. The argument concludes with the assertion
that if barriers to sex information are eliminated and if sex is demystified
through widespread sex education programs, then pornography would lose
its function and attraction.

The commission suggests that existing empirical data show no
relation between the availability of explicit sexual materials and increased

rates of deviant behaviors (crime, delinquency, emotional disorder, or other sexual deviance). Furthermore, it argues that obscenity laws and attempts at censorship are usually ineffective and when applied sometimes constitute an unjust infringement on individual freedom. The commission also asserts that the availability of explicit sexual information, in their opinion, does not exert an important influence on sexual morality. Finally, it concludes that the laws that promote censorship of pornography present a greater danger to society than the actual existence of pornography.

The second article is a minority statement of the commission which asserts that the majority report constitutes a "magna carta" for pornographers. The authors of the minority report feel that pornography has an eroding effect on society, on public morality, on respect for human worth, on attitudes toward the family, love, and culture. They assert that the commission was irresponsible when it implied that pornography is harmless because in their opinion the data is scanty and slanted. The dissenting commissioners call for a vigorous legal campaign against pornography by all levels of government.

Irving Kristol argues that almost all people accept the need for public officials to establish a limit to self-expression at some point. He argues that our culture must avoid nihilism if it is to survive. If everything is permissible, then the very basis of moral order is eliminated. Kristol asserts that pornography is objectionable not because it sexually excites, but instead because it debases vital human relationships. He argues that when sex is treated in a profane way by making it a public spectacle, it is degenerated from a human relationship to a mere animal connection. Kristol suggests that women suffer the worst degradation in this situation because most pornography is produced by men for men about women. Thus it could be considered a most vulgar form of sexual exploitation. Kristol suggests that the popularity will not be reduced by attempting to remove its mystique through legalization. He asserts that pornography would become more popular with increased availability because it provides a regressive sexual pleasure that results in a self-reinforcing neurosis. Kristol believes that pornography damages our cultural life since it occupies a large part of the literary market while providing an unsatisfactory substitute for more substantial cultural forms.

In the last article of this section Ned Polsky argues that pornography promotes the maintenance of social organization. Polsky asserts that it provides a harmless opportunity for the fulfillment of deviant sexual needs. He suggests that the existence of pornography actually supports the societal institutionalization of legitimate sex within marriage by providing vicarious sexual fulfillment that drains off other illegitimate sexual desires. Still, society officially defines pornography in a negative fashion in order to maintain a restrictive societal definition of legitimate sex. Thus pornography remains stigmatized, but little is done to eliminate it from newsstands and bookstores.

Non-Legislative Recommendations

THE COMMISSION ON OBSCENITY
AND PORNOGRAPHY

The Commission believes that much of the "problem" regarding materials which depict explicit sexual activity stems from the inability or reluctance of people in our society to be open and direct in dealing with sexual matters. This most often manifests itself in the inhibition of talking openly and directly about sex. Professionals use highly technical language when they discuss sex; others of us escape by using euphemisms—or by not talking about sex at all. Direct and open conversation about sex between parent and child is too rare in our society.

Failure to talk openly and directly about sex has several consequences. It overemphasizes sex, gives it a magical, nonnatural quality, making it more attractive and fascinating. It diverts the expression of sexual interest out of more legitimate channels, into less legitimate channels. Such failure makes teaching children and adolescents to become fully and adequately functioning sexual adults a more difficult task. And it clogs legitimate channels for transmitting sexual information and forces people to use clandestine and unreliable sources.

The Commission believes that interest in

sex is normal, healthy, good. Interest in sex begins very early in life and continues throughout the life cycle although the strength of this interest varies from stage to stage. With the onset of puberty, physiological and hormonal changes occur which both quicken interest and make the individual more responsive to sexual interest. The individual needs information about sex in order to understand himself, place his new experiences in a proper context, and cope with his new feelings.

The basic institutions of marriage and the family are built in our society primarily on sexual attraction, love, and sexual expression. These institutions can function successfully only to the extent that they have a healthy base. Thus the very foundation of our society rests upon healthy sexual attitudes grounded in appropriate and accurate sexual information.

Sexual information is so important and so necessary that if people cannot obtain it openly and directly from legitimate sources and through accurate and legitimate channels, they will seek it through whatever channels and sources are available. Clandestine sources may not only be inaccurate but may also be distorted and provide a warped context.

Note: From *The Report of the Commission on Obscenity and Pornography,* U.S. Government Printing Office, Sept. 1970.

The Commission believes that accurate, appropriate sex information provided openly and directly through legitimate channels and from reliable sources in healthy contexts can compete successfully with potentially distorted, warped, inaccurate, and unreliable information from clandestine, illegitimate sources; and it believes that the attitudes and orientations toward sex produced by the open communication of appropriate sex information from reliable sources through legitimate channels will be normal and healthy, providing a solid foundation for the basic institutions of our society.

The Commission, therefore, presents the following positive approaches to deal with the problem of obscenity and pornography.

1. The Commission recommends that a massive sex education effort be launched. This sex education effort should be characterized by the following:

    a) its purpose should be to contribute to healthy attitudes and orientations to sexual relationships so as to provide a sound foundation for our society's basic institutions of marriage and family;

    b) it should be aimed at achieving an acceptance of sex as a normal and natural part of life and of oneself as a sexual being;

    c) it should not aim for orthodoxy; rather it should be designed to allow for a pluralism of values;

    d) it should be based on facts and encompass not only biological and physiological information but also social, psychological, and religious information;

    e) it should be differentiated so that content can be shaped appropriately for the individual's age, sex, and circumstances;

    f) it should be aimed, as appropriate, to all segments of our society, adults as well as children and adolescents;

    g) it should be a joint function of several institutions of our society: family, school, church, etc.;

    h) special attention should be given to the training of those who will have central places in the legitimate communication channels—parents, teachers, physicians, clergy, social service workers, etc.;

    i) it will require cooperation of private and public organizations at local, regional, and national levels with appropriate funding;

    j) it will be aided by the imaginative utilization of new educational technologies; for example, educational television could be used to reach several members of a family in a family context.

The Commission feels that such a sex education program would provide a powerful positive approach to the problems of obscenity and pornography. By providing accurate and reliable sex information through legitimate sources, it would reduce interest in and dependence upon clandestine and less legitimate sources. By providing healthy attitudes and orientations toward sexual relationships, it would provide better protection for the individual against distorted or warped ideas he may encounter regarding sex. By providing greater ease in talking about sexual matters in appropriate contexts, the shock and offensiveness of encounters with sex would be reduced.

2. The Commission recommends continued open discussion, based on factual information, on the issues regarding obscenity and pornography.

Discussion has in the past been carried on with few facts available and the debate has necessarily reflected, to a large extent, prejudices and fears. Congress asked the Commission to secure more factual information before making recommendations. Some of the facts developed by the Commission are contrary to widely held assumptions. These findings provide new perspectives on the issues.

The information developed by the Commission should be given wide distribution, so that it may sharpen the issues and focus the discussion.

3. The Commission recommends that additional factual information be developed.

The Commission's effort to develop information has been limited by time, financial resources, and the paucity of previously existing research. Many of its findings are tentative and many questions remain to be answered. We trust that our modest pioneering work in empirical research into several problem areas will help to open the way for more extensive and long-term research based on more refined methods directed to answering more refined questions. We urge both private and public sources to provide the financial resources necessary for the continued development of factual information so that the continuing discussion may be further enriched.

The Federal Government has special responsibilities for continuing research in these areas and has existing structures which can facilitate further inquiry. Many of the questions raised about obscenity and pornography have direct relevance to already existing programs in the National Institute of Mental Health, the National Institute of Child Health and Human Development, and the United States Office of Education. The Commission urges these agencies to broaden their concerns to include a wider range of topics relating to human sexuality, specifically including encounters with explicit sexual materials.

4. The Commission recommends that citizens organize themselves at local, regional, and national levels to aid in the implementation of the foregoing recommendations.

The sex education effort recommended by the Commission can be achieved only with broad and active citizen participation. Widespread discussion of the issues regarding the availability of explicit sexual materials implies broad and active citizen participation. A continuing research program aimed at clarifying factual issues regarding the impact of explicit sexual materials on those who encounter them will occur only with the support and cooperation of citizens.

Organized citizen groups can be more constructive and effective if they truly represent a broad spectrum of the public's thinking and feeling. People tend to assume, in the absence of other information, that most peoples' opinions are similar to their own. However, we know that opinions in the sexual realm vary greatly—that there is no unanimity of values in this area. Therefore, every group should attempt to include as wide a variety of opinion as is possible.

The aim of citizen groups should be to provide a forum whereby all views may be presented for thoughtful consideration. We live in a free, pluralistic society which places its trust in the competition of ideas in a free market place. Persuasion is a preferred technique. Coercion, repression and censorship in order to promote a given set of views are not tolerable in our society.

Legislative Recommendations

THE COMMISSION ON OBSCENITY
AND PORNOGRAPHY

On the basis of its findings, the Commission makes the following legislative recommendations. The disagreements of particular Commissioners with aspects of the Commission's legislative recommendations are noted below, where the recommendations are discussed in detail. Commissioners Link, Hill, and Keating have filed a joint dissenting statement. In addition, Commissioners Keating and Link have submitted separate remarks. Commissioners Larsen and Wolfgang have filed statements explaining their dissent from certain Commission recommendations. A number of other Commissioners have filed short separate statements.[1]

In general outline, the Commission recommends that federal, state, and local legislation should not seek to interfere with the right of adults who wish to do so to read, obtain, or view explicit sexual materials.[2] On the other hand, we recommend legisla-tive regulations upon the sale of sexual materials to young persons who do not have the consent of their parents, and we also recommend legislation to protect persons from having sexual materials thrust upon them without their consent through the mails or through open public display.

The Commission's specific legislative recommendations and the reasons underlying these recommendations are as follows:

STATUTES RELATING TO ADULTS

The Commission recommends that federal, state, and local legislation prohibiting the sale, exhibition, or distribution of sexual materials to consenting adults should be repealed. Twelve of the 17 participating members[3] of the Commission join in this recom-

From *The Report of The Commission on Obscenity and Pornography*, U.S. Government Printing Office, Sept. 1970.

[1] Commissioners Joseph T. Klapper, Morris A. Lipton, G. William Jones, Edward D. Greenwood and Irving Lehrman.

[2] The term explicit sexual materials is used here and elsewhere in these recommendations to refer to the entire range of explicit sexual depictions or descriptions in books, magazines, photographs, films, statu-ary, and other media. It includes the most explicit depictions, or what is often referred to as "hard-core pornography." The term, however, refers only to sexual *materials*, and not to "live" sex shows, such as strip tease or on-stage sexual activity or simulated sexual activity. The Commission did not study this phenomenon in detail and makes no recommenda-tions in this area. See Preface to this Report.

[3] Commissioner Charles H. Keating, Jr., chose not to participate in the deliberation and formulation of any of the Commission's recommendations.

mendation.[4] Two additional Commissioners[5] subscribe to the bulk of the Commission's Report, but do not believe that the evidence presented at this time is sufficient to warrant the repeal of all prohibitions upon what adults may obtain. Three Commissioners dissent from the recommendation to repeal adult legislation and would retain existing laws prohibiting the dissemination of obscene materials to adults.[6]

The Commission believes that there is no warrant for continued governmental interference with the full freedom of adults to read, obtain or view whatever such material they wish. Our conclusion is based upon the following considerations:

1. Extensive empirical investigation, both by the Commission and by others, provides no evidence that exposure to or use of explicit sexual materials plays a significant role in the causation of social or individual harms such as crime, delinquency, sexual or nonsexual deviancy or severe emotional disturbances.[7] This research and its results are described in detail in the Report of the Effects Panel of the Commission and are summarized above in the Overview of Commission findings, p. 23. Empirical investigation thus supports the opinion of a substantial majority of persons professionally engaged in the treatment of deviancy, delinquency and antisocial behavior, that exposure to sexually explicit materials

has no harmful causal role in these areas.

Studies show that a number of factors, such as disorganized family relationships and unfavorable peer influences, are intimately related to harmful sexual behavior or adverse character development. Exposure to sexually explicit materials, however, cannot be counted as among these determinative factors. Despite the existence of widespread legal prohibitions upon the dissemination of such materials, exposure to them appears to be a usual and harmless part of the process of growing up in our society and a frequent and nondamaging occurrence among adults. Indeed, a few Commission studies indicate that a possible distinction between sexual offenders and other people, with regard to experience with explicit sexual materials, is that sex offenders have seen markedly *less* of such materials while maturing.

This is not to say that exposure to explicit sexual materials has no effect upon human behavior. A prominent effect of exposure to sexual materials is that persons tend to talk more about sex as a result of seeing such materials. In addition, many persons become temporarily sexually aroused upon viewing explicit sexual materials and the frequency of their sexual activity may, in consequence, increase for short periods. Such behavior, however, is the type of sexual activity already established as usual activity for the particular individual.

In sum, empirical research designed to clarify the question has found no evidence to date that exposure to explicit sexual materials plays a significant role in the causation of delinquent or criminal behavior among youth or adults.[8]

2. On the positive side, explicit sexual materials are sought as a source of entertainment and information by substantial numbers of American adults. At times, these materials also appear to serve to

[4] Commissioner Edward E. Elson joins in this recommendation only on the understanding that there will be prior enactment of legislation prohibiting the public display of offensive sexual materials both pictorial and verbal, that there will be prior enactment of legislation restricting the sales of explicit sexual materials to juveniles, and that there be prior public and governmental support for the Commission's nonlegislative recommendations before such repeal is enacted.

[5] Commissioners Irving Lehrman and Cathryn A. Spelts.

[6] Commissioners Morton A. Hill, S.J., Winfrey C. Link, and Thomas C. Lynch.

[7] See footnote 4 in the Overview of Effects.

[8] See footnote 4 in the Overview of Effects.

increase and facilitate constructive communication about sexual matters within marriage. The most frequent purchaser of explicit sexual materials is a college-educated, married male, in his thirties or forties, who is of above average socioeconomic status. Even where materials are legally available to them, young adults and older adolescents do not constitute an important portion of the purchasers of such materials.

3. Society's attempts to legislate for adults in the area of obscenity have not been successful. Present laws prohibiting the consensual sale or distribution of explicit sexual materials to adults are extremely unsatisfactory in their practical application. The Constitution permits material to be deemed "obscene" for adults only if, as a whole, it appeals to the "prurient" interest of the average person, is "patently offensive" in light of "community standards," and lacks "redeeming social values." These vague and highly subjective aesthetic, psychological and moral tests do not provide meaningful guidance for law enforcement officials, juries or courts. As a result, law is inconsistently and sometimes erroneously applied and the distinctions made by courts between prohibited and permissible materials often appear indefensible. Errors in the application of the law and uncertainty about its scope also cause interference with the communication of constitutionally protected materials.

4. Public opinion in America does not support the imposition of legal prohibitions upon the right of adults to read or see explicit sexual materials. While a minority of Americans favors such prohibitions, a majority of the American people presently are of the view that adults should be legally able to read or see explicit sexual materials if they wish to do so.

5. The lack of consensus among Americans concerning whether explicit sexual materials should be available to adults in our society, and the significant number of adults who wish to have access to such materials, pose serious problems regarding the enforcement of legal prohibitions upon adults, even aside from the vagueness and subjectivity of present law. Consistent enforcement of even the clearest prohibitions upon consensual adult exposure to explicit sexual materials would require the expenditure of considerable law enforcement resources. In the absence of a persuasive demonstration of damage flowing from consensual exposure to such materials, there seems no justification for thus adding to the overwhelming tasks already placed upon the law enforcement system. Inconsistent enforcement of prohibitions, on the other hand, invites discriminatory action based upon considerations not directly relevant to the policy of the law. The latter alternative also breeds public disrespect for the legal process.

6. The foregoing considerations take on added significance because of the fact that adult obscenity laws deal in the realm of speech and communication. Americans deeply value the right of each individual to determine for himself what books he wishes to read and what pictures or films he wishes to see. Our traditions of free speech and press also value and protect the right of writers, publishers, and booksellers to serve the diverse interests of the public. The spirit and letter of our Constitution tell us that government should not seek to interfere with these rights unless a clear threat of harm makes that course imperative. Moreover, the possibility of the misuse of general obscenity statutes prohibiting distributions of books and films to adults constitutes a continuing threat to the free communication of ideas among Americans—one of the most important foundations of our liberties.

7. In reaching its recommendation that government should not seek to prohibit consensual distributions of sexual ma-

terials to adults, the Commission discussed several arguments which are often advanced in support of such legislation. The Commission carefully considered the view that adult legislation should be retained in order to aid in the protection of young persons from exposure to explicit sexual materials. We do not believe that the objective of protecting youth may justifiably be achieved at the expense of denying adults materials of their choice. It seems to us wholly inappropriate to adjust the level of adult communication to that considered suitable for children. Indeed, the Supreme Court has unanimously held that adult legislation premised on this basis is a clearly unconstitutional interference with liberty.

8. There is no reason to suppose that elimination of governmental prohibitions upon the sexual materials which may be made available to adults would adversely affect the availability to the public of other books, magazines, and films. At the present time, a large range of very explicit textual and pictorial materials are available to adults without legal restrictions in many areas of the country. The size of this industry is small when compared with the overall industry in books, magazines, and motion pictures, and the business in explicit sexual materials is insignificant in comparison with other national economic enterprises. Nor is the business an especially profitable one; profit levels are, on the average, either normal as compared with other businesses or distinctly below average. The typical business entity is a relatively small entrepreneurial enterprise. The long-term consumer interest in such materials has remained relatively stable in the context of the economic growth of the nation generally, and of the media industries in particular.

9. The Commission has also taken cognizance of the concern of many people that the lawful distribution of explicit sexual materials to adults may have a deleterious effect upon the individual morality of American citizens and upon the moral climate in America as a whole. This concern appears to flow from a belief that exposure to explicit materials may cause moral confusion which, in turn, may induce antisocial or criminal behavior. As noted above, the Commission has found no evidence to support such a contention. Nor is there evidence that exposure to explicit sexual materials adversely affects character or moral attitudes regarding sex and sexual conduct.[9]

The concern about the effect of obscenity upon morality is also expressed as a concern about the impact of sexual materials upon American values and standards. Such values and standards are currently in a process of complex change, in both sexual and nonsexual areas. The open availability of increasingly explicit sexual materials is only one of these changes. The current flux in sexual values is related to a number of powerful influences, among which are the ready availability of effective methods of contraception, changes of the role of women in our society, and the increased education and mobility of our citizens. The availability of explicit sexual materials is, the Commission believes, not one of the important influences on sexual morality.

The Commission is of the view that it is exceedingly unwise for government to attempt to legislate individual moral values and standards independent of behavior, especially by restrictions upon consensual communication. This is certainly true in the absence of a clear mandate to do so, and our studies have revealed no such mandate in the area of obscenity.

The Commission recognizes and believes that the existence of sound moral standards is of vital importance to individuals and to society. To be effective and meaningful, however, these standards must be based upon deep personal commitment flowing from values instilled in the home, in educational

[9] See footnote 4 in the Overview of Effects.

and religious training, and through individual resolutions of personal confrontations with human experience. Governmental regulation of moral choice can deprive the individual of the responsibility for personal decision which is essential to the formation of genuine moral standards. Such regulation would also tend to establish an official moral orthodoxy, contrary to our most fundamental constitutional traditions.[10]

[10] Commissioner Thomas D. Gill has amplified his position with reference to this finding as follows: Legislation primarily motivated by an intent to establish or defend standards of public morality has not always been, as the Report of the Commission would have it, inappropriate, unsound, and contrary to "our most fundamental constitutional traditions."

In fact for at least 140 years after its adoption, the Constitution never appears to have been considered a barrier to the perpetuation of the belief held in the 13 original colonies that there was not only a right but a duty to codify in law the community's moral and social convictions. Granted homogeneous communities and granted the ensuing moral and social cohesiveness implied in such uniformity of interest the right of these solid and massive majorities to protect their own values by legislation they deemed appropriate went unchallenged so long as it did not impinge upon the individual's right to worship and speak as he pleased.

Only in the 20th century has an increasingly pluralistic society begun to question both the wisdom and the validity of encasing its moral and social convictions in legal armour, and properly so, for if all laws to be effective must carry into their implementation the approval of a majority, this is peculiarly and all importantly the case with laws addressed to standards of morality, which speedily become exercises in community hypocrisy if they do not embody the wishes and convictions of a truly dominant majority of the people.

The Commission's studies have established that on a national level no more than 35% of our people favor adult controls in the field of obscenity in the absence of some demonstrable social evil related to its presence and use.

The extensive survey of the prosecutorial offices of this country gives added affirmation of the principle that acceptable enforcement of obscenity legislation depends upon a solid undergirding of community support such as may be and is found in the smaller, more homogeneous communities, but is increasingly difficult to command in the largest urban areas where the divisiveness of life leads to splintered moral and social concepts. In effect this report tells us that where you have substantial community con-

Therefore, the Commission recommends the repeal of existing federal legislation which prohibits or interferes with consensual distribution of "obscene" materials to adults. These statutes are: 18 U.S.C. Section 1461, 1462, 1464, and 1465; 19 U.S.C. Section 1305; and 39 U.S.C. Section 3006.[11] The Commis-

cern you don't require the law, but lacking such concern, the law is a substitute of uncertain effectiveness.

If, then, legal rules controlling human conduct are designed to emphasize and reinforce society's moral convictions only in those areas where the pressures for transgression are the greatest and the resulting social consequences the most serious, there is a notable lack of justification for such intervention in the Commission's findings as to the magnitude of the public's concern and the efficacy of the enforcement of current obscenity laws. As has so often occurred, an approach which was both defendable and workable in one era has become vulnerable and suspect in another.

Fairness, however, requires that despite these formidable considerations something more be said and therein is to be found the primary reason for this individual statement. It is by no means certain that the Commission's national study, accurate as it has every reason to be in presenting a national consensus, has an equal validity in depicting the group thinking of a given geographical area, state, or community. It is believable, therefore, that notwithstanding the findings in the national reports, and quite consistent with them, there well may be found geographical pockets of homogeneous conviction, various regional, state, and local units where the requisite massive majority support essential for the legal codification of community standards does exist. My concurrence in the recommendation for the abolition of obscenity controls for consenting adults is not intended to express my disapproval of the right of any such group, so constituted, to challenge and attempt to override the substantial findings of law and fact which the Commission has determined to be persuasive in order to sustain their own deeply and widely held beliefs: a very considerable body of legislation in this country rests on just such a base of moral and social traditions.

It is a base, however, which is being undercut and eroded by the currents of the time and because this is so it may not now upon fair and objective examination be found to be of sufficient dimensions to sustain its burden.

[11] The broadcasting or telecasting of explicit sexual material has not constituted a serious problem in the past. There is, however, a potential in this area for thrusting sexually explicit materials upon unwilling

sion also recommends the repeal of existing state and local legislation which may similarly prohibit the consensual sale, exhibition, or the distribution of sexual materials to adults.

STATUTES RELATING TO YOUNG PERSONS

The Commission recommends the adoption by the States of legislation set forth in the Drafts of Proposed Statutes in Section III of this Part of the Commission's Report prohibiting the commercial distribution or display for sale of certain sexual materials to young persons. Similar legislation might also be adopted, where appropriate, by local governments and by the federal government for application in areas, such as the District of Columbia, where it has primary jurisdiction over distributional conduct.

The Commission's recommendation of juvenile legislation is joined in by 14 members of the Commission. Two of these[12] feel the legislation should be drawn so as to include appropriate descriptions identifying the material as being unlawful for sale to children. Three members disagree.[13] Other members of the Commission, who generally join in its recommendation for juvenile legislation, disagree with various detailed aspects of the Commission's legislative proposal.

These disagreements are noted in the following discussion.

The Commission's recommendation of juvenile legislation flows from these findings and considerations:

A primary basis for the Commission's recommendation for repeal of adult legislation is the fact that extensive empirical investigations do not indicate any causal relationship between exposure to or use of explicit sexual materials and such social or individual harms such as crime, delinquency, sexual or nonsexual deviancy, or severe emotional disturbances. The absence of empirical evidence supporting such a causal relationship also applies to the exposure of children to erotic materials. However, insufficient research is presently available on the effect of the exposure of children to sexually explicit materials to enable us to reach conclusions with the same degree of confidence as for adult exposure. Strong ethical feelings against experimentally exposing children to sexually explicit materials considerably reduced the possibility of gathering the necessary data and information regarding young persons.

In view of the limited amount of information concerning the effects of sexually explicit materials on children, other considerations have assumed primary importance in the Commission's deliberations. The Commission has been influenced, to a considerable degree, by its findings that a large majority of Americans believe that children should not be exposed to certain sexual materials. In addition, the Commission takes the view that parents should be free to make their own conclusions regarding the suitability of explicit sexual materials for their children and that it is appropriate for legislation to aid parents in controlling the access of their children to such materials during their formative years. The Commission recognizes that legislation cannot possibly isolate children from such materials entirely; it also recognizes that exposure of children to sexual materials may not only do no harm but may, in certain instances, actually facilitate much needed communication between parent and

persons. Existing federal statutes imposing criminal and civil penalties upon any broadcast of "obscene" material do not adequately address this problem because they do not describe with sufficient specificity what material would be prohibited, or under what conditions. Hence, the repeal of these statutes is recommended, upon the understanding that the Federal Communications Commission either already has, or can acquire through legislation, adequate power to promulgate and enforce specific rules in this area should the need arise.

[12] Commissioners Edward E. Elson and Winfrey C. Link.

[13] Commissioners Otto N. Larsen and Marvin E. Wolfgang disagree for reasons stated in their separate statement. Commissioner Morton A. Hill, S.J. disagrees for reasons stated in his separate statement.

child over sexual matters. The Commission is aware, as well, of the considerable danger of creating an unnatural attraction or an enhanced interest in certain materials by making them "forbidden fruit" for young persons. The Commission believes, however, that these considerations can and should be weighed by individual parents in determining their attitudes toward the exposure of their children to sexual materials, and that legislation should aid, rather than undermine such parental choice.

Taking account of the above considerations, the model juvenile legislation recommended by the Commission applies only to distributions to children made without parental consent. The recommended legislation applies only to commercial distributions and exhibitions; in the very few instances where noncommercial conduct in this area creates a problem, it can be dealt with under existing legal principles for the protection of young persons, such as prohibitions upon contributing to the delinquency of minors. The model legislation also prohibits displaying certain sexual materials for sale in a manner which permits children to view materials which cannot be sold to them. Two members of the Commission,[14] who recommend legislation prohibiting sales to juveniles, do not join in recommending this regulation upon display; one member of the Commission[15] recommends only this display provision, and does not recommend a special statute prohibiting sales to young persons.

The Commission, pursuant to Congressional direction, has given close attention to the definitions of prohibited material included in its recommended model legislation for young persons. A paramount consideration in the Commission's deliberations has been that definitions of prohibited materials be as specific and explicit as possible. Such specificity aids law enforcement and facilitates and encourages voluntary adherence to law on the part of retail dealers and exhibitors, while causing as little interference as possible with the proper distribution of materials to children and adults. The Commission's recommended legislation seeks to eliminate subjective definitional criteria insofar as that is possible and goes further in that regard than existing state legislation.

The Commission believes that only pictorial material should fall within prohibitions upon sale or commercial display to young persons. An attempt to define prohibited textual materials for young persons with the same degree of specificity as pictorial materials would, the Commission believes, not be advisable. Many worthwhile textual works, containing considerable value for young persons, treat sex in an explicit manner and are presently available to young persons. There appears to be no satisfactory way to distinguish, through a workable legal definition, between these works and those which may be deemed inappropriate by some persons for commercial distribution to young persons. As a result, the inclusion of textual material within juvenile legislative prohibitions would pose considerable risks for dealers and distributors in determining what books might legally be sold or displayed to young persons and would thus inhibit the entire distribution of verbal materials by those dealers who do not wish to expose themselves to such risks. The speculative risk of harm to juveniles from some textual material does not justify these dangers. The Commission believes, in addition, that parental concern over the material commercially available to children most often applies to pictorial matter.

The definition recommended by the Com-

[14] Commissioners Edward E. Elson and Freeman Lewis believe that segregating that material prohibited for sale to juveniles from that which is available to all would only enhance its appeal. Further, Commissioner Elson believes that juveniles would be protected from viewing sexually explicit materials if the Model Public Display Statute were extended to apply to those places technically private but public in the sense that they offer free and open access to all. Moreover, such an extension would significantly insulate the general public from such materials being thrust upon them without their consent.
[15] Commissioner Morton A. Hill, S.J. See his separate statement for his reasons.

mission for inclusion in juvenile legislation covers a range of explicit pictorial and three-dimensional depictions of sexual activity. It does not, however, apply to depictions of nudity alone, unless genital areas are exposed and emphasized. The definition is applicable only if the explicit pictorial material constitutes a dominant part of the work. An exception is provided for works of artistic or anthropological significance.

Seven Commissioners would include verbal materials within the definition of materials prohibited for sale to young persons.[16] They would, however, also include a broad exception for such textual materials when they bear literary, historical, scientific, educational, or other similar social value for young persons.

Because of changing standards as to what material, if any, is inappropriate for sale or display to children, the Commission's model statute contains a provision requiring legislative reconsideration of the need for, and scope of, such legislation at six-year intervals.

The model statute also exempts broadcast or telecast activity from its scope. Industry self-regulation in the past has resulted in little need for governmental intervention. If a need for governmental regulation should arise, the Commission believes that such regulations would be most appropriately prepared in this specialized area through the regulating power of the Federal Communications Commission, rather than through diverse state laws.

The Commission has not fixed upon a precise age limit for inclusion in its recommended juvenile legislation, believing that such a determination is most appropriately made by the States and localities which enact such provisions in light of local standards. All States now fix the age in juvenile obscenity statutes at under 17 or under 18 years. The recommended model statute also excludes married persons, whatever their age,

from the category of juveniles protected by the legislation.

The Commission considered the possibility of recommending the enactment of uniform federal legislation requiring a notice or label to be affixed to materials by their publishers, importers or manufacturers, when such materials fall within a definitional provision identical to that included within the recommended state or local model juvenile statute. Under such legislation, the required notice might be used by retail dealers and exhibitors, in jurisdictions which adopt the recommended juvenile legislation, as a guide to what material could not be sold or displayed to young persons. The Commission concluded, however, that such a federal notice or labelling provision would be unwise.[17] So long as definitional provisions are drafted to be as specific as possible, and especially if they include only pictorial material, the Commission believes that the establishment of a federal regulatory notice system is probably unnecessary; specific definitions of pictorial material, such as the Commission recommends, should themselves enable retail dealers and exhibitors to make accurate judgments regarding the status of particular magazines and films. The Commission is also extremely reluctant to recommend imposing any federal system for labelling reading or viewing matter on the basis of its quality or content. The precedent of such required labelling would pose a serious potential threat to First Amendment liberties in other areas of communication. Labels indicating sexual content might also be used artificially to enhance the appeal of certain materials. Two Commissioners[18] favor federally im-

---

[16] Commissioners Edward E. Elson, Thomas D. Gill, Joseph T. Klapper, Irving Lehrman, Winfrey C. Link, Thomas C. Lynch, and Cathryn A. Spelts.

[17] Commissioner Thomas D. Gill finds this conclusion acceptable at the present time, but if experience demonstrates that the effective enforcement of juvenile statutes which proscribe written as well as pictorial material is hampered by the problem of *scienter* he believes the labelling statute promises to be an appropriate method of correction and should be tried. Commissioners Irving Lehrman and Cathryn A. Spelts join in this footnote.

[18] Commissioners Edward E. Elson and Winfrey C. Link.

posed labelling in order to advise dealers as clearly and accurately as possible about what material is forbidden for sale to young persons, placing the responsibility for judging whether material falls within the statute on the publisher or producer who is completely aware of its contents and who is in a position to examine each item individually.

Finally, the Commission considered, but does not affirmatively recommend, the enactment by the federal government of juvenile legislation which would prohibit the sale of certain explicit materials to juveniles through the mails. Such federal legislation would, the Commission believes, be virtually unenforceable since the constitutional requirement of proving the defendant's guilty knowledge means that a prosecution could be successful only if proof were available that the vendor knew that the purchaser was a minor. Except in circumstances which have not been found to be prevalent, as where a sale might be solicited through a mailing list composed of young persons, mail order purchases are made without any knowledge by the vendor of the purchaser's age. Certificates of age by the purchaser would be futile as an enforcement device and to require notarized affidavits to make a purchase through the mails would unduly interfere with purchase by adults. The Commission has found, moreover, that at present juveniles rarely purchase sexually explicit materials through the mail, making federal legislative machinery in this area apparently unnecessary.

PUBLIC DISPLAY AND UNSOLICITED MAILING

The Commission recommends enactment of state and local legislation prohibiting public displays of sexually explicit pictorial materials, and approves in principle of the federal legislation, enacted as part of the 1970 Postal Reorganization Act, regarding the mailing of unsolicited advertisements of a sexually explicit nature. The Commission's recommendations in this area are based upon its finding, through its research, that certain explicit sexual materials are capable of causing considerable offense to numerous Americans when thrust upon them without their consent. The Commission believes that these unwanted intrusions upon individual sensibilities warrant legislative regulation and it further believes that such intrusions can be regulated effectively without any significant interference with consensual communication of sexual material among adults.

Public Display

The Commission's recommendations in the public display area have been formulated into a model state public display statute which is reproduced in the Drafts of Proposed Statutes in Section III of this Part of the Commission Report. Three Commissioners dissent from this recommendation.[19]

The model state statute recommended by the Commission (which would also be suitable for enactment in appropriate instances by local government units and by the federal government for areas where it has general legislative jurisdiction) prohibits the display of certain potentially offensive sexually explicit pictorial materials in places easily visible from public thoroughfares or the property of others.[20] Verbal materials are not

[19] Commissioners Otto N. Larsen, Freeman Lewis, and Marvin E. Wolfgang believe that a public display statute specifically aimed at erotic material is unnecessary. Very few jurisdictions have such a statute now. The execution of existing statutes and ordinances concerned with the projection of generally offensive objects, erotic or not, before the public provides all the spatial boundaries on public display of offensive erotica that is needed. Moreover, these three Commissioners believe that the offensiveness which may be caused by undesired exposure to sexual depictions is not so serious in scope or degree to warrant legislative response.

[20] Commissioners Edward E. Elson and Winfrey C. Link believe that the model display statute should be so extended as to apply to those places technically private but public in the sense that they offer free and open access to all. The statute would then cover, for example, retail stores, transportation terminals, and building lobbies. It would then prevent potentially offensive sexually explicit materials from being thrust upon the public unexpectedly at any time.

included within the recommended prohibition. There appears to be no satisfactory way to define "offensive" words in legislation in order to make the parameters of prohibition upon their display both clear and sufficiently limited so as not to endanger the communication of messages of serious social concern. In addition, the fact that there are few, if any, "dirty" words which do not already appear fairly often in conversation among many Americans and in some very widely distributed books and films indicates that such words are no longer capable of causing the very high degree of offense to a large number of persons which would justify legislative interference. Five Commissioners disagree[21] and would include verbal materials in the display prohibition because they believe certain words cause sufficient offense to warrant their inclusion in display prohibitions.

Telecasts are exempted from the coverage of the statute for the same reasons set forth above in connection with discussion of the Commission's recommendation of juvenile legislation.

The recommended model legislation defines in specific terms the explicit sexual pictorial materials which the Commission believes are capable of causing offense to a substantial number of persons. The definition covers a range of explicit pictorial and three-dimension depictions of sexual activity. It does not apply to depictions of nudity alone, unless genital areas are exposed and emphasized. An exception is provided for works of artistic or anthropological significance. The Commission emphasizes that this legislation does not prohibit the sale or advertisement of any materials, but does prohibit the public display of potentially offensive pictorial matter. While such displays have not been found by the Commission to be a serious problem at the present time, increasing commercial distribution of explicit materials to adults may cause considerable offense to others in the future unless specific regulations governing public displays are adopted.

Unsolicited Mailing

The Commission, with three dissents,[22] also approves of federal legislation to prevent unsolicited advertisements containing potentially offensive sexual material from being communicated through the mails to persons who do not wish to receive such advertisements. The Federal Anti-Pandering Act, which went into effect in 1968, imposes some regulation in this area, but it permits a mail recipient to protect himself against such mail only after he has received at least one such advertisement and it protects him only against mail emanating from that particular source. The Commission believes it more appropriate to permit mail recipients to protect themselves against all such unwanted mail advertisements from any source. Federal legislation in this area was enacted just prior to the date of this report as part of the 1970 Postal Reorganization Act. Public Law 91-375, 91st Cong., 2nd Sess., 39 U.S.C. Sections 3010-3011; 18 U.S.C. Sections 1735-1737.

The Commission considered two possible methods by which persons might be broadly insulated from unsolicited sexual advertisements which they do not wish to receive. One approach, contained in the 1970 Postal Reorganization Act, authorizes the Post

---

[21] Commissioners Edward E. Elson, Morton A. Hill, S. J., Winfrey C. Link, Thomas C. Lynch and Cathryn A. Spelts.

[22] Commissioners Otto N. Larsen and Marvin E. Wolfgang. See their separate statement. Commissioner Freeman Lewis dissents for two reasons: (1) that legislation restricting only the mailing of sexually oriented materials when so many other kinds of unsolicited mail also produce offense is bad public policy because it is too particular and too arbitrary; and (2) that the frequency of offense caused by unsolicited sexually oriented mail is demonstrably so minute that it does not warrant either the costs of the requisite machinery for operation and enforcement or the exorbitant expenses which would be forced upon this particular small category of mailers in order to comply. In his opinion, the most effective resolution of this problem is to employ the same technique commonly used for any other kinds of unwanted, unsolicited mail: throw it in the garbage pail.

Office to compile and maintain current lists of persons who have stated that they do not wish to receive certain defined materials, makes these lists available at cost to mailers of unsolicited advertisements, and prohibits sending the defined material to persons whose names appear on the Post Office lists. A second approach, described in detail in the Commission's Progress Report of July, 1969, would require all mailers of unsolicited advertisements falling within the statutory definition to place a label or code on the envelope. Mail patrons would then be authorized to direct local postal authorities not to deliver coded mail to their homes or offices.

In principle, the Commission favors the first of these approaches employed by Congress in the 1970 Postal Reorganization Act. The Commission takes this view because it believes that the primary burden of regulating the flow of potentially offensive unsolicited mail should appropriately fall upon the mailers of such materials and because of its reluctance to initiate required federal labelling of reading or viewing matter because of its sexual content. The Commission believes, however, that under current mail-order practices it may prove financially unfeasible for many smaller mailers to conform their mailing lists to those compiled by the Post Office. Use of computers to organize and search mailing lists will apparently be required by the new law; few, if any, small mailers utilize computers in this way today. If the current lists maintained by the Post Office came to contain a very large number of names—perhaps one million or more— even a computer search of these names, to discover any that were also present on a mailing list sought to be used by a mailer, might be prohibitively expensive. If such were the case, the Commission would believe the second possible approach to regulation to be more consistent with constitutional rights. This approach, however, might place serious burdens upon Post Office personnel. The Commission was not able to evaluate the practical significance of these burdens.

In considering the definition appropriate to legislation regulating unsolicited sexual advertisements, the Commission examined a large range of unsolicited material which has given rise to complaints to the Post Office Department in recent years. A definition was then formulated which quite specifically describes material which has been deemed offensive by substantial numbers of postal patrons. This definition is set forth in the footnote.[23] The Commission prefers this definitional provision to the less precise definitional provision in the 1970 Postal Reorganization Act.

DECLARATORY JUDGMENT LEGISLATION

The Commission recommends the enactment, in all jurisdictions which enact or retain provisions prohibiting the dissemination of sexual materials to adults or young persons, of legislation authorizing prosecutors to ob-

---

[23] Potentially offensive sexual advertisement means:

"(A) Any advertisement containing a pictorial representation or a detailed verbal description of uncovered human genitals or pubic areas, human sexual intercourse, masturbation, sodomy (*i.e.*, bestiality or oral or anal intercourse), direct physical stimulation of unclothed genitals or flagellation or torture in the context of a sexual relationship; or

"(B) Any advertisement containing a pictorial representation or detailed verbal description of an artificial human penis or vagina or device primarily designed physically to stimulate genitals;

"Provided that, material otherwise within the definition of this subsection shall not be deemed to be a potentially offensive sexual advertisement if it constitutes only a small and insignificant part of the whole of a single catalogue, book, or other work, the remainder of which does not primarily treat sexual matters and, *provided further*, that the Postmaster General shall, from time to time, issue regulations of general applicability exempting certain types of material, or material addressed to certain categories of addressees, such as advertisements for works of fine art or solicitations of a medical, scientific, or other similar nature addressed to a specialized audience, from the definition of potentially offensive sexual advertisement contained in this subsection, where the purpose of this section does not call for application of the requirements of this section."

tain declaratory judgments as to whether particular materials fall within existing legal prohibitions and appropriate injunctive relief. A model statute embodying this recommendation is presented in the Drafts of Proposed Statutes in Section III of this Part of the Commission Report. All but two[24] of the Commissioners concur in the substance of this recommendation. The Commission recognizes that the particular details governing the institution and appeal of declaratory judgment actions will necessarily vary from State to State depending upon local jurisdictional and procedural provisions. The Commission is about evenly divided with regard to whether local prosecutors should have authority to institute such actions directly, or whether the approval of an official with state-wide jurisdiction, such as the State Attorney General, should be required before an action for declaratory judgment is instituted.

A declaratory judgment procedure such as the Commission recommends would permit prosecutors to proceed civilly, rather than through criminal process, against suspected violations of obscenity prohibition. If such civil procedures are utilized, penalties would be imposed for violation of the law only with respect to conduct occurring after a civil declaration is obtained. The Commission believes this course of action to be appropriate whenever there is any existing doubt regarding the legal status of materials; where other alternatives are available, the criminal process should not ordinarily be invoked against persons who might have reasonably believed, in good faith, that the books or films they distributed were entitled to constitutional protection, for the threat of criminal sanctions might otherwise deter the free distribution of constitutionally protected material. The Commission's recommended legislation would not only make a declaratory judgment procedure available, but would require prosecutors to utilize this process instead of immediate criminal prosecution in all cases except those where the materials in issue are unquestionably within the applicable statutory definitional provisions.

Withdrawal of Appellate Jurisdiction

The Commission recommends against the adoption of any legislation which would limit or abolish the jurisdiction of the Supreme Court of the United States or of other federal judges and courts in obscenity cases. Two Commissioners[25] favor such legislation, one[26] deems it inappropriate for the Commission to take a position on this issue.

Proposals to limit federal judicial jurisdiction over obscenity cases arise from disagreement over resolution by federal judges of the question of obscenity in litigation. The Commission believes that these disagreements flow in largest measure from the vague and subjective character of the legal tests for obscenity utilized in the past; under existing legal definitions, courts are required to engage in subjective decision-making and their results may well be contrary to the subjective analyses of many citizens. Adoption of specific and explicit definitional provisions in prohibitory and regulatory legislation, as the Commission recommends, should eliminate most or all serious disagreements over the application of these definitions and thus eliminate the major source of concern which has motivated proposals to limit federal judicial jurisdiction.

More fundamentally, the Commission believes that it would be exceedingly unwise to adopt the suggested proposal from the point of view of protection of constitutional rights. The Commission believes that disagreements with court results in particular obscenity cases, even if these disagreements are soundly

[24] Commissioners Morton A. Hill, S.J. and Winfrey C. Link.

[25] Commissioners Morton A. Hill, S.J. and Winfrey C. Link.
[26] Commissioner Cathryn A. Spelts.

based in some instances, are not sufficiently important to justify tampering with existing judicial institutions which are often required to protect constitutional rights. Experience shows that while courts may sometimes reverse convictions on a questionable basis, juries and lower courts also on occasion find guilt in cases involving books and films which are entitled to constitutional protection, and state appeals courts often uphold such findings. These violations of First Amendment rights would go uncorrected if such decisions could not be reversed at a higher court level.

The Commission also recommends against the creation of a precedent in the obscenity area for the elimination by Congress of federal judicial jurisdiction in other areas whenever a vocal majority or minority of citizens disagrees strongly with the results of the exercise of that jurisdiction. Freedom in many vital areas frequently depends upon the ability of the judiciary to follow the Constitution rather than strong popular sentiment. The problem of obscenity, in the absence of any indication that sexual materials cause societal harm, is not an appropriate social phenomenon upon which to base a precedent for removing federal judicial jurisdiction to protect fundamental rights guaranteed by the Bill of Rights.

A Minority Statement in Response to the Report of the Commission on Obscenity and Pornography

MORTON A. HILL AND WINFREY C. LINK

The Commission's majority report is a Magna Carta for the pornographer.

It is slanted and biased in favor of protecting the business of obscenity and pornography, which the Commission was mandated by the Congress to regulate.

The Commission leadership and majority recommended that most existing legal barriers between society and pornography be pulled down. In so doing, the Commission goes far beyond its mandate and assumes the role of counsel for the filth merchant—a role not assigned by the Congress of the United States.

The Commission leadership and majority recommend repeal of obscenity law for "consenting adults." They go on, then, to recommend legislation for minors, public display and thrusting of pornography on persons through the mails.

The American people should be made aware of the fact that this is precisely the situation as it exists in Denmark today. The Commission, in short, is presumptuously recommending that the United States follow

Note: This is a portion of a statement by Hill and Link in response to the Report of the Commission on Obscenity and Pornography.

Denmark's lead in giving pornography free rein.

We feel impelled to issue this report in vigorous dissent.

The conclusions and recommendations in the majority report will be found deeply offensive to Congress and to tens of millions of Americans. And what the American people do not know is that the scanty and manipulated evidence contained within this report is wholly inadequate to support the conclusions and sustain the recommendations. Thus, both conclusions and recommendations are, in our view, fraudulent.

What the American people have here for the two million dollars voted by Congress, and paid by the taxpayer, is a shoddy piece of scholarship that will be quoted ad nauseam by cultural polluters and their attorneys within society.

The fundamental "finding" on which the entire report is based is: that "empirical research" has come up with "no reliable evidence to indicate that exposure to explicit sexual materials plays a significant role in the causation of delinquent or criminal behavior among youth or adults."

The inference from this statement, i.e.,

pornography is harmless, is not only insupportable on the slanted evidence presented; it is preposterous. How isolate one factor and say it causes or does not cause criminal behavior? How determine that one book or one film caused one man to commit rape or murder? A man's entire life goes into one criminal act. No one factor can be said to have caused that act.

The Commission has deliberately and carefully avoided coming to grips with the basic underlying issue. The government interest in regulating pornography has always related primarily to the prevention of moral corruption and *not* to prevention of overt criminal acts and conduct, or the protection of persons from being shocked and/or offended.

The basic question is whether and to what extent society may establish and maintain certain moral standards. If it is conceded that society has a legitimate concern in maintaining moral standards, it follows logically that government has a legitimate interest in at least attempting to protect such standards against any source which threatens them.

The Commission report simply ignores this issue, and regulates government's interest to little more than a footnote—passing it off with the extremist cliche that it is "unwise" for government to attempt to legislate morality. Obscenity law in no way legislates individual morality, but provides protection for public morality. The Supreme Court itself has never denied society's interest in maintaining moral standards, but has instead ruled for the protection of the "social interest in order and morality."

The Commission report ignores another basic issue: the phrase "utterly without redeeming social value." The language has been propagandized by extremists and profit-seekers, and it is so propagandized in this report as being the law of the land. It is not the law of the land, since no Supreme Court ever voiced such an opinion, yet this erroneous concept has been built into the statutes of several states as a result of extremists asserting that it is a necessary "test" enunci-

ated by the Supreme Court. This erroneous concept has led to a vast upsurge in the traffic in pornography in the past four years. The fact is, it is nothing more than an opinion of three judges, binding on no one, neither court nor legislature.

In sum, the conclusions and recommendations of the Commission majority represent the preconceived views of the Chairman and his appointed counsel that the Commission should arrive at those conclusions most compatible with the viewpoint of the American Civil Liberties Union. Both men single-mindedly steered the Commission to this objective.

In the interest of truth and understanding, it should be noted here that the policy of ACLU has been that obscenity is protected speech. Mr. Lockhart, the Chairman of the Commission, has long been a member of the American Civil Liberties Union. Mr. Bender, his general counsel, is an executive of the Philadelphia Civil Liberties Union.

The two million dollars voted by Congress have gone primarily to "scholars" who would return conclusions amenable to the extreme and minority views of Mr. Lockhart, Mr. Bender and the ACLU.

OUR POSITION

We stand in agreement with the Congress of the United States: the traffic in obscenity and pornography is a matter of national concern.

We believe that pornography has an eroding effect on society, on public morality, on respect for human worth, on attitudes toward family love, on culture.

We believe it is impossible, and totally unnecessary, to attempt to prove or disprove a cause-effect relationship between pornography and criminal behavior.

Sex education, recommended so strongly by the majority, is the panacea for those who advocate license in media. The report suggests sex education, with a plaint for the dearth of instructors and materials. It notes that three schools have used "hard-core pornography" in training potential instructors. The report does not answer the question that comes to mind immediately: Will these instructors not bring the hard-core pornography into the grammar schools? Many other questions are left unanswered: How assure that the instructor's moral or ethical code (or lack of same) will not be communicated to children? Shouldn't parents, not children, be the recipients of sex education courses?

Children cannot grow in love if they are trained with pornography. Pornography is loveless; it degrades the human being, reduces him to the level of animal. And if this Commission majority's recommendations are heeded, there will be a glut of pornography for teachers and children.

In contrast to the Commission report's amazing statement that public opinion in America does not support the imposition of legal prohibitions upon the consensual distribution of pornography to adults, we find, as a result of public hearings conducted by two of the undersigned in eight cities throughout the country, that the majority of the American people favor tighter controls. Twenty-six out of twenty-seven witnesses at the hearing in New York City expressed concern and asked for remedial measures. Witnesses were a cross section of the community, ranging from members of the judiciary to members of women's clubs. This pattern was repeated in the cities of New Orleans, Indianapolis, Chicago, Salt Lake City, San Francisco, Washington, D.C., and Buffalo. (And yet, one member of the Commission majority bases his entire position for legalization on the astounding "finding" of the Commission survey that "no more than 35% of our people favor adult controls in the field of obscenity in the absence of some demonstrable social evil related to its presence and use.")

Additionally, law enforcement officers testifying at the Hill-Link hearings were unanimous in declaring that the problem of obscenity and pornography is a serious one. They complained that law enforcement is hampered by the "utterly without redeeming social value" language. The Commission's own survey of prosecuting attorneys indicates that 73% of prosecutors polled said that "social value" is the most serious obstacle to prosecution. The decision not to prosecute is usually a manifestation of this obstacle. This figure and information is strangely missing from the report's "Overview of Findings.'"

We point also to the results of a Gallup poll, published in the summer of 1969. Eighty-five out of every 100 adults interviewed said they favored stricter state and local laws dealing with pornography sent through the mails, and 76 of every 100 wanted stricter laws on the sort of magazines and newspapers available on newsstands.

We believe government must legislate to regulate pornography, in order to protect the "social interest in order and morality."

SUMMARY AND CONCLUSIONS

1. The Commission on Obscenity and Pornography (majority report) is recommending major changes in laws and social policy in an area of controversy, public concern, and also in an area having health and welfare implications for adults and minors (e.g., remove all controls on pornography for adults and children—except in the latter case, pictorial materials).

    The basis for recommending these changes is that the Commission found no empirical scientific evidence showing a causal relationship between exposure to pornography and any kind of harm to minors or adults.

2. However, it should be stated that conclusively proving causal relationships among social science type variables is extremely difficult if not impossible.

Among adults whose life histories have included much exposure to pornography it is nearly impossible to disentangle the literally hundreds of causal threads or chains that contributed to their later adjustment or maladjustment. Because of the extreme complexity of the problem and the uniqueness of the human experience it is doubtful that we will ever have absolutely convincing scientific proof that pornography is or isn't harmful. And the issue isn't restricted to, "Does pornography cause or contribute to sex crimes?" The issue has to do with how pornography affects or influences the individual in his total relationship to members of the same as well as opposite sex, children and adults, with all of its ramifications.

The "burden of proof" or demonstration of no harm in a situation such as this is ordinarily considered to be on the shoulders of he who wishes to introduce change or innovation. It might be noted that in areas where health and welfare are at issue most government agencies take extremely conservative measures in their efforts to protect the public. In the case of monosodium glutamate which was recently removed from all baby food by government order, the evidence against it, in animal studies, was quite weak. However, because the remote possibility of harm existed, measures were immediately taken to protect children from consuming it.

3. The evidence the Commission presents does not clearly indicate "no harm." There are also many areas of "neglect" relative to the Commission's studies of pornography's effects (e.g., no longitudinal studies, no in-depth clinical studies, no porno-violence data, no studies in modeling or imitative learning, etc., etc.).

4. In the Commission's presentation of the scientific evidence there are frequent er-

rors and inaccuracies in their reporting of research results as well as in the basic studies themselves. Frequently, conclusions which are not warranted are drawn inappropriately from data. There is a frequent failure to distinguish or discriminate between studies which are badly flawed and weak and those of exceptional merit. But, most serious of all, data from a number of studies which show statistical linkages between high exposure to pornography and promiscuity, deviancy, affiliation with high criminality groups, etc. have gone unreported. This suggests a major bias in the reporting of results which raises a major issue of credibility of the entire report. Regardless of why it occurred, it suggests that, at the very least, a panel of independent scientists be called in to reevaluate the Commission research and the conclusions which might be validly drawn from it before any major changes occur in laws and social policy regarding pornography's control.

Legal "Findings" of Commission

We vigorously object to the word "findings" with regard to legal issues. Section IV of the majority report is an attempt to foist upon the people and upon the President and the Congress a philosophy of law which is misleading at best.

The section headed letter "C" states that the "prevailing view" in the Supreme Court is that to be classified as obscene an item must meet three—and all three—criteria. These criteria, the report claims, are: (1) the dominant theme of the material, taken as a whole, must appeal to the prurient interest of the average person; (2) the material must be patently offensive according to contemporary community standards; and (3) the material must lack redeeming social value.

This is a misinterpretation of the law, as counsel to the Commission must know, for he originally stated in his Legal Panel Report that *no majority of the U.S. Supreme Court* has ever accepted the proposition that "utterly without redeeming social value" is a "test" for obscenity. To say that an item may not be adjudged obscene if it does not meet all three of these criteria is false. It is exactly the promotion of this canard which has brought us to the deplorable state we are in today in this nation insofar as obscenity is concerned. *No Supreme Court opinion so holds.* In fact, the *Roth* case says the opposite. This is the only case where the Supreme Court gives us a definition of obscenity. The "utterly without redeeming social value" language is assumed to have been built into the *Roth* test by an opinion in the *Memoirs* (Fanny Hill) case of 1966.

However, this was the opinion only of three Justices: Brennan, Warren and Fortas. It was not the opinion of the Court, and so is not the law of the land. It is a three-Justice out of nine opinion, not binding on anyone. In 29 American Jurisprudence 2nd, at Section 195 of the topic "Courts," we find the following:

A decision by an equally divided court does not establish a precedent required to be followed under the stare decisis doctrine. And where the members of the court unanimously or by a majority vote reach a decision, but cannot even by a majority agree on the reason therefore, no point of law is established by the decision and it cannot be a precedent covered by the stare decisis rule.

The Supreme Court of the United States has said in 218 U.S. at 213 that unless a majority of the Supreme Court agrees on an opinion the case cannot become "an authority either in this or in inferior courts."

The *Roth* case gives us only the prurient interest test and this test has not been modified by *any* subsequent Supreme Court decision. In *Roth* the Court said, an item is obscene when to the average person, applying contemporary community standards, the dominant theme of the material taken as a whole appeals to the prurient interest.

This brings us to the Legal Panel Report, prepared by general counsel Bender and staff, with the apparent assistance of Mr. Lockhart, from which the "Legal Findings" section is drawn, and upon which legislative recommendations are based.

The Legal Panel Report should reflect the concepts of the Commission, their conclusions, their interpretations and analysis and their recommendations for legislative action. Instead, the Commission is asked to adhere to ideas, concepts, suggestions, analyses and recommendations prepared by staff members appointed by the Chairman and his general counsel, and reflecting their points of view.

This Bender-Lockhart Panel Report is misleading in many fundamental areas of the law, and so misleads the Commission, so as to cause those members, many of whom are unlearned in the law, to come to fundamentally erroneous conclusions of the state of the law.* We object specifically to the following misleading statements in the Bender-Lockhart Legal Panel Report:

1. "Unless there is a basis for finding that certain sexually explicit materials create such a danger [clear and present danger of significant social harm], therefore, general prohibitions upon the dissemination of 'obscene' speech would appear constitutionally invalid under ordinary principles." We are told on the next page that this analysis was rejected in *Roth* by the Supreme Court. Why then do they state it as a fact and ask the Commission to accept it?

2. Shortly after this, the Panel Report begins to take after the United States

* On September 10, as this dissent was going to press, Mr. Lockhart called Commissioner Gill and instructed him to make certain modifications in these statements so that the Legal Panel Report no longer reads the same as it did when the Commission was influenced by it to vote for the legalization of obscenity at their first meeting of August 11 & 12 and the final meeting of August 26 & 27.

Supreme Court decision in *Roth* and suggests that it is erroneous and should be reversed and in fact has in effect been reversed by the decision in *Stanley v. Georgia* in 1969. They discuss the meaning of *Stanley* vis-a-vis *Roth* as they interpret it and make the following statements:

(a) "Obscenity prohibitions were found constitutional in the *Roth* decision . . . without investigation into or conclusions regarding the actual social effect of the dissemination of obscene materials. It is the conclusion—that obscenity prohibitions regulating what even consenting adults may obtain may be upheld without any indication of social harm—that has been brought into question by . . . *Stanley*."

(b) "*Redrup* may be read as doubting whether *Roth* was actually still the law."

(c) "In *Stanley* . . . the Court threw greatly into doubt the continuing validity of the fundamental premise of the *Roth* case that the dissemination of 'obscene' materials may be prohibited without reference to First Amendment values, and suggested, instead, the strong constitutional significance of the question whether such materials are in fact socially harmful."

(d) "The question of the social effect of obscenity, which *Roth* had deemed irrelevant has assumed critical importance in *Stanley* 'in order to determine whether the state there had a valid regulatory interest sufficient to prohibit private possession of obscene materials.' The Court held in *Stanley* that it did not."

(e) "Prohibitions upon the commercial dissemination of obscenity to consenting adults may interfere with the right of adults to read or see what they wish in their own homes."

(f) "*Stanley* appears to have held that government may not rest prohibitions upon what consenting adults may read or view upon a desire to control their morality."

(g) "It further held that adult prohibitions premised upon a desire to prevent crime or anti-social behavior must, at least, rest upon a solid empirical foundation."

A Commission member, reading these statements and the continual "pounding" of *Stanley v. Georgia* at every opportunity throughout the rest of this panel report, would naturally assume that these statements are true and that *Roth* in some way has been overturned in a very fundamental manner by *Stanley v. Georgia*. But, as a matter of fact, *Roth* has not been overturned. It has been specifically confirmed in *Stanley* at 22 L. Ed. 2d 542, where the Court says:

Roth and the cases following that decision are not impaired by today's holding. As we have said, the states retain broad power to regulate obscenity; that power simply does not extend to mere possession by the individual in the privacy of his own home.

If the Bender-Lockhart Panel Report was intended to give the Commission an unbiased view of the state of the law, why was not the meaning of this phrase expounded? Since *Roth* is still the law of the land, then the following are the true facts (as stated in *Roth*):

(1) It is not necessary to prove that "obscene material will perceptively create a clear and present danger of antisocial conduct or will induce its recipients to such conduct."

(2) That the basis for federal and state proscription for obscenity is "the social interest in order and morality."

It is also to be noted that the Court said its decisions following *Roth* are not impaired.

Our conclusion in Roth . . . that the clear and present danger test was irrelevant to the determination of obscenity made it unnecessary . . . to consider the debate among the authorities whether exposure to pornography caused antisocial consequences."

The *Ginzburg* case was subsequent to *Roth*. Why was it not mentioned? Among other United States Supreme Court decisions subsequent to *Roth* that should have been mentioned are the following, all contradicting the Bender-Lockhart thesis that somehow *Stanley* has changed things:

(1) *Times Film* (1960)
(State has right to censor obscene motion pictures.)
(2) *Freeman v. Maryland* (1965)
(State may require prior submission of motion pictures to a Board of Censors.)
(3) *Ginzburg v. U.S.* (1966)
(State has a valid interest in preventing pandering to "the widespread weakness for titillation by pornography" books and magazines.)
(4) *Mishkin v. New York* (1966)
(State has interest in protecting homosexuals from obscenity.)
(5) *Interstate Circuit v. Dallas* (1968)
(Municipality may enact an ordinance regulating motion pictures for adults as well as children and censoring those obscene.)

Each of the statements made in (a), (b), (c), (e), (f) and (g) above in the Bender-Lockhart Report are incorrect when we look at *Stanley v. Georgia's* reaffirmation of *Roth* and cases thereafter. The statement made in (d) above is misleading that "private possession" is

permissible because it fails to complete the quotation "in the privacy of his home."

It would appear that for purposes of the Bender-Lockhart Panel Report, the "wish is father to the thought." They would like *Stanley v. Georgia* to say what they say it says but that desire is not borne out by the facts of that case.

It is quite clear that *Stanley v. Georgia* stands for a very narrow position and that is that a state may not convict a person of a crime "for mere possession of printed or filmed matter in the privacy of a person's *own home.*" 22 L. Ed. 2d 542. And again, at 22 L. Ed. 2d 551, "the right to be free from state inquiry into the contents of *his library.*" The state has no business "telling a man sitting alone *in his own house,* what books he may read or what films he may watch."

It could not be much clearer that this was the narrow proposition decided. The Court said it *four* times while specifically upholding *Roth* and all subsequent decisions.

3. The Bender-Lockhart Panel Report hits us with two phrases. One appears to be the invention of the authors in lieu of the use of the word "obscene" and that is the phrase "explicit sexual material." The other phrase is the catchword "consenting adults" which is a euphemism to express the authors' position that there are no restraints on "explicit sexual material" as long as "consenting adults" patronize it. Translated simply, it means "Legalize Obscenity for Adults" and the authors of this report should have so labeled it since this is the net effect of their suggestions. Nowhere is it explained that neither of these terms is used in any Supreme Court opinion, nor it is explained that this is the phrase used by those who would have the Court legalize the showing of "I Am Curious (Yellow)" in both Massachusetts and Maryland where it has been held obscene. In fact, there is an amaz-

ing parallel between the Bender-Lockhart Panel Report and the language used in the briefs for the distributors of that potion picture. Both sing the same tune. The Panel Report suggests that adults have "a right to obtain [explicit sexual materials] they wish to see." They cite no justification for setting up this false premise. Certainly *Stanley v. Georgia* never said it. They then proceed to state the motivations of the government in regulating "explicit sexual materials" (which we translate to "obscene"). They fail completely, however, to give the real reason which is the "social interest in order and morality." Having set up two false premises, they then proceed to obfuscate the true situation. There is a bald misstatement of the law when the Panel Report says:

In a series of cases subsequent to *Roth,* the Court made clear that where attempts were made to prohibit only specific distributional activities connected with sexual materials—and not to prevent consenting adults from obtaining material they wished to see— more inclusive definitional standards than that imposed in *Roth* would be permitted to be applied. The first case leading in this direction was *Ginzburg v. United States.* There the Court . . . permitted the conviction of the defendant to stand because he was found to have 'pandered' the materials in an offensive manner rather than merely to have sold them to persons who wished to obtain them. Thus the Court permitted a conviction which it would not have permitted had the defendant merely been engaged in neutral dissemination to consenting persons.

You would assume that Mr. Bender and staff, who ought to know, have told the Commission members what the *Ginzburg* case held. Nothing could be further from the truth. As they ought to know, this is *not* what *Ginzburg* held, since:

(a)   The term "consenting adults" is

nowhere used or implied in that case.

(b)   The Court did not say anything about *Ginzburg* not having "merely sold them to persons who wished to obtain them." It didn't mention that at all.

(c)   The implication that the case stands for the right to receive "obscenity" by consenting adults is misplaced. The Court said in *Ginzburg* that the materials *were not* "obscene in the abstract."

4.   The Bender-Lockhart Panel Report suggests that "some of" the federal mailing statute may be unconstitutional under *Stanley.* This is another nonsequitur. The mailing statute has nothing to do with invading a man's home.

5.   The implication on page 13 that there is something in *Redrup* which proves a theory that "consenting adults" have a right to receive obscenity is also misplaced. *Redrup* found the materials not to be obscene.

6.   On page 16, the Bender-Lockhart Panel Report states that: "*Stanley v. Georgia,* if given full effect, would mean . . . that the individual's right to see materials of his own choice may only be overcome where there is a substantial social basis for government regulation. As a result, many applications of general prohibitions may no longer be permissible. The *Roth* standard for determining the 'obscene' retains potential validity only in those areas where *Stanley* permits general prohibitions to apply."

Now, if this problem were not so important to our country, the immediate reaction to such a non-sequitur from *Stanley v. Georgia* would be to shrug it off as ridiculous. There is absolutely nothing in *Stanley* to warrant this misinformation.

"*Roth* is supreme," says *Stanley*—not the other way around. *Stanley* cannot be exploited or expanded to help the pornographers in this fashion.

7. Eventually, the Legal Panel Report abandons the position that *Fanny Hill* has modified the *Roth* test and engages in the business of counting Justices who have adopted the "patently offensive" test. Four of these six Justices are no longer on the Court so this maneuver fails. The footnote reference to Black and Douglas also fails since they have never enunciated this standard. The reference to Stewart and Harlan refers to federal cases only. The reference to the American Law Institute standard is misleading since that Institute never used the phrase "patently offensive."

8. Again, the Panel Report abandons its original claim that the *Roth* test included an "utterly without redeeming social value" element, and now tries to give new dignity to the opinion of three Justices (two of whom, if we use his technique, we should note are no longer on the Court) by calling it a plurality opinion. As we point out in our discussion of *Fanny Hill,* under the decisions of the United States Supreme Court, an opinion of three Justices is no precedent, does not establish the law and does not bind either the United States Supreme Court or "any inferior court."

9. The Legal Panel Report finally admits that *Memoirs* "utterly without redeeming social value" "test" is not a test at all, not having been adopted by a majority, but they suggest that it is nice to incorporate the same in statutes because Black and Douglas are on the bench and this is two strikes against you. They state, "So long as at least three other Justices employ the three-part test," no application of a general prohibition which does not employ this test will be upheld on appeal. What kind of specious reasoning is this? The Bender-Lockhart Legal Panel Report seems so intent on keeping this unnecessary language in our statutes (which contradicts *Roth*—see our comments under

Memoirs case) that they employ the scare tactics that you only need two more people against you and you lose. Is this what our statutes should be based on in this vital area? Is this what this Commission was formed for, "to estimate percentages"? Fortas and Warren are gone, leaving only Brennan who adheres to this pernicious concept. Presumably then, eight out of nine Justices will adhere to *Roth,* which rejects this so-called test and says that once it is obscene by the *Roth* test (which has no social value language), then it is proscribable. But this is not our function. We are to interpret *Roth* honestly and give the country an honest definition of obscenity. Such a definition does not include the "Brennan" so-called "test." It is to be noted that the Legal Panel Report does not quote the recent decisions in Maryland, Massachusetts and Arizona that say that there is no "social value" test in *Roth* (see our comments in Appendix under *Fanny Hill*) nor do they say that New York is proposing repeal of this part of their statute (see our remarks under *Fanny Hill*).

10. The Bender-Lockhart Panel Report states that the Supreme Court believes that the *Roth* standard does not permit a finding of obscenity to be made under a prohibition of what consenting adults may obtain with regard to a large class of pictorial material. Again we note that there is no opinion of the Supreme Court that supports this statement that somehow "consenting adults" are a separate class under the *Roth* standard. That phrase is not used in any Supreme Court opinion.

Conclusions

We submit: That the Commission majority has not carried out the mandates of Congress.

We submit: That its legislative recommendations should be excluded from consideration by the Congress and States, since they are not responsive to the mandate of Congress to regulate the traffic in pornography. It is irrelevant legislation and deserves condemnation as inimical to the welfare of the United States, its citizens and its children.

We submit: That the purpose of the Commission's report is to legalize pornography.

In the pursuit of the mandates of the Congress, and in compliance therewith we have made a review of the law and the decisions of the United States Supreme Court and have analyzed the same in detail. This review is attached as Appendix I. In the light of that review and comment thereunder, and in view of our other mandates, we make the following recommendations.

Recommendations

1. RECOMMENDED TEST OR DEFINITION OF OBSCENITY

A thing is "obscene" if, by contemporary community standards, and considered as a whole, its predominant appeal is to the prurient interest. As a matter of public policy, anything which is obscene by this definition shall be conclusively deemed to be utterly without redeeming social importance. Any slight social value in such obscenity shall be deemed outweighed by the social interest in order and morality.

"Prurient interest" is defined as a shameful or morbid interest in nudity, sex or excretion which goes substantially beyond customary limits of candor in description or representation of such matters. If it appears from the character of the material or the circumstances of its dissemination that the subject matter is designed for, or directed to, a specially susceptible audience, the subject matter shall be judged with reference to such audience. When the subject matter is distributed or exhibited to minors who have not attained their 18th birthday, the subject matter shall be judged with reference to an average person in the community of the actual age of the minor to whom such material is distributed or exhibited. In all other cases, the subject matter shall be judged with reference to the average person in the community.

Comment. This formulation is taken from the *Roth* case which is the only case in which the Supreme Court defined obscenity and the *Ginzburg* case, in which the Supreme Court accepts the concept of variable obscenity as it applies to minors. It rejects the suggestion of three of the nine Justices that "utterly without redeeming social value" is a test for obscenity, since the Supreme Court has never adopted this suggestion. In fact, it is this unnecessary "test" that has caused the flood of hardcore pornography in motion pictures, books, magazines and other publications.

A complete review of the lack of constitutional necessity for this so-called "test" is found in Appendix I in our comments under the *Memoirs* (*Fanhy Hill*) case.

The *Roth* test, it is claimed by some, is subjective. Upon examination, however, it is plain that the individual juror is not instructed to apply his subjective concept of what is obscene, but to determine something objective, *viz.* "the prurient interest of the average person." This is very similar to what juries are called upon to do in negligence cases where the juror is asked to determine if a person used that degree of care that a "reasonably prudent man" would use. This determination has never been thought to be subjective nor too impractical or difficult to apply. We have confidence in the ability of the Anglo-Saxon jury system to determine obscenity if properly instructed. (See Judge's charge in *Roth* case Appendix 1.)

Our recommendations are squarely based on the concept that the State has, as the Supreme Court says, a right to enact obscenity legislation based on the "social interest in morality." There is a distinction that should be made between individual morality and the level of general morality which the state needs to protect.

A person's beliefs and practices depend on what he relies on for an authority as to what is right and best. As children grow up, they come under various authorities' influences: parents, relatives, friends, teachers, writers, actors, celebrities, clergymen and a host of others. They are also influenced in various ways by other forces of good and evil.

At every point in life a person has a certain moral character. It is the sum total of what he then believes and practices in the area of right and wrong. This overall moral character is constantly changing under the interplay of the aforementioned influences. Thus if a person accepts higher standards, his moral character improves; if he accepts lower standards, his moral character deteriorates.

Not only does every individual reflect a certain moral character, but so does every group of individuals, a club, a city, a state, or even a nation—*the essence of which is determined by a general consensus of individual standards*. It is, stated another way, the distillation of all the individual moralities or the *level* of morality generally. It is this level, this distillation, this average, this essence, which the state has an interest in protecting. The state protects this level from falling and creates an atmosphere by which it can rise. The obvious morals protected are chastity, modesty, temperance, and self-sacrificing love. The obvious evils being inhibited are lust, excess, adultery, incest, homosexuality, bestiality, masturbation and fornication.

A discussion of the background of the other aspects of this definition may be found in our comment on the Model State Obscenity Statute in Appendix II.

2. RECOMMENDED FEDERAL LEGISLATION

We recommend:

(a) That the United States Codes Sections 1461, 1462, 1463, 1464, 1465, of Title 18, and Section 1305 of Title 19, and Section 4006 of Title 39 be amended to define "obscene" in accordance with our recommended definition of obscenity mentioned above.

(b) That so much of our recommended Model State Statute, found in Appendix II, which is suitable for incorporation in these federal statutes be therein incorporated.

(c) We recommend that Congress note that Section 4009 of Title 39, Prohibiting of Pandering Advertisements in the Mails, was specifically upheld by the U.S. Supreme Court in *Rowan v. U.S.*, decided May 4, 1970. This statute, it should be noted, gave a parent the right to require, also, that the mailer stop sending mail to "any of his minor children who have not attained their nineteenth birthday, and who reside with the addressee."

While the decision did not turn on this specific point, it is nevertheless an indication that the Supreme Court will accept at least an age 18, and possibly 19 or older, as a division line between minor and adult in the obscenity field. Certainly under 16 is too low.

(d) We have reviewed anti-obscenity legislation now before Congress which we believe will help, effectively and constitutionally, to regulate obscenity. This review is attached as Appendix III.

(e) We recommend legislation or a Presidential Directive establishing a Division, in the Office of the Attorney General of the United States, under the direction of a Deputy Attorney General of the United States, under lawyers ready and able to assist District

Attorneys throughout the nation in prosecutions against sex exploiters. We have personal knowledge of the fact that district attorneys generally are desperately in need of this type of assistance. The urgent necessity for the same was enunciated in March of 1965 by the presiding Judge of Franklin County, Pa., Judge Chauncey M. Depuy, when he said:

"Whenever a prosecution for obscenity occurs in a county, the well-heeled purveyors of smut act with lightning alacrity to provide high-priced counsel for the defendant. Legal smut specialists are called into the county from the nationwide staff. These professionals soon place the local district attorney's staff, unacquainted with a highly specialized field of law, at a great disadvantage. The average district attorney or assistant is no match for these well-experienced 'pros' who move from county to county and state to state. . . . There is no hope for government to serve the interest of the general citizen in managing this flood of pornography unless a massive effort is made at the Department of Justice level. An effective mechanism must be devised, on a permanent basis, as a division of the department, having . . . highly skilled lawyers ready to be loaned at any time . . . to assist the district attorney in connection with any prosecution against the sex exploiters."

It should be noted that if it is believed that such a mechanism could not be set up on the federal level without enabling legislation, such legislation could be based on the Commerce clause, since most obscenity is transported interstate or imported. A model could be found in language used in the Civil Rights Act of 1964.

(f)   We recommend the establishment, by Federal legislation, of a National Crime Research and Reference Library on the Law of Obscenity. The Library

will be unique, since the Librarian of Congress has indicated that after diligent search, "no reference to any special law library in this area has been found, and . . . such a library would be unique and unduplicated as a single collection."

The purpose of the library will be to service prosecutors nationwide to expedite preparation of cases. It will be available also to the judiciary, behavioral scientists, clergymen, writers and other professionals who can contribute to the effort to stem the flow of obscene material. The district attorneys of New York City are of the unanimous opinion that such a library will prove invaluable to law enforcement agencies. It will contain everything written on the law of obscenity: statutes, ordinances, decided cases, texts, commentaries, etc. It will also contain a section on medical, psychiatric and psychological research relative to obscenity. Law enforcement officials believe that the convenience of finding all precedents, statutes, briefs, etc. in one location will save countless hours in case preparation.

3. RECOMMENDED STATE LEGISLATION

(a)   *Model State Obscenity Statute* Attached to this Report as Appendix II is our recommended Model State Obscenity Statute based on the concept of variable obscenity and taking into consideration all U.S. Supreme Court cases. We believe it is a constitutionally effective statute that will effectively regulate the traffic in obscenity. The suggested statute is explained and annotated in the Appendix.

(b)   We also recommend to the States that they establish, by legislation, a Board of Film Review which would require—

under carefully prescribed rules based on Supreme Court decisions discussed in Appendix I—the submission of all motion pictures for licensing prior to their exhibition. This proposed statute is taken from Maryland Statutes Article 66A which has been revised to comply with *Freeman v. Maryland,* a Supreme Court decision. In our opinion it will withstand constitutional attack. A copy of this proposed Model Statute on Film Review is attached as Appendix IV.

(c) In addition, we suggest that some States might desire to permit local ordinances for the establishment of Film Review Boards, generally, or for the purpose of establishing classification of films as suitable or unsuitable for minors under 18. Such States should enact legislation confirming the existing right of municipalities to adopt such legislation, and permitting them to apply for injunctive relief in the courts; and requiring a prompt judicial determination of the issue. A suggested statute to be used as a model is Section 418A, again of the State of Maryland, found in Appendix V. It should be used as a supplement to any State statute or local ordinance on Film Review or classification. This model should be modified where used in aid of local ordinances to permit the Chief Legal Officer of the municipality, or the Film Review or Classification Board, to apply also for an injunction in the case of motion pictures.

(d) We recommend the employment of the injunctive remedy, found in 22a of the New York Statute or 418A of the Maryland Statute, to supplement the Model State Statute generally. This is a most effective weapon sanctioned by the decisions of the U.S. Supreme Court, and will reach all types of obscenity. See Appendix V.

(e) We recommend that the Attorney General's Office be required to review for possible prosecution any type of suspected obscenity distributed or about

to be distributed, of which he gains knowledge, and which falls into any of the descriptive categories listed below:

(1) The Stag Film
(2) The Sexploitation Film
(3) The Commercial X-rated Film
(4) The Commercial Unrated Film
(5) Advertisements for X and Unrated Films
(6) Underground Sex Publications
(7) Underground Newspapers
(8) Mimeographed Underground Newspapers
(9) Sensational Tabloids
(10) Homosexual Magazines
(11) Sex-violence Magazines
(12) "Spreader" or "Tunnel" Magazines
(13) Teenage Sex Magazines
(14) Pseudo-scientific Sex Publications
(15) So-called Nudist Magazines
(16) Lyrics on Commercially Distributed Rock Records
(17) Sex-action Photographs
(18) Sex-action Records
(19) Sex-action Slides and Tapes
(20) Mail Order Advertisements for the Above
(21) Paperbacks with Themes of Homosexuality, Sado-masochism, Incest, Bestiality
(22) Hardcover Books Devoted to Homosexuality, Sado-masochism, Incest

(f) We advocate the establishment in the office of the Attorney General of each State, a team of one or more skilled attorneys, under the direction of a Deputy Attorney General, to be used to assist in the local prosecutions where intrastate commerce is involved or where federal assistance from the Department of Justice is not readily available.

(g) We advocate the establishment in State Police headquarters of a similar division, working closely with the legal staff just mentioned. The state police have experts in arson, ballistics and other specialties. The formation of a special unit on pornography is long overdue.

(h) We advocate the establishment of a permanent State Commission to examine the laws on obscenity, to make recommendations to the legislature, and recommendations for more effective means of enforcement. A suggested statute is attached in Appendix VI, and is modeled on a statute of the State of Illinois, approved September 6, 1967.

(i) We recommend the establishment of a State Commission to review and classify motion pictures and printed materials for minors. A suggested statute in this respect, based on our review of *Bantam Books v. Sullivan,* is attached as Appendix VII.

(j) As minimum legislation, we advocate elimination of the phrase "utterly without redeeming social value" in any State statute. A suggested statute is attached as Appendix VIII.

4. RECOMMENDED LOCAL ORDINANCES

(a) We recommend a review of existing ordinances in the light of our review of U.S. Supreme Court decisions in Appendix I, and the modifying or amending of same to comply therewith, including the elimination of the phrase "utterly without redeeming social value" whenever found.

(b) We recommend the adoption of local ordinances (wherever the State has not adopted a Film Review Statute) to review motion pictures—based on Maryland Statute recommended above.

(c) On an optional basis, or as part of general ordinance on motion picture review, we recommend a Film Review and Classification Ordinance for minors. The suggested ordinance, attached as Appendix IX, is taken from the recently enacted ordinance in Jersey City and is liberally designed to meet Supreme Court requirements.

(d) We recommend an ordinance designed to protect minors from being exposed, on the highway or street, to drive-in movie scenes of motion pictures that are unsuitable for children. The suggested Ordinance attached as Appendix X has been approved by the United State Court of Appeals for the Fifth Circuit in the case of *Chemline Ind. v. City of Grand Prairie,* decided August 8, 1966, 364 F 2d. 721.

(e) We recommend a local ordinance to penalize the showing of obscene motion pictures, and to penalize the licensee found guilty. See Appendix XII, based on a second ordinance upheld in *Chemline* case above, containing pure *Roth* test.

5. RECOMMENDED PRIVATE ACTION BY THE PUBLIC

(a) We recommend that private citizens join with or form private, nonsectarian, community organizations that take organized but constitutional action against obscenity.

(b) We recommend citizens bring official legal complaints whenever evidence of obscenity comes to their attention.

(c) We recommend that citizens continually urge their municipal, State and federal officials to prosecute obscenity cases. Here, again, this is best accomplished in an organized manner, working through an existing community organization.

Pornography, Obscenity and the Case for Censorship

IRVING KRISTOL

Being frustrated is disagreeable, but the real disasters in life begin when you get what you want. For almost a century now, a great many intelligent, well-meaning and articulate people—of a kind generally called liberal or intellectual, or both—have argued eloquently against any kind of censorship of art and/or entertainment. And within the past 10 years, the courts and the legislatures of most Western nations have found these arguments persuasive—so persuasive that hardly a man is now alive who clearly remembers what the answers to these arguments were. Today, in the United States and other democracies, censorship has to all intents and purposes ceased to exist.

Is there a sense of triumphant exhilaration in the land? Hardly. There is, on the contrary, a rapidly growing unease and disquiet. Somehow, things have not worked out as they were supposed to, and many notable civil libertarians have gone on record as saying this was not what they meant at all. They wanted a world in which *Desire Under the Elms* could be produced, or *Ulysses* pub-

Note: Irving Kristol, "Pornography, Obscenity and the Case for Censorship," *New York Times Magazine,* March 1971. Copyright © by Irving Kristol. Reprinted with permission.

lished, without interference by philistine busybodies holding public office. They have got that, of course; but they have also got a world in which homosexual rape takes place on the stage, in which the public flocks during lunch hours to witness varieties of professional fornication, in which Times Square has become little more than a hideous market for the sale and distribution of printed filth that panders to all known (and some fanciful) sexual perversions.

But disagreeable as this may be, does it really matter? Might not our unease and disquiet be merely a cultural hangover—a "hangup," as they say? What reason is there to think that anyone was ever corrupted by a book?

This last question, oddly enough, is asked by the very same people who seem convinced that advertisements in magazines or displays of violence on television do indeed have the power to corrupt. It is also asked, incredibly enough and in all sincerity, by people—e.g., university professors and school teachers—whose very lives provide all the answers one could want. After all, if you believe that no one was ever corrupted by a book, you have also to believe that no one was ever improved by a book (or a play or a movie). You have to believe, in other words, that all art is morally trivial and that, consequently, all education is morally irrelevant. No one, not even a university professor, really believes that.

To be sure, it is extremely difficult, as social scientists tell us, to trace the effects of any single book (or play or movie) on an individual reader or any class of readers. But we all know, and social scientists know it too, that the ways in which we use our minds and imaginations do shape our characters and help define us as persons. That those who certainly know this are nevertheless moved to deny it merely indicates how a dogmatic resistance to the idea of censorship can—like most dogmatism—result in a mindless insistence on the absurd.

I have used these harsh terms—"dogmatism" and "mindless"—advisedly. I might also have added "hypocritical." For the plain fact is that none of us is a complete civil libertarian. We all believe that there is some point at which the public authorities ought to step in to limit the "self expression" of an individual or a group, even where this might be seriously intended as a form of artistic expression, and even where the artistic transaction is between consenting adults. A playwright or theatrical director might, in this crazy world of ours, find someone willing to commit suicide on the stage, as called for by the script. We would not allow that—any more than we would permit scenes of real physical torture on the stage, even if the victim were a willing masochist. And I know of no one, no matter how free in spirit, who argues that we ought to permit gladiatorial contests in Yankee Stadium, similar to those once performed in the Colosseum at Rome—even if only consenting adults were involved.

The basic point that emerges is one that Prof. Walter Berns has powerfully argued: no society can be utterly indifferent to the ways its citizens publicly entertain themselves.[1] Bearbaiting and cockfighting are

prohibited only in part out of compassion for the suffering animals; the main reason they were abolished was because it was felt that they debased and brutalized the citizenry who flocked to witness such spectacles. And the question we face with regard to pornography and obscenity is whether, now that they have such strong legal protection from the Supreme Court, they can or will brutalize and debase our citizenry. We are, after all, not dealing with one passing incident—one book, or one play, or one movie. We are dealing with a general tendency that is suffusing our entire culture.

I say pornography *and* obscenity because, though they have different dictionary definitions and are frequently distinguishable as "artistic" genres, they are nevertheless in the end identical in effect. Pornography is not objectionable simply because it arouses sexual desire or lust or prurience in the mind of the reader or spectator; this is a silly Victorian notion. A great many non-pornographic works—including some parts of the Bible—excite sexual desire very successfully. What is distinctive about pornography is that, in the words of D. H. Lawrence, it attempts "to do dirt on [sex] . . . [It is an] insult to a vital human relationship."

In other words, pornography differs from erotic art in that its whole purpose is to treat human beings obscenely, to deprive human beings of their specifically human dimension. That is what obscenity is all about. It is light years removed from any kind of carefree sensuality—there is no continuum between Fielding's *Tom Jones* and the Marquis de Sade's *Justice*. These works have quite opposite intentions. To quote Susan Sontag: "What pornographic literature does is precisely to drive a wedge between one's existence as a full human being and one's existence as a sexual being—while in ordinary life a healthy person is one who prevents such a gap from opening up." This definition occurs in an essay *defending* pornography— Miss Sontag is a candid as well as gifted critic—so the definition, which I accept, is neither tendentious nor censorious.

Along these same lines, one can point

[1] This is as good a place as any to express my profound indebtedness to Walter Berns's superb essay, "Pornography vs. Democracy," in the winter, 1971, issue of *The Public Interest.*

out—as C. S. Lewis pointed out some years back—that it is no accident that in the history of all literatures obscene words—the so-called "four-letter words"—have always been the vocabulary of farce or vituperation. The reason is clear; they reduce men and women to some of their mere bodily functions—they reduce man to his animal component, and such a reduction is an essential purpose of farce or vituperation.

Similarly, Lewis also suggested that it is not an accident that we have no offhand, colloquial, neutral terms—not in any Western European language at any rate—for our most private parts. The words we do use are (a) nursery terms, (b) archaisms, (c) scientific terms or (d) a term from the gutter (i.e., a demeaning term). Here I think the genius of language is telling us something important about man. It is telling us that man is an animal with a difference: he has a unique sense of privacy, and a unique capacity for shame when this privacy is violated. Our "private parts" are indeed private, and not merely because convention prescribes it. This particular convention is indigenous to the human race. In practically all primitive tribes, men and women cover their private parts; and in practically all primitive tribes, men and women do not copulate in public.

It may well be that Western society, in the latter half of the 20th century, is experiencing a drastic change in sexual mores and sexual relationships. We have had many such "sexual revolutions" in the past—and the bourgeois family and bourgeois ideas of sexual propriety were themselves established in the course of a revolution against 18th century "licentiousness"—and we shall doubtless have others in the future. It is, however, highly improbable (to put it mildly) that what we are witnessing is the Final Revolution which will make sexual relations utterly unproblematic, permit us to dispense with any kind of ordered relationships between the sexes, and allow us freely to redefine the human condition. And so long as humanity has not reached that utopia, obscenity will remain a problem.

One of the reasons it will remain a problem is that obscenity is not merely about sex, any more than science fiction is about science. Science fiction, as every student of the genre knows, is a peculiar vision of power: what it is really about is politics. And obscenity is a peculiar vision of humanity: what it is really about is ethics and metaphysics.

Imagine a man—a well-known man, much in the public eye—in a hospital ward, dying an agonizing death. He is not in control of his bodily functions, so that his bladder and his bowels empty themselves of their own accord. His consciousness is overwhelmed and extinguished by pain, so that he cannot communicate with us, nor we with him. Now, it would be, technically, the easiest thing in the world to put a television camera in his hospital room and let the whole world witness this spectacle. We don't do it—at least we don't do it as yet—because we regard this as an *obscene* invasion of privacy. And what would make the spectacle obscene is that we would be witnessing the extinguishing of humanity in a human animal.

Incidentally, in the past our humanitarian crusaders against capital punishment understood this point very well. The abolitionist literature goes into great physical detail about what happens to a man when he is hanged or electrocuted or gassed. And their argument was—and is—that what happens is shockingly obscene, and that no civilized society should be responsible for perpetrating such obscenities, particularly since in the nature of the case there must be spectators to ascertain that this horror was indeed being perpetrated in fulfillment of the law.

Sex—like death—is an activity that is both animal and human. There are human sentiments and human ideals involved in this animal activity. But when sex is public, the viewer does not see—cannot see—the sentiments and the ideals. He can only see the animal coupling. And that is why, when men and women make love, as we say, they prefer to be alone—because it is only when you are alone that you can make love, as distinct from merely copulating in an animal and casual way. And that, too, is why those who are voyeurs, if they are not irredeemably sick, also feel ashamed at what they are witnessing. When sex is a public spectacle, a human relationship has been debased into a mere animal connection.

It is also worth noting that this making of sex into an obscenity is not a mutual and equal transaction, but is rather an act of exploitation by one of the partners—the male partner. I do not wish to get into the complicated question as to what, if any, are the essential differences—as distinct from conventional and cultural differences—between male and female. I do not claim to know the answer to that. But I do know—and I take it as a sign which has meaning—that pornography is, and always has been, a man's work; that women rarely write pornography; and that women tend to be indifferent consumers of pornography.[2] My own guess, by way of explanation, is that a woman's sexual experience is ordinarily more suffused with human emotion than is man's, that men are more easily satisfied with autoerotic activities, and that men can therefore more easily take a more "technocratic" view of sex and its pleasures. Perhaps this is not correct. But whatever the explanation, there can be no question that pornography is a form of "sexism," as the Women's Liberation Movement calls it, and that the instinct of Women's Lib has been unerring in perceiving that, when pornography is perpetrated, it is perpetrated against them, as part of a conspiracy to deprive them of their full humanity.

But even if all this is granted, it might be said—and doubtless will be said—that I really ought not to be unduly concerned. Free competition in the cultural marketplace—it is argued by people who have never otherwise had a kind word to say for laissez-faire—

will automatically dispose of the problem. The present fad for pornography and obscenity, it will be asserted, is just that, a fad. It will spend itself in the course of time; people will get bored with it, will be able to take it or leave it alone in a casual way, in a "mature way," and, in sum, I am being unnecessarily distressed about the whole business. The New York Times, in an editorial, concludes hopefully in this vein.

"In the end . . . the insensate pursuit of the urge to shock, carried from one excess to a more abysmal one, is bound to achieve its own antidote in total boredom. When there is no lower depth to descend to, ennui will erase the problem."

I would like to be able to go along with this line of reasoning, but I cannot. I think it is false, and for two reasons, the first psychological, the second political.

The basic psychological fact about pornography and obscenity is that it appeals to and provokes a kind of sexual regression. The sexual pleasure one gets from pornography and obscenity is autoerotic and infantile; put bluntly, it is a masturbatory exercise of the imagination, when it is not masturbation pure and simple. Now, people who masturbate do not get bored with masturbation, just as sadists don't get bored with sadism, and voyeurs don't get bored with voyeurism.

In other words, infantile sexuality is not only a permanent temptation for the adolescent or even the adult—it can quite easily become a permanent, self-reinforcing neurosis. It is because of an awareness of this possibility of regression toward the infantile condition, a regression which is always open to us, that all the codes of sexual conduct ever devised by the human race take such a dim view of autoerotic activities and try to discourage autoerotic fantasies. Masturbation is indeed a perfectly natural autoerotic activity, as so many sexologists blandly assure us today. And it is precisely because it is so perfectly natural that it can be so dangerous to the mature or maturing person, if it is not controlled or sublimated in

[2] There are, of course, a few exceptions—but of a kind that prove the rule. *L'Histoire d'O*, for instance, written by a woman, is unquestionably the most *melancholy* work of pornography ever written. And its theme is precisely the dehumanization accomplished by obscenity.

some way. That is the true meaning of Portnoy's complaint. Portnoy, you will recall, grows up to be a man who is incapable of having an adult sexual relationship with a woman; his sexuality remains fixed in an infantile mode, the prison of his autoerotic fantasies. Inevitably, Portnoy comes to think, in a perfectly *infantile* way, that it was all his mother's fault.

It is true that, in our time, some quite brilliant minds have come to the conclusion that a reversion to infantile sexuality is the ultimate mission and secret destiny of the human race. I am thinking in particular of Normon O. Brown, for whose writings I have the deepest respect. One of the reasons I respect them so deeply is that Mr. Brown is a serious thinker who is unafraid to face up to the radical consequences of his radical theories. Thus, Mr. Brown knows and says that for his kind of salvation to be achieved, humanity must annul the civilization it has created—not merely the civilization we have today, but all civilization—so as to be able to make the long descent backwards into animal innocence.

What is at stake is civilization and humanity, nothing less. The idea that "everything is permitted," as Nietzsche put it, rests on the premise of nihilism and has nihilistic implications. I will not pretend that the case against nihilism and for civilization is an easy one to make. We are here confronting the most fundamental of philosophical questions, on the deepest levels. But that is precisely my point—that the matter of pornography and obscenity is not a trivial one, and that only superficial minds can take a bland and untroubled view of it.

In this connection, I might also point out those who are primarily against censorship on liberal grounds tell us not to take pornography or obscenity seriously, while those who are for pornography and obscenity, on radical grounds, take it very seriously indeed. I believe the radicals—writers like Susan Sontag, Herbert Marcuse, Norman O. Brown, and even Jerry Rubin—are right, and the liberals are wrong. I also believe that those young radicals at Berkeley, some five years

ago, who provoked a major confrontation over the public use of obscene words, showed a brilliant political instinct. Once the faculty and administration had capitulated on this issue—saying: "Oh, for God's sake, let's be adult: what difference does it make anyway?" —once they said that, they were bound to lose on every other issue. And once Mark Rudd could publicly ascribe to the president of Columbia a notoriously obscene relationship to his mother, without provoking any kind of reaction, the S.D.S. had already won the day. The occupation of Columbia's buildings merely ratified their victory. Men who show themselves unwilling to defend civilization against nihilism are not going to be either resolute or effective in defending the university against anything.

I am already touching upon a political aspect of pornography when I suggest that it is inherently and purposefully subversive of civilization and its institutions. But there is another and more specifically political aspect, which has to do with the relationship of pornography and/or obscenity to democracy, and especially to the quality of public life on which democratic government ultimately rests.

Though the phrase, "the quality of life," trips easily from so many lips these days, it tends to be one of those cliches with many trivial meanings and no large, serious one. Sometimes it merely refers to such externals as the enjoyment of cleaner air, cleaner water, cleaner streets. At other times it refers to the merely private enjoyment of music, painting or literature. Rarely does it have anything to do with the way the citizen in a democracy views himself—his obligations, his intentions, his ultimate self-definition.

Instead, what I would call the "managerial" conception of democracy is the predominant opinion among political scientists, sociologists and economists, and has, through the untiring efforts of these scholars, become the conventional journalistic opinion as well. The root idea behind this "managerial" conception is that democracy is a "political system" (as they say) which can be adequately defined in terms of—can be fully reduced to—its mechanical arrangements. Democracy is then seen as a set of rules and procedures, and *nothing but* a set of rules and procedures, whereby majority rule and minority rights are reconciled into a state of equilibrium. If everyone follows these rules and procedures, then a democracy is in working order. I think this is a fair description of the democratic idea that currently prevails in academia. One can also fairly say that it is now the liberal idea of democracy par excellence.

I cannot help but feel that there is something ridiculous about being this kind of a democrat, and I must further confess to having a sneaking sympathy for those of our young radicals who also find it ridiculous. The absurdity is the absurdity of idolatry— of taking the symbolic for the real, the means for the end. The purpose of democracy cannot possibly be the endless functioning of its own political machinery. The purpose of any political regime is to achieve some version of the good life and the good society. It is not at all difficult to imagine a perfectly functioning democracy which answers all questions except one—namely, why should anyone of intelligence and spirit care a fig for it?

There is, however, an older idea of democracy—one which was fairly common until about the beginning of this century—for which the conception of the quality of public life is absolutely crucial. This idea starts from the proposition that democracy is a form of self-government, and that if you want it to be a meritorious polity, you have to care about what kind of people govern it. Indeed, it puts the matter more strongly and declares that, if you want self-government, you are only entitled to it if that "self" is worthy of governing. There is no inherent right to self-government if it means that such government is vicious, mean, squalid and debased. Only a dogmatist and a fanatic, an idolator of democratic machinery, could approve of self-government under such conditions.

And because the desirability of self-gov-

ernment depends on the character of the people who govern, the older idea of democracy was very solicitous of the condition of this character. It was solicitous of the individual self, and felt an obligation to educate it into what used to be called "republican virtue." And it was solicitous of that collective self which we call public opinion and which, in a democracy, governs us collectively. Perhaps in some respects it was nervously over-solicitous—that would not be surprising. But the main thing is that it cared, cared not merely about the machinery of democracy but about the quality of life that this machinery might generate.

And because it cared, this older idea of democracy had no problem in principle with pornography and/or obscenity. It censored them—and it did so with a perfect clarity of mind and a perfectly clear conscience. It was not about to permit people capriciously to corrupt themselves. Or, to put it more precisely: in this version of democracy, the people took some care not to let themselves be governed by the more infantile and irrational parts of themselves.

I have, it may be noticed, uttered that dreadful word, "censorship." And I am not about to back away from it. If you think pornography and/or obscenity is a serious problem, you have to be for censorship. I'll go even further and say that if you want to prevent pornography and/or obscenity from becoming a problem, you have to be for censorship. And lest there be any misunderstanding as to what I am saying, I'll put it as bluntly as possible: if you care for the quality of life in our American democracy, then you have to be for censorship.

But can a liberal be for censorship? Unless one assumes that being a liberal *must* mean being indifferent to the quality of American life, then the answer has to be: yes, a liberal can be for censorship—but he ought to favor a liberal form of censorship.

Is that a contradiction in terms? I don't think so. We have no problem in contrasting *repressive* laws governing alcohol and drugs and tobacco with laws *regulating* (i.e., discouraging the sale of) alcohol and drugs and tobacco. Laws encouraging temperance are not the same thing as laws that have as their goal prohibition or abolition. We have not made the smoking of cigarettes a criminal offense. We have, however, and with good liberal conscience, prohibited cigarette advertising on television, and may yet, again with good liberal conscience, prohibit it in newspapers and magazines. The idea of restricting individual freedom, in a liberal way, is not at all unfamiliar to us.

I therefore see no reason why we should not be able to distinguish repressive censorship from liberal censorship of the written and spoken word. In Britain, until a few years ago, you could perform almost any play you wished—but certain plays, judged to be obscene, had to be performed in private theatrical clubs which were deemed to have a "serious" interest in theater. In the U.S., all of us who grew up using public libraries are familiar with the circumstances under which certain books could be circulated only to adults, while still other books had to be read in the library reading room, under the librarian's skeptical eye. In both cases, a small minority that was willing to make a serious effort to see an obscene play or read an obscene book could do so. But the impact of obscenity was circumscribed and the quality of public life was only marginally affected.[3]

I am not saying it is easy in practice to sustain a distinction between liberal and repressive censorship, especially in the public realm of a democracy, where popular opinion is so vulnerable to demogoguery. Moreover, an acceptable system of liberal censorship is likely to be exceedingly difficult to devise in the United States today, because our

educated classes, upon whose judgment a liberal censorship must rest, are so convinced that there is no such thing as a problem of obscenity, or even that there is no such thing as obscenity at all. But, to counterbalance this, there is the further, fortunate truth that the tolerable margin for error is quite large, and single mistakes or single injustices are not all that important.

This possibility, of course, occasions much distress among artists and academics. It is a fact, one that cannot and should not be denied, that any system of censorship is bound, upon occasion, to treat unjustly a particular work of art—to find pornography where there is only gentle eroticism, to find obscenity where none really exists, or to find both where its existence ought to be tolerated because it serves a larger moral purpose. Though most works of art are not obscene, and though most obscenity has nothing to do with art, there are some few works of art that are, at least in part, pornographic and/or obscene. There are also some few works of art that are in the special category of the comic-ironic "bawdy" (Boccaccio, Rabelais). It is such works of art that are likely to suffer at the hands of the censor. That is the price one has to be prepared to pay for censorship—even liberal censorship.

But just how high is this price? If you believe, as so many artists seem to believe today, that art is the only sacrosanct activity in our profane and vulgar world—that any man who designates himself an artist thereby acquires a sacred office—then obviously censorship is an intolerable form of sacrilege. But for those of us who do not subscribe to this religion of art, the costs of censorship do not seem so high at all.

If you look at the history of American or English literature, there is precious little damage you can point to as a consequence of the censorship that prevailed throughout most of that history. Very few works of literature—of real literary merit, I mean—ever were suppressed; and those that were, were not suppressed for long. Nor have I noticed, now that censorship of the written word has

---

[3] It is fairly predictable that some one is going to object that this point of view is "elitist"—that, under a system of liberal censorship, the rich will have privileged access to pornography and obscenity. Yes, of course they will—just as, at present, the rich have privileged access to heroin if they want it. But one would have to be an egalitarian maniac to object to this state of affairs on the grounds of equality.

to all intents and purposes ceased in this country, that hitherto suppressed or repressed masterpieces are flooding the market. Yes, we can now read *Fanny Hill* and the Marquis de Sade. Or, to be more exact, we can now openly purchase them, since many people were able to read them even though they were publicly banned, which is as it should be under a liberal censorship. So how much have literature and the arts gained from the fact that we can all now buy them over the counter, that, indeed, we are all now encouraged to buy them over the counter? They have not gained much that I can see.

And one might also ask a question that is almost never raised: how much has literature lost from the fact that everything is now permitted? It has lost quite a bit, I should say. In a free market, Gresham's Law can work for books or theater as efficiently as it does for coinage—driving out the good, establishing the debased. The cultural market in the United States today is being preempted by dirty books, dirty movies, dirty theater. A pornographic novel has a far better chance of being published today than a non-pornographic one, and quite a few pretty good novels are not being published at all simply because they are not pornographic, and are therefore less likely to sell. Our cultural condition has not improved as a result of the new freedom. American cultural life wasn't much to brag about 20 years ago; today one feels ashamed for it.

Just one last point which I dare not leave untouched. If we start censoring pornography or obscenity, shall we not inevitably end up censoring political opinion? A lot of people seem to think this would be the case—which only shows the power of doctrinaire thinking over reality. We had censorship of pornography and obscenity for 150 years, until almost yesterday and I am not aware that freedom of opinion in this country was in any way diminished as a consequence of this fact. Fortunately for those of us who are liberal, freedom is not indivisible. If it were, the case for liberalism would be indistinguishable from the case for anarchy; and they are two very different things.

But I must repeat and emphasize: what kind of laws we pass governing pornography and obscenity, what kind of censorship—or, since we are still a Federal nation—what kinds of censorship we institute in our various localities may indeed be difficult matters to cope with; nevertheless the real issue is one of principle. I myself subscribe to a liberal view of the enforcement problem: I think that pornography should be illegal *and* available to anyone who wants it so badly as to make a pretty strenuous effort to get it. We have lived with under-the-counter pornography for centuries now, in a fairly comfortable way. But the issue of principle, of whether it should be over or under the counter, has to be settled before we can reflect on the advantages and disadvantages of alternative modes of censorship. I think the settlement we are living under now, in which obscenity and democracy are regarded as equals, is wrong; I believe it is inherently unstable; I think it will, in the long run, be incompatible with any authentic concern for the quality of life in our democracy.

On the Sociology of Pornography

NED POLSKY

Samuel Johnson once informed James Boswell that he could recite a complete chapter of a book called *The Natural History of Iceland.* The chapter was entitled "Concerning Snakes," and consisted in its entirety of the following: "There are no snakes to be met with throughout the whole island." I can be similarly brief concerning studies on the sociology of pornography: there are no such studies to be met with throughout the whole of sociology.

What we do have, first of all, is an abundance of offhand "sociologizing" about pornography, on the part of contemporary journalists, cultural historians, psychiatrists, literary critics, lawyers, and judges—especially if they are of liberal inclination and don't like censorship. This material isn't worth much. In fact its chief interest for sociologists, as I shall elaborate below, is that the sociological interpretations most often found in it are demonstrably wrong.

Secondly, we have some published data on consumers of pornography and their social backgrounds. The best material of this sort, as on most matters sexual, comes (as you

might expect) from the Institute for Sex Research.[1]

Thirdly, we have a particular sociological theory—I would call it a theory of the upper-middle range—that was not developed to explain the place of pornography in society but nevertheless serves, I think, to explain that place very well.

There are many special aspects of the sociology of pornography, and in what follows I shall not even mention most of them, much less pursue them. Instead, I shall try to spell out how that theory of the upper-middle range gives a sociological overview of pornography within which more specialized investigations might proceed.

In his study of prostitution Kingsley Davis demonstrated, with cogent reasoning and much evidence that I cannot rehearse here, the following main argument: (a) the goals of sexual behavior in man are not inherently social; but (b) societies need to hook sexuality onto social ends, particularly the ends

[1] Cf. Alfred Kinsey, Wardell Pomeroy, and Clyde Martin, *Sexual Behavior in the Human Male* (Philadelphia: W. B. Saunders, 1948), pp. 363, 510; and Kinsey, Pomeroy, Martin, and Paul Gebhard, *Sexual Behavior in the Human Female* (Philadelphia: W. B. Saunders, 1953), pp. 652–72. N. B. that most Kinsey findings on male use of pornography are presented in the volume on females, along with comparative data on females.

of bearing and raising children, by restricting the morally legitimate expression of sex to the institution of the family; and (c) this conflict between sexual inclinations and social requirements is ameliorated by prostitution, which helps to maintain the family as an institution by acting as a safety-valve for the expression of antisocial coitus—i.e., impersonal, transitory, nonfamilial coitus—that cannot be fully suppressed.[2] Davis thus sees the family and prostitution as complementary institutions, each requisite to the other.

I suggest that Davis's theory applies, *mutatis mutandis,* to pornography. Prostitution and pornography occur in every society large enough to have a reasonably complex division of labor; and although pornography develops in only a rudimentary way in preliterate societies (by means of erotic folktales and simple pictorial or sculptural devices), whenever a society has a fair degree of literacy and mass-communication technology then pornography becomes a major functional alternative to prostitution.

In saying that prostitution and pornography are, at least in modern societies, functional alternatives, I mean that they are different roads to the same desired social end. Both provide for the discharge of what society labels anti-social sex, i.e., impersonal, nonmarital sex: prostitution provides this via real intercourse with a real sex object, and pornography provides it via masturbatory, imagined intercourse with a fantasy object.

Although societies use both alternatives, the degree to which one is used in preference to the other seems to vary considerably from one society to the next, in ways and for reasons that remain to be investigated. There is also variation within a given society, of at least two kinds: First, there is variation in what is considered appropriate in different social situations; for example, a group of adolescent boys might collectively visit a prostitute but masturbate to pornography only singly and in private, with group contemplation of pornography serving merely to convey sex information or as the occasion for ribald humor. A second kind of variation has to do with what is considered appropriate in different subcultures. The main such variation in our own society, revealed by the Kinsey data, is that masturbating to pornographic books or pictures is largely a phenomenon of the better-educated classes; at the lower levels of our society, this is generally put down (as is long-term masturbation *per se*), and, conversely, prostitutes are visited much more often.

Prostitution, as Davis noted, presents a great paradox of social life: on the one hand it is so nearly a cultural universal[3] that it seems to fill a need endemic to complex societies, but on the other hand the prostitute is, except in very special circumstances, generally and highly stigmatized. Davis's theory resolves the paradox, and does so in a way that applies equally to pornography: both prostitutes and pornographers are stigmatized because they provide for the socially illegitimate expression of sex, yet their very existence helps to make tolerable the institutionalizing of legitimate sex in the family.

An additional relation between the functioning and the stigmatizing of prostitutes and pornographers, a relation at once more general and more intimate than that given by Davis, may be inferred from the neo-

---

[2] Cf. Kingsley Davis, "Prostitution," in Robert Merton and Robert Nisbet (Eds.), *Contemporary Social Problems* (New York: Harcourt, Brace & World, 1961), pp. 262–88.

[3] [*Addendum, 1968:* Mario Bick has pointed out to me that prostitution and pornography are not fully cross-cultural phenomena, and that Davis and I have been misled simply because these occur in various Eastern societies (such as China, Japan, India) as well as Western ones. Mr. Bick notes that (a) all the examples we can cite are from long-time monetary economies, and (b) in non-monetary, polygynous societies such as those of Africa, prostitution appears to be unknown before European contact and/or urbanization, and erotic depictions do not have the pornographic function they have in monetary economies.]

Durkheimian theory of deviance recently proposed by Kai Erikson. He observes:

> The only material found in a system for marking [moral] boundaries is the behavior of its participants; and the kinds of behavior which best perform this function are often deviant. . . . In this sense, transactions between deviant persons and agencies of social control are boundary-maintaining mechanisms. . . . Each time the group censures some act of deviation it sharpens the authority of the violated norm. . . . [Instances of publicity about deviants, as in the old public parading of them or in the modern newspaper] constitute our main source of information about the normative contours of society.[4]

In Erikson's view, then, one function of prostitutes and pornographers would lie precisely *in* the fact that they are stigmatized.

The use of pornography is by no means limited to its role as an adjunct to masturbation. For example, as already indicated, pornography may sometimes serve rather as a sex instruction manual. (Conversely, a sex instruction manual may serve as pornography.) And sometimes pornography, far from stimulating masturbation, may be used to stimulate real intercourse, as in, say, the case of whorehouse murals from Pompeii to the present. Granted all that, and other uses as well, people given to using pornography do so for the most part as a means of facilitating masturbation. This is the primary use of pornography. It is summed up in the classic definition of pornographic books as "the books that one reads with one hand."

The consumption of pornography is a sort of halfway house between sexual intercourse and erotic response to purely private mental fantasies. Masturbation to pornography is more "social" than masturbation simply to inner pictures, i.e., pornography offers the masturbator erotic imagery that is external to himself, a quasi-real "other" to whom he can more "realistically" respond. That is why even lower-class males fre-

quently use pornography for masturbatory release—and here the Kinsey findings need qualification—when they are deprived of their usual sexual outlets: people in prisons are overwhelmingly from the lower class, and the masturbatory use of pornography is widespread in prisons and a continual headache for any prison administrator who wants to make it one.[5] Sociologists, however, in their fascination with the way prisoners turn toward homosexuality, seem to have neglected the prisoners' turn toward pornography.

As my reference to jailhouse pornography implies, a great deal of pornography exists unpublished, in the form of manuscript writing or drawing. Even outside the prison context, an enormous number—perhaps even the majority—of pornographic works are in manuscript.[6] The important thing to realize about such manuscripts is that mostly they are produced neither for publication nor for circulation as manuscripts, but for self-enjoyment. Here we have a major difference between prostitution and pornography: hardly any man can, as it were, be his own prostitute (although many try, by attempting auto-fellation),[7] but every man can be his own pornographer. Even a good deal of published pornography was written initially to aid the masturbation of the writer. For example, Jean Genet indicates that this was why he wrote *Our Lady of the Flowers*.[8] And

[4] Kai Erikson, "Notes on the Sociology of Deviance," *Social Problems,* Vol. 9 (Spring, 1962) , pp. 307–14.

[5] Cf. Charles Smith, "Prison Pornography," *Journal of Social Therapy,* Vol. 1 (1955), pp. 126–29, and Stanley B. Zuckerman, "Sex Literature in Prison," *ibid.,* pp. 129–31. I cite these articles merely to document the widespread prison use of pornography.

[6] This seems to be the implication of a statement about quantities made in the Kinsey volume on females, *op. cit.,* p. 672. See also Wladimir Eliasberg, "Remarks on the Psychopathology of Pornography," *Journal of Criminal Psychopathology,* Vol. 3 (1942), pp. 715–20, although on other points, as note 20 below may indicate, Eliasberg is unreliable.

[7] Kinsey *et al.* report in their volume on males, *op. cit.,* p. 510, that "a considerable portion" of males attempt auto-fellation, at least in early adolescence, but that it is anatomically impossible for all except two or three males in a thousand.

[8] Cf. Jean Genet, *Our Lady of the Flowers* (New York: Bantam Books, 1964) , e.g., pp. 59–61.

it is apparently to this motivation that we owe the pornography produced by the most noted pornographer of them all, the Marquis de Sade. Here is a letter from Sade to his wife written from prison in 1783—a date, note well, that is several years after Sade had begun writing non-pornographic works but before he had written any pornography:

> I'll bet you thought you had a brilliant idea in imposing a revolting abstinence on me with regard to the sins of the flesh. Well, you were mistaken. You brought my brain to the boiling point. You caused me to conjure up fanciful creatures which I shall have to bring into being.

Over the years that followed, most of them spent in jail, Sade devoted himself to setting down those fanciful creatures on paper. As Albert Camus put it, Sade "created a fiction in order to give himself the illusion of being."[9]

Of course Genet and Sade wrote most of their pornography while in prison. But especially when it comes to sexuality, society imprisons everyone in a number of ways; that is the starting point of Kingsley Davis's argument and mine—and also and originally and profoundly, though Davis is silent on the matter, of Sigmund Freud's. Let us now consider one of those ways—and here my point of departure is Freud rather than Davis—that seems especially germane to our subject.

Prostitution and pornography, as we have seen, allow the expression of antisocial sex— impersonal, transitory, non-familial sex. But both institutions also provide for antisocial sex in another, deeper sense—one that is merely mentioned in passing by Kingsley Davis but is nevertheless a key function of prostitution as well as pornography: these institutions permit "polymorphous perverse" and other sexual behaviors so highly stigmatized as to be labeled deviant even within the institution of marriage and morally inhibited from expression therein.

[9] I take the Sade and Camus quotations from Georges May, "Fiction Reader, Novel Writer," *Yale French Studies*, No. 35, "Sade" (December, 1965), p. 7.

In other words, sex is socialized by being placed in a double constraint—the marital relationship on the one hand and a specified selection of possible sex acts on the other. It is important to see that the function of prostitution and pornography in alleviating the latter constraint is clearly distinct from their providing merely for coitus *per se* (real or imaginary) in an impersonal and transitory relationship.

No real house of prostitution has perhaps approached the logically ultimate one depicted in Genet's play *The Balcony*, where each client buys a custom-made social scene that conforms in all particulars to any wishful sexual fantasy he chooses to select. But many such houses, as well as freelance prostitutes, have specialized in catering to customers who wanted to indulge in sadism, masochism, orgies, intercourse with children, anal or oral intercourse, voyeurism, intercourse with the aid of mechanical contraptions, fetishism, and so on. Among one city's documented examples that come to mind are: London's Victorian houses of child prostitutes, including (a sub-specialty of the house) the providing of prepubescent virgins[10]; the advertisement by London prostitutes, in their *Ladies Directory* of 1959–1960, offering themselves in rubber or leather clothing; and the many more advertisements, in the same periodical, by prostitutes offering "corrective treatment" and signing themselves with such sobriquets as "Ex-governess, strict disciplinarian" and "Miss Whyplash."[11] In a study of 732 American clients of prostitutes (574 clients were married, 158 single), the motivation for patronage that the clients indicated most frequently (78 per cent of the clients) was that they "got something

[10] Cf. W. T. Stead's series of articles, "Maiden Tribute of Modern Babylon," in issues of the *Pall Mall Gazette* for 1885.
[11] Published monthly in Soho, the *Ladies Directory* was transparently disguised as a directory of "models" in an attempt to circumvent the new ban on open soliciting. At least nine issues appeared. The prosecution of its publisher is described in, e.g., the London *Evening Standard* of July 26, 1960.

different" from a prostitute, and 10 per cent of these further volunteered the information that the difference was in the type of sexual act performed.[12] Other studies have shown that even the prostitute having no desire to specialize must learn, and quite early in her career, that she will encounter a goodly share of customers presenting "kinky" or "freaky" sexual requests.[13] There is an enormous amount of this sort of material on prostitution (far more than I have mentioned), but, although most of it was available when Davis wrote, he ignores all of it.[14]

[12] Cf. Charles Winick, "Clients' Perceptions of Prostitutes and of Themselves," *International Journal of Social Psychiatry*, Vol. 8 (1961–62), pp. 289–97.

[13] Cf. John Murtagh and Sara Harris, *Cast the First Stone* (New York: McGraw-Hill, 1957), pp. 180–86; James Bryan, "Apprenticeships in Prostitution," *Social Problems*, Vol. 12, No. 3 (Winter, 1965), pp. 287–97.

[14] There are many other defects in Davis's account of prostitution. Most are matters of detail—e.g., Davis thinks the attempt to control pimps arises only with industrialized societies, though Pompeo Molmenti could have told him that in twelfth-century Venice "pimps were imprisoned, branded, tortured, and banished"—but one is crucial: Davis insists that *promiscuity* is the fundamental defining element of prostitution, with commercial and emotionally indifferent aspects of the role being distinctly secondary. But against this emphasis we can put the following considerations: (1) the typical prostitute undertakes intercourse for money or valuables. (2) Even the untypical prostitute, such as one whose prostitution is a religious duty, works for some remuneration, albeit largely for what the economist calls "psychic income." (3) Davis ignores the fact that nymphomaniacs, free souls, and others who literally "give it away" may be stigmatized by the society but are not generally classified as prostitutes either by law enforcers or by laymen (for example, cf. W. F. Whyte, "A Slum Sex Code," *American Journal of Sociology*, Vol. XLIX [July, 1943], pp. 24–31). (4) Davis also ignores the fact that, conversely, some women not promiscuous in the slightest degree, such as concubines, are usually regarded as special types of prostitutes, although they carry lesser stigma. (5) Davis finds support for his "promiscuity" thesis in the fact that the prostitute's stigma is lessened whenever promiscuity is lessened (as in the case of *geisha*, who were selective about customers); but with equal logic one can note that the prostitute's stigma is lessened whenever she is not "strictly commercial," even if she is highly promiscuous (as in the case of temple prostitutes). A

For our purpose, the point is this: as prostitution goes with respect to perversity, so goes pornography—only more so. Possibly the "more so" derives from the fact that "freaky" sexual interests, being much more highly stigmatized than simple nonmarital coitus, lie closer to total repression or suppression and thus are more often banished strictly to fantasized interaction; possibly other factors account for the difference. In any event, it seems clear that although much pornography depicts sexual relations whose only deviance consists of their nonmarital status, an extraordinary amount of this material offers fantasy involvement in sex acts that society proscribes as "unnatural." The history of pornography provides endless examples, and in this regard it makes no difference whether one thinks of the "hard core" tradition from, say, the *Priapea* of ancient Rome to such current paperbacks as *Perverted Lust Slave*, or of the "art" tradition from, say, Petronius to *Histoire d'O*.

From a sociological standpoint, our society's current distinction between "genuine" or "hard core" pornography and highly erotic art is specious in a more fundamental respect.

In recent years the U.S. federal courts have tended to second and extend the view—a view advanced by defense lawyers, literary critics, *et al.*—that certain extremely erotic books and films are not really pornographic because they show over-all serious artistic intent and/or contain other redeeming social virtues, that is, because they seem not to be simply "dirt for dirt's sake." The courts in various ways have reaffirmed and amplified the doctrine, first set forth clearly in Judge John Woolsey's 1933 decision on Joyce's *Ulysses* and the 1934 confirming opinion of

definition of prostitution that would best fit all these points—while excluding the woman who "marries for money" as well as the girl who consents to intercourse only after a fancy dinner and is, as Kinsey remarks, "engaged in a more commercialized relationship than she would like to admit"—is the following: Prostitution is the granting of nonmarital sex *as a vocation*.

Augustus Hand, that highly realistic descriptions of sex cannot be judged pornographic in isolation, but must be viewed within the context of the work as a whole.[15] And except for a handful of diehard clergymen, our social critics, literary scholars, journalists, and the like—our "sociologizers" about pornography—have fallen in line.[16] But the sociologist, at any rate this sociologist, must disagree with such "contextual" arguments and maintain that a work like, say, Henry Miller's *Tropic of Cancer* is pornographic, whatever else it may be in addition.

Granted that in one type of sociological analysis—what is loosely called the "labelling" approach—pornography is neither more nor less than what the society's decisive power groups say it is at any given time, and if our society now chooses officially to label *Tropic of Cancer* nonpornographic, that's that.[17] Such a conceptual framework does lead to many useful discoveries, along the lines indicated by W. I. Thomas's famous dictum that if people define a situation as real, it is real in its consequences. But this mode of analysis has its limitations, as can be seen when we turn to another and equally legitimate mode, functional analysis, and define pornography in terms of what it actually

does to or for society—what are its particular uses and effects on people, intended or otherwise.[18]

Pornography obviously has many functions; and some of these are not even sexual, e.g., the providing of paid work for pornography producers and sellers, as well as for their professional opponents. But as we have seen, pornography's main function at the societal level (as distinguished from the individual-psychological level) is to help preserve society's double institutionalizing of legitimate sex—within marriage and within a specified few of the possible sex acts—by providing sexual depictions that literally drain off the other, socially illegitimate sexual desires of the beholder. Any sexual depiction (written, recorded, pictorial) that facilitates such masturbatory involvement is thus pornographic. And when pornography is defined in this way, it becomes clear that the courts and the literary critics are wrong, viz., their assumption that pornography and art are mutually exclusive is patently false. For in contemplating naturalistic erotic art, people can and do easily respond to the erotic qualities as such, in utter disregard of the "artistic

---

[15] Judge Woolsey's decision is most readily available in the front matter of the Modern Library edition of *Ulysses*. For Augustus Hand's affirming decision, which languishes unreprinted, see 72 F. (2d) 705.

[16] Among many recent examples of this kind of reasoning, the best known is probably Eberhard and Phyllis Kronhausen's *Pornography and the Law* (New York: Ballantine Books, 1959).

[17] The "labelling" viewpoint, associated with publications in recent years by Edwin Lemert, Howard Becker, John Kitsuse, *et al.*, is actually a reinvention of a viewpoint formulated and applied in sociology at least as far back as Wilhelm Lange-Eichbaum's *The Problem of Genius* (1931), and in the sociology of deviance at least as far back as Frank Tannenbaum's *Crime and the Community* (1938; see Tannenbaum on "the dramatization of evil"). As a "literary" insight into the workings of society its history goes back much further, e.g., the Spanish inquisitor Salazar Frias wrote in 1611 that "there were neither witches nor bewitched until they were written and talked about." The topic is worthy of a Shandean postscript, but I forbear.

[18] As other parts of this essay should indicate, I am hardly arguing for functionalist theory *against* labelling theory, and rather believe that the two theories apply at different levels of analysis and that both have great explanatory power. But unfortunately some "labellers," in their initial zeal for the reinvented theory, fail to see its limitations. They have overly reified W. I. Thomas's dictum, and are in danger of falling into the same trap W. Lloyd Warner fell into when he concluded that social class is "really" what people say it is.

Thomas's insight is true, but only half the truth. The other half is that social life, though profoundly affected by the participants' linguistic interpretation of it, is not identical with or completely determined by such interpretation. In other words, a real situation has some real consequences even if people *don't* define it as real. That fact is often lost sight of by those who take a "labelling" stance (see, for example, my remarks on Korn and McCorkle in Chapter 3). It is never lost sight of by functionalists; in fact, their recognition of it underlies two of the most useful analytic concepts of modern sociology, the concept of latent function and the concept of functional alternatives.

context." The stock of every pornography store confirms this. Thus the user of written pornography, for example, gets his pornography from "hard core" literature or from erotic "art" literature; so far as he is concerned, the only significant difference is that in the latter he usually gets less for his money.[19]

Let me suggest at this point that my readers think back to their early adolescence and recall the so-called "dirty books" that were used for adolescent masturbation. (Rather, I ask males among readers to do this. As the Kinsey data reveal, only a small minority of females are sexually excited by pornography, much less masturbate to it, for reasons largely unknown.[20]) I think most

will be able to recall not only "hard core" pornography, such as the little booklets containing pornographic versions of American comic strips, but also that there were so-called "dirty books" which were really for the most part "clean" and were read for their occasional "dirty pages," such as the books of Erskine Caldwell. At least, that was true not only for my own early adolescence but for that of most every other middle-class boy I knew at the time.

I know of no evidence to indicate that people erotically interested in naturalistic descriptions of sex—whatever their age—are seriously impeded by, or even give much thought to, the over-all non-erotic context in which such descriptions might be embedded; and this applies to highly artistic works as well as any other. Can one seriously maintain, for example, that most of the Americans in Paris who smuggled back copies of *Lady Chatterley's Lover* and *Tropic of Cancer* did so out of interest in the "artistic" or "other social redeeming" qualities of these books rather than out of "prurient interest"? Or when it comes to the people—adolescent or adult—who masturbate to such books, can one seriously claim that they used these works for masturbatory purposes only so long as our society labelled them pornographic and stopped such masturbating when the label changed? Clearly we must modify W. I. Thomas's dictum, which is the "labelling" dictum writ small, to read that if people define a situation as real (erotic X is non-pornographic), it is real in some of its consequences (erotic book X can be sold over the counter) but not in others (people don't stop masturbating to it).

And clearly society has always permitted the dissemination of some kinds of material that are functionally pornographic. In our own society one of the major ways it currently does so, as previously indicated, is to non-label such material as pornographic if it is packaged between significant amounts of non-erotic material—as in, say, the pages of *Playboy*.

The social processes involved in deciding

---

[19] Hanan Selvin has reminded me that the strong erotic appeal, as such, of much erotic art, is also noted in Sir Kenneth Clark's *The Nude*.

[20] Note that theories of the female "role" won't do to explain this, for even when men take on all the female role attributes they can, i.e., become hyper-effeminate homosexuals, they do not give up the male's interest in pornography (though of course the object changes and so their pornography consists of erotic depictions of males). And, conversely, when women take on as many male role attributes as they can, i.e., become tough "butch" lesbians, they do not typically lose the female's disinterest in pornography.

There are indeed many pornographic "lesbian" novels, but they are fakes. They are written by men and bought by men. (Both points have been made to me by Times Square pornography peddlers, and I have confirmed the latter from observation in their stores.) The genuine lesbian novel, whether the inartistic kind such as Radclyffe Hall's *Well of Loneliness* or the artistic kind such as Djuna Barnes's *Nightwood*, does not contain naturalistic description of sex but emphasizes the emotional-psychological aspect of sexual relationships. In this respect it is similar to the romantic literature that heterosexual women enjoy (on the latter, see the Kinsey volume on females, *op. cit.*, p. 670).

Apart from disinterest by females (heterosexual or homosexual) in pornography consumption, and the fact that "lesbian" pornography is actually produced by males for males, it has also been established beyond doubt that heterosexual pornography production by females is very rare. (Cf. Kinsey volume on females, *op. cit.*, p. 672.) Yet Wladimir Eliasberg, *op. cit.*, claims a striking feature of pornographic literature is that one cannot tell whether a man or woman is either the producer or consumer.

which pornography shall be permitted, and even some (though by no means all) of the selective criteria used, are roughly analogous to the way that—as Sutherland showed us—our society permits certain types of criminals, notably businessmen who commit crimes in their corporate capacities, to escape penological consequences and even public stigma.[21] The recent case of the magazine *Eros* notwithstanding, the classier the pornography the more likely it is to be permitted.[22] What is big news about the publisher of *Eros* is precisely what is big news about those price-fixing G.E. officials: such people are rarely the kind who get rapped.

At the same time that society permits the dissemination of pornography, it officially denounces it. There is good reason for it to do both at once: from the desire to maintain a restrictive societal definition of "legitimate" sex, it naturally follows that pornography should be stigmatized and harassed yet tolerated as a safety-valve, in the same way that, as Davis demonstrates, society stigmatizes and otherwise harasses prostitution but never really abolishes it.

And just as Davis indicates for prostitution, the stigma attached to pornography is lessened when pornography is tied to some other socially valued end, such as art or science. One important result is this: when the "situation" being defined by society is a naturalistic depiction of sex, the most real consequence of a definition that labels it something other than pornographic is to increase its pornographic use in the society by reducing the inhibitions on acquiring it.

[21] Cf. Edwin Sutherland, *White Collar Crime* (New York: Holt, Rinehart & Winston, 1949), especially pp. 42ff. Of course there are also special selective factors operating at more mundane levels of pornography production. For example, in the recent case of a Michigan hard-core pornographer who was not only fined $19,000 but sentenced to ten years in prison, I assume that the severity of the sentence was not unrelated to the title of his masterpiece: *The Sex Life of a Cop*. (Cf. New York *Daily News*, April 7, 1966, p. 13, col. 1.)

[22] On the case of *Eros* and the prison sentence given to its publisher, see, for example, *The New York Times*, March 27, 1966, p. 8E, cols. 1–2.

This is obvious from the libraries of countless souls who avidly buy highly erotic works that society labels "art" or "literature" or "science" or "scholarship," but who take care not to buy "real" pornography.

And if the non-labelling of an erotic depiction as pornographic actually increases its pornographic use in the society, *de*-labelling increases such usefulness still more. As any publisher can tell you (I speak as a former publisher), it is much better for sales to have an erotic book that was once labelled pornographic and then got de-labelled than to have one that never got labelled at all. Thus such works as *Lady Chatterley* or *Tropic of Cancer* are, functionally, among our society's most pornographic books of all.

All of this could, as Albert Cohen has suggested to me, simply indicate that many if not most Americans label *Playboy* or erotic art or sexual scholarship as "pornography" even if the courts and others don't. But such an interpretation depends on a dubious double hypothesis—that the courts have largely deluded themselves in claiming to follow community opinion and have also failed to mold opinion. It might still be truer than mine, and only empirical data we don't yet have can settle the question. However, I think it more reasonable to suppose this: If the behavior of people often contradicts their attitudes (and social research is forever stumbling against that one), then it can be just as discrepant with their labelling or definition of the situation, and, moreover, such discrepancy is widespread in areas of life involving socially encouraged hypocrisy and unawareness, as in the case of sex behavior.

An even clearer, and more fundamental, discrepancy between social reality and the social definition or labelling of the situation has to do with highly erotic depictions that make no claim to art or science and are not enwrapped in non-erotic contexts, depictions that society calls "real" or "hard core" pornography or "dirt for dirt's sake." Such a label means that the material is, in the words of Mr. Justice Brennan, "utterly without redeeming social importance." That definition of the situation is obviously upheld by the great majority of our society; it is entertained equally by the courts, by assorted professional experts (such as literary critics and psychiatrists), and by the lay public. It is, nevertheless, mistaken. To the extent that society, in restricting morally legitimate sex to certain specified acts within marriage, cannot count fully on the mechanisms of repression and suppression, to that extent it must provide stigmatized safety-valve institutions such as prostitution and pornography.[23] As Thomas Aquinas put it—he was explaining prostitution—"A cesspool is necessary to a palace if the whole palace is not to smell."[24]

As I mentioned at the beginning of this chapter, there are many special aspects of the sociology of pornography. One involves a hypothesis I am currently testing and for which I have already found a bit of confirmation, namely, that organized crime is more and more associating itself with the production and distribution of hard core pornography, particularly but not exclusively the most profitable part of it, pornographic movies. This would represent a coming together of organized crime's traditional interest in providing illegal goods and services, with a change in American consumption patterns that is having fateful consequences for the technology of pornography: the great increase, over the past fifteen years, in private ownership of 8 mm. movie projectors.

Until roughly 1950, the pornographic movie business consisted largely in renting films for showing at stag dinners, fraternity parties, and the like, but since then it has been increasingly, and is now overwhelmingly, a matter of outright sale of prints to individual customers.[25] Consequently, over the past decade and a half, the pornographic movie business has had one of the highest growth rates of any business in the United States (legal or illegal); and organized crime is now well aware of that fact if the general public is not. It is true that the pornographic movie industry, like the pornography industry generally, is still mostly in the hands of individual entrepreneurs; but if present trends continue, investment in this industry by organized crime may one day reach the takeoff point, that is, the stage where muscle is applied to make independents fall in line or get out.

There are other special hypotheses about the sociology of pornography that need investigating, dozens of them. What I have tried to do here is offer a general framework within which such investigations might be made. [26]

[23] The historical and comparative sociology of the part that "safety-valve" institutions play in social control has yet to be written. We do not even have an adequate general theory of these functions— merely scattered remarks about *panem et circenses*— although Freud has provided many psychological underpinnings for such a theory. Here I note only that in our society major historical changes in safety-valve mechanisms have involved other than sexual institutions; for example, there has been a decrease in displacement of secular goals onto an afterlife (a decline in "pie in the sky" or "opium of the people" functions of religion), and an increase in spectatorship for competitive sports as a means of draining off potential public violence.

[24] This view of prostitution—which, shorn of its moralism, is the essence of Davis's sociological view— can be found in many writers beside St. Thomas, e.g., in Horace's *Satires* and Mary Wollstonecraft's *A Vindication of the Rights of Woman*. Of these functionalist explanations prior to Davis, the ablest are in Bernard Mandeville's "An Inquiry into the Origin of Moral Virtue" (his preface to the 1714 edition of *Fable of the Bees*) and his *A Modest Defence of Publick Stews* (1724).

[25] I am informed by pornography distributors in Soho, London, that a similar shift has taken place in England.

[26] *Addendum:* A detailed scholarly study of mid-Victorian sexuality and pornography, based on the Kinsey collection, was published after this book went to press: Steven Marcus, *The Other Victorians* (New York: Basic Books, 1966). At various places in his book Mr. Marcus discusses the relation of pornography to Victorian society, and his concluding chapter is, in design and in the words of the publisher, "an essay propounding a general theory of pornography as a sociological [i.e., social] phenomenon." In this late note I cannot demonstrate, but only asseverate, that *The Other Victorians* is a prime instance of rubbishy "sociologizing" about pornography, "so-

(Footnote 25 Cont'd.)

ciologizing" of the sort produced by that growing band of American literary critics who believe they are experts on society simply because they live in it.

One brief example: Mr. Marcus seems ignorant of statistical reasoning and, worse, of its possible relevance to his argument. Hence one cannot learn from his book that the Victorian era's tremendous upsurge in the growth rate of pornography publishing, which he finds so strange, was equalled and usually surpassed by increases in growth rates for every other kind of publishing. (Indeed, he even seems innocent of the distinction between growth and growth rate.) Nor can one learn that all this had some relation to England's having perfected, in the first decade of the nineteenth century, the Fourdrinier machine for cheap papermaking, nor the fact that, over the following decades, while England's population grew nearly fourfold its *literate* population grew thirty-two-fold.

Analysis of Values
and
Conflicts of Interest

The majority report of The Commission on Obscenity and Pornography presents arguments and supporting data that reject the definition of pornography as a social problem. Rather, the real social problem, they argue, is the effects of legal restrictions on pornography. The statement of the majority report is consistent with the views of most artists, writers, and libertarians. These groups fear the threat to freedom of expression that censorship represents. The definition of pornography is vague because it is evaluated in subjective and often personal terms. Thus there are no safeguards against zealous censors with very broad definitions of pornography.

The majority report is also supportive of those who believe that the state should not legislate morality. This position suggests that individuals should be allowed to engage in private behaviors that do not inflict harm upon others. People who adopt this stance argue that laws intended to regulate such behavior are unnecessary, unenforceable, and often repressive. This perspective is advocated by many sociologists, liberal reform groups and libertarian conservatives.

Groups like The Commission on Obscenity and Pornography are created to clarify the definition of social problems and to suggest programs to cope with them. Diverse interest groups are often represented on these commissions to promote broad public support for their conclusions and proposals. However, it is often difficult for such diverse groups to reconcile their value differences and conflicting interests. For example, the majority report is primarily an expression of the liberal view of pornography, in particular, that of liberal social scientists. On the other hand, the minority report, which is but one of several dissenting statements, represents a contradictory set of concerns. This report supports individuals and groups who maintain that pornography is harmful to the person and to the community. It suggests that the majority report promotes the interests of the pornographer by recommending the removal of restrictions against pornography. The minority report characterizes the existence of pornography as a significant social problem. It supports police actions, legal charges, and community pressure against the pornographer.

Since publication of the commission report, public policy has been directed increasingly against dissemination and sale of pornography. Few politicians found it in their interest to support a less restrictive public policy. Also recent court decisions have allowed more vigorous local action against pornography.

Kristol's article suggests that pornography is not only degrading and morally offensive, but is a threat to the very basis of society. He maintains that society is founded upon a moral consensus that requires some restraints on individual expression. This view supports those who are concerned with preservation of social order and maintenance of traditional morality. It suggests that the alternative—complete freedom for the individual—ultimately results in nihilism and even anarchy. This position suggests that social order rests upon moral order—that society can exist only when its members accept common moral values that infuse their lives with meaning and impose restrictions on their behavior. Many of those who oppose pornography assert that it represents a significant erosion of moral order that cannot be tolerated if society is to survive. This view has been expressed by many different religious groups and is clearly stressed in the moral philosophy of classical conservatism.

Finally, Polsky suggests that pornography has important, positive social functions, yet it also represents a threat to society. Therefore, he says, it will always exist, but without official societal sanction. This position suggests that the present marginal status of pornography will be maintained. Police groups and politicians often adhere to this view; they often condemn pornography morally, but they seldom take active measures to eliminate it.

2

Institutional
and
Group Social Problems

1

WOMEN AND SEX ROLES:
Should Sex Roles Be Redefined?

In the early 1970s the black movement and the student movement entered a comparatively quiet stage, but during this same period the women's liberation movement gained in popularity. Spokeswomen Germaine Greer and Kate Millett replaced the vocal black radicals and student radicals of the last decade. Unlike the radicals of the 1960s, the women's movement is not generally oriented to revolutionary violence. Instead, its goals focus upon changing the traditional, constrictive definitions of sex roles and eliminating the injustices that unfold from them. The movement has already had a significant impact because it caused thousands of American women to reflect upon their position. Women's liberation is still gaining momentum and could lead to important social changes.

Lucy Komisar's essay is basically the story of the unfulfilled middle-class college girl who wanders into a women's liberation encounter group and is sensitized for the first time to her sex-role related problems. Komisar's article focuses upon the problems that women have encountered because of the sexism endemic to American society. Regardless of their abilities, women have been forced into subordinate and degrading roles and as a result have developed a poor self-image. In this society women are socialized to be secondary to and supportive of men, rather than being oriented to their own self-development. They quickly become dependent on their husbands and vicariously live through their success as well as their children's success, instead of seeking and attaining their own goals. Even if they seek fulfillment outside the home, women find that men are in control and that their chance of finding work worthy of their abilities is remote. Traditionally, men have had the power to define women's roles; this male dominated culture placed women in inferior roles. As a result women come to resent the physical and social power of men. However, liberated women also come to recognize that men are as enslaved in their own achievement-oriented roles as women are in their subordinate positions. Thus, the most frequently articulated goal of the women's liberation movement is the elimination of the rigid sex–role system that enslaves *both* women *and* men.

Marlene Dixon sees the history of women's liberation as a struggle between the traditional feminists (like Komisar) and what she terms the "politicos," or leftists. In Dixon's view, the feminists have gained control of the women's liberation movement and pushed it in some unfortunate directions. For example, Dixon feels that the feminists were misguided in trying to unite all women against a common oppressor. To Dixon, the differences between different classes of women are as great or greater than their common denominator—male oppression. Dixon states, "The ethic of sisterhood also disguises and mystifies the internal class contradictions of the women's movement. Specifically, sisterhood masks the fact that all women do *not* have the same interests, needs, and desires. Working-class women and middle-class women, student women and professional women, black women and white women have more *conflicting* interests than could ever be overcome by their common experience based on sex discrimination." Dixon attributes the failure of the women's movement to two factors: false commonality caused by erroneously describing men as the enemy, and control of the movement by middle-class women, which gives it a middle-class orientation. It is this orientation that prevents the movement from attracting a constituency from outside the middle class.

Dixon also criticizes what she characterizes as the "reactionary feminist philosophy" of the women's liberation movement. While liberal feminists tend to see men as "misguided," the reactionary feminists see all men as the enemy of all women. In its extreme form, it calls for the subjugation, even extermination, of men. It is, in Dixon's view, a withdrawal strategy (in its extreme form calling for separation of the sexes) and not an ideology of revolution. This reactionary philosophy is most attractive to white, middle and lower-middle class, urban women, whose major oppression is psychological oppression by men. But, Dixon points out, the vast majority of women are far more oppressed economically than they are psychologically. Lower-class women worry far more about economic oppression than they do about psychological oppression. According to Dixon, the "woman problem" is not just a woman problem, not is it caused primarily by men. Women's problems are inherent in our economic and social systems and will only be solved when those systems are transformed.

Ann Leffler and Dair Gillespie find little merit in Dixon's position. They accuse Dixon of trying to make it to the top of the left movement by attacking women's liberation and engaging in what they label "middle-class baiting." They argue that many of her facts are wrong and contend that ". . . she prefers innuendo to fact." They do not see an interrelationship between capitalism–imperialism and the oppression of women, and argue that this oppression antedates imperialism. They admit that there are class differences between women. However, they take the position that the oppression by males is a crucial common denominator for all women. Further, they regard internal division and conflict as a natural social process. They view Dixon's efforts as counterproductive, and oriented toward Dixon's own career in the "left," rather than helping women.

The final piece in this section is an acid critique of all of the positions outlined in this section. Helen Lawrenson argues that what liberationists want is not equality, but "the absolute subjugation of men, or even their elimination." Lawrenson denies that women involved in the movement are normal; rather, she labels them "freaks." She denies that women hate men, marriage, and housework. She takes the position that the women's liberation movement distracts us from our real problems: "They might better devote themselves to more socially useful protest: Against the war in Indochina, against nuclear, chemical and biological weapons, against environmental pollution. . . ." She also attacks the movement for being elitist and ignoring the masses of women: "With a rare exception here and there, it is a movement of white, middle-class, college-educated women, and their appeal to the proletariat is minimal."

Lawrenson cannot understand why such a movement is taking place in the United States. She says that its existence would be rational in such places as Spain or Algeria, where women are truly downtrodden. However, in America women control most of the wealth and can be found in almost every occupation. In Lawrenson's view, there are not more women at the top of the occupational world because women do not want to be there. In the end she agrees with Dr. Benjamin Spock's well-known quotation: "If you liberate women in America one more inch, man will be completely subjugated."

The New Feminism

LUCY KOMISAR

A dozen women are variously seated in straight-backed chairs, settled on a couch, or sprawled on the floor of a comfortable apartment on Manhattan's West Side. They range in age from twenty-five to thirty-five, and include a magazine researcher, a lawyer, a housewife, an architect, a teacher, a secretary, and a graduate student in sociology.

They are white, middle-class, attractive. All but one have college degrees; several are married; few are active in social causes. At first, they are hesitant. They don't really know what to talk about, and so they begin with why they came.

"I wanted to explore my feelings as a woman and find out what others think about the things that bother me." Slowly, they open up, trust growing. "I always felt so negative about being a woman; now I'm beginning to feel good about it."

They become more personal and revealing. "My mother never asked me what I was going to be when I grew up." "I never used to like to talk to girls. I always thought women were inferior—I never *liked* women." "I've been a secretary for three years; after that, you begin to think that's all you're good for." "I felt so trapped when my baby was born. I

Note: Lucy Komisar, "The New Feminism," *Saturday Review,* Feb. 1970, pp. 27–30, 55. Copyright 1970, Saturday Review, Inc., and reproduced by permission.

wanted to leave my husband and the child."

Repeated a hundred times in as many different rooms, these are the voices of women's liberation, a movement that encompasses high school students and grandmothers, and that is destined to eclipse the black civil rights struggle in the force of its resentment and the consequence of its demands.

Some of us have become feminists out of anger and frustration over job discrimination. When we left college, male students got aptitude tests, we got typing tests. In spite of federal law, most women still are trapped in low-paying, dead-end jobs and commonly earn less than men for the same work—sometimes on the theory that we are only "helping out," though 42 per cent of us support ourselves or families.

Others have discovered that the humanistic precepts of the radical movement do not always apply to women. At a peace rally in Washington last year, feminists were hooted and jeered off the speakers' platform, and white women working in civil rights or antipoverty programs are expected to defer to the black male ego. Many of us got out to salvage our own buffeted egos. However, most of the new feminists express only a general malaise they were never able to identify.

Nanette Rainone is twenty-seven, the wife

of a newspaperman, the mother of a seven-month-old child, and a graduate of Queens College, where she studied English literature. She married while in graduate school, then quit before the year was out to become an office clerk at *Life* magazine. "I could have known the first day that I wasn't going to be promoted, but it took me eight months to find it out."

She spent the next five months idly at home, began doing volunteer public affairs interviews for WBAI radio, and now produces *Womankind,* a weekly program on the feminist movement.

"I always felt as though I was on a treadmill, an emotional treadmill. I thought it was neurotic, but it always focused on being a woman. Then I met another woman, who had two children. We talked about my pregnancy—my confusion about my pregnancy—and the problems she was having in caring for her children now that she was separated from her husband and wanted to work."

One evening Nanette Rainone's friend took her to a feminist meeting, and immediately she became part of the movement. "The child had been an escape. I was seeking a role I couldn't find on the outside," she says. "Then I became afraid my life would be overwhelmed, and that I would never get out from under and do the things I had hoped to do.

"You struggle for several years after getting out of college. You know—what are you going to do with yourself? There's always the external discrimination, but somehow you feel you are talented and you should be able to project yourself. But you don't get a good job, you get a terrible job.

"I think I was typical of the average woman who is in the movement now, because the contradictions in the system existed in my life. My parents were interested in my education. I had more room to develop my potential than was required for the role I eventually was to assume.

"I don't put down the care of children. I just put down the fixated relationship that

the mother has, the never-ending association, her urge that the child be something so that *she* can be something. People need objective projects. We all feel the need to actively participate in society, in something outside ourselves where we can learn and develop.

"The closest I've been able to come to what's wrong is that men have a greater sense of self than women have. Marriage is an aspect of men's lives, whereas it is the very center of most women's lives, the whole of their lives. It seemed to me that women felt they couldn't exist except in the eyes of men—that if a man wasn't looking at them or attending to them, then they just weren't there."

If women need more evidence, history books stand ready to assure us that we have seldom existed except as shadows of men. We have rarely been leaders of nations or industry or the great contributors to art and science, yet very few sociologists, political leaders, historians, and moral critics have ever stopped to ask why. Now, all around the country, women are meeting in apartments and conference rooms and coffee shops to search out the answers.

The sessions begin with accounts of personal problems and incidents. For years, we women have believed that our anger and frustrations and unhappiness were "our problems." Suddenly, we discover that we are telling *the same story*! Our complaints are not only common, they are practically universal.

It is an exhilarating experience. Women's doubts begin to disappear and are replaced by new strength and self-respect. We stop focusing on men, and begin to identify with other women and to analyze the roots of our oppression. The conclusions that are drawn challenge the legitimacy of the sex role system upon which our civilization is based.

At the center of the feminist critique is the recognition that women have been forced to accept an inferior role in society, and that we have come to believe in our own inferiority. Women are taught to be passive, dependent, submissive, not to pursue careers but to be taken care of and protected. Even those who seek outside work lack confidence and self-esteem. Most of us are forced into menial and unsatisfying jobs: More than three-quarters of us are clerks, sales personnel, or factory and service workers, and a fifth of the women with B.A. degrees are secretaries.

Self-hatred is endemic. Women—especially those who have "made it"—identify with men and mirror their contempt for women. The approval of women does not mean very much. We don't want to work for women or vote for them. We laugh, although with vague uneasiness, at jokes about women drivers, mothers-in-law, and dumb blondes.

We depend on our relationships with men for our very identities. Our husbands win us social status and determine how we will be regarded by the world. Failure for a woman is not being selected by a man.

We are trained in the interests of men to defer to them and serve them and entertain them. If we are educated and gracious, it is so we can please men and educate their children. That is the thread that runs through the life of the geisha, the party girl, the business executive's wife, and the First Lady of the United States.

Men define women, and until now most of us have accepted their definition without question. If we challenge men in the world outside the home, we are all too frequently derided as "aggressive" and "unfeminine"— by women as readily as by men.

A woman is expected to subordinate her job to the interests of her husband's work. She'll move to another city so he can take a promotion—but it rarely works the other way around. Men don't take women's work very seriously, and, as a result, neither do most women. We spend a lot of time worrying about men, while they devote most of theirs to worrying about their careers.

We are taught that getting and keeping a man is a woman's most important job; marriage, therefore, becomes our most important achievement. One suburban housewife says her father started giving her bridal pictures

cut from newspapers when she was six. "He said that was what I would be when I grew up."

Most feminists do not object to marriage per se, but to the corollary that it is creative and fulfilling for an adult human being to spend her life doing housework, caring for children, and using her husband as a vicarious link to the outside world.

Most people would prefer just about any kind of work to that of a domestic servant; yet the mindless, endless, repetitive drudgery of housekeeping is the central occupation of more than fifty million women. People who would oppose institutions that portion out menial work on the basis of race see nothing wrong in a system that does the same thing on the basis of sex. (Should black and white roommates automatically assume the Negro best suited for housekeeping chores?) Even when they work at full-time jobs, wives must come home to "their" dusting and "their" laundry.

Some insist that housework is not much worse than the meaningless jobs most people have today, but there is a difference. Housewives are not paid for their work, and money is the mark of value in this society. It is also the key to independence and to the feeling of self-reliance that marks a free human being.

The justification for being a housewife is having children, and the justification for children is—well, a woman has a uterus, what else would it be for? Perhaps not all feminists agree that the uterus is a vestigial organ, but we are adamant and passionate in our denial of the old canard that biology is destiny.

Men have never been bound by their animal natures. They think and dream and create—and fly, clearly something nature had not intended, or it would have given men wings. However, we women are told that our chief function is to reproduce the species, prepare food, and sweep out the cave—er, house.

Psychologist Bruno Bettelheim states woman's functions succinctly: "We must start with the realization that, as much as women want to be good scientists or engineers, they want first and foremost to be womanly companions of men and to be mothers."

He gets no argument from Dr. Spock: "Biologically and temperamentally, I believe women were made to be concerned first and foremost with child care, husband care, and home care." Spock says some women have been "confused" by their education. (Freud was equally reactionary on the woman question, but he at least had the excuse of his Central European background.)

The species must reproduce, but this need not be the sole purpose of a woman's life. Men want children, too, yet no one expects them to choose between families and work. Children are in no way a substitute for personal development and creativity. If a talented man is forced into a senseless, menial job, it is deplored as a waste and a personal misfortune; yet, a woman's special skills, education, and interests are all too often deemed incidental and irrelevant, simply a focus for hobbies or volunteer work.

Women who say that raising a family is a fulfilling experience are rather like the peasant who never leaves his village. They have never had the opportunity to do anything else.

As a result, women are forced to live through their children and husbands, and they feel cheated and resentful when they realize that is not enough. When a woman says she gave her children everything, she is telling the truth—and that is the tragedy. Often when she reaches her late thirties, her children have grown up, gone to work or college, and left her in a bleak and premature old age. Middle-aged women who feel empty and useless are the mainstay of America's psychiatrists—who generally respond by telling them to "accept their role."

The freedom to choose whether or not to have children has always been illusory. A wife who is deliberately "barren"—a word that reinforces the worn-out metaphor of woman as Mother Earth—is considered neurotic or unnatural. Not only is motherhood not central to a woman's life, it may not be necessary or desirable. For the first time, some

of us are admitting openly and without guilt that we do not want children. And the population crisis is making it even clearer that as a symbol for Americans motherhood ought to defer to apple pie.

The other half of the reproduction question is sex. The sexual revolution didn't liberate women at all; it only created a bear market for men. One of the most talked-about tracts in the movement is a pamphlet by Ann Koedt called "The Myth of the Vaginal Orgasm," which says most women don't have orgasms because most men won't accept the fact the female orgasm is clitoral.

We are so used to putting men's needs first that we don't know how to ask for what *we* want, or else we share the common ignorance about our own physiology and think there is something wrong with us when we don't have orgasms "the right way." Freudian analysts contribute to the problem. The realization that past guilt and frustration have been unnecessary is not the least of the sentiments that draws women to women's liberation.

Feminists also protest the general male proclivity to regard us as decorative, amusing sex objects even in the world outside bed. We resent the sexual sell in advertising, the catcalls we get on the street, girlie magazines and pornography, bars that refuse to serve unescorted women on the assumption they are prostitutes, the not very subtle brainwashing by cosmetic companies, and the attitude of men who praise our knees in miniskirts, but refuse to act as if we had brains.

Even the supposedly humanistic worlds of rock music and radical politics are not very different. Young girls who join "the scene" or "the movement" are labeled "groupies" and are sexually exploited; the flashy pornosheets such as *Screw* and *Kiss* are published by the self-appointed advocates of the new "free," anti-Establishment lifestyle. *"Plus ça change. . . ."*

We are angry about the powers men wield over us. The physical power—women who study karate do so as a defense against muggers, not lovers. And the social power—we resent the fact that men take the initiative with women, that women cannot ask for dates but must sit home waiting for the phone to ring.

That social conditioning began in childhood when fathers went out to work and mothers stayed home, images perpetuated in schoolbooks and games and on television. If we were bright students, we were told, "You're smart—for a girl," and then warned not to appear *too* smart in front of boys— "Or you won't have dates."

Those of us who persisted in reaching for a career were encouraged to be teachers or nurses so we would have "something to fall back on." My mother told me: "You're so bright, it's a pity you're not a boy. You could become president of a bank—or anything you wanted."

Ironically, and to our dismay, we discovered that playing the assigned role is precisely what elicits masculine contempt for our inferiority and narrow interests. *Tooth and Nail,* a newsletter published by women's liberation groups in the San Francisco area, acidly points out a few of the contradictions: "A smart woman never shows her brains; she allows the man to think himself clever. . . . Women's talk is all chatter; they don't understand things men are interested in."

Or: "Don't worry your pretty little head about such matters. . . . A woman's brain is between her legs. . . . Women like to be protected and treated like little girls. . . . Women can't make decisions."

The feminist answer is to throw out the whole simplistic division of human characteristics into masculine and feminine, and to insist that there are no real differences between men and women other than those enforced by culture.

Men say women are not inferior, we are just different; yet somehow they have appropriated most of the qualities that society admires and have left us with the same distinctive features that were attributed to black people before the civil rights revolution.

Men, for example, are said to be strong, assertive, courageous, logical, constructive,

creative, and independent. Women are weak, passive, irrational, overemotional, emptyheaded, and lacking in strong superegos. (Thank Freud for the last.) Both blacks and women are contented, have their place, and know how to use wiles—flattery, and wide-eyed, open-mouthed ignorance—to get around "the man." It is obviously natural that men should be dominant and women submissive. Shuffle, baby, shuffle.

Our "sexist" system has hurt men as well as women, forcing them into molds that deny the value of sensitivity, tenderness, and sentiment. Men who are not aggressive worry about their virility just as strong women are frightened by talk about their being castrating females. The elimination of rigid sex-role definitions would liberate everyone. And that is the goal of the women's liberation movement.

Women's liberation groups, which have sprung up everywhere across the country, are taking names like Radical Women or the Women's Liberation Front or the Feminists. Most start as groups of ten or twelve; many, when they get too large for discussion, split in a form of mitosis. Sometimes they are tied to central organizations set up for action, or they maintain communications with each other or cosponsor newsletters with similar groups in their area.

Some are concerned with efforts to abolish abortion laws, a few have set up cooperative day-care centers, others challenge the stereotypes of woman's image, and many are organized for "consciousness-raising"—a kind of group therapy or encounter session that starts with the premise that there is something wrong with the system, not the women in the group.

The amorphousness and lack of central communication in the movement make it virtually impossible to catalogue the established groups, let alone the new ones that regularly appear; many of the "leaders" who have been quoted in newspapers or interviewed on television have been anointed only by the press.

The one organization with a constitution, board members, and chapters (some thirty-five) throughout the country is the National Organization for Women. Its founding in 1966 was precipitated by the ridicule that greeted the inclusion of sex in the prohibitions against job discrimination in the 1964 Civil Rights Act. (A staff member in the federal Equal Employment Opportunity Commission, which enforces the act, said it took pressure from NOW to get the EEOC to take that part of the law seriously.)

NOW members are not very different from women in other feminist groups, though they tend to include more professionals and older women. In general, they eschew "consciousness-raising" in favor of political action, and they are more likely to demonstrate for job equality and child-care centers than for the abolition of marriage or the traditional family unit.

NOW's president is Betty Friedan, who in 1963 published *The Feminine Mystique,* a challenge to the myth that a woman's place is either in a boudoir in a pink, frilly nightgown, on her hands and knees scrubbing the kitchen floor, or in a late model station wagon taking the kids to music lessons and Cub Scout meetings. (An article that previewed the theme of the book was turned down by every major women's magazine. "One was horrified and said I was obviously talking to and for a few neurotic women." When the book came out, two of these magazines published excerpts and several now have commissioned articles about the movement.)

Today, Betty Friedan says, the movement must gain political power by mobilizing the 51 per cent of the electorate who are women, as well as seeking elected offices for themselves. "We have to break down the actual barriers that prevent women from being full people in society, and not only end explicit discrimination but build new institutions. Most women will continue to bear children, and unless we create child-care centers on a mass basis, it's all talk."

Women are beginning to read a good deal about their own place in history, about the determined struggles of the suffragettes, the isolation of Virginia Woolf, and the heroism of Rosa Luxemburg. The Congress to Unite Women, which drew some 500 participants from cities in the Northeast, called for women's studies in high schools and colleges.

Present are all the accouterments of any social movement—feminist magazines such as *No More Fun and Games* in Boston, *Up from Under* in New York, and *Aphra,* a literary magazine published in Baltimore. (Anne Sexton wrote in the dedication, "As long as it can be said about a woman writer, 'She writes like a man' and that woman takes it as a compliment, we are in trouble.")

There are feminist theaters in at least New York and Boston, buttons that read "Uppity Women Unite," feminist poems and songs, a feminist symbol (the biological sign for woman with an equal sign in the center), and, to denounce specific advertisements, gum stickers that state, "This ad insults women."

With a rising feminist consciousness, everything takes on new significance—films, advertisements, offhand comments, little things that never seemed important before. A few women conclude that chivalry and flirting reduce women to mere sex objects for men. We stop feeling guilty about opening doors, and some of us experiment with paying our own way on dates.

Personal acts are matched by political ones. The National Organization for Women went to court to get a federal ruling barring segregated help-wanted ads in newspapers, and it regularly helps women file complaints before the EEOC and local human rights commissions.

A women's rights platform was adopted last year by the State Committee of the California Democratic Party, and the Women's Rights Committee of the New Democratic Coalition plans to make feminist demands an issue in New York politics. A women's caucus exists in the Democratic Policy Council, headed by Senator Fred Harris.

At Grinnell College in Iowa, students protested the appearance of a representative from *Playboy* magazine, and women from sixteen cities converged on Atlantic City to make it clear what they think of the Miss America Pageant. In New York, a group protested advertisements by toymakers that said "boys were born to build and learn" and "girls were born to be dancers."

Women's caucuses have been organized in the American Political Science, Psychological, and Sociological associations. At New York University, a group of law students won their fight to make women eligible for a series of coveted $10,000 scholarships.

Pro-abortion groups have organized around the country to repeal anti-abortion laws, challenge them in the courts, or openly defy them. In Bloomington, Indiana, New York City, and elsewhere, women's liberation groups have set up cooperative day-care centers, which are illegal under strict state rules that regulate child-care facilities.

Free child care is likely to become the most significant demand made by the movement, and one calculated to draw the support of millions of women who may not be interested in other feminist issues. About four million working mothers have children under six years of age, and only 2 per cent of these are in day-care centers.

Even Establishment institutions appear to reflect the new attitudes. Princeton, Wil-liams, and Yale have begun to admit women students, though on an unequal quota basis— and not to the hallowed pine-paneled halls of their alumni clubhouses.

Nevertheless, most people have only a vague idea of the significance of the new movement. News commentators on year-end analysis shows ignored the question or sloughed it off uncomfortably. One said the whole idea frightened him.

Yet, the women's movement promises to affect radically the life of virtually everyone in America. Only a small part of the populations suffers because it is black, and most people have little contact with minorities. Women are 51 per cent of the population, and chances are that every adult American either is one, is married to one, or has close social or business relations with many.

The feminist revolution will overturn the basic premise upon which these relations are built—stereotyped notions about the family and the roles of men and women, fallacies concerning masculinity and femininity, and the economic division of labor into paid work and homemaking.

If the 1960s belonged to the blacks, the next ten years are ours.

Public Ideology and the
Class Composition of
Women's Liberation (1966-1969)

MARLENE DIXON

The present essay is an attempt to trace the development of ideology in the Women's Movement and its inter-relationship with the class composition of the movement from 1966–1969. No attempt is made to wrestle with the present day complexity of ideological positions nor the controversy which presently surrounds them.[1] The purpose is rather to sketch the broad outlines of the major public ideologies as they evolved to 1969, the last year of what might be termed a women's united front.

UNITY

In the early growth stages of any protest movement unity is an overriding necessity.

Note: Marlene Dixon, "Public Ideology and the Class Composition of Women's Liberation (1966–1969)," *Berkeley Journal of Sociology,* Vol. 16, 1971–1972, pp. 149–167. Reprinted by permission of the Berkeley Journal of Sociology.
[1] For example, there is no discussion of the influence of the rise of Gay Liberation within the women's movement, since the subject requires a paper in itself. Nor is the alternative left-socialist ideology systematically presented.

This was particularly true of the women's movement, since the status of women had deteriorated so markedly since the 1930's (and anti-woman propaganda had so discredited earlier women's movements) that there existed almost no widespread recognition that discrimination against women was a social evil. As far as the dominant culture was concerned, discrimination against women was a positive good, sanctioned by God and biology. Thus, the first upsurge of women's protest since the decline of the suffrage movement began with only a tiny band of activists and militants whose early demands for equality were met with ridicule from The Powers and greeted with fearful denials and a sense of personal threat by the vast majority of women. The ideology of the new movement was primarily dictated by the necessities of early organizing, and those necessities were to gain legitimacy and recruits, which required, above all, unity.

As a consequence of the need for unity there developed a public ideology based upon feminism, sisterhood, and opposition to discrimination. However, the outwardly uniform public ideology masked a very bitter internal debate (in the years roughly from 1966–1969) between what were called "Politicos" (representing a range of left-wing politics) and the "Feminists". The feminists tended to reject left wing politics in favor of a feminist "women's politics" uncontaminated by "male dominated" ideologies of revolution. (It was pointed out by some that Marx was a *man,* and therefore, Marxism could hardly be trusted.) [2]

As this essay attempts to outline, many forces were at work to drive the left-wing radical women into a relatively isolated position within Women's Liberation. However, very early, as a result of the need for outward unity and legitimacy, and because of the internal nature of the debate between politicos and feminists, the balance of power was shifted to the feminists. Internally, the politicos had been discredited by the attacks of leftist sects (e.g., from Progressive Labor, Trotskyists, S.D.S., etc.). After all, ridicule was one thing, but *attack* quite another.[3] The political content of the attacks (that the women's movement was divisive, racist and reformist) was in "leftese" and was therefore incomprehensible to most women. The fact of being attacked outweighed any merit contained within the criticism (and there was considerable merit if one overlooked why the attack was being made, and by *whom* it was made). At this time if a politico even sounded left-wing she could be, and most often was, denounced as anti-woman, male-identified, and a dupe and tool of the "male-dominated" movement. In any case, political debates were "oppressive" to non-political sisters.

[2] There is truth in the suspicion; cf. Juliet Mitchell, *Women, The Longest Revolution* (New England Free Press).

[3] Much of the attack against Women's Liberation was in fact motivated by dogmatism and gross male chauvinism with its interest in retaining the predominance of male-dominated middle class culture—but not all of the attack. It is clear, in retrospect, that the left wing sects (with the exception of S.D.S.) also attacked because they took the women's movement very seriously, which put them ahead of the political police and the counter-insurgency boys in understanding what was afoot

Externally, the articulation of a left analysis (or at least one that was easily recognizable as left) frightened women away and antagonized liberals. Because women were, by and large, indifferent to politics (and as unconsciously anti-communist as every other "apolitical" American), left-political agitation, which they didn't understand, bored them or scared them or both. What women did understand was daily life at home or on the job (i.e., personal troubles) and the evils of discrimination, which the Civil Rights movement had finally succeeded in having generally condemned as un-American.[4] Antagonizing liberals was held by many to be an unwise strategy. It was felt that recognition of the legitimacy of women's demands for equality was dependent upon wrenching support from the liberal male establishment. This was particularly true of the National Organization of Women, which greatly feared being publicly contaminated by too close a connection with "bra-burning," left-leaning Women's Liberation.[5]

Another influential factor weakening the over-all position of radical women at this time was the isolation of the politicos from the larger left-wing movement. Left women had rebelled against the male chauvinism and male dominance in the Civil Rights Movement, the S.D.S., etc., so that they were not only engaged in a struggle with the liberal feminists, but also with the male-leadership hierarchies of the wider movement. The results of these conflicts were threefold: (1) many left women who might have become agitators within the women's movement were unwilling to accept the ostracism which would be inflicted on them if they were known participants in Women's

[4] Exploitation, the very heart of the Free Enterprise System (a nice way of saying Capitalism) remains all-American. Thus we have a situation of "equal exploitation" as the basis of a liberal utopia.

[5] N.O.W. however was not at all adverse to trying to drum up Women's Liberation legions to support all of their programs, to which end they engaged in considerable intrigues—and when rebuffed gave out injured cries of "unsisterliness."

Liberation;[6] (2) left women who had embraced Women's Liberation often became so demoralized in, and consequently embittered by, the larger left that they opposed *any* collaboration with male-dominated organizations (and often, with men in general); (3) finally, many left-wing women formed small, all-female left feminist groups (this was particularly characteristic of New York) marked from their inception with a bitter sectarian militance.

All of these factors taken together meant that from 1966 to 1969 the women's movement recruited new members and struggled to gain public recognition on the basis of its liberal, public ideology, a peculiar amalgamation of a feminist ideology, a demand for equality of opportunity, and a mystique of sisterhood. It is to this public ideology and its class character that we shall now turn.

SISTERHOOD

The stress of the early and primitive ideology of Women's Liberation was on psychological oppression and social and occupational discrimination. The politics of psychological oppression and the injustice of discrimination were aimed at altering the consciousness of women newly recruited to the movement in order to transform personal discontent into political militancy. Women, being in most cases without a political vocabulary, could more easily respond to the articulation of emotions. (This, of course, explains the impassioned personal nature of the polemical literature.) Furthermore, women of almost any political persuasion, or lack of one, could easily adopt the straightforward demand for social equality. Explaining the necessity for the abolition of social classes, the complexities of capitalism and its necessary evolution into imperialism, and the like, was a much more formidable task, and often elicited more hostility than sympathy.

The stress on discrimination and the adoption of the "black analogy" (demonstrating that the process of discrimination and oppression was almost identical for blacks and women)[7] was aimed directly at the liberal core of American politics. The demand for equality was a socially legitimate protest demand whereas advocating social revolution was not. Furthermore, sex discrimination affected all women, irrespective of race or class (although the fact that it did not affect all women in the same way or to the same degree was often absent from discussion). The primacy of those ideologies of oppression and discrimination and the absence of ideologies condemning exploitation facilitated the recruitment of large numbers of women, but they were predominantly from the middle class.

The politics of oppression and the politics of discrimination became amalgamated and popularized in the ethic of sisterhood. Sisterhood invoked the common oppression of all women, the common discrimination suffered by all. Sisterhood was the bond, the strength, the glory of the women's movement; it was the call to unity, based on the idea that common oppression creates common understanding and common interests upon which all women (transcending class and race lines) could unite to bring about a vast movement for social justice—after first abolishing the special privileges enjoyed by all men. Sisterhood became a moral imperative: disagreements were to be minimized, no woman was to be excluded from the movement (not even

---

[6] Another very important reason why many women stayed in the male dominated left was that they simply could not accept the public ideology of Women's Liberation, i.e., simply could not bring themselves to equate obtaining day care centers with an active struggle against American imperialism in Viet Nam. The animosity of the liberal and reactionary feminists made life intolerable for women who would not compromise their anti-imperialism.

[7] The "black analogy" is no analogy at all, since the process of discrimination and exploitation under American imperialism is the same. *What is not the same is the outcome:* in *no way* are racism and sexism *the same thing.* Racism is a thousand times more virulent and imposes suffering unknown to any white person, e.g., the genocide in Viet Nam by American militarism.

Jackie Onassis, said some, for are not *all* women oppressed by men?) ; all sisters were to love other sisters, all sisters were to support all sisters. The years 1968–1969 were a veritable orgy of sisterly communion.[8]

The ethic of sisterhood operated in a powerful way to assure unity in the movement. It included the proscription against public attacks against any women; the outward united front position of Women's Liberation and the National Organization of Women; and the proscription against making public the internal ideological struggle that was even then in progress. Sisterhood, and the sentiments of unity it fostered, did help to protect the movement from acutely destructive sectarianism in the early years, and it certainly did provide enormous psychological strength and support to women who were openly rebelling for the first time in their lives.

Yet the ethic of sisterhood also disguised and mystified the internal class contradictions of the women's movement. Specifically, sisterhood temporarily disguised the fact that all women do *not* have the same interests, needs, and desires. Working class women and middle class women, student women and professional women, black women and white women have more *conflicting* interests than could ever be overcome by their common experience based on sex discrimination. The

illusions of sisterhood lasted as long as they did because Women's Liberation was a white, middle class movement. The voice of poor and working class women was heard only infrequently, while the racism of white, middle class women permitted them to reject the criticism and reservations expressed by black women.

The collapse of sisterhood has not resulted from any broadening of the class base of the movement, which remains middle and lower-middle class. It has resulted from growing political divergence, particularly because of the emergence of ideologies of feminism which are openly reactionary. Perhaps even more importantly, it has collapsed because women have failed to create human relationships that differ from those of the society at large. Just as the men most skilled at verbal persuasion and personal aggressiveness were the "powers" in the male-dominated movement, the women most skilled at emotional manipulation have come to dominate the vast collection of cliques that make up the women's movement.[9] Struggles for power are intrinsically oppressive, and they can become very ugly, and a lot of people get hurt. Somewhere in that process, sisterhood died.

FEMINISM

The ideologies which may be termed "Feminist" are many and varied. For purposes of parsimony, only two versions, liberal and radical reactionary feminism, will be discussed. However, it is important to remember that until 1969 there were at least three basic feminist tenets which almost everyone accepted. These were: (1) First priority must be placed upon the liberation of women; (2) action programs ought to put first priority

[8] If all this sounds ironically bitter, that's because it is largely directed against my own one-time belief that women could transcend class and race lines to form a single, radical movement. The psychological roots of these goings-on were related to the joy of being liberated from self-contempt, and a sense of belonging somewhere, at last, in one's own right. The political roots were in the ostracism and general ugliness that one suffered from the male-dominated left. In retrospect, I can only comprehend it as a sort of madness—yet, a derangement far preferable to the present with its cloying hypocrisy and vicious slander. At any rate, I can at least say in self-consolation that I always maintained that Jackie ought to be expropriated. (This exception considerably dampened my sisterly feelings.) Many of us came out of the Civil Rights movement with an abiding detestation of liberals and never did reflect sisterly sentiment toward N.O.W.

[9] The whole question of the internal structure of the movement is urgent, but it is also difficult and complicated. Above all, what is needed is a critique of the "anti-elitist" ideology and its manipulation in the struggle for power. Such a discussion is unfortunately beyond the scope of this article.

upon woman-centered issues (sometimes extended to demand the boycott of any actions which were not woman-centered, e.g., anti-R.O.T.C. demonstrations);[10] (3) any revolution that did not entail the liberation of women was of no interest to women, or ought to be repudiated by women.[11]

Underlying the nominal agreement on basic tenents of feminism, two contradictory lines of analysis were present from the inception of the movement. One line stemmed from the assertion that "men are the enemy" and that the primary contradiction was between men and women. The politicos' analysis argued that the system (and the "system" could mean different things, e.g., internal class contradictions, imperialism, etc.) was the cause of the oppression of women—in which some men were the enemy but most men were dupes, bribed through their privileged position over women to divide the people's struggle. In other words, male chauvinism, like racism, was false consciousness.

The first analysis has the merit of simplicity, since locating the enemy presents no problem; the second analysis has the merit of being correct, but the disadvantage of being complicated.

One can immediately see that the second analysis, pointing to class and property relations as the source of the oppression of women is much more difficult to propagandize than the first. In everyday life what all

women confront is the bullying exploitation by men, particularly if they are middle class and unmarried. From the job to the bedroom, men are the enemy. But men are not the same *kind* of enemy to all women. For a middle class woman, particularly if she has a career or is planning to have a career, the primary problem is to free women from the male dominance which is maintained through institutionalized discrimination. It is not class exploitation, but the system of sexual inequality that is the primary source of middle class female protest. Consequently, it is reform of the existing system which is required, not the revolutionary abolition of existing property relations and, with them, existing class privileges.

The fact that the fight against discrimination was essentially a liberal reform program was for a time mystified by the assertion that the equalization of the status of women would bring about a "revolution" because it would alter the structure of the family and transform human relationships (which were held to be perverted through the existence of male authoritarianism).[12] However, equalization of the status of women is not, nor will it be, the cause of the decomposition of the nuclear family. The organization of the family is a result of the existing economic structure. The claim that status equalization would bring about "revolution" is of the same order as the claim made by the Suf-

---

[10] This position was tactically incorrect because it isolated the women's movement; it was politically incorrect because it did not understand the interrelationship between the oppression of women and imperialism. The basis for the refusal to join forces was a rejection of male opportunism—the desire to use women to fight their battles for them. It is the old familiar story of reactionary male chauvinism fostering reactionary feminism.

[11] Conscious and unconscious anti-communism was greatly fostered by the latter point, as it was often argued that since women in Russia, Cuba, Viet Nam and China were not "liberated" then socialism and communism ought to be rejected by women. Lack of any adequate knowledge of these revolutions made such arguments sound convincing, even though the allegation is false. Cf. Jack Beldon, *China Shakes the World*, and Wilfred Burchett, *Viet Nam North*.

[12] The belief that women were superior to men, that they were equipped with greater empathy, lovingness, and virtue (an ideology also held by the Suffragists) was widely accepted by women. For middle class women it is far from the truth. Social hypocrisy, gossip, slander, emotional manipulation, envy, jealousy, disloyalty, extreme individualism (especially in competition for men) are the necessary results of a socially powerless and dependent position. Women's Liberation sought, through the small group, to change some of these traits in women, but as the ideology of the "emotional and ethical superiority" of women spread, it was no longer necessary to carry through the difficult process of self-change. Women, celebrating themselves, refused to confront the results of a secondary status in their own behavior. The result is that the women's movement is oftentimes more of a hell than the old male dominated movement used to be.

fragists that giving women the vote would usher in an era of world peace. Ideologically, the claims for the revolutionary results stemming from the equalization of the status of women were a compromise worked out between the liberals and the radicals within the movement. This compromise enabled the liberals to co-opt the revolutionary rhetoric of the left.

Feminism, based upon the assertion that "men are the principal enemy," in turn branched into liberal feminism and what may be termed "radical reactionary feminism." Liberal feminists do not openly admit that their ideology is a variant on "men are the enemy." Instead they adopt the forgiving, maternalistic view that men are "misguided" and that through education and persuasion (legal if need be) men can be brought around to accepting the equalization of the status of women. Since the question of the origins of injustice and the roots of social power are never very strong elements in any liberal ideology, there is little besides legislative reforms and education to fall back on.[13]

Reactionary feminism takes as its fundamental tenet the proposition that "all men are the enemies of all women," and in its most extreme form, calls for the subjugation, sometimes the extermination, of all men. The common thread in all reactionary feminist positions is a conception of the world which requires the separation of the sexes. Men become the existential enemy, the symbol of violence, oppression and evil. Women, on the other hand, are conceptualized as

nurturant and good. In any confrontation between good and evil, evil is triumphant. The only solution is the isolation of the principal of good, to avoid its destruction or contamination by evil. The clearest statement of such a philosophical vision is presented by ideologies which call for the end to all sexual relationships between men and women, including a rejection of the childbearing function of women. In a sense, there *is* an enemy within: sexuality and reproduction itself. If men represent evil, then escape from evil, and the affirmation of good, can only occur if the source of contact, the biological imperative itself, is rejected.

Reactionary feminism is in some respects similar to a nationalist position: it conceptualizes women as a people, and as a people they must be separated from the others, the oppressor nation—men. Taken to its logical conclusion, demanding a complete separation of the sexes must lead either to extermination of the oppressor or else to "nationhood." Of course, reactionary feminism rarely follows its position to its logical conclusions. Reactionary feminism is not an ideology of revolution. At best, it is an ideology which supports women in a present day withdrawal from both men and political activism in order to create, in effect, a feminine counterculture. In its most militant forms, reactionary feminism is an ideology of vengeance, which justifies women's hatred of men, and which expresses itself in rejection of the hated object. It is also a profound statement of despair, which sees the cruelty and ugliness of present relationships between men and women as immutable and inescapable.

Reactionary feminism may be politically confused, but it powerfully expresses the experience and feeling of a whole segment of the female population. Reactionary feminism found its greatest stronghold in New York (the cruelest city), but the phenomenon is found in all large American cities. Masses of women, born into the middle class, often well educated, flood the offices as clerks, telephone operators, low-level editors, typists and secretaries. They are poorly paid, their jobs are

---

[13] The discussion of social class and the question of discrimination and legislative reform should not lead one to reject legislative reform. Such reforms as would limit the current abuses of working women are real gains, and worth fighting for. The challenge is to make it clear that legislative reforms are a very minor element in necessary changes, that work to the greater advantage of middle class people. It is possible to support efforts for legislative change, but only if a left set of demands, reflecting class interests, are not submerged and lost in the struggle. It is necessary, as the old socialists used to say, to be in the same march on occasion, but aways under one's own banner.

not respected, and they have little job se-curity. The humiliations heaped upon their heads at work are nothing compared to what happens in the sexual marketplace, where competition for men is ferocious, and where men exploit the situation to the fullest.[14] The root of reactionary feminism is in the sexual exploitation of women and so finds its strongest base among these unmarried, mid-dle class women in the large cities. Its strength lies in the fact that it does express and appeal to the psychological oppression that is far worse than the conditions of eco-nomic exploitation experienced by these women.

The great weakness of all left-wing ideo-logies in women's liberation as a middle class movement was that they never adequately understood or spoke to the realities of sexual exploitation. Even uncompromising leftist women will sit to one side with a soft smile and narrowed eyes while a reactionary fem-inist has the floor, for the anger runs deep and the wounds are daily re-opened. Further-more, the mechanical repetition of "socialism first and then women's liberation" or the even more idiotic claim that socialism by itself would accomplish the liberation of women, was so patently false, so remote from the inner turmoil experienced by women, that it discredited left-wing analysis all the more.

The fact is that socialism will *not* guaran-tee the liberation of women, and the U.S.S.R. is an example of that simple fact. Socialism, without question, improves the material con-ditions of women, and creates new opportun-ities, but one might argue that the same can as easily be accomplished under capitalism.

The inability or unwillingness to talk about communist society and the social revolution, which must be built on the foundation of an economic revolution, led to the early rejec-tion of a "socialist" utopia, and left the way clear for the spread of reactionary ideologies.

It should be clearly understood that reac-tionary feminism is a middle and lower-mid-dle-class phenomenon. Even though working class, and especially poor, women experience male chauvinism as more exploitative and of-ten far more brutal, they also find it much easier to see the ways in which men are op-pressed. These women are able to understand the sources of aimless violence. They know at first hand the ravages of unemployment and enforced pauperization that create the psy-chological despair which is a class component of male chauvinism. The anti-male line was always repugnant to many poor and working class women, especially Black women, and kept many of these women from being able to relate to Women's Liberation in any way (no matter how much they were prepared to improve life for themselves and for their children—including struggling against male chauvinism in their own men). The daily experience with acute exploitation makes it very clear that it is not men who are the enemy, but the wealthy who are the enemy.

Another ideological weakness in the women's movement is embodied in the as-sertion that "women will make the revolu-tion." "Women will make the revolution" can mean two quite different things: one is, quite literally, that women will make the revolution because men are too corrupt, too self-interested and too bound up in the op-pression of people, especially females, to *ever* be trusted as allies. This position stems from conceptualizing men as the primary enemy. The second position involves a two-stage argument: (1) there exists a contradiction between men and women based upon a monopoly of social power in the hands of men; thus, the first step is to create a power base for women which will equalize the power relationships between men and

[14] Many novels, films, and plays have depicted this world. Unfortunately, the authors were primarily men, and little suspected the feelings of hatred and bitterness that women so carefully disguised. The quintessence of that hatred and bitterness was the genius of Valerie Solanis. It is also reflected in a well-known cartoon in which a lovely woman con-templates a heap of human bones with an expression of sublime satisfaction. The caption reads: "He asked her to eat him and she did."

women; (2) men and women will then be able to relate to each other from the base of their own power, represented for women by an autonomous women's movement. The internal contradictions may thus be resolved and class struggle undertaken on the basis of an equal partnership in the form of alliances and coalitions. However, these steps are not seen as discrete, one following the other, but evolving dialectically through organization and practice.

The problem with the notion that *only* women will make the revolution is that it overlooks what it most often points out: women are only half of the population. If it isn't likely that the men are going to do it alone, it isn't likely that the women are either. Furthermore, all women are *not* going to make the revolution: lady psychologists are not going to return to the factory; rich women are not going to give up their elegant houses to go on welfare; and the middle class housewife is not going to become a professional revolutionary.

The whole ideology of "women alone are going to make the revolution" is cloaked in mysticism, invoking an ill-defined vision of woman's "exotic powers" that can somehow bring about the just society in a way totally different from your common, garden variety, "male-dominated" revolution. Violence is *male*, therefore the women's revolution will not be violent, it will be—what? It has not as yet been demonstrated that hexing the ruling class can stop a bullet, discourage the police, shorten a prison sentence, or overthrow the system. The mysticism of "special powers" is much more gratifying than a dismal theory which does not see the superiority of women, but instead describes a painfully unglamorous process requiring objective social and economic conditions, hard work, total commitment, hard thinking (which is in any case "elitist"), effective organizing, the capacity to seize power, and a lot of luck.

The importance of the slogan, "women will make the revolution," was that it articulated the experience of many movement women. After nearly two years of "women's caucuses" many new left women had decided that the realities of male chauvinism made it absolutely necessary to form a separate and autonomous women's movement. This decision was thus a direct result of understanding the roots of male chauvinism, i.e., that the basis of the unequal relationship between men and women was power, not attitudes.

The autonomous movement did create power where little had existed before, and created a new consciousness of the subjugation of women, as well as raising profound issues about the nature and organization of the entire left movement in the United States. However, it should never be forgotten that leftist women were literally forced to create an independent movement. Every attempt to organize within existing left organizations degenerated into the most disgusting forms of tokenism and male liberalism.[15] The autonomous movement inevitably became isolated from the struggles of the existing left-wing movements, particularly as the hostility of men, feeling their privileges threatened, became insufferable.

From a position of relative weakness, left women were, and still are, often helpless to stem the tide of either liberalism or reaction. Again, it is a case of reactionary male chauvinism creating a reactionary women's movement. The lessons from "women will make the revolution" are clear: the basis of the oppression of women is power, and the resolution of the contradiction is not a matter of moral persuasion or individual therapy. Male privilege is not given up voluntarily, it must be taken away. Overall the saga of Women's Liberation testifies most clearly to a paramount truth: a progressive revolutionary movement cannot contain within itself the contradictions of oppression, inequality and special privilege.

[15] One example of this is the revolting and lamentable history of the women's caucus within the New University Conference.

CLASS

Women's Liberation focused almost exclusively upon psychological oppression and sexual exploitation as compared with the National Organization of Women's emphasis on liberal reform measures. In part this distinction can be explained by the fact that Women's Liberation was first a student, and then a student-age, movement. The youthful constituency of Women's Liberation faced different problems than those of the older, married, and largely professional women in N.O.W. Furthermore, the revulsion with liberal politics which is characteristic of modern student movements was also typical of Women's Liberation. The program actually undertaken by Women's Liberation primarily reflected the problems of younger women: the need for legal abortion (since many unmarried young women were oppressed by unwanted pregnancies and the brutalizing experience of obtaining an illegal abortion); the demand for day care centers by those young women who did have children, but whose husbands, just starting out in their careers, could not provide the resources which would free a restless young wife from the drudgery of constant child care; the creation of women's centers and small group meetings to provide young women with a "place of their own" in which to socialize, to work for their social demands, or to help women in distress.

Women's Liberation began to reach a somewhat wider constituency, as young, unmarried, non-student women began to be recruited into the movement; agitation at the workplace began in a very modest way around modest issues: an end to being forced to wait on the boss with coffee; the right to dress as one pleased; better pay and better hours. With the cooling of hostility between women in the S.D.S. and Women's Liberation, and with prison experience on the part of the young politicos, the problems of women prisoners were raised, thus establishing some of the first real links with third

world and poor women. In addition, the gay community, suffering from universal legal and social persecution, tends to be a very mixed and egalitarian society. Thus the rise of gay liberation and the open participation of lesbians in Women's Liberation also brought working class influence to the movement. Nonetheless, the major issues and the major concerns were, and remain, predominantly reflective of the life-styles and needs of unmarried, youthful, middle and lower-class women.

An emphasis upon economic exploitation, which could have begun to reveal the internal class contradictions within the women's movement, was almost totally absent from the ideological mainstream of Women's Liberation. Rather, Women's Liberation politics were dominated by problems of psychological oppression and sexual exploitation. This is not surprising since the major oppression experienced by middle class women is not material, but sexual and psychological. Given the almost exclusive attention to sexual exploitation and its accompanying psychological oppression, the result was to focus not upon white male supremacy, but upon its product, the practice of male chauvinism; not upon the need for revolutionary social and economic changes, but upon individualized struggles between men and women concerning the oppressive attitudes and objective sexual and social privileges of men. Furthermore, emphasis upon male chauvinism had the effect of privatizing the contradiction between men and women, and transmuting the conflict into problems of personal relationships, rather than politicizing the conflict as part of the overall capitalist system of economic and class exploitation.

The result was the production of an ideology unique to Women's Liberation, one which focused upon the individual relationships between men and women, and between women and women (cf. Shulamith Firestone's analysis). This ideology is an important component of radical reactionary feminism. It is strongly related to the widespread adoption of lesbian relationships as a means of escaping the male-female relationship, and it is also the ideological basis for the small group.

The small group was the method used by Women's Liberation to organize women. Literally thousands of small groups sprang up all over the country, because they were ideally suited to women. The group form of organization stressed personal face-to-face relationships, honesty, emotions and direct experience. Women were encouraged to speak and to participate in an atmosphere that was intimate and non-threatening. The origin and key importance of the small group is to be found in the fundamental tenet of Women's Liberation: "organize around your own oppression." There were many foundations for such a position. First, the major task faced by early organizers was to get women to admit that they were, in fact, feeling oppressed. The socialization of women includes a vast superstructure of rationalization for women's secondary status. The superstructure of belief is reinforced through inducing guilt and fear as a response to rebellion against women's traditional role; in addition, women are raised to be very conservative, to cling to the verities of the hearth, and to have a limited and unquestioning acceptance of things as they are. However, it soon became apparent that under the surface crust of submission, an enormous frustration, anger, and bitterness had built up in countless women—they were suffering from what Betty Friedan called "an illness without a name." Women's Liberation gave the illness a name, an explanation, and a cure. The cure was the small group and the method was what the Chinese Communists call "Speaking Bitterness." The bitterness, once spoken, was almost overwhelming in its sheer emotional impact.

The small group was supposed to have been the path to sisterhood, that unity expressed in empathic identification with the suffering of all women, moving from sisterhood to politics, and from politics to revolution. The leftist women understood that women could only be organized through an understanding of their own subjective oppression. The small group, with its intimate exchange of experience, helped to unlock a woman's feelings from the straight-jacket of the conventional ideologies of "women's place." Leftist women came to believe that because the oppression of all women was a reality which cross-cut class and race lines, women could be brought to a political understanding of the need for cross-class unity through an understanding of their personal oppression. Thus the small group was originally visualized as a means of political education, as well as personal development and discovery. In time, however, politics almost entirely disappeared from the small group, as it became more and more a source of social and psychological support. It is quite possible that for the majority of women in Women's Liberation, membership in a small group represents the full extent of their participation. Rivalries, disputes, and feuds have often developed between small groups in the same city. These, along with ideological divisions between present day politicos and feminists, frequently have the effect of making even the minimal functioning of a women's center impossible.

Having as their goal the radicalization of the Women's Liberation constituency, radical women talked a great deal about the common source of oppression, hoping to foster that "empathic identification" that would provide the bridge to cross-class unity. There was, however, much less talk about the fact that the common oppression of women *has different results in different social classes.* What leftists did not take into account was the fact that middle class women do not *want* to identify with their class inferiors; they do not care, by and large, what happens to women who have problems different from their own. Middle class women greatly dislike being reminded that they are richer, better educated, healthier, and have better life chances than most people.

The class position of almost all recruits to Women's Liberation led to a translation of "organize around your own oppression" to "organize around your own interests".[16] Middle class women used this maxim to justify their own class interests and to justify ignoring the mass of lower and working class women. They rationalized that "ending our oppression will end theirs." That is, the fight against discrimination would equalize the status of all women. Most serious of all, middle class women defended their massive racism by replying to Black criticism, whether by men or by women, "we are not only 'also' oppressed, we are 'equally' oppressed." The way was then open for the expression of classic white racism. In most cases, the blacks and the Black struggle simply became invisible. Gestures of liberal tokenism and liberal rhetoric were made now and then to placate white guilt.[17]

In sum, the numerous instances where the small group changed from its original consciousness-raising function into a mechanism for social control and group therapy were results of the predominantly middle class character of Women's Liberation. The fact that there were so few women who were directly experiencing material deprivation, poverty, threats of genocide or enforced pauperization—that is, who were not driven by conditions of objective exploitation and deep social oppression—made it almost inevitable that the search for cultural and lifestyle changes would be substituted for radical and revolutionary politics. The relative wealth and privilege of middle class people makes it possible for them to envision a good life within the system as it is, even to create such a life through counter-culture forms such as communal living or adopting lesbianism as a way to short circuit male sexual exploitation. The transition from self-understanding to altruistic identification and cross-class unity thus never occurred within the small group because the real basis for radicalization, i.e., objective exploitation and oppression, was absent.

In retrospect it all becomes painfully clear. From the self-interested position of a middle class woman, Viet Nam can be written off as "penis" war which women, who will never be soldiers, should ignore in order to press for liberation on the sexual front. Imperialism is a wicked trick on the part of male chauvinist, domineering elites, and their female dupes, which women should ignore while fighting for day-care centers for students and faculty. Racism is a cry which is nothing more than a nasty conspiracy by Black men to sabotage the efforts of white liberationists—and thus can be ignored while forging ahead with the abortion protests at the legislature. The exploitation of working class men and women is little more than "commie cant."

NEW DIRECTIONS

Women's Liberation, despite its rhetoric, pretensions, and brave beginning, has outwardly become what it really is, indeed, what it had to be: a reactionary middle class reform movement. Nonetheless, the movement has accomplished a great deal, much of which is not merely middle class reform. Women have won recognition for the justness of their cause; the left wing movement in the United States has been de-mystified, revealed as a shoddy copy of the alienated and anti-human competitive careerism of the bourgeois world; the broad outlines of the liberating ideas of Women's Liberation are slowly spreading to Third World groups and filtering into the working class; thousands of women now have a chance for a better life; large numbers of

[16] This attitude can be summed up in a comment made to me in Washington, D. C., by a woman professor: "We have to take care of our own problems first"—she might well have added, first, last and always. The most notorious example of such middle class self-interest was the struggle over the equal rights amendment, which would have advantaged professional women at the expense of working women.

[17] It should never be forgotten that whites and middle class people have a good deal to feel guilty about.

women have been politically mobilized who were before passive and conservative.

However, at the present time leftist women within the women's struggle, especially those women who have worked within the autonomous movement, are faced with the hard reality that Women's Liberation, as an autonomous movement, has failed to express the radical energy that was expected. The causes of this failure rest basically with the class composition of the movement itself, but there has also been a failure of ideology and a failure of practice.

Left-wing women have not as yet fused feminism and revolutionary social change into a coherent whole which has the capacity to organically link the women's struggle with class struggle. Left-wing women have not as yet constructed a program of action which expresses both feminist interests and class interests. Women have fallen into a tragic and paradoxical trap. In building an autonomous movement, women have forced themselves to become as limited in practice as are women in the larger culture.

The larger culture dictates that women shall be concerned only with home and family, "women's concerns"; in the same way, Women's Liberation became limited, almost exclusively, to "women's concerns." Part of the reason for this limitation was male dominance in the Left. The insurgency of women and their challenge to male domination in leadership was answered by segregating women into a "woman's "bag." ("Go over there and do day care, that is *your* place.") The result is that women do not understand that they, as women, have just as total a stake in the conduct of American militarism and imperialism as does every citizen of this country; that every issue on the left is also a woman's issue. The first step towards a new direction would be to refuse, absolutely refuse, to be caught in the trap of so-called "women's issues." The existence of an auton-

omous movement does not demand the segregation of women. I mean by segregation that in the movement today *women are still permitted to express themselves freely only in the women's movement.* The larger movement refuses, even today, the recognition of women's rightful political role. Establishing a separate women's power base failed in its confrontation with the Left; the autonomous movement became a ghetto. It trivialized the women's struggle, and severely limited the range of women's political action.

The crucial question is that of practice: what form will organizing take in the future; what constituencies will be given priority? If, in fact, much of the present crisis stems from the predominantly middle class character of Women's Liberation, it seems clear that agitation among women must extend into the working and lower classes. This means a shift in priority to working with women's unions, working women, welfare organizations, and similar kinds of organizational efforts. The problems presented by shifting the class priorities in the women's movement (not to be confused with Women's Liberation) are exactly the same problems that face all cadres (who are drop-outs from the middle class). Just as the larger movement is going to have to learn to solve these problems, women will have to learn to solve them. Such problems have been solved in the past in revolutionary movements, and it can be done again.

In the end, it is clear that a revolutionary movement will only emerge from a revolutionary constituency. If women want to work to bring about the liberation of women and the liberation of all people, then women must relocate themselves as a central part of the overall struggle. They must rediscover their own central political role and become a part of, and serve, the people who will be the leading forces for revolutionary change.

A Feminist Reply: We Deny the Allegations and Defy the Allegator

ANN LEFFLER AND DAIR L. GILLESPIE

According to Marlene Dixon, Women's Liberation is a flop. Its middle-class constituency, by definition morally degenerate, doomed from the start to liberal and even reactionary politics: this, despite the heroic efforts of politicos to protect the revolutionary tiara their bourgeois sisters seemed intent upon tarnishing.

Now, we don't want to alarm anyone, but rumors have reached us that it is not ability which advances you, but how well you play the game. It has even been whispered by slanderous extremists that the same process applies to the left and to Women's Liberation as well. If this is true, Dixon is on the right track. Substituting rancor for rigor, susurrus for substance, histrionics for history, and "middle-class" for depravity, she moves like a rook through the labyrinthine twists of what others might consider complex intellectual issues.

Note: Ann Leffler and Dair L. Gillespie, "A Feminist Reply: We Deny the Allegations and Defy the Allegator," *Berkeley Journal of Sociology*, Vol. 16, 1971–1972, pp. 168–179. Reprinted by permission of the Berkeley Journal of Sociology.

HISTORY: CANT AND RECANT

Dixon's historical account—the 1971 version at least—depicts politico women as the intimidated underdogs of the early movement. Actually, from its beginnings until at least 1968, Women's Liberation was oriented toward and intimately linked with the left. Most leaders during this period were the wives, lovers, and ex's of male celebrities. This factor so strongly permeated Women's Liberation *weltanschauungen* that many movement women still turn to the left for ideology and intimate contacts.[1] Talk of

[1] Coming out of the Civil Rights Movement, Women's Liberation members often sought similar legitimacy from the Black left, for both moral and political points with white men. The very use of the Black analogy demonstrates this. The "sisterhood" concept was also taken from the Black movement. In effect, the movement women were saying to Blacks, "See—we, too, have suffered. Accredit us." From the beginning, the women's movement has been very sensitive to charges of racism, and almost all its major campaigns, e.g., those for child care, Joan Bird, Erika Huggins, Angela Davis, welfare rights support, have in part been attempts to as-

"dialectical materialism," "manifestos," "capitalism," and "oppression" larded early women's gatherings. The original name of the movement, the "Women's Liberation Front," was deliberately copied from the N.L.F., designed to shock middle-class liberal sensibilities and to reassure the left.

Dixon claims ridicule from "The Powers" and a need for legitimacy dictated early movement ideology. (p. 149) Who were "The Powers"? From whom did the movement want to "gain legitimacy"? Certainly not the capitalists of imperialistic Amerikkkkka: until 1969, they ignored Women's Liberation completely. When Marlene Dixon speaks of "The Powers," she really means the left; and when she speaks of women who sought legitimacy, she really means they sought it from the left.[2] True, early Women's

Liberation writings and speeches frequently criticized male radicals. Of the "you done me wrong" genre, these attacks revealed a fervent hope that left brothers, faced with the dastardy of their deeds, would make room for women in the steering committees of radical politics. So much for her account of the source of Women's Liberation ideology.

RED HERRINGS

She's no better on politico prescriptions than politico history, telling us only what opinion to hold about left analyses. They were dialectical, altruistic, complicated, and correct.

Well, all right. It makes a pretty package. But if Dixon's own analysis is any indication, there's nothing much inside. Her caveats on the proper revolution amount to warmedover vulgar Marxist slogans, with a dash of humanism for the "apolitical" palate. A proper revolutionary avoids emotional manipulation (154); refrains from both intra- and internecine struggles for power (153, 163); cools it with the "social hypocrisy, gossip, slander, emotional manipulation, envy, jealousy, disloyalty, and extreme individualism" (156); and has good human relation-

---

suage white guilt. Far from "rejecting the criticism and reservations expressed by black women" (p. 154), Women's Liberation has eagerly solicited them: and the harsher the better. In fact, any Black woman who fails to deliver is likely to be dismissed as a "Tom," black bourgeois," or nut. The Black movement for its part, in effect rewarded for refusal to grant legitimacy credentials, has consistently maintained a condescending attitude towards the women's movement; and the more the Blacks raise charges of racism, the more slavishly women turn to them for approval.

This is not to imply that the women's movement is not racist. It is merely to say that Dixon's cries of racism are an old counter in an old game. Women's Liberation as now constituted is no more and no less racist than any other white left-of-center organization.

Blacks' and women's experiences differ: of course. Just the same, certain structural similarities generally characterize oppressed situations. If we, following Dixon, call exploration of these similarities "racist," we must abandon all efforts to understand social phenomena common to powerless groups. Creating a sociology of oppression then becomes impossible.

[2] The 1968 Chicago conference, the only national Women's Liberation conference held in this country, is a good example. "The defensiveness that characterized the workshops and plenary sessions was the expression of an overriding anxiety about being able to justify the existence of a women's movement. The Invisible Audience present at the Chicago conference were the very 'male heavies' who had done so much to bring about the existence of a radical

women's female liberation movement." (p. 21) ". . . The strategy that the leftist women adopted for the Chicago conference was to develop a 'politics' with sufficient analytical merit to force the men to recognize the legitimacy of the women's movement, a tactic which has paid off in the [Left] Movement by 1969. Socialism, Revolution, Capitalism were thick in discussion." (p. 27)

"The ideology of the radical women was, by and large, an academic exercise in the art of the 'intellectual male heavy' in the Movement. The radical women were decimated by the invisible male audience. Thus, the real split among the women hinged upon the significant audience that women addressed: other women, or [Left] movement men." (p. 28) "On Women's Liberation," *Radical America*, by Marlene Dixon, Vol. IV, No. 2 (February 1970).

We do not object to Dixon's changing her opinions of certain historical facts. We do, however, object to her changing the facts themselves.

ships (154). A correct revolutionary platform does not criticize socialist governments
(155); does not focus on personal troubles
(like exploitation in the workplace) (158,
161); does not make modest demands (like
better pay and hours) (161); does not demand succor for its own petty problems, over-
looking real social oppression (151); does
not call all men the enemy, even if it seems
apparent that they are (155, 158); and is
altruistic (165). A perfect revolutionary
strategy shrinks from Jackie Onassis (153),
middle-class housewives (160), "unmarried,
youthful, middle and lower-middle class women" (162); enlists the poor and working
class (159); appeals to those "directly experiencing material deprivation, poverty,
threat of genocide, or enforced pauperization" (164); and does not rely on a potential base of only 50% of the population to
make a revolution (160). To make the revolution, one should return to the factory, give
up her elegant house, or go on welfare (160).

Some of her humanistic prescriptions are
utterly irrelevant to any human group, since
moral imperatives, as she herself pointed out
in the concept of "sisterhood," just don't cut
it. Others, such as the requirements for a
good revolutionary, seem sociologically naive
in the extreme. Regardless of a movement's
constituency, it would be unique not to find
therein struggles for control and their psychological concomitants—gossip, jealousy,
disloyalty, pettiness, etc. To blame such behavior upon middle-class domination of the
movement indicates a startling ignorance
about normal social processes.[3] Even to suggest that movement rivalry results from its
female composition pushes our credulity too
far. Power conflicts are unique neither to
women, nor to the middle-class, nor to a
combination of the two. Yes indeed, "struggles for power are intrinsically oppressive,
and they can become very ugly, and a lot of
people get hurt." But does Dixon really think
they can be eliminated?

[3] We suggest that she read Michels' *Political Parties*
for a better understanding of such processes.

Still she claims that middle-class ideological domination caused the movement's down-
fall. In addition to power struggles, she says,
three other class-related factors contributed
to the collapse of "sisterhood." First, recruitment appealed to the least common denominator. That is, (a) it recruited on the basis
of gender; and (b) it aimed at altering the
apolitical consciousness of women, thus transforming personal discontent into political
militancy. Second, the middle-class ideology
of Women's Liberation attacked personal oppression and sexual exploitation, not economic exploitation. Third, it camouflaged
class contradictions among women.

There are two problems with her first
criticism. Dixon assumes that gender recruitment attracted to the movement women who
were per force middle-class, apolitical, and
in general just plain dumb. For example,
she states: "Because women were, by and
large, indifferent to politics (and as unconsciously anti-communist as every other 'apolitical' American), left-political agitation,
which they didn't understand, bored them or
scared them or both." (p. 151) "Women,
being in most cases without a political vocabulary, could more easily respond to the
articulation of emotions. (This, of course,
explains the impassioned personal nature of
the polemical literature.)" (p. 152) ". . .
Women are raised to be very conservative, to
cling to the verities of the hearth, and to
have a limited and unquestioning acceptance
of things as they are." (p. 163) Communi-
cating with the intellectually deficient
(middle-class) recruits forced politicos to
"talk down," thereby diluting the revolutionary complexity of Women's Liberation.
Actually, one would have a hard time, even
if one were so inclined, to prove women are
any dumber than members of other movements. Perhaps Dixon's hypothetical dilution
problem can be attributed to whoever shares
her belief that women are stupid. Anyway,
early Women's Liberation literature evi-
dences no lack of political vocabulary, particularly of the left variety.

Further, politicos, Dixon among them,

consistently equate "politics" and "political debates" with the left movement line. To discuss anything else was considered nonpolitical from the very beginning. (The common phrase is, we believe, "she has no politics.") And in this definition lay a politico problem. New feminists, apolitical, dumb, and uppity, insisted that Women's Liberation analysis move beyond "leftese" to explore structural problems of all women as a group. Consequently, feminists refused to become mere support troops for such issues as attacks on imperialism.[4] This bitterly disappointed politicos. Their former followers began to criticize both their analyses and their liberal hope that the male-dominated left would accept individual women as legitimate leaders on left issues. That this remains the final hope of politicos is clear from Dixon's conclusion, which calls on women to "relocate themselves as a central part of the over-all struggle, rediscover their own central role," and chastises the "larger movement" for failure to recognize women's rightful political role. Thus, politico disgruntlement—feminists rejected the male left movement (not the working class, protestations to the contrary notwithstanding); they are in fact ward-heelers, wanting from women mainly a push up into left leadership circles. Thus Dixon: "The autonomous movement did create power where little had existed before, and created a new consciousness of the subjugation of women, as well as raising profound issues about the nature and organization of the entire left movement in the United States." (p. 160) Where did it create power? In which groups this new consciousness? Raised issues profound to whom? Wo-

men's position in the society-at-large has not changed. Upward mobility restrictions have relaxed only in the left.

Thus it is by no means clear that gender-based recruitment attracted either extraordinarily dumb or extraordinarily apolitical women. No: the politico failure was a failure to control movement actions and to circumscribe movement goals. That the failure was avoidable, reprehensible, or in any way connected with gender recruitment is at best moot. Sisterhood failed in this sense because politicos couldn't get their own way.

The second reason for the collapse of the sisterhood concept, according to Dixon, was "the primacy of these ideologies of oppression and discrimination and the absence of ideologies condemning exploitation" (p. 153). She states: "The root of reactionary feminism is in the sexual exploitation of women, and so finds its strongest base among these unmarried, middle class women in the large cities. Its strength lies in the fact that it does express and appeal to the psychological oppression that is far worse than the conditions of economic exploitation experienced by these women." (p. 158)

Dixon uses "sexual exploitation" in two senses throughout the paper. The first refers to the exploitation of women in sexual encounters; the second, to the economic exploitation of women as a gender. She continually confuses the two. For example, she clearly delineates the exploitation of women as a gender: "Masses of women, born into the middle class, often well educated, flood the offices as clerks, telephone operators, low level editors, typists, and secretaries. They are poorly paid, their jobs are not respected, and they have little job security." (p. 158) But she expects us to take her word for it that female psychological oppression (evidently connected with the exploitation of women in sexual encounters) is far worse than female economic exploitation, for "the humiliations heaped upon their heads at work are nothing compared to what happens in the sexual marketplace, where competition for men is ferocious, and where

---

[4] This is not to say feminists supported imperialism, or even were apathetic about it. But radical movements in general are perenially short of resources: money, time, and members. Priorities must be set, and women are clearly the only ones around willing to work on women's issues. Further, in coalitions with older, more powerful movements, new movements have a discouraging tendency to get co-opted. For feminists to suspect left coalition proposals was eminently wise.

men exploit the situation to the fullest."
(p. 158)

However, it seems to us that the two are
intricately linked, the warp and woof of
sexism. It is clear, even from Dixon's analysis,
that unmarried women are exploited in the
workplace. Their alternative is the nuptial
rat-race: that is, ferocious competition for
men, who exploit the situation to the fullest.
Nor does housewivery bring freedom. There
is no way to escape male exploitation—either
at work, or in husband-hunting, or in the
family. The psychological oppression of women is the direct result of our socio-economic
position. How, then, we ask Dixon, is the
psychological oppression of women any worse
than the economic exploitation? Does it
merely *seem* so because theory has not yet
clearly linked the two? Then it would seem
her duty, as a Marxist, to clarify the connection rather than deny the basic economic
exploitation of clerical and service workers.
Just what does Dixon mean by economic exploitation as opposed to psychological oppression and sexual exploitation? Is economic
exploitation confined to the proletariat?
Should we eliminate all clerical and service
workers (the major proportion of women
workers) from the working class? It seems
that is middle-class baiting,[5] without even a
clear notion of what she means by "middle-
class." And there are questions of empirical
fact as well. Is the women's movement more
middle-class than the male left? Is it middle-
class at all? What is middle-class? Is the
bourgeoisie predominantly young and single?
Where do housewives fit in? Part-time workers? Even assuming that her analysis of certain aspects of the ideology is correct—is
there any data that connects this ideology to
middle-class background, or must we yet
again take her word for it? And in light of
the fact that feminists began discussing class
at least as early as the politicos—how is it

that politicos but not feminists can transcend
middle-class backgrounds?[6]

The oppression/discrimination account of
sisterhood's collapse is nothing but a collection of undefined and contradictory concepts, linked by fiat. We are not told what
"oppression" is, nor "discrimination," nor
"exploitation," nor "middle-class"; their
connections with each other, with feminists,
and with the failure of sisterhood remain
unclear.

The third reason sisterhood flopped, she
says, was that it disguised and mystified the
internal class contradictions of the women's
movement, i.e., "the fact that all women do
not have the same interests, needs, and desires. Working class and middle class women,
student women and professional women,
black women and white women have more
conflicting interests than could ever be overcome by their common experience based on
sex discrimination." (p. 154) In other words,
women have so few common experiences and
problems that they can never constitute a
political movement in their own interests.
Yet even Marx recognized that there were
differences in the interests of the working
class. "The same would hold for the infinite
fragmentation of interests and positions
which the division of labor produces among

---

[5] Racist-baiting, middle-class baiting, single-women
baiting, youth-baiting, housewife-baiting, anti-communist baiting—a fine example of "hard thinking."

[6] Feminist newspapers today (*Ain't I a Woman?*, for
example) still excel in articles exploring the contradictions of class within the movement. Left wing
papers (such as *Rat* and *Off Our Backs*) have only
recently begun to discuss class and mainly in descriptions of working class women, not analyses of
class as a potentially divisive factor within the
women's movement.

The New York Feminists (formed in October
1969) were one of the first groups to include class
problems explicitly in their early analyses. They were
also, incidentally, the first group to revive the old
19th century term "feminism" and to legitimate it
for current movement usage. The term, at least until
1968, carried a faint air of fanaticism and anachro-
nism. True, the Feminists began in 1969, which brings
us to the edge of the time limits Dixon claims to be
describing; but in fact, she is as careless with her
dating as with her data, mainly describing in her
article events from 1968 to the present.

workers as among capitalists and land-owners. . . ." (Marx, 1953) This fragmentation of working class interests would hold so long as the working class did not consciously recognize the common interests of the entire class, i.e., did not attain true consciousness. "In so far as the identity of [worker] interests does not produce a community, national association, and political organization—they do not constitute a class. [Such groups in a common situation] are therefore unable to make their class interests heard in their own name. . . ." (Marx, 1946) Is the analysis really so different for women? There are divisions among both the working class and women. Yet she thinks class solidarity is possible while gender solidarity is not. We have no grounds to believe her. Sisterhood may have collapsed, but not for the reasons she gives.

Since she prefers innuendo to fact, and since her reconstruction of feminist ideology is haphazard, we don't know exactly which groups she considers when she discusses feminism. There seem to be four criteria for identifying feminists: (1) the belief that men are the enemy; and consequently (2) an emphasis on sexual and personal relationship complaints; (3) a preference for the small group as the basic structural unit of Women's Liberation; and (4) the goal of separation from men, or female nationhood.

At times she evidently considers the National Organization for Women the main source of liberal feminist thought. Unfortunately, if the belief that men are the enemy is the criterion, N.O.W. is no more feminist than John Jacob Jingleheimer Smith. Its members trace female subordination to inequitable laws; job-market policies, especially at the upper levels of the job-market; and sex-role stereotyping. Since this stereotyping affects both sexes, N.O.W. considers men also oppressed by sexism, and its goal is androgynous equality. As for focusing on sexual and personal relationships, N.O.W. rarely discusses them. And it avoids the small-group structure in favor of business meetings and a traditional organizational

hierarchy. Under no criterion is its ideology feminist.[7]

It is true that of the women's groups which *do* consider men the enemy, many use a small-group structure. However, it is by no means confined only to those who consider men the enemy. Small groups were developed in New York Radical Women, a leftist group, in 1968; the first Berkeley Women's Liberation group, also Leftist, used them in 1969 as its main organizing technique and structure-of-preference. Nor did all feminists approve their use.

As for sexual and personal relationships, left women do not cede the floor when feminists raise these issues: they jostle for the mike, being at least as fond of the topics as anyone else.[8] Again, many feminists do not consider these to be paramount women's issues, but rather useful indicators of a much more deeply rooted structural problem.

Finally, the goal of separation, and, at last, a genuine distinction between leftists and feminists: no leftist group has ever advocated it. The only trouble is, neither do many "reactionary" feminists. It marks what one of the authors, one and one-half years ago, criticized as a "cultural nationalist" faction

---

[7] We must warn the reader that we are using the term "feminist" as it was developed from 1968–1970. Simple self-identification doesn't work, since with the word's current media popularity, N.O.W., leftist, and I-don't-give-a-damn women often call themselves "feminists"; so do some men. This unfortunate popularity has robbed the word of most of its descriptive power.

   Incidentally, feminism never did and still does not dominate Women's Liberation—ideologically, organizationally, publicly, or privately; and it is not, *pace* Dixon, eagerly snatched up by bargain-basement ideology shoppers.

[8] "Theirs [politicos] has been a profoundly a-political, personalized struggle, one devoted to personal liberation. It is ironic that radical women, so wrapped up in their sex lives and Movement careers, so obsessed with personal liberation, have been unble to see the contradiction in turning to attack (as utopian, apolitical and bourgeois) women who are doing no more than the same thing, only with more boldness, originality and courage. . . ." Marlene Dixon, "On Women's Liberation," *Radical America*, Vol. IV, No. 2 (February 1970), p. 33.

within feminist ranks. And this faction has been criticized, until very recently, mainly by other feminists; left women, noting its resemblance to the once radically chic counter-culture and "cultural revolution," participated in many of its activities and adopted some of its proposals. A final point: the identification of all men as the enemy does not necessarily imply social segregation; it merely implies that if anyone is to be on top, it should be women. One need not go so far as to imagine male extermination or to dismiss the "biological imperative." Men have managed to retain power for lo, these many years, without such elaborate structures. There is no reason for women to assume that *we* will need them. We must only attain power, the rest follows. After several decades of being without institutionalized violence, men will learn to accept their subordination as reasonable and just.

So we are left with only one criterion for discovering whether or not your sister has married a feminist: the belief that men are the enemy. Dixon thinks this belief necessarily fuels sexual and personal relationship obsessions, small groups, and female separatism. She's wrong. Feminism did cause trouble in Women's Liberation, but not these particular troubles.

SAYING YES TO BOYS WHO SAY NO

Why then no movement unity, if her reasons for sisterhood's collapse are false? What *was* so bad about feminists?

Politico ideology and strategy serve certain political functions. First, we have noted throughout this essay that politicos have always faced left for assurance and legitimacy. Dixon states that first priority upon woman-centered issues was tactically incorrect because it isolated the women's movement (p. 155). From whom did it isolate the women's movement? From poor and working class women, the constituency the politicos

wanted to attract? What is her evidence? Did it in fact isolate the movement from other women, or was it from the male left?

The politicos have consistently stated that it is not men who are the enemy. It is the system which is the enemy—be it capitalist, imperialist, or what have you—the further removed the better. "It was politically incorrect because it did not understand the interrelationship between the oppression of women and imperialism." (p. 155) We hate to be apolitical, unsophisticated, emotionally manipulative, and reactionary, but we'd really like to have the interrelationship clarified. It seems to us the oppression of women antedates imperialism. But if the left and Women's Liberation can be made to agree on a common enemy, the career chances of politico women in the left will be much improved.

Politicos have asserted continuously that women are apolitical if they do not concern themselves primarily with theoretical and practical problems of the male left. If women's politics do not feed into the left formula, women do not have "politics"—either good or bad.

The plan of the politicos is spelled out clearly:

1) There exists a contradiction between men and women based upon a monopoly of social power in the hands of men: thus, the first step is to create a power base for women which will equalize the power relationships between the men and women;

2) Men and women will then be able to relate to each other from the base of their own power, represented for women by an autonomous women's movement. The internal contradictions may thus be resolved and the class struggle undertaken, on the basis of an equal partnership in the form of alliances and coalitions. However, these steps are not seen as discrete, one following the other, but evolving dialectically through organization and practice. (p. 159)

Ward-heeling again: plans such as this are mainly attempts to use the women's movement as political leverage within the left establishment. Where else will men and women be able to relate to each other from the base of their own power (represented for women by an autonomous women's movement), how else do "thousands of women have a chance now for a better life" (p. 165) —certainly not in the family or in the office or factory.

All right. So women are to work for the left. Nothing's wrong with that, if you happen to be one of those sharing "equal partnership" in the class struggle. But the left, like every other hierarchy, has room at the top for only a few. If all women were to aim for or have equal access to the positions left women covet, the game would be blown. The efforts of the left women rest precisely upon women having an autonomous movement (because aspiring leaders do need an independent power base at times), and in having its rank and file happily accepting a subordinate position within it. Most Women's Liberation members gain nothing from such a plan but the vicarious satisfaction of watching their star rise in the heaven, go to secret meetings with the heavies of the "larger movement," or make the left Chautauqua circuit. It was their revolt against this strategy, and consequently against left Women's Liberation leadership, that made feminists troublesome to politicos. If she thinks working-class and middle-class women have a lot of different interests, she should consider the differences between the stars and the rank and file.

To politicos: We ask not that you give up your male orientation, not even that you give up your male; we ask only that you take your boot from off your necks. Either come along, or get out of the way.

NOTES

1. Karl Marx, *Das Kapital*. (New Edition Berlin: 1953), Vol. III, pp. 941 ff.
2. ———, *Eighteenth Brumaire of Louis Bonaparte*. (New Edition Berlin: 1946), p. 104.

The Feminine Mistake

HELEN LAWRENSON

You might have to go back to the Children's Crusade in 1212 A.D. to find as unfortunate and fatuous an attempt at manipulated hysteria as the Women's Liberation movement. For six months I have been reading their literature and listening to their strident speeches, and I had hoped that by now these sick, silly creatures would have huffed and puffed themselves out.

Instead, the movement is spreading, not only in America but in Europe; more and more women are letting themselves be worked up to a splenetic frenzy of hatred for men; and the latter, in cowardly panic lest they be labeled male chauvinists, are ignominiously making placatory noises. Male magazine editors, to a mouse, have jumped on the bandwagon, and every militant feminist with a typewriter is banging away on it. The books they produced last year sold so well that many bookstores have set up special Women's Lib sections in anticipation of increasing demand for the more than a dozen titles steaming off the presses this winter, with more to come, all contracted for by leading male publishers who fell over each other to compete for the authors. Last summer, the New York Shakespeare Festival put on a Women's Lib musical gawkishly entitled *Mod Donna*, written by two females and described as dealing with "women's sexual subjugation to Penis Power"; a group called the Feminist Repertory Theatre produced plays containing such fustian lines as "Have you made my body the incubator of your artificial passion?"; and actress Barbara Harris promised to direct a dramatic presentation of selected feminist writings from Susan B. Anthony on down, a theatrical event to be awaited with muted anticipation. The commercial lampreys of the cinema world will surely not be dilatory in latching on, just as they did with the youth revolution, so that before long we can expect to see a spate of films exploiting Women's Lib in different versions—comic, serious, sexy, and, of course, Cary Grant and Katharine Hepburn in the geriatric version.

It's a phony issue and a phony movement. Demands for equal political and legal rights, for child-care centers and equal pay for equal work are reasonable enough—although even in these areas some of the more belligerent feminists tend to go off the beam—but these have been submerged in a hair-raising emotional orgy of hatred as vicious as it is ludicrous, directed at love, marriage, children,

Note: Helen Lawrenson, "The Feminine Mistake," *Esquire*, Jan. 1971, pp. 82–83, 146–147, 153–154. Reprinted by permission of *Esquire* magazine © 1971 by Esquire, Inc.

the home, and encompassing en route, with wild catholicity, the penis, the Pill, false eyelashes, brassieres, Barbie dolls, Freud, Dr. Spock, the Old Left, the New Left, detergent advertisements, and such despicable male gallantries as opening doors for women and helping them on with their coats. What they are demanding is not equality but the absolute subjugation of men, or even their elimination.

These are not normal women. I think they are freaks. Besides, they are dead wrong in their assumption that most women detest men, marriage and housework so much they can't wait to be liberated from them so they can rush out to work all day in factory, shop or office. Where do they get this lunatic idea that women had rather work for a boss than stay at home and run their own domain? All orthodox Lib members seethe with bile at the thought of housework, to which they constantly refer as "shitwork," and rant continuously about the dreadful degradation of cooking meals, making beds, bathing babies. But the average normal woman derives a very basic happiness from performing these tasks. Most women have a strong nesting instinct and they *like* taking care of their homes. It may get tiresome at times but it sure as hell beats working. They get satisfaction from cooking special dishes to please their families, from polishing their best furniture and washing their grandmother's china, from planning new curtains or refurbishing an old chair. Even if they own nothing valuable or grand, what they have are Their Own Things and they enjoy taking care of them. Housework is not degrading, and there is nothing demeaning about caring for your home, your husband, your children. Besides, who do these Women's Lib characters think ought to do this "degrading" housework? Other women? Their husbands? One of them, Caroline Bird, in an article in *Signature,* the Diners Club magazine, suggests an end to the family system, which might be replaced by some sort of commune, and adds, "If women are totally liberated, more men and women would remain single," thus ignoring the fact that most women *want* to get married. Discussing the effect on industry, she writes, "The market for nursery furniture and child gear would taper off" (What? No more little pink or blue crib mattresses with bunnies and kittens on them?), and prophesies that "convenience foods" (whatever they are) and takeout-food shops would replace home-cooked meals and that "Home furnishings would give way to portable or disposable furniture." *Disposable furniture.* Can she really be kidding herself that this is what women want in their homes?

The worst thing about the movement is that it is distracting the attention of thousands of women from more urgent and important questions. They should get their priorities straight. Instead of yapping about men treating them as "sex objects" (and, personally, I have always *liked* being treated as a sex object), they might better devote themselves to more socially useful protests: against the war in Indochina, against nuclear, chemical and biological weapons, against environmental pollution, to name a few of the more obvious. Or the exploitation of migrant workers, the oppression of the blacks, the American Indians, the Alaskan Eskimos. Or any one of at least several hundred other projects more immediate and more deserving than the issue of whether or not women should do housework and let men whistle at them in the streets. There is only so much time and energy that each person has available to devote to causes. To try to persuade people to concentrate this time and energy on something as capricious and spurious as Women's Lib is not only wasteful but truly evil.

Estimates of Women's Lib active membership in the U.S.A. have varied widely from 10,000 to 500,000, but their peripheral influence is far greater. There is at least one organized group in more than one hundred cities in twenty-nine states. The movement as a whole takes in feminist societies ranging from N.O.W. (National Organization for Women, one hundred twenty chapters and a constantly increasing membership), founded in 1966 by the vociferously assertive Betty Friedan, author of *The Feminine Mystique* (published in 1963, it has sold 1,500,000 paperback copies), to groups called Redstockings, Radical Feminists, Radical Mothers, Bread and Roses, Bitch, Older Women's Liberation, Sisters of Lilith, Radical Lesbians, W.I.T.C.H. (Women's International Terrorist Conspiracy from Hell), Gallstones, S.A.L.T. (Sisters All Learning Together), and even S.C.U.M. (Society for Cutting Up Men, whose most activist member might be said to have been Miss Valerie Solanas, the lady who shot up Andy Warhol).

With a rare exception here and there, it is a movement of white, middle-class, college-educated women, and their appeal to the proletariat is minimal. In all their obsessive yammering about the injustice of not allowing women to do men's work, they aren't thinking of the average working-class jobs. No, these women have in mind bank presidents, Supreme Court justices, chairmen of the board or any other job which means Top Boss. (What they seem to ignore is that not all men can get these jobs, either.) They talk a lot about freeing working-class women from housework and, actually, women in different parts of the world have done just about everything at one time or another, but what woman in her right mind wants to go out and build subways or load cargo or mine coal? Nor do all women dream of becoming president of U.S. Steel (or even ambassador to Italy, so they can settle Trieste). Certainly not the average American woman, black or white. Rose Mary Byrd, a member of the Black Panthers, referring to Women's Lib groups, has said that while black men and women *together* are "fighting the whole power structure, those white chicks are talking about individual hang-ups like getting jobs"; and she added that "hating someone because he's a man is a way-out trip. . . . When they talk about myths of orgasm their minds are on the moon . . . the main thing they can't put up with is themselves."

That is exactly what they do talk about incessantly. Instructions on how to start a Women's Lib group in your own community advise you to get together eight to fifteen women who will meet once a week at each other's houses, presumably to discuss the iniquity of men. A topic should be selected for each week, and samples given include the questions: Why did you marry the man you did? What was your first sex experience? Do you pretend to have an orgasm?

One of their favorite subjects in these rap sessions is the clitoris, according to reports in their various publications. One woman didn't know she had one; one thought hers was a mistake, a strange growth; one cried, "Why didn't my mother tell me about it?"; and another, worried about the quality of her orgasms, "talked to eighteen women, not counting my mother, and after a lot of hemming and hawing they agreed with me. The only two who did not were Europeans. *They laughed.*" (Italics mine.) This one's husband, who at first had been "interested in my problem," she said, had then grown "surly," hardly surprising if he discovered she was discussing their sex life all over the neighborhood.

One of their inspirational guide-books is *The Myth of The Vaginal Orgasm,* a 4000-word pamphlet written in 1968 by Anne Koedt (now writing a book on—what else?— "female sexuality") which has become widely quoted in Women's Lib circles, although it scarcely represents an original idea. In 1967, *I Accuse,* by Mette Ejlersen of Denmark, was a best seller throughout Scandinavia and was later translated into English. Miss Ejlersen states that previous sex books —she cites as examples the *Kama Sutra, The Perfumed Garden* and Dr. Van de Velde's *Ideal Marriage*—were written by men and therefore are nothing but ignorant male fantasies. Reading both Miss Ejlersen and Miss Koedt, one wonders how men have managed to bumble through the sex act all these centuries, considering that they apparently got it all wrong.

Women don't need them anyway, if you believe the Women's Lib leaders, whose views are made clear in the following quotes.

Ti-Grace Atkinson: "Love has to be destroyed. It's an illusion that people care for each other." Abby Rockefeller: "Love between a man and a woman is debilitating and counterrevolutionary." Roxanne Dunbar: "Sex is just a commodity, a programmed activity. It is not a basic need." Miss Dunbar was the first Lib leader publicly to advocate the right for women to masturbate. (So who's stopping them?)

Of their various publications, *It Aint Me Babe,* printed in Berkeley, California, is the most entertaining—in a lurid way. One eye-catching cover was a photograph of a giant penis decorated with the Stars and Stripes and protruding from a garbage can. Usually, the editorial contents feature long, explicitly detailed accounts of unhappy sexual experiences with "super-pig supremacists" (husbands) and complaints about the latter's egregious behavior around the house. (Example given: husbands ignore wives' conversation and when wives say, "You're not listening," husbands reply, "What do you mean I'm not listening? I'm just looking at the paper.") In one issue, husbands were referred to as "the Hitlers in our homes," and the writer asks, "how was he [Hitler] different from nearly any man women know?"

A publication issued by W.I.T.C.H. makes the scientific statement, "Women are more human than men," while one of its contributors writes, "Of course, I can't discount the possibility that men are genetically flawed; but we need more time to be sure."

When not bending over a smoking typewriter, the Sisters, as they call themselves, can often be found harassing their enemy, Man, in one way or another. Groups of them have invaded the office of the San Francisco *Chronicle,* Grove Press (where several were arrested and Ti-Grace claimed she was forcibly stripped), and the *Ladies' Home Journal,* where at least a hundred marched into the office of Editor John Mack Carter and stayed eleven hours, demanding that he resign and hand over the magazine to an all-woman staff which they would be willing to

select. (Mr. Carter capitulated to the extent of agreeing to let them write a nine-page supplement for a later issue.) One of their objections to women's magazines is that printing recipes is an insult to their sex, an assumption which can be listed among their major fallacies. The truth is that almost all women enjoy reading recipes, even women who don't do much cooking, as the combined circulation of the two leading women's magazines—some 15,000,000—plus the enormous sales of all types of cookbooks should clearly prove. If Women's Lib members don't like reading recipes, let them curl up with *Barron's Financial Weekly* but leave the rest of us to our homely pleasures.

In San Francisco, Women's Lib members charged into a conference of male psychiatrists and in the ensuing melee, according to a written report by one of the Sisters, the psychiatrists "were shown up as the anal-repressives they are." One Sister, the report continued, claimed a white-haired doctor "manhandled" her, shook his fist at her, and shouted, "Shut up, you bitch," while all the other psychiatrists cheered. In Minnesota, women of the Twin Cities Female Lib held a joint meeting with men to discuss the movement, but concluded that men cannot be talked to rationally on the subject because "they think with their cocks." In New York, groups took over the Statue of Liberty and unfurled a banner reading "Women of the World, Unite," attempted to force their way into Men Only clubs and bars, and took to whistling at men on the streets, under the mistaken notion that they were thereby demonstrating what an insulting custom it is. I have never in my life known a woman of any age, old or young, who didn't feel flattered by wolf whistles, but to Women's Lib members this is one more nauseating indication of men's degenerate tendency to treat women as sexual objects. As a Boston Lib publication put it, "We will not be leered at, smirked at, whistled at by men enjoying their private fantasies of rape and dismemberment." (One is tempted to comment that the ladies have nothing to worry about, in view of the fact that their total lack of humor is almost equaled by a paucity of carnal appeal.)

There is some of this whistling going on in European Women's Lib movements, too, especially in Holland, where the feminists call themselves Dolle Minas, or Crazy Minas. (They chose the name in honor of Wilhelmina Trucker, a nineteenth-century Dutch feminist.) At their 1970 congress, they urged abolition of "the myth that the father is the head of the family," and groups of them roamed the streets whistling at men and pinching men's bottoms. They claim a membership of 1500, with affiliated groups in Belgium, Germany, and England. France, as might be expected, lags behind, despite Simone de Beauvoir. Frenchwomen are too conscious of their femininity and too skillful at exploiting it to welcome an anti-men movement, although Evelyne Sullerot, forty-five, blonde, rather pretty, and reeking with charm, has written a successful book, *Demain les Femmes,* now translated into seven languages, which appeals to housewives to help reorganize society and participate more in political and civic life.

In England the movement has been picking up speed in the past year. Women's Liberation Workshop in London publishes a newsletter called *Shrew* (formerly *Harpies Bizarre;* they reprinted *The Myth of The Vaginal Orgasm*) and their members frequently appear on television to complain about the drudgery of the housewife ("Every day she has to buy the food and prepare it, when it could be done better in a communal setup") or the education of girls ("Girls are encouraged to think that they should fulfill their biological functions"). On one program, a Women's Lib representative stated that "having children is automatically assumed the responsibility of the mother and that's one of the things we'd like to see changed." Mai Zetterling, an ardent women's rights advocate, gave a talk at a London movie theatre showing her feminist film, *The Girls,* and denounced the demoralizing effects of the cosmetics advertisements. "Lipstick

containers are phallic," she said. More than a dozen groups have sprung up since 1969, and early in 1970 they held a three-day conference in Oxford, where their ancillary activities included the painting of slogans, among them my favorite slogan of the year: Phalluses are Fascist.

In practically any other country than the United States, a feminist movement for political, legal and economic rights would make more sense, especially, say, in a country like Spain, or in Algeria, where veiled women lead an almost medieval existence, or in sections of Africa, or even South America.

It is most interesting to note that Oriental and Asian women, traditionally submissive in their bondage to men, are becoming emancipated without any blather about sex warfare and without losing one iota of their celebrated charm. In Thailand, fifty-four percent of the labor force is female, but whether they work as bricklayers or bank managers, they still remain of their own volition responsible for every home activity. Most of them are delectably pretty, and even their campaigners for women's rights display no overt animosity toward men. Two of the only three women prime ministers in the world are in Ceylon and India, supposedly bastions of male supremacy, but both Mme. Bandaranaike and Mme. Gandhi combine political expertise with femininity of person and manner, doubtless having ascertained that you catch more flies with molasses than with vinegar. If Women's Lib wants someone more in their own particular style, they can take Mrs. Golda Meir (and welcome to her).

American women have more freedom and more material advantages than any other women on earth. They are also notorious for their tendency to dominate their menfolk. As Dr. Spock remarked when he appeared on British television a few months ago, "If you liberate women in America one more inch, man will be completely subjugated." Sentiments like this have aroused the rage of Women's Lib groups: one of their publications portrayed him as a penis (obviously the most hateful object they could imagine) in a drawing, and a *Newsweek* journalist talking to Lib groups reported that they hissed at the mention of his name.

He was only confirming what many psychiatrists and sociologists have said previously. Dr. Theodore S. Weiss, formerly a senior psychiatrist of the New York City Department of Hospitals, once told me, "America is becoming a matriarchy." The American wife, he claimed, treats her husband as a combination of problem child and indentured servant. She expects him to be escort, meal ticket, handyman, errand boy and mother's helper. She is always trying to remodel and improve him. She supervises his manners and language, dictates how he shall dress, what friends he shall have, and how he shall spend his leisure time. Customarily, it is she who determines the decor of their home, the extent of their social orbit, and where they go on holidays. In public, she does not hesitate to interrupt him, contradict him, or attempt to regulate his habits. ("Don't give him any more to drink. He's had enough.") If he rebels, she nags him, bosses him, belittles him and tries to make him feel so inadequate that he would no more think of asserting his male authority as head of the family than he would dare wipe his hands on the guest towels in the bathroom. Increasingly, he suffers from nervous breakdowns, ulcers, premature heart attacks, insomnia, alcoholism. On the other hand, American women not only live longer than their men but they own more than fifty percent of the money in the country, they have sixty-five percent of the savings accounts, they control fifty-seven percent of listed securities, have title to seventy-four percent of suburban homes, and according to The New York Sunday *Times,* control about eighty-seven and a half percent of the total buying power.

So what are they bitching about? Careers? If a woman is sufficiently ambitious, determined *and* gifted, there is practically nothing she can't do. We have been judges, legislators, bank presidents, college presidents, publishers, ambassadors, doctors, lawyers, scientists, Cabinet members, auditors, bond traders, tax experts, bullfighters, bartenders, plumbers, taxi drivers, riveters and even, some twenty-odd years ago, six percent of the total number of the country's paperhangers. At the present time, we have a woman Director of the Mint, U.S. Treasurer, Chairman of the Federal Maritime Commission, as well as a couple of ambassadors. There is only one woman Senator but ten women in the House. That there are not more of us in the top echelons is due to personal choice rather than denial of opportunity. The main life interest of the average woman quite simply lies in other directions: love, marriage, children, home. Men start work with the intention of working all their lives, often with the goal of rising to the top. The majority of women take their first jobs with the intention of working only until they get married, or, if they continue after marriage, until they have children. There are 29,500,000 women in the U.S. labor force today and those of that number who continue to work after marriage usually do so for reasons more economic than feminist. A Department of Labor questionnaire some years ago asked the motives of married women workers. The typical answer was: "Because my husband does not earn enough to support our family with the cost of living what it is." They did not say: "Because I'm just crazy about the factory assembly line."

There is, too, the matter of ability—or talent. (I'm not going into the question of genius here, although certainly the absence of any female equivalent to Beethoven, Shakespeare, Leonardo da Vinci or all the other great composers, writers and painters cannot be blamed on male oppression.) If women have it and are sufficiently dedicated to its advancement, they can make the grade. They do not always have it, or if they do, they sometimes lack the driving urge, the single-minded perseverance to exploit it. Furthermore, as far as politics go, whatever makes the feminists think that women could run the world any better than men? We got the vote, kiddo, and a fat lot of good we've done with it.

What they want is Everything—and they can't even agree on that. Although most of the groups who demonstrated last August on the fiftieth anniversary of the women's suffrage constitutional amendment listed free abortions among their demands, Women, Inc. of San Francisco, opposes abolition of the abortion laws, while Roxanne Dunbar, a leading Liberation spokeswoman, has been quoted as saying she feels support of abortion reform is "basically racist." Nor do they approve of the Pill, which they have denounced as "the final pollution, the exact analogue of DDT," or of douches—"another billion-dollar industry off our bodies"—while at the same time they attack the supposed hardships of motherhood. For years, feminists have railed against the sexual freedom of men and the double standard in morals, but now that the sexual revolution is here, they don't like it. Robin Morgan, a founder of W.I.T.C.H., is only one of those who claim that the new sexual freedom "never helped us—just made us more available," and someone else has written, "Women have gone from private property to public property—she's fair game." (This brings to mind the same question I had when I read Sally Kempton's statement, "In my adolescence I screwed a lot of guys I didn't much like." Doesn't it ever occur to any of these girls that they can always say No?) Some of them are even against the newly acclaimed clitoral orgasm: "The hullabaloo over the female clitorally stimulated orgasm has further done nothing to liberate women because male domination of all women has not changed. Men are heard gloating over the power trip of 'I can make my girl go off like a machine gun.'"

To these women, a man is always wrong, no matter what. Although some feminists speak glowingly of the examples of communal nurseries and equality of work in Communist countries, others claim that "socialism in Cuba, China, the Soviet Union is a more advanced stage of male supremacy in which the means of production are owned by all men collectively." Many Lib members quit American radical groups because women

had to type, answer telephones, run mineograph machines and get coffee when what they thought they should have been doing, of course, was making the speeches and dictating the policy. As one of them has written, "The average student male wants a passive sex object . . . while he does all the fun things [like getting his head clubbed?] and bosses her around . . . he plays either bigshot male executive or Che Guevara—and he is my oppressor and my enemy." A manifesto issued on the West Coast by Redstockings refers to revolutionary groups as all "run by men and, consequently, interested in destroying us." Another complaint cites the "male supremacy rampant in white, male, anti-war groups" and says that women must "begin to demand control of these groups." (Note —not equal rights but *control*.)

Women like these will never be satisfied, no matter what rights they gain, because they are incapable of coming to terms with their own natures as females. Many of the Lib leaders are divorced or separated from their husbands (one deserted her husband and baby when the child was only one year old); many are childless; many more state flatly that they never want children or marriage. Those are their problems, but they should not try to impose them on other women, nor should they blame men for their own deficiencies. In nature, the basic, primary function of women is to mate for the purpose of reproduction. Everything else has been superimposed, and women deny this at their peril. No matter what kind of political, economic or social setup we may have in the future, nothing is going to change the biological facts. Kate Millett can claim that gender identity is imposed by society, not genes, till she's blue in the face, but this doesn't make it true, as several anthropologists and psychiatrists have recently remarked. Even Simone de Beauvoir, topdrawer member of feminist hagiology, has written, "The division of the sexes is a biological fact, not an event in history." After treating us to a survey of the sex habits of ants, termites (did you know that a termite queen lays up to 4000 eggs a day? Well, now you do) and toads, she works her way up to birds, fishes and mammals and admits that "it is unquestionably the male who takes the female—she is *taken . . .* the male deposits his semen, the female receives." Even among female humans, she says, the "reproductive function is as important as the productive capacity." This doesn't mean that she approves of marriage or motherhood. Speaking with all the assurance of one who has experienced neither, she feels that "the tragedy of marriage is not that it fails to assure woman the promised happiness—there is no such assurance in regard to happiness—but that it mutilates her. . . . Real activities, real work, are the prerogative of her man . . . she is betrayed from the day he marries her." This contempt for the wife-mother role is as major a Women's Lib theme as hatred of men (the producer of a Lib radio program on New York's WBAI claimed that "to be a woman is to be nothing" and described the lives of housewives and mothers as "nothingness, total nothingness"). Simone thinks that marriage should be prohibited as a career for women. Man should free woman, she writes, and "give her something to *do* in the world" (a statement which could only have been written by a nullipara), although even she confesses that women enjoy marketing and cooking: "there is a poetry in making preserves . . . cooking is revelation and creation; and a woman can find special satisfaction in a successful cake." (She'd better retract that or they'll tear off all her buttons and drum her out of the movement.)

Women also dearly love cosmetics and it is idiotic for Lib members to say they should renounce them because they are degrading. Women enjoy using makeup, trying out new kinds, playing around with it. They always have, primarily to make themselves desirable in the eyes of men (a goal which is anathema to Lib members) and, secondarily, for the sheer pleasure of self-adornment. Women's Lib sneers at this and their members plaster stickers reading "This Ad Insults Women" across posters which play up feminine sex

appeal. It is an insult, they say, to assume that women are thinking of sex when they buy soap or perfume (Oh, but they are, honey) and in many cities Lib groups have publicly burned lipsticks, false eyelashes, bras and girdles, along with assorted objects like wedding certificates, birth-control pills, a Barbie doll and a book by Norman Mailer. (They lambaste Mailer and D. H. Lawrence as "male supremacist sexists," but have a kind word for Jean Genet.) The Barbie doll was included because they consider that "toys are, like abortion laws, deadly earnest instruments of women's oppression" dreamed up by fiendish male toy manufacturers who foist dolls, miniature stoves, refrigerators, mops and brooms on innocent and helpless little girl children. This, of course, is piffle. Little girls play with dolls, etc. because they love them, just as they love helping around the kitchen, dreaming of the day when they will be housewives and mothers, themselves. Why not? There is probably no career in the world as basically rewarding for a woman, from an emotional and psychological point of view, as that of wife and mother. And what about love? Even the most emancipated career woman can fall in love; and love is not only when the bush becomes the burning bush, but it is also caring more about someone else than you do about yourself. When a woman falls madly in love with a man, she *wants* to wait on him and please him and be bossed by him and make a home for him and bear his children. Anyone who says otherwise is talking rubbish.

Women's Lib members who, for whatever personal reasons, find this idea loathsome are bucking nature. Women are the lunar sex. They do menstruate and they do have the babies. This is not the fault of men. It is asinine, as well as useless, to try to reverse the genders or to mount a venomous hate campaign against men for fulfilling the role for which nature made them. Men and women today should be working together to try to make the earth a better and a safer place. Any movement that tends to set them against each other by drumming up false sexual controversies is stupid and wrong. I cannot even feel sorry for these neurotic, inadequate women, because they are so appallingly selfish. They shriek about the monotony of housework with never a thought for the millions of men working their balls off at far more monotonous jobs in order to support their wives and children. Housework in America, despite all the labor-saving gadgets and easily prepared foods, may be boring at times, but it can't compare with the ego-destructive, soul-deadening boredom of standing in one spot on an assembly line, repeating one motion over and over, all day, every day.

Come off it, girls. Who is kidding whom? Besides, hasn't it ever dawned on you that whatever equality women get is given to them by men? So you see, no matter how you slice it, it's the same old sex game. Liberate me, daddy, eight to the bar.

Analysis of Values
and
Conflicts of Interest

Komisar is a vocal supporter of feminist groups struggling to free
themselves from rigidly defined and oppressive sex roles. She speaks for many
women who are frustrated in their traditional role, and who desire redefinition
of it in order to transform themselves into more fully developed human
beings. Komisar's paper also reflects the interests of male supporters of the
feminist movement—men who have strong beliefs in equality; who want
more active, independent mates; and who feel that women have many
resources that go unused because of their present role.

Dixon is an opponent of the feminist movement because she believes it
represents only the interests of white middle-class women. Dixon considers
criticism of oppressive social and economic institutions far more important
than the discussion of the condition of women. Dixon is a supporter of
revolutionary groups who believe the redefinition of sex roles should be part
of a broad transformation of society. She attempts to represent the underclass
of this society. However, Leffler and Gillespie, both spokeswomen for feminist
groups, assert that Dixon is acting out of self-interest. They argue that her
inaccurate critique of feminism reflects her desire to improve her personal
position in the left movement. On the other hand, Leffler and Gillespie assert
that their feminist perspective reflects the interests of women, regardless of
their class status. This assertion is certainly debatable, but it can be justly
argued that they do represent, at least indirectly, women who feel trapped
by and alienated from the traditional women's role. Finally, Leffler and
Gillespie can be considered the direct representatives of women's liberationist
groups actively attempting to transform this role.

Helen Lawrenson articulates the position of many women who do not feel
oppressed by their traditional role. She speaks for those who believe marriage,
housework, and child care are meaningful and fulfilling preoccupations
which are being threatened by women's liberation. They are often women
who have invested their lives in these activities and have found them
rewarding. Thus, Lawrenson considers the traditional women's role to be

desirable rather than a social problem. She believes that if feminist groups realized their goals it would result in a social problem—the subjugation of men.

Lawrenson supports the status quo and the maintenance of the traditional role of women. This stance coincides with that of many men who benefit from this situation. These men frequently argue that women are more natural in this role and that males are more comfortable with those who fit it well. Others who take a more extreme position believe that women's liberation is the first step in women's defeminization that will eventually lead to the elimination of differences between the sexes. These persons say that they oppose women's liberation because they do not think women should become men or vice versa. Feminists assert that all of these arguments help keep women in their subordinate position.

As we stated above, many women agree with Lawrenson's position. In fact, there are organized women's groups that not only support the traditional role of women, but who advocate male dominance. Feminists assert that these women are so alienated that they lack any conception of their actual interests. On the other hand, the anti-feminists assert that feminists are so disordered and so masculinized that they no longer have the ability to adapt to their natural role. Obviously, these analyses rest on contradictory interests and conflicting class values concerning the role of women.

2

RACE:

Heredity, Intelligence Differences Between Races—Fact or Myth?

There has been a great deal of debate in the social sciences concerning the relationship between IQ and race. This controversy has sometimes tended towards emotionalism with resulting charges of racism and countercharges of anti-intellectualism. Those who accept the idea that IQ is largely genetically determined believe that existing ameliorative programs for the poor and black are doomed to failure unless they are reorganized to take into account native intelligence differences. Those who oppose this idea, and feel IQ is a result of environmental factors, assert that such an action would serve to rationalize oppression and fix black people in their lowly social-economic situation. This section includes a number of articles by prominent social scientists embroiled in this debate. This debate is a critical one because its eventual outcome may have long-term effects on public policy towards minorities.

This section opens with a statement by Arthur Jensen, who sparked the emergence of this controversy. His 1969 article suggested that IQ may be largely determined by genetic factors. In the article included here, Jensen does not restate the evidence on this issue; howver, he does present his political position with respect to it. He argues that the goal of science should be "truth" and that we must not be dissuaded from this goal because our findings might be misunderstood, misused, or put to evil and inhumane ends. Thus, the social scientist must continue to seek the "truth" about the relationship between IQ and race irrespective of its possible effects on social policy. Jensen urges that we seek the truth, then turn our attention to those who would use the findings for their own ends. Jensen feels that we should accept scientific findings, not ideology. He sums up his position on the IQ–race controversy in this way:

> *I have always advocated dealing with persons as individuals, and I am opposed to according differential treatment to persons on the basis of their race, color, national origin, or social-class background. But I am also opposed to ignoring or refusing to investigate the causes of the well-established differences among racial groups in the distribution of educationally relevant variables, particularly IQ. Purely environmental explanations of racial differences in intelligence will never gain the status of scientific knowledge unless genetic theories are put to the test and disproved by evidence.*

Jensen's article is followed by three pieces which question his position. Kagan summarizes his position in this way: "In my view, a person's score on a contemporary IQ test has a poor relation to his ability to think logically and coherently. Moreover, the psychological trait 'intelligence'—now unfortunately equated with the IQ score—has become a primary explanation for the unequal access to power in our society." Kagan argues that the IQ test is a product of white, middle-class society, but is used to rank everyone in society. This obviously gives the white, middle-class a great advantage over other classes and races. This class further ensures its chances of success by having its own members administer these tests. Their instructions and mannerisms are more meaningful to white, middle-class subjects of the test than those from any other group. Kagan asserts that the genetic explanation of IQ is unsubstantiated. However, this position is already used by some to justify the current distribution of power in society.

McClelland equates the IQ test with the ancient Mandarin Chinese language: In both cases dominant groups manipulate symbols in order to keep other groups out of power. Furthermore, leisure time is needed to learn the rules of either of these games and only the elite have the time to do it. McClelland feels that IQ tests only predict one's ability to take such tests and earn scholastic grades (which he feels are derived from successes on the same types of tests). Nevertheless, IQ scores are being used to create a new type of aristocracy. In order to counter this, McClelland suggests a lottery system for the selection of employees complemented by extensive training and weeding out of those who do not possess the desired and necessary characteristics. He also suggests alternate abilities such as the ability to communicate, as a basis for selection.

Light offers an enlightening argument against those who have argued for a strong relationship between race and IQ. He points out that in 1925 in Britain it was common to argue that Jews were inferior mentally. Since then, of course, this has been shown to be fallacious. Similarly, prior to 1960 it was felt that Catholics were mentally inferior since they generally scored lower on intelligence tests. Despite this, Light recognizes that evidence from twin studies indicates that there is some support for the genetic position. Given this contrary evidence, Light suggests three conclusions:

1. Intelligence, as measured by IQ tests, is somewhat heritable.
2. There is no way to estimate the true relative effect of heredity and environment.

3. There is no foundation in the data for the conclusion that observed differences between social groups mean that IQ scores are largely genetic.

The debate then shifts to four replies to the position enunciated by McClelland. Jensen offers a ten-point rebuttal to McClelland, with some of his more important positions being the following:

1. Intelligence tests do, in fact, predict socially and occupationally significant criteria.
2. Intelligence tests do not reflect only the accidents of cultural and social privilege.
3. McClelland downgrades the importance of cultural, social class, and linguistic factors in biasing the IQ testing procedure.

Eysenck argues that McClelland must have been humoring his audience. "I am led to believe this because he never mentions the tremendous support given the hypothesis of an inherited general factor of mental ability by factor analysis and other studies, by genetic studies of identical and fraternal twins, or by educational research." Eysenck accepts the view that whatever is measured by IQ testing has a strong hereditary bias and that those with higher IQ's are more successful in life..

Shockley calls McClelland's position "unsearch dogmatism." He refers to it in this way because McClelland rejects the desirability of research on genetic factors in regard to intelligence and social problems. He feels that research into this question is rejected because it offends the egalitarian–environmental mentality. Shockley is the most extreme of those who urge research into the relationship between IQ and heredity. Shockley is afraid of dysgenic trends because those who have more children tend to have lower IQ's. He urges the consideration of a "thought experiment" about a "voluntary-sterilization bonus plan." Those with low IQ's would be rewarded for being sterilized. Although he favors such action, Shockley claims that we "need not fear . . . the horrors of Nazi 'eugenics.'"

Finally, Kenneth Clark does not reject the possibility of a linkage between IQ and race. Rather he argues that our society places too much emphasis on IQ testing. The solution is not, as McClelland suggests, a lottery, but to develop different types of tests for different abilities, jobs, etc.

Ethical Forum: I.Q. and Race

INTRODUCTION [1]

This issue of *The Humanist* presents what we believe to be a most important symposium on intelligence, I.Q., and race. In July/August 1969, January/February 1970, and in subsequent issues of *The Humanist* we published a critical discussion of H. J. Eysenck's view that there are genetic differences in intelligence between blacks and whites. In this issue we again present a discussion of the case for and against I.Q. tests.

Arthur R. Jensen is considered the leading proponent of the view that intelligence (as measured by I.Q.) is basically inherited. Since publishing his view in the *Harvard Educational Review* (1969), he has come under heavy attack. Some well-meaning people believe that even to investigate the relationship between race and intelligence is immoral. In his article, "The Ethical Issues," Professor Jensen claims that what is at issue is the freedom of scientists to inquire and publish, even on topics considered sensitive in a moral and political milieu. If the progress of the black man in America is to continue, he argues, we need to know all the facts.

Note: The following eight articles first appeared in *The Humanist,* Jan./Feb. 1972, and are reprinted by permission.
[1] Introduction written by the editors of *The Humanist.*

Does this mean that there is a difference in intelligence between Negroes and Caucasians? Are the I.Q. tests—which show an average disparity of 10 to 15 points in scores of blacks and whites—reliable? If the tests are to be accepted, how is this difference to be explained? Is it caused by deficiencies in the environment, and can these be corrected by compensatory education (like Head Start) and other social programs? On the other hand, if the explanation is genetic, what should be our social policy, if any, and what are the implications for our democratic ideals?

There are those who dissent from Jensen's position. They believe that all the evidence is not in, and, further, that I.Q. tests are unreliable as measures of competence. This position was informally argued by David C. McClelland, noted Harvard psychologist, at a symposium sponsored by the Union Graduate School. Because we thought it a provocative statement, we asked him for permission to publish an edited version of his remarks. Subsequently, this was sent out to various writers in the field of race and intelligence. Jerome Kagan also raises serious questions about I.Q. and intelligence, and his article is published along with McClelland's discussion as part of "The Case Against I.Q. Tests." Richard Light takes a moderate position, believing that the development of human intelligence is too complex to be investigated fully by the instruments we have now.

In "The Case for I.Q. Tests," Arthur R. Jensen, H. J. Eysenck, and William Shockley, leading exponents of the view that there are racial and genetic differences in intelligence, defend the validity of the I.Q. tests against McClelland. Kenneth E. Clark defends the testing of ability as socially useful, but believes that we overemphasize abstract analytical thinking and verbal skills in the standard I.Q. tests.

The Humanist is committed to two principles: We believe in an open society and the free mind, and we are committed to the improvement of the condition of disadvantaged groups in our society. We hope that these two aims are not mutually exclusive. Whatever the causes or explanations for differences between the races, if they indeed exist, it is clear that we have a continuing moral obligation to the further progress of minorities. But in order to do this we must leave open the doors of free inquiry. Perhaps those most committed to helping the black man should be in the forefront of free and unrestricted research into the social and biological determinants of human behavior.

The Ethical Issues

ARTHUR R. JENSEN

The range of ethical issues concerning research and research applications in human genetics is so great that I will not even attempt to review it here. It involves diverse questions about raising human embryos in "test tubes," the use of artificial insemination in human research, the cross-fostering of fetuses, and direct alteration of chromosomes and genes by what is now called genetic surgery, and goes all the way to questions of eugenics and population quantity and quality control.

But the most frequently heard objection to further research into human genetics, particularly research into the genetics of behavioral characteristics, is that the knowledge gained might be misused. I agree. Knowledge also, however, makes possible greater freedom of choice. It is a necessary condition for human freedom in the fullest sense: I therefore completely reject the idea that we should cease to discover, to invent, and to know (in the scientific meaning of that term) merely because what we find could be misunderstood, misused, or put to evil and inhumane ends. This can be done with almost any invention, discovery, or addition to knowledge. Would anyone argue that the first caveman who discovered how to make a fire with flint stones should have been prevented

from making fire, or from letting others know of his discovery, on the grounds that it could be misused by arsonists? Of course not. Instead, we make a law against arson and punish those who are caught violating the law. The real ethical issue, I believe, is not concerned with whether we should or should not strive for a greater scientific understanding of our universe and of ourselves. For a scientist, it seems to me, this is axiomatic.

An important distinction, often not made or else overlooked, is that between scientific research and the specific use of the research findings in a technological application with a highly predictable outcome. The classic example is the atomic bomb. Should Einstein have desisted from the research that led to $e = mc^2$? Nuclear physics can, of course, be misused. But it need not be. For it can also be used to cure cancer and to provide electric power. Moral decisions involve the uses of knowledge and must be dealt with when these are considered. Before that, however, my own system of values holds that increasing knowledge and understanding is preferable to upholding dogma and ignorance.

In a society that allows freedom of speech and of the press, both to express and to criticize diverse views, it seems to me the social responsibility of the scientist is clear. He must simply do his research as competently and carefully as he can, and report his methods, results, and conclusions as fully and as accurately as possible. When speaking as a scientist, he should not introduce personal, social, religious, or political ideologies. In the bizarre racist theories of the Nazis and in the disastrous Lysenkoism of the Soviet Union under Stalin, we have seen clear examples of what happens when science is corrupted by servitude to political dogma.

For the past two years, I have been embroiled in debate over my article "How Much Can We Boost I.Q. and Scholastic Achievement?" *(Harvard Educational Review,* 39, 1969, pp. 1–123) . Though there are many possible grounds for raising ethical questions concerning research and publication on the genetic aspect of human abilities, in this case I think a block has been raised because of obvious implications for the understanding of racial differences in ability and achievement. Serious consideration of whether genetic as well as environmental factors are involved has been taboo in academic, scientific, and intellectual circles in the United States. But despite taboo, the question persists. My belief is that scientists in the appropriate disciplines must finally face this question squarely and not repeatedly sweep it under the rug. In the long run, the safest and sanest thing we can urge is intensive, no-holds-barred inquiry in the best tradition of science.

We must clearly distinguish between research on racial differences and racism. Racial implies hate or aversion and aims at denying equal rights and opportunities to persons because of their racial origin. It should be attacked by enacting and enforcing laws and arrangements that help to insure equality of civil and political rights and to guard against racial discrimination in educational and occupational opportunities. But to fear research on genetic racial differences, or the possible existence of a biological basis

for differences in abilities, is, in a sense, to grant the racist's assumption: that if it should be established beyond reasonable doubt that there are biological or genetically conditioned differences in mental abilities among individuals or groups, then we are justified in oppressing or exploiting those who are most limited in genetic endowment. This is, of course, a complete non sequitur. Equality of human rights does not depend upon the proposition that there are no genetically conditioned individual differences or group differences. Equality of rights is a moral axiom: It does not follow from any set of scientific data.

I have always advocated dealing with persons as individuals, and I am opposed to according differential treatment to persons on the basis of their race, color, national origin, or social-class background. But I am also opposed to ignoring or refusing to investigate the causes of the well-established differences among racial groups in the distribution of educationally relevant traits, particularly I.Q. Purely environmental explanations of racial differences in intelligence will never gain the status of scientific knowledge unless genetic theories are put to the test and disproved by evidence.

There is a perhaps understandable reluctance to come to grips scientifically with the problem of race differences in intelligence —to come to grips with it, that is to say, in the same way that scientists would approach the investigation of any other phenomenon. This reluctance is manifested in a variety of "symptoms" found in most writings and discussions of the psychology of race differences. These symptoms include a tendency to remain on the remotest fringes of the subject, to sidestep central questions, and to blur the issues and tolerate a degree of vagueness in definitions, concepts, and inferences that would be unseemly in any other realm of scientific discourse. Many writers express an unwarranted degree of skepticism about reasonably well-established quantitative methods and measurements. They deny or belittle facts already generally accepted—accepted, that is, when brought to bear on inferences outside the realm of race differences—and they demand practically impossible criteria of certainty before even seriously proposing or investigating genetic hypotheses, as contrasted with extremely uncritical attitudes toward purely environmental hypotheses. There is often a failure to distinguish clearly between scientifically answerable aspects of the question and the moral, political, and social-policy issues; there is a tendency to beat dead horses and to set up straw men on what is represented, or misrepresented, I should say, as the genetic side of the argument. We see appeals to the notion that the topic is either too unimportant to be worthy of scientific curiosity, or is too complex, or too difficult, or that it will be forever impossible for any kind of research to be feasible, or that answers to key questions are fundamentally "unknowable" in any scientifically acceptable sense. Finally, we often see the complete denial of intelligence and race as realities, or as quantifiable attributes, or as variables capable of being related to one another. In short, there is an altogether ostrich-like dismissal of the subject.

I believe these obstructive tendencies will be increasingly overcome the more widely and openly the subject is researched and discussed among scientists and scholars. As some of the taboos against open discussion of the topic fall away, the issues will become clarified on a rational basis. We will come to know better just what we do and do not yet know about the subject, and we will be in a better position to deal with it objectively and constructively through further research.

In recent years, however, we have witnessed more and more the domination of ideologically motivated environmentalist dogma concerning the causes of large and socially important differences in average educational and occupational performance among various subpopulations in the United States, particularly those socially identified as racial groups. For example, the rate of occurrence of mental retardation, with I.Q.'s below 70 plus all the social, educational, and occupa-

tional handicap that this implies, is six to eight times higher in our Negro population than in the rest of the population. According to research sponsored by the National Institute of Health, as many as 20 to 30 per cent of the black children in some of our largest urban centers suffer severe psychological handicaps. Yet the Government *has* not supported, *does* not, and *will* not, as of this date, support any research proposals that could determine whether or not any genetic factors are involved in this differential rate of mental handicap. To ignore such a question, in terms of our present knowledge, I submit, may not be unethical—but it is, I believe, short-sighted, socially irresponsible, and inhumane.

More important than the issue of racial differences per se is the probability of dysgenic trends in our urban slums. The social-class differential in birthrate appears to be much greater in the Negro than in the white population. That is, the educationally and occupationally least able among Negroes have a higher reproductive rate than their white counterparts, and the most able segment, the middle class, of the Negro population have a lower reproductive rate than their white counterparts. If social-class intelligence differences within the Negro population have a genetic component, as in the white population, this condition could both create and widen genetic intelligence differences between Negroes and whites. The social and educational implications of this trend, if it exists and persists, are enormous. The problem obviously deserves thorough investigation by social scientists and geneticists and should not be ignored or superficially dismissed because of well-meaning wishful thinking. I find myself in agreement with Professor Dwight Ingle, who has said, "If there are important average differences in genetic potential for intelligence between Negroes and non-Negroes, it may be that one necessary means for Negroes to achieve true equality is biological." The possible consequences of our failure to seriously study these questions may well be viewed by future generations as our society's greatest injustice to Negro Americans.

Carl Jay Bajema, a Harvard geneticist and researcher on population trends who is frequently cited by my critics in support of their notion that there are no dysgenic trends to worry about (based on his earlier, limited research), now has this to say (in *Bio-Science*, 29, 1971, pp. 71–5):

> The overall net effect of current American life-styles in reproduction appears to be slightly dysgenic—to be favoring an increase in harmful genes which will genetically handicap a larger proportion of the next generation of Americans. American life-styles in reproducton are, in part, a function of the population policy of the United States. What will be the longe-range genetic implications of controlling or not controlling population size in an industrialized welfare state democracy such as America? . . . [He concludes:] . . . Each generation of mankind faces anew the awesome responsibility of making decisions which will affect the quantity and genetic quality of the next generation. A society, if it takes its responsibility to future generations seriously, will take steps to insure that individuals yet unborn will have the best genetic and cultural heritage possible to enable them to meet the challenges of the environment and to take advantage of the opportunities for self-fulfillment present in that society.

Finally, some persons who call themselves environmentalists tend to cast the issues of genetic research on intelligence and race as a battle between the good guys and the bad guys. I resent this. The simple-minded morality play in which I have been wittingly or unwittingly cast in the role of villain has presented the issue of ethics as if ethical behavior were the sole possession of the environmental dogmatists, and as if those of us who would suggest looking into genetic factors were ethical and moral pariahs! One rather prominent psychologist publicly made libelous and defamatory statements about my article in the *Harvard Educational Review*, and for nearly two years, repeated attempts have failed to elicit either a substantiation or a retraction of the charges.

"Knowledge can be misused, but this does not excuse efforts to block inquiry and debate or to deny laymen in a democratic society the right to know. Closed systems of belief can also be misused, and ignorance is a barrier to progress. All possible causes for people's being disadvantaged should be investigated, and hopefully the application of knowledge to their advancement will be guided by moral principle" (Professor Dwight Ingle in *Perspectives in Biology and Medicine*, 10, 1967). In my view, society will benefit most if scientists treat these problems in the spirit of scientific inquiry rather than as a battlefield upon which one or another preordained ideology may seemingly triumph.

The Case Against I.Q. Tests:
The Concept of Intelligence

JEROME KAGAN

The concept of intelligence is among the most confused in our repertoire of ideas. Ambiguity surrounds its definition, etiology, and social significance. A central issue is to what degree scores on standard intelligence tests reflect a generalized quality of memory and reasoning that is not limited to a particular cultural setting. In my view, a person's score on a contemporary I.Q. test has a poor relation to his ability to think logically and coherently. Moreover, the psychological trait "intelligence"—now unfortunately equated with the I.Q. score—has become a primary explanation for the unequal access to power in our society.

To state my own view briefly: The white, middle-class Western community, like any moderately isolated social group, has created over the years a specialized vocabulary, reservoir of information, and style of problem-solving summarized under the concept "intelligence." Since possession of these skills is a rite of passage to positions of power and wealth in the society, many have been easily seduced into concluding that those without power or wealth are of fundamentally different intellectual competence. This view ignores the fact that children's access to the experiences necessary to acquire the valued

intellectual skills differs enormously by social classes. But our society has been doing this for so long that the faulty logic has gone unnoticed. We are much like the Bushman mothers who believe that a child will not walk unless he is placed erect in sand from the earliest weeks of life. Since no Bushman mother bothers to test this hypothesis, and all children walk by 18 months, the false idea continues to live.

Let me state the issue in kernel form: Every society, or large cohesive group within a society, recognizes that in order to maintain stability a small group must possess some power over the much larger citizenry. This power can be inherited, awarded, attained, or seized. In actual practice, this lean and rather raw description is usually disguised by a clever strategy—much like a magician's wrist movement—that makes select psychological traits symbolic of highly valued, status-conferring attributes. Those who possess these traits are inevitably those to whom power is given.

At other times and in other places, sexual abstinence, sexual potency, hunting skill, a capacity for silent meditation, good soldiering, or efficient farming have been the basis for ranking men and dividing them into unequal groups. Tenth-century Europe awarded power to those who were assumed to be more religious than their brothers. The presumption of a capacity for more intense religiosity provided a rationale for the fact that a privileged few were permitted entry into marble halls, and allowed the larger society to accept it. Contemporary American society uses intelligence as one of the bases for ranking its members. We celebrate intelligence the way the Islamic Moroccans celebrate the warrior-saint.

Moreover, the cultural similarity extends to our explanations of the unequal distribution of either intelligence or saintliness. The majority of Americans believe that children are born with differing intellectual capacities and that as a result some are destined to assume positions of status and responsibility. A much smaller group believes that this psychological capacity has to be attained through the right combination of early experience and will. These opposing hypotheses are identical in substance to the two interpretations of differential "capacity for religiosity" held by Muslims in Morocco and Indonesia. The Moroccans believe that some are born with a greater capacity for strong and intense religious experience. The Javanese believe it is attained following long periods of meditation. And they, like we, discover the small proportion of their population that fit the description of the pure, and allow them ascent.

We are not contesting the obvious fact that individuals really do differ in regard to the psychological traits valued by our society. But we lack sufficient information about the causes of these differences.

Let me try to support this rather strong statement by partially analyzing what an intelligence test is made of. The widely publicized announcement that 80 per cent of intelligence is inherited and 20 per cent environmentally determined is based on information from two similarly constructed standardized I.Q. tests invented by Caucasian middle-class Western men, at the request of Caucasian middle-class Western men, for Caucasian middle-class Western men to use for ranking everyone in the society.

The most important set of test questions (important because scores on this set have the highest correlation with the total I.Q.) asks the testee to define words of increasing rarity. Rarity is a relative quality, depending always on the language community one selects as referent. "Shilling" is a rare word for the American child, but so is "joint." The test constructors decided that rarity would be defined with respect to the middle-class Caucasian experience. And a child reared in a middle-class home is more likely to learn the meaning of "shilling" than the meaning of "joint." If contemporary black psychologists had accepted the assignment of constructing the first part of the intelligence test, they probably would have made a different choice.

A second set of questions poses the child some everyday problem and asks him what he would do in that situation. For example, one question asks a 7-year-old, "What should you do if you were sent to buy a loaf of bread and the grocer said he didn't have any more?" Clearly, this question assumes a middle-class urban or suburban environment with more than one grocery store within safe walking distance of the home, for, believe it or not, the only answer for which maximum credit is given is, "I would go to another store." It is not surprising that rural and ghetto children are less likely to offer that answer. I recently examined a set of protocols on poor black children living in a large Eastern city and found that many of them answered, "Go home"—a perfectly reasonable and even intelligent answer for which they were not given credit. One task that does not favor middle-class white children asks the testee to remember a list of four or five numbers read at the rate of one per second. This test usually yields minimal differences among class and ethnic groups in the United States.

These biases in the selection of questions comprise only part of the problem. There is also a serious source of error in the administration of the test. White middle-class examiners usually administer the tests to children of different linguistic backgrounds. The test protocols of the black children mentioned above, gathered by well-intentioned, well-trained examiners, indicated that the children often misunderstood the examiner's pronunciation. When asked to define the word "fur" some said, "That's what happens when you light a match." Clearly, the child had understood the word to be "fire," but he received no credit. Similarly, when requested to define "hat," some children said, "When you get burned," indicating that they perceived the word as "hot." Again, they received no credit.

Many other sources of error could be documented, but even these few examples suggest that the I.Q. test, the basis for Arthur Jensen's argument and for the statement that 80 per cent of I.Q. is inherited, is a seriously biased instrument. It almost guarantees that middle-class white children will obtain higher scores than any other group of children in the country, and that the more similar the experiences of two people, the more similar their scores should be.

Most citizens, however, are unaware both of the fundamental faults in the I.Q. test and of the multiple bases for differences in tested intelligence. But like the Greeks, Islamic Moroccans, and medieval Christians, we too need a rational basis for the awarding of power and prizes. Intelligence is our modern substitute for saintliness, religiosity, courage, or moral intensity, and, of course, it works. It works so well that when we construct an intervention project, be it a major effort like Head Start or a small study run by a university scientist, we usually evaluate the effect of the intervention by administering a standard intelligence test or one very similar to it, a practice reflecting the unconscious bias that a child's I.Q. must be the essential dimension we wish to change.

What implications are to be drawn from this acerbic analysis of the I.Q.? The first may seem paradoxical, considering our apparently hostile critique of the I.Q. test. Despite the injustice inherent in awarding privilege, status, and self-esteem to those who possess more of some attribute the society happens to value, this practice seems to be universal, perhaps because it is necessary. Power—and we mean here benevolent power—probably has to be held unequally. Therefore the community must invent a complex yet reasonable rationale that will both permit and explain the limited distribution of this prized resource. Knowledge of Western language, history, and customs is one partial basis. But let us be honest about the bases for this arbitrary decision and rid ourselves of the delusion that those who temporarily possess power are biologically more fit for this role because their brains are better organized. Sir Robert Filmer made this argument in 1680 to rationalize the right of kings to govern, and John Locke's political philosophy was shaped on a brilliant critique of Filmer's thesis.

We do not deny that biological differences, many of them inherited, exist between and within ethnic and racial groups. But we do not think that inherited characteristics like eye color or tendency to perspire entitle anyone to special favor. Similarly, we should reflect on the wisdom of using 15-point differences on a culturally biased test—regardless of the magnitude of the genetic contribution to the I.Q.—to sort some children into stereotyped categories, thus impairing their ability to become mayors, teachers, or lawyers. It is possible to defend the heretical suggestion that for many contemporary occupations—note that I did not say all—I.Q. should not be the primary attribute by which a candidate is judged. Of course, biological factors determine a person's muscle mass, brain size, and adrenalin secretion under stress. But let us not unfairly exploit these hard-won facts to rationalize the distribution of secular power, which is a political and sociological dimension. That is using fair science for dark deeds that she is ill-prepared to carry out.

Those who insist that I.Q. is inherited base their conclusion on a mathematical model of heritability which assumes that the statistical variation in I.Q. scores is additive, some of it due to genetic and some to environmental factors. That assumption is questionable and has been criticized by many psychologists and mathematicians. Hence, all one can say at the moment is that the genetic contribution to I.Q. is still unknown. A second fact has also led some to conclude that intelligence is controlled in a major way by genetic factors: American blacks, who are of a different gene pool than whites, have lower I.Q. scores. We have argued that the 10-to-5–point average difference between American blacks and whites is likely to be due to the strong cultural biases in the I.Q. test. Hence, given the current knowledge no one can be sure of the determinants of variation in I.Q. score, a conclusion that is even more true of intelligence itself.

I.Q. Tests and Assessing Competence

DAVID C. McCLELLAND

DEBUNKING I.Q. TESTS

There has always been a tendency on the part of certain people who are good at manipulating symbols to use this capacity to exclude other people from positions of power in society. For example, to insure their dominant position, the Chinese intelligentsia invented a language, Mandarin Chinese, that could be learned by only a very small part of the population. Our society has a comparable system for defending power, and it is supported oddly enough by the standard antidemocratic argument for "pure" knowledge and "pure" understanding. (In contrast, the people who usually threaten the intelligentsia are practical people.) We call our system intelligence testing. I have been very much concerned about it for a long time, because it has become like a game of Chinese checkers or chess. The landed gentry have plenty of time to learn to play chess

Note: These remarks were taped at an informal seminar sponsored by the Union Graduate School. They were intended to be provocative and to stimulate discussion. The audience were students who needed to have some of their assumptions questioned. The remarks accordingly are not documentated; nor are they offered as a complete scholarly presentation of Dr. McClelland's point of view—*The Editors.*

and other fun and games that poor people don't have time to master. Then they turn around and say that if you can't play chess, you can't belong to the élitist system. Unfortunately, the game in this country is becoming almost as effective as it was with the Chinese.

At one time, in order to get into the Chinese civil service, a person had to pass some extremely rigorous and extensive examinations. Of course, only certain people in certain families had the leisure time necessary to learn the rules of the games being tested and to develop their playing skills. In our own society, the so-called intelligence movement has been extended to an extraordinary number of things. We demand good performance on similar tests as an important qualification for all sorts of jobs and positions. Consequently we also discriminate against people who haven't had the chance to learn the games that have been selected. We can look at this practically, moreover, and ask the businessman's utilitarian question: "So what, so if you play chess and these other wonderful games so beautifully—what does that mean? What else can you do?" As far as I can determine, the justification for the use of tests is almost completely circular. There is no evidence that they predict anything more useful than one's ability to take other intelligence tests. Yes, they may also predict grades, but grades, of course, involve the same kinds of tests. I'd like to give a simple example of how the system works.

I have been serving as a member of a governor's commission appointed to deal with the problem of discrimination in the civil service of Massachusetts. To determine a person's qualifications for a job in the civil service, Massachusetts uses an intelligence-scholastic-aptitude type of test for all positions except maybe that of janitor. We have been especially concerned with the one that must be passed to become a policeman. An applicant has to play the analogies game; a typical item is the following: "Lexicon is to dictionary as policeman is to (check one of the four alternatives)." Now in order to qualify to be a cop, you have to score 70 on this test. (Where they get the number 70, I don't know, and they don't know. It's just one of those games that they play.) But if you're a black resident of Roxbury, chances are you haven't been exposed to words like "pyromaniac," "lexicon," and so on. There are several consequences of this simple fact.

First, by definition, a person is less intelligent if he can't play the game these people have made up. He doesn't know the words or the rules. Second, as a result, the person naturally doesn't qualify to be a cop or anything else in Massachusetts, and there is therefore a high and significant correlation between intelligence and occupational level. We've all seen tables showing that people in lower occupations have lower I.Q. scores, while those in higher occupations have higher scores. This guy who can't be a policeman because he can't play the I.Q.-test game is contributing to those tables. He can't do the intelligence test, so all he can be is a janitor, whereas people who play the games well can become policemen and enter higher-level jobs. The test itself thus becomes part of an élitist mechanism to discriminate against the disadvantaged. What we have is a very vicious circle that insures poor people don't get better jobs. Still a third thing

that happens is that the test-taker gets mad, angry, upset. This establishes a nice correlation between intelligence and human adjustment. If you have low intelligence-test scores, you are more apt to be neurotic. Of course, you may be neurotic because you can't get a job, and you can't go to school, and so on. But the correlation is there—by dint of what we may call "incestuous validity," that is, you correlate the thing with itself.

I have been very much concerned about these methods and have been trying to figure out how they could be attacked in some way that would offer a reasonable chance of success. The traditional attack against an élite's discriminatory devices is utilitarian: "Look, there is no evidence that the test has anything to do with being a better cop or a worse cop. No one has shown that those who score higher in the so-called intelligence test make better cops." In Massachusetts, this argument forms the basis of a lawsuit that will probably prevent the test from being used. Furthermore, there's very little evidence that high intelligence-test scores predict success in any other occupation. Even really creative research scientists do not score higher. This has been shown in the United States and, independently, in England; it's been shown repeatedly.

All the evidence, however, does not prevent educational institutions from saying, "Doing well on these kinds of tests means that you will do well in our school." A fundamental problem, then, is whether we can allow educational institutions to ruin society by insisting that only the people who go to their schools should have access to higher positions in the society. Surely the schools become an oppressive mechanism when they select and distribute only people with certain types of talent into various types of jobs and the talents, like chess playing, are not really related to performing well in the jobs. In some cases, there may even be an inverse relationship between the two abilities.

What is really odd is that the tests have often been justified on the grounds that they are more democratic than other means of selection. There's an especially nice historical irony here. Testing got its start because it was supposed to prevent nepotism, such as getting sons of alumni into Yale. It was supposed to be a democratic mechanism. Instead, it has become much more oppressive than the method it was designed to replace. Under the old method, even if you did happen to get sons of alumni who were not very good at taking this type of test, they would still be able to get into college. For the new type of aristocracy, however, testing selects more rigorously than genes.

During my years of searching for ways to measure different types of human competence, I have argued for things like tests with answers that are known to the people who are trying to do well on them. (Another trick of the oppressing classes is to keep the answers a secret: You don't learn the mistakes you've made; you guess at how to improve your performance.) Teachers are in a somewhat peculiar position because the psychologists do not allow them to understand very much about what's going on. They know that some of the kids have high S.A.T. scores, but they don't really know how to teach a person to get a high score. I think it was Tim Leary who suggested to me the idea of teaching people to cheat on intelligence tests; that is, you give out the answers. The argument is that if you really know how to do the problems, you are more intelligent by definition; so we ought to teach the definitions and produce as many intelligent people as possible. I've been very much interested in developing measures that teachers could use to achieve this goal. Unfortunately, I haven't been able to get the kind of support I need to develop them into practical form.

Question: Meaning financial support?
McClelland: Yes.
Question: You have a design that might work?
McClelland: We have all kinds of designs, measures, and things we think are

important. We need support to put them into a practical format. Then people could write in and say, "Hey, send me a copy." I now get many requests of this sort, but I can't fill them.

Question: Given that block, how do we attack the system? How do we stop people from using the tests?

McClelland: One way is by lawsuit, like the one I mentioned previously. If I could think of a good one, I'd go ahead with it. The problem is that in most cases, which are concerned with education, you can't win a lawsuit, because the schools have a good defense; namely, that the tests discriminate validly insofar as grades are concerned. The testing service says that it has tests to predict how well people will do in the schools—and that is perfectly true. Since that's all they claim, the schools rather than the tests are the major problems. And because of that, the lawsuit is a method that won't work.

Question: What about the Massachusetts case that you mentioned?

McClelland: That's a different problem. We can probably win that one, because we can show that the tests do not predict police performance. We cannot show that they don't predict school performance, however, because the schools use the same type of tests. They could stop using them, but that might threaten their methods, their traditions, their status quo, and so on. On the other hand, Bowdoin College has stopped using the S.A.T., although it did it for the wrong reason. The decision shows how strange things can happen. They had the teachers pick out those whom they regarded as the ideal Bowdoin students, then discovered that there was no relationship between the test scores and the people whom the teachers had selected. So they dropped the tests. Although that's probably not a reason I would like to use for dropping them, it might be better than I think.

Comment: The school with which I'm associated, and which used the S.A.T. initially, has found it to be totally invalid because the structure and the ends of the schools are not academic, but educational in a broader and more varied sense. They don't want S.A.T. scores anymore; they have other criteria for selection. Whether what you're saying will help generally, however, I don't know. I can see traditional educational institutions saying that they're not interested in looking for creepy, weird people.

Also, for reasons somewhat different from those already mentioned, Mexican-American parents in California have brought an injunction against the State Board of Education to prohibit administering these kinds of standardized tests to their children. Their reasons are linguistic.

McClelland: I think they can probably make that case stick. The problem is gaining recognition of ghetto dialect as a separate language, and that's not going to be hard to prove in court. It can be demonstrated by taking a white, middle-class person and putting him in the ghetto to try to figure out what's going on. As a matter of fact, some black students are now inventing tests in ghetto dialect, and even high scorers on the S.A.T. couldn't pass them. But what do you prove by all that? It's a kind of gamesmanship that really isn't getting at the issue.

AN ALTERNATIVE: THE LOTTERY PLUS INTENSIVE TRAINING

Question: Could the tests be proved unconstitutional? Wouldn't a state university or other state organizations using them be particularly susceptible to a charge of discrimination? And what about an alternative?

McClelland: I think that question has to be examined in light of an interesting problem concerning American values. In talking with the civil-service people in Massachusetts, we had to confront the following question: "All right, suppose we don't use this test. We still have 4,000 applicants for 50 jobs in the Boston police department. How do we choose 50 people?" A judge will also want an answer to that question. He'll want to know what other workable method is free of discrimination. We don't want to open jobs to patronage.

After all, that's why the civil-service system was started: We wanted to make certain that whoever got elected didn't appoint all his relatives and friends to public jobs. Moreover, we want to fill the jobs with the best persons possible.

I've recommended an alternative to the present system, but it goes so much against American values, even against most liberals' values, that it would be difficult to implement. My solution is a lottery. Let's do it by chance. That avoids patronage, gives minority groups a break, and saves money. But how does it get the best people for the jobs? I think the answer is to pick a few more people than needed and then put everyone through very intensive training. Lots of evidence suggests that people may start out without the characteristics necessary for a job, but they can and do learn.

Let's look more closely at the problem. A lottery would likely produce, for example, a certain number of candidates for the police force who were very prejudiced against blacks. Since we don't want those people on the force, we ought somehow to screen them out. But we do not have to use preliminary tests. What we can do is to intensively train those selected by lot and at the end of two weeks throw out the ones who still show prejudice against blacks. We do not accept the idea that bigotry is something in the genes; that we can screen 4,000 people for it. We believe we can get rid of it. We also know, however, that we will not succeed with everyone; that there are some people from whom we can't eradicate prejudice. They will be dropped out at the end of the training and told, "Sorry, this was one of our objectives and you didn't make it." What is important here is that no one has been prejudged on the basis of a test that may bear no relationship whatsoever to the demands of the job and that, beyond this, allows no opportunity for learning. In effect, we use training itself as a screening device.

It's like the process a person must go through to get a license to drive a car. We don't predetermine that only people whose fathers have owned cars will be licensed. No, we try to train everyone of normal physical capacity to drive, but at the end we may screen out some uncoordinated idiots we don't ever want on the road. We just wouldn't give them a license at the end of their training.

Americans nonetheless would feel very uncomfortable about using a lottery to pick people for important positions. If they're picking a social worker, they want to insure that they're getting a person who is sympathetic. My point is that we can probably train most people to be sympathetic, and train for various other functions and characteristics that we're now trying to select by test. The few who can't be trained may be eliminated at the end of the training period. Using intelligence tests to pick social workers is also a way of picking by lot; it's just less obvious and less equitable. As I've mentioned, however, these arguments notwithstanding, there are few people who would opt for a lottery system.

Question: Don't we do it when lives are at stake; that is, when we pick juries?

McClelland: That system begins by trying to eliminate people who are prejudiced.

Question: No, people are picked out of the phone book; names are put into a pot and drawn by lot. I think there's an analogy between that and your suggestions. But there is and probably will continue to be resistance against selecting people for jobs by lottery. Do you have any notion why—particularly when it is perhaps the most politically democratic idea ever invented, one the Greeks used when they conceived the system we call democracy?

McClelland: Well, as I've already said, I think the idea of meritocracy, which is the basis of our present system, was conceived as an anti-aristocratic point of view. The idea was that people would be selected on the basis of qualification and merit, not on the basis of pedigree or connections. So how do you defend yourself against somebody who asks, "Don't you believe in getting the best qualified person to do the job?" You have to say, "Yes." At least I do.

Comment: But there is a vein of American thought and practice—it's usually identified with the Jeffersonian tradition—that you can train anybody.

McClelland: That's interesting. You give me a little hope. But I'd like to see somebody try to win that case somewhere. I know there are lots of opportunities for all of us to try it. Are you picked by lot in this program [Union Graduate School for the Union for Experimenting Colleges and Universities]?

Answer: No.

McClelland: Then start here. You're all saying let somebody else pick by lot. You could abolish the admissions office. It's much cheaper not to have one. You wouldn't need so much staff and paperwork!

MEASURING COMPETENCE

Question: You said something about alternative measures of competence. Could you lay out a few of them?

McClelland: I have a general list of things that I think are more important than some of what we now measure. I think, for example, more of our tests should involve measuring a person's ability to communicate, since that's often part of our criteria for successful behavior in a position. I remember an application from a black student who was editor of his college newspaper. He enclosed articles he had written, but his Miller Analogies score was unbelievably low. The Miller Analogies test, as you may know, is supposed to predict a person's ability to reason and think straight. We had evidence he could do this, since he had written the articles. But I couldn't get that guy into Harvard because they said it would be unfair to him: He wouldn't do what he had demonstrated he could do well, because the test predicted that he couldn't do it. By the way, I've known people who scored high on the Miller tests, but were terrible at writing a reasoned piece of discourse.

I can draw a similar illustration from an experience in Ethiopia. We were there to evaluate the effect of Peace Corps teachers on Ethiopian high-school students. One of the big arguments going on was whether the students were being taught English well enough to enable them to pass the Cambridge examination. This fill-in-the-blanks test for proficiency in English is based, believe it or not, on *The Vicar of Wakefield*. I don't know if you've read the book recently, but it contains the weirdest vocabulary in terms of usable English. The American Peace Corps teachers rebelled. "First," they said, "this is the wrong vocabulary, second, we want to know if the kids can use the language, not whether they can fill in the blanks to show they know English grammar."

The problem became political; accusations were made that students taught by the Peace Corps were flunking the exam. So we invented a different one. We had students write little themes or stories, and we also probed for motivational changes. The design was not so much to check correctness of spelling and grammar, but to look for what we called fluency, that is, the ability to communicate reasonably well. We coded for, among other things, the complexity of the sentences. And we found that the students taught by the Peace Corps were really much better at writing complex sentences than were other students—primarily, I think, because their teachers spoke English as a native language. In other words, the Ethiopians were learning from the American teachers how to think and communicate in a language rather than how to memorize the rules of its grammar. I think that we need more teaching and tests of this sort.

Psychology Today published a test that fascinates me because it illustrates a communication skill in which I have long been interested. It's a card game that requires you to communicate emotions. The card tells you which part of the body you have to use in order to do this. I'm sure some people are good at it and some people are bad at it. It's an important human skill. Why isn't it just as important as the Miller Analogies? I don't know if the game works. I've never played it. But I'm sure it's fun.

Question: All right, you've named one type of competence. Do you have other suggestions?

McClelland: Yes. Much competence depends upon what are known as personality variables. One of the important ones in kids is the ability to delay, it's sometimes called reflective ability, as opposed to impulsiveness. This is a quality that I would want in cops, for instance, to lessen the chance of their literally jumping the gun. Waiting long enough to size up the situation is a very valuable human trait. It can be taught to young kids or to adults training to be policemen.

Another important competence is learning to set a moderate goal. We stress this in our achievement-motivation training. Unfortunately, kids are often taught in school to choose goals that are either too easy (so that they get A's) or too difficult (so that they'll be rewarded for shooting high). We try to correct problems that arise from this kind of teaching.

We must also work with ego development. The concept bothers me, as it does most American psychologists, because I'm not sure there are genuine stages to it. American educators, however, have always wanted to develop people to higher levels so that they can adapt better. Paul Costa and I have been working on a measure of ego development with four stages, corresponding more or less to those described by Erik Erikson. The first is that of compliance or waiting; Erikson sometimes calls it hope-trust—the oral stage, if you want to think of it in traditional psychoanalytic terms. Within each stage there are four levels. For instance, level two of stage one is essentially compliance with whatever the teacher wants after a kind of minimal objection has been made. Stage two is rebellion, that is, assertion of individual will. This represents an improvement in ego development, although, since it makes trouble for them, most teachers see it as a nuisance. The third, or phallic, stage is one of curiosity. A person begins to reflect on what is going on. The fourth involves generativity or committed action. Costa has developed a rough measure of these stages. He has found, using the measure, that a more democratic, participatory type of school program tends to raise people on the scale of ego development. Most of the kids in a program of this type reflect later stages of ego development, whereas kids from the traditional schools are still primarily at stage one, passive and compliant.

Comment: But surely these stages are not hierarchical.

McClelland: I agree. The problem, however, is that if you have stages of one, two, three, and four, everybody, teachers included, begins thinking automatically that stage four is better than stage one. We might all deny it but how do you stop thinking that way if you talk about development? I don't know. That's why I'm a little worried about using the concept when discussing the types of competence about which we should be concerned. Nvertheless, I think it's a welcome alternative to academic I.Q. games.

HOW DO MOTIVATORS MOTIVATE?

In the last 10 years, most of my time has been spent trying to teach achievement motivation to businessmen and students. Those of us engaged in this effort have now concluded that we probably haven't been teaching motivation after all. We've been effective in making kids better students and making businessmen better businessmen, but we're not sure that we've been changing motivation so much as teaching people how to better manage their lives. Through a program emphasizing self-study, we teach participants about the achievement syndrome, about how to analyze their problems, to find out their wishes, their wants, and their goals; we also teach them to plan for the future. Mastering this is comparable to developing what we call a cognitive skill.

There is a bank in Atlanta that requires this training as part of a system by which they're trying to develop black men who want to get into business and own property— just the way whites do. Recently I asked some people who had participated in the program a year ago what they thought the motivation course had done for them. None spoke of increased motivation, which was the purpose of the course. Rather, they said it taught them to look at themselves more carefully, to see that certain of their problems were in themselves rather than in the world, and, based upon their evaluation, to set goals that they had a reasonable chance of achieving. That's an excellent measure of competence.

Intelligence and Genes

RICHARD J. LIGHT

At least three questions generally arise in discussions of I.Q. tests. One is precisely what such tests measure. A second is how social stratification is related to I.Q. scores, and what are the consequences of these relationships. The third question—the one I intend to focus on here—concerns the potential role of genetic differentiation in I.Q.'s within and between social groups.

In 1925, Karl Pearson, one of Britain's most creative and methodologically sophisticated statisticians, wrote about Jewish immigrants: "Taken on the average, and regarding both sexes, this alien Jewish population is somewhat inferior both physically and mentally to the native population." The context of Pearson's assertion was that this alleged inferiority was genetic. In both America and Britain today, however, it is quite well known that Jews score as high on intelligence tests as the majority non-Jewish population.

Prior to 1960, Catholics in America scored lower than non-Catholics on standardized intelligence tests. In the 1930's, a genetic explanation was put forth to account for the observed differences. Since 1960, however, the distribution of intelligence-test scores for American Catholics has duplicated the non-Catholic score distribution almost exactly.

These two historical examples illustrate that a genetic explanation for differences of intelligence-test scores between social groups can be mistaken.

Consider now two research findings relating genes and intelligence. First, there exist four studies of identical twins reared apart—one conducted in America, two in England, and one in Denmark. These four studies, involving a total of 122 twin pairs, showed essentially that identical twins reared apart had much more similar I.Q. scores than pairs of children selected at random. Since identical twins share the same genes, the studies imply that genetic variation explains some intelligence variation (the data suggest approximately 75 per cent).

A second group of five studies examined pairs of unrelated foster children raised in the same families. They found that a relatively low proportion (approximately 25 per cent) of I.Q.-score variation was explained by environmental factors: Foster children score only slightly closer together than pairs of children selected at random. If pairs of unrelated foster children raised in the same family are presumed to be exposed to similar environments, and if environmental effects are very "important," then I.Q. scores for each pair of these children should be quite close together. They are not.

We thus have two sets of conflicting findings. History tells us that two social groups who at one time had a lower mean I.Q. than that of the "general population" no longer lag behind. More specifically, the genetic explanations for these gaps have been discredited. Yet at the same time, evidence from the twin studies indicates that a large genetic component of intelligence in fact exists. What can we reasonably conclude?

I believe that only three conclusions are warranted. First, intelligence (as measured very specifically by I.Q.-test scores) appears to be somewhat heritable: That is, a genetic component to intelligence exists. Second, we have no way of estimating with reasonable scientific accuracy the true proportion of variation in I.Q. scores explained by genetic factors. The statistical procedures used in the twin studies do not represent intellectual development as a dynamic process, over time, but provide only a snapshot at a single point in time. In addition, it is important to remember that heritability is not a single fixed number for all people, but varies among populations because it depends upon the social structure within the population. Third, any assertion that observed differences between social groups' mean I.Q. scores are largely genetically based simply has no foundation in data.

Why can't the estimate I mention in conclusion two be made more definitively? Because I.Q. tests given to twin pairs, and to children generally, can lead to misestimates of heritability. The additive linear statistical model used to estimate heritability does not allow for changes due to outside stimulative factors in a child's I.Q. performance over time. It simply has no way of detecting such factors. For example, imagine that a mother has two children. Suppose that it was possible to measure their "intelligence genes" at birth, and that child A's genetic I.Q. capacity was 99, and child B's was 101—a small but real genetic difference. Now, assume that the mother, like many mothers, enjoys interacting with the more verbal, more responsive, "brighter" child. When

she talks to this "brighter" child, she is reinforced by his response; he in turn is reinforced by her response; and so on. The opposite happens with the less "bright" child; he is less reinforced. It is then possible that the observed I.Q.'s for these two children when they are, say, six weeks old will differ by more than two points. In this event, a tiny genetic effect will have been magnified substantially by an environmental effect. Measuring children's I.Q. at a single point in time does not enable us to identify such features of children's growth and development; yet such features probably have an impact upon the formation of intelligence.

Why can't the assertion I refer to in conclusion three be made more definitively? Because the *interaction* between genetic endowments and environments can lead to incorrect explanations of performance differences between social groups. For example, imagine that a large group of fat people and a large group of thin people are born at a certain point in time, and that the two groups have identical distributions of intelligence genes. Suppose also that in general fat people are treated less well than thin people. We may then find such differential treatment reflected in the groups' intelligence scores. Specifically, we may find that fat people have a lower mean I.Q. than thin people. Further, this may be construed as a genetic effect due to fatness or thinness.

But this genetic-difference interpretation would be wrong. What has happened is that a genetic-environmental interaction (the way society reacts to fat people versus thin people) has transformed what is really an environmental factor into a seemingly consistent genetic difference between social groups. Thus, in terms of heritability estimates, the heritability of intelligence might be accurately estimated as high for fat people, high for thin people, and there would still be a difference between the mean I.Q. scores of the two groups.

The implication of these arguments is simply that the development of human intelligence is a complex time-dependent process. We do not understand very well how I.Q. tests reflect a genetic component of intelligence, as any genetic component will interact with a person's environment. Further, differences in I.Q.-score distributions between social groups can be artificially created by the genetic-environmental interaction operating over time. There is an illusory attractiveness in the "simple explanation" that the existence of genetic differences in intelligence *within* social groups implies genetic differences *between* social groups. The difficulty with such simple explanations is that history often proves them wrong. Electrical engineers have found that they need detailed time-dependent models to describe complex circuit and network behavior. Surely we need models at least as sensitive when we try to describe even more complex human behavior.

The Case for I.Q. Tests:
Reply to McClelland

ARTHUR R. JENSEN

Readers of *The Humanist* ought to realize that many arguments against I.Q. tests ignore a large number of scientifically established facts. Below I have listed some of those that seem most germane; except the first, all items are amply substantiated by research published in scientific journals. *Note:* Unless explicitly specified, the following points pertain only to standard intelligence tests. Although such tests take a number of different forms (for example, verbal and nonverbal, group and individual, and so on), not *all* tests are intelligence tests.

1. The level of technology needed to maintain the standard of living enjoyed in North America and Europe, given · their present populations, demands that a substantial proportion (say, 15 per cent) of the population possess a high level of the kind of mental ability measured by intelligence tests. We could get along without this kind and amount of intelligence in the population only if we drastically reduced population size and returned to a simple agrarian way of life or became hunters and gatherers of food, as in primitive societies. The present population could not be sustained without the technology (food production, transportation, health services, sanitation, and so on)

and the kinds of brains needed to maintain it. Thus, to denigrate intelligence is to abandon civilization as we know it.

2. Intelligence tests do, in fact, predict socially and occupationally significant criteria. I.Q. is in a sense a measure of a person's ability to compete successfully in the world of work in all known civilized societies. When the "man in the street" is asked to rank various occupations in order of their "prestige," "desirability," and so on, it turns out that the rank order of the average I.Q. of persons in those occupations closely corresponds to the rank order of their desirability. For example, most of the practical business executives to whom McClelland refers have an average I.Q. that places them above approximately 96 per cent of the rest of the population.

3. Persons would still differ in intelligence even if there were no intelligence tests. Any merit system based on performance reveals these differences. I.Q. tests reveal the same differences to the extent that the performance involves mental capabilities. They are not intended to predict performance based on physical capacities or on special talents such as artistic and musical ability. Bright persons and dull persons were recog-

nized long before intelligence tests came into existence, and there has always been a marked relationship between mental characteristics and occupational attainments. Throwing out intelligence tests will not improve a person's intelligence or reduce differences between persons, just as throwing away the thermometer will not cure a patient's fever.

4. The use of intelligence tests in the armed forces shows that they are highly correlated with the kinds and levels of skills for which men can be trained and the time they need to achieve certain levels of skill. Reversing the assignments of recruits in mental Categories I and IV would guarantee the greatest snafu in military history.

5. Intelligence tests do not reflect only the accidents of cultural and social privilege; they get at some quite basic biological capacity underlying the ability to reason, to organize and utilize one's knowledge, and so on. Hereditary or genetic factors account for more of the I.Q. differences among persons than do cultural and environmental factors. In the white European and North American populations, where this has been studied most extensively, it has been found that genetic factors are about twice as important as environment as a cause of individual differences in I.Q.

6. Intelligence is positively related to other nonintellectual traits of personality and character that are also involved in competing successfully for what most persons in our society—rich or poor, black or white—regard as the "good things in life."

7. Various intelligence tests differ in their degree of "culture loading." Contrary to popular belief, blacks perform *better* on the *more* culture-loaded than on the more culture-free tests. (The opposite is true for other minorities.) Blacks also do better on verbal than on nonverbal tests. Thus, on some nonverbal I. Q. tests, about 85 per cent

of American blacks score below the average for whites, while the culturally very different Arctic Eskimos score on a par with white norms. This shows that higher scores on these tests do not depend upon having experienced a white, middle-class American background.

8. Just as no one has been able to make up a test of mental ability that favors younger children (say, 10-year-olds) over older children (say, 12-year-olds), so no one has been able to make up a test that favors persons of low socioeconomic status over persons of middle- and upper-class status. If the reasons for social-class intelligence differences were due to status-biased content, it should be possible to make tests that reverse the differences. Yet, despite many attempts, no one has succeeded in devising such tests.

9. Language and dialect do not have the importance in intelligence tests attributed to them by popular belief, especially where nonverbal I.Q. tests are used. Urban black children tested on the Stanford-Binet I.Q. Test by a black tester using ghetto dialect do not score appreciably higher than when the test is administered in standard English. Children who are born deaf, though scoring poorly on verbal tests because of their severe language deprivation, score no differently from children with normal hearing on the nonverbal tests.

10. College aptitude tests, such as the S.A.T., predict college grades for blacks as well as for whites, for rich as well as for poor. The tests are color-blind. Black individuals and white individuals, rich or poor, with the same I.Q. can be expected to perform equally well in school or on the job—insofar as the job depends upon intellectual ability. In predicting a person's scholastic performance, knowledge of his race or social class adds little or nothing to what is predicted by his I.Q.

Don't Talk Nonsense

H. J. EYSENCK

Debunking can be a very useful activity, but it is best performed by people who have some expert knowledge of the subject in question. What Professor McClelland has to say about I.Q. tests leads me to conclude that he was having his interviewers on. I am led to believe this because he never mentions the tremendous support given to the hypothesis of an inherited general factor of mental ability by factor analytic and other statistical studies, by genetic studies of identical and fraternal twins, or by educational research. The simplistic notions advocated by him that the abilities tested are simply learned skills of no importance to anything serious are so far removed from the facts that it is difficult to take them seriously. Consider a simple fact. Identical twins separated very early in life, and brought up in entirely different environments (differing as widely as environments do in our type of society) are nevertheless very close in measured I.Q. Sir Cyril Burt found them slightly less similar than identical twins brought up together; James Shields found his sample slightly more similar than identical twins brought up together. In these and all other studies reported in the literature, identical twins brought up in separation were much more alike with respect to intelligence than were fraternal twins. McClelland does not even mention

these facts, which are completely destructive of his views. This is hardly commensurate with scientific integrity. There are many other, similar facts emerging from genetic studies; it would be impossible to rehearse them all here. Whatever is measured by I.Q. tests has a strong hereditary basis (the most widely accepted figure is 80 per cent, but at the moment a fair margin of error almost certainly attaches to any such estimate). To give the impression that this is not so is factually inaccurate and misleading.

McClelland also gives the impression that high I.Q. is unimportant. He fails to mention the large literature that suggests otherwise. Admittedly there are occasions when the use of intelligence tests as selection devices can be mistaken; it may not be definitely established that dull cops are not as good as bright cops. This may be due in part to the difficulties attaching to assessment of success and failure in certain occupations. Where the criterion is poor, a selection device that is working perfectly well may not correlate with this poor criterion. This may suggest that we ought to improve the criterion, rather than that we should get rid of the selection device. Not knowing the facts of the particular example cited by McClelland, I cannot say; he may be right in this particular instance. But in general the evidence is overwhelming that people with higher I.Q.'s succeed better in life (that is to say, in any occupation requiring intelligence—they may not do so well as baseball pitchers, or jazz musicians, or movie actors) than do people with low I.Q.'s. Note the way in which McClelland tries to support an unsupportable case. "Even really creative research scientists do not score higher [on these tests]," he says, suggesting to the listener who is not an expert that such people have I.Q.'s around the mean. But this is simply untrue. What is true is that in a highly selected group of well-above-average I.Q. dons, there is little correlation between I.Q. and achievement in original scientific research. Those who do succeed are nevertheless well above the mean of the whole population.

Consider the following table of data collected from some 40 thousand adults and children. (The data were collected by Sir Cyril Burt in his long-continued studies.) Note two facts that stand out very clearly. In the first place, there is a perfect correlation between social status and I.Q. The higher the social status, the higher, on the average, is the I.Q. of those in that occupation. In the second place, note the fact of regression. The children of people in the highest occupations regress toward the mean and have much lower I.Q.'s than their parents, while the children of people in the lowest occupations regress upward, that is, have higher I.Q.'s than their parents. The first effect gives the lie to McClelland's notion that I.Q. is unrelated to important variables in everyday life. Social status would seem to qualify as something quite important. The second effect gives the lie to his notion that the environmental variables are all-important. If they were, why do the children of successful, high-I.Q. people regress downward, while those of unsuccessful, low-I.Q. people regress upward? This makes genetic sense (you find the same effect with such strongly hereditary variables as height), but it makes no sense at all for a whole-hogging environmentalist.

TABLE 1		
Occupation:	Adult IQ:	Child IQ:
Upper Professional	140	121
Lower Professional	131	115
Clerical	116	108
Skilled	108	105
Semiskilled	98	99
Unskilled	85	93

McClelland fulminates against school and university examinations. One wonders: When he is crossing a bridge in a raging tempest, would he not prefer this bridge to have been designed by an architect who passed his examination with flying colors, rather than by one who flunked out of school? And would he not prefer to be operated on by a doctor who stood at the top of his class, rather than by a dropout who failed all his exams? As a student, did he not prefer to be taught by a professor who was successful in his academic career, rather than by someone who had never managed to get his B.A.? It seems to me that McClelland is guilty of *trahissón des savants*—putting up a case that he knows to be not only weak, but false. Popularizers must try to counter, if they can, facts that go against their idiosyncratic notions. The Royal Society has a good motto, *"Nullius in verba,"* which, if I may translate rather freely, means: "Don't talk nonsense, professor; look at the figures." And if you don't know what the figures say, you might dip into my book *The I.Q. Argument*—you'll find them there.

The Apple-of-God's-Eye Obsession

WILLIAM SHOCKLEY

Who can say how far this seed of self-awareness and self-transfiguration that is within us may in ages to come extend down the corridors of the cosmos . . . ? For the law of the gene is ever to increase, and to evolve to such forms as will more effectively manipulate and control materials outside itself so as to safeguard and promote its own increase. And if the mindless gene has thereby generated mind and foresight, and then advanced this product from the individual to the social mind, to what reaches may not we and our heirs, the incarnations of that social mind, be able, if we will, to carry consciously the conquests of life?

HERMAN JOSEPH MULLER
The Humanist (*Number 6, 1955*)

"Foresight" and "the social mind"—these two evolutionary outcomes of the "mindless gene," eloquently described by the geneticist Muller four years before he retired as president of the American Humanist Association, are, I believe, now in danger. Sound thinking by the social mind is threatened by wishful thinking resulting from what I call the "Apple-of-God's-Eye Obsession." This is how I interpret Dr. McClelland's expressed viewpoint. My comment on his article consists of the answers to three questions: (1) What is the "Apple-of-God's-Eye Obsession"? (2) Are viewpoints "debunking I.Q. tests" distorted because those who hold them have succumbed to this obsession? (3) Do such distorted viewpoints prevent humanistic application of foresight by the social mind?

To answer the first question: What I call the "Apple-of-God's-Eye Obsession"—"God" meaning for some people the proper socio-biological order of the universe—is a theologico-scientific delusion. True believers in this obsession hold that God has designed nature's laws so that good intentions suffice to ensure humanity's well-being—a belief that satisfies a human need for self-esteem. Any evidence counter to man's claim to be the apple of God's eye strikes a central blow at his self-esteem, and provokes retaliation reminiscent of the prompt execution of a Greek messenger bearing ill tidings of defeat in battle. The parallel becomes clearer in historical perspective: Both Galileo and Darwin created new knowledge incompatible with the then-cherished belief that humanity has a unique place in the universe. Either the new knowledge had to be rejected or else the Apple-of-God's-Eye Obsession had to be painfully revised.

In my opinion, Dr. McClelland is avoiding this kind of painful revision—as applied to his beliefs about human genetic disadvantages—when he expresses distorted views of I.Q. tests, typified by this clause: ". . . the test itself becomes part of an élitist mechanism to discriminate against the disadvantaged." What does Dr. McClelland propose to to replace élitist discriminatory tests? A two-week intensive training period with rejection of "those who still show prejudice against blacks." Didn't Tim Leary, whom Dr. McClelland credits with suggesting how to cheat on I.Q. tests, suggest cheating on prejudice tests? Does Dr. McClelland believe any disadvantages can be genetic?

Dr. Muller's article warned of genetic disadvantages and the dysgenic threat posed by "artificial saving of lives under modern civilization" with "accumulation" of detrimental genes: "But if we grant that man will achieve adequate control over his numbers and will advance to untold reaches in his social evolution, all this progress must still rest on a crumbling biological basis unless not merely the quantity but also the quality of that basis is vigilantly taken care of." Dr. Muller's concern that the ". . . quality of that [biological] basis is vigilantly taken care of" stimulates research motivation. "Unsearch dogmatism"—my contrasting phrase—rejects the possibility of research on genetic factors in intelligence and social problems.

To answer the second question, I propose that unsearch dogmatism and unsound viewpoints flourish because the theory that intelligence is largely determined by the genes and that races may differ in distribution of mental capacity offends equalitarian-environmentalism—an important feature in the contemporary version of the Apple-of-God's-Eye Obsession. The preponderance of the world's intellectual community resists the fact that nature can be cruel to the newborn baby. Nevertheless, the baby too often gets an unfair shake from a badly loaded parental genetic dice cup. Some features of racial differences are the acme of unfairness. Yet my own research inescapably leads me to conclude that they exist: Perhaps nature has color-coded groups of individuals so that we can pragmatically make statistically reliable and profitable predictions of their adapt-ability to intellectually rewarding and effective lives.

The remainder of this comment concentrates on my third question. The tone of Dr. McClelland's article clearly dismisses my dismal conclusion that genetics plays a role in the disadvantages of our nation's black minority. In my opinion, Dr. McClelland succumbs to the Apple-of-God's-Eye Obsession so far as to reject facts that are well established for white populations about heritability of I.Q. and the correlation of I.Q. with successful living. He thereby avoids even traces of doubt about the racial-equality facet of equalitarian-environmentalism.

My own position on I.Q. was expressed in a paper contributed at the most recent meeting of the National Academy of Sciences. In A. R. Jensen's compilation of 122 pairs of separately reared white identical twins, the value for all nongenetic contributions is only 18 per cent. I showed that if environment contributed as much as 30 per cent of the I.Q. variance, then the probability is only 0.0005 that chance produced a figure as low as 18 per cent. I find, for 46 of these twin pairs, that an increase of one social class in Sir Cyril Burt's scale of six classes improved I.Q. by only one point on the average.

My research on I.Q. and race gives the estimate that for Negro populations, with average I.Q.'s in the 70-to-90 range, each additional 1 per cent of Caucasian ancestry raises average I.Q. by one point. In 1920 Dr. Muller anticipated my independently conceived method, suggesting the study of human psychological traits by the marker method and the use of blood antigens. Did "unsearch dogmatism" bury Muller's suggestion for 46 years? What harm has lack of sound diagnosis caused?

A humanist is morally obligated to face these issues. An alternative is such future self-condemnation as this: "Whether I knew or did not know, or how much or how little I knew is totally unimportant when I consider what horrors I ought to have known about and what conclusions were the natural ones to draw from the little I did know."

Who wrote these words? About what? Albert Speer in his *Memoirs of the Third Reich,* when he was forced to admit the extremity of his own evasion of the inhumanity of Dachau.

The failure of our intellectuals—exemplified by Dr. McClelland's article—to respond to Dr. Muller's warnings on dysgenics by seeking out the truth about genetic factors in human behavior brings to mind Herbert Spencer's words: "The profoundest of all infidelities is the fear that truth will be bad."

Our nation need not fear that "bad" truth will provoke the horrors of Nazi "eugenics." The lesson to be learned from Nazi history is not that eugenics is intolerable. Since 1935 Denmark has carried out programs with clearly positive eugenic implications. (Although a cause-and-effect relationship is uncertain, it is noteworthy that Denmark's per capita homicide rate has dropped since World War II and is less than 2 per cent of Washington, D.C.'s rising rate—20 per cent higher in 1971 than in 1970.) The real lesson of Nazi history was anticipated 140 years before Hitler, when the Bill of Rights incorporated into our Constitution the First Amendment guaranteeing freedom of speech and of the press. Only the most anti-Teutonic racist can believe the German people to be such an evil breed that they would have tolerated the concentration camps and gas chambers if a working First Amendment had permitted exposure and discussion of Hitler's final solution—the extermination of the Jews.

The First Amendment makes is safe for us in the United States to try to find humane eugenic measures. As a step in such research, I propose as a *thinking exercise* a voluntary-sterilization bonus plan:

Bonuses would be offered for sterilization. Income-tax payers would get nothing. Bonuses for all others, regardless of sex, race, or welfare status, would depend on best scientific estimates of hereditary factors in disadvantages such as diabetes, epilepsy, heroin addiction, arthritis, and so on. At a rate of a thousand dollars for each point below 100 I.Q., 30 thousand dollars put in trust for a 70 I.Q. moron, potentially capable of producing 20 children, might return 250 thousand dollars to tax payers in reduced costs of mental retardation care. Ten per cent of the bonus in spot cash might put our national talent for entrepreneurship into action.

In Honolulu, on September 29, 1971, John G. Veneman, Under Secretary of Health, Education, and Welfare, rejected this thinking exercise:

> And the more I thought about [the voluntary-sterilization bonus plan], the less I liked that idea. All my instincts told me that the way to attack mental retardation is at its roots—not through its victims. For many years I was a fruit grower in California. And I've learned that you begin with good rich soil—not with the fruit.

He did not mention seed quality. This substitution of instinct for scientific analysis, and emphasis on environmental soil to the exclusion of genetic seed quality, reminded me of Lysenko in Russia who, as Stalin's favorite, insisted that his Soviet biologists had discovered how to transform species—wheat into rye, pines into firs, and so on. Lysenkoism was a disaster in Russian agriculture.

If, as many thinking citizens fear, our welfare programs are unwittingly—with the highest of motives—selectively downbreeding the poor of our slums by encouraging the least foresighted, with the weakest social minds, to be the most prolific, then the consequences will be tragic for both blacks and whites—but proportionately so much worse for our black minority that a form of genetic enslavement may result, provoking extremes of racism with resultant agony for everyone. I believe that in demanding objective diagnosis and in proposing the voluntary-sterilization bonus plan as a thinking exercise, I am acting in the best interests of all our citizens regardless of race.

My position is that humanity has an obligation to use its intelligence to diagnose and to predict. Foresight by the social mind, Dr.

Muller's humanistic objective, can then prevent the human agonies of a "crumbling biological basis." To be healthy, the social mind must reject false premises—no matter how idealistic. I value the opportunity to counter the distorted viewpoint, noble in intent but potentially disastrous in effect, of Dr. McClelland's article.

The Social Uses of Testing

KENNETH E. CLARK

This symposium should bring into public view a growing discontent among test specialists generated by unalterable and incontrovertible evidence that their products—tests of intelligence and of special aptitudes—yield results disliked by most people, including themselves. Persons from poorer neighborhoods, persons whose parents are uneducated, persons who hold the most menial jobs or whose parents hold menial jobs, score *on the average* well below the more fortunate members of our society. Most notably, blacks obtain scores that are, on the average, considerably below those obtained by whites.

McClelland sees the continuance of poverty and underemployment in neglected parts of our society as resulting from the use of tests to support discriminatory practices. This is hard to believe, since such tests have been widely used for scarcely three generations, while the phenomena he decries have existed for centuries. And in the earliest years of intelligence testing in this country, Terman and his collaborators observed the same differences in test scores for various segments of society.

In addition to blaming the tests, McClelland goes on to blame the schools. He wants to abandon the tests: Happily, he makes no such proposal for schools. His ultimate solution is to select employees by lot, and then to let them be fired if they fail to measure up to the employer's standard—whatever that might be. One standard that he proposes is essentially political: A person whose belief system did not fit the standards set for a job would necessarily be discharged. The fact that he specifies absence of bigotry, or "sympathy," as the basis for such judgment only obscures the essence of his argument without changing it.

McClelland touches only lightly on the fact that in various job settings some people do succeed while others fail. Nonetheless, he obviously believes that there are differences in persons' abilities to perform on the job, for he indicates that he has been trying to devise some tests to predict performance. His illustrations emphasizing beliefs and attitudes are deceptive, however, and suggest a social order that most of us would abhor. In a sensible society, success or failure on a job should be determined by performance, not belief. It is essential to conduct performance reviews so as to eliminate the influence of the supervisor's value system. Such a procedure must be fully open and documented. Supervisors must be required to support their judgments with objective evidence that can be examined and reviewed. Otherwise hidden discrimination against any unpopular or denigrated segment of the population cannot be reduced. What purpose is served by writing laws to prevent violation of the civil and human rights of employees in the absence of such objective measures of performance?

Tests of ability exist that will predict performance; David McClelland's statement about this matter should be more precise. A better statement would be: "Many, many jobs require abilities other than those measured by tests of general intelligence. The widespread use of tests of general intelligence to screen applicants for jobs, without any examination of the relationship between test scores and job performance, will harm those persons who have less schooling, who come from poorer neighborhoods, and who have parents with little education."

McClelland has drawn attention to an important point: Our society places far too much reliance on abstract analytical thinking with a strong verbal component. We set as models the liberally educated elite, and downgrade the important roles to be played by all the others whose ingenuity and service is essential to the smooth running of our society. As a result many people elect occupations in which their performance is mediocre, when choice of a different occupation would have made possible a more satisfying life and a greater sense of accomplishment. McClelland is certainly correct when he points up the need to pay more attention to the man of practical affairs and less attention to the scholar. It is unfortunate that he identifies as villain the psychological tests that may in the long haul aid in the accomplishment of the very goals he outlines.

A wider variety of occupations should have greater prestige and greater attractiveness to young persons. We have, moreover, a wide variety of tests to predict success in many of these occupations. They can be used in counseling young persons to help them find the particular areas in which their talents lie. To condemn a person to a life of poverty or to assume that he will be unattractive to employers because he has "a low I.Q." is to disregard the fact that each individual has a wide range of abilities, weaknesses as well as strengths. Sophisticated developments in test procedures have emphasized this characteristic of human beings and have not relied on a single measure of "general intelligence."

Our tests of ability do need improvement. Tests presumed to measure different abilities too frequently yield the same results—this is one of McClelland's complaints. If tests measure only a general characteristic, then it should also follow that employees are generally good or generally poor. We know that this is not so: Frequently a change of job will transform a failure into a fully satisfactory employee. Tests that are good predictors of performance should be very helpful in advising employees to make such changes.

We must recognize and openly admit that we shall always have persons who are less able, and that such persons will exist in different segments of our society. Knowing this, how can we help every member of our society employ his own talents so that he can lead a fruitful and satisfying life? By assigning people to tasks by lot? By abandoning any notion that people differ? By firing people from jobs to which they should not have been assigned in the first place? By saying that tests were the culprits? Let us hope not. Tests can be used to assay the sincerity and integrity of job performance review in order to assure that hidden forms of discrimination and bigotry are eradicated from all segments of our society. Should we find prejudice in the tests, or in the schools, or in the world of work, let us eradicate it where we find it, rather than assume that our tests must be giving us a false picture of human nature.

When we discover that our good intentions run up against obstacles related to the nature of man himself, we ought not to flail at the devices that helped us to discover this. Rather, we should use the added knowledge to search for new ways of attaining our social goals.

Analysis of Values
and
Conflicts of Interest

Scientists who believe in the existence of systematic, hereditary racial differences in intelligence claim that the response to their ideas has been overwhelmingly ideological, not scientific. They, too, find accusations of racism and fascism to be repugnant and, in their case, unwarranted. In reaction, these scientists assert that they are persecuted for merely pursuing truth. Although their precise conceptions of the relationship between intelligence and race vary, Jensen, Eysenck, and Shockley all claim to be operating according to the ideals of scientific inquiry. They speak as members of the scientific community who believe that the "good society" is one in which inquiry is uninhibited by political constraints and reason triumphs over ideology. These scientists deny that they are simply serving their own professional interests, but are acting in the interests of all who believe that science serves human needs. Thus, if there are hereditary differences between the races, it is better to be cognizant of them than to remain ignorant. Knowledge of the nature and extent of these differences would permit the development of more effective programs to cope with racial problems.

The idea that intelligence and race are related is not new. Many nineteenth and early twentieth century social scientists and social philosophers theorized that European, particularly northern European, racial groups were superior in intelligence to other groups. They asserted that the difficulties that other racial groups encountered in adapting to and succeeding in European and North American societies were the result of their inherent inferiority. This belief system legitimated the economic exploitation, discrimination, and generally oppressive treatment suffered by these minorities. From this perspective the lowly social-economic position of American blacks was considered the result of native inability, rather than racial oppression.

Although many who support the notion of hereditary intelligence differences genuinely disclaim any prejudice on their part toward racial minorities and decry discriminatory treatment of them, the hereditarian stance may still have racist consequences. In other words, such "scientific" research may be used by groups and individuals to mask their prejudices and rationalize their opposition to racial equality. Critics argue that academic legitimation of racial differences in intelligence reinforces the beliefs of the majority group in the validity of their claims to power and thus serves to maintain and perpetuate inequalities that currently exist in American society. Such research thus serves to reinforce inegalitarian beliefs and to legitimize discriminatory treatment of racial minorities.

Kagan, Light, and McClelland argue that evidence supporting hereditary racial differences in intelligence is weak and incomplete. These critics not only assert that the role of heredity in intelligence has not been clearly established, but they also believe that there is little evidence that IQ is predictive of success in activities of everyday life (e.g., in the business world). In other words, even if hereditary IQ variations among the races could be proven, they may have little relationship to differences in the groups' social and economic positions. The critics imply that IQ tests are employed— usually unconsciously—to perpetuate the status quo. They argue that advocates of hereditary differences in IQ (as well as those who expend great effort in empirical research on the topic) often join in an unwitting alliance with the groups that profit from social inequality. They suggest that scientists such as Jensen, Eysenck, and Shockley, although well intentioned, are technologists providing blocks for a new caste system based on IQ—a caste system controlled by wealthy, well-educated groups who are most able at manipulating cognitive symbols.

Those who oppose the idea of hereditary differences in intelligence are often strong advocates of social equality. They believe that the ideal society is one in which all individuals have equal access to opportunity and resources. This position is shared by all egalitarians, many minority groups, and many others who promote progressive social change. However, scientists like Shockley criticize persons, especially social scientists, who adopt this egalitarian position dogmatically. They believe that rigid egalitarians who oppose research which might disprove their ideology harm disadvantaged minority groups by preventing inquiry that could generate new and more effective programs to help them.

It is obvious that arguments supporting hereditary intelligence differences between the races support the interests of those who desire to maintain racial inequality. It is equally clear that critics of this position support the interests of egalitarians who want to eliminate racial inequality. However, despite the obvious ideological implications of the two positions, there are also methodological aspects that should be considered separate from ideology. For example, the question of whether IQ tests really measure what they claim is an empirical and methodological question. The answers to this question, while having ideological overtones, can and should be judged in a scientific rather than in an ideological fashion.

3

WELFARE:

Problem of the Rich or of the Poor?

Many Americans find the public welfare system to be one of the country's most disturbing social problems. From their point of view, welfare is a gift of federal, state, and local funds to the unemployed, particularly the unemployed members of minority groups. This gift, or charity, is specifically irritating to the middle-American who works hard and is taxed heavily to support welfare programs. He simply cannot understand why these people are willing to accept money from the government rather than work to support themselves. Furthermore, many Americans suggest that a high percentage of those who receive doles do so fraudulently. They believe that there are thousands of "welfare chiselers," who waste public money on alcohol, big cars, and Florida vacations.

This section opens with an article by Gordon Tullock. It is Tullock's thesis that the level of public and private "charity" affects the number of people who work or, conversely, do not work (the unemployment rate). Tullock argues: "As the real value of welfare, charity and unemployment rises, more and more people can be expected to find the combination of such benefits and leisure more attractive than the best available combination of income and work . . . it could be fairly unambiguously predicted that raising the rate of *dole* (italics ours) would increase unemployment." The implication of this is that given the right conditions, people would rather remain idle than work. A further implication is that the dole must be kept at a minimum if we are to reduce unemployment. If the dole is high, people will find welfare more attractive than work. The image of the poor being imparted here is that of a group of indolents for whom jobs are available, but who would rather remain at home than go to work because of the generosity of the government. Of course, Tullock admits that ". . . all of this is a hypothesis for which no empirical testing has yet been undertaken."

Herbert Gans offers a very different analysis of the source of the welfare problem. In opposition to Tullock, who sees the problem in welfare

payments that reduce a person's motivation to work, Gans argues that the source
of the problem lies in the economy: ". . . which simply does not need all the
unemployed looking for work at a living wage and which cannot provide
for all the working poor who require higher wages to support their families."
On the basis of this analysis, Gans suggests that the economy needs to be
restructured so that it produces full employment at a living wage. A lesser
alternative is to attempt to change public attitudes so that the government
will provide the poor with a decent income, rather than the pittance they
now receive. This change of attitude should also eliminate the stigma and
degradation presently involved in receiving welfare. Gans criticizes the present
image of the welfare recipient as a chiseler. Citing evidence, Gans argues,
among other things, that most welfare recipients do not cheat and that most
would rather work than receive welfare. The problem is that the economy
is incapable of providing an adequate number of jobs.

Although Gans prefers replacement of the entire system of welfare
for the poor, he also examines the present system and states ways of
improving it. He suggests job training for the poor along with the creation
of jobs, such as the paraprofessions. The paraprofessions maintain a low
enough status not to threaten job incumbents, but have enough future
promise to attract and hold trainees. Gans also urges the creation of low
status jobs that can be filled without training. Here the government would
be the employer of last resort, hiring the unskilled for *badly needed* public
works projects. Gans sees these as dead-end jobs and therefore only a temporary
measure. However, if they are adequately paid, their limitations would
be less of a problem. To open lower level jobs in private industry, Gans urges
such things as promoting skilled craftsmen to master-status positions,
encouraging older employees to retire early by offering them extra pensions,
and eliminating the minimum wage for such positions to encourage employers
to create these new jobs. With respect to this last point, Gans recommends
that the government pay the difference between what the employer pays and
the legal minimum (which he would set far higher than the present minimum
wage). Gans is also in favor of income in lieu of work, or in support of
underpaid work. In effect, he supports guaranteed annual income.

Finally, Gans recognizes another method to reduce welfare eligibility:
". . . stating residence and other punitive requirements, cut benefits to
absolute subsistence levels and force recipients to work at starvation wages."
Although Gans recognizes that this alternative is attractive to many
Americans, he points out the grave danger that this approach would lead to
greater polarization and conflict with untold costs to future generations.

The final two articles in this section focus on welfare for the non-poor.
Tussing argues that there are two welfare systems in American society: "One
is well-known, it is explicit, poorly funded, stigmatized and stigmatizing, and
is directed at the poor. The other, practically unknown, is implicit, literally
invisible, is nonstigmatized and nonstigmatizing and provides vast but
unacknowledged benefits to the non-poor—whether working class, middle class,
or well-to-do." Tax advantages, oil depletion allowance, farm parity, and social
security are examples of welfare for the non-poor. Tussing points out five
basic differences between the two welfare systems:

1. Welfare for the non-poor is supported at a far higher level than welfare for the poor.
2. Welfare for the non-poor is concealed; welfare is open for the poor. Phrases which are defined as positive are reserved for non-poor welfare while negative phrases are attached to poor welfare. Welfare to the non-poor receives such labels as "parity," "insurance," compensation," and "compulsory saving." Welfare for the poor is labelled "relief," "welfare assistance," or "charity."
3. Welfare for the non-poor tends to be controlled federally, while welfare for the poor is controlled by local authorities.
4. Welfare for the poor discourages incentive for becoming self-supporting, thrifty, and interested in maintaining a regular family.
5. There is much greater intervention in the family life of the poor welfare recipient than the non-poor.

Stern focuses specifically on welfare for the rich. He shows how money from oil or real estate, stock market bonanzas, and interest on state or local bonds are exempted in whole, or in part, from taxation. He discusses the case of J. Paul Getty, who in the early 1960s earned a reported $300,000 a day, but paid only a few thousand dollars in taxes. He paid only as much taxes as a middle-income engineer or college professor. In effect, Getty was receiving a $70 million welfare check. The rich receive lavish welfare returns while the poor are confronted with penny-pinching at all government levels.

Paying People Not to Work: A New Look at Welfare

GORDON TULLOCK

Modern explanations of massive unemployment, particularly that unstable form of unemployment which used to be referred to as cyclical, have largely depended upon the assumption that labor wages are sticky.

Recently, Professor Armen Alchian of UCLA proposed a not unreasonable explanation for the apparent stickiness of wages. Alchian argues that it takes time for people to discover through the costly process of searching for a job, that the market price of their services has declined generally—not just at one specific firm or locale. During a continual price deflation, as occurred in the early 1930s, the worker eventually realizes that the wage offer he refused a few months ago was the best opportunity available. But when the worker returns to that employer he finds the offer has fallen, and the search process begins anew. This explanation—the "Alchian effect" —seems undeniably correct as far as it goes; but the phenomenon would appear to be too weak to explain such things as the Great Depression. That is, small fluctuations in

unemployment could easily be explained by the Alchian effect, but massive and persistent unemployment, I think, cannot. Further, even for the small fluctuations in unemployment, we might prefer to have additional explanations. It is the point of this article to suggest an alternative explanation.

Circumstances usually require exchanging a certain amount of work for a certain income (this trade-off between work and income can be illustrated by a standard "indifference curve" diagram). In most modern countries, however, there is an alternative. In general, some type of charity—private or government—is available for the person who is not working.

It is fairly obvious that the level of the charitable payment would affect the number of people who are working. As the real value of welfare, charity, and unemployment benefits rises, more and more people can be expected to find the combination of such benefits and leisure more attractive than the best available combination of income and work. Needless to say, different individuals have different preferences with respect to work and leisure; hence, one would expect that, with a given basic wage rate, various levels of the dole would end up putting different people on welfare. It could be fairly un-

Note: Gordon Tullock, "Paying People Not to Work: A New Look at Welfare," *National Review,* Aug. 1973, pp. 831, 854. Reprinted with permission of National Review, 150 East 35 Street, New York, New York 10016.

ambiguously predicted that raising the rate of dole would increase unemployment.

This, of course, is the lesson of the work that has already been done showing correlation between relief payments and unemployment, and correlation between unemployment insurance and unemployment. But a good deal of cyclical and historical unemployment can be explained in the same manner. (In the 1840s Tocqueville explained the existence of unemployment in England—while it was no problem in France, Spain, and Portugal—by the fact that relief existed only in England.)

Suppose, for example, that a change occurs in the value of a currency. For simplicity, let us assume the currency increases in value very sharply, as it did between 1929 and 1933. Under these circumstances, nominal wages fall, although real wages may not because each dollar buys more goods. Under these circumstances, the rise in value of the money would amount to an increase in the real value of the dole. With the dole at a higher level, a certain number of people would choose to be unemployed because that was the best alternative available to them. Similarly, an inflation lowering the value of the money would lower the value of the dole in real terms; hence, more people would move off the dole and into work. It would appear that those very conservative bankers who insisted, in 1931, that England's government must lower the dole may have been correct after all.

This hypothesis implies that there is a high correlation between unemployment and the percentage of average wages currently being paid to those who are unemployed. In practice, the hypothesis might be quite difficult to test because data on average wages may not be very accurate in cyclical changes. It may be that various minor changes in work rules and conditions of work are resorted to by management *before* they change the nominal wage rates; hence, changes in real wages are not entirely reflected in the data. It is also likely that low-income workers will move to the dole first. This would affect the average wage for the rest. Even more important, in most countries the unemployment compensation schemes are quite complex and different people obtain different amounts depending on relatively arbitrary criteria.

Consider the recent history of England: Before 1911, there was substantially no government unemployment relief, and unemployment insurance was offered by labor unions. Under these circumstances, the labor unions were compelled to cut their wages in times of contraction, and unemployment was seldom protracted or severe. Then the government took over unemployment insurance and apparently set the rate too high. As a result, throughout the 1930s—in other respects a quite prosperous period for England—there was considerable unemployment.

After World War II, as a result of a combination of inflation and rising living standards, the rate paid the unemployed was low enough that virtually no one was interested in living on the dole. Under the circumstances, there was practically no unemployment in England from 1945 to 1966. This in spite of the fact that the English economy was an almost classic example of a series of very short, macro-induced inflations and deflations, the stop-and-go economy of the 1950s. In 1966, England introduced a reformed unemployment compensation scheme that provided a great deal more income to the average unemployed worker. Since that time, England has had a substantial number of unemployed. Once again, there are macroeconomic explanations for the unemployment but I think taking the entire period from 1900 to 1972 and running a correlation would show that unemployment compensation would match up better than the standard fiscal and monetary variables with the degree of unemployment.

It has always seemed a little odd to me that the West European countries and, for that matter, Japan had so little unemployment in the post-1945 period. The theory that their macro policy was more aggressively Keynesian than the United States' seemed absurd (particularly in the cases of West

Germany and Japan). Nevertheless, low unemployment was characteristic of all of these economies. It is my opinion that what actually happened is that their minimum unemployment insurance had, in essence, been reduced to an unattractive value by inflation, with the result that no one was much affected by it. The fact that they had very little in the way of minimum-wage requirements (and, in the case of England, none at all) probably helped also.

If this explanation of unemployment is correct, the results would, indeed, be ironic. It would imply that the long, high unemployment in the 1930s was, to a large extent, the *result* of the very extensive measures undertaken by many governments to provide relief for the unemployed. The remedy was actually the cause. The initial burst of unemployment in the Thirties can be put down to the Alchian effect; the continuation of it may have been the result of the unem-

ployment-compensation measures available.

As I said above, all of this is a hypothesis for which no empirical testing has yet been undertaken. If the hypothesis turns out to be correct, then it has policy implications, but they are not as strong as might be suspected. It would be perfectly possible to argue that our present rates of welfare are proper and that we wish to give people a minimum utility level resulting from the combination of the present welfare payment and resulting leisure. With this set of preferences, the basic policy recommendation would simply be that we worry less about unemployment. On the other hand, it might be that with the demonstration that unemployment is caused by the unemployment-relief system, we might decide to modify that system in order to provide more employment and a lower utility floor. The ultimate decision, then, would be a matter of values, not of science.

Three Ways to Solve
the Welfare Problem

HERBERT J. GANS

When the Nixon Administration's Family Assistance Plan was shelved by the last Congress at the end of 1970, 15 per cent of New York City's population, 25 per cent of Newark's population and 6 per cent of all Americans—about 12.5 million people—were on welfare, and since then their number has continued to rise faster than expected. One would therefore think that national and local task forces would be searching for other solutions to the welfare problem. But the White House—though it is still planning to revive FAP, as welfare experts now call it—is preoccupied with revenue sharing. And Mayor Lindsay and Congressman Wilbur Mills, the Chairman of the House Ways and Means Committee, who are trying in different ways to have the Federal Government take over welfare, are worrying about who pays the bill. None of the programs, FAP included, can do much about the welfare problem itself. That problem is really in the heart of the American economy, which simply does not need all the unemployed looking for work at a living wage and which

Note: Herbert J. Gans, "Three Ways to Solve the Welfare Problem," *New York Times,* March 1971 © 1971 by The New York Times Company. Reprinted by permission.

cannot provide for all the working poor who require higher wages to support their families. Ultimately, therefore, an end to the welfare problem requires either remaking the economy so that it produces full employment at a living wage, or altering public beliefs about welfare so that the Government will provide the unneeded and underpaid with a decent income.

Had it passed, the Family Assistance Plan would have aided some of the cities and states caught in a budget squeeze by constantly rising welfare costs, for it increased Federal sharing in welfare expenditures; but it would not have resulted in either jobs or decent incomes for the poor. It did establish the salutary and much-needed principle of a guaranteed annual income for all Americans, but the guarantee came only to about $2,300 for an otherwise penniless family of four ($1,600 plus $700 worth of food stamps), an amount higher than present welfare benefits in only eight states. The plan would not have improved the lot of welfare recipients in the remaining states, although it would have helped the working poor (or underemployed) with wage supports until their income reached $3,940.

It could be argued, of course, that once the

principle of a guaranteed income became law, the guarantee, now far below the Federal poverty line of $3,800, would eventually be raised, but perhaps FAP would also have established a new and lower poverty line for a long time to come, for while Government benefits are usually raised over the years, this is not the case with programs for the poor. Thus, Social Security benefits, which are paid mainly to the nonpoor, have gone up, but Medicaid benefits have gone down and, although the Federal Government established the principle of building decent housing for the poor in the late nineteen-thirties, the number of public housing units actually built has been declining for 15 years.

THE PROBLEM

When an economy cannot provide work for everyone, some people have to be excluded from the labor force. The American economy excludes the sick, the blind and the old, even though some may be able to work; it discourages wives and mothers from working, and it keeps the young out as long as possible, only partly so that they can obtain more education. It also excludes people without the proper job skills, work habits and sometimes skin color, or employs them only if they are willing to accept very low wages. Many of the excluded are compensated directly by government for being left out, but unemployed men are often left without help after unemployment compensation runs out unless they desert from or are rejected by their families, the wives and children then becoming eligible for Aid to Families of Dependent Children, or A.F.D.C.

A.F.D.C. was established for widows and orphans, but during the Depression it also began to help separated, divorced and unmarried mothers. Even then the caseload was less than half a million, but after World War II it began to climb. By 1956, there were more than two million recipients; by 1963, almost four million, and since then the number has increased at an even faster rate, to five million in 1967, six and a half million in 1968, and more than eight and a half million by December, 1970.

Why the A.F.D.C. rolls should increase so spectacularly is still being debated by experts and critics. Initially, the most common explanation was the onset of unemployment, with women applying for help when their jobless husbands deserted—sometimes just to make their wives eligible for aid—or when separated or divorced women lost their jobs. As the numbers continued to increase during the period of nearly full employment in the mid-sixties, however, other explanations were offered. Daniel Patrick Moynihan, who, as the President's Counselor, fought tirelessly for FAP, argued in the now-famous Moynihan Report that the increase was stimulated not just by unemployment but also by the disintegration of the black family, the ravages of slavery having created a matriarchal family which rejected its men even without economic cause. He pointed out that the A.F.D.C. rolls were going up while black unemployment was coming down. But no one knows how long it takes for a man who has lost his job to leave his family and for the family to apply for A.F.D.C. Besides, actual joblessness in the ghetto is considerably higher than that counted in official unemployment figures and may not come down even when the rest of society is prospering.

In recent years, the rise in the number of A.F.D.C. recipients has also been explained by (or blamed on) actions of the Supreme Court, which invalidated residence requirements that had postponed eligibility for newly arrived poor people in many states; the Federal Government, which, through a program known as A.F.D.C.–U., made benefits available with a jobless man in the house; overly liberal local welfare agencies which were letting too many people on the rolls; and various ghetto organizations, notably the National Welfare Rights Organization, which were urging poor women to claim their welfare rights. These explanations are not supported by the available evidence, however. Most A.F.D.C. recipients, even those newly on the rolls, are long-time residents of these communities; the A.F.D.C.–U. program has been activated in only 25 states and only on a small scale, and the rolls have risen all over the country, even where welfare agencies follow restrictive practices and welfare mothers are not being organized. The increasing militancy in the ghetto may have led more women to claim A.F.D.C. without organized encouragement, however, particularly as recent studies suggest that they feel less stigma about doing so than middle-class observers thought (or thought they should). In addition, as Frances Piven and Richard Cloward demonstrate in a forthcoming book, the welfare rolls have historically been expanded to dampen political militancy among the poor, and the middle nineteen-sixties were the years of the long hot summer.

The rise in the rolls is also due to a concurrent rise in the benefits paid to recipients, for whenever benefits go up people with incomes below the new benefit become eligible. The benefits were increased during the sixties because they had been abysmally low before, and today they still average only about $180 a month for a family, but there are other reasons as well. As the Federal Government reimbursed a larger proportion of total welfare outlays to cities and states, they in turn may have raised benefits because A.F.D.C. recipients are, after all, voters, and as they become more numerous, politicians are naturally more aware of their needs.

Even so, the increase in benefits affects the rolls only when income from work fails to increase at the same rate, but wage levels among the working poor have been sluggish in recent years and have not kept up with the rising benefits. Consequently, as Martin Rein has pointed out, more people are entitled to A.F.D.C. and others are discouraged from looking for a poorly paid job if they can obtain more and steadier income from A.F.D.C., particularly in cities where they can take part-time work on the side without losing benefits. For example, in New York City, a welfare mother can earn $2,000 from

such work and still obtain $3,386 in addition from A.F.D.C.; in Chicago, A.F.D.C. will give her about $2,600; in Wilmington and Phoenix, about $1,800. (The high New York and Chicago payments stem largely from liberal state welfare supplements, but neither they nor the privilege of retaining income from work are available in most other states.) Although there is no evidence that many women in the liberal states have given up full-time jobs to go on welfare, it is possible that they may simply have stopped looking for poorly paid jobs.

Nevertheless, unemployment continues to be a major cause of the increase in A.F.D.C. benefits, the rolls having gone up more sharply than ever in the last year, and the proportion of white applicants is higher as well. In a recession, the low-wage and temporary jobs on which so many poor people exist are the first to disappear, for when the affluent take shorter vacations and businessmen entertain less often, even on expense accounts, maids, dishwashers and others are quickly laid off. If the recession continues, particularly at the lower levels of the economy, which respond least quickly to Federal economic expansion policies, the rolls are likely to continue to rise. They may even do so if the recession ends, for as far as one can tell, 30 to 50 per cent of the women who may be eligible for A.F.D.C. have never applied, partly because they are too proud, but mainly because they do not know they are eligible. Welfare agencies do not advertise their programs, leaving it to the initiative of potential recipients to find out whether they are entitled to it.

Unlike the sick and disabled, whose exclusion from the economy is not thought to be their own fault, A.F.D.C. recipients are often blamed for going on welfare. Over the years, the AF.D.C. recipient has come to be pictured as a Southern black woman who has moved to a Northern city paying high welfare benefits, getting rid of her husband to become eligible for welfare and having illegitimate children to obtain more money. Her absent husband has been accused of shirking his family responsibilities, of being unwilling to work at unpleasant jobs or to work at all, and of wanting to live off his wife's welfare income. Recipients have been characterized as cheaters and welfare workers as permissive bleeding hearts unwilling to cut ineligibles off the rolls. In the last couple of years, public dissatisfaction with A.F.D.C. has escalated further, for welfare is becoming the largest and fastest-growing item in many municipal budgets, New York's included.

Actually, the popular image of welfare recipients is quite similar to that of the poor generally, and reflects a widespread hostility, especially toward the black poor. For a long time this image was also nurtured by lack of information about A.F.D.C. recipients, but now a number of studies exist which show that image to be largely incorrect. To begin with, recipients probably cheat less than affluent income-tax filers, for a recent New York experiment in which welfare applicants claimed their eligibility by personal affidavits without the usual income investigation showed that only 2 per cent had misrepresented their assets, and the latest HEW study on the subject shows a 4 per cent cheating rate. Even in supposedly liberal New York, case workers have not become very liberal in doling out benefits, and their decisions are always checked by supervisors whose job it is to make sure that no extra money is paid out.

Also, about a quarter of the applicants are still denied entry to the rolls and others continue to be dropped for not obeying the welfare workers. And recent studies in poor communities indicate that many A.F.D.C. recipients continue to live a crisis-ridden existence, trying to make ends meet and protecting their children from the hazards of growing up in slum housing and addict-ridden streets.

As for the characteristics of A.F.D.C. recipients, almost half are white, although almost 45 per cent are black, a high proportion considering that only 10 per cent of the total population is black but not so high considering that about a third of the poor and 42 per cent of poor children are black. Few recipients move to cities with high benefits just to get on A.F.D.C.; most come to find jobs. Nor do they want to be on A.F.D.C.; indeed, all the studies suggest that, like other Americans, they would much rather work for a living—and almost a third *are* working, often in part-time jobs. Many go on A.F.D.C. only intermittently, the average period being two to three years, and remarkably few raise children who go on welfare when they become adults. The largest proportion of women have been separated from their husbands a long time before going on A.F.D.C., though few are divorced, divorce being a luxury they could not afford until the Office of Economic Opportunity started to provide free legal services.

Most welfare recipients do not have illegitimate children, but in cities like Chicago and New York about a third of black recipients are unmarried mothers, even though only a few have children with more than one father. Illegitimacy has always been high among the poor, mainly because they could not afford abortions, and it has been higher among blacks because forced marriage to legitimize children, the reason for less illegitimacy among poor whites, has not been considered a viable solution. When unemployment rates for young blacks are between 25 and 40 per cent, men shy away from marriage even when they become fathers, and the women are understandably reluctant to marry men with little prospect of becoming breadwinners. Even so, a new study by Phillips Cutright demonstrates again that increases in A.F.D.C. rolls or benefits do not stimulate an increase in illegitimacy.

The distinguishing characteristic of most A.F.D.C. recipients is, of course, family breakup, but this, too, is only another symptom of their economic difficulties. While about two-thirds of all poor families stay together, family breakup has also always been frequent among the poor, particularly when men have not been able to obtain steady jobs.

A man's role in the family and his self-respect are based mainly on his ability as a breadwinner, and when he fails repeatedly he may eventually either desert or be pushed out by his wife, especially if she has a steadier source of support through work or welfare. This pattern of family breakup was prevalent in the past among white immigrant groups during hard times, despite their reputation for family stability. And despite the popular belief that family breakup is today a predominantly black phenomenon, it is found in poor white and Puerto Rican areas, too, and all over the world wherever men lack steady work and women have more reliable sources of income.

Sociological studies also indicate that most of the men want steady work and would remain with their families if they could get it. The popular stereotype has it that deserters are nonchalant "swingers" enjoying a trouble-free existence, but in reality, they are depressed men whose repeated failure in the job market has sapped their self-confidence. Some manifest their depression by the rejection of all responsibility, some by escape into alcohol, others by pursuing sexual success when economic success is impossible to achieve.

True, in recent years some men have become reluctant to accept low-paying jobs, but they do so knowing that they cannot support their families with such jobs and fearing that they will lose the jobs eventually anyway and suffer further loss of self-confidence. Younger men—and women—are now sometimes unwilling to accept unpleasant or dead-end jobs, but this is true of young people at all income levels, except perhaps for some hippies, and that unwillingness almost always ends when the young people become parents. Undoubtedly there are shirkers among the poor, but they can also be found among the rich, who are called playboys, and among the rest of the population, for every office and factory numbers a few people who loaf on the job. Except among the poor, however, shirkers usually manage to stay employed despite their reluctance to exert themselves.

The fact that welfare now supports about 15 per cent of New York's population when the city's official unemployment rate stands at 5 per cent might suggest that there are many more shirkers among the poor. Actually the welfare percentage is higher because it includes children while the unemployment figure includes only the labor force. Even so, if one adds to the officially unemployed the people who have, after repeated failure, given up looking for work, and are therefore no longer counted as being in the labor force, the real unemployment rate is probably at least twice the official rate.

Moreover, familial breakup may also be caused by the man's bringing home a wage too small to support his family. The working poor with full-time jobs make up more than a quarter of Americans now living below the poverty line, and it is possible that the A.F.D.C. rolls also include some families whose breadwinner, though employed, left his family because he could not support it properly on wages of $60 to $80 a week—and such wages are still being paid to many men in New York.

Until recently, America has ignored the working poor, perhaps because of the belief that if men have jobs they can solve their other problems. The inaccuracy of this belief is well illustrated by Kenneth Clark's 1964 study of Harlem in which he found a higher correlation between social pathology and under-employment than unemployment. As he concluded, "Apparently the roots of pathology in central Harlem lie not primarily in unemployment . . . [but] in the low status of the jobs held by the residents of the community."

THE SOLUTIONS

New solutions to the welfare problem are difficult to invent, for there are really only two alternatives: decently paid and steady jobs for those who can work and income in lieu of work for those who cannot. Providing the jobs also boils down to two alternatives: job training for the skilled blue-collar and white-collar worker most likely to be available in our type of economy—that is, fitting the unskilled, whether employed or unemployed, to a job; or finding decently paid unskilled work for them—that is, creating jobs to fit the people.

Job training has been under way since the mid-sixties as part of the War on Poverty, but so far without much success. Training the unskilled is a new idea and effective techniques are still lacking, particularly to persuade fearful and inexperienced trainees to stick with the program and employers and co-workers to be patient with them. More often, however, job training has failed because, despite all the statistics about vacancies in skilled work, the jobs have just not been available. Off-the-job training did not work because the trainers had no access to jobs or had access only to dead-end jobs, and these neither made use of the training nor could long hold the trainees.

As a result, manpower experts began to emphasize on-the-job training, which guarantees a job at the end of a course, as is normally the case with executive training schemes, but such guarantees are more difficult to make in the factory than in the executive suite. For example, after the ghetto uprisings, companies which worried about the fate of plants near the ghettos hired and trained some of the so-called hardcore unemployed, but as Federal grants for this program ran out, the danger of further ghetto disturbances passed and the recession began, many of those hired were jobless again.

Trainees, particularly those earmarked for the better jobs, also ran into opposition from older workers, who objected that they had put in long years at lower-paying levels and saw no reason why newcomers should not pass the same hurdles. Older workers were also unhappy about the newcomers because they were black, sometimes brought ghetto militancy with them and were thought to be taking jobs away from friends and relatives of the older men, as they sometimes did when companies hired only trainees, who were,

after all, being subsidized by the Government.

One type of job training which has been somewhat more successful has involved paraprofessionals, men and women who were trained as aides to teachers, doctors, nurses and other professionals. This program has achieved as much success as it has because Government funds were available both to create the jobs and to train people for them, but even professionals feared that the paraprofessionals might invade their turfs, so that too many paraprofessional jobs became dead-end.

Nevertheless, job-training efforts ought to be stepped up, particularly in the paraprofessional occupations, for they can offer dignified and steady work. But job training alone is not enough; more jobs must be created for the trainees, of low enough status not to threaten incumbent workers and yet with enough future promise to attract and hold trainees.

The second alternative, to create jobs that unskilled workers can fill at once without training, would be simpler and faster. Although this approach could be used in private industry, particularly if the Government stopped granting tax write-offs for labor-saving machinery and put a punitive tax on further automation, it may be impossible to fight technological progress. Consequently, the Government ought to become the "employer of last resort," hiring the unskilled for public-works programs. This is perhaps still the easiest way to make new jobs, and almost every community needs to build new hospitals, rebuild its sewers, clean up its waterways and construct more public housing. Unfortunately, these jobs would be mostly dead-end, thus providing only a temporary solution, although if the jobs were well paid, their "dead-endness" might be less of a detriment. (Low pay is just one of the shortcomings of the job-creation scheme recently announced by the Administration.)

But there is a different approach to job creation, which might not result in as much opposition from incumbent workers or so many dead-end jobs, for rather than adding new workers at the bottom, as do most present schemes, it would make changes at the top. What I have in mind is promoting the most skilled workers in factories and offices to a master status, like the master teacher who ranks above ordinary teachers, moving all other workers up a notch, letting the unemployed and under-employed fill the vacancies that develop at the bottom and allowing them to work their way up in the traditional manner.

Private enterprise would have no incentive to undertake such a scheme, and much of its cost would have to be borne by the Federal Government, but the unions might well give it political support because it would mean raises for present workers and new union members as well. Another version of this approach would have the Government offer special extra pensions to all older employed workers willing to retire a bit earlier than they planned, move younger workers into vacated slots and again place the unemployed and underemployed at the bottom. Both of these top-down approaches could also be used in Government employment.

Another approach to job creation, which has long been advocated by conservative economists and politicians, is to abolish the minimum wage so that private enterprise can make new jobs by cutting its labor costs. Presumably all kinds of new manufacturing and service employment could spring up if workers were available at $1 to $1.50 an hour. Abolishing the minimum wage would, however, be disastrous; it should, in fact, be raised from the present $1.60 an hour (which is below the poverty line) to $2.50 and more in high cost-of-living areas. Still, an experiment might be set up to allow employers to create genuine new jobs at less than minimum wages, with the Government paying wage supplements to the new workers to bring their total pay up to the minimum wage I have proposed. Such an experiment would undoubtedly be politically popular, for it would get people off the dole and help

low-wage industries and regions of the country. The scheme might, of course, create mostly dead-end jobs, although the wage supplements could be continued at decreasing rates if the newly created jobs were upgraded.

Even so, the experiment ought to be tried only long enough to discover if it would establish viable new jobs, for it has potentially dangerous possibilities. Among other things, it could lead to a stampede of presently under-employed people to the new jobs, and it would create havoc with existing wage levels in any case. It would also subsidize employers who exploit their workers when they could actually pay higher wages; it might motivate employers to cheat by not hiring more skilled workers, and it would encourage or perpetuate inefficient firms which can survive only by paying low wages. Appropriate limitations would have to be established to exclude the exploiters and cheaters, but in a period when new jobs are scarce it may be desirable to maintain inefficient employers as long as they provide new jobs and Government can supplement wages so that the new workers can support their families properly.

The main trouble with job-creation schemes is that they require large governmental subsidies—one reason why job training, which is less costly, has been so popular in Washington, and why the President last year vetoed a pioneering new manpower bill which included funds to create jobs. With unemployment remaining high, however, the Administration has just reversed itself and now proposes to establish 200,000 "last-resort" public service jobs. Unfortunately, 200,000 is just a drop in the bucket, and the pay is to be "at least $1.20 an hour," far below the present minimum wage.

While the President's action is a break with Republican tradition, the Government has long been creating new jobs in an indirect fashion; the Army has always been an employer of last resort for poor boys, and Department of Defense appropriations, Government tax write-offs and other subsidies have established many new industrial jobs at Government expense.

The Government is also moving into job maintenance, funding retraining programs for jobless engineers, subsidizing bankrupt railroads, stimulating highway construction and continuing with the supersonic plane at least in part to prevent the further disappearance of jobs. Given the political power of the Pentagon, the incumbent workers and their unions, however, it is not likely that Washington will soon create large numbers of well-paid jobs for poor people with less political clout, particularly when their work problems are popularly conceived to be their own fault.

Unless such new jobs are created deliberately or found in some other way, the unemployed and the working poor must be supported through some form of income grant until employment at a living wage is available, and that grant should go to the men wherever possible so that further family breakup can be avoided. Unfortunately, giving able-bodied men incomes for not working violates a fundamental American belief that they should earn only by laboring, and whenever pollsters ask the public to choose between guaranteeing the poor jobs or incomes, a large majority always prefers the former.

In practice, this belief has already been rejected, at least by Government, for it is much easier to send checks to the jobless or their wives than to bring new jobs into being. Moreover, the belief that people should not be paid if they do not work puts the blame for poverty on the poor, whereas the blame really belongs on the economy which cannot use them at a living wage.

While that economy has produced more affluence for more people than any other in history, it has never produced full employment at a living wage, except perhaps in World War II. In fact, unemployment and underemployment are natural byproducts of the American economy, just as pollution is a byproduct of current methods of industrial production. The economy can produce relative affluence for perhaps two-thirds of the population (although real affluence for no more than a quarter) because it is free to exclude or underpay the remainder and pass the burden for their upkeep to government, just as it has traditionally passed the burden for removing pollution to government. But if the excluded and unpaid, who are citizens and taxpayers like everyone else—and actually pay a higher proportion of their income in taxes than anyone else[1]—had to be incorporated into the economy as full members, they would reduce the affluence of the majority.Consequently, if the poor indirectly subsidize the affluent by being kept from participation in the economy, the affluent ought to subsidize the poor in return by income in lieu of work.

Opponents of this position will argue that before we resort to paying without requiring work, the poor ought to be forced to take the jobs they are now reluctant to take, whatever the wage; in a similar vein, whites who came up the hard way have insisted that the black poor ought to make it the same way instead of going on welfare.

This argument ignores three facts: that the blacks came up in harder ways than anyone else, having worked as slaves for no pay whatever, that they have often been pushed out of better jobs or kept in the worst ones by discrimination, and that they nevertheless keep trying to come up, as the kinds of jobs held by the working poor and welfare recipients will attest. As for the young people who now sometimes refuse to follow this route, they have absorbed the same values concerning job satisfaction and mobility as every other young American. One can rail against their having learned the prevailing American

[1] A Council of Economic Advisers study showed that in 1965 people earning less than $2,000 paid 44 per cent of their incomes in taxes, as compared to 38 per cent for those earning $15,000 or more, and 27 per cent for those earning betwen $2,000 and $15,000; Federal payroll taxes for Social Security and state and local sales and property taxes are all regressive. Of course, many poor people get their taxes and more back through welfare and other payments, but still, in 1965, the total tax payments by the under-$2,000 group were higher than total national expenditures for public assistance.

job standards, of course, but then one cannot complain if they protest, through demonstrations and civil disturbance, that they are not allowed to share in the prevailing American standard of living.

The most potent argument against giving people incomes without working continues to be the matter of work incentive, the popular belief that if someone can obtain income without working he or she will not seek work. Indeed, historically A.F.D.C. and other welfare benefits have been kept low so that the incentive to work is not eliminated. Nevertheless, there is considerable reason to believe that work incentive would not be affected by income in lieu of work. For one thing, welfare recipients do **work** and want to work; for another, people **work** not only for the income but to gain satisfaction or at least to keep busy, and most important to retain their self-respect.

Among already employed **people,** pay raises seem to increase work **incentive** and striving for further raises, and when industrial firms institute short workweeks even without a loss in pay, many of the workers generate additional work incentive and moonlight on a second job. Moreover, current O.E.O. experiments which pay a negative income tax to a sample of poor families are showing that instead of being content with the O.E.O. funds, these families are increasing their earnings from other sources.

Consequently, the popular belief about income and work incentive may be upside down, and if poor people have a sufficient income to start with, their desire to do better may enhance their incentive to work and to get off the dole. Conversely, forcing them to get by on the lowest welfare grant possible may keep them so busy with day-to-day survival that they lack the energy, morale and hopefulness to look for work. In fact, the only instance in which an income grant will discourage people from working or looking for a job occurs when the work pays less or when it is unpleasant, unsteady and unable to provide self-respect. Thus, income grants may increase reluctance among the poor to

perform the underpaid "dirty work" which they are now forced to perform where welfare benefits are too low for survival.

Still, giving people incomes instead of jobs is not the happiest solution, for as long as work is a measure of being needed and a major source of self-respect, long-term unemployment will be socially and psychologically debilitating, and being on the dole has much the same effect. But if the economy cannot make decent jobs available, an income grant should be considered a reward for staying out of the economy, just as war veterans are rewarded for their services to the nation.[2] Furthermore, if the old and disabled are entitled to a decent income without working, so are people unable to find work, and if A.F.D.C. mothers are entitled to incomes so that they can raise their children properly, so are unemployed or under-employed men, for they play an equally important role in the family.

In all justice, an income in lieu of work or in support of underpaid work ought to come out of the profits of the same private economy that excludes people, for if a company increases its profits by firing or underpaying workers, it should pay the cost of supporting them, just as polluters should be required to pay the costs to others of their pollution. Since American tradition seems to require that government pay for these by-products of the economy, however, the income grant will have to be government's responsibility.

The best way of providing such a grant would be to revive the Family Assistance Plan, but with a higher guaranteed income, such as the $5,600 proposed by Senator Eugene McCarthy last year. A guarantee at this level would not only eliminate poverty at one fell swoop but would also solve the problems of the working poor; it might win political support from more Americans than

[2] A majority of the Supreme Court has decided that welfare payments are still charity, although Justice Douglas pointed out, rightly, that income subsidies going to the affluent are not designated by a similarly pejorative term.

the original plan. Persuading Congress and the more affluent taxpayers of the wisdom of a $5,600 guarantee is likely to be difficult, however, and there are already indications that only the most minimal Family Assistance Plan will have a chance of passage in the new Congress.

In fact, Congressman Mills, who supported FAP last year, has proposed putting the welfare program under the aegis of the Federal Government instead. Although his plan is also intended as a substitute for revenue-sharing, it will either freeze or reduce welfare rolls and benefits (Mr. Mills is no friend of the welfare recipient), and it eliminates FAP's provisions to help the working poor.

If a $5,600 FAP is out of the question for political reasons, I would favor two other strategies: first, to develop a diversified program of multiple-income grants instead of relying on a single grant like A.F.D.C. or FAP; and second, to extend the grants not only to the poor and working poor but also to near-affluent, moderate-income Middle America. Unlike a single-income grant, which draws all of the political animus toward the poor, a program of diversified grants scatters the opposition, and if one part of the program is rejected by Congress, others can still be considered. Grants that bring benefits to Middle Americans will enroll political support from many of the potential beneficiaries.

If the Nixon Administration is successful in reviving last year's $2,300 FAP (which it has just resubmitted to Congress at $2,200) or if the Mills plan becomes law, a program of additional multiple-income supports might include the following:

• New local versions of the present A.F.D.C. program, which, whatever its many faults, has the virtue of being in existence and sending out checks. Indeed, as Nathan Glazer pointed out last year, in New York A.F.D.C. has in some respects become an income grant now that some of the more punishing features (for example, the regulations taxing away all work income, prohibit-

ing payments when there is a man in the house, etc.) have been abolished.

• A family allowance, to go to every family with children, rich or poor, to aid parents in paying the costs of raising their children. Many European countries and Canada have long paid family allowances—and despite popular belief, without an increase in the birth rate. Technically speaking, a family allowance is not even an anti-poverty measure, partly because the allowance is normally high enough by itself to provide escape from poverty (although there is no reason it could not be set higher), but mainly because it goes to every family, even if affluent parents would return most of the allowance through taxes. This latter feature makes it inefficient but gives it the great political virtue of appealing to a huge constituency, not just the poor.[3]

• Wage supports, like those proposed in the Family Assistance Plan and like the wage supplements I suggested earlier to create new jobs, to go to all presently employed working poor until they, too, earn $5,600 or, better still, $6,600, the annual income which is, according to a recent Gallup poll, the minimum a family of four needs to get along.

• Housing assistance for families who cannot afford to pay the going and constantly increasing costs of housing. This subsidy would be quite popular with the sizable number of people, the children of the World War II baby boom who are about to have youngsters of their own and will need some financial help in obtaining housing, for at present only the most affluent third of the population can afford the housing being built. Rent subsidies would have to be accompanied by

[3] A more efficient substitute would award parents too poor to pay Federal income tax the $625 deductions for children that now provide a family subsidy to taxpayers, but this negative family allowance would go only to the poor and would not help moderate-income Americans.

builder subsidies and public housing programs to make sure that more housing is built, however; otherwise rents will just be raised to absorb the subsidies wherever housing is in short supply.

• Student supports, to pay children from low-income and moderate-income families to finish high school and go on to college or technical school so they will have an equal opportunity in the skilled labor market of the future. The Government already subsidizes college students, and there is no reason why it should not also help less affluent youngsters at lower levels of schooling.

Many other subsidies could be included under a multiple program—for example, longer-term unemployment compensation, Social Security for every old person and national health insurance for all. It might also be useful to try some new ones—for example, a migration allowance to enable people to move out of areas where jobs are scarce, a car grant to make it possible for the poor and working poor to obtain automobiles in areas which will not build mass transit and free or cheap antipoverty insurance, a scheme proposed by Amitai Etzioni to insure people against becoming poor, which might be especially useful for the many families who fall temporarily below the poverty line.

THE COST

My proposal for multiple income grants carries a heavy price tag; the cost of the $5,600 FAP alone has been estimated at $20-billion, and it might go as high as $60-billion if workers are given wage supports to bring them closer to the national median income, $10,000. In comparison, the Nixon Administration's FAP would cost only about $5-billion a year, as does the current Federal share of A.F.D.C. payments. The other grants, which would pay lesser amounts but to more people, would be equally costly, although

they would be needed less urgently if a $5,600 FAP became the law of the land. My earlier suggestions for job creation and wage supplements would be even costlier, but more of the outlay would be returned to the Government through higher taxes generated by economic growth.

Proposals that cost $20-billion or more naturally raise the question of who is to pay for them, although this question might not be raised quite so belligerently in the case of multiple grants which go to a sizable portion of the population. Moreover, the first question might lead to a second one that has long needed asking: Who is—and who should be—subsidized by the Government, either directly or through tax exemptions?

Most subsidies now go to producers and employers rather than employees or consumers, although not all are by any means undesirable. Many enable producers to compete in the world market and to provide jobs for American workers, but others allow entrepreneurs and speculators to make unreasonable profits. Even the subsidies for ordinary citizens go to those needing them least—for example, stockholders, investors pursuing capital gains and homeowners. Moreover, the big corporations pile up undistributed profits in good times, the rich continue to pay less of their income taxes than the rest and the very rich almost nothing at all, so that, in effect, their share of Government costs is paid by the taxpayers of moderate and lesser income. (Incidentally, these taxpayers might think differently about the subsidies and tax benefits for which they pay if they were also called welfare programs; if the oil depletion allowance were described as the Oil Producers' Public Assistance Program, or we talked about the Tobacco Growers' Dole, Aid to Dependent Airlines or Supplementary Benefits to Purchasers of Tax-Exempt Bonds.)

Joseph Pechman has recently observed that if unnecessary producer subsidies and tax exemptions that benefit mainly the rich and very rich were eliminated, the Government could raise $25-billion more a year in taxes, enough to pay for much of a $5,600 FAP.

Furthermore, since those who benefit from the exclusionary consequences of the economy should subsidize those who suffer from them, the Government should levy an income-equalization tax surcharge (much like the equalization payments the Government now gives to poorer states and cities) on the most affluent 20 per cent of the population, those earning $15,000 or more. An additional $500 tax on people earning $15,000, with progressively higher surcharges for the most affluent, would bring in about $10-billion a year.

Even less affluent people might be willing to pay somewhat higher taxes if they could obtain directly some of the grants I have described, and some tax moneys should be available for equalization purposes if the President withdraws all troops and weapons from Indochina. Subsidies that go to people of low income might also be a good investment for the Government, for they would spend the money on goods and services they cannot afford now, thus stimulating more economic growth than corporate tax write-offs for labor-saving technology.

There is a third solution to the welfare problem which I have not mentioned so far: to reduce welfare eligibility through reinstating residence and other punitive requirements, cut benefits to absolute subsistence levels and force recipients to work at starvation wages. This solution seems to have generated considerable political interest of late, judging by the various restrictive amendments added to FAP by conservative Senators last fall and by an earlier unsuccessful attempt by a House Committee to overturn Supreme Court rulings on residence and a man-in-the-house and to freeze total welfare expenditures. Public support for this solution may not be lacking, either, for cutbacks in the welfare budget are being demanded in many communities, and New York's public employes, who are seeking higher salaries, are asking, as did one fireman: "If the city has $2-billion a year for the bums on welfare, how come they have no dough for us?"

Although one might be saddened by the attempts of the near affluent to improve their incomes at the expense of the poor, they are just being rational, for taking from the poor requires only a reallocation of already available public monies, whereas taking from the rich would probably require new taxes on them, which would never be levied if past performance is any guide. Besides, asking the poor to pay more or get less is a time-honored American tradition, though it also exists in Europe and even in some socialist countries.

It is possible that this tradition may have to end, however, for the poor of today are not quite like the poor of yesteryear, as I indicated earlier, they are beginning to obtain some political influence, at least in the larger cities. Restrictive measures against A.F.D.C. recipients might also stoke the ever-present anger in the ghetto, but most poor people are not militant, and the most immediate effect of a welfare cutback would be more family breakups and an increase in various pathologies in poor neighborhoods, with higher bills for more police protection, prisons, hospitals and the like.

Still, the major effect of restrictive measures will be on the country as a whole, for pushing the poor further out of the economy and into the underclass that Gunnar Myrdal identified some years ago will add to the polarization of American society. Fortunately or unfortunately, polarization can continue for a long time without serious deleterious consequences for the rest of the population; after all, many generations passed before whites began to feel the effects of slavery. Eventually, however, such effects do surface, and society will have to make political and economic changes to deal with them. We are still paying for the effects of slavery, and if things go on the way they are our descendants may not get all the bills for polarization until the 22nd century.

The Dual Welfare System

A. DALE TUSSING

The differences between poor people's and regular welfare programs are systematic and significant. They mean minimal survival for poor people, and reasonable comfort for non-poor; they mean degradation for poor people, and dignity for non-poor; and most important, they imply continued poverty and dependence for many poor, and continued security and apparent self-reliance for the non-poor.

Two welfare systems exist simultaneously in this country. One is well known. It is explicit, poorly funded, stigmatized and stigmatizing, and is directed at the poor. The other, practically unknown, is implicit, literally invisible, is nonstigmatized and non-stigmatizing, and provides vast but unacknowledged benefits to the non-poor—whether working class, middle class or well-to-do.

Despite the attention given to programs for the poor, they are dwarfed by the programs for the non-poor. As Gordon Tullock has observed. "Almost all standard discussions of redistribution imply that it is normally from the rich to the poor. Some such redistribution does indeed go on, but it is a

Note: A. Dale Tussing, "The Dual Welfare System," *Society,* Jan./Feb. 1974, pp. 50–57. Published by permission of Transaction, Inc. from *Society,* Vol. 11, No. 2. Copyright © 1974 by Transaction, Inc.

trivial phenomenon compared to the redistribution within the middle class. I find the concentration of discussion of redistribution upon the very minor phenomenon of redistribution from the wealthy to the poor and the general ignoring of the major phenomenon—redistribution back and forth within the middle class . . . remarkable."

The legitimacy of one's income and, especially, one's position in the overall distribution of income, are central preoccupations in America. No welfare programs are inherently legitimate in the United States, where the dominant ideology of individualism still appears to reject the welfare state in principle (while applying it in practice—a conflict of some significance). In the view of many people, job-holders are members of and contributors to society; non-job-holders are not. Job-holding legitimates one's political role, as well. In local, state and national politics, more is heard today about "taxpayers" than about "citizens."

Other socially legitimate sources of income exist, but their legitimacy traces directly or indirectly to someone's job. For instance, one can *save* out of one's earnings to provide for one's own retirement, either with a bank or some formal pension scheme. Similarly, one can provide through savings or insurance for an income while sick, or for one's family when one is "no longer there." Virtually all private provisions of this sort are automatically legitimate.

When a recently urbanized and industrialized America found that it could no longer rely on the old, traditional, nongovernmental forms of income protection and maintenance (the extended family, the community and systems of obligation) and had to create a governmental welfare apparatus, a major problem was that American ideology opposed such welfare devices in principle. If both the need for welfare programs *and* the ideology were to be satisfied, either the ideology would have to change, or the *form* and *name* of welfare programs would have to be carefully designed to make them seem to fit the ideology. In particular, they would have to have (or seem to have) a productivity basis.

Two systems were created. Clair Wilcox has labeled the explicit transfer parts of them "social insurance" and "public charity." "Social insurance," the heart of the welfare system for the non-poor, has been constructed to be legitimate, to protect the integrity and dignity of the people involved. To a large extent, this legitimacy is provided by some form of camouflage—by protective nomenclature such as "parity," "compensation" and even "social insurance"; by the paraphernalia of private programs, such as Social Security account numbers; and by burying welfare programs in tax laws.

"Public charity," or the welfare system for the poor, has been constructed to be illegitimate. Thus it too leaves the ideology intact. The illegitimacy of poor people's welfare is multifold. There is, first, the illegitimacy of dependency—living off the incomes of others. Second, there is the separate illegitimacy of apparent idleness, and the usual association with sin. And third, there is the inherent illegitimacy of government spending, financed by taxation. Most welfare programs for non-poor people either do not take the form of government spending (tax relief to some increases others' taxes, but most people do not consider a loophole comparable with an expenditure item), or use earmarked payroll taxes and segregated trust funds, and are thought of, and officially treated as, generically different from spending out of the general revenues of government.

Three examples illustrate the importance of the *form* of a program, and the association of form (rather than content) with legitimacy.

In 1968, Wilbur Cohen, then Secretary of Health, Education and Welfare, advocated a program of "income insurance," as preferable to a guaranteed income, negative income taxes and similar schemes, to cover unemployment as well as more chronic poverty. Cohen pointed to the greater acceptance of Social Security and other programs financed by payroll taxes and with separate trust funds. He argued that the poverty gap could be closed in America—that there were no "economic" reasons that we couldn't afford to redistribute income to eliminate poverty altogether—that the only barriers were "psychological."

In New York State, union members on strike have been eligible to draw public assistance checks. In one upstate city, a prominent labor leader, an outspoken foreign-policy hawk and vehement critic of public assistance recipients, found his membership receiving benefits, and was asked for a justification, both in light of his general antipathy for public assistance, and in light of the argument that public assistance was created to help the poor survive, not to underwrite strikes. His response was that his union members had for years been taxpaying members of the community, and were now only drawing on a fraction of what they had paid in. By contrast, he argued, regular welfare recipients were *less* entitled to public assistance, since they had not (he said) been taxpayers. He was in effect converting the program into a contributory one—for his members, but not for the poor. In both cases, changed perceptions converted a welfare program to a contributory basis, and thereby made it legitimate.

The third example concerns the Brannan Plan, which provides for farm products to be sold for whatever prices they bring in the market while farmers' incomes are supplemented by government checks. Farmers opposed this plan, despite its general superiority to the price-support programs (no storage costs, lower food prices) because a subsidy through the market was less explicit and therefore more legitimate than a direct cash transfer. Opponents used words like "socialism" to describe the Brannan Plan. More revealing still, some said they "didn't need charity." Only when farm surpluses turned into shortages in 1973 was a Brannan Plan-type program seen by farmers as preferable.

SOCIAL SECURITY—A CLOSER LOOK

Legitimacy of welfare programs for the non-poor is provided by some form of camouflage, and acceptability requires changing the form, not the content, of welfare programs. The classic case of a legitimate welfare program is Old-Age and Survivors and Disability Insurance under Social Security. Social Security has existed for more than 35 years, and has covered millions of beneficiaries. And yet it is almost uniformly misunderstood. Its protective camouflage consists in part of widespread mythology.

The details of the Old-Age and Survivors and Disability Programs are as follows: effective 1974 (but subject to change), there is an employee tax of 5.85 percent on the first $12,000 of payroll income, and an identical tax paid by the employer. Economists believe that the employer share is passed on to the employee, in the form of a lower wage rate, so that it is fair to say that there is a tax of 11.70 percent on the first $12,000 of payroll income. There is a rough relationship between the amount a worker pays in, and the amount to which he is entitled, but only a rough one. Each person is given an account number, and a record is kept of his

tax contributions. Each year's benefits (approximately $40 billion annually in the early 1970s) are paid from that year's tax contributions. In addition, there has typically been a small surplus, so that over the years a balance has built up in the Old-Age and Survivors and Disability Insurance trust funds of about $45 billion (as of 1972).

Many people conclude from these details that the Old-Age and Survivors and Disability Insurance system is not a welfare program at all, but is merely a compulsory pension or compulsory saving scheme. As recently as June 1971, NBC newsman David Brinkley, commenting on a news items which stated that Social Security was the largest program of government payments to persons, said, "Social Security is not a government payment to individuals. It is just the government giving the people's own savings back to them."

A second, somewhat more subtle myth, often appears in the conservative press—that Social Security is inefficient, and that individuals could do better by saving on their own through banks and other investments than through a government program. The argument runs as follows: if a man were to "tax" himself at current Social Security payroll tax rates (employer and employee shares combined) and to deposit the proceeds in a savings account, and at age 65 were to stop paying and start drawing a "pension," he would do better (on the average—age of death is, of course, unknown) than under present Social Security benefits.

The argument contains a serious conceptual error: it misunderstands the nature of Social Security by comparing present benefit levels and present tax rates. Yet no one will spend a lifetime paying present tax rates, and then retire and receive present benefit levels. The fact is that tax rates have been rising throughout the existence of Social Security, and that benefit levels have been rising even faster. The fact is also that Social Security payments are, on the average, well over four times the amount paid in by each taxpayer (counting employer and employee shares, and interest) rather than slightly less than he could earn from a bank on the same payments.

How is it possible for a trust-funded program to pay out over four times as much to each beneficiary as he paid during his working life? Three things makes this possible: a rising population and work force, which means that more people will always be currently paying taxes than will be receiving benefits; a rising aggregate income level; and rising tax rates. Could a private pension program do the same thing—relying on growth in the number of clients, and paying out more to each retired person than what he has paid in, together with earned interest? Obviously not. Only a government unit can be completely confident of its ability to continue growing, as only a government has the power to tax.

Social Security is not, then, essentially a scheme by which individuals pay into a fund, from which they later withdraw. Instead, it is a scheme by which those who are now employed are taxed to pay benefits to those who are now unemployed. It is a transfer at this time rather than across time. It is a welfare program, not a savings program.

The resemblance between Social Security and private, funded pension programs is illusory in other ways, too. In a funded pension program, the more you pay in, other things being equal, the more you get. The later in life you enter the program, other things being equal, the less you get. And your eligibility is not typically affected by your eligibility for other pension benefits. None of this is necessarily true with Social Security. As Professor Milton Friedman has written,

> . . . the relationship between individual contributions (that is, payroll taxes) and benefits is extremely tenuous. Millions of people who pay taxes will never receive any benefits attributable to those taxes because they will not have paid for enough quarters to qualify, or because they receive payments in their capacity as spouse. Persons who pay vastly different sums over

their working lives may receive identically the same benefits. Two men or two women who pay precisely the same taxes at the same time may end up receiving different benefits because one is married and the other is single.

Because private pension programs are a form of individual saving, in which beneficiaries receive what they have paid in, together with interest, but less administration costs, private pension programs *do* save for their members, and in fact, acquire massive amounts of stocks and bonds. Over the years, Old-Age and Survivors and Disability Insurance members have paid in more in payroll taxes than have been paid out to beneficiaries, and by 1972 the Social Security Trust Funds had acquired $45 billion in U.S. government securities. Since both own billions in assets, ownership of Treasury securities makes Social Security resemble a funded pension program in still another way. But that ownership actually reflects another *dis*similarity.

These trust funds' ownership of over $45 billion worth of U.S. government securities in 1972 meant that one agency of the federal government (the U.S. Treasury) owed money to another agency (the Social Security Trust Funds). (The other dozen trust funds—most of which, like Railroad Retirement, Medicare and Unemployment Compensation, are linked to welfare programs along the lines of Social Security—owned an additional $40 billion in U.S. government securities.) Since almost every year, receipts exceed payments, the assets of these trust funds continue to grow, though they are far lower than would be necessary to place the system on the same actuarial footing as a private insurance company.

To the extent that Social Security taxes exceed benefit payments, and the excess is "lent" to the U.S. Treasury, Social Security taxes are actually being used to finance expenditures on defense, interior, agriculture, foreign affairs and the rest of the budget. The "lending" is merely a bookkeeping entry. The earmarking of these taxes turns out to be less than perfect—present about $2 billion a year. The point is not that Social Security taxpayers are being bilked, their money being siphoned off into the Treasury. They receive over four times, on the average, what they have paid in—hardly a bilking. The point is, instead, that the Social Security system is not a segregated, quasi-private, compulsory insurance scheme, but rather a government welfare program, fully integrated in fact if not in form with the other functions of the government.

This fact makes it all the more important that Old-Age and Survivors and Disability Insurance payroll taxes are America's most regressive major tax—exempting interest, profit, rent, capital gains, and all payroll income over $12,000, and with no allowance for number of dependents. Moreover, the higher one's income, the larger the ratio of the benefits received to the taxes paid. Friedman has called Social Security "the poor man's welfare payment to the middle class."

DIFFERENCES BETWEEN THE SYSTEMS

There are five major differences between the welfare programs for the non-poor, and those for the poor. They are: the amounts of money involved; the camouflage, or lack of it, in making the programs appear to be something else; the level of government—federal, state and local—involved in administering the program; varying incentive and distributional side-effects of the programs; and the degree of intervention into personal and family life.

LEVELS OF SUPPORT

Both in the aggregate and on a per-person basis, the welfare system for the non-poor provides more liberally than that for the poor. Side-by-side comparisons are hazard-

ous, because coverage from program to program varies according to circumstances (for example, age, number of children and so forth) because the specifications of welfare for the poor and non-poor are different, because there are state-to-state differences in a number of programs, and because some recipients have dual coverage. Nonetheless, the following comparisons are revealing. In March 1973, the average unemployment compensation recipient received $256.76 per month; the average family receiving General Assistance (including, among others, families of those unemployed persons who are ineligible for unemployment compensation) received $114.15. The average retired worker received $164.30 from Old-Age Assistance under Social Security, while the average recipient of Old-Age Assistance under public assistance received $78.65. On the whole, the excess of non-poor over poor welfare programs seems to be in the 20 to 30 percent range for most programs, though some items go up to 100 percent or more.

There are interesting differences even within public assistance. The amount per person averaged as follows in March 1973: Aid to the Blind—$110.10; Aid to the Permanently and Totally Disabled—$106.55; Old-Age Assistance—$78.65; General Assistance—$68.81; and Aid to Families with Dependent Children—$54.20. (As of 1974, benefits for aged, blind and disabled are the same.)

Far more dramatic differences than these exist. In Mississippi the average monthly Aid to Families with Dependent Children payment per recipient was only $14.39. In that same state, a corporate farm, Eastland, Inc., owned by the family of a U.S. senator, received over $250,000 annually in various farm subsidies.

Our welfare systems do not distribute benefits on the basis of need. Rather, they distribute benefits on the basis of legitimacy. Poor people are viewed as less legitimate than non-poor people, and among the poor, those who are disabled, blind and old are seen as more legitimate than those in the

General Assistance or Aid to Families with Dependent Children categories—both heavily dominated by minority group members, including ghetto mothers and their children, and even including small numbers of unemployed men.

Implied here is a social judgment that—rhetoric to the contrary notwithstanding—America's poor are poor because they *should* be poor. This judgment takes the following form. Most non-poor Americans would probably be willing to agree that poor people are poor because of circumstances rather than lack of merit, except that to do so would also imply that they themselves were comfortable, affluent or rich because of circumstances rather than because of merit. Poor people are not necessarily thought to be inferior. Rather, non-poor people are thought to be superior. The success/failure, deserving/undeserving distinctions lead us to create categories of assistance which on the surface appear to be functional, but which on deeper examination prove to be moral and ideological rationalizations. Poverty reflects inadequate performance; and high levels of welfare support for the poor would be tantamount to rewarding sin.

CONCEALMENT OF THE WELFARE NATURE OF THE PROGRAM

By and large, welfare programs for the poor are obvious, open and clearly labeled, and those for the non-poor are either concealed (in tax laws, for instance) and ill understood, or are clothed in protective language and procedures (such as "parity," "social security" and "unemployment insurance," for instance), or both ("tax relief," for instance).

Whether a person is poor or not can often be determined by the names of his welfare programs. If his programs are called "relief," "welfare," "assistance," "charity" or the like, he is surely poor; but if they are called "parity," "insurance," "compensation" or "compulsory saving," he is surely a member of the large majority of non-poor persons who do not even think of themselves as receiving welfare payments.

The degree of concealment in turn influences the level of support, in a number of ways. First, welfare programs for the poor, being more noticed, are more in the public eye. Concealed and camouflaged programs are more likely to escape the wrath of taxpayers' groups. The deductibility of interest on home mortgages and of property taxes, known as "tax expenditure" items, cost the federal government $2.4 billion and $2.7 billion, respectively, in 1971. These tax deductions for home owners serve as a massive "rent supplement" for homebuyers. Either, if acknowledged as such, would be the largest single housing program in the federal government. Together they are more than quadruple the size of all programs combined for housing poor people—including public housing, rent supplements, assistance in purchase of homes and all others. Yet they are all but unknown, except as computations on one's income tax return. According to U.S. Treasury figures, 85 percent of the benefits from these provisions go to taxpayers with over $10,000 of adjusted gross income, while less than .01 percent go to those with adjusted gross incomes of $3,000 or less.

In the eyes of many Americans, the openness of poor people's welfare reinforces the sense that the poor are undeserving. Poor people are viewed as idle and dependent (characteristics often attributed to even the most hard-working and independent); and the publicity given to public assistance and to public assistance recipients is likely to (and often is calculated to) reinforce this impression.

This difference in concealment permits taxpayers to demand and legislators to provide differential levels of support without being conscious of discriminating. Those who have convinced themselves that they are wholly independent and self-reliant, in spite of vast camouflaged welfare programs, will not feel they have provided less generously for poor people. In their opinion, they have provided only for poor people.

The degradation and humiliation involved in some poor people's programs, and the sense of failure in life which is instilled in those who accept poor people's welfare, makes poor people strive mightily to "stay off welfare." This is undoubtedly a major reason that the majority of those legally eligible for public assistance do not receive it at all. The number who decline to claim special tax deductions and other tax preferences in order to preserve their dignity is by contrast surely quite small.

The techniques used for concealment of welfare programs for the non-poor often provide for automatic increases in amount as the years go by. This is especially true of "tax expenditures," which require no annual appropriations, but only that the same tax structure remain intact with higher and higher levels of income.

LEVEL OF GOVERNMENT

The third difference between welfare for the poor and welfare for the non-poor concerns the level of government involved. Welfare programs for the non-poor tend to be federally financed and federally administered, with decisions on eligibility and on levels of support made nationally, with but two exceptions (unemployment compensation and workmen's compensation), and those exceptions involve federal-state partnerships. Programs for the poor, on the other hand, while they may be partially or almost totally supported by federal funds, are characteristically administered as local programs, primarily by county welfare departments (or as state programs in those states where welfare departments are state operated). Even the War on Poverty efforts of the Office of Economic Opportunity and such related programs as Model Cities are tied to local government and local politics.

There is one important and revealing exception to this statement. In 1969, President Nixon proposed a major revamping of the public assistance system, including federal administration and a federally determined minimum payment level, for all four federally aided groups—families with dependent children, the aged, the blind and the disabled.

For nearly four years the Congress labored, and in 1972 it completed its work. The major changes were all rejected, and a bill was passed which made few departures. The most significant of these was the federalization, effective 1974, of a combined program, called Supplementary Security Income, replacing three federally aided state and local programs: Old-Age Assistance, Aid to the Blind and Aid to the Permanently and Totally Disabled. Benefit levels in the new Supplementary Security Income program are, however, lower than those of a number of states in the antecedent Old-Age Assistance, Aid to the Blind and Aid to the Permanently and Totally Disabled programs. Since states are permitted to supplement the federal payments (making the federal benefit the floor or minimum payment), and since a number of states are expected to do so in order not to reduce payments, even the 1972 legislation does not fully federalize assistance to these groups. Benefit levels still depend on state decisions, and state taxes are still involved.

The public assistance system is now left with three levels of federalization: the new, semi-federalized Supplementary Security Income program, for the most "deserving" poor—the aged, blind and disabled; the federally aided program, Aid to Families with Dependent Children, with eligibility and support-level decisions made by the states, and with state and local administration—viewed by many people as the "ghetto mother" program; finally, there is no federal contribution at all for General Assistance, which covers the least socially legitimate of all dependent poor, unemployed single and childless married persons, and unemployed fathers. It is clear that the degree of federalization, like level of support, depends on legitimacy or worthiness. All three of these degrees of federalization are in contrast to the complete federal control, administration and financing of such regular, mainstream welfare programs as Old-Age and Survivors and Disability Insurance under Social Security.

With these partial exceptions, the rule consistently applies: programs for the non-poor are federal; programs for the poor are state and/or local. This fact increases the exposure of poor people's welfare (not only because these programs are subject to local decisions, closer to home and easier to see, but because poor people's welfare legislation will be debated and acted upon on at least two and probably three levels of government, when the Congress, the state legislature, and the local council or board of supervisors passes on public assistance, housing, food and other programs). Poor people's welfare is limited, simply because it is tied to inelastic local and state revenue sources, such as the property tax, while the regular welfare system can provide vast benefits, since it is tied to the overproductive federal tax system.

Local and state administration of poor people's welfare means controls over the size of the population of the poor in given areas. Just as many cities, counties and states compete with one another to attract and keep industry and high-income population, so also do they (with less fanfare, of course) compete to discourage or drive away low-income population. Before Department of Agriculture reforms prompted by the Poor People's March and Resurrection City, hundreds of counties, primarily in the South, refused to participate in surplus food distribution, and a few openly stated their motive: to drive away once-needed farm workers, tenant farmers and sharecroppers, made unnecessary when technology affected agriculture. Competition to get rid of poor people is not limited to the South. A city councilman in a northern city, commenting on the council's recent negative vote on a public housing issue, was quoted as saying that the majority would be delighted to build more public housing for the city's poor, except that construction of public housing would merely attract more people to the community. Suburbs have steadfastly refused (with, since 1971, Supreme Court approval) to provide public housing. And, despite the fact that residence requirements for public assistance were declared unconstitutional in 1969, states continue to adopt them and enforce them.

This direction of thought has some apparent logic. In most cases, poor people's welfare programs will require state and/or local tax money; and even where they don't, taxes paid by poor people will not cover the costs of their public education, police, fire and other services. However one feels about the morality of trying to drive away people for purely economic gain, no amount of local competition to get rid of them will reduce the national total of poor people; it just affects their geographic distribution. In fact, there is good reason to believe that these policies increase the amount of poverty. Since they reduce the mobility of poor people, such people are unlikely to be able to leave unpromising regions to move to growing and prosperous ones. At the same time, low levels of services and support to poor people trap them into poverty's vicious circle.

INCENTIVE AND DISTRIBUTIONAL SIDE-EFFECTS

Poor people's welfare programs discourage poor people from becoming self-supporting, from being thrifty and from maintaining a regular family life. The regular welfare system frequently provides nothing to those with the greatest need, and then provides increasing benefits as need declines. The best-known disincentives to the poor are in the public assistance program, particularly in Aid to Families with Dependent Children. The manner in which most recipients are covered provides that every dollar they earn reduces their assistance check by a dollar. If a family is entitled to $150 per month, and the family earns nothing, it will get a check for $150; if it earns $50, it will get a check for $100; and so forth. This means that, in effect, there is a "tax" of 100 percent on earned income. Since businessmen with marginal tax rates of far less complain of the disincentive effects of taxation, it should hardly be surprising that the motivation of someone with a tax rate of 100 percent should be affected adversely.

In some poor people's welfare programs, the effective marginal tax rate may even exceed 100 percent. This is true wherever a food-stamp, public housing, medical care or other program has a fixed eligibility threshold—an income level above which families or individuals become ineligible to participate in the program. A family may find that any further increases in its income will force it to leave public housing, and pay a rent increase which exceeds the pay increase; force it off food stamps, increasing the grocery budget by more than the pay increase; and force it out of other programs as well.

The Work Incentive program for certain Aid to Families with Dependent Children parents reduces the effective tax rate from 100 percent to 66.67 percent. President Nixon's proposed welfare reforms would have reduced the rate to 50 percent. These lower rates still remain high enough to discourage effort. While recent research indicates that this kind of disincentive is less potent than was once thought, it nonetheless constitutes an added burden on the poor, a "sandbagging" of those who need no such handicaps.

There are other kinds of disincentives in poor people's welfare. The best known is the incentive to break up the family. In a majority of states, Aid to Families with Dependent Children, the largest public assistance program, is available only where there are no employable, unemployed adults in the household. In practice, this has meant

that virtually all such families are headed by husbandless mothers. Chronically unemployed husbands often must desert their families in order for the families to become eligible for assistance.

Mainly because of their concealment, many mainstream welfare programs provide in ways which are inversely related to need. The most glaring examples are found in welfare programs buried in the tax laws. The general proposition is: the dollar value to the taxpayer of any item which reduces his taxable income, whether it is a deductible expense, a dependents' exemption or an exclusion (nontaxable income item), is equal to the size of that item multiplied by the marginal tax rate applicable to that taxpayer. A $100 deduction for someone in the 25 percent marginal tax bracket is "worth" $25.00. With a progressive income tax, the dollar value of any given deduction, exemption or exclusion rises as income rises.

The simplest example of the inverse relation to need is the extra dependents' exemption allowed those over 65. The extra $750 exemption is worth nothing to the person whose taxable income is so low that he pays no taxes; it is worth $105 (14 percent of $750) to a person in the 14 percent bracket, a person with up to $1,000 taxable income; and it is worth $525 to a person in the highest, 70 percent bracket, for families with over $200,000 in taxable income. The added exemption is worth the least to those with the most need, and the most to those with the least need.

Even though the amount of this extra dependents' exemption is the same for all people, its value to the taxpayer rises as income rises. This effect is aggravated whenever the amount of the deduction or exclusion itself rises with income.

The "income-splitting" provision (husband-wife joint tax returns) also provides benefits which increase with income. The effect of the joint return provision is to double the size of each tax bracket. The 14 percent rate applies to 0-$500 for single persons and 0-$1,000 for married couples filing jointly. The 15 percent bracket is $501-$1,000 for single persons, and $1,001-$2,000 on the joint return, and so on. The greatest benefit comes at the highest end of the income scale, because the brackets are much wider (for example, $100,000-$200,000). People with high incomes are, in effect, paid thousands of dollars to be married (which helps explain why many rich persons are well known for having wife after wife, or husband after husband—they formalize their affairs, for tax reasons). As incomes decline, so do the tax advantages of being married. And when the family is so poor as to qualify for public assistance, they instead are paid to break up!

There are ways to design income tax provisions, using credits instead of exemptions, and using such devices as disappearing deductions, to avoid making their benefits inverse to need. The regressive effects that are found in U.S. law are not inherent in progressive taxes. The regressive effects are a by-product of the concealment of these implicit welfare programs. Can anyone believe that the American people would permit Congress to establish an explicit old-age pension which paid nothing to those with zero income or only Social Security or public assistance income, paid $105 to a person with $1,000 in income, and $525 to someone with over $200,000 a year? The same question might be asked of farm programs, which also pay inversely to the size of the farm operation, and hence presumably inversely to need.

INTERVENTION INTO PERSONAL AND FAMILY LIFE

A final distinction between the regular or non-poor welfare system and that for poor people is the degree of intervention into personal and family life. Programs for the non-poor make little or no intrusion into sensitive family decisions; programs for the poor exact, as the price of assistance, an element of control and a surrender of autonomy.

Control over the family's budget is control over important family decisions. Whenever someone can tell you what to buy, he is really telling you how to live. The poor people's welfare system does so in two ways: by providing goods instead of money (public housing, medical care, uplifting symphony concerts for ghetto kids and so forth), and by controlling the use of money transfers (through vouchers, such as food stamps, or through close administrative supervision, as in Aid to Families with Dependent Children).

Another way that poor people's welfare weakens autonomy is that people change behavior and family characteristics to become or stay eligible. Can anyone doubt that one reason that there are so many husbandless mothers who head poor families is that the government has for years paid husbandless mothers? Can anyone doubt that some poor people have children because most states do not provide assistance for childless single or married people, no matter how impoverished? President Nixon's family assistance reform proposals would correct the first but not the second of these. It would reduce assistance by a crucial $500 a year for mothers who did not work, unless they had preschool-age children. Who can doubt that some mothers, faced with the choice between required employment out of the home, and having another baby in order to continue to have pre-school children, will choose the latter? Such choices are not coldly calculated. Rather, the government subtly influences such decisions by determining the environment and reward system in which decisions are made. In precisely the manner described by former Selective Service Director Lewis Hershey, in his famous "channelling" memorandum, just as college students were led to think that becoming engineers or clergymen was their own decision, so poor people are led to think that having children or breaking up a home is theirs.

A third invasion of personal privacy is that

various bureaucrats in the poor people's welfare system actually monitor the behavior of their "clients." Public assistance caseworkers, public housing tenant-relations officers and social workers in a variety of agencies view their role as anything from mere advisor and family friend through parent- or husband-surrogate to warden. Mothers have had assistance checks held up because they were seen in bars. Families have been evicted from housing because of delinquent children. Families have been denied surplus food because they owned a television set.

By contrast, the use of Social Security or Unemployment Compensation checks is never monitored. Though families get a dependent's exemption in the income tax for each minor child, no one checks to make sure the family spends at least as much as the exemption on the child. Home buyers who have drunken orgies will not have their F.H.A. loan insurance revoked. Farmers may spend their farm surplus money as they please.

This double standard makes liars and cheaters out of the stronger poor people, and psychologically dependent grown-up children of the weaker ones. Neither characteristic is conducive to personal development. Moneylessness is only one side of chronic poverty, and the larger and more difficult problem is powerlessness. While some poor people's welfare programs attack this powerlessness, a great many of them aggravate it. An important consequence of stunting independence and reinforcing dependence is to keep many poor people poor.

The differences between poor people's and regular welfare programs are systematic and significant. They mean minimal survival for poor people, and reasonable comfort for non-poor; they mean degradation for poor people, and dignity for non-poor; and most important, they imply continued poverty and dependence for many poor, and continued security and apparent self-reliance for the non-poor.

America's dual welfare system is unique in the world, at least in degree. In other developed countries, while there is persistent debate between the advocates of "universal" and of "selective" social welfare programs, the former win out far more frequently than they do in the United States, where virtually every welfare, health, housing and employment program is designed specifically either for the poor or the non-poor.

We have noted the harmful effects of this dual approach. Separate programs for the poor are typically inferior; they involve demoralizing stigmata; and they tend to be built on assumptions which attribute poverty to defects in the poor. Their structures tend, whether accidentally or not, to inhibit economic and personal development among the poor.

Worse than all of these is the fact that the segregation of social welfare programs has separated, or seemed to separate, the interests of the rest of society. This separation helps account for a mutual hostility between the poor and lower-income non-poor, notably the working class, which has been enormously destructive to the interests of both. It is hard to believe that much progress can be made against poverty in America as long as this separation and hostility persist.

Uncle Sam's Welfare Program for the Rich

PHILIP M. STERN

Most Americans would probably be intensely surprised to find, in their morning newspaper, headlines such as this one:

Congress Sets $16-Per-Year
Welfare Rate for Poor Families,
$720,000 for Multimillionaires

Or this one:

Nixon Asks $103-Billion
Budget Deficit, Doubling
Previous Red-Ink Record

The story behind the first of these headlines (the second will be explained later) might read this way:

Washington, April 16—Congress completed action today on a revolutionary welfare program that, reversing traditional payment policies, awards huge welfare payments to the super-rich but grants only pennies per week to the very poor.

Under the program, welfare payments averaging some $720,000 a year will go to the nation's wealthiest families, those with annual incomes of over a million dollars.

Note: Philip M. Stern, "Uncle Sam's Welfare Program for the Rich," *New York Times*, April 1972. © 1972 by The New York Times Company. Reprinted by permission.

For the poorest families, those earning $3,000 a year or less, the welfare allowance will average $16 a year, or roughly 30 cents a week.

The program, enacted by Congress in a series of laws over a period of years, has come to be called the Rich Welfare Program, after its principal sponsor, Senator Homer A. Rich. In a triumphant news conference, Senator Rich told newsmen that the $720,000 annual welfare allowances would give America's most affluent families an added weekly take-home pay of about $14,000. "Or, to put it another way," the Senator said, "it will provide these families with about $2,000 more spending money every day."

The total cost of the welfare program, the most expensive in the nation's history, amounts to $77.3-billion a year.

Political analysts foresee acute discontent not only among the poor, but also among middle-income families making $10,000 to $15,000 a year. For them, welfare payments under the Rich plan will amount to just $12.50 a week, markedly less than the weekly $14,000 paid to the very rich.

Reporters asked Senator Rich whether wealthy families would be required to work in order to receive their welfare payments, a common eligibility requirement with many welfare programs. Senator Rich seemed puzzled by the question. "The rich? Work?" he asked. "Why, it hadn't occurred to me." Congressional experts advised newsmen that the program contains no work requirement.

Admittedly, the above "news story" sounds implausible, if not unbelievable. Yet the story is essentially true. The facts and figures in it are real. Such a system is, in fact, part of the law of the land. Only the law isn't called a welfare law. It goes by the name of "The Internal Revenue Code of 1954, as Amended"—the basic income-tax law of the United States.

Who gets how much of the "tax welfare" payments from the major "tax preferences"— the loopholes? Until recently, one could only make, at best, an educated guess. But in January, two tax experts at the Brookings Institution in Washington, D.C., Joseph A. Pechman and Benjamin Okner, made a computer analysis of information from actual tax returns (furnished on computer tape, without taxpayer names, by the I.R.S.). Using this data, plus other information from economic surveys, they came up with answers that might astound, or even anger, put-upon taxpayers.

On a per-family basis, a breakdown of the average tax savings of Americans—our "tax welfare" program—looks like this:

Yearly Income	Yearly "Tax Welfare"
Over $1,000,000	$720,000
$500–1,000,000	$202,000
$100–500,000	$41,000
$50–100,000	$12,000
$25–50,000	$4,000
$15–20,000	$1,200
$10–15,000	$650
$5–10,000	$340
$3–5,000	$48
Under $3,000	$16

Since a tax law takes money from people, rather than paying money to them, what connection does the tax law have with the topsy-turvy welfare system in the news story? The connection lies in the way Congress has played fast and loose with the 16th Amendment to the Constitution, and with the principle of basing taxes on "ability to pay."

The 16th Amendment, which authorized the first United States income tax, empowered Congress to tax "incomes, *from whatever sources derived.*" (Italics mine.) That expresses the Gertrude Stein-ish notion that a dollar is a dollar is a dollar and that, regardless of its source, the dollar endows its lucky recipient with 100 cents of "ability to pay" for food, shoes for the baby, a fraction of a yacht—or for taxes. Hence, in fairness, all dollars, no matter what their origin, should be taxed uniformly. But Congress has decreed differently. It has decreed that dollars earned in an oil or real-estate venture, in a stock market bonanza, or in interest on a state or local bond, while undeniably effective in buying food, shoes or yachts, are somehow reduced in potency when it comes to paying taxes—for Congress has exempted such dollars, in whole or in part, from taxation.

The American tax system, which stipulates that rates rise as a person's affluence grows, also holds that a billionaire like oilman Jean Paul Getty—with a reported income of $300,000 *a day*—is better "able to pay" taxes than an impoverished Kentucky coal miner. In fact, under the tax rates supposedly applicable to all citizens, Mr. Getty's $100-million annual income endows him with an "ability to pay" about $70-million to the Internal Revenue Service (on the premise that he should be able to make do on the remaining $30-million each year). But since Mr. Getty's dollars come largely from oil ventures, they are not, by Congressional fiat, taxed like other dollars. In consequence, according to what President Kennedy told two United States Senators, Mr. Getty's income tax in the early sixties came nowhere near $70-million. It amounted to no more than a few thousand dollars—just about the amount a middle-income engineer or professor would pay.

Now compare the notion of excusing Jean Paul Getty from paying $70-million in taxes —taxes that an equally wealthy non-oil man would legally have to pay—with the notion that Mr. Getty is receiving a $70-million Federal welfare check. In both cases the consequences are that:

Mr. Getty is $70-million richer.

The United States Treasury is $70-million poorer than if the full tax had been paid.

The rest of the taxpayers are obliged to pay an added $70-million to make up the difference.

Thus the net effect of a "tax forgiveness" is identical to that of a direct Federal hand-out.

The Brookings study concludes that of the $77.3-billion in tax "handouts," just $92-million goes to the six million poorest families in the nation, while 24 times that amount—$2.2 *billion*—goes to just 3,000 families (those with incomes of more than a million dollars a year). Coincidentally, that $2.2-billion is just the amount Congress voted last year for food stamps for 14.7-million hungry Americans. Moreover, five times that amount in the form of "tax welfare" went to families earning more than $100,000 a year.

The disparity between the "tax welfare" for the wealthy and that granted the poor is even more breathtaking in the case of the "tax preferences" involving so-called "capital gains"—the profits on sales of stocks and bonds, land, buildings and other kinds of property. When a person cashes in such profits during his lifetime, he pays no more than half the usual tax. Even more striking, all the gains in the value of property a person holds until death are not taxed at all. Some $10-billion entirely escapes taxation in that manner every year.

Since to have capital gains you have to own property (i.e., have the surplus cash to buy same), it's not surprising that only one taxpayer in 12 is able to report any gains, and that three-quarters of such gains are

enjoyed by the wealthiest 9 per cent of America's taxpayers. Thus, all but the super-rich have a right to be envious, if not startled, by the Brookings figures on the "tax welfare" payments—the average per family tax savings—granted capital-gains recipients:

Yearly Income	Yearly "Tax Welfare" From Capital Gains
Over $1,000,000	$641,000
$500–1,000,000	165,000
$100–500,000	23,000
$20–25,000	120
$5–10,000	8
$3–5,000	1

These Federal handouts to the wealthy reach the astounding total of nearly $14-billion a year. But even that sum is dwarfed by the tax benefactions that Uncle Sam bestows on all but our poorest citizens the instant they are pronounced man and wife, a happy moment that carries with it the privilege of filing a joint return. The Brookings study reveals, startlingly, that the annual total of this giveaway to married couples comes to $21.5-billion.

Some, noting that the Environmental Protection Agency will only be permitted to spend one-fourteenth that amount next year, have difficulty discerning how this $21.5-billion matrimonial "tax dole" benefits the national welfare. If it is supposed to be an incentive to marriage, it is a strange one indeed, since it shows a total indifference to the marital status of the poor, who derive no financial benefit from this tax giveaway whatever. Instead, it offers increasingly generous benefits the higher a couple's income goes, in brackets where it matters little whether two can indeed live as cheaply as one. Two-thirds of this marital "tax welfare" goes to taxpayers making more than $20,000 a year, and less than 3 per cent goes to the hardest-pressed married couples—those making less than $10,000 a year. These are the average per-family matrimonial tax savings.

Yearly Income	Yearly "Tax Welfare" to Married Couples
Under $3,000	$0
$3–5,000	72 cents
$5–10,000	$24
$25–50,000	$1,479
$100–500,000	$8,212
Over $1,000,000	$11,062

Dramatically top-heavy tax largess flows to the super-rich via the fiction, in the tax law, that the $5-billion of interest on state and local bonds is totally nonexistent. Not only is such interest income untaxed; it doesn't even have to be reported on tax returns. Ownership of such bonds is, understandably, reserved to financial institutions and wealthy individuals, in part because only they have the spare cash to buy such bonds, and in part because these bonds bear comparatively low interest rates that are attractive only to persons in high tax brackets.

As a result, the per-family tax benefactions from this loophole are almost insultingly low for the un-moneyed: an average of only 80 cents a year for families earning $5,000 to $10,000, and just $24 a year even for those in the $25,000-50,000 bracket. But the financial blessing is handsome indeed for the wealthy—$36,000 a year for families with incomes of over $1-million—and it is even more spectacular for the big banks. In 1970 this tax feature saved the Bank of America an estimated $58-million.

All these profligate handouts to the un-needy would be far more publicly apparent if the billions lost to the Treasury through the loopholes came to be regarded in the same jealous, penny-pinching way as the direct outlays that the President requests and Congress votes every year. If that had been

the case this past January, newspapers might well have carried a news story such as the following:

WASHINGTON, April 16—President Nixon today sent Congress the most startling budget in history, calling for a Federal deficit of no less than $103-billion, more than twice as high as any previous deficit in American history.

This colossal deficit resulted from Mr. Nixon's inclusion in his annual budget, for the first time, of not only direct outlays from the Treasury but also what the President calls "tax expenditures." These are sums the Treasury does not collect because of various exceptions and preferences embedded in the nation's tax laws. For the current year, such sums amounted to more than $77-billion, Mr. Nixon said:

"It is time the American people faced up to the truth," Mr. Nixon said in his budget message. "Every dollar in taxes that some individual or industry is excused from paying is just as much of a drain on the Treasury, and contributes just as much to Federal deficits, as a dollar appropriated by the Congress and spent directly from the Treasury.

"For example," Mr. Nixon said, "nearly $10-billion in 'tax expenditures' is granted every year to stimulate home ownership. This ought to be part of the budget of the Department of Housing and Urban Development if we are to get an honest picture of how much we, as a nation, are really spending on America's housing problems."

Of course there was no such fiscal candor in Mr. Nixon's January Budget message; nor had there been in those of his predecessors in both parties. But the housing example is a good one, for almost assuredly, few if any of the housing specialists in HUD—and few of our elected representatives—are aware that a tax-subsidy program Congress has enacted for homeowners operates in the following manner:

Three families—the Lowlies (who make $7,000 a year), the Comfortables (with a $50,000 income) and the Opulents (they make $400,000 a year)—ask HUD for help in paying the 7 per cent mortgage interest on homes that each family wants to buy. HUD's response is different in each case.

• To the Opulents, HUD replies: "HUD will be delighted to pay 5 per cent mortgage interest for you, so that when you buy your mansion, you only need pay 2 per cent mortgage interest."

• To the Comfortables: "HUD will pay half the interest charges, so you can borrow toward your house at 3.5 per cent."

• To the Lowlies: "We're terribly sorry, but the most we can do is pay 1 per cent interest for you, so if you want to borrow to buy that house, you'll have to pay 6 per cent"

That seemingly inhumane result, which flows from the tax deductibility of mortgage interest payments, is inherent in the nature of any tax deduction in a tax system such as ours where tax rates get higher as income rises. It works this way: say Opulent has a taxable income of $400,100. This puts him in the top tax bracket of 70 per cent and it means that he has to pay a tax of $70 on the top $100 of his income. Mr. Lowly, on the other hand, has a taxable income of $7,100, placing him in the 19 per cent tax bracket; this imposes a tax of $19 on the top $100 of his more modest income.

Now suppose that each spends $100 on mortgage interest which, being tax-deductible, reduces the taxable income of each by $100. That step lowers Mr. Opulent's tax by $70; that is, $70 that would have gone to Uncle Sam, where it not for the tax deduction, has been diverted to Mr. Opulent's bank account. Uncle Sam has, in effect, footed the bill for $70 of Mr. Opulent's mortgage interest. But in the case of Mr. Lowly, the $100 deduction only lowers his tax by $19. Only $19 is diverted from Uncle Sam to Mr. Lowly's bank account.

Not only does Mr. Opulent get a bigger bang for each tax-deductible buck than Mr. Lowly does, but also Mr. Opulent far outstrips his counterpart in the *number* of bucks he spends yearly for tax-deductible purposes. Mr. Opulent's average annual de-

ductions for mortgage interest, for example, are about $4\frac{1}{2}$ times as large as Mr. Lowly's. According to the Brookings study, the benefits from the various "tax preferences" enjoyed by homeowners (over home renters) come to just 66 cents a year for the least pecunious taxpayers. But the benefits amount to 10,000 times as much—over $6,000 a year—for the nation's wealthiest and best-housed families.

The price tag attached to this inverted subsidy program is enormous: $9.6-billion a year. This is more than twice HUD's total budget and more than 50 times HUD's direct outlays for housing assistance. Clearly, if the $9.6-billion were part of HUD's budget, HUD officials would be embarrassed if they tried to justify a program that gave 66 cents of aid to the neediest citizen and $6,000 to the wealthiest. But since the inequity is embedded in the tax laws, involving no visible outlays, HUD, the President and the Congress are all spared the embarrassment of annually accounting for this expensive and irrational subsidy. Instead, the $9.6-million drain on the Treasury will continue just as long as Congress fails to change the law, and Congressional *inaction* is demonstrably easier to come by than affirmative Congressional action.

The same is true of the tax favors enjoyed by oil companies and investors, which entail an annual "expenditure" of a billion and a half dollars (supposedly to encourage development of our oil resources). But that sum appears nowhere in the Interior Department's natural resources budget. Perhaps if it did, Secretary of the Interior Rogers C. B. Morton would be spurred to cut back or end this huge "outlay," especially since a recent Government-commissioned study showed that the returns on the $1.5-billion were a meager $150-million in additional oil exploration. Any direct subsidy program with a 90 per cent waste factor would hardly warm Congressional hearts when it came up for annual approval; but oil's multibillion-dollar tax subsidy is spared that discomfiture.

Translating tax loopholes into "tax expenditures" (i.e., treating the revenues that leak out through the loopholes as if they were direct outlays) can make even the most unexceptionable features of the tax laws seem questionable. Tax expert Stanley Surrey has explained the effect of that most worthy of all tax features, the deduction for contributions to charity:

Suppose that one Horace Pauper writes the Government as follows: "I am too poor to pay an income tax, but the Salvation Army helped me in a time of need and I am contributing $5 to it. Will the Government also make a contribution?" The response: "Dear Mr. Pauper: We appreciate your generosity and sacrifice, but in this situation we cannot make the contribution you request."

Suppose that at the same time, Herman Greenbacks, nouveau millionaire, writes to say that of his $500,000 income, he has decided to send $3,000 to the Society for the Preservation of Hog-Calling in Arkansas. He wants to know if the Government will help. Reply: "We will be delighted to be of assistance and are at once sending a Government check for $7,000 to the Hog-Calling Society."

Here again, this strange situation results from the fact that when a taxpayer in the 70 per cent bracket such as Mr. Greenbacks gives $10,000 to charity, it reduces his tax by $7,000—i.e., it diverts $7,000 from the United States Treasury to the charity. But for Horace Pauper, who has no taxable income to be affected by his generous deduction, there is no tax saving and the Government's role is zero.

As if the Greenbacks-Pauper contrast weren't irrational enough, the charitable-deduction feature of the tax law could even give rise to a third situation. Let us say that Roger Croesus, heir to the huge Croesus fortune, writes the Government to say that he is selling $2-million in stocks inherited from his grandfather, since he wants to raise cash to pay his taxes and also to buy a yacht. Croesus adds that he feels the Antique Car Society of America is a worthy institution, and that while he has decided not to con-

tribute to the Society himself, he is writing to inquire if the Government has any interest in doing so. In this case, the Government writes as follows:

"Dear Mr. Croesus: We will be delighted to send a $2-million contribution to the Antique Car Society and we will be glad to say that the contribution is in your name. Moreover, in appreciation of your thoughtfulness in suggesting this fine idea to us—and confident that your new yacht will need outfitting—we are sending you a check for $100,000, tax-free, of course."

That unbelievable feat could be accomplished if Mr. Croesus, a taxpayer in the 70 per cent bracket, were to give to the cause of antique cars $2-million of stock that was virtually valueless when he inherited it. His tax saving (i.e., the Treasury's contribution) includes $1,400,00 of income tax from the deduction, plus the avoidance of $700,000 in capital gains tax, for a total of $2,100,000—or, $100,000 more than his $2-million gift. The result: even after the Treasury has, in effect, paid for his entire contribution, he still enjoys a $100,000 cash profit.

But such quirks in the tax law are overshadowed by the even more gaping tax loopholes we've already discussed, as revealed in the Brookings Institution study. During the coming months, the Brookings findings will take on immense importance if, as expected, the Nixon Administration proposes major revenue-raising through a so-called "value-added tax," or VAT. The VAT is a tax on the "value added" to any product, at each stage of its manufacture or distribution, as that product makes its way to the consumer through various middlemen. Since the VAT is, in essence, a hidden national sales tax, it tends to place a relatively heavy share of the burden on lower- and middle-income taxpayers—a far heavier share than would be the case if the same amount of revenue were raised by closing existing loopholes in the tax law. The Brookings study documents that fact in dramatic fashion.

For example, the $13-to-$16-billion in additional revenue the Administration is reportedly considering raising from a VAT coincides almost exactly with the $13.7-billion the Brookings study estimates would be raised by ending the favored taxation on capital gains. Tax reformers can offer a battery of arguments for ending this tax preference, which wholly bypasses 11 out of 12 taxpayers. First, it violates the Basic American Virtues, not to mention elementary standards of fairness, by rewarding the "work" done by *money* vastly more than the work done by men. Why should an already-wealthy multimillionaire pay less tax on, say, a million-dollar stock-market profit—for which he did not an iota of work—than does an industrious professional person who earns a fraction of that amount by personal ingenuity, talent and plain sweat?

Second, capital gains represent by far the most gaping escape hatch for the very rich, allowing them to pay, on the average, only half what the Federal tax rates indicate they should. Third, ending the capital-gains preference would at one stroke narrow, or close, a variety of tax escape-routes available to only a few selected taxpayers guided by ingenious tax lawyers. Examples of such escape routes are corporate executives' stock options, and tax shelters for high-salaried doctors and other professional men who invest in—but usually never see—cattle farms, or kiwi-nut groves, and the like.

Finally, the dire predictions about the drying up of capital that invariably greet any proposal to alter the taxation of capital gains are, at the least, greatly exaggerated. This is evidenced by the economy's apparently tremorless adjustment to a 10 per cent increase in the capital gains tax enacted in 1969, as well as by the fact that 95 per cent of corporations' capital needs are met through plowed-back profits and borrowings, and only 5 per cent from stock issues.

The search for alternatives to the VAT is also likely to increase pressure to end or modify the tax exemption of state and local bonds (it's part of Edmund Muskie's otherwise-moderate tax-reform program, for example). While zealously cherished by hard-pressed governors and mayors as an inexpensive means of public borrowing (the tax-free status allows these bonds to carry below-average interest rates), the tax exemption is a grossly inefficient means of subsidizing state and local borrowing costs. Students of the subject calculate that about half this annual $1.2 billion "tax expenditure" is, in effect, wasted, and that both tax justice and governmental economy would be served by replacing the tax exemption with a direct-subsidy program.

The inefficiency of the bond-interest exemption is typical of such "tax expenditures," which, ironically, are spared the traditional scrutiny for "efficiency" that pinch-penny Congressmen usually require of direct-spending programs.

In enacting multi-billion-dollars tax "incentives" for corporate exports and plant investment, Congress wastefully granted the incentives to exports and to plant outlays that most corporations would have made anyway—rather than confining the benefits to *increases* in those activities. Thus, those tax incentives are windfalls to corporations that merely export or invest as usual. Similarly, the oil-depletion allowance, supposedly designed to reward risk-taking, not only goes to the venturesome oil driller but also is freely dispensed to the fortunate landowner —who permits a successful well to be drilled on his property, but who risks absolutely nothing in doing so.

Tax favors granted to the lowly as well as to the mighty often produce both inequity and inefficiency. Take, for example, the additional $750 personal exemption that Congress has voted the aged and the blind. For nonagenarian Charles Stewart Mott, who is said to be worth more than $300-million, that exemption allows him a saving of $525 a year. But for a retiree in St. Petersburg who qualifies for the lowest tax bracket, it saves only $105. And the exemption gives no relief whatsoever to, say, an ancient and impoverished sharecropper whose meager income would not be taxable anyway.

That same perversity applies to the regular exemption available to each taxpayer and his dependents. While its supposed purpose is to spare poor families from being taxed on what they need to meet "some minimum essential living costs," the exemption nonetheless confers some $4-billion in tax handouts to families making over $15,000 a year. Some Congressional reformers have proposed replacing the exemption with a flat $150 cut in *taxes* for each dependent. This would be applicable equally to the St. Petersburg bench-sitter and to the nonagenarian multimillionaire. That step alone— which would increase the taxes of those who earn $10,000 or more, while reducing the taxes of those who are less affluent—would increase Federal revenues by nearly $2-billion a year.

Other long-standing "loopholes for the many" are rarely examined with a critical eye, even though they represent immense "tax expenditures" justified by little rhyme or reason. For example, about $10-billion in interest accruing on life-insurance policies is exempt from taxation; this annual "tax expenditure" amounts to $2.7-billion. Nonbusiness personal itemized deductions (for major-medical expenses, charitable contributions, taxes, interest and the like) excuse another $10-billion from taxation, and the price tag for this is over $4-billion annually. Another rarely discussed but major untaxed item is the return on a homeowner's investment in his own house; this takes the form of rent the homeowner is spared paying to a landowner, rent which the homeowner, in effect, pays to himself. The total of this untaxed "income" amounts to an estimated $15.5-billion annually; failure to tax it represents an unconscious decision on the part of Congress to spend more than $4-billion annually on aid to homeowners—with, as usual, far more comfort to mansion-dwellers than to Levittowners.

The basic question raised by the Brookings study is whether the unreviewed annual "tax welfare" of over $77-billion makes sense in a time of budgetary deficits averaging $30-billion a year, and in a time when we are plagued with "social deficits" (in housing, health and the like) of vastly greater proportions. The Brookings experts propose

an essentially preference-free, or "no-loophole," tax system. That would open up some choice that the present sieve-like system forbids: it would make it possible to raise added revenues that could be applied to the nation's social needs. Or it could make possible a massive tax-rate reduction; Drs. Pechman and Okner say that in a no-loophole system, the present levels of Federal revenues could be collected with tax rates ranging from 7 to 44 per cent, instead of the present 14 to 70 per cent. Or there could be a combination of both revenue-raising and rate-reduction. But whatever the choice, a preference-free system would put an end to irrational multibillion-dollar "tax expenditures" that continue to be perpetuated as long as Congress fails to act. It would also put an end to a tax system that is highly manipulable by the well-to-do (such as the 112 people with incomes over $200,000 who contrived to pay no tax whatever in 1970, despite the supposed Congressional effort in 1969 to stop such taxlessness) but that leaves largely helpless the vast majority of taxpayers whose taxes are withheld from their paychecks and whisked away before they even see the money.

What are the prospects for significant tax reform? On a strictly nose-count basis, the cause should be a popular one, especially when it comes to ending such preferences as capital gains (from which just one taxpayer in 12 benefits), or the multibillion-dollar tax favors to large corporations. But past loophole-closing efforts have provoked concentrated lobbying pressure on Congress while generating little public enthusiasm. So, as the Brookings study shows, the tax system is clearly not based on a popular nose count.

Some reformers, however, believe that the tactic President Nixon seems ready to pursue in support of his value-added tax—holding out the bait of using the VAT proceeds to relieve hard-pressed property-taxpayers—may at long last create the vocal "constituency" that could prod Congress into genuine reforms. Offering the proceeds of loophole-closing to reduce property taxes could, in effect, steal Mr. Nixon's bait. Indeed, the prospect of the value-added tax has prodded some legislators who were not heretofore enlisted under the reform banner to search for popular alternatives to the VAT.

Reportedly, under pressure from apparent Democratic successes with the tax-reform issue in the early Presidential primaries, Mr. Nixon is considering sweeping reforms instead of the value-added tax. But if he does propose a VAT, it could set off the most basic debate about the tax system in many years and, ironically—despite Treasury Secretary Connally's openly expressed indifference to tax reform ("It leaves me cold") — he and the Nixon Administration might inadvertently give the reform cause the biggest boost it has had in many years.

Analysis of Values
and
Conflicts of Interest

Tullock suggests that large welfare doles to the poor might contribute to the forces producing high levels of unemployment. He implies that reduced welfare payments should motivate people to seek work and therefore reduce unemployment. Tullock, like many opponents of the welfare system, believes that people work because they are compelled by necessity. If people can achieve their material needs by obtaining welfare, they will have little incentive to work.

Many working-class and middle-class people support Tullock's position because they resent having to contribute to the support of those who do not work. However, despite such attitudes, persons in these groups are always vulnerable to becoming welfare recipients themselves. An illness, disability, death, or long layoff from work can suddenly sensitize these people to the importance of welfare. In these cases and in periods of prolonged economic crisis many people who normally oppose welfare realize that the welfare system also supports their interests.

On the contrary, the wealthy and the powerful are rarely forced to suffer the indignity of receiving welfare and therefore find it in their interests to oppose it. Wealthy conservative spokesmen often express vehement arguments against welfare. This deflects public attention from the financial practices of the rich and toward the high costs of welfare and alleged abuses of its recipients. Conservatives describe their opposition to welfare in different terms, arguing that it destroys the will to work and the competitive ethos. They assert that if these motivations are lost, the American economy will crumble and everyone will suffer.

Gans assumes that the vast majority of people want to work rather than receive welfare. This is to be expected in a society that places such a high social importance and moral value upon work. Gans suggests that the welfare problem could be solved if jobs are provided for everyone. Furthermore, he believes that those who remain needy should be given adequate welfare without unnecessary red tape or punitive requirements. Gans represents the interests of welfare recipients and lower-income people who are likely to become welfare recipients. His position also supports the values of many change-oriented persons, social scientists, welfare workers, and minority people. Their ideal society is one which attempts to eliminate poverty or at least takes measures to ease the degradation of the poor.

Lucrative welfare programs also serve more selfish interests. They provide increased support for persons employed in the administration of welfare. Moreover, when there is strong public support for welfare, there are usually lucrative resources available for social researchers who study the poor and evaluate welfare programs. Conservatives feel that little money should be used for these purposes. They often assert that much of the money appropriated for welfare never reaches the poor, but is wasted in administrative and bureaucratic organization of welfare programs.

The articles by Tussing and Stern emphasize a different and more costly form of welfare—welfare for the rich. They describe the massive tax loopholes and advantages that are available to the rich. These permit a small percentage of the population to control most of the nation's wealth. These articles define concentrated wealth and the forces that maintain it, rather than poor peoples' welfare as a social problem. Radicals taking this position often argue that the normal functioning of capitalist economic institutions produce both poverty and high tax burdens for workers. To correct these inequities they propose redistribution of wealth in the context of broad institutional change. There are also liberal groups who call for large scale tax reform and redistribution of wealth. According to liberals such proposals will benefit almost everyone because they would reduce poverty, taxes, and conflict between the classes, without causing the painful readjustments of revolutionary change. The articles by Tussing and Stern provide support for individuals and groups who profess egalitarian values and believe that economic equality is a crucial element of a good society. They also serve the interests of a larger group of poor and middle-income people who would desire to have their tax burden and material deprivation reduced.

4

EDUCATION:
Should We Deschool Society?

One of the most important controversies in the area of education is the debate between the supporters of the current system of schooling and those, such as A. S. Neill and Paul Goodman, who seek to establish radical alternatives to that school system. Lately, a new voice has been raised in the debate over education, articulating a new position in the controversy. The new voice belongs to Ivan Illich and his position is a simple one—disestablish school. Illich argues, in the first article in this section, that we are witnessing the end of the age of schooling. He feels that reformers who are trying to patch up the current system are on the wrong track. He argues that such palliatives as courses in Women's Liberation, increased student participation, and group therapy methods only postpone the confronting of the really grave issues. The reason for Illich's opposition to reformism lies in his feeling that these reforms do not affect what he calls the school's "hidden curriculum." Among the aspects of this hidden curriculum are the ideas that one must spend a number of years in school to acquire his civil rights, a society's development depends on improved schooling, one must learn from professionals, and what one learns is economically valuable. This hidden curriculum serves to alienate the student from the learning process by changing the meaning of "knowledge" from a term that designates intimacy, intercourse, and life experience into one that designates a commodity served in professionally packaged products, marketable entitlements, and abstract values.

In the article included here Illich is more concerned with the shape of society after it is deschooled than he is with arguing that schools should be eliminated. He recognizes that school as an institution cannot be eliminated without adverse consequences for society. He seems even more wary of a future society without schools, but which educates using more subtle, programmed devices. Thus Illich is not content with doing away with schools; he wants to go further and deschool culture. Deschooling culture involves a wide variety of activities including integration of education and living, individual freedom to learn (and not to learn), and the measuring of educational success by performance on a specific job rather than in abstraction. In a sense, then, Illich's proposal is even more radical than abolishing schools, he wants to radically change our cultural attitudes toward learning and knowledge. To do this he suggests the creation of an educational free market. Everyone regardless of class, race, or sex must be given access to the "things, places, processes and records" necessary for learning. Furthermore, knowledge must be freed from special languages and specialized teachers. Incentives must be given to skilled individuals to encourage them to share their knowledge with students. Illich is suggesting that the traditional barriers between the intellectual and those not guided by the intellect be destroyed. Finally, each man should bear the responsibility for the limits within which this knowledge and these tools can be used.

Gintis suggests that Illich's approach is overly simplistic and distorts the true role education plays in American society. He suggests that Illich treats the educational institution in abstraction from the rest of the social system. He argues that one can neither understand nor transform the process of learning and education without considering the nature of the broader social structure in which it is embedded.

Gintis congratulates Illich for recognizing that our present educational system treats knowledge as a commodity, that the knowledge delivery system (school) treats individuals as mere recipients of products, and finally that these delivery systems induce and reinforce a passive consumerism. However, Gintis criticizes Illich for suggesting that this system can be changed by eliminating the school rather than through transformation of the social and economic relations that produce the school.

Gintis argues that the social system in American society is perpetuated because its people are motivated by a desire to accumulate commodities. He argues that this is necessary in any capitalist society. According to Gintis the school performs an important function by socializing the child into this kind of motivational structure. The school has a crucial role in helping with the production of willing consumers who fit into the system. Gintis argues that the present/social system could never be deschooled because the school is too important to the maintenance of the system. Deschooling would cause such great chaos that the powerful groups in society would soon reinstitute schools.

Sidney Hook considers Illich's deschooling position as extremist and irresponsible. Hook suggests that this position is characteristic of the new left since it calls glibly for radical change rather than intelligent reform. He does not believe that the casual, chance educational encounters of a deschooled society would provide a reasonable alternative to the present method of education. Hook does not accept the idea that the young always learn something useful from their experience. In fact, some degree of training is necessary for one to be able to organize his experience so that valuable new learning can take place. Hook asserts that it is absurd to contend that a child could become aware of his needs, especially those that involve long-term considerations, by exposure to raw, unstructured sense data. He insists that the young do not know what they need to learn. In order to learn they need supervision and direction from those who are wiser. Hook also believes that a sequential organization of subject matter and a structured acquisition of skills has more benefits than disadvantages.

Hook argues that Illich's conception of learning is based completely on chance, since the child is left to his own initiative. He suggests that we have no reason to believe that the child will be drawn to the things that are educationally beneficial rather than those things which could do him harm. Thus the unguided child may want to come in contact with live wires and drugs as well as great books and important ideas. Furthermore, children may, because of their background, avoid the educationally beneficial. For example, in this society many children might consciously avoid children of other racial, ethnic, or religious backgrounds. Hook concludes that the remedy for poor schooling is better schools, not the abolition of schools.

The Alternative to Schooling

IVAN ILLICH

For generations we have tried to make the world a better place by providing more and more schooling, but so far the endeavor has failed. What we have learned instead is that forcing all children to climb an open-ended education ladder cannot enhance equality but must favor the individual who starts out earlier, healthier, or better prepared; that enforced instruction deadens for most people the will for independent learning; and that knowledge treated as a commodity, delivered in packages, and accepted as private property once it is acquired, must always be scarce.

In response, critics of the educational system are now proposing strong and unorthodox remedies that range from the voucher plan, which would enable each person to buy the education of his choice on an open market, to shifting the responsibility for education from the school to the media and to apprenticeship on the job. Some individuals forsee that the school will have to be disestablished just as the church was disestablished all over the world during the last two centuries. Other reformers propose to replace the universal school with various new systems that would, they claim, better

Note: Ivan Illich, "The Alternative to Schooling," *Saturday Review,* June 1971, pp. 44–48, 59, 60. Copyright 1971 by Saturday Review Co. First appeared in Saturday Review 1971. Used with permission.

prepare everybody for life in modern society. These proposals for new educational institutions fall into three broad categories: the reformation of the classroom within the school system; the dispersal of free schools throughout society; and the transformation of all society into one huge classroom. But these three approaches—the reformed classroom, the free school, and the worldwide classroom—represent three stages in a proposed escalation of education in which each step threatens more subtle and more pervasive social control than the one it replaces.

I believe that the disestablishment of the school has become inevitable and that this end of an illusion should fill us with hope. But I also believe that the end of the "age of schooling" could usher in the epoch of the global schoolhouse that would be distinguishable only in name from a global madhouse or global prison in which education, correction, and adjustment become synonymous. I therefore believe that the breakdown of the school forces us to look beyond its imminent demise and to face fundamental alternatives in education. Either we can work for fearsome and potent new educational devices that teach about a world which progressively becomes more opaque and forbidding for man, or we can set the conditions for a new era in which technology would be used to make society more simple and transparent, so that all men can once again know the facts and use the tools that shape their lives. In short, we can disestablish schools or we can deschool culture.

In order to see clearly the alternatives we face, we must first distinguish education from schooling, which means separating the humanistic intent of the teacher from the impact of the invariant structure of the school. This hidden structure constitutes a course of instruction that stays forever beyond the control of the teacher or of his school board. It conveys indelibly the message that only through schooling can an individual prepare himself for adulthood in society, that what is not taught in school is of little value, and that what is learned outside of school is not knowing. I call it the hidden curriculum of schooling, because it constitutes the unalterable framework of the system, within which all changes in the curriculum are made.

The hidden curriculum is always the same regardless of school or place. It requires all children of a certain age to assemble in groups of about thirty, under the authority of a certified teacher, for some 500 to 1,000 or more hours each year. It doesn't matter whether the curriculum is designed to teach the principles of fascism, liberalism, Catholicism, or socialism; or whether the purpose of the school is to produce Soviet or United States citizens, mechanics, or doctors. It makes no difference whether the teacher is authoritarian or permissive, whether he imposes his own creed or teaches students to think for themselves. What is important is that students learn that education is valuable when it is acquired in the school through a graded process of consumption; that the degree of success the individual will enjoy in society depends on the amount of learning he consumes; and that learning *about* the world is more valuable than learning *from* the world.

It must be clearly understood that the hidden curriculum translates learning from an activity into a commodity—for which the school monopolizes the market. In all countries knowledge is regarded as the first necessity for survival, but also as a form of currency more liquid than rubles or dollars. We have become accustomed, through Karl Marx's writings, to speak about the alienation of the worker from his work in a class society. We must now recognize the estrangement of man from his learning when it becomes the product of a service profession and he becomes the consumer.

The more learning an individual consumes, the more "knowledge stock" he acquires. The hidden curriculum therefore defines a new class structure for society within which the large consumers of knowledge—those who have acquired large quantities of knowledge stock—enjoy special privileges, high income, and access to the more powerful tools of production. This kind of knowledge-capitalism has been accepted in all industrialized societies and establishes a rationale for the distribution of jobs and income. (This point is especially important in the light of the lack of correspondence between schooling and occupational competence established in studies such as Ivar Berg's *Education and Jobs: The Great Training Robbery*.)

The endeavor to put all men through successive stages of enlightenment is rooted deeply in alchemy, the Great Art of the waning Middle Ages. John Amos Comenius, a Moravian bishop, self-styled Pansophist, and pedagogue, is rightly considered one of the founders of the modern schools. He was among the first to propose seven or twelve grades of compulsory learning. In his *Magna Didactica,* he described schools as devices to "teach everybody everything" and outlined a blueprint for the assembly-line production of knowledge, which according to his method would make education cheaper and better and make growth into full humanity possible for all. But Comenius was not only an early efficiency expert, he was an alchemist who adopted the technical language of his craft to describe the art of rearing children. The alchemist sought to refine base elements by leading their distilled spirits through twelve stages of successive enlightenment, so that for their own and all the world's benefit they might be transmuted into gold. Of course, alchemists failed no matter how often they tried, but each time their "science" yielded new reasons for their failure, and they tried again.

Pedagogy opened a new chapter in the history of Ars Magna. Education became the search for an alchemic process that would bring forth a new type of man, who would fit into an environment created by scientific magic. But, no matter how much each generation spent on its schools, it always turned out that the majority of people were unfit for enlightenment by this process and had to be discarded as unprepared for life in a man-made world.

Educational reformers who accept the idea that schools have failed fall into three groups. The most respectable are certainly the great masters of alchemy who promise better schools. The most seductive are popular magicians, who promise to make every kitchen into an alchemic lab. The most sinister are the new Masons of the Universe, who want to transform the entire world into one huge temple of learning. Notable among today's masters of alchemy are certain research directors employed or sponsored by the large foundations who believe that schools, if they could somehow be improved, could also become economically more feasible than those that are now in trouble; and simultaneously could sell a larger package of services. Those who are concerned primarily with the curriculum claim that it is outdated or irrelevant. So the curriculum is filled with new packaged courses on African Culture, North American Imperialism, Women's Lib, Pollution, or the Consumer Society. Passive learning is wrong—it is indeed—so we graciously allow students to decide what and how they want to be taught. Schools are prison houses. Therefore, principals are authorized to approve teach-outs, moving the school desks to a roped-off Harlem street. Sensitivity training becomes fashionable. So we import group therapy into the classroom. School, which was supposed to teach everybody everything, now becomes all things to all children.

Other critics emphasize that schools make

inefficient use of modern science. Some would administer drugs to make it easier for the instructor to change the child's behavior. Others would transform school into a stadium for the educational gaming. Still others would electrify the classroom. If they are simplistic disciples of McLuhan, they replace blackboards and textbooks with multimedia happenings; if they follow Skinner, they claim to be able to modify behavior more efficiently than old-fashioned classroom practitioners can.

Most of these changes have, of course, some good effects. The experimental schools have fewer truants. Parents do have a greater feeling of participation in a decentralized district. Pupils, assigned by their teacher to an apprenticeship, do often turn out more competent than those who stay in the classroom. Some children do improve their knowledge of Spanish in the language lab because they prefer playing with the knobs of a tape recorder to conversations with their Puerto Rican peers. Yet all these improvements operate within predictably narrow limits, since they leave the hidden curriculum of school intact.

Some reformers would like to shake loose from the hidden curriculum, but they rarely succeed. Free schools that lead to further free schools produce a mirage of freedom, even though the chain of attendance is frequently interrupted by long stretches of loafing. Attendance through seduction inculcates the need for educational treatment more persuasively than the reluctant attendance enforced by a truant officer. Permissive teachers in a padded classroom can easily render their pupils impotent to survive once they leave.

Learning in these schools often remains nothing more than the acquisition of socially valued skills defined, in this instance, by the consensus of a commune rather than by the decree of a school board. New presbyter is but old priest writ large.

Free schools, to be truly free, must meet two conditions: First, they must be run in a way to prevent the reintroduction of the hidden curriculum of graded attendance and certified students studying at the feet of certified teachers And, more importantly, they must provide a framework in which all participants—staff and pupils—can free themselves from the hidden foundations of a schooled society. The first condition is frequently incorporated in the stated aims of a free school. The second condition is only rarely recognized, and is difficult to state as the goal of a free school

It is useful to distinguish between the hidden curriculum, which I have described, and the occult foundations of schooling. The hidden curriculum is a ritual that can be considered the official initiation into modern society, institutionally established through the school. It is the purpose of this ritual to hide from its participants the contradictions between the myth of an egalitarian society and the class-conscious reality it certifies. Once they are recognized as such, rituals lose their power, and this is what is now beginning to happen to schooling. But there are certain fundamental assumptions about growing up—the occult foundations—which now find their expression in the ceremonial of schooling, and which could easily be reinforced by what free schools do.

Among these assumptions is what Peter Schrag calls the "immigration syndrome," which impels us to treat all people as if they were newcomers who must go through a naturalization process. Only certified consumers of knowledge are admitted to citizenship. Men are not born equal, but are made equal through gestation by Alma Mater.

The rhetoric of all schools states that they form a man for the future, but they do not release him from his task before he has developed a high level of tolerance to the ways of elders: education *for* life rather than *in* everyday life. Few free schools can avoid doing precisely this. Nevertheless they are among the most important centers from which a new life-style radiates, not because of the effect their graduates will have but, rather, because elders who choose to bring up their children without the benefit of properly ordained teachers frequently belong to a radical minority and because their preoccupation with the rearing of their children sustains them in their new style.

The most dangerous category of educational reformer is one who argues that knowledge can be produced and sold much more effectively on an open market than on one controlled by school. These people argue that most skills can be easily acquired from skill-models if the learner is truly interested in their acquisition; that individual entitlements can provide a more equal purchasing power for education. They demand a careful separation of the process by which knowledge is acquired from the process by which it is measured and certified. These seem to me obvious statements. But it would be a fallacy to believe that the establishment of a free market for knowledge would constitute a radical alternative in education.

The establishment of a free market would indeed abolish what I have previously called the hidden curriculum of present schooling —its age-specific attendance at a graded curriculum. Equally, a free market would at first give the appearance of counteracting what I have called the occult foundations of a schooled society: the "immigration syndrome," the institutional monopoly of teaching, and the ritual of linear initiation. But at the same time a free market in education would provide the alchemist with innumerable hidden hands to fit each man into the multiple, tight little niches a more complex technocracy can provide.

Many decades of reliance on schooling has turned knowledge into a commodity, a marketable staple of a special kind. Knowledge is now regarded simultaneously as a first necessity and also as society's most precious currency. (The transformation of knowledge into a commodity is reflected in a correspondence transformation of language. Words that formerly functioned as verbs are becoming nouns that designate possessions. Until recently dwelling and learning and even healing designated activities. They are now usually conceived as commodities or services to be delivered. We talk about the manufacture of housing or the delivery of medical care. Men are no longer regarded fit to house or heal themselves. In such a society people come to believe that professional services are more valuable than personal care. Instead of learning how to nurse grandmother, the teen-ager learns to picket the hospital that does not admit her.) This attitude could easily survive the disestablishment of school, just as affiliation with a church remained a condition for office long after the adoption of the First Amendment. It is even more evident that test batteries measuring complex knowledge-packages could easily survive the disestablishment of school—and with this would go the compulsion to obligate everybody to acquire a minimum package in the knowledge stock. The scientific measurement of each man's worth and the alchemic dream of each man's "educability to his full humanity" would finally coincide. Under the appearance of a "free" market, the global village would turn into an environmental womb where pedagogic therapists control the complex navel by which each man is nourished.

At present schools limit the teacher's competence to the classroom. They prevent him from claiming man's whole life as his domain. The demise of school will remove this restriction and give a semblance of legitimacy to the life-long pedagogical invasion of everybody's privacy. It will open the way for a scramble for "knowledge" on a free market, which would lead us toward the paradox of a vulgar, albeit seemingly egalitarian, meritocracy. Unless the concept of knowledge is transformed, the disestablishment of school will lead to a wedding between a growing meritocratic system that separates learning from certification and a society committed to provide therapy for each man until he is ripe for the gilded age.

For those who subscribe to the technocratic ethos, whatever is technically possible must be made available at least to a few whether they want it or not. Neither the privation nor the frustration of the majority counts. If cobalt treatment is possible, then the city of Tegucigalpa needs one apparatus in each of its two major hospitals, at a cost that would free an important part of the population of Honduras from parasites. If supersonic speeds are possible, then it must speed the travel of some. If the flight to Mars can be conceived, then a rationale must be found to make it appear a necessity. In the technocratic ethos poverty is modernized: Not only are old alternatives closed off by new monopolies, but the lack of necessities is also compounded by a growing spread between those services that are technologically feasible and those that are in fact available to the majority.

A teacher turns "educator" when he adopts this technocratic ethos. He then acts as if education were a technological enterprise designed to make man fit into whatever environment the "progress" of science creates. He seems blind to the evidence that constant obsolescence of all commodities comes at a high price: the mounting cost of training people to know about them. He seems to forget that the rising cost of tools is purchased at a high price in education: They decrease the labor intensity of the economy, make learning on the job impossible or, at best, a privilege for a few. All over the world the cost of educating men for society rises faster than the productivity of the entire economy, and fewer people have a sense of intelligent participation in the commonweal.

A revolution against those forms of privilege and power, which are based on claims to professional knowledge, must start with a transformation of consciousness about the nature of learning. This means, above all, a shift of responsibility for teaching and learning. Knowledge can be defined as a commodity only as long as it is viewed as the result of institutional enterprise or as the fulfillment of institutional objectives. Only when a man recovers the sense of personal responsibility for what he learns and teaches can this spell be broken and the alienation of learning from living be overcome.

The recovery of the power to learn or to

teach means that the teacher who takes the risk of interfering in somebody else's private affairs also assumes responsibility for the results. Similarly, the student who exposes himself to the influence of a teacher must take responsibility for his own education. For such purposes educational institutions—if they are at all needed—ideally take the form of facility centers where one can get a roof of the right size over his head, access to a piano or a kiln, and to records, books, or slides. Schools, TV stations, theaters, and the like are designed primarily for use by professionals. Deschooling society means above all the denial of professional status for the second-oldest profession, namely teaching. The certification of teachers now constitutes an undue restriction of the right to free speech: the corporate structure and professional pretensions of journalism an undue restriction on the right to free press. Compulsory attendance rules interfere with free assembly. The deschooling of society is nothing less than a cultural mutation by which a people recovers the effective use of its Constitutional freedoms: learning and teaching by men who know that they are born free rather than treated to freedom. Most people learn most of the time when they do whatever they enjoy; most people are curious and want to give meaning to whatever they come in contact with; and most people are capable of personal intimate intercourse with others unless they are stupefied by inhuman work or turned off by schooling.

The fact that people in rich countries do not learn much on their own constitutes no proof to the contrary. Rather it is a consequence of life in an environment from which, paradoxically, they cannot learn much, precisely because it is so highly programmed. They are constantly frustrated by the structure of contemporary society in which the facts on which decisions can be made have become elusive. They live in an environment in which tools that can be used for creative purposes have become luxuries, an environment in which channels of communication serve a few to talk to many.

A modern myth would make us believe

that the sense of impotence with which most men live today is a consequence of technology that cannot but create huge systems. But it is not technology that makes systems huge, tools immensely powerful, channels of communication one-directional. Quite the contrary: Properly controlled, technology could provide each man with the ability to understand his environment better, to shape it powerfully with his own hands, and to permit him full intercommunication to a degree never before possible. Such an alternative use of technology constitutes the central alternative in education.

If a person is to grow up he needs, first of all, access to things, to places and to processes, to events and to records. He needs to see, to touch, to tinker with, to grasp whatever there is in a meaningful setting. This access is now largely denied. When knowledge became a commodity, it acquired the protections of private property, and thus a principle designed to guard personal intimacy became a rationale for declaring facts off limits for people without the proper credentials. In schools teachers keep knowledge to themselves unless it fits into the day's program. The media inform, but exclude those things they regard as unfit to print. Information is locked into special languages, and specialized teachers live off its retranslation. Patents are protected by corporations, secrets are guarded by bureaucracies, and the power to keep others out of private preserves—be they cockpits, law offices, junkyards, or clinics—is jealously guarded by professions, institutions, and nations. Neither the political nor the professional structure of our societies, East and West, could withstand the elimination of the power to keep entire classes of people from facts that could serve them. The access to facts I advocate goes far beyond truth in labeling. Access must be built into reality, while all we ask from advertising is a guarantee that it does not mislead. Access to reality constitutes a fundamental alternative in education to a system that only purports to teach *about* it.

Abolishing the right to corporate secrecy —even when professional opinion holds that this secrecy serves the common good—is, as shall presently appear, a much more radical political goal than the traditional demand for public ownership or control of the tools of production. The socialization of tools without the effective socialization of know-how in their use tends to put the knowledge-capitalist into the position formerly held by the financier. The technocrat's only claim to power is the stock he holds in some class of scarce and secret knowledge, and the best means to protect its value is a large and capital-intensive organization that renders access to know-how formidable and forbidding.

It does not take much time for the interested learner to acquire almost any skill that he wants to use. We tend to forget this in a society where professional teachers monopolize entrance into all fields, and thereby stamp teaching by uncertified individuals as quackery. There are few mechanical skills used in industry or research that are as demanding, complex, and dangerous as driving cars, a skill that most people quickly acquire from a peer. Not all people are suited for advanced logic, yet those who are make rapid progress if they are challenged to play mathematical games at an early age. One out of twenty kids in Cuernavaca can beat me at Wiff 'n' Proof after a couple of weeks' training. In four months all but a small percentage of motivated adults at our CIDOC center learn Spanish well enough to conduct academic business in the new language.

A first step toward opening up access to skills would be to provide various incentives for skilled individuals to share their knowledge. Inevitably, this would run counter to the interest of guilds and professions and unions. Yet, multiple apprenticeship is attractive: It provides everybody with an opportunity to learn something about almost anything. There is no reason why a person should not combine the ability to drive a car, repair telephones and toilets, act as a midwife, and function as an architectural draftsman. Special-interest groups and their disciplined consumers would, of course, claim that the public needs the protection of a professional guarantee. But this argument is now steadily being challenged by consumer protection associations. We have to take much more seriously the objection that economists raise to the radical socialization of skills: that "progress" will be impeded if knowledge—patents, skills, and all the rest—is democratized. Their argument can be faced only if we demonstrate to them the growth rate of futile diseconomies generated by any existing educational system.

Access to people willing to share their skills is no guarantee of learning. Such access is restricted not only by the monopoly of educational programs over learning and of unions over licensing but also by a technology of scarcity. The skills that count today are know-how in the use of highly specialized tools that were designed to be scarce. These tools produce goods or render services that everybody wants but only a few can enjoy, and which only a limited number of people know how to use. Only a few privileged individuals out of the total number of people who have a given disease ever benefit from the results of sophisticated medical technology, and even fewer doctors develop the skill to use it.

The same results of medical research have, however, also been employed to create a basic medical tool kit that permits Army and Navy medics, with only a few months of training, to obtain results, under battlefield conditions, that would have been beyond the expectations of full-fledged doctors during World War II. On an even simpler level any peasant girl could learn how to diagnose and treat most infections if medical scientists prepared dosages and instructions specifically for a given geographic area.

All these examples illustrate the fact that educational considerations alone suffice to demand a radical reduction of the professional structure that now impedes the mutual relationship between the scientist and the majority of people who want access to science. If this demand were heeded, all men could learn to use yesterday's tools, rendered more effective and durable by modern science, to create tomorrow's world.

Unfortunately, precisely the contrary trend

prevails at present. I know a coastal area in South America where most people support themselves by fishing from small boats. The outboard motor is certainly the tool that has changed most dramatically the lives of these coastal fishermen. But in the area I have surveyed, half of all outboard motors that were purchased between 1945 and 1950 are still kept running by constant tinkering, while half the motors purchased in 1965 no longer run because they were not built to be repaired. Technological progress provides the majority of people with gadgets they cannot afford and deprives them of the simpler tools they need.

Metals, plastics, and ferro cement used in building have greatly improved since the 1940s and ought to provide more people the opportunity to create their own homes. But while in the United States, in 1948, more than 30 per cent of all one-family homes were owner-built, by the end of the 1960s the percentage of those who acted as their own contractors had dropped to less than 20 per cent.

The lowering of the skill level through so-called economic development becomes even more visible in Latin America. Here most people still build their own homes from floor to roof. Often they use mud, in the form of adobe, and the thatchwork of unsurpassed utility in the moist, hot, and windy climate. In other places they make their dwellings out of cardboard, oildrums, and other industrial refuse. Instead of providing people with simple tools and highly standardized, durable, and easily repaired components, all governments have gone in for the mass production of low-cost buildings. It is clear that not one single country can afford to provide satisfactory modern dwelling units for the majority of its people. Yet, everywhere this policy makes it progressively more difficult for the majority to acquire the knowledge and skills they need to build better houses for themselves.

Educational considerations permit us to formulate a second fundamental characteristic that any post-industrial society must pos-

sess: a basic tool kit that by its very nature counteracts technocratic control. For educational reasons we must work toward a society in which scientific knowledge is incorporated in tools and components that can be used meaningfully in units small enough to be within the reach of all. Only such tools can socialize access to skills. Only such tools favor temporary associations among those who want to use them for a specific occasion. Only such tools allow specific goals to emerge in the process of their use, as any tinkerer knows. Only the combination of guaranteed access to facts and of limited power in most tools renders it possible to envisage a subsistence economy capable of incorporating the fruits of modern science.

The development of such a scientific subsistence economy is unquestionably to the advantage of the overwhelming majority of all people in poor countries. It is also the only alternative to progressive pollution, exploitation, and opaqueness in rich countries. But, as we have seen, the dethroning of the GNP cannot be achieved without simultaneously subverting GNE (Gross National Education—usually conceived as manpower capitalization.) An egalitarian economy cannot exist in a society in which the right to produce is conferred by schools.

The feasibility of a modern subsistence economy does not depend on new scientific inventions. It depends primarily on the ability of a society to agree on fundamental, self-chosen anti-bureaucratic and anti-technocratic restraints.

These restraints can take many forms, but they will not work unless they touch the basic dimensions of life. (The decision of Congress against development of the supersonic transport plane is one of the most encouraging steps in the right direction.) The substance of these voluntary social restraints would be very simple matters that can be fully understood and judged by any prudent man. The issues at stake in the SST controversy provide a good example. All such restraints would be chosen to promote stable and equal enjoyment of scientific know-how.

The French say that it takes a thousand years to educate a peasant to deal with a cow. It would not take two generations to help all people in Latin America or Africa to use and repair outboard motors, simple cars, pumps, medicine kits, and ferro cement machines if their design does not change every few years. And since a joyful life is one of constant meaningful intercourse with others in a meaningful environment, equal enjoyment does translate into equal education.

At present a consensus on austerity is difficult to imagine. The reason usually given for the impotence of the majority is stated in terms of political or economic class. What is not usually understood is that the new class structure of a schooled society is even more powerfully controlled by vested interests. No doubt an imperialist and capitalist organization of society provides the social structure within which a minority can have disproportionate influence over the effective opinion of the majority. But in a technocratic society the power of a minority of knowledge capitalists can prevent the formation of true public opinion through control of scientific know-how and the media of communication. Constitutional guarantees of free speech, free press, and free assembly were meant to ensure government by the people. Modern electronics, photo-offset presses, time-sharing computers, and telephones have in principle provided the hardware that could give an entirely new meaning to these freedoms. Unfortunately, these things are used in modern media to increase the power of knowledge-bankers to funnel their program-packages through international chains to more people, instead of being used to increase true networks that provide equal opportunity for encounter among the members of the majority.

Deschooling the culture and social structure requires the use of technology to make participatory politics possible. Only on the basis of a majority coalition can limits to secrecy and growing power be determined without dictatorship. We need a new environment in which growing up can be classless, or we will get a brave new world in which Big Brother educates us all.

Toward a Political Economy of Education: A Radical Critique of Ivan Illich's Deschooling Society

HERBERT GINTIS

The author critiques Ivan Illich's Deschooling Society, *arguing that, despite his forthright vision of the liberating potential of educational technology, Illich fails to understand fully how the existing educational system serves the capitalist economy. Gintis evaluates and rejects the book's major thesis that the present character of schooling stems from the economy's need to shape consumer demands and expectations. Instead, he offers a production orientation which maintains that the repressive and unequal aspects of schooling derive from the need to supply a labor force compatible with the social relations of capitalist production. Gintis concludes that meaningful strategies for educational change must explicitly embrace a concomitant transformation of the mechanisms of power and privilege in the economic sphere.*

Ivan Illich's *De-Schooling Society*,[1] despite

Note: Herbert Gintis, "Towards a Political Economy of Education," *Harvard Educational Review,* Vol. 42, Feb. 1972, pp. 70–96. Copyright © 1972 by President and Fellows of Harvard College, and reproduced by permission.
[1] Ivan Illich, *Deschooling Society* (New York: Harper & Row, 1971).

its bare 115 pages, embraces the world. Its ostensible focus on education moves him inexorably and logically through the panoply of human concerns in advanced industrial society—a society plainly in progressive disintegration and decay. With Yeats we may feel that "things fall apart/The center cannot hold," but Illich's task is no less than to discover and analyze that "center." His endeavor affords the social scientist the unique and rare privilege to put in order the historical movements which characterize our age and define the prospects for a revolutionary future. Such is the subject of this essay.

This little book would have been unthinkable ten years ago. In it, Ivan Illich confronts the full spectrum of the modern crisis in values by rejecting the basic tenets of progressive liberalism. He dismisses what he calls the Myth of Consumption as a cruel and illusory ideology foisted upon the populace by a manipulative bureaucratic system. He treats welfare and service institutions as part of the problem, not as part of the solution. He rejects the belief that education constitutes the "great equalizer" and the path to personal liberation. Schools, say Illich, simply must be eliminated.

Illich does more than merely criticize; he conceptualizes constructive technological alternatives to repressive education. Moreover, he sees the present age as "revolutionary" because the existing social relations of economic and political life, including the dominant institutional structure of schooling, have become impediments to the development of liberating, socially productive technologies. Here Illich is relevant indeed, for the tension between technological possibility and social reality pervades all advanced industrial societies today. Despite our technological power, communities and environment continue to deteriorate, poverty and inequality persist, work remains alienating, and men and women are not liberated for self-fulfilling activity.

Illich's response is a forthright vision of participatory, decentralized, and liberating learning technologies, and a radically altered vision of social relations in education.

Yet, while his *description* of modern society is sufficiently critical, his *analysis* is simplistic and his program, consequently, is a diversion from the immensely complex and demanding political, organizational, intellectual, and personal demands of revolutionary reconstruction in the coming decades. It is crucial that educators and students who have been attracted to him—for his message does correspond to their personal frustration and disillusionment—move beyond him.

The first part of this essay presents Illich's analysis of the economically advanced society —the basis for his analysis of schools. Whereas Illich locates the source of the social problems and value crises of modern societies in their need to reproduce alienated patterns of *consumption,* I argue that these patterns are merely manifestations of the deepest workings of the economic system. The second part of the essay attempts to show that Illich's over-emphasis on consumption leads him to a very partial understanding of the functions of the educational system and the contra-dictions presently besetting it, and hence to ineffective educational alternatives and untenable political strategies for the implementation of desirable educational technologies.

Finally, I argue that a radical theory of educational reform becomes viable only by envisioning liberating and equal education as serving and being served by a radically altered nexus of social relations in *production.* Schools may lead or lag in this process of social transformation, but structural changes in the educational process can be socially relevant only when they speak to potentials for liberation and equality in our day-to-day labors. In the final analysis "de-schooling" is irrelevant because we cannot "de-factory," "de-office," or "de-family," save perhaps at the still unenvisioned end of a long process of social reconstruction.

THE SOCIAL CONTEXT OF MODERN SCHOOLING: INSTITUTIONALIZED VALUES AND COMMODITY FETISHISM

Educational reformers commonly err by treating the system of schools as if it existed in a social vacuum. Illich does not make this mistake. Rather, he views the internal irrationalities of modern education as reflections of the larger society. The key to understanding the problems of advanced industrial economies, he argues, lies in the character of its consumption activities and the ideology which supports them. The schools in turn are exemplary models of bureaucracies geared toward the indoctrination of docile and manipulable consumers.

Guiding modern social life and interpersonal behavior, says Illich, is a destructive system of "institutionalized values" which determine how one perceives one's needs and defines instruments for their satisfaction. The process which creates institutional values insures that all individual needs—physical, psychological, social, intellectual, emotional, and spiritual—are transformed into demands for goods and services. In contrast to the "psychological impotence" which results from institutionalized values, Illich envisages the "psychic health" which emerges from self-realization—both personal and social. Guided by institutionalized values, one's well-being lies not in what one *does* but in what one *has* —the status of one's job and the level of material consumption. For the active person, goods are merely means to or instruments in the performance of activities; for the passive consumer, however, goods are ends in themselves, and activity is merely the means toward sustaining or displaying a desired level of consumption. Thus institutionalized values manifest themselves psychologically in a rigorous fetishism—in this case, of commodities and public services. Illich's vision rests in the negation of commodity fetishism[2]:

> I believe that a desirable future depends on our deliberately . . . engendering a life style which will enable us to be spontaneous, independent, yet related to each other, rather than maintaining a life style which only allows us to make and unmake, produce and consume. (*De-Schooling Society*, hereafter *DS*, p. 52)

Commodity fetishism is institutionalized in two senses. First, the "delivery systems" in modern industrial economies (i.e., the suppliers of goods and services) are huge, bureaucratic institutions which treat individuals as mere receptors for their products. Goods are supplied by hierarchical and impersonal corporate enterprises, while services are provided by welfare bureaucracies which enjoy ". . . a professional, political and financial monopoly over the social imagination, setting standards of what is valuable and what is feasible. . . . A whole society is initiated into the Myth of Unending Consumption of services" (*DS*, p. 44) .

Second, commodity fetishism is institutionalized in the sense that the values of passive

consumerism are induced and reinforced by the same "delivery systems" whose ministrations are substitutes for self-initiated activities.

> . . . manipulative institutions . . . are either socially or psychologically "addictive." Social addiction . . . consists in the tendency to prescribe increased treatment if smaller quantities have not yielded the desired results. Psychological addiction . . . results when consumers become hooked on the need for more and more of the process or product. (*DS*, p. 55)

These delivery systems moreover "both invite compulsively repetitive use and frustrate alternative ways of achieving similar results." For example, General Motors and Ford:

> . . . produce means of transportation, but they also, and more importantly, manipulate public taste in such a way that the need for transportation is expressed as a demand for private cars rather than public buses. They sell the desire to control a machine, to race at high speeds in luxurious comfort, while also offering the fantasy at the end of the road. (*DS*, p. 57)

This analysis of addictive manipulation in private production is, of course, well-developed in the literature.[3] Illich's contribution is to extend it to the sphere of service and welfare bureaucracies:

> Finally, teachers, doctors, and social workers realize that their distinct professional ministrations have one aspect—at least—in common. They create further demands for the institutional treatments they provide,

---

[2] Illich himself does not use the term "commodity fetishism." I shall do so, however, as it is more felicitous than "institutional values" in many contexts.

[3] See for instance: Herbert Gintis, "Commodity Fetishism and Irrational Production," (Cambridge, Mass.: Harvard Institute for Economic Research, 1970); "Consumer Behavior and the Concept of Sovereignty," *American Economic Review*, forthcoming; "A Radical Analysis of Welfare Economics and Individual Development," *Quarterly Journal of Economics*, forthcoming; John K. Galbraith, *The New Industrial State* (Boston: Houghton Mifflin, 1963); Herbert Marcuse, *One Dimensional Man* (Boston: Beacon Press, 1964).

faster than they can provide service institutions. (*DS*, p. 112)

The well-socialized naturally react to these failures simply by increasing the power and jurisdiction of welfare institutions. Illich's reaction, of course, is precisely the contrary.

THE POLITICAL RESPONSE TO INSTITUTIONALIZED VALUES

As the basis for his educational proposals, Illich's overall framework bears close attention. Since commodity fetishism is basically a psychological stance, it must first be attacked on an individual rather than political level. For Illich, each individual is responsible for his/her own demystification. The institutionalization of values occurs not through external coercion, but through psychic manipulation, so its rejection is an apolitical act of individual will. The movement for social change thus becomes a cultural one of raising consciousness.

But even on this level, political action in the form of *negating* psychic manipulation is crucial. Goods and services as well as welfare bureaucracies must be *prohibited* from disseminating fetishistic values. Indeed, this is the basis for a political program of deschooling. The educational system, as a coercive source of institutionalized values, must be denied its preferred status. Presumably, this "politics of negation" would extend to advertising and all other types of psychic manipulation.

Since the concrete social manifestation of commodity fetishism is a grossly inflated level of production and consumption, the second step in Illich's political program is the substitution of leisure for work. Work is evil for Illich—unrewarding by its very nature—and not to be granted the status of "activity":

> . . . "making and acting" are different, so different, in fact, that one never includes the other. . . . Modern technology has increased the ability of man to relinquish

the "making" of things to machines, and his potential time for "acting" has increased. . . . Unemployment is the sad idleness of a man who, contrary to Aristotle, believes that making things, or working, is virtuous and that idleness is bad. (*DS*, p. 62)

Again, Illich's shift in the work-leisure choice is basically apolitical and will follow naturally from the abolition of value indoctrination. People work so hard and long because they are taught to believe the fruits of their activities—consumption—are intrinsically worthy. Elimination of the "hard-sell pitch" of bureaucratic institutions will allow individuals to discover *within themselves* the falsity of the doctrine.

The third stage in Illich's political program envisages the necessity of concrete change in social "delivery systems." Manipulative institutions must be *dismantled,* to be replaced by organizational forms which allow for the free development of individuals. Illich calls such institutions "convivial," and associates them with leftist political orientation.

> The regulation of convivial institutions sets limits to their use; as one moves from the convivial to the manipulative end of the spectrum, the rules progressively call for unwilling consumption or participation. . . . Toward, but not at, the left on the institutional spectrum, we can locate enterprises which compete with others in their own field, but have not begun notably to engage in advertising. Here we find hand laundries, small bakeries, hairdressers, and—to speak of professionals—some lawyers and music teachers. . . . They acquire clients through their personal touch and the comparative quality of their services. (*DS*, p. 55–6)

In short, Illich's Good Society is based on small scale entrepreneurial (as opposed to corporate) capitalism, with perfectly competitive markets in goods and services. The role of the state in this society is the prevention of manipulative advertising, the development of left-convivial technologies compatible with self-initiating small-group welfare institutions (education, health and medical services, crime prevention and rehabilitation, community development, etc.) and the provisioning of the social infrastructure (e.g., public transportation). Illich's proposal for "learning webs" in education is only a particular application of this vision of left-convivial technologies.

ASSESSING ILLICH'S POLITICS: AN OVERVIEW

Illich's model of consumption-manipulation is crucial at every stage of his political argument. But it is substantially incorrect. In the following three sections I shall criticize three basic thrusts of his analysis.

First, Illich locates the source of social decay in the autonomous, manipulative behavior of corporate bureaucracies. I shall argue, in contrast, that the source must be sought in the normal operation of the basic *economic* institutions of capitalism (markets in factors of production, private control of resources and technology, etc.),[4] which consistently sacrifice the healthy development of community, work, environment, education, and social equality to the accumulation of capital and the growth of marketable goods and services. Moreover, given that individuals must participate in economic activity, these outcomes are quite insensitive to the preferences or values of individuals, and are certainly in no sense a reflection of the autonomous wills of manipulating bureaucrats

[4] Throughout this paper, I restrict my analysis to *capitalist* as opposed to other economic systems of advanced industrial societies (e.g., state-socialism of the Soviet Union type). As Illich suggests, the *outcomes* are much the same, but the *mechanisms* are in fact quite different. The private-administrative economic power of a capitalist elite is mirrored by the public-administrative political power of a bureaucratic elite in state-socialist countries, and both are used to reproduce a similar complex of social relations of production and a structurally equivalent system of class relations. The capitalist variety is emphasized here because of its special relevance in the American context.

or gullible consumers. Hence merely ending "manipulation" while maintaining basic economic institutions will affect the rate of social decay only minimally.

Second, Illich locates the *source* of consumer consciousness in the manipulative socialization of individuals by agencies controlled by corporate and welfare bureaucracies. This "institutionalized consciousness" induces individuals to choose outcomes not in conformity with their "real" needs. I shall argue, in contrast, that a causal analysis can *never* take socialization agencies as basic explanatory variables in assessing the overall behavior of the social system.[5] In particular, consumer consciousness is generated through *the day-to-day activities and observations* of individuals in capitalist society. The sales pitch of manipulative institutions, rather than *generating* the values of commodity fetishism, merely *capitalize* upon and *reinforce* a set of values derived from and reconfirmed by daily personal experience in the social system. In fact, while consumer behavior may seem irrational and fetishistic, it is a reasonable accommodation to the options for meaningful social outlets *in the context* of capitalist institutions. Hence the abolition of addictive propaganda cannot "liberate" the individual to "free choice" of personal goals. Such choice is still conditioned by the pattern of social processes which have historically rendered him or her amenable to "institutionalized values." In fact, the likely outcome of de-manipulation of values would be no significant alteration of values at all.

Moreover, the ideology of commodity fetishism not only *reflects* the day-to-day operations of the economic system, it is also *functionally necessary* to motivate men/women to accept and participate in the system of alienated production, to peddle their (potentially) creative activities to the highest bidder through the market in labor, to accept the destruction of their communities, and to

[5] Gintis, "Consumer Behavior and the Concept of Sovereignty."

bear allegiance to an economic system whose market institutions and patterns of control of work and community systematically subordinate all social goals to the criteria of profit and marketable product. Thus the weakening of institutionalized values would in itself lead logically either to unproductive and undirected social chaos (witness the present state of counter-culture movements in the United States) or to a rejection of the social relations of capitalist production along with commodity fetishism.

Third, Illich argues that the goal of social change is to transform institutions according to the criteria of "non-addictiveness," or "left-conviviality." However, since manipulation and addictiveness are not the sources of social decay, their elimination offers no cure. Certainly the implementation of left-convivial forms in welfare and service agencies—however desirable in itself—will not counter the effects of capitalist development on social life. More important, Illich's criterion explicitly accepts those basic economic institutions which structure decision-making power, lead to the growth of corporate and welfare bureaucracies, and lie at the root of social decay. Thus Illich's criterion must be replaced by one of democratic, participatory, and rationally decentralized control over social outcomes in factory, office, community, schools, and media. The remainder of this essay will elucidate the alternative analysis and political strategy as focused on the particular case of the educational system.

ECONOMIC INSTITUTIONS AND SOCIAL DEVELOPMENT

In line with Illich's suggestion, we may equate individual welfare with the pattern of day-to-day *activities* the individual enters into, together with the personal *capacities*—physical, cognitive, affective, spiritual, and aesthetic—he or she has developed toward their execution and appreciation. Most individual activity is not purely personal, but is based on social interaction and requires a social setting conducive to developing the relevant capacities for performance. That is, activities take place within socially structured domains, characterized by legitimate and socially acceptable roles available to the individual in social relations. The most important of these activity contexts are work, community, and natural environment. The character of individual participation in these contexts—the defining roles one accepts as worker and community member and the way one relates to one's environment—is a basic determinant of well-being and individual development.

These activity contexts, as I shall show, are structured in turn by the way people structure their *productive relations*. The study of activity contexts in capitalist society must begin with an understanding of the basic economic institutions which regulate their historical development.

The most important of these institutions are: 1) *private ownership* of factors of production (land, labor, and capital), according to which the owner has full control over their disposition and development; 2) *a market in labor,* according to which a) the worker is divorced, by and large, from ownership of non-human factors of production (land and capital), b) the worker relinquishes control over the disposition of his labor during the stipulated workday by exchanging it for money, and c) the price of a particular type of labor (skilled or unskilled, white-collar or blue-collar, physical, mental, managerial, or technical) is determined essentially by supply and demand); 3) *a market in land,* according to which the price of each parcel of land is determined by supply and demand, and the use of such parcels is individually determined by the highest bidder; 4) income determination on the basis of the *market-dictated returns to owned factors* of production; 5) *markets in essential commodities*—food, shelter, social insurance, medical care; and 6) *control of the productive process by owners of capital* or their managerial representatives.[6]

Because essential goods, services, and activity contexts are marketed, income is a prerequisite to social existence. Because factors of production are privately owned and market-determined factor returns are the legitimate source of income, and because most workers possess little more than their own labor services, they are required to provide these services to the economic system. Thus control over the developing of work roles and of the social technology of production passes into the hands of the representatives of capital.

Thus the activity context of work becomes alienated in the sense that its structure and historical development do not conform to the needs of the individuals it affects.[7] Bosses determine the technologies and social relations of production within the enterprise on the basis of three criteria. First, production must be flexibly organized for decision-making and secure managerial control from the highest levels downward. This means generally that technologies employed must be compatible with hierarchical authority and a fragmented, task-specific division of labor.[8] The need to maintain effective administrative power leads to bureaucratic order in production, the hallmark of modern corporate organization. Second, among all technologies and work roles compatible with secure and flexible control from the top, bosses choose those which minimize costs and maximize profits. Finally, bosses determine

[6] The arguments in this section are presented at greater length in Gintis, "Power and Alienation," in *Readings in Political Economy*, ed. James Weaver (Boston, Mass.: Allyn and Bacon, forthcoming, 1972) and "Consumer Behavior and the Concept of Sovereignty."

[7] This definition conforms to Marxist usage in that "alienation" refers to *social processes*, not psychological states. For some discussion of this term in Marxist literature, see Gintis, "Power and Alienation," and "Consumer Behavior and the Concept of Sovereignty."

[8] See the essay by Stephen Marglin, "What Do Bosses Do?" unpublished, Dept. of Economics, Harvard University, 1971.

product attributes—and hence the "craft rationality" of production—according to their contribution to gross sales and growth of the enterprise. Hence the decline in pride of workmanship and quality of production associated with the Industrial Revolution.

There is no reason to believe that a great deal of desirable work is not possible. On the contrary, evidence indicates that decentralization, worker control, the reintroduction of craft in production, job rotation, and the elimination of the most constraining aspects of hierarchy are both feasible and potentially efficient. But such work roles develop in an institutional context wherein control, profit, and growth regulate the development of the social relations of production. Unalienated production must be the result of the revolutionary transformation of the basic institutions which Illich implicitly accepts.

The development of communities as activity contexts also must be seen in terms of basic economic institutions. The market in land, by controlling the organic development of communities, not only produces the social, environmental, and aesthetic monstrosities we call "metropolitan areas," but removes from the community the creative, synthesizing power that lies at the base of true solidarity. Thus communities become agglomerates of isolated individuals with few common activities and impersonal and apathetic interpersonal relations.

A community cannot thrive when it holds no effective power over the autonomous activities of profit-maximizing capitalists. Rather, a true community is *itself* a creative, initiating, and synthesizing agent, with the power to determine the architectural unity of its living and working spaces and their coordination, the power to allocate community property to social uses such as participatory child-care and community recreation centers, and the power to insure the preservation and development of its natural ecological environment. This is not an idle utopian dream. Many living-working communities do exhibit architectural, aesthetic, social, and ecological integrity: the New England town, the Dutch village, the moderate-sized cities of Mali in sub-Saharan Africa, and the desert communities of Djerba in Tunisia. True, these communities are fairly static and untouched by modern technology; but even in a technologically advanced country the potential for decent community is great, given the proper pattern of community decision mechanisms.

The normal operation of the basic economic institutions of capitalism thus render major activity contexts inhospitable to human beings. Our analysis of work and the community could easily be extended to include ecological environment and economic equality with similar conclusions.[9]

This analysis undermines Illich's treatment of public service bureaucracies. Illich holds that service agencies (including schools) fail because they are manipulative, and expand because they are psychologically addictive. In fact, they do not fail at all. And they expand because they exist as integral links in the larger institutional allocation of unequal power and income. Illich's simplistic treatment of this area is illustrated in his explanation for the expansion of military operations:

> The boomerang effect in war is becoming more obvious: the higher the body count of dead Vietnamese, the more enemies the United States acquires around the world; likewise, the more the United States must spend to create another manipulative institution—cynically dubbed "pacification"—in a futile effort to absorb the side effects of war. (DS, p. 54)

Illich's theory of addiction as motivation proposes that, once begun, one thing naturally leads to another. Actually, however, the purpose of the military is the maintenance of aggregate demand and high levels of employment, as well as aiding the expansion of international sources of resource supply and capital investment. Expansion is not the result of addiction but a primary characteristic of the entire system.[10]

Likewise from a systematic point of view, penal, mental illness, and poverty agencies are meant to contain the dislocations arising from the fragmentation of work and community and the institutionally determined inequality in income and power. Yet Illich argues only:

> . . . jail increases both the quality and the quantity of criminals, that, in fact, it often creates them out of mere nonconformists . . . mental hospitals, nursing homes, and orphan asylums do much the same thing. These institutions provide their clients with the destructive self-image of the psychotic, the overaged, or the waif, and provide a rationale for the existence of entire professions, just as jails produce income for wardens. (DS, p. 54)

Further, the cause of expansion of service agencies lies *not* in their addictive nature, but in their failure even to attempt to deal with the institutional sources of social problems. The normal operation of basic economic institutions progressively aggravates these problems, hence requiring increased response on the part of welfare agencies.

THE ROOTS OF CONSUMER BEHAVIOR

To understand consumption in capitalist society requires a *production* orientation, in contrast to Illich's emphasis on "institutionalized values" as basic explanatory variables. Individuals consume as they do—and hence acquire values and beliefs concerning consumption—because of the place consumption activity holds among the constellation of available alternatives for social expression. These alternatives directly involve the qual-

9 See Michael Reich and David Finkelhor, "The Military-Industrial Complex," in *The Capitalist System*, ed. Richard C. Edwards, Michael Reich, and Thomas Weisskopf (New York: Prentice-Hall, 1972).

10 See Gintis, "Power and Alienation," for a concise summary.

ity of basic activity contexts surrounding social life—contexts which, as I have argued, develop according to the criteria of capital accumulation through the normal operation of economic institutions.

What at first glance seems to be an irrational preoccupation with income and consumption in capitalist society, is seen within an activity context paradigm to be a logical response on the part of the individual to what Marx isolated as the central tendency of capitalist society: the transformation of all complex social relations into impersonal *quid-pro-quo* relations. One implication of this transformation is the progressive decay of social activity contexts described in the previous section, a process which reduces their overall contribution to individual welfare. Work, community, and environment become sources of pain and displeasure rather than inviting contexts for social relations. The reasonable individual response, then, is a) to disregard the development of personal capacities which would be humanly satisfying in activity contexts which are not available and, hence, to fail to demand changed activity contexts and b) to emphasize consumption and to develop those capacities which are most relevant to consumption *per se*.

Second, the transformation of complex social relations to exchange relations implies that the dwindling stock of healthy activity contexts is parceled out among individuals almost strictly according to income. High-paying jobs are by and large the least alienating; the poor live in the most fragmented communities and are subjected to the most inhuman environments; contact with natural environment is limited to periods of *vacation*, and the length and desirability of this contact is based on the means to pay.

Thus commodity fetishism becomes a *substitute* for meaningful activity contexts, and a *means of access* to those that exist. The "sales pitch" of Madison Avenue is accepted because, in the given context, it is true. It may not be much, but it's all we've got. The indefensibility of its more extreme forms

(e.g., susceptibility to deodorant and luxury automobile advertising) should not divert us from comprehending this essential rationality.

In conclusion, it is clear that the motivational basis of consumer behavior derives from the everyday observation and experience of individuals, and consumer values are not "aberrations" induced by manipulative socialization. Certainly there is no reason to believe that individuals would consume or work much less were manipulative socialization removed. Insofar as such socialization is required to *stabilize* commodity fetishist values, its elimination might lead to the overthrow of capitalist *institutions*—but that of course is quite outside Illich's scheme.

THE LIMITATIONS OF LEFT-CONVIVIAL TECHNOLOGIES

Since Illich views the "psychological impotence" of the individual in his/her "addictedness" to the ministrations of corporate and state bureaucracies as the basic problem of contemporary society, he defines the desirable "left-convivial" institutions by the criterion of "non-addictiveness."

Applied to commodities or welfare services, this criterion is perhaps sufficient. But applied to major contexts of social activities, it is inappropriate. It is not possible for individuals to treat their work, their communities, and their environment in a simply instrumental manner. For better or worse, these social spheres, by regulating the individual's social activity, became a major determinant of his/her psychic development, and in an important sense define *who* he/she is. Indeed, the solution to the classical "problem of order" in society[11] is solved only by the individual's becoming "addicted" to his/her social forms by *participating through*

---

[11] Talcott Parsons, *The Structure of Social Action* (New York: Free Press, 1939).

them.[12] In remaking society, individuals do more than expand their freedom of choice—they change *who they are,* their self-definition, in the process. The criticism of alienated social spheres is not simply that they deprive individuals of necessary instruments of activity, but that in so doing they tend to produce in all of us something less than *we intend to be.*

The irony of Illich's analysis is that by erecting "addictiveness vs. instrumentality" as the central welfare criterion, he himself assumes a commodity fetishist mentality. In essence, he posits the individual *outside* of society and using social forms as instruments in his/her preexisting ends. For instance, Illich does not speak of work as "addictive," because in fact individuals treat work first as a "disutility" and second as an instrument toward other ends (consumption). The alienation of work poses no threat to the "sovereignty" of the worker because he is not addicted to it. By definition, then, capitalist work, communities, and environments are "non-addictive" and left-convivial. Illich's consideration of the capitalist enterprise as "right-manipulative" only with respect to the consumer is a perfect example of this "reification" of the social world. In contrast, I would argue that work is *necessarily addictive* in the larger sense of determining who a man/women is as a human being.

The addictive vs. instrumental (or, equivalently, manipulative vs. convivial) criterion is relevant only if we posit an essential "human nature" prior to social experience. Manipulation can then be seen as the perversion of the natural essence of the individual, and the de-institutionalization of values allows the individual to return to his/her essential self for direction. But the concept of the individual prior to society is nonsense. All individuals are concrete persons, uniquely developed through their particular articulation with social life.

The poverty of Illich's "addictiveness" criterion is dramatized in his treatment of technology. While he correctly recognizes that technology can be developed for purposes of either repression or liberation, his conception requires that the correct unalienated development of technological and institutional forms will follow from a simple aggregation of individual preferences over "left-convivial" alternatives.

The same analysis which I applied to the atomistic aggregation of preferences in the determination of activity contexts applies here as well: there is no reason to believe that ceding control of technological innovation and diffusion to a few, while rendering them subject to market criteria of success and failure, will produce desirable outcomes. Indeed this is *precisely* the mechanism operative in the private capitalist economy, with demonstrably adverse outcomes. According to the criterion of left-conviviality, the historical development of technology in *both* private and public spheres will conform to criteria of profitability and entrepreneurial control. Citizens are reduced to *passive consumers,* picking and choosing among the technological alternatives a technological elite presents to them.

In contrast, it seems clear to me that individuals must exercise direct control over technology in structuring their various social environments, thereby developing and coming to understand their needs through their exercise of power. The control of technical and institutional forms must be vested directly in the group of individuals involved in a social activity, else the alienation of these individuals from one another becomes a *postulate* of the technical and institutional development of this social activity—be it in factory, office, school, or community.

In summary, the facile criterion of left-conviviality must be replaced by the less immediate—but correct—criterion of *unalienated social outcomes:* the institutionally mediated allocation of power must be so

---

[12] Karl Marx, *The Economic and Philosophical Manuscripts of 1844* (Moscow: Foreign Language Publishing House, 1959) and Karl Marx and Friedrich Engels, *The Germany Ideology* (New York: International Publishers, 1947).

ordered that social outcomes conform to the wills and needs of participating individuals, and the quality of participation must be such as to promote the full development of individual capacities for self-understanding and social effectiveness.

SCHOOLING: THE PRE-ALIENATION OF DOCILE CONSUMERS

> Everywhere the hidden curriculum of schooling initiates the citizen to the myth that bureaucracies guided by scientific knowledge are efficient and benevolent. . . . And everywhere it develops the habit of self-defeating consumption of services and alienating production, the tolerance for institutional dependence, and the recognition of institutional rankings. (*DS*, p. 74)

Illich sets his analysis of the educational system squarely on its strategic position in reproducing the economic relations of the larger society. While avoiding the inanity of reformers, who see "liberated education" as compatible with current capitalist political and economic institutions, he rejects the rigidity of old-style revolutionaries, who would see even more repressive (though different) education as a tool in forging "socialist consciousness" in the Workers' State.

What less perceptive educators have viewed as irrational, mean, and petty in modern schooling, Illich views as merely reflecting the operation of all manipulative institutions. In the first place, he argues, the educational system takes its place alongside other service bureaucracies, selling a manipulative, pre-packaged product, rendering their services addictive, and monopolizing all alternatives to self-initiated education on the part of individuals and small consenting groups.

Yet, argues Illich, schools cannot possibly achieve their goal of promoting learning.

For as in every dimension of human experience, learning is the result of personal *activity*, not professional ministration:

> Most learning is not the result of instruction. It is rather the result of unhampered participation in a meaningful setting. Most people learn best by being 'with it,' yet school makes them identify their personal, cognitive growth with elaborate planning and manipulation. (*DS*, p. 39)

Thus, as with all bureaucratic service institutions, schools fail by their very nature. And true to form, the more they fail, the more reliance is placed on them, and the more they expand:

> Everywhere in the world school costs have risen faster than enrollments and faster than the GNP, everywhere expenditures on school fall even further behind the expectations of parents, teachers, and pupils. . . . School gives unlimited opportunity for legitimated waste, so long as its destructiveness goes unrecognized and the cost of palliatives goes up. (*DS*, p. 10)

From the fact that schools do not promote learning, however, Illich does not conclude that schools are simply irrational or discardable. Rather, he asserts their central role in creating docile and manipulable consumers for the larger society. For just as these men and women are defined by the quality of their *possessions* rather than of their *activities*, so they must learn to "transfer responsibility from self to institutions. . . ."

> Once a man or woman has accepted the need for school, he or she is easy prey for other institutions. Once young people have allowed their imaginations to be formed by curricular instruction, they are conditioned to institutional planning of every sort. 'Instruction' smothers the horizon of their imaginations. (*DS*, p. 39)

Equally they learn that anything worthwhile is standardized, certified, and can be purchased.

Even more lamentable, repressive school-ing forces commodity fetishism on individ-uals by thwarting their development of personal capacities for autonomous and initiating social activity:

> People who have been schooled down to size let unmeasured experience slip out of their hands. . . . They do not have to be robbed of their creativity. Under instruc-tion, they have unlearned to "do" their thing or "be" themselves, and value only what has been made or could be made. . . . (DS, p. 40)

Recent research justifies Illich's emphasis on the "hidden curriculum" of schooling. Mass public education has not evolved into its present bureaucratic, hierarchical, and authoritarian form because of the organiza-tional prerequisites of imparting cognitive skills. Such skills may in fact be more efficiently developed in democratic, non-repressive atmospheres.[13] Rather, the social relations of education produce and rein-force those values, attitudes, and affective capacities which allow individuals to move smoothly into an alienated and class-stratified society. That is, schooling reproduces the social relations of the larger society from generation to generation.[14]

[13] The literature on this subject is immense. Illich himself is quite persuasive, but see also Charles E. Silberman, *Crisis in the Classroom* (New York: Ran-dom House, 1970), for a more detailed treatment.

[14] Gintis, "Contre-Culture et Militantisme Politique," *Les Temps Modernes* (February, 1971) "New Work-ing Class and Revolutionary Youth," *Social Revolu-tion* (May, 1970); and "Education and the Charac-teristics of Worker Productivity," *American Economic Review* (May, 1971); David Cohen and Marvin Lazer-son, "Education and the Corporate Order," *Socialist Revolution*, March 1972; Clarence Karrier, "Testing for Order and Control," *Education Theory*, forth-coming; Michael B. Katz, *The Irony of Early School Reform* (Cambridge, Mass.: Harvard University Press, 1968) and "From Voluntarism to Bureaucracy in American Education," *Sociology of Education*, forth-coming, 1972; Joel Spring, "Education and Progres-sivism," *History of Education* (Spring, 1970); and Robert Dreeben, *On What Is Learned in Schools* (Reading, Mass.: Addison-Wesley, 1968).

Again, however, it does *not* follow that schooling finds its predominant function in reproducing the social relations of *consump-tion per se*. Rather, it is the social relations of *production* which are relevant to the form and function of modern schooling.

A production orientation to the analysis of schooling—that the "hidden curriculum" in mass education reproduces the social rela-tions of production—is reinforced in several distinct bodies of current educational re-search. First, economists have shown that education, in spite of providing a properly trained labor force, takes its place along-side capital accumulation and technological change as a major source of economic growth.[15] Level of educational attainment is the major non-ascriptive variable in further-ing the economic position of individuals.

Second, research shows that the type of personal development produced through schooling and relevant to the individual's productivity as a worker in a capitalist enter-prise is primarily *non-cognitive*. That is, profit-maximizing firms find it remunerative to hire more highly educated workers at higher pay, essentially *irrespective* of differ-ences among individuals in cognitive abilities or attainments.[16] In other words, two indi-viduals (white American males) with identical cognitive achievements (intelli-gence or intellectual attainment) but differ-ing educational levels will not command, on the average, the same income or occupational status. Rather, the economic success of each will correspond closely to the average for his educational level. All individuals with the same level of educational attainment tend

[15] See Edward F. Denison, *The Sources of Economic Growth in the United States and the Alternatives Before Us* (New York: Committee for Economic De-velopment, 1962) and Theodore Schultz, *The Eco-nomic Value of Education* (New York: Columbia University Press, 1963).

[16] This surprising result is developed in Gintis, "Edu-cation and the Characteristics of Worker Produc-tivity," and is based on a wide variety of statistical data. It is validated and extended by Christopher Jencks *et al.*, *Education and Inequality* (New York: Basic Books, forthcoming, 1972).

to have the same expected mean economic success (racial and sexual discrimination aside). This is not to say that cognitive skills are not necessary to job adequacy in a technological society. Rather, these skills either exist in such profusion (through schooling) or are so easily developed on the job that they are not a criterion for hiring. Nor does this mean that there is no correlation between cognitive attainments (e.g., IQ) and occupational status. Such a correlation exists (although it is quite loose),[17] but is almost totally mediated by formal schooling: the educational system discriminates in favor of the more intelligent, although its contribution to worker productivity does not operate primarily *via* cognitive development.[18]

Thus the education-related worker attributes that employers willingly pay for must be predominantly *affective* characteristics—personality traits, attitudes, modes of self-presentation and motivation. How affective traits that are rewarded in schools come to correspond to the needs of alienated production is revealed by direct inspection of the social relations of the classroom. First, students are rewarded in terms of grades for exhibiting the personality characteristics of good workers in bureaucratic work roles—proper subordinancy in relation to authority and the primacy of cognitive as opposed to affective and creative modes of social response—above and beyond any actual effect they may have on cognitive achievement.[19] Second, the hierarchical structure of schooling itself mirrors the social relations of industrial production: students cede control over their learning activities to teachers in the classroom. Just as workers are alienated from both the *process* and the *product* of their work activities, and must be motivated

by the external reward of pay and hierarchical status, so the student learns to operate efficiently through the external reward of grades and promotion, effectively alienated from the process of education (learning) and its product (knowledge). Just as the work process is stratified, and workers on different levels in the hierarchy of authority and status are required to display substantively distinct patterns of values, aspirations, personality traits, and modes of "social presentation" (dress, manner of speech, personal identification, and loyalties to a particular social stratum),[20] so the school system stratifies, tracks, and structures social interaction according to criteria of social class and relative scholastic success.[21] The most effectively indoctrinated students are the most valuable to the economic enterprise or state bureaucracy, and also the most successfully integrated into a particular stratum within the hierarchical educational process.[22]

Third, a large body of historical research indicates that the system of mass, formal, and compulsory education arose more or less directly out of changes in productive relations associated with the Industrial Revolution, in its role of supplying a properly socialized and stratified labor force.[23]

17 See, e.g., Jencks *et al.*
18 For more extensive treatment, see Jencks *et al.* and Gintis, "Education and the Characteristics of Worker Productivity."
19 For an analysis of relevant data and an extensive bibliography, see Gintis, "Education and the Characteristics of Worker Productivity," and "Alienation and Power," diss., Harvard University, 1969.

20 This phenomenon is analyzed in Claus Offe, *Leistungsprinzip und Industrielle Arbeit* (Frankfort: Europaïsche Verlaganstalt, 1970).
21 See Merle Curti, *The Social Ideas of American Educators* (Chicago: C. Scribners Sons, 1935); Gintis, "Contre-Culture et Militantisme Politique"; Gorz, "Capitalist Relations of Production and the Socially Necessary Labor Force," in *All We Are Saying . . .*, ed. Arthur Lothstein (New York: G. P. Putnam's Sons, 1970) and "Technique, Techniciens, et Lutte de Classes"; Samuel Bowles, "Unequal Education and the Reproduction of the Social Division of Labor," in *The Capitalist System*, ed., Edwards, Reich, and Weisskopf; and "Contradictions de L'enseignement Superieure" *Les Temps Modernes*, Aout-Sept., 1971; and David Bruck, "The Schools of Lowell," honors thesis (unpublished), Harvard University, 1971.
22 This statement is supported by the statistical results of Richard C. Edwards, Diss., Department of Economics, Harvard University, in progress.
23 Katz, *The Irony of Early School Reform* and "From Voluntarism to Bureaucracy in American Education"; Lawrence Cremin, *The Transformation*

The critical turning points in the history of American education have coincided with the perceived failure of the school system to fulfill its functional role in reproducing a properly socialized and stratified labor force, in the face of important qualitative or quantitive changes in the social relations of production. In these periods (e.g., the emergence of the common school system) numerous options were open and openly discussed.[24] The conflict of economic interests eventually culminated in the functional re-orientation of the educational system to new labor needs of an altered capitalism.

In the mid- to late 19th century, this took the form of the economy's need to generate a labor force compatible with the factory system from a predominantly agricultural populace. Later, the crisis in education corresponded to the economy's need to import peasant European labor whose social relations of production and derivative culture were incompatible with industrial wage-labor. The resolution of this crisis was a hierarchical, centralized school system corresponding to the ascendance of corporate production. This resolution was not without its own contradictions. It is at this time that the modern school became the focus of tensions between work and play, between the culture of school and the culture of immigrant children, and between the notion of meritocracy and equality. Thus while Illich can *describe* the characteristics of contemporary education, his consumption orientation prevents him from understanding how the system came to be.

It seems clear that schools instill the values of docility, degrees of subordination corresponding to different levels in the hierarchy of production, and motivation according to external reward. It seems also true that they do not reward, but instead penalize, creative, self-initiated, cognitively flexible behavior. By inhibiting the full development of individual capacities for meaningful individual activity, schools produce Illich's contended outcomes: the individual as passive receptor replaces the individual as active agent. But the articulation with the larger society is *production* rather than *consumption*.

If the sources of social problems lay in consumer manipulation of which schooling is both an exemplary instance and a crucial preparation for future manipulation, than a political movement for de-schooling might be, as Illich says, "at the root of any movement for human liberation." But if schooling is both itself an *activity context* and preparation for the more important activity context of work then personal consciousness arises not from the elimination of outside manipulation, but from the experience of solidarity and struggles in remolding a mode of social existence. Such consciousness represents not a "return" to the self (essential human nature) but a *restructuring* of the self through new modes of social participation; this prepares the individual for itself.

Of course this evaluation need not be unidirectional from work to education. Indeed, one of the fundamental bases for assessing the value of an alternative structure of control in production is its compatibility with intrinsically desirable individual development through education. Insofar as Illich's left-convivial concept is desirable in any ultimate sense, a reorganization of production should be sought comfortable to it. This might involve the development of a vital craft artistic/technical/service sector in production organized along master-apprentice or group-control lines open to *all* individuals. The development of unalienated work technologies might then articulate harmoniously with learning-web forms in the sphere of education.

But a recognition of production has other goals as well. For example, any fore-

of the School (New York: Alfred A. Knopf, 1964); Raymond E. Callahan, *Eduction and the Cult of Efficiency* (Chicago: University of Chicago Press, 1962); Curti; Bowles, "Unequal Education and the Reproduction of the Social Division of Labor"; Spring; Cohen and Lazerson.
[24] See David B. Tyack, *Turning Points in American Educational History* (Boston: Ginn & Co., 1967); and Katz.

seeable future involves a good deal of socially necessary and on balance personally unrewarding labor. However this work may be reorganized, its accomplishment must be based on individual values, attitudes, personality traits, and patterns of motivation adequate to its execution. If equality in social participation is a "revolutionary ideal," this dictates that all contribute equally toward the staffing of the socially necessary work roles. This is possible only if the hierarchical (as opposed to social) division of labor is abolished in favor of the solidary cooperation and participation of workers in control of production. Illich's anarchistic notion of learning webs does not seem conducive to the development of personal characteristics for this type of social solidarity.[25]

The second setting for a politics of education is the *transitional society*—one which bears the technological and cultural heritage of the capitalist class/caste system, but whose social institutions and patterns of social consciousness are geared toward the progressive realization of "ideal forms" (i.e., revolutionary goals) . In this setting, the social relations of education will themselves be transitional in nature, mirroring the transformation process of social relations of production.[26] For instance, the elimination of boring, unhealthy, fragmented, uncreative, constraining, and otherwise alienated but socially necessary labor requires an extended process of technological change in a transitional phase. As we have observed, the repressive application of technology toward the formation of occupational roles is not due to the intrinsic nature of physical science nor to the requisites of productive efficiency, but to the political imperative of stable control from the top in an enterprise. Nevertheless the shift to automated, decentralized, and worker-controlled technologies require the continuous supervision and cooperation of workers themselves. Any form this takes in a transitional society will include a constant struggle among three groups: managers concerned with the development of the enterprise, technicians concerned with the scientific rationality of production, and workers concerned with the impact of innovation and management on job satisfaction.[27] The present educational system does not develop in the individual the capacities for cooperation, struggle, autonomy, and judgment appropriate to this task. But neither does Illich's alternative which avoids the affective aspects of work socialization totally, and takes technology out of the heads of learners.

In a transitional setting, liberating technologies cannot arise in education, any more than in production, spontaneously or by imposition from above. The social relations of unalienated education must evolve from conscious cooperation and struggle among educational administrators (managers), teachers (technicians) , and students (workers), although admittedly in a context of radically redistributed power among the three. The outcome of such a struggle is not only the

---

[25] The main elements in Illich's left-convivial "learning web" alternative to manipulative education are all fundamentally dispersive and fragmenting of a learning community: (1) Reference Services to Educational Objects—which facilitate access to things or processes used for formal learning. Some of these things can be reserved for this purpose, stored in libraries, rental agencies, laboratories, and showrooms like museums and theaters; others can be in daily use in factories, airports, or on farms, but made available to students as apprentices or on off-hours. (2) Skill Exchanges—which permit persons to list their skills, the conditions under which they are willing to serve as models for others who want to learn these skills, and the addresses at which they can be reached. (3) Peer-Matching—a communications network which permits persons to describe the learning activity in which thy wish to engage, in the hope of finding a partner for the inquiry. (4) Reference Services to Educators-at-Large—who can be listed in a directory giving the addresses and self-descriptions of professionals, paraprofessionals, and free-lancers, along with conditions of access to their services.

[26] Bowles, "Cuban Education and the Revolutionary Ideology," *Harvard Educational Review*, 41 (November 1971).

[27] Marco Maccio, "Parti, Technicien, et Classe Ouvriere dans la Revolution Chinoise," *Les Temps Modernes*, (August–Septmber, 1970), and Gorz "Techniques, Techniciens et Lutte de Classes."

positive development of education but the fostering of work-capacities in individuals adequate to the task of social transition in work and community life as well.[28]

The inadequacy of Illich's conception of education in transitional societies is striking in his treatment of China and Cuba. It is quite evident that these countries are following new and historically unprecedented directions of social development. But Illich argues the necessity of their failure from the simple fact that they have not de-schooled. That they were essentially "de-schooled" *before* the revolution (with no appreciable social benefits) does not faze him. While we may welcome and embrace Illich's emphasis on the social relations of education as a crucial variable in their internal development toward new social forms, his own criterion is without practical application.

The third setting in which the politics of education must be assessed—and the one which would most closely represent the American reality—is that of capitalist society itself. Here the correspondence principle implies that educational reform requires an *internal failure* in the stable reproduction of the economic relations of production. That is, the idea of liberating education does not arise spontaneously, but is made possible by emerging contradictions in the larger society. Nor does its aim succeed or fail according as its ethical value is greater or less. Rather,

success of the aim presupposes a correct understanding of its basis in the contradictions in social life, and the political strategies adopted as the basis of this understanding.

The immediate strategies of a movement for educational reform, then, are political: a) understanding the concrete contradictions in economic life and the way they are reflected in the educational system; b) fighting to insure that consciousness of these contradictions persists by thwarting attempts of ruling elites to attenuate them by co-operation; and c) using the persistence of contradictions in society at large to expand the political base and power of a revolutionary movement, that is, a movement for educational reform must understand the social conditions of its emergence and development in the concrete conditions of social life. Unless we achieve such an understanding and use it as the basis of political *action*, a functional reorientation will occur vis-a-vis the present crisis in education, as it did in earlier critical moments in the history of American education.

In the present period, the relevant contradiction involves: a) blacks moved from rural independent agriculture and seasonal farm wage-labor to the urban-industrial wage-labor system; b) middle-class youth with values attuned to economic participation as entrepreneurs, elite white-collar and professional and technical labor, faced with the elimination of entrepreneurship, the corporatization of production, and the proletarianization of white-collar work [29]; and c) women, the major sufferance of ascriptive discrimination in production (including household production) in an era where capitalist relations of production are increasingly legitimized by their sole reliance on achievement (non-ascriptive) norms.[30]

---

[28] The theory of political organization which takes *contradictions* among the interests of the various groups participating in the control of a social activity context as central to social development, underlies my argument. This theory is well developed in Chinese Communist thought, as presented in Mao Tse Tung, "On Contradiction" in *Selected Works* (Peking: Foreign Language Press, 1952), and Franz Schurmann, *Ideology and Organization in Communist China* (Berkeley: University of California Press, 1970). In terms of this "dialectical theory of political action," the reorganization of power in education in a transitional society must render the contradictions among administrators, teachers, and students *non-antagonistic*, in the sense that the day-to-day outcomes of their struggles are the positive, healthy development of the educational system, beneficial to all parties concerned.

[29] Bowles, "Contradictions de L'enseignement Superieure," and Gintis, "Contre-Culture et Militantisme Politique" and "New Working Class and Revolutionary Youth."

[30] For a general discussion of these issues, see Edwards, Reich, and Weisskopf, ed., *The Capitalist System*.

This inventory is partial, incomplete, and insufficiently analyzed. But only on a basis of its completion can a successful educational strategy be forged. In the realm of contradictions, the correspondence principle must yet provide the method of analysis and action. We must assess political strategies in education on the basis of the single—but distressingly complex—question: will they lead to the transitional society?

I have already argued that de-schooling will inevitably lead to a situation of social chaos, but probably not to a serious mass movement toward constructive social change. In this case the correspondence principle simply fails to hold, producing at best a temporary (in case the ruling elites can find an alternative mode of worker socialization) or ultimately fatal (in case they cannot) breakdown in the social fabric. But only if we posit some essential pre-social human nature on which individuals draw when normal paths of individual development are abolished, might this lead in itself to liberating alternatives.

But the argument over the sufficiency of de-schooling is nearly irrelevant. For schools are so important to the reproduction of capitalist society that they are unlikely to crumble under any but the most massive political onslaughts. "Each of us," says Illich, "is personally responsible for his or her own de-schooling, and only we have the power to do it." This is not true. Schooling is legally *obligatory,* and is the *major means of access* to welfare-relevant activity contexts. The political consciousness behind a frontal attack on institutionalized education would necessarily spill over to attacks on other major institutions. "The risks of a revolt against school," says Illich,

> . . . are unforseeable, but they are not as horrible as those of a revolution starting in any other major institution. School is not yet organized for self-protection as effectively as a nation-state, or even a large corporation. Liberation from the grip of schools could be bloodless. (*DS,* p. 49)

This is no more than whistling in the dark.

The only presently viable political strategy in education—and the precise *negation* of Illich's recommendations—is what Rudi Deutchke terms "the long march through the institutions," involving localized struggles for what Andre Gorz calls "non-reformist reforms," i.e., reforms which effectively strengthen the power of teachers vis-a-vis administrators, and of students vis-a-vis teachers.

Still, although schools neither can nor should be eliminated, the social relations of education *can* be altered through genuine struggle. Moreover, the experience of both struggle and control prepares the student for a future of political activity in factory and office.

In other words, the correct immediate political goal is the nurturing of individuals both liberated (i.e., demanding control over their lives and outlets for their creative activities and relationships) *and* politically aware of the true nature of their misalignment with the larger society. There may indeed be a bloodless solution to the problem of revolution, but certainly none more simple than this.

CONCLUSION

Illich recognizes that the problems of advanced industrial societies are institutional, and that their solutions lie deep in the social core. Therefore, he consciously rejects a partial or affirmative analysis which would accept society's dominant ideological forms and direct its innovative contributions toward marginal changes in assumptions and boundary conditions.

Instead, he employs a methodology of total critique and negation, and his successes, such as they are, stem from that choice. Ultimately, however, his analysis is incomplete.

Dialectical analysis begins with society as is (thesis), entertains its negation (antithesis), and *overcomes* both in a radical reconceptualization (synthesis). Negation is a form of demystification—a drawing away from the immediately given by viewing it as a "negative totality." But negation is not without presuppositions, is not itself a form of liberation. It cannot "wipe clean the slate" of ideological representation of the world or one's objective position in it. The son/daughter who acts on the negation of parental and societal values is not free—he/she is merely the constrained negative image of that which he/she rejects (e.g., the negation of work, consumption order, and rationality is not liberation but negative un-freedom). The negation of male dominance is not women's liberation but the (negative) affirmation of "female masculinity." Women's liberation in dialectical terms can be conceived of as the overcoming (synthesis) of male dominance (thesis) and female masculinity (antithesis) in a new totality which rejects/embodies both. It is this act of overcoming (synthesis, consciousness) which is the critical and liberating aspect of dialectical thought. Action lies not in the act of negation (antithesis, demystification) but in the act of overcoming (synthesis/consciousness).

The strengths of Illich's analysis lie in his consistent and pervasive methodology of negation. The essential elements in the liberal conceptions of the Good Life—consumption and education, the welfare state and corporate manipulation—are demystified and laid bare in the light of critical, negative thought. Illich's failures can be consistently traced to his refusal to pass *beyond* negations —beyond a total rejection of the appearances of life in advanced industrial societies—to a higher synthesis. While Illich should not be criticized for failing to *achieve* such a synthesis, nevertheless he must be taken seriously to task for mystifying the nature of his own contribution and refusing to step—however tentatively—beyond it. Work is alienating—Illich rejects work; consumption is unfulfilling—Illich rejects consumption; institutions are manipulative—Illich places "nonaddictiveness" at the center of his conception of human institutions; production is bureau-

cratic—Illich glorifies the entrepreneurial and small-scale enterprise; schools are dehumanizing—Illich rejects schools; political life is oppressive and ideologically totalitarian—Illich rejects politics in favor of individual liberation. Only in one sphere does he go beyond negation, and this defines his major contribution. While technology is in fact dehumanizing (thesis), he does *not* reject technology (antithesis). Rather he goes beyond technology *and* its negation towards a schema of liberating technological forms in education.

The cost of his failure to pass beyond negation in the sphere of social relations in general, curiously enough, is an implicit affirmation of the deepest characteristics of the existing order.[31] In rejecting work, Illich affirms that it *necessarily* is alienating—reinforcing a fundamental pessimism on which the acceptance of capitalism is based; in rejecting consumption, he affirms either that it is inherently unfulfilling (the Protestant ethic), or would be fulfilling if unmanipulated; in rejecting manipulative and bureaucratic "delivery systems," he affirms the *laissez-faire* capitalist model and its core institutions; in rejecting schools, Illich embraces a commodity fetishist cafeteria-smorgasbord ideal in education; and in rejecting political action, he affirms a utilitarian individualistic conception of humanity. In all cases, Illich's analysis fails to pass beyond the given (in both its positive and negative totalities), and hence affirms it.

The most serious lapse in Illich's analysis is his implicit postulation of a human "essense" in all of us, preceding all social experience—potentially blossoming but repressed by manipulative institutions. Indeed, Illich is logically compelled to accept such a conception by the very nature of his methodology of negation. The given is capitalist (or state socialist) socialization—

[31] Indeed to stop one's analysis at negation normally leads to implicit affirmation. For a discussion of this, see "The Affirmative Character of Culture," in Herbert Marcuse, *Negations* (Boston: Beacon Press, 1968).

repressive and dehumanizing. The antithesis is no socialization at all—individuals seeking independently and detached from any mode of social integration their personal paths of development. Such a view of personal growth becomes meaningful in human terms only when anchored in some absolute human standard within the individual and anterior to the social experience that it generates.

In such a conception of individual "essence," critical judgment enters, I have emphasized, precisely at the level of sensing and interpreting one's pre-social psyche. This ability requires only demystification (negation); hence a methodology of negation is raised to a sufficient condition of a liberating social science. Dialectical analysis, on the other hand, takes negation (demystification) as the major *precondition* of liberation, but not its sufficient condition. Even the most liberating historical periods (e.g., the Reformation, the French and American Revolutions), despite their florid and passionately idealistic rhetoric, in fact responded to historically specific potentials and to limited but crucial facets of human deprivation. Dialectical analysis would view our present situation as analogous and, rejecting "human essence" as a pre-social driving force in social change, would see the central struggle of our era as specific negations *and their overcoming* in localizable areas of human concern—while embracing the ideologies that support these struggles.

The place of critical judgment (reason) in this analysis model lies in a realistic-visionary annihilation of both existing society *and* its negation-in-thought in a new, yet historically limited, synthesis. I have argued that this task requires as its point of departure the core economic institutions regulating social life—first in coming to understand their operation and the way in which they produce the outcomes of alienating work, fragmented community, environmental destruction, commodity fetishism, and other estranged cultural forms (thesis), and then in entertaining how we might negate and overcome them through political action and personal consciousness. Illich, in his next book, might leave the security and comfort of negation, and apply his creative vitality to this most demanding of tasks.

Illich's De-Schooled Utopia

SIDNEY HOOK

We are beginning to understand that the rhetoric of revolutionary extremism is not simply a put-on or a form of exhibitionism or an outburst of politicalised aesthetic fury that titillates the pent-house *rentiers* of the New Left. Not only have ideas consequences, words have consequences, too, even if the ideas they express are vague and somewhat incoherent. The inflammatory language of the Black Panthers and the blood-chilling manifestos of the Weathermen may be empty of serious content. There can be little doubt, however, that they have had a profound effect on the behavior of some of their initiates. The terrorism of the word—even revolutionary bull—prepares the way for the terrorism of the deed.

Something analogous is observable in the field of education. Paralleling the extremist position and inflated rhetoric of the revolutionist decrying the possibility of democratic social reform is the development of extremist positions in education decrying the possibility of intelligent school reform. Here, too, what was listened to with indulgence as an exaggerated expression of a universally shared dissatisfaction with the present state of schooling is beginning to have practical consequences. The existence of the school itself and the system of compulsory public education has come under fire in the United States. The professional teachers and their organisations are becoming the scapegoats of our discontent. Permanent tenure is under fierce attack in many quarters as primarily a shelter for incompetence at public expense. At the same time we are told that everyone has a natural birthright not only to learn to learn but to teach. Every citizen is not only equally concerned with education, he is equally an authority about what should be learned and how. Those educational authorities, especially the professional teachers and administrators, who are dubious about this are really authoritarians masking themselves as adepts in the pseudo-science of pedagogy. In the interest of freedom we must abolish schools whose inhibiting and demoralising effects on the personalities of their charges are worse than those of our military and penal systems.

The most recent expression of this view is found in a slight volume, *De-schooling Society* by Ivan Illich.[1] It is a book whose absurd extremism warrants little attention from anyone endowed with a normal portion of common sense. The only reason for taking

Note: Sidney Hook, "Illich's De-Schooled Utopia," *Encounter,* Jan. 1972, pp. 53–57. Reprinted with the permission of the author and publisher.

[1] *De-schooling Society.* By Ivan Illich. Calder & Boyars, £1.95; Harper & Row, $5.95.

it seriously is that some of its positions are influencing the new radical critics of American education who, without subscribing to Illich's panacea, are accepting some of his assumptions about schools and schooling to fortify their attacks on current educational theory and practice and on professional teachers as "buttresses of the Establishment." Also disquieting is the fact that Illich's views seem to have won the endorsement of some officials of educational Institutes who purvey advice for liberal fees to the school systems of the nation.

Illich's thesis is a simple one—so simple that the reader hesitates for a moment in concluding that he really means what he writes. But he does. Our schools are unmitigatedly bad. All of them? Well, almost all. Then why not try to improve schooling by taking as a model the best schools? This is hopeless, a trap, says Illich. The "hidden curriculum" of schooling, of any formal schooling, inspires the "myth" that certified teachers—bureaucrats all—can use scientific knowledge to impart "humane and efficient" education. The only remedy is to abolish all formal schools and with it all compulsory education.

What do we put in its stead? Reliance upon "self-motivated" learning, upon the processes of self-education in freedom through natural association with those who already possess skills and knowledge or who are willing to cooperate in a quest for them. This will be facilitated by four interrelated networks or "learning webs." The first will make accessible to children and students the necessary things and processes (in libraries, museums, theatres, factories and farms); the second will facilitate the exchange of skills among learners; the third is called "peer-matching": persons will advertise their educational needs or interests "in the hope of finding a partner" for mutual advantage; and, finally, diligent use will be made of a Yellow Book of self-selected and self-advertised Educators-at-Large who will list their skills and addresses and the price of their services.

The only thing clear about the operation of these networks is that the government will pay the costs. Left completely vague is the answer to the question: Who will supervise and direct this educational experience and provide for the sequential organisation of subject matters and acquisition of skills without which no discipline can be mastered? Something like the invisible hand that guarantees the harmonious adjustment of the needs of buyers and sellers in the free market is presupposed. But even less than the free market in commodities, the free market in education may not meet genuine and desirable needs while gratifying some that are not so desirable. Some of the proposals for peer-matching are suggestive of the techniques used by genteel and literate prostitutes in arranging assignations through the columns of literary periodicals. Although Illich admits that his networks of learning may be abused, he is convinced that the perils of schooling are far worse because of their restrictions on the freedom of natural self-motivated learners. How the child who is not self-motivated is to learn is left unexplained.

It is not only the school which in Illich's view prevents "personal, creative and autonomous interaction" among learners and teachers but all the major institutions of society: the state, the church, the army, the medical services, the political party, the media, the family as we know it.

Not only education but the society as a whole needs de-schooling.

One would imagine therefore that before any significant change in education can be effected we would need a total social and cultural revolution. Nonetheless Illich holds that the de-schooling of education can succeed in relative independence of the other equally necessary "de-schoolings."

Despite the extremism of his position Illich writes with an astonishing confidence and dogmatism, piling one questionable statement upon another in reckless disregard of evidence, logic, and common sense.

Middle class parents commit their children to a teacher's care to keep them from learning what the poor learn on the streets.

But parents—poor ones no less than those of the middle class—usually commit their children to schools and teachers in the hope that they will learn what they can't learn at home or in the street. (Illich seems unaware that a child who is well taught at home is not compelled to attend school.)

Teachers more often than not obstruct such learning of subject matters as goes on in a school.

In order to know this Illich would have to know how much reading, writing, arithmetic, geography, history, etc. most children learn *without* benefit of any schooling. Since he does not and cannot know this today, his remark simply slanders school teachers whose dedication to their students is no less than his own. Teachers are painted as monsters sadistically exploiting and oppressing children whose "chronological age disqualifies [them] from safeguards which are routine for adults in a modern asylum—madhouse, monastery, or jail." They need the constitutional protection of the First and Fifth Amendments!

Why should all schools, not merely authoritarian ones but those that are avowedly liberal and progressive, be charged with totalitarian oppressiveness? Because they all operate with the idea that "one person's judgment should determine what and when another person must learn." Yet, surely, when the other person is a growing child and not an adult an informed and sympathetic determination of what and when he should learn is no more improper than determining what and when he should eat. What is wrong is the imposition of the same learning (or feeding) schedules on children independently of their special needs and interests. But there is a world of difference between individualising the curriculum and, as Illich proposes, abolishing it.

Actually it is both foolish and cruel to rely for education on the casual, chance encounters of the young. Illich's assurance that the young always learn something from their experiences or become aware of their needs through raw, unstructured experience is not less absurd than his implied view that with respect to health they should be liberated from the ministrations of compulsory medical care. The young are no more always aware of what they need to know in order to grow to their full powers than they are always aware of what to do and what to avoid to achieve health. In either case what they don't know may sometimes cripple them for life. If they waited until they experienced an acute need before learning certain things, they would discover what so many foolish adults have discovered who waited to see a doctor until they had an acute need for one, *viz.*, that it was too late or costly to remedy what ailed them.

The basic question in education, explicitly denied by Illich and other New Left critics, is: "what should individuals learn" in modern society in order more readily to achieve their maximum growth as persons? The basic problem in teaching on every level (except the graduate school) is how to motivate the individual to learn joyfully yet thoroughly what he should learn—as well as what he wants to learn—until he is mature enough to take over the direction of his own education. This, of course, is a gradual process that recognises that each learner has individual needs as well as common needs.

For Illich and those he has influenced, on the other hand, the planning of new educational institutions must start with the question: "What kind of things and people might learners want to be in contact with in order to learn?" A parent who actually lived up to Illich's dictum might well find himself in difficulties with the Society for the Prevention of Cruelty to Children (if that worthy group hasn't also been abolished). Children might want to be in contact with anything from live wires and drugs to the glazed ridges of tenement roofs; they may never recover from the effects of learning about them and kindred things. Conversely, they might *not* want to be in contact with children of different races, religions, or nationalities. And yet such experiences of mixing and contact might be necessary to cure them of their prejudices and helpful in avoiding the stereotyped judgments of their elders. On Illich's view whether anyone learns anything worthwhile is purely a matter of chance. On a more sensible view, our world is too dangerous to take such chances.

The flaws in this smart, silly book can be traced to a number of assumptions explicitly made by Illich but also widely held by other romantic critics of the school system who draw back from his extremist remedies. He assumes that because children learn to speak their own language casually without going to school and without explicit instruction, they learn most other things in the same way. To be sure, children have learned to speak and walk without schooling or explicit instruction since the emergence of man from more primitive species, but all human history testifies that they do not learn to read and write as effortlessly. Before compulsory schooling was introduced the vast majority of mankind remained illiterate. Illich holds no brief for illiteracy but he assumes that literacy can be more readily acquired by abolishing schools and relying upon the casual operation of his networks to effect mastery of elementary skills. To claim that we will all learn from and teach one another as need and interest manifest themselves is to invoke pious hope that flies in the face of overwhelming evidence. Not everyone who knows something, even when he knows it well, can teach it, not to mention teach it effectively. Not everyone who is able to teach is willing or in a position to do so. Even speech depends upon the models imitated and can be immensely improved by proper schooling.

Further, some skills are best learned in youth, like writing and arithmetical computation, as well as certain habits of work,

and of thoughtfulness for others. Anyone who has seen a grown man, who has been raised in some foreign culture where no ball games were played, writhe as he vainly tries to throw a ball, understands the point. Accidents have been known to happen when persons who never having learned when children to differentiate automatically between left and right paused too long at the shouted advice to turn out of the path of an oncoming car.

Illich "hopes" that education will improve after society is de-schooled. But his conception of "hope" indicates that he has not liberated himself from metaphysical superstition. He sharply contrasts "expectation" with "hope," and downgrades the former because it means "reliance upon results which are planned and controlled by man." Schooling is a form of expectation, since it uses plans and controls, and is therefore bad. Hope "means trusting faith in the goodness of nature." It is interference with nature and human nature that produces evil. Disease presumably is the product of medicine, not the consequence of natural causes. If Illich had the courage of his hope, he would opt for the free market as well as for education free of schools in order to avoid any kind of planning and controlling of the economy.

Illich has a flair for drawing absurd conclusions from truisms. "We have all learned most of what we know outside the school." From which he infers that schools are therefore unnecessary. But unless the kind of learning is specified, it is just as true to say that most of what we learn outside of school we learn *because* of the skills, knowledge and training we learned in school. Obviously, since formal schooling is comparatively recent, human beings have learned most things, for better or worse, in the course of living. In a sense they always will. But having an experience is not *ipso facto* educational. Schooling can make a difference to what we bring to an experience to make it educationally significant. Illich pretends that "schools are designed on the assumption that there is a secret to everything in life" and that only teachers hold the key to it. The truth is that the assumptions of modern schooling are much more modest. They are: that much knowledge and many skills are interesting and useful in helping people cope with their experience and in enhancing the quality of their lives that they can be learned by systematic schooling more easily than by casual encounters with things and persons or by reliance on "the goodness of nature"; that the acquisition of knowledge and mastery of skills requires a grasp of sequential order in subject matter; that teachers can be helpful in the process of learning until students are in a position intelligently to choose their own patterns of growth.

Illich disputes all this. He claims that schools and teachers prevent children from learning by chaining them to alternating routines of trivial play and drill. According to him we tend to romanticise what we have learned in schools. No one, he claims, really learned how to read in school. We learned outside of school from parents or older siblings or from the boy across the way. He leaves unexplained how, in the U.S.A., entire generations of children of immigrant parents who could neither speak, read nor write English, learned English more or less adequately. He has read about all the weaknesses of the American public school; but he is ignorant of its achievements.

The animus against school teachers extends to a point where he resents and deplores reliance upon official certification by the state of the capacity to teach or to practice any profession. For all his talk about autonomy and independence and creative rediscovery in education he bemoans the passing of "personal discipleship." The Yellow Book of Educators-at-Large will probably have a special supplement on Gurus. Not unaware of the dangers, he nonetheless would abandon all official restraints or controls on those who hold themselves out to be healers of the sick in mind and body. Their expertise would be determined by popularity polls of students, patients, and clients. "The right to teach any skill"—including surgery and engineering?—"should come under the protection of free speech." For him academic freedom is not the right of *qualified* and administrative interference. Academic freedom is a human right; it does not have to be earned. His open society therefore would be an open society for medical and educational quacks without any safeguards for their victims that intellectual skepticism, the by-product of effective teaching, can produce. Never mind the casualties! Of course, schools of medicine, engineering and education today have their casualties, too. But the remedy for poor schools is better schools, not their abolition.

What makes Illich's proposal to abolish schools gratuitously foolish is that some of his suggested webs of learning, with appropriate revisions and safeguards, are in use today as supplementary aids to basic schooling. Compulsory education is an institution, not a process of learning. Students can no more be compelled to learn than to love. Compulsory education expresses the responsibility of society to all its children, especially where parental responsibility is absent. It does not go on forever. By the time students have reached the school-leaving age, they should be in a position to choose freely and intelligently the kind of continuing education, in school or out, they wish to pursue.

The meeting of extremes in politics is an old story. The voice of Bernadine Dohrn and the Weathermen is hardly distinguishable from that of Charles Manson and his family. In education the mindless Right which opposes public education sounds very much like some factions among the mindless Left. For both the state is always the enemy whose interference with the natural order must be resisted even if it is the order of anarchy. The case in general for compulsory education, not necessarily through one kind of school or any formal school, is even better than the case for compulsory vaccination which in Illich's eyes must also appear as an abridgement of human freedom and a betrayal of hope "in the goodness of nature." In a democratic community the right to learn is a human right. The community owes a responsibility to all children to provide them with the opportunities to develop their powers to make informed and reflective choices not only for the sake of their survival but its own. Under certain circumstances this responsibility may override the rights of parents who are either indifferent or hostile to their children's development.

It is significant that in democratic societies schools are not restricted. Nor is it fortuitous that sophisticated apologists of oppressive régimes in the past have been hostile to universal compulsory education out of fear that "the lower classes," having caught glimpses of the great legacies of human culture, would seek to enlarge their share of it. Nothing would please those who are opposed to desegregation in American education today more than the abolition of compulsory schooling. Like so many other contemporary reactionaries on the new Left, Illich talks a great deal about freedom but neglects the principles of intellectual authority and organization necessary to negotiate the conflicts of freedom. The result is that his free society is one in which everyone is free "to do one's thing" no matter if the consequences result, as in all anarchist utopias that rely on the goodness of nature, in the universal loss of hard-won freedoms.

Analysis of Values
and
Conflicts of Interest

Many persons who are disaffected with modern society call for its decentralization. Conservatives decry the threat of big government, while radicals argue that corporate power should be drastically reduced. People of many different political affiliations oppose what some sociologists refer to as "institutionalism." They feel that peoples' lives are becoming increasingly dominated by the dictates of impersonal bureaucratic institutions—both private and public. Individuals and groups that embrace this view believe that society should be changed so that it becomes more sensitive to the needs of the individual, and less likely to impose bureaucratic restrictions.

Illich believes that the school is an oppressive, bureaucratic institution; its very existence is to him a social problem. He implies that the school is the primary institution of bureaucratized society, because it transmits to the child values that promote bureaucratic organization. In other words, school robs children of initiative, instills in them an acquiesence to authority, and teaches them to passively accept external control. Illich implies that the school and the attitudes that support structured schooling must be eliminated before more extensive social change can be realized. He shares the values of those who believe that society needs to be changed and humanized. His ideas about deschooling are a program for this change. Illich also represents the more specific interests of frustrated educators who believe that the present system of education is a failure. Few of these critics agree that school should be completely eliminated, but many concur with the main thrust of Illich's critique and seek to discover new methods to promote authentic learning.

Gintis agrees with much of Illich's critique, but disagrees with his solution. Gintis, a Marxist, believes that economic institutions must first be changed if broader social transformation is to take place. Because Marxists argue that the institutions providing for persons' material needs are the most important, they reason that efforts to reform other institutions must come after or in concert with economic change. The Gintis article is supportive of the groups that advocate radical socioeconomic change. Radicals often consider the social criticism of humanists like Illich to be fragmented and diversionary. They argue that these critiques only serve to divert attention away from the major problem, capitalism.

There is another kind of interest that has not been discussed. Sociologists belong to various schools than can be considered interest groups. Membership in such a group, even if it is indirect and identificational, affects the style and content of sociological analysis. For example, Gintis belongs to the Marxist School and his emphasis on mode of production and alienation reflects major concerns of this School. Illich, Hook, and most of the other contributors to this book are also associated with schools or groups that express internal agreement on assumptions about man and society, on methods of data collection, and on conceptual approaches. Members of a School are awarded recognition by their peers on the basis of their ability to do quality work within the limits of the accepted mode of analysis. This reward structure naturally affects the interpretation of supposed social problems.

Most Americans believe that the educational system provides people with a better understanding of themselves and the world about them. People who so value education usually support schooling, because schooling and education are generally equated. Hook expresses the majority view of the school by describing it as a necessary institution that should be improved and made stronger rather than eliminated. According to his view, the child should not be left to himself to determine what should be learned. Instead, he implies that the child should be taught what is considered socially useful so that he can become a successful and constructive member of society. Hook enunciates values that uphold the traditional function of schooling and in doing so he represents those who are concerned with the maintenance of social order, which the school promotes by transmitting social rules, values and traditions to the child. Hook's position also supports the groups who have a direct interest in perpetuating schools—teachers, administrators, and others who are engaged in the process of schooling. It should be pointed out that Hook has been associated in recent years with a number of groups who have opposed radical activities in schools and universities because it might lower educational quality.

5

GOVERNMENT SURVEILLANCE:

Conducted in the National Interest or Threat to Individual Freedom?

The morality of government officials has been called into question on more than one occasion. The indictment and conviction of numerous high officials in the Nixon administration over the Watergate affair marked the high point of this phenomenon. However, the debate over the continued government surveillance of private citizens poses even graver questions. The computerization and easy retrieval of information on a massive number of American citizens has made it increasingly possible for government officials to intrude on the privacy of citizens. Given the past and present occurrences of immorality in government, we should be sensitized to the possibility of misuse of information accumulated on private citizens.

This section includes the testimony of various government officials, private organizations, and citizens before the Subcommittee on Constitutional Rights of the Senate Committee on the Judiciary. Although it focuses on computerized government data banks, questions are also raised about other forms of government surveillance.

This section opens with a description of federal data banks. It is pointed out that government information gathering has been expanding since the first decennial census in 1790, but in recent years the addition of the computer has added a significant new dimension to the problem. The computer has made possible the creation of a national instant recall data bank ". . . incorporating dossiers of 'cradle-to-grave' information on every United States citizen." A large number of government agencies currently have data banks which ". . . can be rapidly transmitted, upon request, to authorized agencies and individuals throughout the country." The scope of the present federal activity includes employee records, military records, and information on private citizens from many sources including security risk data, the census and internal revenue reports.

The debate over the efficacy of wide-ranging data collection on private individuals follows the brief introductory discussion. Presented initially are arguments in favor of current government methods. John Volpe, former United States Secretary of Transportation, discusses the National Driver Register. This is a ". . . record of individuals whose licenses have been denied, terminated, or withdrawn, except for withdrawals of less than six months or for moving violations." This seemingly innocuous list takes on menacing proportions when Volpe points out that it contains over two million names. The potential threat increases when he admits that there have been errors in the past in the use of the list. However, Volpe contends that he is aware of the potential threat to individual privacy, but argues that the register saves lives, it does not destroy them.

Robert Froehlke, former United States Assistant Secretary of Defense, discusses the collection of military data on civilians in the 1960s. He argues that this collection of data, which was *officially* ended in 1970, was a direct result of the racial and anti-war disorders of the 1960s. He asserts that in 1967 the military was confronted with the possibility of simultaneous involvement in twenty-five disorders and needed information to aid in the commitment and deployment of federal troops. In the early years of the 1960s, data were collected through liaison work and the public media, but soon moved to direct agent observation. This activity increased following the Detroit riots. Froehlke asserts that this activity was never prohibited by any federal or state law. Froehlke claims that the data collected was not used ". . . to the prejudice of any individual or organization. It is difficult to perceive how the constitutional rights or even the right of privacy could be impinged by collection of such information."

Arguing the Justice Department's position, William Rehnquist contends that there is a need to maximize various investigative techniques, including modern data processing ". . . in combating organized crime, preventing acts of violence, controlling civil disorders where appropriate, and enforcing numerous federal statutes." He contends that the Justice Department is aware of the threat to individual rights, but he *rejects* ". . . the suggestion that the mere potential for abuse of these technological advances is a sufficient reason in itself to dispense with their use in the investigation and prosecution of crime." The real vice is not surveillance per se, but the surveillance of things that are not the department's business. Rehnquist, too, recognizes that there have been "isolated" abuses, but he feels that we can rely in the future on the "self-discipline" of the Executive Branch.

Former Senator Sam Ervin argues against the existence of government data banks. His view is that more and more people are expressing themselves politically and becoming involved in political activities. Modern technology has provided them with a more efficient way of registering their views, but it has also placed in government hands more efficient ways of recording that dissent. What is recorded is immutable and stays with the individual throughout his life, no matter what changes the individual himself goes through. Modern technology has ". . . given the government the power to take note of anything whether it be right or wrong, relevant to any purpose or not, and to retain it forever." Ervin recognizes that even if the people collecting such data are not malevolent, there are potential areas of trouble such as collecting information that is none of the government's business, keeping it too long, making it part of a network of data systems, not giving the individual the right to know the information is there, to review it, and to know the use to which it is put. Ervin concludes that these data systems, when misused, can lead to "the worst sort of tyranny."

The then-Democratic representative from New York, Edward Koch, focuses on the problem of military surveillance. He points out that the military apparently collected data on Illinois public officials like Senator Stevenson, Judge Kerner, and Congressman Mikva. He argues that it is apparent that ". . . the Army expanded its role to maintain records about, and to spy on, citizens who might conceivably be unsympathetic to present government policies." He supports legislation to limit surveillance and is sensitive to the problems raised by Sam Ervin. For similar reasons, Ralph Stein, a former Army intelligence officer who was engaged in domestic intelligence in 1967 and 1968, contends that ". . . the military must be permanently removed from the domestic intelligence picture."

The American Friends Service Committee attacks a wide range of government surveillance and data collection activities. They describe a variety of ways in which the government has spied on its citizens. They conclude: "America must be guaranteed that it will become neither a police state nor a garrison state and that current activities leading to such developments will be stopped and reversed." Similarly, the American Civil Liberties Union attacks what it labels the "police state mentality." They feel that our society simply cannot function if its citizens believe that they are being observed and recorded. They conclude that we must balance potential gains in law enforcement against the costs to freedom.

The last article by Nat Hentoff considers the issue of surveillance in its broadest possible terms. He discusses surveillance of all types and contends that we are embarking on a grim path that can lead to a *1984* world in which Big Brother is watching from birth to death.

Controversy Over Federal
"Data Banks"

INTRODUCTION [1]

A recurring subject of congressional discussion in recent years has been the question of the extent to which the Federal Government may collect and utilize files of personal information on private individuals. In the present 92nd Congress, hearings conducted earlier this year before the Senate's Constitutional Rights Subcommittee have sought to examine the overall Federal information-gathering role and to assess its scope and implications. The hearings are expected to result, later in the session, in broad legislative proposals which would impose rigorous collection and dissemination standards for such information files and establish a "watchdog" agency to protect individuals against Federal data-collection practices which may imperil basic rights of privacy.

Dating from the first decennial census in 1790, the governmental information-gathering role has expanded as government itself has grown. Today, the accumulation of data on individuals for a variety of governmental purposes has become a major activity of many Federal agencies.

Note: Congressional Digest, 1971, pp. 225–30, 256.

[1] Introduction written by the editors of *Congressional Digest.* Reproduced by permission.

A significant new dimension has been added in recent years with the development of high-speed data retrieval systems, many based on computer technology—a trend which has led some public officials to predict the ultimate establishment of a national computerized data bank incorporating dossiers of "cradle-to-grave" information on every United States citizen.

These developments, together with advances in the field of communications, have given rise in a number of Federal establishments to creation of so-called "data banks"—mechanized or computerized files of instantly available information which can be rapidly transmitted, upon request, to authorized agencies and individuals throughout the country.

In certain areas of government—perhaps most notably that of crime control—the benefits of such systems have been widely acknowledged. In some other areas, however, where their application is less clearly identified with public safety or national security, collections of personal data have been subject to frequent and growing criticism.

Such criticism has emphasized, among other objections, the compulsory nature of much information-gathering; the maintenance of non-criminal files on individuals of which the subjects are unaware; and the inability of individuals in many instances to learn the contents of records concerning them or to correct or update allegedly inaccurate information they may contain.

Defending the use of data banks are many officials of government, particularly in the Executive Branch, who are charged with highly complex and frequently sensitive responsibilities in an era when disruption of government has become an overt tool of dissident individuals and groups. Arguing for their necessity to the national interest in the government of a large and mobile society, many who oppose rigorous curtailment of the present governmental role maintain that existing safeguards, properly observed, adequately protect the privacy rights of individuals without impairing what is regarded as a vital role played by data banks in the operation of the Federal Government.

The issue, whose underlying subject area has been chosen by the Speech Association of America as this year's intercollegiate debate topic, is neither simple nor clear-cut. Nor are the volume of personal data presently in government files and the related questions of necessity and propriety of such activity easily assessible.

In consequence, as will be seen in this month's Pro & Con discussion, debate over the subject ranges across a broad spectrum of viewpoints. Fundamental questions of how to manage the growing Federal banks of data on individuals—whether to condone them in present form, to curtail and regulate some or all of them, or whether to abolish some information-gathering activities outright—are expected to receive increasing attention in Congress in the months ahead.

THE SCOPE OF PRESENT FEDERAL ACTIVITY

Records maintained by elements of the Federal Government on individuals vary from agency to agency both as to volume and to scope of information recorded. Such differences reflect, among other factors, particular functions performed by agencies involved,

provisions of Federal law which specify responsibilities and programs administered by such agencies, national security implications of the agency's mission and, in some instances, differences in administrative philosophy among the Federal agencies and departments involved.

Civilian Personnel Records

A fundamental class of records maintained throughout the Federal Government incorporates information of various types on its own employees. Commonly included in Federal personnel dossiers are employment applications, pay and leave records, proficiency reports and promotion records, results of physical examinations, and information relative to the security clearance status appropriate to the employee and his position. Basic employee information generally includes name, date of birth, social security number, educational background, professional qualifications, grade, date of rank or grade, job assignment, job-related experience and, where applicable, disciplinary actions to which he has been subjected.

Military Records

The above elements of information, applicable to civilian employees, are repeated in somewhat modified form in the case of present and former members of the Armed Forces. Data pertinent to service personnel having current duty or standby status is maintained in active files of the Department of Defense or other appropriate agency. Records of former military personnel are maintained in several records repositories in various parts of the country and, in limited form, in the files of the Veterans Administration. Additionally, as will be noted below under "Defense," combined Department of Defense files reflecting investigations and security clearance status include military personnel who have been the subject of actions related thereto.

Information on Private Individuals

In recent years increasing attention has been focused on the extent to which agencies of the Federal Government maintain records on individuals who are not government employees. Some such records are of general "security" nature, identifying persons who have received various levels of security clearance or those who for various reasons are not regarded as eligible for Federal employment or for benefits under certain Federal programs. Other records relate to law enforcement, identifying criminal suspects, wanted persons, arrested or convicted individuals, and those engaged in or associated with organized crime.

A further, and much vaster, class of records is general in nature. Some files falling under this category—those records maintained by the Census Bureau, the Bureau of Internal Revenue, the Social Security Administration, among others—include highly detailed information on individual citizens.

No overall picture is available which in practicable form would reflect the full scope of Federal information-gathering on individuals. The analysis which follows, taken from a staff summary and related documents prepared by the Senate Committee on Constitutional Rights, consists of a selected list of Federal agencies and records maintained by them; it is intended to be illustrative rather than definitive.

Omitted are descriptions of personal information maintained by regulatory agencies (FCC, FTC, SEC, AEC, among others) and by agencies such as the Small Business Administration which maintain what are broadly classed as applicant financial records. Also omitted are records of such departments as Agriculture, Labor, and the Post Office, although data banks are employed in some degree in connection with the work of each.

CIVIL SERVICE

The Security Investigations Index consists of approximately 10,250,000 index cards listing every personnel investigation made by the Commission and other agencies since 1939. Cards show, for the person named, when an investigation was made, what agency made it, and where the investigative file is located. Information is derived from agencies making the investigations listed; information from the index is available on request to any personnel or security official having a bona fide employment or investigative interest in the individual.

The Security File consists of approximately 2,120,000 index cards containing lead information to persons who might be proven ineligible for government clearance because of questioned loyalty or subversive activities. The file primarily involves private citizens, and is developed from published hearings of Federal and State legislative committees, public investigative bodies, reports of investigation, publications of subversive organizations, and various other newspapers and periodicals. The file is used extensively by investigative and intelligence officials of various Federal agencies, particularly in connection with national agency checks, inquiry cases, and full field investigations in connection with Federal employment.

COMMERCE

In addition to a data bank on departmental personnel, four non-intelligence-oriented compilations of records are maintained on individuals: data on seafaring personnel; the National Defense Executive Reserve (1,500 entries); Merchant Marine Academy Students, including 32 items of information on each of some 13,000 graduates of the Academy, principally designed to reflect current employment status.

Decennial Census: The fourth, and numerically largest data bank maintained by the Federal Government on a current basis, is the nation's decennial census records. The Bureau of the Census maintains on microfilm all census records from 1909 to date, ranging in growing increments from 76 million persons enumerated in 1900 to approximately 204 million counted in the 1970 census. The scope of information gathered has varied over the years; since 1940 a housing census has been included. The most comprehensive census undertaken from the standpoint of personal information gathered was that completed in 1970. The Bureau produces and makes public extensive compilations of statistical data based on the decennial censuses; individual information is available only to the individual concerned or to his legal heirs.

Patent Office. Data banks maintained by the Patent Office include information on patents and the identities of those holding them, but do not contain personal information.

DEFENSE

In addition to military service records and civilian personnel files maintained by the Department, a locator file, shortly to be computerized, exists as the Defense Central Index of Investigations. The Index identifies by individual name the location of files concerning an unspecified number of present and former service personnel, civilian employees, and contractor personnel.

Included in departmental records are approximately seven million Army investigative files relating to security, loyalty, or criminal investigations concerning the above classes of persons.

The Defense Supply Agency additionally maintains an index file of approximately 1.5 million personnel cards detailing security clearance information for individuals employed by contractors engaged in classified work for the Department of Defense and eleven other Federal agencies. Information included is vital statistics, clearance sought, investigation conducted, and action taken; where adjudicative action has been taken, reason for issuance or denial of a clearance as well as information on the individual's background, personal life, personality, habits, etc., are included. Information in the file is made available on a need-to-know basis by the above user agencies; clearance status information only is made available to cleared contractors concerning persons actually or potentially in their employ.

HEW

Among the extensive records on individuals maintained by component agencies of the Department of Health, Education and Welfare, two groups are considered major information systems: the National Center for Health Statistics (NCHS) and the Social Security Administration's (SSA) data systems. Additionally, the Department provides financial support to a number of computerized data banks operated by State and local governments, public school systems, colleges and universities, and health and welfare organizations.

The NCHS, considered a key component of the Federal statistical system, provides statistical intelligence on vital events, health, injury, illness, impairments, use of medical, dental, hospital and other health care services, and on facilities and manpower providing these services. HEW reports that, while much of the "input" into the system is individual-oriented, with persons identified, confidentiality is maintained by authorizing release of information only in summary or statistical form which does not identify individuals by name.

SSA Data Systems are so extensive as to render statistics concerning their scope largely meaningless. Data banks maintained contain information on all individuals issued a social security account number, beneficiaries of the major social welfare programs conducted under authority of the Social Security Acts, and earnings information on those subject to social security taxes, among other categories of data. The records of SSA in Fiscal 1970, for example, were affected by receipt of 375 million individual items of data on earnings of social security number holders, over 17 million hospital bills for reimbursements under Medicare hospital insurances, and about 44 million bills for doctors' and related health services covered under the medical insurance part of Medicare.

HUD

Among the records maintained by elements of the Department of HUD which include information on individuals are two basic groups:

Insurance Inventories: An automated file with 4.5 million entries showing home insurance in force, containing mortgagee's name, unpaid balance, and a fiscal record of his account. A second file of 800,000 entries shows mortgage insurance in force on projects. A third file with 400,000 entries lists information on defaulted home improvement loans, including the name of the defaulting borrower. Additional records concern participation shares and mortgage note servicing.

Individual Characteristics: This group of records includes a 60,000-entry file developed by low-rent tenant surveys, including names of tenants. A 720,000-entry file identifies sponsor organizations and their corporate officers participating in FHA multi-family housing programs. A 350,000 card index lists

individuals or firms which have been the subject of or prominently mentioned in investigations since 1954.

JUSTICE

Civil Disturbance System. The system, used as an intelligence aid for planning purposes as well as on-the-scene information for use in police operations during a disorder, consists of two fully automated files. The Subject File contains information on approximately 13,200 persons involved in civil disturbances; the Incident File contains records of about 14,000 events that have developed into civil disorders or have had the potential for such a disorder. The Incident File contains descriptions of the event without listing names.

The Subject File contains name, age or date of birth, sex, race, home city and State, aliases, and criminal record. A code number cross-indexes the Subject File with the Incident File, which does not contain personal data.

Only the Justice Department has direct access to the files. Information is made available on a need-to-know basis to other Federal agencies and law enforcement bodies. The system is utilized to respond to requests for information by the Attorney General or his principal assistants in connection with either prosecutive functions or for intelligence evaluation. Additionally, information is provided any concerned Federal official on a need-to-know basis about potential disorders so that adequate preparations can be made to prevent or contain such activity.

Organized Crime Intelligence System. A computerized file and card index, the latter containing some 400,000 cards referring to approximately 200,000 names, the system includes financial information, participation in illegal organizations, business connections, associations, habits, or any other data on the the individual listed of possible future value in investigations, prosecutions, or intelligence analysis. Information has been gathered by Federal investigative agencies in the normal conduct of their business or in response to specific notification of interest. Only the Department of Justice has direct access to the system, although at departmental discretion, information may be made available to State and local law enforcement agencies involved in investigation of organized crime. Primary use of information is by strike forces and attorneys of the Organized Crime Section.

Bureau of Narcotics and Dangerous Drugs. Addict Files. These identify approximately 70,000 persons reported by Federal, State, and local agencies as illicitly using a narcotic drug. Information includes name, criminal identification number, city and State of birth, date of birth, sex, race, drug cures, drug used, length of use, original reason for use, reporting agency and city, and date reported. Information is obtained from arrest records maintained by law enforcement agencies at all levels. Data is available on request to Federal, State and local enforcement agencies for law enforcement purposes in the form of statistical data only. Identifying data is available only to those agencies which originated the file. Data is made available in statistical form to the Congress and other Federal agencies as well as State and local enforcement and health agencies.

Defendant Statistical Program. Records identify approximately 2,900 individuals arrested by the Bureau of Narcotics and Dangerous Drugs for violations of drug laws. Information is obtained from the individual following his arrest and includes particulars of his arrest, past criminal and/or drug record, and related data. Information is published in statistical form only for the use of Congress, other Federal agencies, and the public.

Federal Bureau of Investigation. Fingerprint and Criminal Indentification Files. A

national clearinghouse for such records, the files presently contain approximately 199 million fingerprint cards—at present visually classified, manually searched, and divided into criminal and civil file sections. In the criminal group, 19 million individuals are represented; the civil file is comprised of cards on 67 million persons—Federal employees and applicants, Armed Forces personnel, civilian employees in National Defense industries, aliens, and persons desiring to have their fingerprints on file for identification purposes.

Fingerprint cards contain the name, signature, and physical description of the person fingerprinted; information concerning the reason for fingerprinting; identity of contributing agency; date printed; and, where applicable, the charge and disposition or sentence. Some cards contain the residential address, occupation and employment of the person fingerprinted.

Identification records, compiled from fingerprint cards contain the identity of the contributors of the cards; names and aliases of the subject of the record; agency identifying numbers; dates of arrests and/or incarcerations; charges; and dispositions. No other information concerning an individual's background, personal life, personality or habits is included in these records.

Fingerprint cards are submitted by over 14,000 contributors representing local, State and Federal law enforcement agencies, including penal institutions, the Federal Government, and organizations authorized by State laws to contribute fingerprints for official purposes.

The FBI's records are furnished to authorized officials of the Federal Government, the States, cities, and penal and other institutions for their official use only. Written record is maintained of each dissemination of an identification record, including the date disseminated and the identity of the receiving agency.

The FBI began computerization of Federal criminal offender identification records on May 1, 1970. Later that year the Attorney

General directed the FBI to establish a nationwide computerized system for the exchange of criminal history information between the FBI and the States for the benefit of all law enforcement arms—police, prosecutions, courts, probations, and corrections. The goal of this project is a computerized national index of criminal history records concerning serious offenders which can be queried over communication lines by remote law enforcement computer terminals, utilizing computer and communication facilities presently serving the FBI National Crime Information Center.

National Crime Information Center. The NCIC is the FBI's computerized index containing information on wanted persons and stolen and/or missing property. Information concerning individuals is retained only in the Wanted Person File which contains records of warrants and descriptive data on the persons wanted. The file is completely computerized with extensive communications networks among local, State, and Federal law-enforcement agencies who may enter records directly into the index from type-writer-like terminal devices in their respective departments. Such arrests are immediately available in response to query by other agencies participating in the system.

Information in the Wanted Person File relates to individuals for whom Federal warrants are outstanding or for individuals who have committed or have been identified with an offense classified as a felony or serious misdemeanor for whom the jurisdiction originating the entry has been issued a warrant. Probation or parole violators with outstanding warrants are also entered in the National Crime Information Center. Law enforcement agencies in the Federal Government, the 50 States, District of Columbia, Puerto Rico, and Canada have direct on-line access to the computer records; the system is used to identify suspects and apprehend fugitives.

Descriptive data recorded includes name, sex, race, nationality, date of birth, height, weight, hair color, FBI number, NCIC fingerprint classification, miscellaneous identification numbers, Social Security number, driver's license data, offense for which warrant was issued and date of warrant, and data identifying license plates and automobiles associated with the wanted person.

Known Professional Check Passers File. The FBI's PROCHEK is a tape storage of records containing information on approximately 2,000 prolific bad-check passers. Information includes a description of the individual (age and appearance), his method of operation, and the check format (how his bad checks are customarily filled out).

Information is collected from existing FBI investigative records, and is accessible only to FBI personnel involved in official investigations concerning bad checks.

Immigration and Naturalization Service. Alien Reports File. This file is maintained in the district offices and designated suboffices of I&NS, and contains reports submitted by aliens in the United States each year during the month of January. A total of 4,247,377 aliens reported their addresses during January 1970.

Records contain the individual's name, date and place of birth, country of nationality, date and place of entry into the United States, immigration status at time of entry, length of time for which admitted, and U.S. and foreign addresses.

The file is designed to serve mainly as a locator. Only security and enforcement agencies of the Federal Government have access to information from this system. Its major use is to answer inquiries relating to an individual's immigration status and location of any relating files.

Master Index. Maintained in the central offices of I&NS, this index contains names and other identifying characteristics of the approximately 40 million persons admitted to or excluded from this country since 1952, as well as sponsors of record. Records contain the individual's name and date and place of birth, country of nationality, date and place of entry into the U.S., immigration status at time of entry, case file number, and location of the office holding the individual's file.

The file is designed primarily as a locator, used solely by security and enforcement agencies of the Federal Government.

Nonimmigrant Index. This index contains names and other identifying characteristics of approximately 500,000 individuals admitted to the United States for temporary periods of time, and who must eventually depart from this country. Only security and enforcement agencies of the Federal Government have access to information from the index, whose primary function is to assist in the control of aliens during the periods of their temporary stay in this country.

SELECTIVE SERVICE

No data bank as such is maintained, although some information is being computerized at the national headquarters level at the present time. Basic information maintained is data on individual registrants, filed by individuals at local board offices; information on registration, classification, physical examinations, and induction maintained by local boards and State headquarters; data maintained at national headquarters relating to special studies and that obtained from State offices for inclusion in semi-annual reports to the Congress. All above files are used exclusively by the Selective Service System; no information is routinely included on background, personal life, personality, or habits of registrants.

STATE

Passport Office. "Lookout File." The Lookout File is a completely computerized file of approximately 243,135 individuals who have been placed in the file for a variety of reasons: defectors, expatriates, and repatriates whose activities or background demand further inquiry (3,805 persons) ; wanted in connection with criminal activity (6,710) ; outstanding court order restricting travel or involvement in custody or desertion case (2,245) ; indebtedness to U.S. (8,680) ; Organized Crime and Rackets list (7,312) ; known or suspected communist or subversive (14,860) ; loss of U.S. citizenship (110,572) ; delinquent or suspected delinquent in military obligations (800) ; not U.S. citizen and not clear ever possessed U.S. citizenship (13,891) ; previous passport issued on insufficient evidence (12,987) ; miscellaneous or reason unknown and there is lookout (9,925) .

The principal use of the Lookout File is to identify those passport applications which require other than routine adjudication in determining eligibility. In addition, whenever an application is "flagged," the original source of the lookout is notified that the individual has applied for a passport.

Requests for additions to the file are received from various sections of the State Department, other government agencies, and, in the limited category of child custody cases, from an interested parent or guardian. Direct access to the file is limited to personnel in the Department of State involved in passport matters whose official duties require access. When an individual whose name is in the file applies for a passport, this fact is provided to requesting agencies.

TRANSPORTATION

National Highway Safety Bureau. National Driver Register Service. The National Driver Register Service is a computerized record of the names of persons whose license to drive has been denied, terminated or temporarily withdrawn by a State or political subdivision thereof. Approximately 2.6 million individuals are identified by name, alias, physical characteristics, social security number, date and place of birth.

Information comes from voluntary reports submitted by State officials from their files. Access to information in the Register is limited to Federal agencies, States, and political subdivisions of States, and only with respect to an individual applicant for a motor vehicle operator's license. The brochure describing the Register, however, envisions its use by other than driver license administrators. Examples given include police, prosecutors, judges, school administrators, insurance firms, and transportation companies.

A printout on each name requested by an authorized agency will include the personal information above noted, as well as the reason for license revocation, the date the license was withdrawn, the date the person is eligible to have it restored, and the date of restoration (where reported) .

TREASURY

Customs Bureau. The Customs Bureau maintains a computerized data bank of suspect information which is available on a 24-hour basis to Customs agents and inspectors throughout the United States. Some 3,000 suspect records derived from informer, fugitive, and suspect lists maintained at U.S. ports of entry are presently included, with plans to expand the proportions and use of the data bank. The file is used to identify suspect persons and vehicles at various ports of entry into the U.S., and includes name and address, social security number, citizenship, race, sex, date of birth, physical description, driver's license, suspect category, vehicle information, aliases, known associates, and "remarks." Information in the file is available on a need-to-know basis to law enforcement agencies.

Internal Revenue Service. A comprehen-

sive data bank is maintained by IRS in the the form of tax returns filed by every taxliable individual and corporate entity in the United States. IRS data can be made available to:

1. Executive departments and establishments of the Federal Government in connection with matters officially before the requestor. Information may be used as evidence in any proceeding conducted by or before any department or establishment of the U.S. to which the U.S. is a party. Data is obtained by written request on the part of such Federal agencies, and is made available in accordance with rules which vary somewhat as they pertain to different agencies.
2. Committees of the Congress upon written request indicating authorization in the form of a properly-adopted Committee resolution.
3. States, the District of Columbia, Puerto Rico, and U.S. possessions when requested by the chief executive official of such jurisdiction to assist in the administration of local tax laws. Available to the States for this purpose since 1935, tax information concerning all citizens of a given State has been made available in recent years on magnetic tape to facilitate comparison of returns and identification of non-filers. In 1968, 26 States and the District of Columbia utilized this service; in 1969 the District and 30 States did so.

Other IRS data reflects tax audits, payment status of non-withheld income received by taxpayers, and administrative and judicial actions undertaken against individual and corporate taxpayers.

A further compilation of personal data maintained by IRS lists individuals who have registered firearms in compliance with Federal law as well as licensed dealers and others required to be licensed under Title I (State Firearms Control Assistance) of the Gun Control Act of 1968. Information from this file is considered in the public domain, and is available upon written request.

Secret Service. Among the information collected and maintained on a partially computerized basis by the United States Secret Service is that considered "protective" in nature, counterfeiting and forgery information, and data on gold and "gold coins." Scope of such data banks is not made public, but includes information derived from other Federal agencies on a continuing basis in areas of concern to the Secret Service.

Information affecting the Service's responsibility, for protecting the President and other designated persons includes:

"A. Information pertaining to a threat, plan or attempt by an individual, a group, or an organization to physically harm or embarrass the persons protected by the U.S. Secret Service, or any other high U.S. Government official at home or abroad.

"B. . . . pertaining to individuals, groups, or organizations who have plotted, attempted, or carried out assassinations of senior officials of domestic or foreign governments.

"C. . . . concerning the use of bodily harm or assassination as a political weapon. This should include training and techniques used to carry out the act.

"D. . . . on persons who insist upon personally contacting high Government officials for the purpose of redress of imaginary grievances, etc.

"E. . . . on any person who makes oral or written statements about high Government officials in the following categories: (1) threatening statements, (2) irrational statements, and (3) abusive statements.

"F. . . . on professional gate crashers.

"G. . . . pertaining to 'Terrorist' bombings.

"H. . . . pertaining to the ownership or concealment by individuals or groups of caches of firearms, explosives, or other implements of war.

"I. . . . regarding anti-American or anti-U.S. Government demonstrations in the United States or overseas.

"J. . . . regarding civil disturbances."

Information files are, as noted above, maintained on persons and incidents involving counterfeiting of U.S. or foreign obligations (currency, coins, stamps, bonds, U.S. Treasurer's checks, Treasury securities, Department of Agriculture food stamps coupons, etc.), as well as forgery, alteration, or fraudulent negotiation of U.S. Treasurer's checks and U.S. Government bonds.

VETERANS

In addition to a data bank on its own employees, the VA maintains two such banks affecting an unspecified number of the estimated 28 million veterans now living.

The first of these contains data on beneficiaries of various VA benefits, with special reference to eligibility for benefits and location. The second consists of data on veterans who are patients, and includes relevant medical records and information on eligibility for medical care.

Such records are available only for the use of the Veterans Administration; information is made available to other government agencies only in the form of statistical summaries, although some information is made available in form identifying individuals—lists of disabled veterans to veterans organizations, for example, as well as lists of holders of government insurance policies for specified users and purposes.

Is the Present Scope of Collecting Data on Private Individuals Necessary to the National Interest?

HON. JOHN A. VOLPE

"No doubt many of the disclosures of the past several months have increased everyone's awareness and concerns over the use of data banks. There can be no question that the more efficient we become at gathering information of all kinds, the more insistent we must be against invasions of individual privacy. I assure you that the Department of Transportation will continue to be sensitive to this issue, and that at no time will we knowingly allow data collection or dissemination which violates the constitutional safeguards upon which our personal liberties are guaranteed.

"At the outset I would like to emphasize two important points with respect to the National Driver Register that differentiate it from many federally operated data banks.

"First, the Federal Government is not the source or the originator of the data contained in the Register. The information stored in the Register is not the work product of government agents in the field, nor is it the result of surveillance of unsuspecting

Note: John A. Volpe, *Congressional Digest*, 1971, pp. 232, 234, 236. Reproduced by permission. From testimony given before the Subcommittee on Constitutional Rights of the Senate Committee on the Judiciary on March 11, 1971, concerning operations of the National Driver Register.

individuals. The Register is simply a depository for State-collected and State-furnished information which is part of a State's public record. In most States, this record is available to anyone who requests it.

"Secondly, the Federal Government makes no use of this data, except in a very limited area provided for by law.

"A National Driver Register was first suggested in a 1959 report by the Secretary of Commerce to the House Public Works Committee on the federal role in highway safety. In that report, it was pointed out that one million driver licenses issued by the States had been revoked.

"Originally, the idea of a Register had been suggested by State officials, who pointed out that individuals with a revoked license in one State were acquiring a new one in another.

"The legislation establishing the Register was enacted in 1960, and provided for a listing of all individuals who had their licenses revoked for driving while intoxicated or because of a conviction of a traffic violation involving loss of life. In 1961, the legislation was amended to change the term 'revoked' to 'terminated or temporarily withdrawn' to make the act mirror State practices. It was again amended in 1966 to allow for the recording of denials and withdrawals, not just denials and withdrawals for driving while intoxicated or being convicted of a traffic offense resulting in a fatality. Under the legislation a Federal agency only has access to the information in regard to the issuance of a U.S. Government motor vehicle operator's permit.

"The Register is a data retrieval system maintained by the National Highway Traffic Safety Administration. It is, in essence, a set of magnetic tapes which contain a record of individuals whose licenses have been denied, terminated or withdrawn, except for withdrawals of less than six months for non-moving violations. It currently contains the records of approximately 2.2 million persons. Each State, on a form specified by the National Highway Traffic Safety Administration, submits records of such denials and withdrawals which are transferred to the tape. However, the applicability of the information provided by the Register to a particular license applicant is left to the State.

"The forms for data recording and retrieval used by the Register require the name and physical features of the individual, his license number and/or social security number, and the reason for, and duration of, the revocation. Approximately half of the States supply social security numbers to the Register.

"A number of safeguards are in effect to insure the security of the information submitted by the States. Only specified State sources may submit a revocation notice, and printouts from the Register may only be sent to specifically designated State and Federal officials. The Register staff periodically checks with States to verify the number of records submitted by that State to the Register. The Register also provides special pre-addressed, franked envelopes and special containers to the States to be used for all submissions. Special format punch cards and magnetic tape are also supplied to the State.

"Further, Register personnel are carefully instructed as to their responsibilities, and all have received clearances. The Register offices have special locks, and Register personnel, rather than normal cleaning crews, clean their offices. Obsolete records are destroyed by burning in the presence of Register personnel and computer tapes are erased before being sent to the States for additional information.

"As indicated above, printouts from the Register are available only to designated State and Federal officials, and only in connection with an application for a motor vehicle license or permit. To my knowledge there have been two exceptions to this requirement. In 1965 the FAA requested and received a correlation between individuals holding FAA pilot's licenses and entries in the Register. In 1968, a study was made by the National Institute of Mental Health, in cooperation with the State of Maryland and the National Highway Safety Bureau, to determine the correlation between individuals whose licenses were suspended for drunken driving in Maryland and individuals who sought help in Maryland for alcoholism. We must admit that both these instances involved a misapplication of the law and should not have taken place. Since those instances occurred, Register personnel have been strongly instructed to grant information from the Register only to designated State and Federal officials. And, I have been assured that there have been no cases since 1968 in which these instructions have been disregarded.

"The Register receives a daily average of 3,000 reports of license denials and withdrawals. States, to varying degrees, query the Register when they receive an application for a driver's license. The Register receives daily 65,000 inquiries, and sends approximately 650 reports of probable driver record identifications to the States. There are two runs made to match data, 90 days apart. This is to eliminate the problem of someone applying for a new license in a State before his revocation from another State has been entered in the Register. After the second run, the request for information is destroyed.

"There are, in actuality, two files maintained. There is an active file to which the designated State and Federal officials have access. This file is purged quarterly by directive of the NHTSA of all records over five years old except in the case of violations requiring mandatory revocations under the Uniform Motor Vehicle Code. The records in this latter instance are erased after seven years. There is also an inactive file, consisting of data deleted from the active file, which is retained for one year thereafter to answer possible State questions concerning the removal of the file. After this additional one year, this record is also destroyed. There are no circumstances under which this data can be reentered into the Register.

"The accuracy of the information in the Register is essentially a State responsibility, since the data is prepared and submitted by the State from its own records. We have cautioned the States to advise us immediately of any errors or alterations in their submissions. There is no practical way in which the National Highway Traffic Safety Administration can independently review or evaluate for accuracy the substance of the records submitted by the States.

"As I have said, the Federal Government is not the source of any information contained in the Register. We merely maintain a summary file of State records related to driver license denials, withdrawals and revocations. There is no information in the Register which cannot be obtained by direct inquiry to nearly all States.

"The law does not provide that an individual be notified when his name has been entered in the Register. Obviously, however, and individual is notified and aware of the revocation of his State driver's license or the denial of his application for a license under normal State procedures. Further, the only use by a State or Federal agency of the information in the Register is in connection with license applications. In these instances, the individual is made aware of the basis of the action taken with respect to his application. We believe he can at that point correct any errors in the information obtained from the Register.

"Let me speak now of the way maintaining the Driver Register directly helps to lessen the death on our highways. I need not remind this Committee that the *annual* deaths on this nation's highways exceed the *total* number of Americans killed during the entire history of the war in Vietnam. Because of the danger of allowing some individuals access to our highways the States have established a suspension or withdrawal system for those convicted of serious motor vehicle offenses. There would be little good in this system if an individual, after having his license revoked in one State, could immediately go to another State and obtain a new license. It was to combat this problem that the National Driver Register was established.

"Through the Register, a State can query other States to guard against issuing what can only be called a license to kill.

"From our experience with the Driver Register, we have determined that it would be desirable to expand its use somewhat. We have under consideration legislation which will accomplish the following expansion of the purposes for which States may apply for information from the Register.

"First, it will allow an employer to determine if an applicant for employment as a driver has a history of license revocations. Effective January 1, 1971, such a determination required of employers by regulation of the Bureau of Motor Carrier Safety. Under existing practices, it is necessary for the employer to contact each State in which an applicant for employment is licensed in order to make that determination.

"Secondly, the amendment we will propose will allow a judge, prior to imposing sentence on an individual convicted of a motor vehicle offense, to query the Register. This will allow for more effective sentencing of first, second, or multi-offenders.

"We believe that the National Driver Register in no way constitutes an invasion of an individual's privacy. The Federal Government does not collect personal data, merely official and publicly available State records. Finally, and more importantly, the National Driver Register doesn't destroy lives, it saves them."

HON. ROBERT F. FROEHLKE

"Within the past year, there has been a focus of official and public attention on the fact that for a period of time during the 1960's the Military Services were engaged in the collection and analysis of information on persons and organizations not affiliated with the Department of Defense. Clearly there is no precedent for the scope and intensity of information collection and analysis related to the civilian communities which occurred in the period in question. The character and extent of information collection undertaken by the military and the curtailment of this activity during the past two years can only be understood if related to the circumstances which initially led to the military involvement.

"The collection, storage, and analysis of information related to the civilian community has been the focal point of current discussion and concern. This informational aspect of military involvement is only a part of, and inseparably related to, the more direct and comprehensive involvement of the Military Services in civil disturbances, namely the prepositioning or actual use of military forces to cope with violence in civilian communities.

Note: Robert F. Froehlke, *Congressional Digest,* 1971, pp. 236, 238, 240, 242, 244. Reproduced by permission. From testimony given before the Subcommittee on Constitutional Rights of the Senate Committee on the Judiciary on March 2, 1971, in the course of hearings on Federal data banks.

"The history of the United States contains a number of instances when civilian authorities used National Guard or Federal troops in connection with domestic disturbances. Article IV, Section 4, of the Constitution of the United States provides: 'The United States shall guarantee to every State in this Union a Republican Form of Government, and shall protect each of them against Invasion; and on Application of the Legislature, or of the Executive (when the Legislature cannot be convened) against domestic Violence.'

"As early as 1795, the Congress passed statutes implementing this Constitutional provision. Currently applicable enabling statutes including Sections 331, 332 and 333 of Chapter 10 of the United States Code.

"Between 1786 and 1921, Federal military forces were used in connection with domestic disturbances approximately 30 times, according to a list compiled by the War Department for the Senate. Approximately seven of these instances occurred in the aftermath of the Civil War. Some five of them occurred in territories, rather than in states.

"It is apparent that prior to 1960 instances of civil disturbances necessitating the use of Federal troops were sufficiently infrequent and isolated as to preclude any necessity for detailed contingency planning by Federal civilian or military authorities. Therefore, there was no need for collection of information to assist in such contingency planning.

"In the early 1960's incidents of civil disturbances, unfortunately, increased in frequency and intensity. Federal troops were deployed in Oxford, Mississippi, in 1962 and 1963. Federal troops were again committed in Tuscaloosa and Huntsville, Alabama, in June 1963. Federal troops were deployed, although not committed, in Birmingham, Alabama, in June 1963 and were pre-positioned, but again not committed, in Washington, D.C., in August 1963. Federal troops were deployed during the Selma-Montgomery, Alabama, march of 1965. During this period, there were also a number of other instances of civil disturbances which occasioned alerts but not deployments of Federal troops.

"Officials charged with responsibility for the commitment, deployment, or potential deployment of Federal troops in this period foresaw and expressed the need for improved planning in connection with Federal activities and participation in assistance to States and local communities during civil disturbances.

"Prior to the summer of 1967, the involvement of the Military Services in collection of civil disturbance information could be characterized as minimal but increasing. July and August of 1967, however, marked a turning point.

"In mid July, Federal troops were alerted for Newark, New Jersey, in connection with large-scale disorders which were occurring there. The riots in Detroit began on July 23 and continued until July 31. Federal troops were committed. Shortly after the beginning of the Detroit riots, the Secretary of Defense created a Civil Disturbance Task Force under the Chairmanship of the Under Secretary of the Army. This was an interdepartmental task force and included membership from the White House and the Department of Justice, as well as other agencies.

"During the riots in Detroit in July 1967, Mr. Cyrus Vance, who had previously served as Deputy Secretary of Defense, was the personal representative of the President and the senior Federal official in Detroit. In Sep-

tember 1967, Mr. Vance filed an extensive report.

"In response to the increasing frequency and intensity of civil disorders, the Army's experience in Detroit, and to Mr. Vance's after-action report, the Department of the Army undertook through a task group to evaluate the roles and functions of the active Army and of Reserve component units in urban riots. This task group subsequently became the Army Civil Disturbance Committee. It made numerous recommendations which resulted in the formulation and issuance of a comprehensive civil disturbance plan on February 1, 1968.

"Through the period 1965–1968, there was a crisis-oriented attitude with respect to civil disorders. During the entire period, and particularly in 1967 and 1968, heavy emphasis was placed by civilian and military officials at the highest levels of Government on improving the preparedness of the Federal Government structure, including the military, for dealing with multiple, large-scale, concurrent civil disturbances.

"It is significant that around 1967, the character of the major disturbances underwent a change. Prior to this point in time, the civil disturbances had largely arisen in connection with racial matters, and had apparently been precipitated by a chance incident. Later, although racial incidents continued, a new potential for major civil disturbances also arose. This potential centered on planned and usually pre-announced assemblies of persons from across the nation to protest the war. Many of the potential participants in these pre-announced assemblies announced their intention to disrupt the government. It was the cumulative impact of these developments which led to the Army being asked to plan for possible commitment of Federal troops in as many as 25 major cities concurrently.

"On April 10, 1968, the National Advisory Commission on Civil Disturbances, known as the Kerner Commission, filed its report. This Commission reported that the Army Staff Task Group had conducted a study on which the Commission had relied heavily.

The Commission commended the Army for undertaking this overall review. One of the Commission's recommendations was:

"'The Commission further recommends that Federal-State planning should ensure that Federal troops are prepared to provide aid to cities not presently covered by the Army's "planning packet" effort.'

"It is also significant to note that a Commission finding stated that 'the absence of accurate information, both before and during disorder, has created special control problems for police.'

"It was against this general background, and in this period of crisis, that the involvement of the Military Services in collection and analysis of information on civilians and organizations not affiliated with the Department of Defense occurred. These so-called intelligence activities were only one facet of the overall planning and operations required from the Military Services in connection with civil disturbances.

"Although all of the Military Services were subjected to requirements connected with information collection related to civil disturbances, the Department of the Army had the responsibility for the principal effort. The other military departments had a collateral role consisting primarily of responding to intelligence requirements developed by the Army planners to the extent the other Services possessed information which filled the specified need.

"The involvement of Army investigative and related counterintelligence organizations in the collection and utilization of information related to civil disturbances had its genesis in 1963. At that time, after several deployments of Federal troops, the Chief of Staff of the Army was designated as Executive Agent for the Joint Chiefs of Staff to command Federal troops committed to civil disturbances. Concurrent with this designation, the investigative and counterintelligence organizations of the Army, at that time organic components of the several Continental Armies, were assigned the mission of briefing the personal representative of the Army Chief of Staff on the scene. In addition,

directives specified that upon the issuance of an executive order by the President committing Federal troops in connection with the civil disturbances, the investigative and related counterintelligence units in that particular Continental Army area immediately came under the operational control of the personal representative of the Chief of Staff of the Army.

"From 1963 to 1965, the investigative and related counterintelligence units of the Continental Armies had the mission, in connection with civil disturbances, of being prepared to provide initial briefings to the Commander at the time of commitment of Federal troops by the President. In addition, they were to be prepared thereafter to provide the informational needs of the Task Force Commander during the period of troop commitment. In order to prepare for the requirement of an initial briefing, civil disturbance information began to be collected. The collection means which were authorized by directives of the Continental Army Command were by liaison and reviewing the public media. Generally direct, agent observation could be resorted to in an emergency situation by authority of the Continental Army Commander. Covert collection was prohibited without the specific approval in each case of the Commander, Continental Army Command, after coordination with the Federal Bureau of Investigation as provided in the Delimitations Agreement.

"On January 1, 1965, the United States Army Intelligence Command was activated. It included all Army investigative and counterintelligence units in the United States which had formerly been parceled out among the various Continental Armies. It did not, of course, include the tactical units assigned to combat operations organizations. The same policies authorizing and restricting methods of collection which previously pertained were incorporated into the directives of the Intelligence Command. The Commander of the United States Army Intelligence Command reserved to himself the authority to approve any covert collection.

"As early as 1963, there are records of complaints about the failure, or inability, of the Army's investigative and counterintelligence units to provide adequate civil disturbance information prior to the commitment of Federal troops. In retrospect, it is clear that such Army units could not satisfy the requirements for civil disturbance information by authorized collection means, namely, liaison and public media review.

"The number and variety of requirements for specific information related to civil disturbance continued to increase through 1967. Following Detroit, direct agent observation was increasingly used to fill requirements.

"Let me emphasize, however, that even during this period a small proportion of the total time and effort of personnel assigned to investigative and counterintelligence organizations was used for collection or processing of civil disturbance information. The great majority of investigative personnel were at all times engaged in the routine personnel background investigations.

"It is also evident that both civil and military authorities continued to be dissatisfied with the quality and quantity of civil disturbance information provided.

"The increased concern, activity and planning led to the issuance of the comprehensive Army Civil Disturbance Plan in January 1968. On February 1, 1968, the Intelligence Annex to the Civil Disturbance Plan was issued. The Intelligence Annex contained a one page list of general essential elements of information, and there was limited tasking by specific units and types of units.

"In the first six months of 1968, however, the level of riots continued high and at an even greater intensity. It was in this period that the extensive riots following the assassination of Dr. Martin Luther King occurred. Official concern grew. Law enforcement agencies, including Federal agencies, made known to the high civil authorities their lack, in quantity and quality, of the necessary resources to cope with the increasing demands for information. As a consequence, a more comprehensive and detailed intelligence document was issued on May 2,

1968. This was the Department of Army Civil Disturbance Information Collection Plan. It was classified Confidential. It was rescinded on June 9, 1970 and declassified on February 24, 1971.

"This Civil Disturbance Information Collection Plan provided that predisturbance information would be obtained by drawing on other Federal as well as State and local forces. These forces secure such data in the course of carrying out their primary duties and responsibilities. It further provided that United States Army Intelligence Command personnel would not be directly used to obtain civil disturbance information unless specific direction to do so had been received from Headquarters, Department of Army. Covert operations by United States Army Intelligence Command personnel were prohibited without the prior approval and direction of the Assistant Chief of Staff of Army for Intelligence.

"This collection plan contained the following preamble:

"It is recognized that Army assistance to local or state authorities in peacetime, as well as in wartime emergency, is a long standing tradition in our country. In most instances in the past, such assistance was rendered with a minimum of advance information concerning the situation. The current civil disturbance situation dictates a change in the degree to which the Army must seek advance information concerning potential and probable trouble areas and trouble makers.

"'The Army is well aware that the overwhelming majority in both the anti-war and the racial movements are sincere Americans. It also realizes that in both groups there is a small but virulent number who are out to tear America apart. During demonstrations and disturbances these are the activists that control the violent action. These are people who deliberately exploit the unrest and seek to generate violence and terror for selfish purposes. If the Army must be used to quell violence it wants to restore law and order as quickly as possible and return to its normal protective role—to do this it must know in advance as much as possible about the well springs of violence and the heart and nerve causes of chaos. To do less means the professional violence purveyors will have a better chance to achieve their end aims—law breaking, social disintegration, chaos, violence, destruction, insurrection, revolution.

" 'In obtaining the information called for in this plan the Army seeks only to collect that needed to exercise honest and sound judgment of the measures to be taken in suppressing rampant violence and restoring order—to assure that only the mildest effective measures are exercised—to insure that no overstepping of the degree of force or circumscription needed is applied—to conserve military resources and to avoid infringement on the responsibility and authority of civil government agencies—to insure pervasive vigilance for the fundamental rights of private citizens by the selective and enlightened use of force in restraint against those who are truly violating the rights of their fellow citizens.'

"The Collection Plan directed specific tasking of organizations within the Army to provide civil disturbance information In addition, it contained a standing request for pertinent information which might be obtained by the Department of the Navy, Department of the Air Force, the Defense Intelligence Agency and other Department of Defense agencies. In addition, it requested civil disturbance information from a number of non-DOD Federal agencies and offices.

"This Collection Plan received wide distribution including the Office of the Secretary of Defense, the National Security Council, and the Department of Justice.

"This Civil Disturbance Information Collection Plan imposed requirements in extensive detail in four categories: predisturbance activities, activities during civil disturbance, post disturbance activities and international activities related to civil disturbance. The requirements were both comprehensive and detailed, and, in the light of experience, substantially beyond the capability of military intelligence units to collect.

They reflected the all-encompassing and uninhibited demand for information directed at the Department of the Army.

"Despite the limitations in the Civil Disturbance Information Collection Plan on the methods of collection, it is apparent that many of the requirements which the United States Army Intelligence Command was asked to satisfy could not conceivably be collected by liaison or public media-type collection. It is highly improbable that many of the requirements listed could be obtained by other than covert collection. Indeed, many of these requirements could not be satisfied by any collection means and certainly not with the resources available. So comprehensive were the requirements levied in the Civil Disturbance Information Collection Plan that any category of information related even remotely to people or organizations active in a community in which the potential for a riot or disorder was present, would fall within their scope. Information was sought on organizations by name or by general characterization. Requirements for information were even levied which required collection on activities and potential activities of the public media, including newspapers and television and radio stations.

"In summary, the Department of Army Civil Disturbance Information Collection Plan was widely distributed throughout the Federal Government, and to officials of each State government. It expressed the need and desire for every conceivable type of information related to civil disturbances and the people and organizations who were or might become involved in civil disturbances.

"The civil disturbance information collection activities of the Military Services were all integrally connected to the use or potential use of Federal troops. This information collected was obviously considered necessary and essential to the effective use of Federal military forces in connection with the widespread riots and domestic disorders occurring in this period.

"In none of the documents of record, however, during this period of crisis do we find a specific legal rationale for this use of military resources to collect civil disturbance information. Indeed, it would be surprising, had such a rationale been prepared, since the information collection was so inseparably a part of the total use of Federal troops. In order to carry out the President's order and protect the persons and property in an area of civil disturbance with the greatest effectiveness, military commanders must know all that can be learned about that area and its inhabitants. Such a task obviously cannot be performed between the time the President issues his order and the time the military is expected to be on the scene. Information gathering on persons or incidents which may give rise to a civil disturbance and thus commitment of Federal troops must necessarily be on a continuing basis. Such is required by Sections 331, 332 and 333 of Title 10 of the U.S. Code since Congress certainly did not intend that the President utilize an ineffective Federal Force.

"It is worthy of note that none of the activities referred to above were prohibited by Federal or State law. Two cases have been decided in the lower Federal courts where action has been brought by individuals seeking to enjoin collection by military organizations of civil disturbance type information on persons and organizations not affiliated with the Department of Defense. One suit, the *ACLU et al. v. Westmoreland et al.* was recently heard in the Federal District Court in Chicago. This action was ordered dismissed by the District Judge and that order is now on appeal. In the other case, *Tatum et al. v. Laird et al.*, the court dismissed plaintiff's motion for a preliminary injunction on the grounds that plaintiff failed to state a cause of action and showed no unconstitutional action and alleged no unlawful action on the part of defendants. The appeal from the order of the District Court has been argued before the Court of Appeals and a decision on the appeal is pending.

"Since no use of civil disturbance information was made or intended to be made

that would result in any action to the prejudice of any individual or organization, it is difficult to perceive how the Constitutional rights or even the right of privacy could be impinged by the collection of such information. Even were the individual rights of some individuals indirectly affected, however, the Supreme Court has repeatedly held that such rights of individuals are not absolute but are under certain conditions subject to incidental limitations upon their exercise. *United States* v. *O'Brien* (1968)

"The records reveal that little, if any, direction and guidance was provided to the Military Services from the White House or the Department of Justice in written form. There were, of course, the several Executive Orders, which during the period committed Federal troops to assist in controlling major disorders. Numerous memoranda of record of inter-agency group meetings at the White House and elsewhere, however, demonstrated that the highest level of civilian officials participated.

"In a number of instances during this period, the potential for disorders was perceived from announced intentions of various organizations to promote mass demonstrations of large numbers of people from all over the country for demonstrations in a specific city, often Washington, D.C. Some demonstration leaders publicly announced their intent to disrupt the functions of government. Information was desired on the numbers of persons from a variety of organizations from many locations across the country who might attend such demonstrations. No organization had sufficient trained personnel of the types needed to collect such information except organizations within the Military Services.

"The records clearly indicate that military resources were employed because civilian agencies—Federal, State and local—had demonstrated a lack of capability to provide the quantity and types of information believed to be necessary effectively to cope in a timely fashion with the emergency then prevailing."

HON. WILLIAM H. REHNQUIST

"I am pleased to discuss the constitutional and statutory sources of the investigative power of the Executive branch of the government generally, and of the Department of Justice in particular. This authority has properly been construed by the Executive to include the use of a wide variety of investigative techniques, among which are modern data processing systems.

"The Department of Justice is convinced of the necessity to maximize the potential of these devices in combating organized crime, preventing acts of violence, controlling civil disorders where appropriate, and enforcing the numerous Federal statutes. At the same time, the Department is aware of the potential for injury to individuals which could result from unauthorized collection or unnecessary dissemination of such data. We believe that full utilization of advanced data processing techniques is by no means inconsistent with the preservation of personal privacy. We reject the suggestion that the mere potential for abuse of these technological advances is a sufficient reason in itself to dispense with their use in the investigation

Note: William H. Rehnquist, *Congressional Digest*, 1971, pp. 244, 246, 248. Reproduced by permission. From testimony given before the Subcommittee on Constitutional Rights of the Senate Committee on the Judiciary on March 9, 1971, in the course of hearings on Federal data banks.

and prosecution of crime. The Department believes that careful attention to the potential for abuse will enable us to improve methods for preventing these abuses without significantly impairing the value of data processing techniques as an important tool of law enforcement.

"The functions and organization of the Department of Justice are outlined in the provisions of Part II of Title 28, United States Code and regulations promulgated thereunder.

"With regard to the collection and dissemination of records, section 534 of Title 28 provides as follows:

" ' (a) The Attorney General shall—
   " ' (1) acquire, collect, classify, and preserve identification, criminal identification, crime, and other records; and
   " ' (2) exchange these records with, and for the official use of, authorized officials of the federal government, the states, cities, and penal and other institutions.
" ' (b) The exchange of records authorized by subsection (a) (2) of this section is subject to cancellation if dissemination is made outside the receiving departments or related agencies.
" ' (c) The Attorney General may appoint

426

officials to perform the functions authorized by this section.'

"Section 534 is the primary statutory source of authority for data collection, analysis and dissemination.

"In addition, 5 U.S.C. 301 provides in part that:

" 'The head of an Executive department . . . may prescribe regulations for . . . the custody, use and preservation of its records, papers and property. . . .'

"We believe these statutes authorize broad discretion over the control of investigative information that is collected and stored manually or electronically.

"While there is obviously no justification for surveillance of any kind that does not relate to a legitimate investigative purpose, the vice is not surveillance *per se,* but surveillance of activities which are none of the government's business.

"The Federal Bureau of Investigation uses both undercover agents and paid informers in its criminal intelligence activities. In many cases, arrest and prosecution of lawbreakers can be effected only through the use of such persons. Utilization of the full panoply of lawful investigative techniques is consistent with the oft-expressed desire of this administration to vigorously enforce the Federal criminal law. It is our view that the computer is a useful aid in coordinating criminal intelligence gathering and fulfilling the overall purpose of efficient law enforcement. Thus far, we have only recently begun to use electronic data processing. Therefore, it has been of only limited use to date in the investigation and prosecution of crime. Yet we are beginning to realize that the computer with its ability to store, analyze, and quickly retrieve vast amounts of data can be of immense help to law enforcement administration.

"Although we are anxious to increase the effectiveness of law enforcement through the use of technology, we do not propose to ignore the increased potential for abuse that arises from the expanded capability we will have to make complex analyses of investigative data. Indeed, we believe that stringent physical and personnel security measures can greatly reduce the risk of improper access and dissemination so that it poses no greater threat to personal privacy than manual data storage.

"The function of gathering intelligence relating to civil disturbances, previously confided to the Army, has since been transferred to the Internal Security Division of the Justice Department. No information contained in the data base of the Department of the Army's now defunct computer system has been transferred to the Internal Security Division's data base. However, in connection with the case of *Tatum* v. *Laird,* now pending in the United States Court of Appeals for the District of Columbia Circuit, one print-out from the Army computer has been retained for the inspection of the court. It will thereafter be destroyed.

"The data being stored and analyzed by the Internal Security Division relates to specific incidents in which there is evidence that a law has been or may be broken. The information is obtained primarily from FBI reports.

"To date the data base of the Internal Security computer has been used to determine the probability of civil disorder in various geographical areas of the country. For example, the computer might be queried concerning acts of violence that have occurred in a given city over a certain period of time. With the decrease in urban disorder and the corresponding increase in individual acts of destruction, such as bombing, there has been a shift in the use of the data base toward preventing and solving these kinds of crime.

"With regard to the question of whether the constitutional rights of individuals were violated by government surveillance in cases where there was not probable cause to believe that a particular individual had committed a crime, the responsibility of the Executive branch for the execution of the law extends not merely to the prosecution of crime, but to the prevention of it. Given the far-flung responsibilities of the Executive branch for law enforcement, and the large complements of personnel required to discharge these responsibilities, it would scarcely be surprising if there were not isolated examples of abuse of this investigative function. Such abuse may consist of the collection of information which is not legitimately related to the statutory or constitutional authority of the Executive branch to enforce the laws, or it may consist of the unauthorized dissemination of information which was quite properly collected in the first instance.

"I know of no authoritative decision holding that either of these situations amounts to a violation of any particular individual's constitutional rights. I think the courts have been reluctant, and properly so, to enter upon the supervision of the Executive's information gathering activities so long as such information is not made the basis of a proceeding against a particular individual or individuals. But the fact that such isolated Executive excesses may not be a violation of individual rights does not mean that they are proper, and it does not mean that appropriate steps should not be taken to prevent their reoccurrence. Departmental regulations of the Department of Justice forbid any employee or former employee to produce any material contained in the files of the Department, or to disclose any information relating to material contained in files of the Department, without prior approval of the Attorney General. This regulation is intended to preserve the confidentiality of information contained in departmental files, and to make certain that it will not be disseminated to unauthorized persons.

"With the additional investigative capabilities made available by technological advances, it will undoubtedly be necessary to be vigilant against possible violations of this regulation. Physical security precautions must be improved in order to assure both those within and without the Department that unauthorized personnel do not have access to confidential information. Those in the Executive branch generally, including the Department of Justice, must make certain that law enforcement intelligence gathering is limited to those areas in which the Executive branch has constitutional or statutory responsibility for law enforcement.

"I think it quite likely that self-discipline on the part of the Executive branch will provide an answer to virtually all of the legitimate complaints against excesses of information gathering. No widespread system of investigative activity, maintained by diverse and numerous personnel, is apt to be perfect either in its conception or in its performance. The fact that isolated imperfections are brought to light, while always a reason for attempting to correct them, should not be permitted to obscure the fundamental necessity and importance of Federal information gathering, or the generally high level of performance in this area by the organizations involved.

"In saying this, I do not mean to suggest that the Department of Justice would adamantly oppose any and all legislation on this subject. Legislation which is carefully drawn to meet demonstrated evils in a reasonable way, without impairing the efficiency of vital Federal investigative agencies, will receive the Department's careful consideration. But it will come as no surprise, I am sure, for me to state the Department will vigorously oppose any legislation which, whether by opening the door to unnecessary and unmanageable judicial supervision of such activities or otherwise, would effectively impair this extraordinarily important function of the Federal Government."

HON. SAM J. ERVIN, JR.

"In recent months, with the discovery of each new Federal data bank and data system, public concern has increased that some of the Federal Government's collection, storage, and use of information about citizens may raise serious questions of individual privacy and constitutional rights.

"Our Nation is predicated on the fundamental proposition that citizens have a right to express their views on the wisdom and course of governmental policies. This involves more than the currently popular notion of a so-called right to dissent. Our system cannot survive if citizen participation is limited merely to registering disagreement with official policy: the policies themselves must be the product of the people's views. The protection and encouragement of such participation is a principal purpose of the first amendment.

"More than at any other time in our history, people are actively expressing themselves on public questions and seeking to participate more directly in the formulation of policy. Mass media have made it easy for

Note: Sam J. Ervin, Jr., *Congressional Digest,* 1971, pp. 233, 235, 237, 239. Reproduced by permission. From remarks delivered on the floor of the U.S. Senate on September 8, 1970, announcing the scheduling of hearings before the Subcommittee on Constitutional Rights of the Senate Judiciary Committee on the subject of "Federal Data Banks and the Bill of Rights."

large numbers of people to organize and express their views in written and oral fashion. Rapid means of transportation have aided our mobile population to move easily to sites of central and local authority for the purpose of expressing their views more publicly. The freedom of our form of government and the richness of our economy have made it possible for individuals to move about freely and to seek their best interests as they will in vocations and avocations of their choice, or indeed, to pursue none at all for a time, if that is what they wish. If modern technology has provided citizens with more efficient means for recording their dissent, or for registering their political, economic, or social views, it has also placed in the hands of executive branch officials new methods of taking note of that expression of views and that political activity. For these reasons, those individuals who work actively for public causes are more visible than ever before.

"These new sciences have accorded those who control government increased power to discover and record immutably the activities, thoughts and philosophy of an individual at any given moment of his life. That picture of the person is recorded forever, no matter how the person may change as time goes on. Every person's past thus becomes an inescapable part of his present and future. The computer never forgets.

"To be sure, recordkeeping is nothing new

in the history of government; nor indeed is the habit all governments and all societies have of surveillance, black-listing and subtle reprisal for unpopular political or social views. Men have always had to contend with the memories of other men. In the United States, however, we are blessed with a Constitution which provides for due process of law. This applies to the arbitrary use of the recordkeeping and information power of government against the individual.

"Despite these guarantees, the new technology has been quietly, but steadily, endowing officials with the unprecedented political power which accompanies computers and data banks and scientific techniques of managing information. It has given Government the power to take note of anything whether it be right or wrong, relevant to any purpose or not, and to retain it forever. Unfortunately, this revolution is coming about under outdated laws and executive orders governing the recordkeeping and the concepts of privacy and confidentiality relevant to an earlier time.

"These developments are particularly significant in their effect on the first amendment to our Constitution.

"No longer can a man march with a sign down Pennsylvania Avenue and then return to his hometown, his identity forgotten, if not his cause.

"No longer does the memory of the authorship of a political article fade as the pages of his rhetoric yellow and crumble with time.

"No longer are the flamboyant words exchanged in debate allowed to echo into the past and lose their relevance with the issue of the moment which prompted them.

"No longer can a man be assured of his enjoyment of the harvest of wisdom and maturity which comes with age, when the indiscretions of youth, if noticed at all, are spread about in forgotten file cabinets in basement archives.

"Instead, today, his activities are recorded in computers or data banks, or if not, they may well be a part of a great investigative index.

"How do these things come about? It would be unfair, perhaps, to attribute suspicious political motives, or lack of ethics to those responsible for any one program or for any group of programs for collecting and storing personal information about citizens. Frequently, they just grow over the years. Sometimes, executive department data banks are either merely good faith efforts at fulfillment of specific mandates from Congress; or they are based on what some officials think to be implied mandates to acquire information necessary for Congress to legislate. If so, then Congress has no one to blame but itself when such programs unnecessarily threaten privacy or other rights. But it then has an even greater responsibility for acting, once its own negligence is discovered.

"Perhaps the most such officials can be charged with is overzealousness in doing their job within narrow confines, to the exclusion of all other considerations.

"Sometimes the issue of threats to individual rights is presented only after a data system has developed, and only after practical problems are raised which were not envisioned on paper.

"At times, due process may be threatened by the failure of the computer specialists to consider only the information on a person absolutely essential for their programming.

"There are political reasons also. One is the failure of heads of executive departments and agencies to mind their own stores and stay out of the business of other agencies. Each department does not need to seize the total man when it administers a program; only those portions of him necessary for the job. Another reason is the tendency of executive branch officials in the interest of political expediency and shortcuts to law and order goals, to seize upon the techniques of data banks, intelligence gathering, and surveillance activities as a substitute for hard-hitting, practical law enforcement work by the proper agencies, and for creative administration of the laws.

"All of these excuses will not help the law-abiding citizen who, at the whim of some official, is put into an intelligence-type data bank which is part of a network of inquiry for all manner of governmental purposes.

"No one would deny that the Government of such a populous and farflung country should not avail itself of the efficiency offered by computers and scientific data management techniques. Clearly, Government agencies must, as Congress has charged them, acquire, store, and process economically the information it obtains from citizens for administrative purposes. There is an ever-increasing need for information of all kinds to enable the Congress to legislate effectively and the executive branch to administer the laws properly.

"Furthermore, there is an obvious need in such a complex mobile society for recording and documenting amply the official relationship between the individual and his government.

"More and more frequently, misguided individuals are resorting to violence and violation of the law. Communities are faced with rising crime rates. Local, State and Federal Government have a right and a duty to know when a person has a legal record of violation of the law which, under the law, would deny him certain rights or benefits. They should be able to ascertain these matters quickly.

"There are always some problems of accuracy and confidentiality with such records, especially when automated. It is not the carefully designed individual law enforcement data banks which concern the public. Rather, the subcommittee study is revealing that data programs which have aroused the most apprehension recently are those—

"Which bear on the quality of first amendment freedoms by prying into those protected areas of an individual's personality, life, habits, beliefs, and legal activities which should be none of the business of Government even in good causes:

"Which are unauthorized, or unwarranted for the legitimate purpose of the agency;

"Which keep the information they acquire too long, and which by the very retention of unknown data may intimidate the individual subject;

"Which are part of a network of data systems;

"Which make little, if any provision for assuring due process for the individual in terms of accuracy, fairness, review, and proper use of data, and thereby may operate to deny the individual rights, benefits, privileges, reputation, which are within the power of government to influence, grant or deny.

"There is growing concern that the zeal of computer technicians, of the systems planners, and of the political administrators in charge of the data systems threatens to curtail the forces of society which have operated throughout our history to cool political passions and to make our form of government viable by allowing a free exchange in the marketplace of ideas.

"The new technology has made it literally impossible for a man to start again in our society. It has removed the quality of mercy from our institutions by making it impossible to forget, to forgive, to understand, to tolerate. When it is used to intimidate and to inhibit the individual in his freedom of movement, associations, or expressions of ideas within the law, the new technology provides the means for the worst sort of tyranny. Those who so misuse it to augment their own power break faith with those founders of our Constitution who, like Thomas Jefferson, swore upon the altar of God eternal hostility against every form of tyranny over the mind of man.

"It has become dangerously clear in recent times that unless new controls are enacted, new legal remedies are provided, and unless Federal officials can be persuaded to exercise more political self-control, this country will not reap the blessings of man's creative spirit which is reflected in computed technology. Rather, if the surveillance it encourages is allowed to continue without strict controls and safeguards, we stand to lose the spiritual and intellectual liberty of the individual which have been so carefully nourished and so valiantly defended, and which our Founding Fathers so meticulously enshrined in the Constitution.

"I say this out of my conviction that the undisputed and unlimited possession of the resources to build and operate data banks on individuals, and to make decisions about people with the aid of computers and electronic data systems, is fast securing to executive branch officials a political power which the authors of the Constitution never meant any one group of men to have over all others. It threatens to unsettle forever the balance of power established by our Federal Constitution.

"Our form of government is the fruition of an ideal of political, economic, and spiritual freedom which is firmly rooted in our historical experience. Basic to its fulfillment has always been the monumental truth that such freedom is truly secure only when power is divided, limited, and called to account by the people. For this reason the central Government was divided into three separate and equal branches.

"For this reason, the bill of rights was added to secure certain areas of liberty against incursion by Government and the exercise of Federal power was limited to certain purposes.

"For this reason, we cherish and protect the legal freedom of each citizen to develop his mind and personality and to express them free of unwarranted governmental control.

"I differ with those who say that there are no existing checks on this developing power of computer technology, for I believe they already exist in our form of Government. The guarantees are established in our Constitution.

"It is my hope that the hearings and study by the Constitutional Rights Subcommittee will add a unique and valuable dimension to the public and congressional dialog on the role of data banks, information systems, and computers in our constitutional form of government."

HON. EDWARD I. KOCH

"The reports of military surveillance of civilians to ascertain so-called political reliability is a fearful omen to those who cherish traditional American values of freedom and privacy. For the first time in our history it appears that the military is creating a permanent apparatus for its possible involvement in domestic politics. This new orientation of the Pentagon, combined with the technological advances made in the area of data storage and retrieval, is fraught with danger and can be stopped, if at all, only by effective and immediate Congressional action.

"The Army's surveillance operations in Illinois, where Members of Congress' and other public officials were apparently the subjects of spying, is only the most recent dramatic example of the danger we face. But as hearings before this Subcommittee and other

Note: Edward I. Koch, *Congressional Digest*, 1971, pp. 237, 239. Reproduced by permission. From testimony given before the Subcommittee on Constitutional Rights of the Senate Committee on the Judiciary on February 23, 1971, in the course of hearings on Federal data banks. Rep. Koch is sponsor, in the House of Representatives, of H.R. 854, a proposal to establish comprehensive checks on the collection and use by the Federal Government of data on private citizens.

studies have demonstrated, the Army is not the only culprit. All of our governmental agencies appear to be competing to compile the most extensive set of dossiers on American citizens. The Transportation Department, the Civil Service Commission, the Justice Department, the Department of Housing and Urban Development, the State Department, the Treasury, the Department of Health, Education and Welfare and others are all engaged in similar activities.

"So long as we have a large governmental structure, and so long as the military apparatus is a major economic and administrative factor in American life, we will always have governmental—and military—records and investigations of American citizens.

"Second, we know enough about bureaucracy—public and private—to know that bureaucrats feed upon the expansion of power and information. With respect to military surveillance, it appears that from an initial mandate merely to prepare contingency plans to deal with authorized involvement in riot situations, the Army expanded its role to maintain records about, and to spy on, citizens who might conceivably be unsympathetic to present governmental policies.

"Third, modern computer technology

permits the most extensive collection and retrieval systems for information.

"Fourth, the best way to prevent the erosion of liberties is to establish as many countervailing forces as we can on the abuse of power.

"HR 854 would, I believe, establish such a countervailing system which would act as a check, to a large degree self-executing, on this type of governmental recordkeeping. Under this bill, each agency which maintains records concerning any individual—including records which may be retrieved by reference to the individual's name—must (1) notify the individual that such a record exists; (2) notify the individual of all transfers of such information; (3) disclose information from such records only with the consent of the individual or when legally required; (4) maintain a record of all persons inspecting such records; (5) permit the individual to inspect his records, make copies of them, and supplement them. I have introduced a similar bill, HR 841, to cover records of the House Committee on Internal Security.

"This bill would not require the destruction of legitimate governmental records, for we all recognize that records must be kept. It provides exceptions in the case of national security, investigations for purposes of criminal prosecutions and safeguards for informers and the like. Certainly it will cause, at least initially, some inconvenience to government officials. But this is a cost eminently worth paying for the benefits of creating such a system of protection.

"One of the most successful methods of enforcing legal rights in this country is to create private remedies and rights of action. It is, of course, important to have a vigilant Congress and courageous journalists as a check on arbitrary executive power. But in the long run it might be even more important to establish firmly a right in each individual to protect his own privacy.

"First, by letting citizens know what government records say about them, millions of individuals will have a first-hand and personal involvement in what their government is doing.

"Second, the implementation of this bill will necessarily reveal patterns of government operations which are detrimental to individual liberties. For example, if this bill had been law during the Army's surveillance in Illinois, Senator Stevenson, Judge Kerner and Congressman Mikva and other officials would have been notified that dossiers were being maintained about them; they could have blown the whistle on this operation immediately.

"Third, this bill, if enacted, would have a powerful deterrent effect on government agencies. There would be a strong new disincentive for the establishment of files on individuals; where records are maintained officials would treat them with more respect than presently is the case and would be inclined to weed out irrelevant, incorrect and dubious material.

"HR 854 is not the whole answer. Some types of surveillance and data collection should be forbidden absolutely—and I put Army surveillance of civilian political activity in that category. But in light of the immediate and pervasive threat to our liberties through the cancerous expansion of data collection, I strongly recommend the enactment of HR 854 as a step that the Congress can take now to make concrete its commitment to the right of privacy."

AMERICAN FRIENDS SERVICE COMMITTEE

"In our view, each living person has dignity and value and has certain inalienable rights which must be preserved if that dignity and value are to be respected. To preserve these rights, all levels of government, and indeed of society at large, must refrain from activity that either destroys these rights or undermines them so that they later collapse or become the more easily destroyed. We believe that such activity has progressed to a very damaging point already and must be stemmed promptly, as a first step in the reinforcing and upholding of those rights. There is very much that must be done if all Americans are to live in the secure knowledge that all other Americans are mutually concerned for the honoring of the rights of each. But, though that is a historic ideal, to which we regularly attest our belief, realism compels us to recognize that it is more a goal than a reality and that what we actually face today is not the challenge to achieve our American democratic faith in practice for all but to reverse a trend which threatens to destroy or undermine the rights of many, if not all Americans.

"We wish to state clearly what we think

American Friends Service Committee, *Congressional Digest,* 1971, pp. 239, 241, 243. Reproduced by permission. From a statement presented on February 25, 1971, before the Subcommittee on Constitutional Rights of the Senate Committee on the Judiciary in the course of hearings on Federal data banks.

must be self-evident to all who believe in American ideals:

"1) Civilian government agencies (federal, state or local) have the right to gather information about private individuals and groups only when it is essential to their specific responsibilities.

"2) Military departments (Army, Navy, Air Force) have no right to maintain surveillance and intelligence-gathering on civilians and civilian activities.

"3) Any governmental system permitting the routine exchange of information among agencies is vulnerable to abuse and prone to become oppressive. All information gathered by an agency relevant to its responsibilities should be available to the subject person but otherwise confidential and not available to any other public agency or individuals or private bodies except through due process of law.

"If these principles are not practiced, the sluice gate is opened and modern technology takes the flood of facts and orders them to suit, not the liberty of the people, but the ambitions of agencies and departments and thus leads to the expansion of intentionally limited powers and to the replacement of threat of replacement of liberty by repression.

"We believe that it should be the highest priority for the Congress to act in support of American rights and liberty, against the silent and subrosa dissipation of rights of

privacy and against the invalidation or sub-
version of the rights of assembly, press,
speech, and dissent by means of secret or
even brazen surveillance, data storage and
information exchange between different
governmental units.

"We therefore support the efforts of this
subcommittee to write legislation protecting
the rights of citizens and giving them adequate recourse against abuses—which, under
today's practices, are rights and recourse
which may depend on the willingness of
governmental agencies and departments to
forego voluntarily practices they wish to conduct or practices others are urging on them.
Someone must speak and act for the relatively
resourceless U.S. civilian who may never
know, as things now stand, when or whether
he is the subject of government scrutiny or
why certain things happen or do not happen
to him.

"Let us consider AFSC experiences. I
should note that the experiences I now report
refer, as far as I know, to municipal police
activity and the FBI. But I stress that the
civilian does not know whether anonymous
men in plainclothes are from the police, FBI,
Army, Navy, Air Force or Marines. It is
known, on the other hand, that police information is available to the FBI and FBI
information is available to the Armed Services.

"1) One of our staff members served on
the Steering Committee of the New Mobilization to End the War in Vietnam. Another
serving on that committee was a house guest
on one occasion of the AFSC man. At the
Chicago Conspiracy trial, the house guest
was identified as a member of the Chicago
police force.

"2) At a peace meeting in Philadelphia,
a YMCA building security guard was observed taking literature from the literature
table. When pressed for his purpose, he told
an AFSC staff member that he had been
instructed to do so by the FBI.

"3) At a lawful public rally in New York
City, an AFSC speaker saw a television camera pointed at him. It was identified as the
instrument of the New York Police Department.

"4) A national network television broadcast (April 30, 1970) showed Police Commissioner Rizzo of Philadelphia discussing his
department's political intelligence files. Eight
persons and six organizations were named or
their names were exhibited as being peace
and anti-war demonstrators. What is the
effect on political and civil liberty when a
citizen's name may be broadcast publicly by
the police from coast to coast in a derogatory
manner?

"5) In Philadelphia a young man of
Puerto Rican ancestry, who had volunteered
in an AFSC summer work project, was apprehended by police for a traffic violation.
He was hustled to the police station, questioned about literature and posters in his
car, about his political beliefs and about
whether or not he had attended the Black
Panther convention in Philadelphia. During
three hours, he was given no opportunity to
call a lawyer nor was he questioned about the
alleged traffic violation.

"6) I can personally describe occasions in
Seattle, Washington (where I worked for
AFSC for four years) when I attended out-
door meetings on the Vietnam war. Men who
were readily acknowledged to be policemen
were taking both crowd photographs and
close-ups of individuals. The impact which
this had on individuals was significant. Some
people hid behind other people. Some turned
away. Some refused to hide themselves or
their faces. I asked myself whether these were
the ones of whom the police and sometimes
the press have scoffed that they like to have
their pictures taken.

"These instances are only the thinly disguised and readily identifiable actions of
police and government agents gathering data
on citizens who were engaged in lawful and
legitimate—and by our standards—patriotic
and praiseworthy activities. What of the volume of such surveillance which is successfully
disguised and unidentifiable? What sense
does the citizen have that his government
honors and respects him?

"We ask: What information will a free society permit to accumulate without the individual's consent or even without his knowledge or any recourse against the practice? After all, it is now possible to use a laser beam to eavesdrop on a conversation a mile away behind a closed window. Behind what closed window may freedom and liberty be exercised without the threat of government intervention? Where in America is privacy possible?

"Now let us turn from the police, FBI and other government agencies to the Armed Services. It has been recorded in the press that the Army, Navy and Air Force have conducted surveillance on the lawful activities of civilians. In the case of the Army, it has been reported in the public press not only that the Army built up files on the political activities of civilians but also that such organizations as the American Friends Service Committee, the American Civil Liberties Union, the Center for the Study of Democratic Institutions, Clergy & Laymen Concerned About Vietnam, and the New Mobilization Committee to End the War in Vietnam were among the direct objects of such investigation. The American Friends Service Committee was alarmed by these reports for two reasons:

"1) The Constitution and the laws of the United States consistently make it clear that the military establishment of the United States is under the control of the civilian authorities chosen freely by the people rather than the reverse. The Army has no right whatever to launch and maintain a broad program of surveillance over and investigation into the activities and affairs of civilians or civilian organizations.

"2) The concerns, aims and purposes of the AFSC arise out of our deep concern for peace, justice and freedom achieved, maintained and fulfilled through nonviolence. For the American military to gather information regarding the activities of the AFSC (which are carried out openly and without any secrecy whatever) not only suggests to us that the American military usurped the authority which properly belongs to the representatives of the people but also that in the minds of at least some of the military there is something pernicious and suspect about an organization which for more than 50 years has consistently opposed war, repression and racism and has attempted to serve the victims.

"America must be guaranteed that it will become neither a police state nor a garrison state and that current activities leading to such developments will be stopped and reversed."

AMERICAN CIVIL LIBERTIES UNION

"Government surveillance of the individual is not a new phenomenon. The governmental process of gathering, storing, retrieving and disseminating data on individuals has always existed—and has always been recognized as a significant threat to the functioning of a free society. What is new, however, is the incredible advances in technology which have enabled governmental agencies to achieve surveillance undreamed of only a few years ago.

"Innovations in electronic and photographic techniques have made possible the collection of vast amounts of data on the day to day activities of all citizens, without so much as an inkling that the data collection is occurring.

"Innovations in computer technology have made possible the storage, retrieval and dissemination of personal dossiers on millions of Americans. Thus, the practical deterrents of cost and storage space can no longer be relied upon to check the growth of a national dossier system.

"The wedding of sophisticated information storage and dissemination systems has created, for the first time, a very real danger

Note: Burt Neuborne, Staff Attorney. American Civil Liberties Union, *Congressional Digest*, 1971, pp. 243, 245, 247, 249, 251. Reproduced by permission. From testimony given before the Subcommittee on Constitutional Rights of the Senate Committee on the Judiciary on February 23, 1971, in the course of hearings on Federal data banks.

that the sense of privacy which has traditionally insulated Americans against the fear of state encroachment will be destroyed and be replaced, instead, by a pervasive sense of being watched. The emergence of such a police state mentality could mean the destruction of our libertarian heritage.

"Civil libertarians are often asked why they regard unrestricted governmental surveillance of the individual as an evil. After all, it is said, if a person has done nothing wrong, what has he to fear from governmental surveillance?

"The simple answer to such a question is that a libertarian democratic society simply cannot exist, unless its citizens are encouraged to act free from an all encompassing sense of being observed and recorded. The tone of life and spontaneity of spirit which characterizes a free society cannot survive in an atmosphere where all deviations from the norm are immediately noted by the State and stored for future reference. The 'chilling effect' of pervasive surveillance will inevitably destroy any society's capacity for dissent, non-conformity and heterodoxy. Subtract those elements from a libertarian democracy and you have totalitarianism.

"From the very beginnings of the Republic we have recognized that a sense of anonymity *vis a vis* the government was a practical precondition to the proper functioning of a political democracy.

"Even the debates over the ratification of the Constitution were carried on anonymously in the Federalist Papers and Anti-Federalist Papers.

"It has been estimated that between 1789–1809, six Presidents, fifteen cabinet members, twenty Senators and thirty-four Congressmen published anonymous political material.

"In *Talley v. California* (1960), the Supreme Court protected the critical role which a sense of anonymity plays in the free exercise of our political freedom by invalidating a California ordinance prohibiting the dissemination of anonymous political leaflets. The Supreme Court stated:

"Anonymous pamphlets, leaflets, brochures and even books have played an important role in the progress of mankind. Persecuted groups and sects from time to time throughout history have been able to criticize oppressive practices and laws either anonymously or not at all. The obnoxious press licensing law of England, which was also enforced on the Colonies, was due in part to the knowledge that exposure of the names of printers, writers and distributors would lessen the circulation of literature critical of the government. The old seditious libel cases in England show the lengths to which government had to go to find out who was responsible for books that were obnoxious to the rulers. John Lilburne was whipped, pilloried and fined for refusing to answer questions designed to get evidence to convict him or someone else for the secret distribution of books in England. Two Puritan Ministers, John Penry and John Udal, were sentenced to death on charges that they were responsible for writing, printing or publishing books. Before the Revolutionary War colonial patriots frequently had to conceal their authorship or distribution of literature that easily could have brought down on them prosecutions by English-controlled courts. Along about that time the Letters of Junius were written and the identity of their author is unknown to this day. Even the Federalist Papers, written in favor of the adoption of our Constitution, were published

under fictitious names. It is plain that anonymity has sometimes been assumed for the most constructive purposes.'

"In *NAACP v. Alabama* (1958), the Supreme Court refused to permit Alabama to compel disclosure of the membership list of the Alabama NAACP.

"In *Griswold v. Connecticut* (1965), the Supreme Court explicity recognized a constitutional right of privacy emanating from the penumbral application of the fundamental rights guaranteed by the First, Third, Fourth, Fifth and Ninth Amendments to the Constitution. The Court noted that the First Amendment erected a zone of privacy protecting freedom of speech and association; the Third Amendment erected a zone of privacy against governmental quartering of troops; the Fourth Amendment erected a zone of privacy against unreasonable searches and seizures; and the Fifth Amendment erected a zone of privacy in the area of interrogation.

"The Supreme Court in *Griswold,* therefore, accelerated the trend of *NAACP v. Alabama* and *Talley v. California* in recognizing that a libertarian society, as we know it, cannot exist unless its citizens enjoy a sense of privacy.

"The evolution of privacy as a constitutional imperative continued in the Supreme Court with the decision in *Stanley v. Georgia* (1969). In *Stanley,* the Court invalidated a Georgia statute rendering it criminal to possess pornography. The decision of the *Stanley* Court was explicitly founded upon the inherent limitations on the States' power to inquire into the 'private' lives of its citizenry.

"The evolution of privacy as a right of constitutional dimensions received its most recent Supreme Court recognition in *Wisconsin v. Constantineau* (1971). In *Constantineau,* the Supreme Court invalidated a Wisconsin statute which permitted the 'posting' by Police Chief of names of persons to whom the sale of liquor was forbidden. The Court explicitly recognized limitations on the ability of the State to collect and to disseminate potentially derogatory information about individuals.

"The acceptance by the Supreme Court in *Talley, NAACP v. Alabama, Griswold, Stanley* and *Constantineau,* of the existence of privacy as a constitutional right renders the widespread surveillance practices currently engaged in at all levels of government of highly questionable legality. Simply, if it was unconstitutional for Alabama to compel the disclosure of the NAACP membership lists, it would be equally unconstitutional for it to assemble the identical information by photographing NAACP meetings. If it was unconstitutional for California to outlaw anonymous political activity by statute, it is equally unconstitutional for it to achieve the identical result via sophisticated surveillance. It it was unconstitutional for Wisconsin to assemble and disseminate derogatory information about individuals without any procedural safeguards, it is equally unconstitutional for it to engage in the identical practice via surveillance.

"Before the technological revolution in information gathering and storage, physical searches and interrogation constituted the primary forms of governmental surveillance. Our society evolved the Fourth Amendment protection against unreasonable searches and seizures and the Fifth Amendment protection against compulsory self-incrimination as the primary devices to safeguard the sense of privacy from those surveillance techniques. Given the revolution in surveillance techniques, however, the Fourth and Fifth Amendments, as they have been traditionally viewed, fail to afford sufficient protection against burgeoning State surveillance techniques which threaten to destroy the veil of privacy needed to insulate the dissenter, the non-conformist and the unorthodox from the fear of sanction.

"We must, therefore, evolve new safeguards if libertarian values are to be secure in the latter half of the 20th century.

"First, we must evolve a modern concept of the roles of the Fourth and Fifth Amendments in regulating surveillance.

"Second, we must evolve substantive limitations upon the government's use of the 'new' surveillance, especially in the areas of politically sensitive activity.

"Finally, we must evolve procedural guarantees which minimize the potential for abuse inherent in any system of governmental surveillance.

"When surveillance consisted primarily of physical searches, the Fourth Amendment provided a staunch bulwark for our right of privacy. Unfortunately, however, the Supreme Court has failed to extend the Fourth Amendment's prohibition against unreasonable and warrantless searches to be coextensive with modern notions of government surveillance. Despite a brilliant dissent by Mr. Justice Brandeis in 1928 in the *Olmstead* case, the Supreme Court failed to extend the scope of the Fourth Amendment to encompass wiretapping. In 1967, the Supreme Court abandoned this restrictive interpretation and held that wiretapping did constitute a 'search' under the Fourth Amendment. *Katz v. United States* (1967). Nevertheless, despite the fact that the sophisticated surveillance techniques currently in vogue involve equally intrusive searches, substantial confusion continues as to the role of the Fourth Amendment in controlling modern electronic and photographic searches.

"It is increasingly apparent that the Fourth Amendment must be read to protect individuals from all unreasonable and warrantless surveillance. In short, no surveillance should be permitted if it fails to satisfy the strictures of the Fourth Amendment.

"Thus, prior to utilizing any modern surveillance, an appropriate official should be required to appear before a magistrate and give sworn testimony that probable cause exists that the proposed surveillance will uncover specific evidence of a designated serious crime; that the surveillance is directed at a specific individual and that no less drastic means exist to obtain the evidence in question. The warrant would authorize surveillance for a limited period, and would not be renewable except upon a showing of strong probability that evidence of a serious crime would be uncovered.

"In each instance in which court approved surveillance of any kind failed to uncover evidence, a report to that effect would be required to the authorizing magistrate, and unless he ruled to the contrary, to the individual against whom the surveillance was directed.

"Finally, all material obtained pursuant to court authorized surveillance would be required to be destroyed unless actually introduced as evidence in a criminal matter.

"In connection with any criminal prosecution, a defendant would be entitled to a copy of all surveillance directed against him, to determine whether the fruits of unlawful surveillance are involved in his case.

"Any evidence obtained in violation of such Fourth Amendment surveillance procedures would be inadmissible under the doctrine of *Mapp v. Ohio* (1961).

"The recent assertion by Attorney General Mitchell of power to engage in warrantless electronic surveillance and wiretapping in situations involving 'national security' is, of course, an immense danger to the free exercise of our political freedoms. The traditional existence of a narrow exception for warrantless surveillance of foreign intelligence operations has been dramatically extended by the Attorney General into a *carte blanche* to engage in electronic surveillance of Americans whenever he deems it important from a national security standpoint.

"We must recognize, however, that even if we imposed a fully developed set of Fourth Amendment controls across the spectrum of modern surveillance, we would have only begun to deal with the problem. In addition to Fourth Amendment controls, a set of substantive limitations must be imposed upon the nature and scope of the information gathering and storage process.

"Modern surveillance consists primarily of watching devices, such as cameras and lenses; listening devices such as wiretaps or electronic bugs; and the widespread use of undercover agents who infiltrate and report upon certain groups. Each technique carries with it particular dangers, especially to the robust exercise of First Amendment freedoms. Be-fore any technique is resorted to, a form of social accounting must be considered to determine whether the danger to the basic tenets of our society inherent in the particular technique outweighs its value as a law enforcement device.

"Thus, for example, in assessing the desirability of wiretapping, one must question whether the results justify the massive destruction of privacy caused by even court supervised wiretapping. For example in New Jersey during 1970, court approved taps on over 24,000 separate conversations involving over 19,000 persons produced only two convictions—each for a gambling offense. Often the tap is placed upon a public telephone, thus ensnaring large numbers of totally unconnected persons in the surveillance net.

"As Mr. Justice Holmes eloquently said in his dissent in *Olmstead:* '[I]t is better sometimes that crime should go unpunished than that the citizen should be liable to have his premises invaded, his desks broken into, his private books, letters and papers exposed to prying curiosity, and to the misconstructions of ignorant and suspicious persons.'

"If we are to continue to tolerate wiretapping and eavesdropping we must take a long hard look at the reality of their impact and decide whether the concomitant massive loss of privacy is worth it.

"In assessing the social accounting aspects of watching devices a second set of considerations comes into play. Watching devices have been utilized with increasing frequency to monitor and to record the identities of persons engaging in lawful political activities. Thus, the New York City Police Department attempted to videotape last year's May Day celebration in Union Square, ostensibly to provide classroom footage for a course in crowd control. Only a court order prevented the videotaping. Police in Toledo, Ohio, photographed peace demonstrators and are alleged to have shown the pictures to the demonstrators' employers. FBI agents openly take moving picture footage of demonstrations as a matter of course. Police in Richmond, Virginia, photographed the license plates of demonstration participants.

"If we are to continue to tolerate the use of watching devices, we must balance their unique propensity for political surveillance against any alleged law enforcement benefit.

"Finally, in assessing the use of undercover agents, especially in the area of political associations, the devastating effect of infiltration upon free association must be weighed. The 'chilling effect' of the fear of infiltration is an ever present danger.

"We have witnessed a distressing tendency for each organ of government to attempt to develop an independent surveillance network.

"The most glaring example of the proliferation of surveillance organs is the repeated disclosure of military intelligence operations designed to gather dossiers on civilian political figures.

"In addition to the Military Intelligence dossier system, virtually every other arm of government, including the Passport Section of the Department of State, is busy gathering dossiers on individual Americans. If we are to avoid a national dossier system, legislation narrowly circumscribing the persons authorized to gather, store, retrieve and disseminate information must be enacted. Surveillance activities, including data storage, should be confined strictly to designated law enforcement officials.

"The surveillance process should be confined to individuals who are suspected of actually engaging in, or being about to engage in, serious crime.

"Blanket data collection of persons engaged in controversial political activity should be absolutely prohibited. Such data collection is currently so widespread as to be epidemic.

"The police force of virtually every city in America contains a department the major function of which is the compilation of dossiers on political activists.

"Unless specific prohibitions against the blanket surveillance of Americans engaged in protest activities are enacted, the sense of anonymity which the Supreme Court sought to preserve in *NAACP v. Alabama* and

Talley v. California will be irretrievably lost.

"There currently exists no check on the nature of the information being fed into our existing dossier system.

"First, legislation absolutely prohibiting the gathering or storage of information relating to lawful political activities is desperately needed.

"The common practice of monitoring demonstrations in order to permanently record the participants is so widespread that the FBI brazenly photographs demonstrators without fear of criticism. A recent meeting of the Suffolk County Chapter of the New York Civil Liberties Union was tape recorded by the Suffolk County Police Department without permission. During the 1967 March on Washington, military intelligence agents, disguised as demonstrators, were instructed to photograph demonstration leaders. When the photographs were developed, the New York agents had photographed the New Jersey agents and vice versa.

"Another common surveillance practice involves the compilation of membership lists in controversial political groups. Although *NAACP v. Alabama* precludes the government from requiring the disclosure of membership lists in controversial organizations, modern surveillance techniques attempt to attain the identical end covertly.

"Second, legislation outlawing the storage or dissemination of hearsay or anonymous derogatory information is desperately needed. Current practices invite the inclusion of anonymous, subjective characterizations of an individual. Such information must be excluded.

"Third, legislation regulating the storage and dissemination of arrest records is desperately needed. Current surveillance techniques provide for the wide dissemination of all arrest records, even those occurring many years ago.

"The practice of permitting the dissemination of arrest records is a self-defeating process which has the effect of fencing out arrested persons from society. The existence of an arrest record renders it virtually impossible for a member of an ethnic or racial minority to find a decent job. Despite the presumption of innocence, an arrest record acts as a punishment which stigmatizes an individual for life.

"Much of the folklore of this Nation turns on the concept of putting a person's past behind him and beginning a new life. This Nation was settled by waves of immigrants who chose to begin a 'new life' in the new world. The vastness of the Nation and the existence of the frontier posed numerous opportunities for a fresh start.

"Given modern technology, however, it has become virtually impossible for any citizen to escape from his past. As surely as the scarlet letter was once branded on the flesh, our computers now impose an electronic brand upon us. There is no escape from our past; no opportunity for a fresh start. Truly, we live imprisoned in a web of imperishable data.

"'We must evolve a social procedure, analogous to the economic bankruptcy process, whereby an individual can gain a 'discharge' from his past. Just as the commercial process could not function without a procedure enabling participants to attempt a fresh start, the social system cannot function without a procedure enabling individuals to obliterate the residue of their past errors. That procedure was once the simple expedient of moving to a new town. A shrinking world has destroyed that procedure; and we must evolve a new one. Thus, an informational statute of limitations should be an integral part of any surveillance system, automatically expunging 'stale' information after a given period.

"Even the imposition of careful substantive limitations upon the surveillance process cannot remove its capacity for abuse. In order to minimize that capacity, the surveillance process must be hedged with rigorous procedural safeguards.

"Every person about whom personal data is being stored by the Government must be notified of that fact and must be permitted access to his dossier to check its accuracy and propriety. An individual, upon receipt of a notice of dossier compilation, must be permitted an opportunity to challenge the propriety of the maintenance of a dossier.

"Notice of a request for personal information must be given to an individual prior to its dissemination. The notice must describe the putative information recipient and summarize the requested information. An individual, upon receipt of such a notice, must be afforded an opportunity to challenge the proposed dissemination.

"An individual must be afforded an expeditious opportunity to challenge the accuracy or propriety of information contained in his dossier. Such an opportunity should take the form of an 'accuracy hearing' or 'propriety hearing' at which an individual could rebut the contents of his dossier and move for its expunction. Such a procedure would be highly useful to remove 'stale' information from a dossier.

"To the extent information is gathered in violation of the expanded Fourth Amendment or the substantive statutory limitations imposed upon surveillance, it should be subject to an 'exclusionary rule' and stricken from the records.

"To the extent information is disseminated in violation of procedural and substantive safeguards, an individual should have the option of either recovering his actual damages or settling for a statutory liquidated amount.

"As with almost every field of technological advance, we are faced in the area of surveillance with the dilemma of controlling the technological Frankensteins we have created. In the industrial area, production technology threatens the physical ecology of our continent; in the political area, surveillance technology threatens the psychological ecology of the democratic spirit. If we are to survive as a libertarian society, we must insure that the delicate sense of freedom which is dependent upon a commitment to individual privacy is not destroyed in the often spurious name of 'efficiency.'"

If You Liked "1984," You'll Love 1973

NAT HENTOFF

Welcome to postconstitutional America, where big brother's spies, bugs and data banks keep tabs on you from birth to death.

In New York, a 22-year-old woman has been fighting a Civil Service Commission order that she be fired from her job as a substitute postal clerk. The commission has learned from the FBI files that this woman—exercising her First Amendment rights—had taken part in a campus demonstration at Northwestern University in 1969. She was also, according to the FBI, a member at that time of Students for a Democratic Society—a legally constituted organization.

In Philadelphia, former mayors James Tate and Richardson Dilworth have charged that the present mayor, ex-police chief Frank L. Rizzo, is tapping their telephones. And Kent Pollock, an investigative reporter for *The Philadelphia Inquirer*, claims that his private life has been investigated ever since he wrote a story on police corruption. Greg Walter, on the staff of the same paper, has also been critical of Rizzo and of the police department. As a result, Walter charges, "Persons who are close to me, persons who

Note: Nat Hentoff, "If You Liked '1984,' You'll Love 1973," *Playboy*, 1973, pp. 147, 148, 156, 178, 182, 184–186. Originally appeared in *Playboy* magazine; copyright © 1973 by Playboy.

were contacts of mine in . . . Philadelphia have been questioned extensively about my sex life, my drinking habits and God knows what all. And this information is all filed away."

In Cleveland, a recent issue of *Point of View,* a local investigatory publication, quotes a police officer who was sympathetic to the administration of Carl Stokes when the latter was mayor of Cleveland. According to the officer, Stoke's staff knew that the mayor's private office was bugged and that its phones were tapped by the Cleveland police, many of whom were quite hostile to the city's first black mayor. But Stoke's staff felt, the maverick cop explained, "that if they brought the Cleveland police intelligence unit in to remove the bugs, they would have removed five and put in ten." The staff also decided that hiring a private firm to do the bug-clearing and wire-tap-removing job wasn't worth it, since the cost would persistently recur. I checked out the story with a source very high in Stoke's administration and he confirmed it. "I will authorize you to say," my source added, "but without revealing my name, that while Carl Stokes was mayor of Cleveland, he never held any really important meetings in his private office. He always used rooms in different hotels, and he would call those hotels at a moment's notice, just prior to the time the room was needed for the meeting. That way, the Cleveland police didn't have time to bug that particular room or put taps on its phones."

In Milwaukee, a letter from an ordinary, apolitical citizen appeared in the letters column of the July 1, 1971, Milwaukee Journal:

> I never used to look at our country from the political aspect, for I have always felt secure. But now I do, and I am confused. . . . I have been involved in a situation which tends to make me raise grave doubts. Recently, a friend and I were walking down Brady Street around midnight. While stopping for a DON'T WALK sign, we heard a series of clicks. Looking around, we saw an unmarked police car with one officer inside. He had his camera aimed at us and was taking pictures. I rather believed in the law, but this action caused me to wonder. Why was it done? Does someone have an answer?

In October 1972, *The New York Times,* in a lead editorial, tried to provide part of the answer by describing the chilling atmosphere that the Nixon Administration has created not only on the Federal level but also through the encouragement its practices give to state and local officials. "The President and his men," the *Times* pointed out, "have injected into national life a new and unwelcome element—fear of Government repression, a fear reminiscent of that bred by the McCarthyism of 20 years ago. The freedom of the press . . . the right to privacy, the right to petition and dissent, the right of law-abiding citizens to be free of surveillance, investigation and harassment—these and other liberties of the individual are visibly less secure in America today than they were four years ago." The *Times,* accordingly, supported McGovern. You know who won and by how much.

One explanation for the indifference of the majority of the electorate to the danger that we are approaching what former New

Jersey Democratic Congressman Cornelius Gallagher has called "postconstitutional America" is that many Americans have come to *accept* such ominous phenomena as the precipitous rise in dossier collecting and spying by local, state and Federal secret police. The majority has surely not welcomed the prevalence of secret surveillance, but the practice is considered a normal fact of late-20th Century life in the U.S.

In view of the lack of public concern about the rise of secret surveillance, along with the increasing sophistication of surveillance technology, Justice Louis Brandeis' 1927 dissent in *Olmstead vs. United States*—the first time the Supreme Court declared judicially authorized wire tapping to be constitutional—is all the more powerful today. "The makers of our Constitution," he wrote, "conferred, as against the Government, the right to be let alone—the most comprehensive of rights and the right most valued by civilized men."

The extent to which our right to be let alone has been eroded has been made appallingly clear by Michael Sorkin, an investigative reporter for *The Des Moines Register,* in a detailed account that appeared in the September 1972 issue of *Washington Monthly.* The FBI, he writes, is well into the process of compiling "the largest single depository of information ever gathered about U.S. citizens by their Government." The FBI's data bank is fed by a computerized network designed to receive and store information from all 50 states through 40,-000 Federal, state and local agencies. The raw material is coming in with increasing speed and, by 1975, some 95 percent of the nation's law-enforcement agencies will be hooked into the mammoth privacy-shredding machine.

The National Crime Information Center in Washington is the central depository of such information, with the names of millions of Americans—many of them never charged with a crime—neatly filed away. It is likely to contain the names and records of all those ever arrested for any cause, since the master computer is not required to show if an arrest led to indictment or trial, let alone to conviction. Since an estimated 50,000,000 Americans now have arrest records of one sort or another, you have one chance in four of being in the data bank once it's fully hooked up across the country. And since the probability of a black urban male's being arrested at least once before he dies is estimated to be as high as 90 percent, the data bank is going to be exceptionally well integrated.

In this respect, it's essential to realize that in 20 to 30 percent of arrests, the police never bring charges; they drop cases for a diversity of reasons, such as lack of evidence and mistaken identification. Furthermore, according to the 1969 FBI Uniform Crime Reports, of 7,500,000 people arrested that year for all kinds of criminal acts, excluding traffic offenses, more than 1,300,000 were never prosecuted or charged and 2,200,000 were acquitted or had the charges against them dismissed. Yet in those millions of cases in which an arrest doesn't lead to conviction, only eight states have statutes providing for expungement of records of arrest without conviction. And of those eight, only one provides for the expungement of records for a person with a previous conviction.

The harm of having arrest records centrally available for checking by government and private employers is incalculable. As a 1971 study by the President's Commission on Federal Statistics has emphasized, "An applicant [for a job] who lists a previous arrest faces at best a 'second trial' in which, without procedural safeguards, he must prove his innocence; at worst the listing of the arrest disqualifies him per se." One recent study of employment agencies in the New York area, for example, revealed that 75 percent would refuse an applicant with an arrest record, even though the arrest hadn't led to a conviction.

But much more than arrest records are in the national data bank and in the burgeoning files of state and local police. First of all, thanks to a decision made by the late

J. Edgar Hoover and by John Mitchell, when the latter was Attorney General, there is no requirement that *any* of the raw materials in the electronic surveillance network be evaluated for accuracy. This means that even if you haven't been arrested, derogatory information about you can be supplied to the data bank with no check as to its reliability.

A 1971 study by the Law Enforcement Assistance Administration, which provides Federal funds for the FBI data bank, noted that half of the 108 computer projects already in existence at that time were collecting data on "potential troublemakers." (The Justice Department keeps copious records on persons who are "violence prone" and on other "persons of interest" for national security reasons.) The LEAA study recommended legislation to restrict and monitor the use of such information, but not a single copy of that study was given to Congress.

Since the FBI's computer network now operates without legislative restraint concerning privacy, each state decides what kind of information it will put into the network, and many states are alarmingly permissive as to what they allow cities to supply to state data banks—information that is then forwarded to the National Crime Information Center.

"Kansas City," *Washington Monthly* points out, "is feeding its computer the names of area dignitaries such as councilmen, judges and other municipal leaders; parolees; adults and juveniles with arrest records; people with a history of mental disturbance (would Thomas Eagleton have been listed?) or who have confronted or opposed law-enforcement personnel in the performance of their duties; college students known to have participated in disturbances; suspects in shoplifting cases; and people with outstanding parking-ticket warrants."

Welcome to Washington, all ye who would exercise your First Amendment right "to petition the Government for a redress of grievances." During the first week of May

1971, nearly 13,000 people protesting the killings of students at Kent State by the National Guard, were swept up in dragnet arrests by Washington police with the enthusiastic support—and direction—of the Nixon Justice Department. It was the largest mass bust in American history, and only 128 of those arrested were found guilty after trial. Administration officials have said that such mass arrests will take place again, under similar circumstances; and, in that event, the arrest records of all those caught in the net will be included in the national data bank.

On the state level, some states say they may limit access to their computer files to law-enforcement officers only. Other states may decide to make the information available to anyone willing to pay a fee, a course Iowa is now contemplating. It must be emphasized, moreover, that unless legislation is enacted to the contrary, each state can determine whether its raw files will include data going beyond criminal matters—into such areas as records of applicants for Civil Service jobs.

Let us suppose, however, that somehow you don't end up in the FBI's computerized central files, with its circuits to and from state data banks. You're not safe yet. There are many other data banks in the process of interfacing—that is, exchanging information with one another. As of this writing, Federal investigators already have access to 264,000,000 police records, 323,000,000 medical histories, 279,000,000 psychiatric reports and 100,000,000 credit files. Among their sources are the files of the Secret Service, the Civil Service Commission, the Department of Health, Education and Welfare (hospitals are required to forward to HEW the confidential records of patients receiving Medicare and Medicaid benefits), the Department of Housing and Urban Development, the Census Bureau and the Internal Revenue Service.

If you've been under the illusion that your Federal tax returns are held in strict confidence, you may be disquieted to learn that they are available not only to state tax officials but to any select committee of the House or the Senate—and to anyone else authorized by Executive order. The University of Missouri's Freedom of Information Center reports that "between 1953 and 1970, 53 of those orders were issued, two of the chief beneficiaries being the old House Un-American Activities Committee and the Senate Committee on Internal Security."

A statement of dissent, even by a prominent American, can lead to his harassment through release of his income-tax returns to investigatory agencies. A distinguished professor of government, long a critic of the war in Vietnam, was puzzled and disturbed when, over a period of years, his income-tax returns were intensively reviewed by Internal Revenue agents, while evidence accumulated that other agencies of the Government were privy to those returns. Finally, a former White House assistant, whose conscience had been bothering him about the dogging of the professor, admitted to the victim that it had all come about on direct orders from Lyndon Johnson.

Nor, by any means, are dossiers and data banks a creation only of the Government. In a 1971 report for the American Civil Liberties Union, Ralph Nader focused on how very private information about you can be collected even if you're not a dissenter or a freak of one kind or another, and even if you escape the various Federal data banks. By way of illustration, Nader wrote, "When you try to buy life insurance, a file of . . . intimate information about you is compiled by the 'inspection agency.' The insurance company not only finds out about your health, it also learns about your drinking habits (how often, how much, with others or alone, and even what beverage), your net worth, salary, debts, domestic troubles, reputation, associates, manner of living and standing in the community. The investigator is also asked to inquire of your neighbors and associates whether there is 'any criticism of character or morals.' The 'inspection agency' that obtains this information puts it into a dossier and saves it. The agency may later make another investigation for an insurance company, or for an employer, a prospective creditor or a landlord. In fact, the agency will probably make this personal information available to anyone who has five dollars and calls himself a 'prospective employer.' "

Private credit bureaus have similar masses of data on individuals and they, as well as insurance companies, will open their files to agents of the Federal Government. In January 1972, Edward Brennan, Jr., vice-president of TRW Credit, a completely computerized national credit-reporting company, admitted on an ABC special, Assault on Privacy, that the Fair Credit Reporting Act "now makes it mandatory that we supply information to . . . police departments and any Governmental agency that has a legitimate reason for accessing." All told, the more than 2500 credit-reporting companies in the country have files on at least 110,000,000 Americans. Some files are limited only to credit information; others contain more about your personal habits, finances, medical history and life style than your closest friends may know.

With all these private and Government computers exchanging information about millions of Americans—probably including you—we may be approaching a time when, as former Attorney General Ramsey Clark has warned, "a person can hardly speak his mind to any other person without being afraid that the police or someone else will hear what he thinks. Because of our numbers and the denseness of our urban society, it will be difficult enough in the future for us to secure some little sense of privacy and individual integrity. We can trap ourselves, we can become the captives of our technology, and we can change the meaning of man as an individual."

Why do we stand by as our privacy is raped? Why do we acquiesce as the rapidly growing quantity of information being fed to and distributed by the FBI data bank threatens to become what Senator Charles Mathias, a liberal Republican from Mary-

land, calls "the raw materials of tyranny"? Part of the answer is fear: a national fear, born in the late Sixties, of demonstrators, of blacks, of students, of muggers. The national desire, an almost desperate desire—as Richard Nixon accurately reads it—is for order. In this kind of climate, the majority of the people are much more concerned with their safety than with civil liberties—not only those of others but their own.

A seminal Congressional reaction to the fears of the populace was the Omnibus Crime Control and Safe Streets Act of May 1968. The bill, with only four Senators and 17 Representatives voting against it, sharply limited the rights of criminal defendants and greatly broadened the permissible use of bugging and wire tapping by the Government. During debate on the measure, then-Senator Ralph Yarborough, who later was not one of the four to vote against the bill, declared that "the Senate has opened a Pandora's box of inquisitorial power such as we have never seen in the history of this country." Senator Hiram Fong, who *did* vote against the bill (together with Philip Hart, Lee Metcalf and John Sherman Cooper), added: "I am fearful that if these wire-tapping and eavesdropping practices are allowed to continue on a widespread scale, we will soon become a nation in fear—a police state."

Two years later, in an amendment to the Organized Crime Act, Congress authorized the FBI to keep centralized criminal records, thereby leading to the establishment of the FBI's data bank. During the same year, Congress passed a drug bill permitting police to break into any place without warning if they had a court order and if they believed that a preliminary knock on the door might result in the destruction of evidence. Commenting on this "no-knock" bill in *The New York Times,* columnist Tom Wicker asked: "How long will it be before agents come bursting without warning into the houses of political dissidents, contending under this law that any other procedure would have resulted in the destruction of pamphlets, documents and the like, needed by society to convict?"

As Congress yielded to the fear of its constituents, the Supreme Court—ultimate protector of our privacy, along with our other constitutional rights and liberties—became markedly less sensitive to the need for safeguarding the Bill of Rights. As Nixon began to appoint new Justices—there are now four Nixon selections on the Court—the egalitarian spirit of the Warren Court began to be reversed.

A significant, though little noted, decision by what can now be called the Burger Court was handed down in December 1970. By a 5–4 majority, the Court ruled that state courts could use, in criminal proceedings, hearsay evidence that would not be admissible in Federal courts. If fear in this country —including fear of dissenters—intensifies, state criminal charges of conspiracy can, under this ruling, be brought against political defendants on the basis of secondhand testimony from secret police agents who don't want their identities publicly revealed.

As *The New Yorker* made clear, "The Sixth Amendment to the Constitution gives defendants in criminal cases the right to confront witnesses against them, and, by extension, this (with a few exceptions) rules out hearsay evidence, since the person who makes the accusation, not the person who heard it secondhand, is the one to be confronted." This Burger Court ruling narrows every citizen's liberties, particularly since, as *New Yorker* emphasized, "93 percent of all criminal cases are tried in stat courts. . . . The decision places 93 percent of all defendants, guilty and innocent alike, at a severe disadvantage.

During its 1971–1972 term, the Supreme Court handed down an equally dangerous decision, maintaining that it was no longer necessary in state criminal trials to have a unanimous jury verdict. As Melvin Wulf, legal director of the American Civil Liberties Union, has pointed out: "The decision . . . effectively abolishes the need for a jury to agree that the prosecution has proven guilt beyond a reasonable doubt."

Another Burger Court decision that is disheartening to civil libertarians allows police to stop and frisk people on the street under circumstances that, as Wulf points out, "come nowhere near satisfying the Fourth Amendment's 'probable cause' standard for arrest." It is now, therefore, much easier for the police to intimidate dissenters —and "possible" dissenters—by literally putting them against the nearest wall.

Yet another ominous ruling by the Burger Court has made further inroads on the right to refuse to testify before a grand jury or a trial jury on the Fifth Amendment ground of possible self-incrimination. This right has been steadily eroded in recent years as witnesses have been compelled to accept immunity from prosecution and thereby testify or be held in contempt of court. Under the Burger Court decision, that kind of pressure from the Government has been considerably strengthened. The forced witness used to be given transactional immunity, which meant that the Government couldn't prosecute him for anything connected with his compelled testimony. Now a witness can be forced to testify in return for only *use* immunity, which means that though the Government can't use his own testimony or any leads from it to build its case against him, he can still be prosecuted. But how will it be possible to prove that a subsequent lead that the Government does use against a witness wasn't developed, however obliquely, from something he said under forced testimony?

It used to be that dissenters, whether under grand-jury pressure or not, had recourse to the press to reveal information they believed to be in the public interest or to give their side of a case in which the Government was prosecuting them or associates of theirs. In such cases, the dissenting source often didn't want to be identified, for fear of Government retaliation, and he would talk only to a reporter whom he trusted not to reveal his identity. This way for dissenters and others to get information to the public has been seriously limited by another Burger Court decision. In the case of New York Times reporter Earl Caldwell, the Court declared—with all four of the Nixon appointees in the majority—that a reporter does not have a constitutional right to protect his sources.

The effect of the Caldwell decision is already evident. In Caldwell's own case, he has burned the tapes and notes he had collected for a book he was preparing on the Black Panther Party. This material, which had not appeared in the Times, had been obtained by a pledge of confidentiality, and Caldwell didn't want to take the chance that, under repeated threats of being jailed, he might finally break that pledge. The burning of his tapes and notes is both a loss to history and a denial of the public's First Amendment right to get information about public issues.

Another illustration of the increasing willingness of Government to subvert the Bill of Rights has been the pressure against Beacon Press and its parent church organization, the Unitarian Universalist Association. On October 22, 1971, Beacon published the so-called Senator Gravel edition of the Pentagon papers. These were public documents that Senator Gravel had inserted into the records of a Senate subcommittee he heads. Sevens days after publication, FBI agents, acting for the Justice Department's Internal Security Division, appeared at the bank in which the Unitarian Universalist Association has its accounts. The agents had a Federal grand-jury subpoena calling for delivery of all of the church's records—not just those of Beacon Press—including copies of each check written and each check deposited by the church group between June first and October 15, 1971.

Every church member throughout the country who sent a check to the Unitarian Universalist Association during that time is now in the FBI files, and I have information that donations to the church have declined following the news of the FBI's collection of its bank records. The experience of this church group indicates that we may be coming closer to a state in which, as Justice William O. Douglas has warned, "our citizens will be afraid to utter any but

the safest and most orthodox thoughts; afraid to associate with any but the most acceptable people. Freedom as the Constitution envisages [it] will have vanished."

Meanwhile, as Government pressure against the press and against dissenters intensifies, with Justice Douglas increasingly among the minority in Supreme Court decisions concerning basic civil liberties, the technology to make this a pervasively watched society continues to advance. There are the inviting possibilities, for instance, of closed-circuit TV. Last year, the Committee on Telecommunications of the National Academy of Engineering prepared a study about which you might not have been informed on television or in your local paper. The study, paid for by the Justice Department, recommended 24-hour television surveillance of city streets.

It's already happening. Among the cities that now have or soon will have 24-hour uninterrupted surveillance of a downtown area are Hoboken, New Jersey; Mount Vernon, New York; Saginaw, Michigan; and San Jose, California. Any city, if it has the money, can do it, because so far there are no laws against electronic surveillance of large public areas. The immediate purpose of keeping watch in this way on the citizenry is to cut down street crime. But among other consequences of having the police department's unblinking eye on certain parts of a city is that demonstrators converging in those areas can be photographed and their identities filed for future use—all from police headquarters.

The psychological effects—and the dangers to the Bill of Rights—of increasing police surveillance of public areas have been analyzed in a probing and disturbing article in the winter 1972 issue of *Columbia Human Rights Law Review*, published by students at the Columbia University School of Law: "To begin with," says the *Review*, "police can use a . . . surveillance system to read a pedestrian's lips or to read documents in his possesion. More generally, police can direct the cameras to observe . . . people in their apartments in cars or on the streets . . . One might reasonably fear that police abuse of the system would lead to increased dossier building. In a way not presently practicable, the police could use wide-scale surveillance systems to track associational ties and mark the day-to-day habits of revolutionaries, activists, homosexuals and other people of police interest. . . . To the extent that America adopts the ethic of a watched society, we inevitably lose the sense of participatory democracy and trust that privacy nourishes."

Among other coming surveillance attractions in the watched society is spying by helicopter. New York City recently completed a two-year test of this avant-garde way of by-passing the Bill of Rights. The cost was $490,000. But the wonders of surveillance by helicopter aren't limited to the police departments of such big cities as New York. Kettering, Ohio, a suburb of Dayton, has a population of 70,000 who can occasionally see two police helicopters equipped with siren, public-address system, searchlights, radio—and a portable video-tape camera.

With the market for police visual-surveillance equipment booming—or, rather, zooming—manufacturers are zestfully promoting their spying wares. In a characteristic sales pitch, Eugene G. Fubini, former vice-president for research at IBM and now a private consultant, told those attending a National Law Enforcement Symposium: "Wouldn't you like to be able to frisk every citizen without him knowing he is being frisked? . . . You can put multidimensional magnetometers in turnstiles and movie theaters and lots of other places. Let me try another one: You could put on all bridges and parkways a device which reads license plates and automatically matches them against a list."

We are well into what the Lawyers' Committee for Civil Rights Under Law calls a "police-industrial complex" that will serve "to increase an already extensive, easily abused police capability for surveillance, harassment and interference with noncriminal activities." And what the police see and record will be filed and then hooked into

local, state and Federal data banks. In September 1972, conservative columnist James J. Kilpatrick wrote: "For many years, politically active Americans have been wondering: Were they suffering a kind of paranoia, or was Big Brother really watching them? Answer: He was watching."

Now, every year, Big Brother watches and puts into dossiers more and more of what we're doing and saying. A grimly reasonable case can be made that University of Michigan Law School Professor Arthur R. Miller was being prescient rather than fanciful in 1971 when he speculated in his book *The Assault on Privacy*: "The identification number given to us at birth might become a leash around our necks and make us the object of constant monitoring through a womb-to-tomb computer dossier."

Most of us already have such an identification number. It's our Social Security card. As Senator Sam Erwin has noted, although the Social Security card states on its face that it's not to be used for identification purposes (except for Social Security and income-tax needs), citizens have to submit their Social Security numbers on job applications, voter-registration affidavits, credit applications, telephone records, arrest records, military records, driver's licenses and many other forms. In fact, there is a move in Congress that would make Professor Miller's prophecy come true. On March 2, 1972, the Senate Finance Committee voted to require that every child be issued a Social Security card upon entering the first grade. Not to be outdone, Representative Martha Griffiths, Democrat from Michigan, proposed that it be assigned at birth.

Widespread use of a single number of identification, Senator Ervin adds, can hasten Government maintenance of extensive computerized data banks of information on all of us. The Social Security number alone, he points out, could be the single, common key required "to link computers, enabling them to talk among themselves, promiscuously combining accurate, inaccurate and incomplete information about nearly all

Americans. . . . Decisions affecting a person's job, retirement benefits, security clearance, credit rating or many other rights may be made without benefit of a hearing or confrontation of the evidence."

Despite such omens of *1984*, it would be foolish and foolhardy to simply allow post-constitutional America to come into being without fighting to keep and to regenerate *this* Constitution. There *are* ways to do more than privately keen over the drifting away of the Bill of Rights. One way is through the courts. With regard to political surveillance by secret police, for example, at least 30 suits have been brought by the A.C.L.U., as of January 1973, that challenge spying on political activities by the FBI, the National Guard, state and local police departments. More will surely be filed by the A.C.L.U. and other civil-liberties organizations in the months ahead.

The main thrust in most of these court actions is to force disclosure of how dossiers on individuals and organizations are opened and nurtured, on whom they are kept and to whom their contents are distributed. A corollary request for relief is that the secret police be forbidden from then on to gather information for political dossiers and be required to destroy those they already have.

A characteristic suit of this nature has been brought by the Civil Liberties Union of Southern California against the Los Angeles Police Department. The C.L.U. charges in its complaint that the police keep files on a variety of organizations—church, political, educational—and on individuals associated with these groups, even though neither the police department nor any police officer "has any information that such group or person has committed, will commit or intends to commit any criminal offense."

That case and others like it are still in the courts. There has been one significant triumph in this area, along with one seeming victory that turned into a defeat because of what Nixon has done to the Supreme Court. The defeat, which is not terminal (other cases can still be brought, despite this particular Supreme Court decision), concerns a case brought against then–Secretary of Defense Melvin Laird by Arlo Tatum, a Quaker, and other plaintiffs who charged that the United States Army had been secretly keeping track on their lawful civilian political activities. Tatum and his associates in the suit had long and publicly opposed the war in Vietnam, and that made them fodder for Army spies, who, according to Senator Ervin, had kept tabs until at least 1969 on more than 100,000 civilians and organizations.

In April 1971, a U.S. Court of Appeals sent the case (*Laird vs. Tatum*) back to the lower Federal district court that had denied relief to Tatum and his associates. The Court of Appeals disagreed with the lower court's findings, declaring that the plaintiffs did have a case and that it ought to be heard. The Court of Appeals, moreover, stressed the danger of the country of Army political surveillance of civilians and went on to order that the following facts be determined: "The nature of the Army domestic intelligence system . . . specifically the extent of the system, the methods of gathering the information, its content and substance, the methods of retention and distribution, and the recipients of the information. . . . Whether the existence of any overbroad aspects of the intelligence-gathering system . . . has or might have an intimidating effect on appellants or others similarly situated."

In sum, just what the hell was the Army up to by spying on civilian political activity? Did all those dossiers really have any relationship to the Army's responsibility for handling such massive civilian disorders as might arise? Or was the Army just collecting whatever it could find about potential troublemakers, even though they had done nothing unlawful? After all, said the Court of Appeals, "To permit the military to exercise a totally unrestricted investigative function in regard to civilians, divorced from the normal restrictions of legal process and the courts, and necessarily coupling sensitive information with military power, could create a dangerous situation in the Republic."

But, we have been told, the Army no longer spies on civilians, so why stir up a dead issue? Yet, as Senator Ervin noted in May 1972, "It's going to be impossible to destroy all the information the Army has gathered. Our investigations show that while the Army was engaged in spying on civilians, it interchanged information that it collected with the FBI and with local law-enforcement agencies throughout the United States, and there is no way we can run that down and get it out of their files."

Therefore, the issues raised in *Laird vs. Tatum* are hardly dead. Accordingly, the Court of Appeals decision could have been a stunning breakthrough toward letting the citizenry see some of the inner workings of the total national political surveillance system, of which the Army secret police is one branch. Most unfortunately, the Supreme Court thought otherwise. The Government having appealed the Court of Appeals decision, the High Court dismissed *Laird vs. Tatum* in June 1972. The vote was 5–4 and in the majority were all four Nixon's appointees, including the redoubtable William Rehnquist, who participated in the decision even though he had been directly involved in the issue at the core of this suit while he was in the Justice Department and testified before Senator Ervin's Subcommittee on Constitutional Rights, that he opposed any limitation on Government surveillance of any citizen.

The majority of the Court, in *Laird vs. Tatum*, declared that it isn't enough to claim that being spied on has a "chilling effect" on the exercising of your First Amendment rights. You have to be more specific and show palpable injury directly resulting from political surveillance—loss of a job or loss of income, for example. In his vehement dissent, Justice Douglas wrote: "This case is a cancer in our body politic. It is a measure of the disease which afflicts us. Army surveillance, like Army regimentation, is at war with the principles of the

First Amendment. Those who already walk submissively will say there is no cause for alarm. But submissiveness is not our heritage. The First Amendment was designed to allow rebellion to remain as our heritage. The Constitution was designed to keep Government off the backs of the people. The Bill of Rights was added to keep the precincts of belief and expression, of the press, of political and social activities free from surveillance. The Bill of Rights was designed to keep agents of Government and official eavesdroppers away from assemblies of people. The aim was to allow men to be free and independent and to assert their rights against Government. There can be no influence more paralyzing of that objective than Army surveillance. When an Intelligence officer looks over every nonconformist's shoulder in the library or walks invisibly by his side in a picket line or infiltrates his club, the America once extolled as the voice of liberty heard around the world no longer is cast in the image which Jefferson and Madison designed, but more in the Russian image."

Several lower Federal court decisions since *Laird vs. Tatum*, fortunately, indicate that the door is far from closed to attempts, through the courts, to expose Government ferrets gnawing at the Bill of Rights. In Philadelphia, a Federal judge refused to dismiss a suit against the local police department for keeping files on all known demonstrators in that city. And on October 25, 1972, a Federal judge in the state of Washington settled a suit by ten antiwar demonstrators against the police of the city of Longview who had taken pictures of antiwar marches in the fall of 1969. That court order requires destruction of all police photographs of the plaintiffs, who in turn have agreed to drop their claim for damages.

So the court route to protect our Constitution—and ourselves—from the secret police is being used. Future suits will focus on specific harm—direct or indirect—resulting from police surveillance, such as the disruption of lawful organizations by police infiltrators.

Some of these cases will be lost; but there is reason to believe that others can be won. Even a losing case may produce a dissenting opinion that later guides both lawyers and judges in other jurisdictions.

In addition to continuing the battle in the courts, the campaign against the secret police can also be waged by legislation. Among a number of bills now pending in Congress to stem the assault on privacy is New York Congressman Edward Koch's Federal privacy act, which requires that each Government agency maintaining records on any individual must: notify the person that such a record exists; disclose such records only with the consent of the individual; maintain an accurate record of all persons to whom any information is divulged and the purposes for which it was given to them; permit the individual on whom there is a record to inspect it, make copies of it and supplement it; remove erroneous information of any kind and notify all agencies and persons to whom the erroneous material has been transferred that it has been removed.

Although it's a useful start, there are weaknesses in the Koch bill—a basic flaw being its exclusion from the privacy safeguards of records "specifically required by Executive order to be kept secret in the interest of national security." The Government cannot safely be allowed to simply pronounce the words "national security" and thereby seal off whatever it wills. At the very least, in any court case under a privacy act, the burden of proof has to be on the Government to justify any attempt to keep secret the records maintained on an individual or a group.

Another fundamental weakness in the Koch bill is its exclusion from privacy protection of "investigatory files compiled for law-enforcement purposes, except to the extent that such records have been maintained for a longer period than reasonably necessary to commence prosecution." As I have indicated, that clause would leave unprotected the swiftly growing mass of data being collected by Federal agencies and states and cities for the FBI data bank at the National Crime Information Center. And Koch's attempt to mitigate that clause in his bill by the term "reasonably necessary" is so broad and vague as to be useless.

The intent behind the bill, nevertheless, is commendable—as is Congressman Koch's recognition that "most types of surveillance and data collection should be forbidden absolutely." Again, at the very least, no Government agency should have the right, for one example, to engage in political surveillance of lawful activities. But other kinds of legislation—state as well as Federal—will be necessary, along with persistent court actions, to safeguard privacy against the myriad secret police. Even so limited a Federal privacy act as the Koch bill, however, could become a catalytic force in creating public pressure for stronger legislation.

If the Koch bill, or one similar to it, can be passed, the provision that everyone on whom records are kept must be so informed might well startle at least some of the populace from sleep as their liberties are being computerized away. Under such a law, huge numbers of Americans would have to be informed that dossiers with their names on them are in some agency's files (and thereby, through computer interfacing, are likely to be in *many* agencies' files). Accordingly, a tougher Federal privacy act might conceivably follow the passage of a relatively mild bill if enough citizens were stirred to anger on finding out that they, too—not just extremists and other freaks—are in the secret police files.

It is also important to provide, by law, for the erasure of a considerable amount of material now in state and Federal files that has no business being there—ranging from the names of dissenters who have lawfully used their First Amendment rights to information gathered by credit bureaus about the private lives of citizens applying for charge accounts. Absolute erasure is impossible, because some Federal agencies and police departments are likely to squirrel away some files for vague future use. But at least the doctrine in law that certain information harmful to an individual should be erased will place the secret police on notice that their retention of illegal raw files can subject them to a court suit if a citizen finds out about it.

A strong rationale for erasure is provided by privacy expert Alan Westin: "Look at the way the property system has established rights in our capitalist system," he writes. "You wipe out records of bankruptcy, for example, and it is part of the commercial system that after a certain period of time we simply do not continue to record certain kinds of commercial failures because we want to encourage people to come back into business. The same thing should be true of our personal records and our personal privacy."

I believe that no state or local agency, whether supported by Federal funds or not, has the constitutional right to invade any individual's privacy—at the very least without his knowing about it and then being able to take action against it. Furthermore, since private agencies—such as credit bureaus—exchange information with Government agencies, they, too, should be included in laws regulating their collection and distribution of information.

An even stronger supplementary safeguard has been proposed by attorney Richard Miller, as reported in the University of Missouri's Freedom of Information Bulletin: "He would like to see state laws providing that public agencies, private firms and agents in the business of gathering and distributing personal data be liable to injured parties for passing out false information or knowingly disseminating true information for a defamatory purpose."

This liability, I would emphasize, should also extend to Federal agencies and personnel in the data-collecting and data-distributing business. The liability, moreover, should consist of money damages for the injured party and sanctions against those, whether public or private agents, who are found to have caused the injury. When private citizens start collecting damages because they've been abused by secret police and other information gatherers, and when some of these secret agents are demoted or otherwise punished for mugging the Bill of Rights, the zeal to snoop may well be markedly diminished.

Finally, on Federal, state and local levels, there should also be independent commissions to make sure that new laws safeguarding privacy are being enforced. The Lawyers' Committee for Civil Rights Under Law restricts its recommendation to a national independent commission that would conduct audits and spot checks and would report to Congress. But independent state and local commissions also ought to be functioning in a similar way, and they should report to state and local legislative bodies. These commissions, as the Lawyers' Committee recommends, "should include constitutional lawyers, representatives of citizens' groups and other civilians."

In the meantime, even children are no longer immune to the omnipresent eye of surveillance. An unintentionally chilling press release was issued by Eastman Kodak Company last year. It concerns the Polk County, Florida, school system, which has an enrollment of 60,000 students and, according to Kodak, "operates more schools in more towns than any other system in the United States. It controls 58 elementary schools, 14 junior highs, ten senior highs and one vocational-technical school." If we don't do something to stop the national drift, here is an augury of what may be ahead for more Americans than just these Polk County students:

SURVEILLANCE CAMERAS HELP ADMINISTRATORS MAINTAIN ORDER IN FLORIDA SCHOOLS

Bartow, Florida—Smiles and friendly greetings now far outnumber scowls and random left hooks among junior and senior high school students throughout Polk County, Florida. That's because their actions are being recorded on film, and if anyone does anything to seriously disrupt school routine, the odds against establishing an alibi are far from even.

W. W. Read, superintendent of the Polk County School Board, emphasizes that this is by no means a snooping operation. Although the cameras operate . . . during school hours, the film is processed and viewed only when disruptions have occurred. Although the super-8 surveillance cameras have been in use only a short time, Read reports that their psychological impact already has reduced disruptive incidents, and they already have had a definite effect on the total tenor at the schools.

You bet.

Liberation News Service asked some of the kids how they felt about the era of smiles, friendly greetings and surveillance cameras that had come upon the Polk County school system. Said a subversive senior high school student, who probably reads Jefferson and Thoreau on the sly: "In any type of trouble, everybody the camera photographs is sent to the office. After all, they can't tell who caused the trouble, because they don't have sound cameras. They don't know who said what to whom, and anyway, the instigation of trouble might just happen to fall during the 30 seconds [per minute] that the camera isn't photographing." Said another student: "Nothing has changed but the amount of subterfuge and fear. It's like being in jail for six hours a day."

But school, after all, is supposed to be preparation for adult life. And the Polk County school system may already be shaping the subdued citizens of postconstitutional America.

Analysis of Values
and
Conflicts of Interest

The section on government surveillance and data collection on private
citizens sensitizes us to conflicts that result from attempts to preserve both
order and freedom. Volpe, Froehlke, and Rehnquist speak as representatives
of government agencies engaged in the process of maintaining order. They
consider collection and storage of data on private citizens necessary for the
efficient functioning of their respective offices. Agents of the government feel
that limited and proper use of such data banks should not threaten honest
citizens. They often assert that population growth makes maintenance of
order a more complex and difficult task. Vastly increased numbers of criminals
make improved methods of data collection, storage, and retrieval indispensable
to agents of social control.

Arguments favoring the right to collect and store data on private citizens
not only promote the interests of government and police, but also support
similar claims of other groups, such as credit bureaus and corporations. These
private organizations argue that their collection of data on customers and
employees is for strictly legitimate purposes. Like government officials they
assert that demands of modern society make this data collection and storage
a necessity. Most organizations that already have broad data collection
privileges desire to maintain them. Thus, they are likely to find the Volpe,
Froehlke, and Rehnquist papers supportive because these statements define
covert data collection practices a social benefit rather than a social problem.

The Volpe, Froehlke, and Rehnquist articles also reflect the values of
thousands of ordinary citizens who believe that the government and police
need every instrument possible to deal with rising crime rates and dangerous
radicals. They believe that it is in their interest to support the use of such
methods because they are designed for use against lawbreakers and not honest
citizens. Thus only lawbreakers would benefit if covert surveillance
techniques were not legal for government and police agencies.

Ervin, Koch, the American Friends Service Committee, the American
Civil Liberties Union, and Hentoff consider government surveillance and
data storage on private citizens a serious threat to freedom. They believe that

there are no reliable safeguards against misuse of this data once it is collected. Citizens are vulnerable to abuses of overzealous police or even worse to those of corrupt public officials using the data for political advantage. Proponents of this position argue that events related to the Watergate scandal have proven their fears valid. They assert that freedom can be preserved only if government and other bureaucratic agencies are prevented from spying and making other covert interventions into lives of citizens. Ervin, Koch, the American Friends Service Committee, the American Civil Liberties Union, and Hentoff represent persons who value the right of privacy. This value is shared by many conservative, liberal, and radical groups. Recently they all have expressed fear and antipathy toward impersonal government agencies that wield great power and express a lack of concern for individual rights. However, the revelations of Watergate have similarly sensitized many apolitical citizens who do not belong to any of these groups. These persons now feel that it is in their interest to limit the state's power to covertly collect and store data on private citizens.

6

ECOLOGY:
Is There an Ecological Crisis?

In the late 1950s and early 1960s Americans began to fear the negative effects of atomic weapon testing upon man and the environment. This new concern was stimulated further by the publication of Rachel Carson's *The Silent Spring,* which dealt with the destructive consequences of the uncontrolled use of pesticides. Later in the decade these interests culminated in the ecology movement. Environmentalists argued that we were in an "ecological crisis," that was threatening man's very existence upon the planet. These concerned people won a considerable number of supporters by sensitizing a large segment of the American public to ecological problems. The environmentalists even succeeded in bringing about some legislative changes geared to control pollution and protect the environment. However, there has always been considerable opposition to this movement. The opposition feels that the environmentalists have generated hysterical and unfounded fears about pollution. They believe that this could result in overly restrictive legislation that would seriously hinder industrial development and prosperity.

This section begins with a futuristic scenario written by one of the founders of the ecology movement, Paul Ehrlich. This article was completed when public consciousness about ecological problems was at its peak in the late 1960s. It depicts the 1970s as a decade of possible ecological disaster. In an attempt to motivate the public into action, Ehrlich begins by saying: "The end of the ocean came late in the summer of 1979. . ." He goes on to make a number of dire predictions about what could happen in the 1970s. Many of Ehrlich's predictions have not yet occurred. However, ecologists like Ehrlich still believe that these dangers are impending if we do not institute changes to protect our environment. From this point of view, Ehrlich's prediction that 1979 would bring the end of the ocean needs only to be postponed a little. Ecological abuses continue, and some have even begun to increase again under the guise of the energy crisis. The conditions making ecological disaster a *possibility* continue to exist.

John Maddox, a theoretical physicist, attacks Ehrlich as well as other ecologists whose positions constitute what he considers to be a "doomsday syndrome." Maddox does not feel that these ecologists are wrong, but rather that they tend to simplify and exaggerate. Certainly the events of the last few years support Maddox on this point, especially in terms of some of Ehrlich's predictions. What Maddox is afraid of, however, is that instead of motivating people to needed action, the doomsday syndrome will lead them to the fatalistic position that there is nothing they can do to avert the impending cataclysm. He feels that the alarm created by Ehrlich and his colleagues is not conducive to the discovery of rational solutions to our ecological problems. Additionally, the doomsdayers may well alienate the devolping nations by arguing that prosperity is associated with ecological disaster. Since the developing nations are seeking prosperity, they would be put in the uncomfortable position of being forced to ignore ecological problems.

This section concludes with an article by Murray Bookchin, in which he looks at the ecological crisis as only part of a much broader problem. To Bookchin, ecological decay is a problem that has threatened the world since ancient times. What is new, today, is that the decay in the environment is intimately connected to the decay in the existing social structure of capitalist society. Despite this view, Bookchin does not downgrade the significance of the ecological crisis. In fact, he sees it as a threat to "the very capacity of the earth to sustain advanced forms of life." Although he shares a crisis view with Ehrlich and his supporters, Bookchin sees such things as pollution control as insignificant palliatives. Similarly, he does not see the basic fault, or solution, lying in technology or population growth. Rather, in his view, ". . . the roots of the problem lie precisely in the coercive basis of modern society. Modern capitalist society not only converts men into commodities to be bought and sold on the labor market, it also converts every aspect of nature into a similar commodity which is . . . to be manufactured and merchandized wantonly."

Eco-Catastrophe!

PAUL EHRLICH

In the following scenario, Dr. Paul Ehrlich predicts what our world will be like in ten years if the present course of environmental destruction is allowed to continue.

The end of the ocean came late in the summer of 1979, and it came even more rapidly than the biologists had expected. There had been signs for more than a decade, commencing with the discovery in 1968 that DDT slows down photosynthesis in marine plant life. It was announced in a short paper in the technical journal, *Science*, but to ecologists it smacked of doomsday. They knew that all life in the sea depends on photosynthesis, the chemical process by which green plants bind the sun's energy and make it available to living things. And they knew that DDT and similar chlorinated hydrocarbons had polluted the entire surface of the earth, including the sea.

But that was only the first of many signs. There had been the final gasp of the whaling industry in 1973, and the end of the Peruvian anchovy fishery in 1975. Indeed, a score of other fisheries had disappeared quietly from over-exploitation and various eco-catastrophes by 1977. The term "eco-catas-

Note: Paul Ehrlich, "Eco-Catastrophe!" *Ramparts,* Sept. 1969, pp. 24–28. Copyright 1969 by *Ramparts* magazine. Reproduced by permission of the editors.

trophe" was coined by a California ecologist in 1969 to describe the most spectacular of man's attacks on the systems which sustain his life. He drew his inspiration from the Santa Barbara offshore oil disaster of that year, and from the news which spread among naturalists that virtually all of the Golden State's seashore bird life was doomed because of chlorinated hydrocarbon interference with its reproduction. Eco-catastrophes in the sea became increasingly common in the early 1970's. Mysterious "blooms" of previously rare microorganisms began to appear in offshore waters. Red tides—killer outbreaks of a minute single-celled plant—returned to the Florida Gulf coast and were sometimes accompanied by tides of other exotic hues.

It was clear by 1975 that the entire ecology of the ocean was changing. A few types of phytoplankton were becoming resistant to chlorinated hydrocarbons and were gaining the upper hand. Changes in the phytoplankton community led inevitably to changes in the community of zooplankton, the tiny animals which eat the phytoplankton. These changes were passed on up the chains of life in the ocean to the herring, plaice, cod and tuna. As the diversity of life in the ocean diminished, its stability also decreased.

Other changes had taken place by 1975. Most ocean fishes that returned to fresh water to breed, like the salmon, had become extinct, their breeding streams so dammed up and polluted that their powerful homing instinct only resulted in suicide. Many fishes and shellfishes that bred in restricted areas along the coasts followed them as onshore pollution escalated.

By 1977 the annual yield of fish from the sea was down to 30 million metric tons, less than one-half the per capita catch of a decade earlier. This helped malnutrition to escalate sharply in a world where an estimated 50 million people per year were already dying of starvation. The United Nations attempted to get all chlorinated hydrocarbon insecticides banned on a worldwide basis, but the move was defeated by the United States. This opposition was generated primarily by the American petrochemical industry, operating hand in glove with its subsidiary, the United States Department of Agriculture. Together they persuaded the government to oppose the U.N. move—which was not difficult since most Americans believed that Russia and China were more in need of fish products than was the United States. The United Nations also attempted to get fishing nations to adopt strict and enforced catch limits to preserve dwindling stocks. This move was blocked by Russia, who, with the most modern electronic equipment, was in the best position to glean what was left in the sea. It was, curiously, on the very day in 1977 when the Soviet Union announced its refusal that another ominous article appeared in *Science*. It announced that incident solar radiation had been so reduced by worldwide air pollution that serious effects on the world's vegetation could be expected.

Apparently it was a combination of ecosystem destabilization, sunlight reduction, and a rapid escalation in chlorinated hydrocarbon pollution from massive Thanodrin applications which triggered the ultimate catastrophe. Seventeen huge Soviet-financed Thanodrin plants were operating in underdeveloped countries by 1978. They had been part of a massive Russian "aid offensive" designed to fill the gap caused by the collapse of America's ballyhooed "Green Revolution."

It became apparent in the early '70s that the "Green Revolution" was more talk than substance. Distribution of high yield "miracle" grain seeds had caused temporary local spurts in agricultural production. Simultaneously, excellent weather had produced record harvests. The combination permitted bureaucrats, especially in the United States Department of Agriculture and the Agency for International Development (AID), to reverse their previous pessimism and indulge in an outburst of optimistic propaganda about staving off famine. They raved about the approaching transformation of agriculture in the underdeveloped countries (UDCs). The reason for the propaganda reversal was never made clear. Most historians agree that a combination of utter ignorance of ecology, a desire to justify past errors, and pressure from agro-industry (which was eager to sell pesticides, fertilizers, and farm machinery to the UDCs and agencies helping the UDCs) was behind the campaign. Whatever the motivation, the results were clear. Many concerned people, lacking the expertise to see through the Green Revolution drivel, relaxed. The population-food crisis was "solved."

But reality was not long in showing itself. Local famine persisted in northern India even after good weather brought an end to the ghastly Bihar famine of the mid-'60s. East Pakistan was next, followed by a resurgence of general famine in northern India. Other foci of famine rapidly developed in Indonesia, the Philippines, Malawi, the Congo, Egypt, Colombia, Ecuador, Honduras, the Dominican Republic, and Mexico.

Everywhere hard realities destroyed the illusion of the Green Revolution. Yields dropped as the progressive farmers who had first accepted the new seeds found that their higher yields brought lower prices—effective demand (hunger plus cash) was not sufficient in poor countries to keep prices up. Less progressive farmers, observing this, refused to make the extra effort required to cultivate the "miracle" grains. Transport systems proved inadequate to bring the necessary fertilizer to the fields where the new and extremely fertilizer-sensitive grains were being grown. The same systems were also inadequate to move produce to markets. Fertilizer plants were not built fast enough, and most of the underdeveloped countries could not scrape together funds to purchase supplies, even on concessional terms. Finally, the inevitable happened, and pests began to reduce yields in even the most carefully cultivated fields. Among the first were the famous "miracle rats" which invaded Philippine "miracle rice" fields early in 1969. They were quickly followed by many insects and viruses, thriving on the relatively pest-susceptible new grains, encouraged by the vast and dense plantings, and rapidly acquiring resistance to the chemicals used against them. As chaos spread until even the most obtuse agriculturists and economists realized that the Green Revolution had turned brown, the Russians stepped in.

In retrospect it seems incredible that the Russians, with the American mistakes known to them, could launch an even more incompetent program of aid to the underdeveloped world. Indeed, in the early 1970's there were cynics in the United States who claimed that outdoing the stupidity of American foreign aid would be physically impossible. Those critics were, however, obviously unaware that the Russians had been busily destroying their own environment for many years. The virtual disappearance of sturgeon from Russian rivers caused a great shortage of caviar by 1970. A standard joke among Russian scientists at that time was that they had created an artificial caviar which was indistinguishable from the real thing—except by taste. At any rate the Soviet Union, observing with interest the progressive deterioration of relations between the UCDs and the United States, came up with a solution. It had recently developed what it claimed was the ideal insecticide, a highly lethal chlorinated hydrocarbon complex with a special agent for penetrating the external skeletal armor of insects. Announcing that the new pesticide, called Thanodrin, would truly produce a Green Revolution, the Soviets entered into negotiations with various UDCs for the construction of massive Thanodrin factories. The USSR would bear all the costs; all it wanted in return were certain trade and military concessions.

It is interesting now, with the perspective of years, to examine in some detail the reasons why the UDCs welcomed the Thanodrin plan with such open arms. Government officials in these countries ignored the protests of their own scientists that Thanodrin would not solve the problems which plagued them. The governments now knew that the basic cause of their problems was overpopulation, and that these problems had been exacerbated by the dullness, daydreaming, and cupidity endemic to all governments. They knew that only population control and limited development aimed primarily at agriculture could have spared them the horrors they now faced. They knew it, but they were not about to admit it. How much easier it was simply to accuse the Americans of failing to give them proper aid; how much simpler to accept the Russian panacea.

And then there was the general worsening of relations between the United States and the UDCs. Many things had contributed to this. The situation in America in the first half of the 1970's deserves our close scrutiny. Being more dependent on imports for raw materials than the Soviet Union, the United States had, in the early 1970's, adopted more and more heavy-handed policies in order to insure continuing supplies. Military adventures in Asia and Latin America had further lessened the international credibility of the United States as a great defender of freedom —an image which had begun to deteriorate rapidly during the pointless and fruitless Viet-Nam conflict. At home, acceptance of the carefully manufactured image lessened dramatically, as even the more romantic and chauvinistic citizens began to understand the role of the military and the industrial system in what John Kenneth Galbraith had aptly named "The New Industrial State."

At home in the USA the early '70s were traumatic times. Racial violence grew and the habitability of the cities diminished, as nothing substantial was done to ameliorate either racial inequities or urban blight. Welfare rolls grew as automation and general technological progress forced more and more people into the category of "unemployable." Simultaneously a taxpayers' revolt occurred. Although there was not enough money to build the schools, roads, water systems, sewage systems, jails, hospitals, urban transit lines, and all the other amenities needed to support a burgeoning population, Americans refused to tax themselves more heavily. Starting in Youngstown, Ohio in 1969 and followed closely by Richmond, California, community after community was forced to close its schools or curtail educational operations for lack of funds. Water supplies, already marginal in quality and quantity in many places by 1970, deteriorated quickly. Water rationing occurred in 1723 municipalities in the summer of 1974, and hepatitis and epidemic dysentery rates climbed about 500 per cent between 1970–1974.

Air pollution continued to be the most obvious manifestation of environmental deterioration. It was, by 1972, quite literally in the eyes of all Americans. The year 1973 saw not only the New York and Los Angeles smog disasters, but also the publication of the Surgeon General's massive report on air pollution and health. The public had been partially prepared for the worst by the publicity given to the U.N. pollution conference held in 1972. Deaths in the late '60s caused by smog were well known to scientists, but the public had ignored them because they mostly involved the early demise of the old and sick rather than people dropping dead on the freeways. But suddenly our citizens were faced with nearly 200,000 corpses and massive documentation that they could be the next to die from respiratory disease. They were not ready for that scale of disaster. After all, the U.N. conference had

not predicted that accumulated air pollution would make the planet uninhabitable until almost 1990. The population was terrorized as TV screens became filled with scenes of horror from the disaster areas. Especially vivid was NBC's coverage of hundreds of unattended people choking out their lives outside of New York's hospitals. Terms like nitrogen oxide, acute bronchitis and cardiac arrest began to have real meaning for most Americans.

The ultimate horror was the announcement that chlorinated hydrocarbons were now a major constituent of air pollution in all American cities. Autopsies of smog disaster victims revealed an average chlorinated hydrocarbon load in fatty tissue equivalent to 26 parts per million of DDT. In October, 1973, the Department of Health, Education and Welfare announced studies which showed unequivocally that increasing death rates from hypertension, cirrhosis of the liver, liver cancer and a series of other diseases had resulted from the chlorinated hydrocarbon load. They estimated that Americans born since 1946 (when DDT usage began) now had a life expectancy of only 49 years, and predicted that if current patterns continued, this expectancy would reach 42 years by 1980, when it might level out. Plunging insurance stocks triggered a stock market panic. The president of Velsicol, Inc., a major pesticide producer, went on television to "publicly eat a teaspoonful of DDT" (it was really powdered milk) and announce that HEW had been infiltrated by Communists. Other giants of the petro-chemical industry, attempting to dispute the indisputable evidence, launched a massive pressure campaign on Congress to force HEW to "get out of agriculture's business." They were aided by the agro-chemical journals, which had decades of experience in misleading the public about the benefits and dangers of pesticides. But by now the public realized that it had been duped. The Nobel Prize for medicine and physiology was given to Drs. J. L. Radomski and W. B. Deichmann, who in the late 1960's had pioneered in the documentation of the long-term lethal effects of chlorinated hydrocarbons. A Presidential Commission with unimpeachable credentials directly accused the agro-chemical complex of "condemning many millions of Americans to an early death." The year 1973 was the year in which Americans finally came to understand the direct threat to their existence posed by environmental deterioration.

And 1973 was also the year in which most people finally comprehended the indirect threat. Even the president of Union Oil Company and several other industrialists publicly stated their concern over the reduction of bird populations which had resulted from pollution by DDT and other chlorinated hydrocarbons. Insect populations boomed because they were resistant to most pesticides and had been freed, by the incompetent use of those pesticides, from most of their natural enemies. Rodents swarmed over crops, multiplying rapidly in the absence of predatory birds. The effect of pests on the wheat crop was especially disastrous in the summer of 1973, since that was also the year of the great drought. Most of us can remember the shock which greeted the announcement by atmospheric physicists that the shift of the jet stream which had caused the drought was probably permanent. It signalled the birth of the Midwestern desert. Man's air-polluting activities had by then caused gross changes in climatic patterns. The news, of course, played hell with commodity and stock markets. Food prices skyrocketed, as savings were poured into hoarded canned goods. Official assurances that food supplies would remain ample fell on deaf ears, and even the government showed signs of nervousness when California migrant field workers went out on strike again in protest against the continued use of pesticides by growers. The strike burgeoned into farm burning and riots. The workers, calling themselves "The Walking Dead," demanded immediate compensation for their shortened lives, and crash research programs to attempt to lengthen them.

In was in the same speech in which President Edward Kennedy, after much delay, finally declared a national emergency and called out the National Guard to harvest California's crops, that the first mention of population control was made. Kennedy pointed out that the United States would no longer be able to offer any food aid to other nations and was likely to suffer food shortages herself. He suggested that, in view of the manifest failure of the Green Revolution, the only hope of the UDCs lay in population control. His statement, you will recall, created an uproar in the underdeveloped countries. Newspaper editorials accused the United States of wishing to prevent small countries from becoming large nations and thus threatening American hegemony. Politicians asserted that President Kennedy was a "creature of the giant drug combine" that wished to shove its pills down every woman's throat.

Among Americans, religious opposition to population control was very slight. Industry in general also backed the idea. Increasing poverty in the UDCs was both destroying markets and threatening supplies of raw materials. The seriousness of the raw material situation had been brought home during the Congressional Hard Resources hearings in 1971. The exposure of the ignorance of the cornucopian economists had been quite a spectacle—a spectacle brought into virtually every American's home in living color. Few would forget the distinguished geologist from the University of California who suggested that economists be legally required to learn at least the most elementary facts of geology. Fewer still would forget that an equally distinguished Harvard economist added that they might be required to learn some economics, too. The overall message was clear: America's resource situation was bad and bound to get worse. The hearings had led to a bill requiring the Departments of State, Interior, and Commerce to set up a joint resource procurement council with the express purpose of "insuring that proper consideration of American resource needs be an integral part of American foreign policy."

Suddenly the United States discovered that it had a national consensus: population control was the only possible salvation of the underdeveloped world. But that same consensus led to heated debate. How could the UDCs be persuaded to limit their populations, and should not the United States lead the way by limiting its own? Members of the intellectual community wanted America to set an example. They pointed out that the United States was in the midst of a new baby boom: her birth rate, well over 20 per thousand per year, and her growth rate of over one per cent per annum were among the very highest of the developed countries. They detailed the deterioration of the American physical and psychic environments, the growing health threats, the impending food shortages, and the insufficiency of funds for desperately needed public works. They contended that the nation was clearly unable or unwilling to properly care for the people it already had. What possible reason could there be, they queried, for adding any more? Besides, who would listen to requests by the United States for population control when that nation did not control her own profligate reproduction?

Those who opposed population controls for the U.S. were equally vociferous. The military-industrial complex, with its all-too-human mixture of ignorance and avarice, still saw strength and prosperity in numbers. Baby food magnates, already worried by the growing nitrate pollution of their products, saw their market disappearing. Steel manufacturers saw a decrease in aggregate demand and slippage for that holy of holies, the Gross National Product. And military men saw, in the growing population-food-environment crisis, a serious threat to their carefully nurtured Cold War. In the end, of course, economic arguments held sway, and the "inalienable right of every American couple to determine the size of its family," a freedom invented for the occasion in the early '70s, was not compromised.

The population control bill, which was passed by Congress early in 1974, was quite a document, nevertheless. On the domestic front, it authorized an increase from 100 to 150 million dollars in funds for "family planning" activities. This was made possible by a general feeling in the country that the growing army on welfare needed family planning. But the gist of the bill was a series of measures designed to impress the need for population control on the UDCs. All American aid to countries with overpopulation problems was required by law to consist in part of population control assistance. In order to receive any assistance each nation was required not only to accept the population control aid, but also to match it according to a complex formula. "Overpopulation" itself was defined by a formula based on U.N. statistics, and the UDCs were required not only to accept aid, but also to show progress in reducing birth rates. Every five years the status of the aid program for each nation was to be re-evaluated.

The reaction to the announcement of this program dwarfed the response to President Kennedy's speech. A coalition of UDCs attempted to get the U.N. General Assembly to condemn the United States as a "genetic aggressor." Most damaging of all to the American cause was the famous "25 Indians and a dog" speech by Mr. Shankarnarayan, Indian Ambassador to the U.N. Shankarnarayan pointed out that for several decades the United States, with less than six per cent of the people of the world had consumed roughly 50 per cent of the raw materials used every year. He described vividly America's contribution to worldwide environmental deterioration, and he scathingly denounced the miserly record of United States foreign aid as "unworthy of a fourth-rate power, let alone the most powerful nation on earth."

It was the climax of his speech, however, which most historians claim once and for all destroyed the image of the United States. Shankarnarayan informed the assembly that the average American family dog was fed more animal protein per week than the average Indian got in a month. "How do you justify taking fish from protein-starved Peruvians and feeding them to your animals?" he asked. "I contend," he concluded, "that the birth of an American baby is a greater disaster for the world than that of 25 Indian babies." When the applause had died away, Mr. Sorenson, the American representative, made a speech which said essentially that "other countries look after their own self-interest, too." When the vote came, the United States was condemned.

This condemnation set he tone of U.S.–UDC relations at the time the Russian Thanodrin proposal was made. The proposal seemed to offer the masses in the UDCs an opportunity to save themselves and humiliate the United States at the same time; and in human affairs, as we all know, biological realities could never interfere with such an opportunity. The scientists were silenced, the politicians said yes, the Thanodrin plants were built, and the results were what any beginning ecology student could have predicted. At first Thanodrin seemed to offer excellent control of many pests. True, there was a rash of human fatalities from improper use of the lethal chemical, but, as Russian technical advisors were prone to note, these were more than compensated for by increased yields. Thanodrin use skyrocketed throughout the underdeveloped world. The Mikoyan design group developed a dependable, cheap agricultural aircraft which the Soviets donated to the effort in large numbers. MIG sprayers became even more common in UDCs than MIG interceptors.

Then the troubles began. Insect strains with cuticular restraint to Thanodrin penetration began to appear. And as streams, rivers, fish culture ponds and onshore waters became rich in Thanodrin, more fisheries began to disappear. Bird populations were decimated. The sequence of events was standard for broadcast use of a synthetic pesticide: great success at first, followed by removal of natural enemies and development of resistance by the pest. Populations of crop-eating insects in areas treated with Thanodrin made steady comebacks and soon became more abundant than ever. Yields plunged, while farmers in their desperation increased the Thanodrin dose and shortened the time between treatments. Death from Thanodrin poisoning became common. The first violent incident occurred in the Canete Valley of Peru, where farmers had suffered a similar chlorinated hydrocarbon disaster in the mid-'50s. A Russian advisor serving as an agricultural pilot was assaulted and killed by a mob of enraged farmers in January, 1978. Trouble spread rapidly during 1978, especially after the word got out that two years earlier Russia herself had banned the use of Thanodrin at home because of its serious effects on ecological systems. Suddenly Russia, and not the United States was the bête noir in the UDCs. "Thanodrin parties" became epidemic, with farmers, in their ignorance, dumping carloads of Thanodrin concentrate into the sea. Russian advisors fled, and four of the Thanodrin plants were leveled to the ground. Destruction of the plants in Rio and Calcutta led to hundreds of thousands of gallons of Thanodrin concentrate being dumped directly into the sea.

Mr. Sankarnarayan again rose to address the U.N., but this time it was Mr. Potemkin, representative of the Soviet Union, who was on the hot seat. Mr. Potemkin heard his nation described as the greatest mass killer of all time as Shankarnarayan predicted at least 30 million deaths from crop failures due to overdependence on Thanodrin. Russia was accused of "chemical aggression," and the General Assembly, after a weak reply by Potemkin, passed a vote of censure.

It was in January, 1979, that huge blooms of a previously unknown variety of diatom were reported off the coast of Peru. The blooms were accompanied by a massive die-off of sea life and of the pathetic remainder of the birds which had once feasted on the anchovies of the area. Almost immediately another huge bloom was reported in the Indian ocean, centering around the Seychelles, and then a third in the South Atlantic off the African coast. Both of these were accompanied by spectacular die-offs of marine animals. Even more ominous were growing reports of fish and bird kills at oceanic points where there were no spectacular blooms. Biologists were soon able to explain the phenomena: the diatom had evolved an enzyme which broke down Thanodrin; that enzyme also produced a breakdown product which interfered with the transmission of nerve impulses, and was therefore lethal to animals. Unfortunately, the biologists could suggest no way of repressing the poisonous diatom bloom in time. By September, 1979, all important animal life in the sea was extinct. Large areas of coastline had to be evacuated, as windrows of dead fish created a monumental stench.

But stench was the least of man's problems. Japan and China were faced with almost instant starvation from a total loss of the seafood on which they were so dependent. Both blamed Russia for their situation and demanded immediate mass shipments of food. Russia had none to send. On October 13, Chinese armies attacked Russia on a broad front. . . .

A pretty grim scenario. Unfortunately we're a long way into it already. Everything mentioned as happening before 1970 has actually occurred; much of the rest is based on projections of trends already appearing. Evidence that pesticides have long-term lethal effects on human beings has started to accumulate, and recently Robert Finch, Secretary of the Department of Health, Education and Welfare expressed his extreme apprehension about the pesticide situation. Simultaneously the petrochemical industry continues its unconscionable poison-peddling. For instance, Shell Chemical has been carrying on a high-pressure campaign to sell the insecticide Azodrin to farmers as a killer of cotton pests. They continue their program even though they know that Azodrin is not only ineffective, but often increases the pest density. They've covered themselves nicely in an advertisement which states, "Even if an overpowering migration [sic] develops, the flexibility of Azodrin lets you regain control fast. Just increase the dosage according to label recommendations." It's a great game —get people to apply the poison and kill the natural enemies of the pests. Then blame the increased pests on "migration" and sell even more pesticide!

Right now fisheries are being wiped out by over-exploitation, made easy by modern electronic equipment. The companies producing the equipment know this. They even boast in advertising that only their equipment will keep fishermen in business until the final kill. Profits must obviously be maximized in the short run. Indeed, Western society is in the process of completing the rape and murder of the planet for economic gain. And, sadly, most of the rest of the world is eager for the opportunity to emulate our behavior. But the underdeveloped peoples will be denied that opportunity—the days of plunder are drawing inexorably to a close.

Most of the people who are going to die in the greatest cataclysm in the history of man have already been born. More than three and a half billion people already populate our moribund globe, and about half of them are hungry. Some 10 to 20 million will starve to death this year. In spite of this, the population of the earth will increase by 70 million souls in 1969. For mankind has artificially lowered the death rate of the human population, while in general birth rates have remained high. With the input side of the population system in high gear and the output side slowed down, our fragile planet has filled with people at an incredible rate. It took several million years for the population to reach a total of two billion people in 1930, while a second two billion will have been added by 1975! By that time some experts feel that food shortages will have escalated the present level of world hunger and starvation into famines of unbelievable proportions. Other experts, more optimistic, think the ultimate food-population collision will not occur until the decade of the 1980s. Of course, more massive famine may be avoided if other events cause a prior rise in the human death rate.

Both worldwide plague and thermonuclear war are made more probable as population growth continues. These, along with famine, make up the trio of potential "death rate solutions" to the population problem—solutions in which the birth rate-death rate imbalance is redressed by a rise in the death rate rather than by a lowering of the birth rate. Make no mistake about it, the imbalance will be redressed. The shape of the population growth curve is one familiar to the biologist. It is the outbreak part of an outbreak-crash sequence. A population grows rapidly in the presence of abundant resources, finally runs out of food or some other necessity, and crashes to a low level or extinction. Man is not only running out of food, he is also destroying the life support systems of the Spaceship Earth. The situation was recently summarized very succinctly: "It is the top of the ninth inning. Man, always a threat at the plate, has been hitting Nature hard. It is important to remember, however, that nature bats last."

The Doomsday Syndrome

JOHN MADDOX

The environmentalists, a leading British scientist charges, may be the most insidious of all plunderers of our planet. Using "a technique of calculated overdramatization," they have deflected attention from the genuine ecological issues we face and blinded us to solutions that exist now.

Prophets of doom have multiplied remarkably in the past few years. It used to be commonplace for men to parade on city streets with sandwich boards proclaiming, "The End of the World is at Hand!" They have been replaced by a throng of sober people—scientists, philosophers, and politicians—proclaiming that there are more subtle calamities just around the corner. The human race, they say, is in danger of suffocating itself by overbreeding, of poisoning itself with pollution, of undermining its essential character by tampering with heredity and of weakening the basic structure of society through too much prosperity.

The questions that these latter-day doomsayers have raised are complex and interesting; the spirit in which they are asked is usually too jaundiced for intellectual com-

fort. Too often, reality is oversimplified or even ignored, so that there is a danger that much of this gloomy foreboding about the immediate future will accomplish the opposite of its intention. Instead of alerting people to important problems, the "doomsday syndrome" may be as much a hazard to human survival as any of the environmental conundrums society has created for itself.

Nobody doubts the sincerity of the contemporary prophets of calamity, and nobody would disagree that modern society is confronted with important tasks that must be tackled with a sense of urgency. In advanced societies machinery must be devised for the more equitable treatment of the poor and the disadvantaged. Urban life, although better than it used to be, surely leaves much room for improvement. Even where medical care is excellent, ways of preventing untimely death and unnecessary disease remain to be discovered. And in less-developed societies there are the more basic tasks of providing people with adequate food, housing, and schooling. These are difficult problems, but they are capable of solution in the foreseeable future if enough time and money are spent on them. By contrast, the questions the doomsayers generally raise are rhetorical ones, either because they are based on incorrect premises or because they are unanswerable with the knowledge we possess at the present moment. The risk is that too much preoccupation with the threat of distant calamity will lead to a kind of quietism by diverting our attention from good works that might be accomplished now.

The doomsday cause would be more telling if it were more securely grounded in facts, as well as better informed by a sense of history and an awareness of economics. The major defect in the argument that calamity is just around the corner is its imprecision. Some doomsayers fear that the burning of fuel on the scale to which modern industry is accustomed will wreck the earth's climate, but few meteorologists are able unambiguously to endorse such prophecies. Others fear that the use of pesticides will irrevocably damage the human race, but that is an overdramatic statement of the need to carefully regulate the way in which such chemicals are sprayed on crops. Still others fear that modern biology, with its artificially fertilized eggs and its detailed understanding of genetic processes, will create a race of robots, but such a concern flies in the face of the past five centuries of medical history, for the most part a consistent record of humane endeavor. In short, the weakness of the doomsday prophecies is that they are exaggerations. Many of them are frighteningly irresponsible.

The flavor of these prophecies of disaster is well illustrated by the work of Dr. Paul Ehrlich, whose book *The Population Bomb* startled a good many people when it was published four years ago. "The battle to feed all of humanity is over," Ehrlich wote. "In the 1970s the world will undergo famines, hundreds of millions of people are going to starve to death in spite of any crash program embarked on now." Ehrlich went on to describe in a somber way the rate at which the population of the world is increasing, the inconveniences that are likely to result therefrom, and some ways of striking a better balance between the population growth and available resources, especially in developing parts of the world.

Nobody will deny that it is important to control, if not the size of a population, then its rate of growth. In advanced societies population control is increasingly becoming an accepted function of good government. In developing countries it is generally recognized as a prerequisite to economic progress. Ehrlich's warning of imminent famines on a massive scale is unrealistic. The truth is that the total production of food on the earth is now increasing much faster than the population. For most of the Sixties, the population of the world grew at about 2 per cent a year, while agricultural production in the same period increased by 2.7 per cent annually. And in the past few years there has been especially encouraging progress in the hard-pressed countries of Southeast Asia and India, where food production has increased nearly twice as fast as population, due largely to the introduction of new strains of wheat and rice. Nor is there any reason to believe that the "green revolution" will slow down in the coming years. Population control is therefore desirable, not as a means of avoiding calamity, but because it can accelerate the steady improvement of the human condition.

Famine is only one of several hypothetical catastrophes that are said to flow from population growth. Ehrlich and other doomsayers argue that high population density produces individual disorientation and increased social tensions. One common argument for supposing that crowding as such is bad for people starts from experiments that have been carried out with laboratory animals, principally rats. The best known experiments, performed by Dr. John B. Calhoun, showed that rats kept in unusually crowded conditions developed all kinds of psychological disturbances—mother rats took to infanticide, males became unnaturally aggressive, and the mortality rate rose. So is it not reasonable to suppose that people living in metropolitan areas will be more disturbed than those who live in rural areas? With growing population densities, will not violence within and between countries become that much more prevalent? These are common suspicions. Dr. Ehrlich and his wife, Anne, in their book *Population, Resources, Environment* write that there are "very high correlations among rates of population growth . . . and involvement in wars."

The trouble is that the analogy between rats and people is at best tenuous—gregariousness of the kind that led to the development of cities thousands of years ago distinguishes the human race from rodents. And the belief that violence and war accompany crowding rests on the most shaky statistical basis. Who, after all, would claim that the Netherlands, the most crowded of all Western European countries, is more given to violence than, say, the United States?

Implicit in these dire warnings of the consequences of population growth is a misleading method of prediction that gives more credit to simple arithmetic than it deserves. If the population of the world is at present doubling every thirty-five years, does it necessarily follow that the population will multiply by a fourfold factor in the next seventy years, so as to reach 14,000 [*sic*] million by the year 2040? In *The Population Bomb* Ehrlich is scornful of those whom he calls "professional optimists . . . who like to greet every sign of dropping birth rate with wild pronouncements about the end of the population explosion." And even in the more soberly written *Population, Resources, Environment,* he chooses to base predictions of the future population of the earth on the most pessimistic calculations appearing in studies funded by the United Nations, which assume that there will be no change in the fertility of women of childbearing age between now and the end of the century. In reality, however, there are already signs that fertility is declining in developing countries in exactly the same way as, but possibly more rapidly than, it declined in Western Europe between fifty and a hundred years ago. One of the strangest features of Ehrlich's description of the population explosion is the bland assumption that the social

forces that have brought about stability in the developed countries—the improvement of the quality of education and medical care, for example—are inapplicable elsewhere. Is it any wonder that the predominantly Western preoccupation with the population explosion seems like patronizing neocolonialism to people elsewhere?

In much the same way that environmentalists worry about the effects of population growth on our physical and psychological well-being, so, too, they decry its effect on natural resources. In the United States, at least, this is an honorable tradition going back to the end of the nineteenth century, when Gifford Pinchot, head of the U.S. Forest Service, wrung his hands over the prospect that timber in this country would be used up in roughly thirty years, that anthracite coal would last for only fifty years, and that other raw materials such as iron ore and natural gas were being rapidly depleted. Seventy years later the same complaints are heard. The environmentalists have coined the phrase "our plundered planet" to express their anxiety about the probability that petroleum will be much less plentiful a century from now and that the time will soon come when high-grade copper ores are worked out. The fallacy in this reasoning is that society has never been uniquely dependent on the balance of raw materials in common use at a particular time. If copper becomes scarce or merely expensive, more aluminum will have to be used in its place. If natural diamonds are expensive, then we will make them synthetically. In any case, although supplies of such raw materials are known to be limited, the point at which they seem likely to be exhausted tends to recede with the passage of time so as to be always just over the horizon. Indeed, despite what the environmentalists say, the present time appears to be one in which forecasts of scarcity are less valid than ever. Petroleum may be much harder to obtain a century from now, but in the past few years scientists have laid the foundations for wresting energy from hydrogen and minerals such as uranium in large quantities, so that future decades will be much better off than anybody could have expected even a decade ago. And, however strange it may seem, the real economic cost of extracting such metals as lead and copper from the ground is still decreasing as exploration and the techniques of mining and metallurgy become more efficient. In terms of their availability at least, the earth's resources are becoming more and more plentiful.

Ecological catastrophe is also high on the list of public fears for the future. As another leading doomsayer, Dr. Barry Commoner, puts it in *The Closing Circle*, ". . . in our unwitting march toward ecological suicide, we have run out of options." What he and the other environmentalists who echo his opinions wish to imply is that the relation between people and the environment is so delicate, and the dependence of the human race on its surroundings so complete, that many of the effects of our activity on the natural world may destroy the capacity of the earth to support life.

One recipe for ecological disaster, for example, holds that pollution of the surface layers of the oceans by insecticides or chemicals may destroy the microscopic plants that turn the energy of sunlight into chemical form, help to support marine life of all kinds, and replenish the oxygen in the atmosphere. Another theorizes that the accumulation of carbon dioxide produced by the burning of fossil fuels may so increase the temperature on the surface of the earth as to transform the present pattern of weather and perhaps even melt the Antarctic ice. Fortunately, these chains of events are by no means inescapable. For one thing, the processes that are supposed to lead to disaster are only imperfectly understood. Moreover, their scale is still puny in relation to the size of the earth's envelope—the ecosphere, as it is, called.

Tiny though the earth may appear from the moon, it is in reality an enormous object. The earth's atmosphere alone weighs more than 5 billion tons, more than a million tons of air for each human being now alive. The water on the surface of the earth weighs more than 300 times as much—in other words, each living person's share of the water would just about fill a cube half a mile square. So while it is not entirely out of the question that human intervention could at some stage bring about changes in the ecosphere, for the time being the vast scale on which the earth is built should be a great comfort to us all.

But even if the human race is unable to harm the ecosphere significantly, is there not a danger that it may destroy itself more directly? In the past few years the nature of biological research has been repeatedly held up as a potential threat to man's survival. Genetic engineering is a somber phrase, no doubt, conjuring up visions of long rows of test-tube babies bred to governmental specifications. But the concept is less frightening when one recalls that horse breeders and plant growers have been practicing it for centuries. And why should communities that have rejected the eugenic devices already available—forced choice of marriage partners, for example, or selective infanticide—throw their principles to the winds now that molecular biology has come along?

Even the quite real prospect of artificially fertilizing human eggs does not contain the seeds of unwelcome social upheaval that many people suppose. The truth is that the most obvious uses of these new techniques are therapeutic, not subversive. To be sure, biological research has raised novel ethical problems. How, for example, does a doctor decide which of several equally needy patients should have access to an artificial kidney machine or receive a kidney that becomes available for transplant? But the fact that these problems are novel is neither an argument against the new techniques nor a justification for the belief that biological research is full unmanageable social dangers. What justification can there be for the supposition that the same medical men who have developed antibiotics for the treatment of infectious diseases and vaccines for its prevention will seize on the new developments to pursue malevolent objectives?

But what of the possibility that science and technology may undermine the integrity of society in much more subtle ways? This is an old fear, of course, which in its crudest form amounts to unregenerate obscurantism. In the past few years the theme has appeared again in a revised and updated form. In his book *Reason Awake,* Dr. René Dubos writes: "Man has always lived in a precarious state, worried about his place in the order of things. In the past he was threatened chiefly by natural forces that he could not control, and he experienced fear because of ignorance of the cosmos and of his own nature. Now threats and fears derive in large measure from science and its technologies, paradoxically the most characteristic products of human reason." And elsewhere he adds, "Most would agree that science and technology are responsible for some of our worst nightmares and have made our societies so complex as to be almost unmanageable."

The flaw in these protestations is that they label technology, and the science from which it springs, as a subversive force in society. It is true, of course, that technical innovations frequently have unexpected consequences. This has always been the case. Who would have guessed fifty years ago that the motor car would create the suburbs of North America? The fact that ocean beaches are so much more crowded now than half a century ago is also a consequence of the tremendous expansion of the automobile industry. But is it sensible to wish that internal combustion engines had not been invented for the sake of avoiding overcrowding at the beaches? Is it not preferable to enjoy the other benefits of the invention and to regulate the crowding of beaches by other means? And in any case, where such developments are in question, is it not entirely misleading to suggest that the automobile industry has grown to its present size for reasons connected with the character of technology and not because

a need for its product became apparent? On issues like this, the doomsday literature is dishonest.

The introduction of the wheel into primitive societies must similarly have been attended by unforeseen developments. Then, as now, the immediate benefits of innovation may be predictable, but the more distant consequences, beneficial or harmful, are harder to foresee. The moral, of course, is that governments have a responsibility to ensure that most of the social consequences of technological progress are positive ones. To pretend with Dr. Dubos that such discrimination is impossible and that all technology is therefore suspect is to suggest that society is powerless to regulate its own affairs. The argument that technology is an all-powerful juggernaut pressing the humanity out of society usually cloaks a pessimistic belief in the impotence of social institutions. The challenge is not to keep science and technology at bay but to control them and, in particular, to make sure that they do not become dehumanizing influences on our lives.

One of the most common misconceptions about technology is that it consists entirely of gigantic, tax-supported programs for sending rockets to the moon. In reality, most technologists work toward much less spectacular objectives—building safer and cheaper bridges, for example, or devising ways of drying coffee wthout loss of flavor. Those who complain about technology and its effects would be on stronger ground if they concerned themselves with devising ways for society to exploit science and technology. The key question is, *Who* says *which* innovations are worthwhile? Some decisions have to be made by individuals in their role as consumers. Others are left to manufacturers. Still others, which have a political flavor in the most general sense, must be taken by governments acting on behalf of the communities they represent. Governments have all too often been unwilling to shoulder their responsibilities. They have, for example, accepted the introduction of jet planes without taking into proper consideration the extra noise such aircraft cause. They have encouraged industrial development without thinking sufficiently about the unavoidable side effects of industry, pollution being chief among them. They have encouraged urbanization without paying enough attention to city planning.

Were these the complaints of the environmentalists, their cause would be entirely laudable. But by slipping into the pretense that science and technology have between them established such a powerful hold on society's development that the survival of the human race may be undermined, they have side-stepped the real issue, which is to guide, not eliminate, technological progress. There is no reason to think that technology will be less valuable in the future than it has been in the past in liberating men and women from drudgery and so improving the quality of their lives. Paradoxically, the environmental message, at least in its crudest form, is self-defeating.

The main reason the message is so often presented so crudely goes back to the origins of the modern environmental movement. The first environmentalists were probably the scientists who, toward the end of World War II, sensed that the development of nuclear weapons posed a grave threat to the human race. In 1945 Dr. J. Robert Oppenheimer, the scientific director of the Los Alamos program that produced the first atomic bomb, made the point with characteristic eloquence: "In some crude sense which no vulgarity, no overstatement can quite extinguish, the physicists have known sin, and this is a knowledge which they cannot lose."

Throughout the Fifties the campaign to ban the testing of nuclear weapons picked up momentum. In the early years of the decade the first test explosions of hydrogen bombs carried the scientists' initial sense of alarm to a far wider spectrum of the population. In 1954, when four Japanese fishermen were killed by radioactive dust from a thermonuclear explosion, the entire world was given a vivid demonstration of the potential destructiveness of nuclear energy. By the late Fifties nuclear weapons tests had become commonplace, and the amount of radioactive fallout was reaching intolerable levels. The discovery of strontium 90 in the skeletons of young children was a powerful assault on the public conscience. With military strategy still dominated by plans for thermonuclear retaliation, it is no wonder that the decade ended with the sense that Doomsday was just around the corner.

At about the same time, ironically, the concern of the early environmentalists with the perils of nuclear explosions to human health began to win wide acceptance, and in 1963 the major powers signed a treaty prohibiting above-ground testing of nuclear weapons. Suddenly, the environmentalists constituted an army that had tasted blood but seemingly had no further battles to fight. The year before, Rachel Carson had published her now-famous study of the misuse of pesticides, *Silent Spring,* thereby launching an entirely new phase of the environmental movement. The problem was that many environmentalists continued to use the same apocalyptic rhetoric they had employed so effectively to express their indignation over the unregulated dissemination of nuclear weaponry—a truly apocalyptic danger—to describe a much more subtle and complex phenomenon.

Miss Carson herself was concerned almost entirely with the way in which insecticides were being used in the United States. Many of her complaints were well founded—it is absurd that insecticides should have been employed to clear insects from inland lakes with such abandon as to kill the fish as well as the insects. Another of her many cautionary tales described how the use of an insecticide similar to DDT against the Japanese beetle in the cornfields of the Middle West made life easier for a still more dangerous pest, the corn borer, which normally was preyed upon by the Japanese beetle. In this and other ways she marshaled enough evidence to demonstrate that pesticides should be more carefully regulated. The most seriously misleading part of her narrative involves the relating of horror stories about the misuse of DDT to create the impression that there are no safe uses for pesticides at all.

Rachel Carson thus set the tone of much subsequent environmental literature by employing a technique of calculated overdramatization. The silent spring itself was an apocryphal season in "a town in the heart of America" created by Miss Carson's fertile imagination. Her book begins with what she calls "a fable for tomorrow." Once,

> all life seemed to live in harmony with its surroundings. . . . But then a strange blight crept over the area and everything began to change. Some evil spell had settled on the community: mysterious maladies swept the flocks of chickens; the cattle and sheep sickened and died. Everywhere was a shadow of death. The farmers spoke of much illness among their families. In the town the doctors had become more puzzled by new kinds of sickness appearing among their patients. There had been several sudden and unexplained deaths, not only among adults but among children, who would be stricken suddenly while at play and die within a few hours.

The calamity, of course, was caused by the use of pesticides. Miss Carson goes on innocently to reveal that "this town does not actually exist, but it might easily have a thousand counterparts in America or elsewhere in the world." By playing this literary trick on her readers, she provided not merely graphic illustration of the fact that excessive amounts of pesticide could kill animals as well as insects but also a sense that excessive use was almost unavoidable.

Paul Ehrlich's *The Population Bomb* is a splendid illustration of how the technique of calculated exaggeration has flourished. After a tautly written account of how "the battle to feed all of humanity" has been lost, sufficiently vivid to have most readers on the edges of their seats, Ehrlich concludes with the smug apology that he, like any scientist,

"lives constantly with the possibility that he may be wrong." However, no harm will be done if *his* argument proves false, Ehrlich continues, for if I am wrong, people will still be better fed, better housed and happier . . . ." The difficulty, of course, is that alarm does not provide the best atmosphere for finding rational solutions to those problems that are truly worrisome. Aesop knew what happened to shepherd boys who cried wolf too often.

Barry Commoner also uses Miss Carson's technique. In his book *Science and Survival*, for example, he writes that "as large a body of water as Lake Erie has already been overwhelmed by pollutants and has in effect died." The truth is now what it was when the book appeared in 1963, namely, that Lake Erie has indeed been seriously afflicted by pollution, for such a shallow body of water could not be expected to remain unchanged under the assault of the vast amount of sewage and industrial effluent that surrounding cities discharge into it. But throughout the 1960s the lake somehow managed to support a thriving fishing industry. In 1970 it yielded 25,000 tons of fish. Nobody can know for certain why the trout have been replaced by other species of fish—is it in fact the sewage or perhaps the influence of the Welland Canal, which, bypassing Niagara, connects Lake Erie to Lake Ontario? By now it seems to have been generally agreed that something must be done to limit the discharge of effluents into Lake Erie, but the proclamation that the lake is already "dead," whatever such a phrase may mean, has probably given Lake Erie more prominence than it deserves. To be fair, in his more recent book, *The Closing Circle*, Commoner does not say the lake is dead but merely that "we have grossly, irreversibly changed the biological character of the lake and have greatly reduced, now, and for the foreseeable future, its value to man." But even this more moderate statement of his position is dubious if the assertion of the irreversibility of the damage is taken at face value.

Implicit in the pessimistic outlook of many ecologists is a common stand on the nature of living things and their relationship with the environment. In *Science and Survival* Commoner has a chapter entitled "Greater Than the Sum of its Parts," which attempts to demonstrate that the properties of living things cannot be explained solely in terms of the properties of the molecules that make them up.

> There is, I believe, a crisis in biology today. The root of the crisis is the conflict between the two approaches to the theory of life. One approach seeks for the unique capabilities of living things in separable chemical reactions; the other holds that this uniqueness is a property of the whole cell and arises out of the complex interactions of the separable events of cellular chemistry. Neither view has, as yet, been supported by decisive experimental proof. The molecular approach has not succeeded in showing by experiment that the subtly integrated complexity and beautiful precision of the cell's chemistry can be created by adding together its separate components. Nor has the opposite approach, as yet, discovered an integrating mechanism in the living cell which achieves the essential coordination of its numerous separate reactions.

In its essence this argument echoes the old nineteenth-century belief in what was then called "life force"—a special quality of livings things—whose credibility has steadily diminished ever since the first laboratory synthesis a century and a half ago of substances usually considered by-products of life. The modern equivalent of this neovitalism holds that the "web of life"—as Darwin termed the way in which different species are linked together by their mutual dependence—is so complicated that it cannot be submitted to the methods of mathematical analysis. This is one of Commoner's arguments. In the trivial sense, of course, the point is incontrovertible—who would seriously set out to calculate the weight of a full-grown locust when it would be much simpler, and probably safer as well, simply to put it on a scale? But this does not imply that the weight of a locust is in principle incalculable, that there are features of the ecosphere that lie beyond the scope of conventional science. Among the environmentalists there is a temptation to emphasize the unity of the living world in circumstances when it would be more appropriate to consider different parts of it separately. After all, the special character of science is its ability to understand complicated problems by breaking them into their constituent parts.

What happens when scientists attempt to examine the world in its entirety is beautifully illustrated by the controversial Club of Rome study published last spring, entitled *The Limits to Growth*. The study, carried out at MIT under the leadership of Dr. Dennis L. Meadows, is based on a computer simulation of the world and purports to show that many of the more gloomy prophecies of the environmentalists can be upheld by mathematical calculations. The computer is programmed with information about the population of the world (for this purpose broken down into three numbers representing the population of children between zero and fifteen, the population of adults of reproductive age, and the population of those whose reproductive life is over), as well as a number indicating the amount of money invested in industrial capital, another indicating the amount of arable land, one that is supposed to stand for the stock of unrenewable resources, and one that is meant to be a measure of pollution. The object of the exercise is to calculate how these and several other interrelated variables will change in the course of time. In my opinion the results fully justify Gunnar Myrdal's description of the study as "pretentious nonsense."

To cite one example, the stock of nonrenewable resources such as minerals will obviously decrease over time at a rate determined in part by the size of the world's population and by the quantity of material consumed each year by a single individual, which is in turn dependent on the amount of industrial output per person and ultimately on the investment in new factories of various kinds. Dr. Meadows and his colleagues calculate that if there is "no major change in the physical, economic, or social relationships that have historically governed the development of the world system," there will come a point in the next century when the diminishing stock of natural resources brings about a decrease of industrial growth, a consequent decrease in the amount of food available per person, and then, in due course, a return to the bad old days of the eighteenth and nineteenth centuries, when the death rate rose sharply because of starvation and even an increasing birth rate was unable to prevent a population decline.

The first thing to be said about such a prediction is that even the best possible computer model is no better than the assumptions about the real world with which it is programmed. And even very large computer models, such as Dr. Meadows's, are never large enough to take into account all the possible relationships between one thing and another. So it is no wonder that the Club of Rome study has been forced to make drastic simplifications that even the extremists in the environmental movement usually manage to avoid.

The most serious error in the study involves something economists call aggregation—the combining of things that ought not to be considered as one. For example, the authors have been compelled by the limitations of their equipment to represent the totality of pollution on the earth by a single number, based on world industrial production. Having lumped pollution and industrial production together, the authors cannot take into consideration the obvious fact that modern technology can control the first without affecting the second at all.

These simplifications, apparently built into the Club of Rome's computer model, make nonsense of the study. To add another example, *The Limits to Growth* represents the world's stock of nonrenewable resources

with a single number. In one particular calculation it was assumed that the amounts of nonrenewable resources in the earth's crust in 1970 were the equivalent of 250 years' supply at the then rate of consumption. On the face of things this was a generous assumption, for the known reserves of a great many common materials such as lead and mercury are unlikely to last nearly so long. But the history of the past few decades has shown clearly enough that relatively scarce materials are constantly being replaced by more common ones—copper, for instance, has been superseded by aluminum in many branches of the electronics industry. Moreover, by representing the present stock of raw materials with a single number, the study has overlooked a cardinal law of economics, which holds that increasing scarcity and, consequently, higher prices would stimulate exploration for new materials and also make it more practical to mine ores of lower quality.

In general, economics is not the strong suit of the environmentalists. And, unfortunately for their case, most of the issues they tend to present as questions of life or death for the human race are essentially questions of economics. Consider urban air pollution. The overriding issue is not whether cleaner air can be provided (we know it can) but how much taxpayers, and in particular the owners of cars and factories, are prepared to pay for that amenity. Exactly the same is true of the noise produced by jets, the overcrowding of beaches, and even the extent to which farmers are allowed to use pesticides. On such issues there is a need for a better understanding of the economics of the communal good.

Because the relationship between communities and their surroundings is often determined by economic considerations, it is not surprising that different communities should have different objectives and that each should strike its own balance between exploitation and conservation. This is another way of saying that only prosperous communities will pay much attention to environmental amenities. One of the more serious dangers of the extremist wing of the environmental movement is that by insisting on the catastrophic implications of present tendencies, it may alienate the countries of the developing world, not yet rich enough to aspire to the kind of pollution-free future on which the more prosperous nations have set their sights. This was plain enough at the United Nations Conference on the Human Environment held in Stockholm last June, where it proved to be extremely difficult to hammer out a common platform, partly because of the inevitable conflict of interest between rich and poor nations.

The extremists have created the false impression that prosperity itself is the enemy. After all, cars are so numerous on the roads of a wealthy nation because its citizens are able to pay for them. And the heaps of aluminum cans that deface a countryside indicate that consumers can afford the added expense of disposable items. But insisting on the relationship between prosperity and pollution obscures the incontrovertible truth that the level of prosperity now common in developed nations has also purchased better health services, educational systems, and a host of other social benefits to which less fortunate nations still aspire. To people in the developing world environmental concerns are simply not of the highest priority.

The political consequences of this tactlessness by people from industrialized societies are serious. The intellectual sins committed by the environmentalists are more serious still. The common justification of their technique of deliberate exaggeration is the claim that it is necessary to stir people up, to get things done. But people are easily anesthetized by overstatement, and there is a danger that the environmental movement will fall flat on its face when it is most needed, simply because it has pitched its tale too strongly.

Toward an Ecological Solution

MURRAY BOOKCHIN

Popular alarm over environmental decay and population did not emerge for the first time merely in the late '60s, nor for that matter is it the unique response of the present century. Air pollution, water pollution, food adulteration and other environmental problems were public issues as far back as ancient times, when notions of environmental diseases were far more prevalent than they are today. All of these issues came to the surface again with the Industrial Revolution—a period which was marked by burgeoning cities, the growth of the factory system, and an unprecedented befouling and polluting of air and waterways.

Today the situation is changing drastically and at a tempo that portends a catastrophe for the entire world of life. What is not clearly understood in many popular discussions of the present ecological crisis is that the very nature of the issues has changed, that the decay of the environment is directly tied to the decay of the existing social structure. It is not simply certain malpractices or a given spectrum of poisonous agents that is at stake, but rather the very structure of modern agriculture, industry and the city. Consequently, environmental decay and ecological catastrophe cannot be averted merely by increased programs like "pollution control" which deal with sources rather than systems. To be commensurable to the problem, the solution must entail far-reaching revolutionary changes in society and in man's relation to man.

To understand the enormity of the ecological crisis and the sweeping transformation it requires, let us briefly revisit the "pollution problem" as it existed a few decades ago. During the 1930s, pollution was primarily a muckraking issue, a problem of exposé journalism typified by Kallet and Schlink's "100 Million Guinea Pigs."

This kind of muckraking literature still exists in abundance and finds an eager market among "consumers," that is to say, a public that seeks personal and legislative solutions to pollution problems. Its supreme pontiff is Ralph Nader, an energetic young man who has shrewdly combined traditional muckraking with a safe form of "New Left" activism. In reality, Nader's emphasis belongs to another historical era, for the magnitude of the pollution problem has expanded beyond the most exaggerated accounts of the '30s. The new pollutants are no longer "poisons" in the popular sense of the term; rather they belong to the problems of ecology, not merely pharmacology, and these do not lend themselves to legislative redress.

What now confronts us is not the pre-

Note: Murray Bookchin, "Toward An Ecological Solution," *Ramparts,* May 1970, pp. 7, 8, 10, 14, 15. Copyright 1970 by *Ramparts* magazine. Reproduced by permission of the editors.

dominantly specific, rapidly degradable poisons that alarmed an earlier generation, but long-lived carcinogenic and mutagenic agents, such as radioactive isotopes and chlorinated hydrocarbons. These agents become part of the very anatomy of the individual by entering his bone structure, tissues and fat deposits. Their dispersion is so global that they become part of the anatomy of the environment itself. They will be within us and around us for years to come, in many cases for generations to come. Their toxic effects are usually chronic rather than acute; the deadly and mutational effects they produce in the individual will not be seen until many years have passed. They are harmful not only in large quantities, but in trace amounts; as such, they are not detectable by human senses or even, in many cases, by conventional methods of analysis. They damage not only specific individuals but the human species as a whole and virtually all other forms of life.

No less alarming is the fact that we must drastically revise our traditional notions of what constitutes an environmental "pollutant." A few decades ago it would have been absurd to describe carbon dioxide and heat as "pollutants" in the customary sense of the term. Yet in both cases they may well rank among the most serious sources of future ecological imbalance and pose major threats to the viability of the planet. As a result of industrial and domestic combustion activities, the quality of carbon dioxide in the atmosphere has increased by roughly 25 per cent in the past 100 years, a figure that may well double again by the end of the century. The famous "greenhouse effect," which increasing quantities of the gas is expected to produce, has already been widely discussed: eventually, it is supposed, the gas will inhibit the dissipation of the earth's heat into space, causing a rise in overall temperatures which will melt the polar ice caps and result in an inundation of vast coastal areas. Thermal pollution, the result mainly of warm water discharged by nuclear and conventional power plants, has disastrous effects on the ecology of lakes, rivers and estuaries. Increases in water temperature not only damage the physiological and reproductive activities of fish, they also promote the great blooms of algae that have become such formidable problems in waterways.

What is at stake in the ecological crisis we face today is the very capacity of the earth to sustain advanced forms of life. The crisis is being drawn together by massive increases in "typical" forms of air and water pollution; by a mounting accumulation of non-degradable wastes, lead residues, pesticide residues and toxic additives in food; by the expansion of cities into vast urban belts; by increasing stresses due to congestion, noise and mass living; by the wanton scarring of the earth as a result of mining operations, lumbering, and real estate speculation. The result of all this is that the earth within a few decades has been despoiled on a scale that is unprecedented in the entire history of human habitation on the planet.

Finally, the complexity and diversity of life which marked biological evolution over many millions of years is being replaced by a simpler, more synthetic and increasingly homogenized environment. Aside from any esthetic considerations, the elimination of this complexity and diversity may prove to be the most serious loss of all. Modern society is literally undoing the work of organic evolution. If this process continues unabated, the earth may be reduced to a level of biotic simplicity where humanity—whose welfare depends profoundly upon the complex food chains in the soil, on the land surface and in the oceans—will no longer be able to sustain itself as a viable animal species.

In recent years a type of biological "cold warrior" has emerged who tends to locate the ecological crisis in technology and population growth, thereby divesting it of its explosive social content. Out of this focus has emerged a new version of "original sin" in which tools and machines, reinforced by sexually irresponsible humans, ravage the earth in concert. Both technology and sexual irresponsibility, so the argument goes, must be curbed—if not voluntarily, then by the divine institution called the state.

The naiveté of this approach would be visible were it not for its sinister implications. History has known of many different forms of tools and machines, some of which are patently harmful to human welfare and the natural world, others of which have clearly improved the condition of man and the ecology of an area. It would be absurd to place plows and mutagenic defoliants, weaving machines and automobiles, computers and moon rockets, under a common rubric. Worse, it would be grossly misleading to deal with these technologies in a social vacuum.

Technologies consist not only of ·the devices humans employ to mediate their relationship with the natural world, but also the attitudes associated with these devices. These attitudes are distinctly social products, the results of the social relationships humans establish with each other. What is clearly needed is not a mindless depreciation of technology as such, but rather a reordering and redevelopment of technologies according to ecologically sound principles. We need an eco-technology that will help harmonize society with the natural world.

The same over-simplification is evident in the neo-Malthusian alarm over population growth. The reduction of population growth to a mere ratio between birth rates and death rates obscures the many complex social factors that enter into both statistics. A rising or declining birth rate is not a simple biological datum, any more than is a rising or declining death rate. Both are subject to the influences of the economic status of the individual, the nature of family structure, the values of society, the status of women, the attitude toward children, the culture of the community, and so forth. A change in any single factor interacts with the remainder to produce the statistical data called "birth rate" and "death rate." Culled from such abstract ratios, population growth rates can easily be used to foster authoritarian controls and finally a totalitarian society, especially if neo-Malthusian propaganda and the failure of voluntary birth con-

trol are used as an excuse. In arguing that forcible measures of birth control and a calculated policy of indifference to hunger may eventually be necessary to stabilize world populations, the neo-Malthusians are already creating a climate of opinion that will make genocidal policies and authoritarian institutions socially acceptable.

It is supremely ironic that coercion, so clearly implicit in the neo-Malthusian outlook, has acquired a respected place in the public debate on ecology—for the roots of the ecological crisis lie precisely in the coercive basis of modern society. The notion that man must dominate nature emerges directly from the domination of man by man. The patriarchal family may have planted the seed of domination in the nuclear relations of humanity; the classical split between spirit and reality—indeed, mind and labor—may have nourished it; the anti-naturalistic bias of Christianity may have tended to its growth; but it was not until organic community relations, be they tribal, feudal or peasant in form, dissolved into market relationships that the planet itself was reduced to a resource for exploitation.

This centuries-long tendency finds its most exacerbating development in modern capitalism: a social order that is orchestrated entirely by the maxim "Production for the sake of production." Owing to its inherently competitive nature, bourgeois society not only pits humans against each other, but the mass of humanity against the natural world. Just as men are converted into commodities, so every aspect of nature is converted into a commodity, a resource to be manufactured and merchandised wantonly. Entire continental areas in turn are converted into factories, and cities into marketplaces. The liberal euphemisms for these unadorned terms are "growth," "industrial society" and "urban blight." By whatever language they are described, the pheonmena have their roots in the domination of man by man.

As technology develops, the maxim "Production for the sake of production" finds its complement in "Consumption for the sake of consumption." The phrase "consumer society" completes the description of the present social order as an "industrial society." Needs are tailored by the mass media to create a public demand for utterly useless commodities, each carefully engineered to deteriorate after a predetermined period of time. The plundering of the human spirit by the marketplace is paralleled by the plundering of the earth by capital. The tendency of the liberal to identify the marketplace with the human needs, and capital with technology, represents a calculated error that neutralizes the social thrust of the ecological crisis.

The strategic ratios in the ecological crisis are not the population rates of India but the production of the United States, a country that produces more than 50 percent of the world's goods. Here, too, liberal euphemisms like "affluence" conceal the critical thrust of a blunt word like "waste." With a vast section of its industrial capacity committed to war production, the U.S. is literally trampling upon the earth and shredding ecological links that are vital to human survival. If current industrial projections prove to be accurate, the remaining 30 years of the century will witness a fivefold increase in electric power production, based mostly on nuclear fuels and coal. The colossal burden in radioactive wastes and other effluents that this increase will place on the natural ecology of the earth hardly needs description.

In shorter perspective, the problem is no less disquieting. Within the next five years, lumber production may increase an overall 20 per cent; the output of paper, five per cent annually; folding boxes, three per cent annually; metal cans, four to five per cent annually; plastics (which currently form one to two per cent of municipal wastes), seven per cent annually. Collectively, these industries account for the most serious pollutants in the environment. The utterly senseless nature of modern industrial activity is perhaps best illustrated by the decline in returnable (and reusable) beer bottles from 54 billion bottles in 1960 to 26 billion today. Their place has been taken over by "one-way bottles" (a rise from 8 to 21 billion in the same period) and cans (an increase from 38 to 53 billion). The "one-way bottles" and cans, of course, pose tremendous problems in solid waste disposal, but they do sell better.

It may be that the planet, conceived as a lump of minerals, can support these mindless increases in the output of trash. The earth, conceived as a complex web of life, certainly cannot. The only question is, can the earth survive its looting long enough for man to replace the current destructive social system with a humanistic, ecologically oriented society.

The apocalyptic tone that marks so many ecological works over the past decade should not be taken lightly. We are witnessing the end of a world although whether this world is a long-established social order or the earth as a living organism still remains in question. The ecological crisis, with its threat of human extinction, has developed appositely to the advance of technology, with its promise of abundance, leisure and material security. Both are converging toward a single focus: At a point where the very survival of man is being threatened, the possibility of removing him from the trammels of domination, material scarcity and toil has never been more promising. The very technology that has been used to plunder the planet can now be deployed, artfully and rationally, to make it flourish.

It is necessary to overcome not only bourgeois society but also the long legacy of propertied society: the patriarchal family, the city, the state—indeed, the historic splits that separated mind from sensuousness, individual from society, town from country, work from play, man from nature. The spirit of spontaneity and diversity that permeates the ecological outlook toward the natural world must now be directed toward revolutionary change and utopian reconstruction in the social world. Propertied society, domination, hierarchy and the state, in all their forms, are utterly incompatible with the survival of the biosphere. Either ecology action is revolutionary action or it is nothing at all. Any attempt to reform a social order that by its very nature pits humanity against all the forces of life is a gross deception and serves merely as a safety valve for established institutions.

The application of ecological principles to social reconstruction, on the other hand, opens entirely new opportunities for imagination and creativity. The cities must be decentralized to serve the interests of both natural and social ecology. Urban gigantism is devastating not only to the land, the air, the waterways and the local climate, but to the human spirit. Having reached its limits in the megalopolis—an urban sprawl that can best be described as the "non-city"—the city must be replaced by a multitude of diversified, well-rounded communities, each scaled to human dimensions and to the carrying capacity of its ecosystem. Technology, in turn, must be placed in the service of meaningful human needs, its output gauged to permit a careful recycling of wastes into the environment.

With the community and its technology sculptured to human scale, it should be possible to establish new, diversified energy patterns: the combined use of solar power, wind power and a judicious use of fossil and nuclear fuels. In this decentralized society, a new sense of tribalism, of face-to-face relations, can be expected to replace the bureaucratic institutions of propertied society and the state. The earth would be shared communally, in a new spirit of harmony between man and man and between man and nature.

In the early years of the 19th century, this image of a new, free and stateless society was at best a distant vision, a humanistic ideal which revolutionaries described as communism or anarchism, and their opponents as utopia. As the one century passed into its successor, the advance of technology increasingly brought this vision into the realm of possibility. The ecological crisis of the late 20th century has now turned the possibility of its early decades into a dire necessity. Not only is humanity more prepared for the realization of this vision than at any time in history—a fact intuited by the tribalism of the youth culture—but upon its realization depends the very existence of humanity in the remaining years ahead.

Perhaps the most important message of Marx a century ago was the concept that humanity must develop the means of survival in order to live. Today, the development of a flexible, open-ended technology has reversed this concept completely. We stand on the brink of a post-scarcity society, a society that can finally remove material want and domination from the human condition. Perhaps the most important message of ecology is the concept that man must master the conditions of life in order to survive.

During the May-June uprising of 1968, the French students sensed the new equation in human affairs when they inscribed the demand: "Be realistic! Do the impossible!" To this demand, the young Americans who face the next century can add the more solemn injunction: "If we don't do the impossible, we shall be faced with the unthinkable."

Analysis of Values
and
Conflicts of Interest

Ehrlich implies that uncontrolled technological development and population growth threaten the very existence of mankind. He makes many dire and frightening predictions that could occur if environmental problems are ignored. Ehrlich does not provide a penetrating causal analysis of environmental abuse. Instead, he describes the possible ecological cataclysm and immediate conditions (e.g. industrial pollution) that might bring it about. Ehrlich's heavily dramatized statement of the possible consequences of overpopulation, pollution, and overexploitation of natural resources is an attempt to raise public consciousness about environmental problems. Those engaged in defining a new social problem often have to go to extremes to convince the public of the problem's gravity. Ehrlich is a spokesman for those who want the state of the environment defined as a major social problem to effect extensive conservation and environmental protection programs. He supports the demands of numerous pressure groups that are struggling for environmental concern and ecological responsibility. Ehrlich's research and polemics have often been used by these groups in their informational, legal, and consciousness-raising activities. However, Ehrlich also represents the interests of a broad band of citizens of all political affiliations who fear that the environment is being destroyed by powerful economic interests that are concerned only about their profit margins.

Bookchin shares Ehrlich's concern about the environment, but sees the problem from a different perspective. Bookchin does not believe that environmental crisis can be avoided simply by creating programs to reduce pollution, cut energy usage, or limit population growth. He suggests that the cause of environmental problems is not simple neglect, but social institutions that fail to emphasize "quality of life" as their first priority. Bookchin, like Ehrlich, advocates ecological reform, but feels that improvement of the environment can succeed only through extensive social change. Bookchin's position supports groups whose first priority is radical change of

485

the entire social structure. He represents the values and interests of Marxist, leftist, and anarchist groups who feel that almost all social problems have their origins in the economic and industrial interests that dominate the modern capitalist state.

Maddox criticizes environmentalists for promoting excessive and unreasonable fears about the state of the environment. He not only questions the accuracy of their analysis, but also criticizes their anti-scientific and anti-technological inclinations. Maddox argues that extreme statements about environmental doom preclude anything but the most drastic and impractical measures to correct ecological problems. Maddox's position reflects the values and interests of persons working in the physical and technological sciences. These persons usually see their work as a contribution toward the improvement of the human condition. Thus, they express resentment of those environmentalists who portray them as culprits aiding in the destruction of the environment. Furthermore, these scientists fear that environmentalist attacks could result in public backlash (legislation) that would threaten or even terminate some forms of scientific research. Maddox promotes the interests of the scientific community by arguing that environmentalists distort reality in their overdramatizations of ecological crisis and in so doing ignore workable solutions to environmental problems offered by science and technology.

Representatives of industrial interests attack the environmentalists in the same way Maddox does. Industrialists admit that there are ecological problems, but assert that environmentalists allow emotion to exaggerate the facts. They also agree that measures need to be taken to prevent environmental abuse, but consider programs proposed by environmentalists to be extreme and impractical. Although Maddox is by no means their representative, public acceptance of his position serves industrial interests. Industry would prefer ecological problems deemphasized to prevent government imposition of strict regulations for protection of the environment. Anti-pollution devices and other environmental controls are costly and reduce corporate profits.

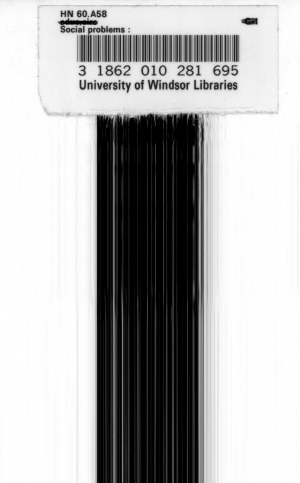